Great Family Vacations

West

"Stapen is a respected travel writer who has done some awfully good books on family travel. They're well researched, very well done."
—*USA Today*

"Stapen provides a reassuring and enthusiastic voice for families on the go."
—*Christine Loomis,* Family Life *magazine*

"The Great Family Vacations series is an inspiration to parents in search of worthy destinations. Stapen is an eminently practical parent and travel expert, down to the fine details. Perhaps even more important, she understands that exploring new places is a thrill that brings families closer together."
—*Alexandra Kennedy, Editorial Director,*
FamilyFun *magazine*

Also by Candyce H. Stapen

Great Family Vacations: South
Great Family Vacations: Midwest and Rocky Mountains
Great Family Vacations: Northeast
Family Adventure Guide: Virginia
Cruise Vacations with Kids: (Prima)
Ski Vacations with Kids: (Prima)

Great Family Vacations

West

Candyce H. Stapen

A Voyager Book

Old Saybrook, Connecticut

Cover photo background: ©1996 PhotoDisc, Inc.
Cover inset photographs: Lori Adamski Peek/©Tony Stone Images; Ken Fisher/©Tony Stone Images; Jess Stock/©Tony Stone Images
Cover design by Schwartzman Design

Library of Congress Cataloging-in-Publication Data is Available.
ISBN 0-7627-0059-9

Manufactured in the United States of America
First Edition/First Printing

To my favorite traveling companions,
Alissa, Matt, and David

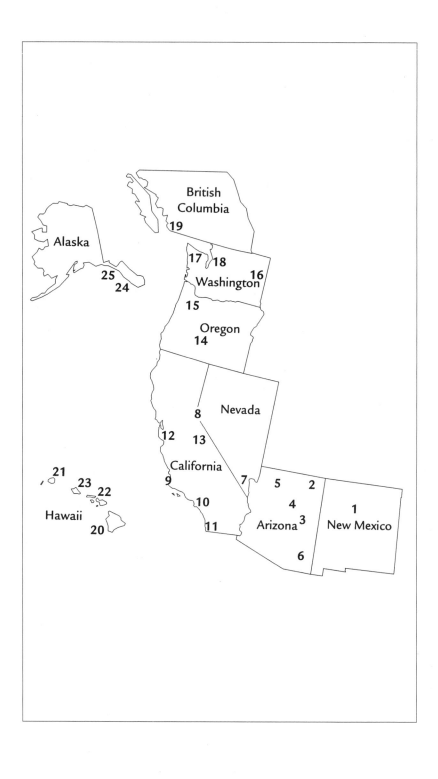

Contents

Acknowledgments

I want to thank my editors, Mace Lewis and Bruce Markot, for their patience and my agent, Carol Mann, for her assistance. I appreciate the hard work of Robert Moll, assistant editor, Deidre Fernandes, editorial assistant, and Carol Eannarino. I also want to thank Dorothy Jordon and Christine Loomis for their companionship on trips and for their support.

Introduction

There is a Chinese proverb that says the wise parent gives a child roots and wings. By traveling with your children you can bestow many gifts upon them: a strong sense of family bonds, memories that last a lifetime, and a joyful vision of the world.

Traveling with your children offers many bonuses for you and your family. These days no parent or child has an excessive amount of free time. Whether you work in the home or outside of it, your days are filled with meetings, deadlines, household errands, and carpool commitments. Your child most likely keeps equally busy with scouts, soccer, music lessons, computer clinics, basketball, and/or ballet. When your family stays home, your time together is likely to be limited to sharing quick dinners and overseeing homework. If there's a teen in your house, an age known for endless hours spent with friends, your encounters often shrink to swapping phone messages and car keys.

But take your child on the road with you, and both of you have plenty of time to talk and be together. Traveling together gives your family the luxury of becoming as expansive as the scenery. Over doughnuts in an airport lounge or dinner in a new hotel, you suddenly hear about that special science project or how it really felt to come in third in the swim meet. By sharing a drive along a country road or a visit to a city museum, your children get the space to view you as a person and not just as a parent.

Additionally, both you and your kids gain new perspectives on life. Children who spend time in a different locale, whether it's a national forest or a city new to them, expand their awareness. For you as a parent, traveling with your kids brings the added bonus of enabling you to see again with a child's eye. When you show a six-year-old a reconstructed Colonial village or share the stars in a Tennessee mountain night sky with a thirteen-year-old, you feel the world twinkle with as much possibility as when you first encountered these sites long ago.

Part of this excitement is a result of the exuberance kids bring, and part is from the instant friendships kids establish. Street vendors save their best deals for preschoolers, and, even on a crowded rush hour bus, a child by your side turns a fellow commuter from a stranger into a friend. Before your stop comes, you'll often be advised of the best toy shop in town and directed to a local cafe with a kid-pleasing menu at prices guaranteed to put a smile on your face.

New perspectives also come from the activities you participate in with your children. Most of these activities you would probably pass up when shuttling solo. Whether it's finding all the dogs in the paintings at the High Museum of Art, playing miniature golf at a resort, or trying horseback riding in a park, you always learn more when you take your kids.

Surprisingly, traveling with your kids can also be cost-effective and practical. By combining or by extending a work-related trip into a vacation, you save money since your company picks up a good part of your expenses. Because tag-along-tots on business trips are an increasing trend, several hotel chains have responded with a range of family-friendly amenities including children's programs, child-safe rooms, and milk and cookies at bedtime.

For all these reasons, traveling with your children presents many wonderful opportunities. It is a great adventure to be a parent, and it is made more wondrous when you travel with your children. You will not only take pleasure in each other's company, but you will return home with memories to savor for a lifetime.

Family Travel Tips

Great family vacations require careful planning and the cooperation of all family members. Before you go you need to think about such essentials as how to keep sibling fights to a minimum and how to be prepared for medical emergencies. While en route you want to be sure to make road trips and plane rides fun, even with a toddler. You want to be certain that the room that is awaiting your family is safe and that your family makes the most of being together. When visiting relatives, you want to eliminate friction by following the house rules. These tips, gathered from a host of families, go a long way toward making your trips good ones.

General Rules

1. Meet the needs of the youngest family member. Your raft trip won't be fun if you're constantly worried about your three-year-old being bumped overboard by the white water the tour operator failed to mention or if your first-grader gets bored with the day's itinerary of art museums.

2. Underplan. Your city adventure will dissolve in tears—yours and your toddler's—if you've scheduled too many sites and not enough time for the serendipitous. If your child delights in playing with the robots at the science museum, linger there and skip the afternoon's proposed visit to the history center.

3. Go for the green spaces. Seek out an area's parks. Pack a picnic lunch and take time to throw a Frisbee, play catch, or simply enjoy relaxing in the sun and people watching.

4. Enlist the cooperation of your kids by including them in the decision making. While family vacation voting is not quite a democracy, consider your kids' needs. Is there a way to combine your teen's desire to be near "the action" with your spouse's request for seclusion? Perhaps book a self-contained resort on a quiet beach that also features a nightspot.

5. Understand your rhythms of the road. Some families like traveling at night so that the kids sleep in the car or on the plane. Others avoid traveling during the evening cranky hours and prefer to leave early in the morning.

6. Plan to spend time alone with each of your children as well as with your spouse. Take a walk, write in a journal together, play ball, share ice cream in the snack shop, etc. Even the simplest of things done together create valuable family memories.

Don't Leave Home Without

1. *Emergency medical kit.* The first thing we always pack is the emergency medical kit, a bag I keep ready to go with all those things that suddenly become important at 3:00 A.M. This is no hour to be searching the streets for baby aspirin or Band-Aids. Make sure your kit includes items suitable for adults as well as children. Be sure to bring:

- aspirin or an aspirin substitute
- a thermometer
- cough syrup
- a decongestant
- medication to relieve diarrhea
- bandages and Band-Aids
- gauze pads
- antibiotic ointment and a physician-approved antibiotic, just in case

- a motion-sickness remedy
- sunscreen
- insect repellent
- ointments or spray to soothe sunburn, rashes, and poison ivy
- something to soothe insect stings
- any medications needed on a regular basis
- tweezers and a sterile needle to remove splinters

    Keep this kit with you in your carry-on luggage or on the front seat of your car.

2. *Snack food.* As soon as we land somewhere or pull up to a museum for a visit, my eleven-year-old daughter wants food. Instead of arguing or wasting time and money on snacks, I carry granola bars with me. She munches on these reasonably nutritious snacks while we continue on schedule.

3. *Inflatable pillow and travel products.* Whether on the road or in a plane, these inflatable wonders help me and the kids sleep. For travel pillows plus an excellent variety of light yet durable travel products including hair dryers, luggage straps, alarms, adaptor plugs for electrical outlets, and clothing organizers, call Magellan's (800–962–4943). TravelSmith (800–950–1600) carries these items as well as clothing, mostly for teens and adults.

4. *Travel toys.* Kids don't have to be bored en route to your destination. Pack books, coloring games, and quiet toys. Some kids love story tapes on their personal cassette players. For innovative, custom-tailored travel kits full of magic pencil games, puzzles, and crafts for children three and a half or older, call Sealed With A Kiss (800–888–SWAK). The packages cost about $35. Surprise your kids with this once you are on the road. They'll be happy and so will you.

Flying with Tots

1. Book early for the seat you like. Whether you prefer the aisle, window, or bulkhead for extra legroom, reserve your seat well in advance of your departure date.

2. Call the airlines at least forty-eight hours ahead to order meals that you know your kids will eat: children's dinners, hamburger platters, salads, etc.

3. Bring food on board that you know your kids like even if you've ordered a special meal. If your kids won't eat what's served at meal

time, at least they won't be hungry if they munch on nutritious snacks.

4. Be sure to explain each step of the plane ride to little kids so that they will understand that the airplane's noises and shaking do not mean that a crash is imminent.

5. Stuff your carry-on with everything you might need (including medications, extra kids' clothes, diapers, baby food, formula, and bottles) to get you through a long flight and a delay of several hours . . . just in case.

6. Bring a child safety seat (a car seat) on board. Although presently the law allows children under two to fly free if they sit on a parent's lap, the Federal Aviation Administration and the Air Transport Association support legislation that would require all kids to be in child safety seats. In order to get a seat on board, the seat must have a visible label stating approval for air travel, and you must purchase a ticket for that seat. Without a ticket, you are not guaranteed a place to put this child safety seat in case the plane is full.

7. With a toddler or young child, wrap little surprises to give as "presents" throughout the flight. These work wonderfully well to keep a wee one's interest.

8. Before boarding, let your kids work off energy by walking around the airport lounge. Never let your child nap just before take-off—save the sleepy moments for the plane.

9. If you're traveling with a lot of luggage, check it curbside before parking your car. This eliminates the awkward trip from long-term parking loaded down with kids, luggage, car-seats, and strollers.

Road Rules

1. Use this time together to talk with your children. Tell them anecdotes about your childhood or create stories for the road together.

2. Put toys for each child in his or her own mesh bag. This way the toys are easily located and visible instead of being strewn all over the car.

3. Avoid long rides. Break the trip up by stopping every two or three hours for a snack or to find a rest room. This lets kids stretch their legs.

4. When driving for several days, plan to arrive at your destination each day by 4:00 or 5:00 P.M., so that the kids can enjoy a swim at the hotel/motel. This turns long hauls into easily realized goals that are fun.

At the Destination

1. When traveling with young children, do a safety check of the hotel room and the premises as soon as you arrive. Put matches, glasses, ashtrays, and small items out of reach. Note if stair and balcony railings are widely spaced or easily climbed by eager tots. Find out where the possible dangers are, and always keep track of your kids.
2. Schedule sightseeing for the morning, but plan to be back at the resort or hotel by early afternoon so that your child can enjoy the pool, the beach, miniature golf, or other kid-friendly facilities.
3. Plan to spend some time alone with each of your children every day. With pre-teens and teens, keep active by playing tennis or basketball, jogging, or doing something else to burn energy.
4. Establish an amount of money that your child can spend on souvenirs. Stick to this limit, but let your child decide what he or she wants to buy.

With Relatives

1. Find out the rules of your relatives' house before you arrive, and inform your kids of them. Let them know, for example, that food is allowed only in the kitchen or dining room so that they won't bring sandwiches into the guest bedroom or den.
2. Tell your relatives about your kids' eating preferences. Let the person doing the cooking know that fried chicken is fine, but that your kids won't touch liver even if it is prepared with the famous family recipe.
3. To lessen the extra work and expense for relatives and to help eliminate friction, bring along or offer to shop and pay for those special items that only your kids eat—a favorite brand of cereal, juice, frozen pizza, or microwave kids' meal.
4. Discuss meal hours. If you know, for example, that grandma and grandpa always dine at 7:00 P.M. but that your pre-schooler and first-grader can't wait that long, feed your kids earlier at their usual time, and enjoy an adult dinner with your relatives later.
5. Find something suitable for each generation that your kids and relatives will enjoy doing together. Look over old family albums, have teens tape record oral family histories, and have grade-schoolers take instant snapshots of the clan.

6. Find some way that your kids can help with the work of visiting. Even a nursery-school age child feels good about helping to clear a table or sweep the kitchen floor.

Family Travel Planners

These specialists can help you assess your family's needs and find the vacation that's best for you.

- *Family Travel Times.* This monthly newsletter offers the latest information on hotels, resorts, city attractions, cruises, airlines, tours, and destinations. Contact Travel With Your Children, 40 Fifth Avenue, New York, NY 10011. For information call (212) 447-5524.
- **Rascals in Paradise.** Specializing in family and small-group tours to the Caribbean, Mexico, and the South Pacific, Rascals' tours usually include nannies for each family and an escort to organize activities for the kids. Call (800) U-RASCAL for more information.
- **Grandtravel.** This company offers a variety of trips for grandparents and grandchildren 7 through 17. Domestic trips include visits to New York, New England, and the Grand Canyon. Foreign destinations include safaris to Kenya. (800) 247-7651.
- **Grandvistas.** Grandparents can take their grandkids on a few trips. Destinations typically include South Dakota, Nevada, and Wyoming. Call (800) 647-0800.
- **Families Welcome!** This agency offers travel packages for families in European cities and New York. With rental of a hotel room or apartment, you receive a "Welcome Kit" of tips on sightseeing, restaurants, and museums. (800) 326-0724.
- **Family Explorations.** Trip destinations include Honduras, Costa Rica, Ecuador, South Africa, and such stateside getaways as Pennsylvania and Maine. (800) WE-GO-TOO.

The prices and rates listed in this guidebook were confirmed at press time. We recommend, however, that you call establishments before traveling to obtain current information.

About the Author

Candyce H. Stapen is an expert on family travel. She appears on many television, cable, and radio shows, including *Good Morning America*, CBS *This Morning*, *Our Home*, WUSA-TV, D.C., and National Public Radio. A member of the Society of American Travel Writers as well as the Travel Journalists Guild, she writes several family travel columns on a regular basis, including columns for *FamilyFun, Vacations, Family.com*, and the *Washington Times*.

Her articles about family travel appear in a variety of newspapers and magazines, including *Ladies' Home Journal, Family Circle, USA Weekend, Better Homes and Gardens, Family Travel Times*, the *New York Post*, the *Miami Herald, Caribbean Travel and Life, Florida Travel and Life*, and *Cruises and Tours*.

Other books by Stapen are *50 Great Family Vacations: Western North America* (Globe Pequot); *Family Adventure Guide: Virginia* (Globe Pequot); and *Cruise Vacations with Kids* (Prima) and *Ski Vacations with Kids* (Prima).

Stapen lives in Washington, D.C., and travels whenever she can with her husband and two children.

ALBUQUERQUE

Albuquerque, New Mexico's largest city (metropolitan area population is about 660,000), was founded as a Spanish colony in 1706 along a wide curve of the Rio Grande. Today, the sprawling city dominated by the Sandia Mountains spreads far beyond the small adobe buildings of what is now called Old Town, a tree-lined historic area of shops, restaurants, and galleries. The Spanish and Native American influences in cooking, music, architecture, and other areas blend with Anglo-American, African American, and Asian cultures, adding zest to Albuquerque life.

There's a lot to see, and most of the time the weather's fine, with sunny days and low humidity. Summers are hot but bearable, brisk winters bring snow to the surrounding mountains, autumn and spring are simply delightful.

GETTING THERE

Albuquerque International Sunport (505-842-4366) is 5 miles south of downtown. **Airport Fast Park** (505-242-5181) operates a shuttle. Taxi service and car rentals are also available. **Amtrak** (800-USA-RAIL) serves Albuquerque Station, 314 First Street S.W.

Greyhound Bus Lines (505-243-4435) is at 300 Second Street S.W. By car, enter town from the north or south on I-25, or from the east or west via I-44.

GETTING AROUND

Since the city is spread out, a car is virtually mandatory. **Sun Tran** is the public bus system; call (505) 843-9200 for information.

WHAT TO SEE AND DO

Museums

Old Town, the picturesque plaza at Rio Grande Boulevard and Route 66, is Albuquerque's original center. What began seventy years before the American Revolution is today a historic area of adobe brick buildings. With recent renovation and new construction, the neighborhoods also bustle with shoppers browsing the hundreds of boutiques and shops. Within walking distance are several museums of special interest to families.

New Mexico Museum of Natural History, 1801 Mountain Road, N.W.; (505) 841-8837. The state's most visited museum is devoted to the natural and physical sciences of New Mexico and the Southwest and is a favorite with kids. A highlight: the Evolator time machine, a one-of-a-kind stand-up theater that simulates an elevator but travels through 38 million years of the state's geologic history.

Other appealing attractions include the Bone Zone, where the impressive fossils of New Mexico's extinct inhabitants include a 25-foot brachiosaurus leg and three life-size skeletal casts of dinosaurs. Hands-on activities take place at the Naturalist Center, where kids are attracted to the active beehive and ant farm. In the New Mexico Seacoast Exhibit, small sharks prowl in a saltwater aquarium. The Dynamax Theater shows larger-than-life films on a 26-foot-tall screen. Check for special exhibits, events, and workshops.

The Albuquerque Museum of Art, History and Science, 2000 Mountain Road N.W.; (505) 243-7255. It's free, so stop in for a peek. Although it's a good way to expose school-age kids to the area's 400 years of local history, from the Spanish Conquistadors to modern times, children either find this place interesting or boring depending on their interest in armor and art. The galleries exhibit authentic arms and armaments from the sixteenth century plus traditional and contemporary art.

The American International Rattlesnake Museum, 202 San Felipe N.W.; (505) 242-6569. Your kids will be either repulsed or delighted (or a little of both) as you walk through a glass-enclosed exhibit featuring the largest live collection of rattlesnake species on public exhibit. Everyone who makes it through gets a certificate of bravery.

Albuquerque at a Glance

- City savvy with a blend of Spanish, Native American, African American, Asian, and Anglo cultures

- Historic adobe brick buildings in Old Town and at nearby pueblos

- Petroglyph National Monument

- Year-round hot-air ballooning

- Albuquerque Convention and Visitors Bureau, (800) 284-2282

The Albuquerque Children's Museum, 800 Rio Grande Boulevard N.W.; (508–842–1537), provides hours of hands-on fun and educational activities for two- to twelve-year-olds. At Creating/Imagining, kids dress up, stage puppet shows, and practice weaving on a giant loom. Weekly Make-It-Take-It art activities allow kids to create their own projects. Other exhibits that encourage creativity and imagination include Bubbles and a Computer Lab.

Another kids-oriented museum is the **Explora! Science Center,** 40 First Plaza/Gallery #68; (505) 842–6188; http://www.explora.edu. Hands-on exhibits and kinetic sculptures have been woven together to make science cool and fun. Visitors can touch a tornado, create a laser show, and compose a musical melody. Kids can take safe experiments for play at home.

Elsewhere in town:

Indian Pueblo Museum, 2401 Twelfth Street N.W.; (505) 843–7270 or (800) 766–4405—outside New Mexico. Part of the Indian Pueblo Cultural Center, this nonprofit organization is owned and maintained by the nineteen area Indian pueblos. The building is patterned after Pueblo Bonito, a well-known ruin in Chaco Canyon in northwestern New Mexico. On the lower level, ancient artifacts reveal the history of the Pueblo Indians. The upper level has alcoves, one for each of the nineteen tribes, which feature changing exhibits, murals, and contemporary art. An area for kids offers a chance to dress up in traditional clothing, grind corn, and take part in other hands-on activities. Each weekend, traditional dance performances and art demonstrations are free to the public. Ask about special events and workshops. The restaurant serves only Native American food. The two most popular items (most kids love them): Indian baked bread and Indian fry bread. Another treat: Their shop features authentic Indian crafts—especially jewelry—at fair prices. Although the Indian Pueblo Museum provides insight into these ancient Native American cultures, you might consider visiting some local pueblos. New Mexico is home to nineteen Indian pueblos, many of which are within an hour's drive of Albuquerque. Ask for more information at the museum's visitor's desk.

The Maxwell Museum of Anthropology, University of New Mexico, University Boulevard (505-277-4405), depicts the history of Native Americans. This museum is ranked as one of the finest of its kind. Ancestors, one of the permanent exhibits, shows the evolution of humans using life-size models that compare Neanderthal and Cro-Magnon man with modern man. Frequently changing exhibits, mainly highlighting Southwestern culture, have included the role of women over the past two centuries and colorful Mexican folk art. Free admission.

Older kids may enjoy strolling around the campus of the **University of New Mexico,** founded around 1889. Some buildings feature distinctive Pueblo Native American architecture, and there are almost 700 acres of gardens, plus several art museums. Call or visit the UNM Visitor Center, 1700 Las Lomas N.E.; (505) 277-1989.

To visit the **National Atomic Museum,** Kirkland Air Force Base at Wyoming Boulevard (505-845-6670), you must get a pass from the military guards at the visitor's center. Whether you're for or against nuclear energy and/or weapons, you and your school-age kids should find this museum both educational and intriguing. Operated by the Department of Energy, the museum—the only one of its kind in the country—has exhibits and films on energy and its many sources, particularly atomic energy. The Manhattan Project that developed, produced, and tested the first atomic bomb, and was centered in New

Spectacular ceremonial dances take place throughout the year at the Indian pueblos of the Rio Grande Valley. (Courtesy Albuquerque Convention and Visitors Bureau)

Mexico, is highlighted. Not everything is portrayed through rose-colored glasses. A fifty-one-minute documentary, *Ten Seconds That Shook the World,* shown four times daily, includes newsreels of the 1930s and 1940s and concludes with Japan's unconditional surrender after the two atom bombings by the United States. The museum also includes a solar-powered TV, interactive exhibits and games, and a tour that explores the development of nuclear weapons. Outside, an ungainly 280mm atomic cannon, the F1015D Thunderchief, is on display. Admission is free; the museum is open daily, except major holidays.

Other Attractions

If your kids aren't afraid of heights, consider a scenic ride up the rugged west side of the Sandia Mountains on the **Sandia Peak Tram,** #10 Tramway Loop N.E.; (505) 856-6419. Up, up, up you go on over Domingo Baca Canyon on the world's longest continuous cable tramway. You may spot bear, bighorn sheep, and mule deer on the slopes below. It's 2.7 miles to the 10,378-foot observation deck on Sandia Peak, where there's an awesome view of Albuquerque and beyond. In summer, tram riders take the Sandia Peak Ski Area chair lift down the other side of the mountain. The 7,500-foot-long double chair lift to the Sandia Peak Ski Area (a popular winter ski facility) goes through spruce, ponderosa pine, and aspen forests. Rentals are available at the ski-lift base for the mountain-bike trails across Cibola National Forest. The chair lift stops running in late afternoon, while the tram continues until sunset. If you take the tram back down, you can purchase packages that include dinner at the High Finance Restaurant atop the peak or at the Pier 66 Restaurant, which overlooks the city from the tram base.

No child fails to be impressed by the more than 15,000 petroglyphs (ancient Indian drawings) on the 17-mile-long West Mesa escarpment that comprises **Petroglyph National Monument,** 6900 Unser Boulevard N.W., 8 miles west of the city; (505) 897-8814 or 873-6620. It's estimated that the petroglyphs were carved somewhere between A.D. 1100 and 1600 by hunting parties who camped at the base of the lava flow of the five now extinct volcanoes. Four easy walking trails wind through the petroglyphs.

Coronado State Park and Monument, 22 miles north of Albuquerque, a mile west of Bernalillo on Highway 44 (505-867-5351), preserves the ruins of the Kuaua Pueblo. Although normally off-limits to non-Indians, this restored kiva (sacred ceremonial chamber) is open to the public. A number of paintings were discovered on the walls; some are reproduced in the kiva, while the originals are in the visitor's center, which offers a superb panorama of the Rio Grande and the Sandia Mountains. There's also a good interpretive trail to follow.

Albuquerque is considered the **Hot Air Balloon Capital** of the World, and its weather makes year-round ballooning both a spectator and participant sport. If you get an urge to take off, there are a number of hot-air-balloon-ride companies (consult Albuquerque Convention and Visitors Bureau—ACVB—for a listing). Be aware that most companies have a minimum age of eight or so, mainly because younger children often get antsy, scared—or simply bored. But older children often love the easy sensation of floating with the breeze.

Parks and Zoos

The Rio Grande Zoo, 903 Tenth Street S.W. (505-764-6200; http://www.abqcvb.org/info/biopark), the largest zoo in the state, merged in the fall of 1996 with the newly constructed **Albuquerque Aquarium** and **Rio Grande Biological Garden** to form the **Albuquerque Biological Park.** At the zoo, more than 1,200 animals live in natural-looking habitats. The African Savannah, tropical rain forest, and primate island are among the highlights of this sixty-acre, top-notch facility.

The Aquarium, 2601 Central Avenue N.W. (505-764-6200), displays 2,855 creatures in twenty-eight tanks. One traces the path of a water drop from the upper Rio Grande as it flows through the canyons, deserts, and valleys of New Mexico, Texas, and Mexico into the Gulf of Mexico. A 285,000-gallon tank houses more than twenty sharks. And visitors get nose to snout with moray eels and rays in the eel cave. A tidal pool demonstrates the effects of the tides and their effects on beaches and sea life.

The 10,000-square-foot conservatory is the showcase of the sixteen-acre Rio Grande Botanic Garden, 2601 Central Avenue N.W.; (505) 764-2000. The conservatory is divided into two houses, a Desert Pavilion, which displays plants from the Chihuahuan and Sonoran deserts, and a Mediterranean Pavilion, which displays tropical plants. There are also several specialty gardens, including a children's fantasy garden. More than 11,000 plant specimens are exhibited on the grounds.

The **Rio Grande Nature Center State Park,** on the east bank of the Rio Grande at Candlearia Road (505-344-7240), contains more than seven acres of woods and park. A partially underground glass visitor's center features exhibits on the Rio Grande's history, ecology, and geology. Nature trails wind through the bosque—or cottonwood trails—along the river.

Theater, Music, and the Arts

Friday and Sunday's *Albuquerque Journal* and Thursday's *Albuquerque Tribune* list cultural happenings in town, or call (800) 284-2282. **Adobe Theater,** 9813 Fourth Street N.W. (505-898-9222), is the city's second-oldest theater. Performances range from comedy to drama to musicals and change monthly. **The Civic Light Opera Association,** 4201 Ellison N.E. (505-345-6577), has been presenting Broadway musicals for more than twenty-five years. Call for performance information. The **New Mexico Symphony Orchestra,** (505) 843-7657. Ticketmaster at Smith's is a citywide computerized ticket agency for all major entertainment events; call (505) TIC-KETS.

Sports

The **Albuquerque Dukes** are the professional baseball Triple-A farm team of the Los Angeles Dodgers and the Pacific Coast League; call (505) 243-1791 for information. Feel the sting of **New Mexico Scorpions Hockey,** Tingley Coliseum, 601 San Pedro N.E.; (505) 232-PUCK or (888) 4-SCORPS. There are thirty-two home games each season.

Shopping

Native American arts and crafts are the specialty here. In the shops of Old Town, you'll find a variety of jewelers and trading posts, art galleries, and gift shops. Kids especially enjoy **La Pinata,** #2 Patio Market, (505) 242-2400, with its bright piñatas, paper flowers, and porcelain dolls. Another favorite is **Rug Rats and Ruffles Children's Shop,** 309 Romero N.W. (505-243-9691), with toys, gifts, dolls, piñatas, and southwestern gear. Don't forget to browse the jewelry and crafts at the **Indian Pueblo Cultural Center.**

At the Wyoming Mall, 2266 Wyoming, a stop at **Planet Fun** (505-294-1099), gives kids ages one to twelve the chance to romp on an acre of life-size toys. There's a special crawling area for toddlers, while older kids can climb and crawl through a huge jungle gym or create a tune on a jumbo piano keyboard like the one from *Big.* There's a glassed-in area for parents, complete with snack bar and TV.

Cottonwood Mall, 10,000 Coors Bypass (505-899-7467), is New Mexico's largest shopping center. Dillards, JC Penney, and Montgomery Ward anchor 134 specialty stores, a food court, and a United Artists Theater. Savings are to be found at the **New Mexico Outlet Center,** 601 West Frontage Road, Algodones; (505) 867-6329. Find brand names for less at Bass, Liz Claiborne, Mikasa, OshKosh, and forty other stores.

SPECIAL EVENTS

Albuquerque hosts a variety of fairs and festivals.

April: Gathering of Nations, cultural festival and Powwow of more than 5,000 Native American dancers, and singers representing more than 300 tribes.

May: Magnifico! Albuquerque Festival of the Arts. Hundreds of events, including Kidfest, a hands-on family festival.

June: New Mexico Arts & Crafts Fair.

Late July: Mountain Discovery Days, Sandia Mountains. Entertainment and arts and crafts.

Early August: Summer festival with food and historical reenactments at El Rancho de las Golondrinas, an old Spanish colonial village, halfway between Albuquerque and Santa Fe.

September: New Mexico State Fair, one of the top ten such fairs in the country.

October: International Balloon Fiesta, a nine-day spectacular from the first through the second weekend of October. Storytellers International, second full week in October, features ghost stories, workshops, and storytelling for all ages.

Late October–Early December: Arts and Crafts fairs throughout the area.

December: Renaissance Fair, a holiday marketplace.

Christmas Eve: Luminaria tour of Albuquerque. The neighborhood streets are lighted with luminarias.

WHERE TO STAY

The Art of Visiting Albuquerque has a comprehensive lodging section, including bed and breakfasts and guest houses. **Accommodations Unlimited, Inc.** (505-291-0215) rents fully furnished luxury apartments and townhouses on a daily basis, complete with linens, phones, and dishes. You'll also find a wide choice of familiar chain motels and hotels.

Casas de Sueños, 310 Rio Grande Boulevard Southwest (505-247-4560), is 1 block from Old Town and adjacent to the Albuquerque Country Club. Some of the casitas in this "House of Dreams," which calls itself a B&B inn, come with a kitchen and fireplace. All have private courtyards.

Fairfield Inn by Marriott, 1760 Menual N.E. (505-889-4000 or 800-228-2800), is an excellent choice in the economy range. The new property, formerly part of the Hilton, has an indoor pool and sauna (and an outdoor pool shared with the Hilton). They serve a complimentary continental breakfast and offer complimentary airport transportation.

Hyatt Regency Albuquerque at Albuquerque Convention Center, 300 Tijeras N.W. (505-842-1234 or 800-233-1234), is one of the state's newest luxury hotels. The property has 395 large guest rooms, fourteen suites, an outdoor pool, a health club and spa, a restaurant, and two lounges. Complimentary airport transportation is offered.

If you want to combine a stay in town with some additional New Mexico fun, book the **Bishop's Lodge,** 3 miles north of Santa Fe on Bishop's Lodge Road, P.O. Box 2367, Santa Fe; (800) 732-2240 or (505) 983-6377. They offer family-style accommodations with horseback riding. Near town, the lodge is close to all the sites and also offers a kids' program from June through Labor Day and over Christmas break, for kids four to twelve.

WHERE TO EAT

Check the official ACVB brochure for a comprehensive restaurant listing. Three nostalgic eateries are sure to appeal to kids and adults. **Owl Cafe,** 800 Eubank N.E. (505-291-4900), a fifties-style diner, has a soda fountain, jukebox, and patio, plus excellent burgers and sandwiches. **66 Diner,** 1405 Central Avenue N.E. (505-247-1421), a former transmission shop, serves up Art Deco decor plus burgers, ribs, and sandwiches. **Yester-Dave's Grill,** 10601 Montgomery (505-293-0033), has a live disc jockey plus vintage cars, and offers ribs, burgers, and sandwiches.

By all means sample the local cuisine, keeping in mind that in New Mexico, the sauce—made with green and red chili peppers grown in the southern part of the state—is what distinguishes local cooking from standard Tex-Mex fare. A good place for enchiladas and other authentic food is at one of the three **Gardunos of Mexico** locations: 10551 Montgomery (505-298-5000); 5400 Academy (505-821-3030); or 8806 Fourth Street N.W. (505-898-2772). There's live mariachi music to add to the fun.

Bella Vista, North Highway 14, Cedar Crest (505-281-3370 or 281-3913), in the foothills of the Sandia Mountains, has a bountiful luncheon buffet. Dinner is served, too.

DAY TRIPS

A visit to this area wouldn't be complete without a trip to an Indian pueblo. The ACVB recommends visiting on a feast day and also recommends being aware of varying rules and restrictions concerning photography, sketching, and tape recording. *The Official Albuquerque Visitors Guide* lists the phone numbers of the various pueblos. **Isleta Pueblo,** fifteen minutes south on I-25 (505-869-3111), has the church of San Augustin, one of the oldest mission churches in the Southwest (1613-1630). The pueblo runs Isleta Lakes Water Recreation area, with picnic grounds and camping facilities.

The pleasures of Santa Fe are only some 55 miles away from Albuquerque, via I-25. A longer, but more scenic, route is the popular **Turquoise Trail** that travels along Route NM-536 (National Scenic Byway) to Sandia Crest (described earlier) and North NM-14 to Santa Fe. Along the way, stop at **The Tinkertown Museum,** 121 Sandia Crest Road (505-281-5233), open April through October, to see carvings and collections that include a miniature Western town, a circus exhibit, and a house made of glass bottles. You can take a detour off the trail south to **Sierra Farms,** corner of Cardinal Road and New Mexico 337 South, Tijeras; (505) 281-5061. It's 15 miles south of I-40, exit 175, about forty-five minutes from Albuquerque. This cheese-making company welcomes visitors year-round. Sundays from 1:00 to 4:00 P.M. is officially Children's Afternoon, when kids help feed baby goats, and families picnic on the grounds. Children are also invited to come after 2:00 P.M. on weekdays, weather permitting, although this visit is more informal than the one on Sunday. Back on the **Turquoise Trail,** restored ghost towns include **Golden,** once a gold-and-turquoise-mining town, and **Cerrillos,** often used as a setting for Western films and filled with small shops selling antiques and other interesting items. While driving the Trail, look for a roadrunner—New Mexico's state bird.

Santa Fe, extremely popular (and crowded) with tourists in July and August, is situated at an altitude of 7,000 feet. Trendy and gentrified,

Santa Fe has a great deal to offer. Start your exploring at the Santa Fe Plaza, which dates from the early 1600s. At one time this area served as a bull ring and the unloading spot for the freight wagons. Now art galleries, shops, and restaurants line the streets. There are several museums in town, but kids may prefer the colorful **Museum of International Folk Art,** about 2 miles from the Plaza, 706 Camino Lejo; (505) 827-6350. Here a fascinating assortment of objects, ranging from toys to religious images, is presented in a pleasant, kid-pleasing setting. Check out the special museum events offered as part of the Saturdays Are for the Kids Program.

If the kids are still game, right behind the museum is another of interest: **Wheelright Museum of the American Indian,** 704 Camino Lejo (505-982-4636), exhibiting works from all Native American cultures. (Kids will like the fact that the building is shaped like a Navajo hogan.) And don't forget the **Santa Fe Children's Museum,** 1050 Old Pecos Trail (505-989-8359), for those hands-on experiences that kids love.

The **Southwest Adventure Group** (800-766-5443) offers more firsthand fun for kids and parents. Their children-only tour of Indian cliff dwellings, for example, comes with permission to climb into the ancient Anasazi homes. The family raft trip on the Rio Grande features regional tales by a Native American storyteller and a taco lunch in the shade of a cottonwood tree.

Call the Santa Fe Visitors and Convention Bureau at (505) 984-6760 or (800) 777-2489 for complete tourist information.

FOR MORE INFORMATION

A number of helpful publications, including the semiannual *Official Albuquerque Visitors Guide,* can be obtained from the **Albuquerque Convention and Visitors Bureau,** 20 First Plaza N.W., Suite 601 (800-284-2282); http://www.abqcvb.org. There are two other tourist information centers: one at the airport, lower level at the bottom of the escalator, open daily from 9:30 A.M. to 5:00 P.M.; and one in Old Town, on Romero N.W., across from the church, open Monday through Saturday at 10:00 A.M. and Sunday 11:00 A.M. to 5:00 P.M. Also check out New Mexico's website at http://128.165.127.126/NewMexico.html.

Emergency Numbers

    Ambulance, fire, police: 911

    Twenty-four-hour emergency room: University Hospital,
        2211 Lomas N.E. (center of town) (505-843-2111);
        Lovelace Medical, 5400 Gibson Boulevard (southern part of
        town) (505-262-7000 or 800-877-7526); or **St. Joseph**
        Medical Center, 601 Grand N.E. (505-848-8000 or
        800-528-8888).

    Poison Control: (505) 843-2551

    Handicapped Transportation Information: (505) 764-6165

    Twenty-four-hour pharmacy: Walgreen's, with branches
        throughout town, including 5001 Montgomery Plaza N.E.
        (Northeast Heights section); (505) 881-5210

PETRIFIED FOREST NATIONAL PARK AND THE PAINTED DESERT

A visit to northeast Arizona's 147-square-mile **Petrified Forest National Park** is a fascinating trip back in time. Despite the name, don't expect to find a forest: The semiarid desert and shortgrass prairie landscape contains little vegetation. The main attraction: the remains of what was a forest some 225 million years ago and is now petrified wood, some of it small brightly colored chips, and some of it enormous prone logs. The Petrified Forest National Park presents the largest collection of petrified wood in the world.

How did it come about? Much of northeast Arizona was a floodplain 225 million years ago. Huge conifer trees that looked like Norfolk Island Pine grew along the meandering river systems. Trees that fell or were washed into the river were quickly covered with silt and mud. The water and sediment provided an oxygen-deprived environment. At the same time, volcanic eruptions jettisoned silica-containing volcanic ash into the air that settled on the land and in the water. When silica was absorbed into the swamp water, tiny quartz crystals formed into the sunken wood, thus "petrifying" it forever. The wood's colors—which include oranges, rusts, deep reds, and yellows, blended with dark white, gray, and tan—shine in the desert.

In the northern part of the park, the **Painted Desert** affords more eye-catching terrain. Here millions of years of erosion have sculpted the sandstone, shale, and clay into colorful pastel layers, many of which reveal fossils of animals that lived millions of years ago. Continuing research reveals fossils of reptiles and amphibians, the early dinosaurs of the Triassic period.

This region of Arizona also offers easy access to **Navajoland** (featured later under Day Trips) and other interesting sites.

GETTING THERE

The closest airport to the area, about 110 miles northeast, is the **Pulliam Municipal Airport,** 6200 South Pulliam Drive, Flagstaff; (520) 556-1234. Car rentals are available at the airport and downtown.

The Flagstaff bus station is **Greyhound/Trailways,** 399 South Malpias Lane (520-774-4573), with connections to the Holbrook station, 2106 Navajo Boulevard (520-524-3832).

Arrivals at the **Amtrak** station, 1 East Santa Fe Avenue, Flagstaff (520-774-8679 or 800-USA-RAIL), can connect to the Winslow station, 300 East Second Street, a little more than 30 miles west of the Park. In Winslow, car rentals are available from **Ames Ford,** 1001 East Third Street (520-289-3354); or **Cake Chevrolet,** 1200 East Second Street (520-289-4681).

By car, enter the Petrified Forest National Park's south entrance by following U.S. 180, about 25 miles from Holbrook. The north entrance is off I-40, 22 miles east of Holbrook.

GETTING AROUND

A car is a must. Driving along the windy, paved 28.6-mile road from either the north or the south is the best way to experience the park. But be sure to get out of your car to look around and explore; the park is closed December 25 and January 1. Winter storms sometimes close the road.

WHAT TO SEE AND DO

We're starting our journey from the south entrance of the **Petrified Forest National Park** (with mileages indicated), though these sights can be accessed from the north as well. There are visitor centers at both entrances.

Begin at the **Rainbow Forest Museum and Visitor Center;** (520) 524-6228. Kids marvel at the early reptile and dinosaur skeletons from the Triassic period and other exhibits that show evidence of bizarre amphibians, ferns, and creepy-crawlies that scampered here some 225 million years ago. The Conscience Wood exhibit contains stolen petrified wood returned with apologies from tourists. Note: Petrified wood is a protected treasure. Each year, the park loses thousands of pounds of it to souvenir-seeking tourists. Don't give in to temptation; you may purchase pieces that come from private lands outside the park in most of the area gift shops.

Your family should do some exploring on foot. The trails near the museum offer easy strolling. Obtain a pamphlet about the **Giant Logs Trail** from the museum. This self-guided trail, which begins behind the museum, winds in a 0.4-mile loop past huge rainbow-colored logs.

The **Long Logs Trail** starts a short distance from the museum. This easy half-mile nature trail gets you close to lots of petrified logs. The mile-long **Agate House Trail,** which branches off from the Long Logs Trail, leads to the Agate House. Ancient Native Americans built this lodging in A.D. 1150 using "bricks" made of petrified wood. Two reconstructed rooms enable you to visualize the house's original size.

From here, head back to the car and drive along the park's north-bound road. As you continue, several worthwhile turnoffs offer both scenic views and welcome chances to stretch your legs. Among them: the **Crystal Forest Trail** (mile 8.1), a paved ¾-mile trail that features some of the most beautiful wood in the park, and the **Jasper Forest** (near mile 9.9) whose overlook provides great views to the west and north. The **Agate Bridge** turnoff (mile 10.1) leads to a petrified log under which the earth has washed away, leaving a natural bridge, which has since been braced with concrete. At the **Blue Mesa** turnoff (mile 12.9, 2½ miles to parking), an overlook and a 1-mile looping interpretive trail show how the now eroding hills were formed.

Bring binoculars to examine the petroglyph-covered **Newspaper Rock** (mile 12.1). From an observation point above, observe this huge

---

Petrified Forest National Park at a Glance

- Formerly a forest, now semiarid desert and shortgrass prairie with rainbow-colored logs and pastel layers of sand

- Navajo and Hopi culture in Navajoland

- Jeep tours through Canyon de Chelly National Monument

- Meteor Crater

- Arizona Office of Tourism, (520) 542-8687

---

sandstone rock, about 30 to 40 feet tall and wide. Petroglyph markings of spirals, snakes, birds, and other figures create a magical effect.

Puerco Pueblo (mile 17.4) was inhabited between A.D. 1100 and 1200 and again around 1300 to 1400. This site, which has undergone some restoration, was once like an apartment complex of today. Approximately one hundred rooms were arranged in a hollow square enclosing a large plaza. This plaza was used by the residents for most daily activities. Several ceremonial chambers, known as kivas, are also located within this square, indicating that the plaza was used for special events, as well. Up to eighty-five people may have lived here at one time. Visitors walk along the trail for an up-close look at the petroglyphs and the pueblo's foundations.

Starting at mile 23.6, several overlooks reveal the **Painted Desert.** The desert appears to change color throughout the day, from red-clay to brown to hazy blue and gray tones. Minerals in the sandstone and clay create this dreamy, yet eerie effect. At mile 26.2, **The Painted Desert Inn** offers eight breathtaking viewpoints of the desert. The inn was built in 1924 with local materials and Native American labor, and it closed in 1962. Now it's a National Historic

A walk along the Long Logs Trail affords great opportunites to see petrified trees.
(National Park Service photo)

Landmark housing exhibits, with artifacts and historical photos, a bookstore, and an information desk.

Stop at the **Painted Desert Visitor Center** (mile 28.1); (520) 524-6228. A film shown every half hour reveals the process of petrification and the history of the park. Rangers are available to answer questions. Other conveniences: a cafeteria, gas station, and gift shop.

Shopping

Desert Oasis sells souvenirs—such as Hopi Indian kachina dolls, turquoise Navajo neckpieces, and pottery—next to the Painted Desert Visitors Center; (520) 524-3756. In Holbrook, find more specialized (and sometimes pricey) Indian boutiques, such as **McGee's Beyond Native Tradition,** 2114 Navajo Boulevard (520-525-1977), which sells Indian jewelry, rugs, and paintings; and **Nakai's Indian Cultural Trade Center,** 357 Navajo Boulevard (520-524-2329), offering a wide range of Native American pottery, rugs, artwork, and dolls. Many shops also sell petrified wood.

SPECIAL EVENTS

For more details on the following, consult the individual tourist bureaus under For More Information.

February: Flagstaff Winterfest, with snow games, Frozen Buns Fun Run, dog sled races, and a carnival.

March: Arizona Ski and Golf Classic, Flagstaff.

June: Holbrook: Old West Days Celebration, with arts and crafts and a Junior Indian Rodeo. Those who do not dress western may get "arrested." Also, Indian Dancing every weekday, Memorial Day to Labor Day. Flagstaff Route 66 Festival with fajitas and chili cook-offs.

July: Fourth of July Holbrook Fire Department Barbecue and fireworks show. The Native American Arts and Crafts Show, Holbrook, features silver work and paintings; Flagstaff Festival of the Arts.

July/August: Navajo County Southwestern Quilt Festival and Doll Show, Holbrook.

August: Navajo County Fair, Holbrook, has a rodeo, midway, and talent shows. Flagstaff Festival in the Pines displays the handiwork of more than 200 craftspeople, plus offers a kid's fun area, live entertainment, and international cuisine.

September: Navajo Nation Tribal Fair (520-871-6478 or 6436), Window Rock, the largest Indian fair in the world, featuring intertribal powwow, rodeo performance, competition, and dance, plus a talent show, midway, and food.

October: The Snow/Bowl Ski Extravaganza Fair, Flagstaff.

December: Flagstaff Symphony's Holiday Spectacular.

WHERE TO STAY

The town of Holbrook, once a popular stop for persons heading out west along Route 66, is the closest city to the **Petrified Forest National Park** in which to find accommodations.

Family choices in Holbrook include the following.

The Comfort Inn, 2602 East Navajo Boulevard; (520) 524-6131. Conveniently located at the exit of I-40, it has a restaurant, pool, and in-room movies. Another familiar name is the **Ramada Inn,** at 2408 Navajo Boulevard; (520) 524-2566.

For a welcome change from typical motels, try the **Wigwam Motel,** 811 West Hopi Drive; (520) 524-3048. Stay in small buildings shaped like wigwams, complete with brightly patterned blankets, old furniture, and air conditioning.

There are no camping facilities in the national park. **Wilderness camping,** however, is allowed with a permit from the Rainbow Forest Museum or Painted Desert Visitor Center. Campers should park vehicles at Kachina Point (near the Painted Desert Visitor Center).

Holbrook campgrounds include **Holbrook Hilltop KOA Campgrounds,** 102 Hermosa Drive (520-524-6689), which offers a pool, showers, cabins, and tent sites, and **O.K. RV Park,** 1576 Roadrunner Road (520-524-3226), with tent sites, showers, and full hookup.

For bed-and-breakfast accommodations, contact the **Arizona Association of Bed and Breakfast Inns,** 3661 North Campbell Avenue; (520) 231-6777 or 622-7167. At press time, the only nearby, family-welcoming bed and breakfasts were in Flagstaff, but call for an updated listing. In Flagstaff, consider **Inn at Four Ten,** 410 North Leroux Street; (520) 774-0088. This recently renovated 1907 building offers nine rooms and moderate rates.

WHERE TO EAT

Inside the park, the **Cougar Café** has a cafeteria-style restaurant next to the Painted Desert Visitor Center; (520) 524-3756. The **Rainbow Forest Curio** (520-524-3138) offers snacks, ice cream, and sandwiches.

In Holbrook, dining choices include Chinese noodles and stir fry at the **Sundown Restaurant,** 915 West Hopi Drive; (520) 524-3785. Try the salad bar and baked goods at the **Roadrunner Cafe,** 1501 East Navajo Boulevard; (520) 524-2787. For burgers, pizza, and chicken wings, head to **Kody's Dugout,** 405 West Hopi Drive; (520) 524-1888. The Mexican food is worth the wait at **Romo's Cafe,** 121 West Hopi Boulevard (520-524-2153), a local favorite.

DAY TRIPS

Travel northward to the Navajo Nation, which spans more than 25,000 square miles of Arizona, Utah, and New Mexico, forming the largest Native American reserve in the United States. The area contains some spectacular desert scenery and the huge Lake Powell. The Navajos, who administer this territory themselves, are generally tolerant of tourists. Visitors must respect the laws and customs of the Navajo people and not treat the Indian reservation as a tourist stop. Photography, for example, is restricted. It is completely forbidden, for instance, to snap shots of the devoutly religious Hopi Indians, whose land is within the boundaries of the Navajo nation; advance permission must be granted for other photos, including taking snapshots or videos of the homes of Navajos. This territory operates on Mountain Standard Time. Have your questions answered in advance of a visit by calling the **Hopi Cultural Center;** (520) 734-2401.

The following are several of Navajoland's highlights. Choose your day-trip opportunities from among these selections, or set aside several days to explore this area. For lodging and other information about Navajoland, contact **Navajoland Tourism Department,** P.O. Box 663, Window Rock, Arizona 86515; (520) 871-6659 or 7371.

From Holbrook, drive northeast on I-40 to U.S. 12N, to the junction of Highway 264 to **Window Rock,** which has been the capital of the Navajo nation since the 1930s. The city gets its name from the doughnut hole-shaped space in the middle of the towering sandstone rock just northeast of Junction 264 and Indian Highway 12. Visit the **Navajo Tribal Museum,** in the Arts and Crafts Enterprise building, next to the **Navajo Nation Inn.** Here you can see elaborate Navajo craftwork displays and learn about the tribe's origins. Visitors may also sit in on the **Navajo National Council Chamber** meetings when in session, or tour the circular chambers where colorful murals adorn the walls. For information call Mr. Harold Morgan; (520) 871-8417 or 6419. Also in town: **Navajo Nation Zoo and Botanical Park,** near the New Mexico state line on Highway 264 (520-871-6574), contains birds of prey, large mammals, and other animals of cultural importance to the Navajo. The area also includes an exhibition center, trails, and examples of traditional dwellings. **The Navajo Nation Inn,** 48 West Highway 264 (520-871-4108 or 800-662-6189), offers comfortable lodging and guided tours of the immediate area and of such day-trip destinations as Canyon de Chelly.

About 30 miles westward, the town of Ganado is the home of the **Hubbell Trading Post,** at the crossroads of U.S. 191 and Highway 264;

(520) 755-3254. The nation's oldest known trading post still in operation, established in 1876, is named after the man who traded coffee, sugar, and supplies with the Native Americans in exchange for their thickly woven blankets and handy trinkets. At this National Historical Monument, many Navajos still purchase groceries and other dry goods. Scheduled guided tours and self-guided tours are available.

U.S. 191 takes you north to the **Canyon de Chelly National Monument,** (520-674-5500), near the city of Chinle (60 miles west of Window Rock). You'll be amazed by the 1,000-foot sandstone walls that shoot up from the ground as you enter. The National Monument encompasses more than 100 miles of these canyons, prehistoric sites, and Navajo cliff dwellings. The Anasazi Indians lived here for years, and now the area is home to Navajos who reside between the canyon walls. The monument includes the beautiful, red sandstone, 26-mile-long **Canyon de Chelly,** adjoining the 35-mile-long **Canyon del Muerto** and **Black Rock and Moment Canyons.** The entrance to Canyon de Chelly is on Navajo Route 64, just past Chinle and a few miles east of U.S. 191. The north and south rim drives incorporate many spectacular overlooks. (Allow about two hours for each rim.) The visitor center (520-674-5500), at the intersection of the rim drives, sells guidebooks. Here you'll also find information on summer ranger-led activities that might include a daily morning canyon hike, an afternoon archaeology/nature walk, daily talks, and campfire programs.

Jeep tours are the only way to thoroughly explore the canyon's interior, which is rich in prehistoric ruins, plant life, and ancient art. From late spring to early fall, **Thunderbird Lodge,** ½ mile from the visitor center (520-674-5841), provides lodging as well as half- and full-day tours. Horseback rides give you another perspective. Two National Park Service authorized outfitters offer hourly guided horse-back tours (extended and overnight rides also available): **Justin's Horse Rental,** at the mouth of Canyon de Chelly (520-674-5678); and **Twin Trail Tours,** North Rim Drive, 9 miles north of the visitor center (520-674-8425).

The Monument Valley, northwest of Canyon de Chelly, near the Utah border and 23 miles north of Kayenta on U.S. 163 (167 miles north of Flagstaff), is the highlight of Navajoland. This landscape of towering buttes and red-tinted desert is spectacular. The red sandstone monoliths, some almost 2,000 feet high, have been the setting for numerous Westerns, such as *Stagecoach* and *Fort Apache.* The valley, which has been preserved by the Navajo, features a 14-mile drive that starts at the visitor center (801-727-3287), where you'll also find an information desk, exhibits, and crafts. For accommodations and jeep tour information, call **Goulding's Lodge;** (801) 727-3231. **Hozhoni Tours** (520-697-8198) and **Roland's Navajo Land Tours** (520-697-3524) offer tours of Monument Valley.

East of the valley, take advantage of the view at the **Four Corners Monument,** ½ mile northwest of U.S. Highway 60 junction in Tee Nos Pos. From here you can see four states: Arizona, Colorado, Utah, and New Mexico.

Glen Canyon and Lake Powell, 122 miles west of the valley along U.S. 160 and AZ 98, is a 196-mile-long man-made canyon lake complete with miles of beach, tucked-away coves, marinas, and lots of water activities. At the Glen Canyon Recreation Area, most of it in Utah, families picnic, scuba dive, water and jet ski, hike, and take a number of excursions to area attractions. Call (520) 645-2471 for more information. (See the Arches National Park and Canyonlands chapter for more of Utah's sight-seeing.)

The massive **Meteor Crater,** 35 miles east of Flagstaff and 20 miles west of Winslow, off I-40 via a 5-mile paved road (520-289-2362), is worth a stop. A plummeting meteorite formed this gigantic hole in the earth 49,000 years ago. The Apollo astronauts trained at this exceptionally well-preserved National Landmark. After taking in the view from the observation tower, visit the **Astronaut Hall of Fame** and enjoy a picnic lunch at Astronaut Park. For longer stays, try the on-site RV park; (520) 289-4002. It's complete with rest rooms and private showers, full hookups, country store, recreation room, and playground.

FOR MORE INFORMATION

Petrified Forest National Park, Office of the Superintendent, Box 2217, Petrified Forest National Park, Arizona 86028; (520) 524- 6228. **Holbrook Chamber of Commerce,** 100 East Arizona Street; (520) 524-6558. **Flagstaff Visitors' Center,** 101 West Santa Fe Avenue; (520)

774–9541 or (800) 842–7293. **Canyon de Chelly National Monument,** P.O. Box 588, Chinle, Arizona 86503; (520) 674–5436. **Arizona Office of Tourism,** 1100 West Washington Street, Phoenix, Arizona 85007; (520) 542–8687. **Navajoland Tourism,** P.O. Box 663, Window Rock, Arizona 86515; (520) 871–6659 or 7371. Check out Arizona's web site at http://arizonaweb.org/enter.html and also http://www.amdest.com/.

Emergency Numbers

Ambulance, fire, police or rescue in most areas: 911

Poison control for these areas: (800) 362–0101

In Holbrook

Fire: (520) 524–3131

Police: 524–3991

Hospital: Community General Hospital, 500 East Iowa; (520) 524–3913

Navajoland Tourism (see above) has literature containing emergency numbers, hospitals, and ranger information for different sections of Navajo territory.

In Flagstaff

Ambulance, fire, police: 911

Hospital: Flagstaff Medical Center, 1200 North Beaver Street; (520) 779–3366

In Canyon de Chelly

Ambulance: (520) 674–5464

Twenty-four-hour emergency pharmacy: Winslow Memorial Hospital, 1501 Williamson Street, Winslow; (520) 289–4691

PHOENIX

Phoenix lures you with much more than golf, although the area's green fairways and those in nearby Scottsdale offer some of the best putting and driving anywhere. But in the city, and just beyond, the legends and colors of the Sonoran Desert beckon, with Native American lore, pastel bluffs and buttes, and bold red mountains. Nearby on the Reservation, the trails fill with the green of creosote against wheat-colored rocks and with the scent of sagebrush. Phoenix is an especially charming winter getaway with mild temperatures—no record-breaking summer highs—and a palette of colors and textures to soothe a dreary winter soul.

GETTING THERE

Just minutes from downtown Phoenix is the **Sky Harbor International Airport.** More than twelve major airlines service Sky Harbor, including **Alaska Airlines** (800-426-0333), **America West** (800-247-5692), **Delta** (800-221-1212), and **Trans World Airlines** (800-221-2000).

Courier Transportation, 1602 South Second Street, Phoenix 85004 (602-232-2222), and **SuperShuttle** (800-331-3565) can take you to your hotel with twenty-four-hour service. **Yellow Cab Co.,** 156 East Mohave Street, Phoenix (602-275-8501), offers taxi service.

GETTING AROUND

A car makes getting around convenient. Because there are more than sixteen car rental agencies, shop around and be choosy. Your options include **Hertz** (800-654-2132); **Advantage Rent-A-Car,** Airport 204 South Street (602-244-0450 or 800-777-5500); **Courtesy Leasing and Rent-A-Car,** 101 North Twenty-fourth Street (800-368-5145), and

Thrifty Car Rental, 4144 East Washington Street (602-244-0311 or 800-367-2277).

The **Transit System** (602-253-5000) runs buses Monday through Saturday and operates the **DASH** shuttle Monday through Friday.

WHAT TO SEE AND DO

Museums and Attractions

Start exploring this odd-but-captivating coupling of city and desert with a trip downtown to the **Heard Museum,** 22 East Monte Vista Road; (602) 252-8848. The museum offers one of the U.S.A.'s best collections of native Southwest artifacts. In this Spanish-style building of courtyards and intimate galleries, the rooms are cool, the colors hot, and the voices and visions clear.

Don't skip the introductory, thirty-minute slide show, a blend of Native American stories set against spectacular countryside shots. In the rooms that follow, the baskets, tapestries, pottery, and jewelry weave these peoples' histories by presenting the art of their lives. Like the Arizona landscape, the textures and designs are both earth-hued subtle and suddenly dramatic. Be sure to browse the second-floor gallery of Navajo rugs, whose geometric patterns echo the earth's contours.

The **kachina gallery,** many of whose Hopi dolls were donated by Senator Barry Goldwater, exudes a special magic, and appropriately so. Kachinas, after all, represent the Native American spirit essences of all the natural things in the world. The room has an eerie quality, enhanced by a background of taped ancient chants. Some of these kachinas, brightly painted and feathered, are sprightly figures; others, intricately carved from cottonwood roots and bearing elaborate headdresses and masks, appear more formidable. By sitting on the benches and studying these figures, you sense the Native American way of seeing the world through the rhythms of ritual and nature.

Before you leave the Heard, stop at the gift shop, an interesting mélange of southwestern items from pricey eagles carved by Native American sculptors to buckles, rugs, and even chili lovers' cookbooks. The children's collection offers an especially nice assortment of native stories.

Phoenix at a Glance

- A charming town with mild temperatures year-round

- Kachina gallery at the Heard Museum

- Hot-air-balloon rides over the colorful Sonoran Desert

- Golf, race cars, basketball, baseball

- Phoenix and Valley of the Sun Convention and Visitors Bureau, (602) 252-5588

Explore the halls of the **Phoenix Art Museum,** 1625 North Central Avenue, Phoenix 85004; (602) 257-1222. The museum is the largest of its kind in the Southwest. From Renaissance to contemporary works, the museum offers hours of viewing pleasure, including paintings, photographs, sculptures, and special exhibits. At times there are Cowboy Artists Shows. Little ones enjoy the children's gallery made just for them.

The **Arizona Science Center,** 600 East Washington (602-716-2000), boasts 350 exhibits, a giant-screen theater, a planetarium, and tons of hands-on activities and presentations. Or, take a trip back in time at the **Phoenix Museum of History,** 105 North Fifth Street (602-256-0033); this museum showcases what Phoenix was like in the old days and how it's preparing for the twenty-first century.

Also worth a visit are the **Arizona Museum for Youth** (602-644-2467) and **Rawhide** (602-563-5600), an authentic 1880s Western town, complete with shoot-outs, stagecoach rides, and more.

Cool off at **Island of Big Surf** (602-947-SURF or 602-947-7873), two and a half acres of ocean in the midst of the desert; swimming, surfing, and other water and sun sports abound.

Allow some time to stroll through **Heritage Square,** Sixth and Monroe streets (602-262-5071), a three-square-block park, with restored Victorian buildings. Plan your visit on a Wednesday, and you can skip the sit-down meal and munch on fresh veggies from local farmers who sell their produce at stalls surrounding the courtyard.

Green Spaces and Zoos

Visit the **Desert Botanical Gardens,** 1201 Galvin Parkway; (602) 941-1225. At these gardens within city limits, the Sonoran flora, and desert habitats worldwide come alive with a thirty-five-acre display of 10,000 plants. All outdoors, this living museum is one of only ten accredited by the American Association of Museums. One visit here dispels the myth that deserts are boring and barren. In the two-hour self-guided walking tour, you discover not only how many shades of green color the desert, but how many shapes flourish there.

The three-acre Sonoran Desert display, heralded by a red rock and a huge acacia, presents such distinct habitats as a saguaro forest, a desert stream area, and a mesquite thicket where the air smells lightly sweet. Look quickly to catch the lizards darting from plant to plant.

You can spend hours roaming around with the lions and tigers at the **Phoenix Zoo,** 455 North Galvin Parkway, Papago Park; (602) 273-1341. With 123 acres and more than 1,200 animals, this is the largest privately owned, self-supporting zoo in the United States. Features include an African savanna, a children's zoo, and a tram ride to see Indonesian Sumatran tigers.

Special Tours

With your cacti-spotting skills honed and your desert eyes widened, venture into the Sonoran expanse. Go through it by jeep, or glide over it in a hot-air balloon. Whatever your angle, the desert boulders, sagebrush, and feathery palo-verde cast a spell as old and potent as the one that lured the prehistoric Hohokam Indians here, the tribe who first settled this river valley centuries ago.

Many companies operate jeep tours and balloon flights. **Cowboy Desert Tours** (602-941-2227 and 941-1555) claims exclusive rights to motor through the Salt River Indian Reservation, which borders the city and belongs now to the Pima/Maricopa tribes.

For a roomful of Indian tradition, tour the **Hoo-Hoogam Ki Museum,** Route 1, Box 216, Scottsdale; (602) 941-7379. Alice Santo, frequently present, is the most interesting part of this one-room display

One of the best ways to explore the many hidden wonders of the Sonoran Desert is on a guided tour on horseback. (Courtesy Phenix and Valley of the Sun/Convention and Visitors Bureau)

of Pima kitchenware and current children's drawings. Santo sits patiently demonstrating the centuries-old skills of Pima basket weaving; she is one of only six Reservation women who still weave. She painstakingly splits willow reeds with her teeth—it took her three years to master this skill—then she twines these thin threads with Devil's Claw to create the ancient black pattern of her tribe.

Next, take to the hills, with its view of **Superstition Mountain,** sacred to the Apache. On these brown hills the Cavalry chased Geronimo and Cochise. From the top of a flat rock, you can imagine the red dust flying as the spirited appaloosas bore these proud Indians in quick pursuit.

A jeep tour reveals up close this beautiful but dusty, and sometimes dastardly, desert. On the nature walk, guides demonstrate how to extract water from a fish-hook cactus, and they caution you to step around the holes that house some of the eleven species of resident rattlesnakes.

But on a desert stroll, you get eye level to a flowering cactus and feel the smooth tops of the boulders. Walk past giant saguaro 30 feet high and 400 years old, and peer at squat hedgehog cactus brightened by pink flowers, jojoba bushes, and prickly pears with pieces munched by javelina wild pigs.

Also try **Goldfield Ghost Town and Mine Tours** (602-983-0333) for a touch of Arizona history.

Hot-Air-Balloon Tours

From a hot-air balloon, the Sonoran floats for miles, taking on a fairytale softness. The desert appears like a broad bowl rimmed by the city's skyscrapers, urban sprawl, and the red mountains. This bird's-eye view is worth the 6:00 A.M. pickup and thirty-minute drive to a dirt field. Wake up in time to watch the spectacular inflation of these huge balloons, 100 feet tall and 75 feet wide. Most accommodate eight people; some smaller ones hold four.

The flight itself is magical, as the balloon leaves the earth so smoothly that you won't be aware of the moment of liftoff unless you look down. All of a sudden you're wafting airborne. The glide is as good as the view. And at 2,000–3,000 feet the desert unfolds delicately, and quietly, becoming a smooth stretch of green, cacti-dotted earth. Below catch sight of jackrabbits hopping for shelter from the balloon's dark shadow.

The trip, expensive at about $175 per person for an hour's flight, is definitely worth the cost when taken with a reputable company. **Unicorn Balloon Company,** 15001 North Seventy-fourth Street, Scottsdale Airport, Scottsdale (602-991-3666), is just one of Phoenix's reputable balloon companies. Sunrise and afternoon flights are available during winter. Sunrise flights are offered in fall and spring. Check the local tourist board and the hotel's concierge for other recommendations. And be wise. Although some operators take two-year-olds aloft, a wicker basket hanging in the sky is no place to hold a squirming kid. Winds change quickly, and balloons land with a bounce and a thud. Board only those children who are unafraid of heights and who, when standing, can see clearly over the basket's rim. At the journey's end, enjoy the traditional champagne toast.

Sports and Recreation

Persons who love race cars will want to find out what's going on at the **Phoenix International Raceway,** 1313 North Second Street, #1300; (602) 252-3833.

In Phoenix sports fans catch up with the **California Angels** on their **Official Spring Training Tour,** 2068 First Street, Livermore, California 94550; (510) 447-1122. Choose a package with lodging, exclusive functions with team members and coaching staff, and preferred game tickets. **The Oakland A's** offer a similar training tour, 2068 First Street, Livermore, California 94550; (510) 373-2432. In season, don't miss seeing the **Arizona Cardinals,** P.O. Box 888; (602) 379-0101. Basketball fans head to the America West Arena, One Phoenix Suns Plaza, 201 East Jefferson Street (602-379-7900), to see the NBA team and pride of the town, the **Phoenix Suns.** Pick up tickets at the box office or at **Select Ticket Service,** 540 West McDowell Road; (602) 254-3300. Watch for the **Arizona Diamondbacks,** who will make their Major League baseball debut in 1998.

Golf lovers have scores of immaculate greens and fairways from which to choose. **Cavecreek,** 15202 North Nineteenth Avenue (602-866-8076), **Encanto,** 2705 North Fifteenth Avenue (602-253-3963), and **Papago,** 5595 East Moreland Street (602-275-8428) are some of the area's public courses. A number of private clubs and hotels offer golf, including **Arizona Biltmore Country Club,** Twenty-fourth Street and Missouri Avenue (602-955-6600); **Gold Canyon Gold Resort** (602-982-9090); **Arizona Golf Resort** in Mesa (602-832-3202 or 800-528-8282); **Marriott's Camelback Inn Resort, Golf Club and Spa,** 5402 Lincoln Drive, Scottsdale (602-948-1700), which has a championship course; and the **Hyatt Regency Ranch Scottsdale,** 7500 Doubletree Ranch Road, Scottsdale (602-991-3388 and 800-233-1234).

Performing Arts and Entertainment

In season, venture down to **Patriots Square Park,** Washington and Central avenues, where you can picnic and enjoy the performances on the outdoor stage.

The **Arizona Theater Company** (602-256-6899), **Arizona Opera** (602-226-7464), **Ballet Arizona,** and the **Actors Theater of Phoenix** all make their home at the **Herberger Theater Center** (602-381-0184).

Undergoing renovation, the 1929 **Orpheum Theatre,** near city hall in downtown Phoenix, was once considered one of the West's most luxurious theaters. When completely renovated, this 1,450-seat playhouse will stage performing arts, film festivals, and children's theater. The **Sundome Center for the Performing Arts,** R.H. Johnson Boulevard, Sun City West (602-584-3118), seats 7,169, making it the largest single-level theater in the United States. Celebrities and various performing art groups regularly take to the stage here. At the **Phoenix Civic Plaza Convention Center and Symphony Hall,** 225 East Adams Street (800-AT-CIVIC), the **Phoenix Symphony Orchestra** plays, and a variety of other events take place. Call for a schedule.

Need more excitement after dark? **America's Original Sports Bar/Phoenix Live!,** 455 North Third Street, offers 40,000 square feet of games. Another Phoenix area winner for after-five entertainment, **The Improvisation,** 930 East University Drive, Tempe (602-921-9877), offers dinner and a comedy revue. Or, the 8-block **Arizona Center** houses more than sixty restaurants, shops, nightclubs, and more.

SPECIAL EVENTS

January: Phoenix Open Golf Tournament (602-870-0163), usually hosted by the Tournament Players Club golf course. Parada del Sol Rodeo; (602) 990-3179.

April: Photo Extravaganza—Carefree/Cave Creek; (602) 488-3381. Capture the blossoms and wildflowers of the desert's spring.

May: Cinco De Mayo Festival (602-262-5025), which celebrates the Mexican victory over French troops in 1862, is a lively and colorful fiesta.

September/October: Jazz on the Rocks (602-282-1985) in Sedona, about two hours from Phoenix, draws crowds from across the Southwest to hear their favorite musicians play. The Arizona State Fair (602-252-6771), one of the most successful in the country, features livestock shows, national performers, games, rides, and more.

November: At the Hot Air Balloon Race and Thunderbird Balloon Classic (602-978-7208), world competitors compete for prizes.

December: The Tempe Festival of the Arts (602-967-4877) brings local and traveling artists and their work to the streets of Tempe.

WHERE TO STAY

The Phoenix/Scottsdale area has a variety of accommodations. Here are some good choices.

The **Hyatt Regency Scottsdale,** 7500 Doubletree Ranch Road, Scottsdale, (602) 991-3388, or for reservations, (800) 233-1234. The Hyatt is a desert oasis with ten swimming pools and championship golf, and it also hosts a children's program on weekends year-round for three- to twelve-year-olds. Program operates Friday 5:00 P.M. to 9:00 P.M., Saturday 9:00 A.M. to 9:00 P.M., and Sunday 9:00 A.M. to 5:00 P.M., and daily in summer and on holidays. Various package plans are available. Regency club rooms come with complimentary breakfast, afternoon snacks, cocktails and hors d'oeuvres, and one hour of free tennis.

The deluxe **Scottsdale Princess,** 7575 East Princess Drive, Scottsdale (602-585-4848 or 800-223-1818), offers weekly Super Team Sports Camps for locals and guests ages five and older Monday through Friday from June to mid-August. Kids play tennis, enjoy pool games, and do arts and crafts. On major holidays, the Princess Kids Klub offers activities for ages five to twelve from 9:00 A.M. to 12:30 P.M. and from 5:30 P.M. to 8:30 P.M.

Red Lion's La Posada Resort, Scottsdale (800-547-8010), rests under the shadow of Camelback Mountain and offers a pool with cascading waterfalls.

The Boulders, P.O. Box 2090, Carefree, Arizona 85377; (800) 553-1717. On 1,300 acres in the Sonoran foothills at Carefree, outside Phoenix, this spacious resort offers desert ambience, fine dining, and a top-rated golf course. All rates include modified American plan. Various packages are available.

The Pointe has two locations in the Phoenix area. Tapatio Cliffs, 11111 North Seventh Street, Phoenix 85020 (602-866-7500); South Mountain, 7777 South Pointe Parkway, Phoenix 85044. For both locations, call (800) 528-0428. Accommodations at these pleasant hotels with a Spanish influence are suites clustered around interior courtyards. Various rates and packages.

The newly renovated all-suite **Pointe Hilton Resort at Squaw Peak,** 7500 North Dreamy Draw Drive (602-977-7777 or 800- 934-1000), comes with a complex of kid-pleasing pools and a year-round children's program for ages four to twelve from 9:00 A.M. to 5:00 P.M.

The **Holiday Inn SunSpree Resort Scottsdale,** 7601 East Indian Bend Road (800–HOLIDAY) offers affordable prices and a children's program.

At press time the **Ritz-Carlton Phoenix,** 2401 East Camelback (602-468-0700 or 800-241-3333), was in the process of extending its Ritz Kids program and standardizing family-friendly amenities at all Ritz hotels. Call for the latest information.

The 1929 classic, **The Arizona Biltmore,** is at Twenty-fourth Street at Missouri; (602) 955-6606 or (800) 228-3000. Partially built under the direction of Frank Lloyd Wright, the hotel is situated on thirty-nine acres and has two PGA golf courses and eight tennis courts. The Kids Kabana, a supervised play program, is offered year-round, daily from 8:00 A.M. to 6:00 P.M. for ages four to twelve. Special programs are added at holidays and in the summer.

In downtown Phoenix, the **Phoenix Crowne Plaza** (602-257-1625) offers moderate rates at a location convenient to the American West Arena, the convention center, and the Algora Center.

Just minutes outside the city is **The Wigwam,** Litchfield Park, Arizona 85340; (800) 327-0396. They provide you with privacy and comfort in guest casitas hidden among an orange-and-palm-tree oasis. A true Southwest luxury resort, The Wigwam has tennis courts, a pool, a health club, horseback riding, and seasonal kids' programs.

WHERE TO EAT

Try **The Good Egg,** 2957 West Bell Road, Phoenix 85023 (602-993-2797), and 906 East Camelback Road, Phoenix 85014 (602-274-5393). They serve up fresh breakfast and lunches straight off the griddle. Omelets and frittatas are some of their specialties. For dinner, try the barbecue landmark of Arizona, **Bill Johnson's Big Apple,** 3757 East Van Buren Street, Phoenix 85008 (602-277-6291), or 3101 West Indian School Road, Phoenix 85017 (602-863-7921). More than three decades of experience make this restaurant an oldie but goody. Authentic Mexican cuisine begins at **Garcia's Mexican Restaurants,** 5509 North Seventh Street at Missouri Avenue, Phoenix 85014

(602-274-1176), or 4420 East Camelback Road, Phoenix 85018 (602-952-8031). For thirty years this has been a top pick in Phoenix for south-of-the-border dishes and atmosphere at reasonable prices. **The Compass Restaurant,** 122 North Second Street, Phoenix 85004 (602-252-1234), offers a menu of southwestern dishes with a breathtaking view of the Valley of the Sun. For a special dinner before you go, visit **Christopher's Bistro,** 2398 East Camelback Road, Phoenix 85016; (602) 957-3214. Voted Best New Chef by *Food and Wine* magazine, Christopher Gross will lure you in with exciting American specialties with a French flair.

DAY TRIPS

For more desert beyond Phoenix, don't miss **Sedona,** 120 miles north of Phoenix on I-17 and Route 179. It is an easy day trip to a dramatically different landscape of red rock mountain ranges. But the road to Sedona, about two hours from Phoenix, is part of the fun.

At 4,000 feet, as you pass **Prescott National Forest,** brackish-colored bushes cover the ground, and yellow "prairie grass" grows in patches. Nearby, make a quick stop at **Montezuma Castle National Monument,** I-17 north to exit 289 (about 25 miles south of Sedona). These well-preserved, four-tiered, limestone cliff dwellings, started in the twelfth century, offer insight into the Hohokam life by the river.

Back on the road, the canyons and cliffs on the Coconino National Forest come into view, as do the buttes surrounding Sedona. Rising in fantastical shapes, separated by stretches of pine, piñon, and sycamore trees, these singular rock formations amaze, and their hues dazzle. Salmon, wheat, rust, and red, these towering mesas and buttes flash with brash streaks of pinks, purples, and grays. This is sheer delight.

Sedona, a town in the heart of Arizona's Red Rock country, is a funky match of old-time western stores, Native American trading posts —try Gordon Wheeler's for some of the more authentic Native American jewelry—art galleries, and spectacular red rock mountains for hiking (see Sedona chapter).

Venture further to experience one of the great natural wonders, the **Grand Canyon,** about five hours drive from Phoenix. The range of colors along the canyon walls, carved into the earth by the Colorado River, offers amazing views year-round. Take a hike through the mighty basin, ride down on the back of a mule, or drive the scenic rim. Take Interstate 17 north to Flagstaff, then Route 180 northwest to the Canyon.

Play cowboy on a six-day backpacking and horseback riding tour of the Superstition Mountains. **American Wilderness Experience,** P.O. Box 1486, Boulder, Colorado 80306 (800-444-0099), offers this trip for ages eighteen and older. Visit cliff dwellings, look for coyote, deer, and rattlesnakes, and camp in tents under the stars.

Take a tour of **Biosphere 2** (520-825-6200), a two-hour drive south. The thirty-one-and-a-half-acre, glass-enclosed environment supports 3,800 species of plants and animals.

FOR MORE INFORMATION

Phoenix and Valley of the Sun Convention and Visitors Bureau, One Arizona Center, 400 East Van Buren Street, Suite 600, Phoenix 85004-2290; (602) 252-5588. Website http://www.ci.phoenix.az.us

Flight Guides West, Inc., 1635 East Myrtle Avenue, Suite 300, Phoenix 85020; (602) 943-4493 for monthly flight guide and airline schedule information.

A Taste of Phoenix, 3370 North Hayden Road, Suite 123-289, Scottsdale 85251; (602) 998-5810 for dining guide.

The Arizona Office of Tourism (800-842-8257), the **Visitor Hotline** (602-252-5588), and **Arizona State Parks** (602-542-4174) all offer visitor information.

Emergency Numbers

  Ambulance, fire, police: 911
  Phoenix Fire Department: (602) 253-1191
  Air Evac Medical Air Transportation: 2630 Sky Harbor
    Boulevard, Phoenix 85034; (502) 244-9327
  Phoenix Police Department: (602) 262-7626
  Poison Control: (602) 253-3334
  Hospitals: St. Joseph's Hospital and Medical Center,
    350 Thomas Road, Phoenix 85013; (602) 285-3000.
    Phoenix Memorial Hospital, 1201 South Seventh Avenue,
    Phoenix 85007; (602) 258-5111
  Doctor Referral: (602) 230-CARE

SEDONA AND OAK CREEK CANYON

Sedona, and the adjacent Oak Creek Canyon area, is a magical landscape of pastel painted bluffs, buttes, and boldly shaped geological formations. Often referred to as "red rock country" because of these mountainous forms, Sedona lures tourists with its beauty, and attracts "New Age" devotees with its "power spots," or vortices where the electrical and magnetic fields emit a special energy often described by devotees as peaceful and calming. These places often coincide with sites sacred to Native Americans.

Native Americans have inhabited Sedona and the surrounding region for centuries. The Anasazi—a Navajo word meaning "the ancient ones"—came here to hunt and fish. You can still visit the remnants of their cliff dwellings and see their pictographs carved into the stone. Later other settlers grew crops such as corn, beans, and squash. In 1876 the first white settlers arrived. Shortly thereafter T.C. Schnebly moved into the area—with only five families as his neighbors. He petitioned the U.S. government for a post office, hoping to establish Schnebly Station or Oak Creek Crossing. The postmaster deemed both names too long for cancellation stamps. However, the shorter Sedona—the name of Schnebly's wife—was accepted. In the 1950s Surrealist painter Max Ernst, perhaps drawn by the area's geographically severe shapes and texture, moved to Sedona. Other artists followed and, over the years, Sedona developed into a recognized artist colony.

Oak Creek Canyon refers to route 89A, a scenic stretch of road that runs between Sedona and Flagstaff.

GETTING THERE

Most visitors arrive in Sedona by car. The city is 120 miles north of Phoenix and 30 south of Flagstaff. Although Sedona has a small airport, 1225 Airport Road; (520) 282-1699, most visitors fly into Phoenix and rent a car in Phoenix or take a shuttle to Sedona. Ground transportation is provided from Phoenix Sky Harbor International airport. A handful of car rental companies operate in Sedona. These include Budget Rent-a-Car (520) 282-4602, and Sedona Car Rentals (520) 282-2227 or (800) 879-5337 are represented in the city.

Getting Around

If you didn't get to Sedona via driving, or if you haven't rented a car, you're not out of luck. The Sedona Trolley (520-282-5400 or 520-282-6826) offers two 50-minute tours of Sedona. Sites include uptown, Tlaquepaque, Gallery Row, Chapel of the Holy Cross, and Boynton Canyon. Each tour costs $6, both are $9. Many tour operators provide excursions to the major regional attractions (see TOURS).

WHAT TO SEE AND DO

The Outdoors—Canyons, Red Rock Mountains, State Parks

Since it's the landscape that lures tourists, plan to spend a good deal of your time in Sedona outdoors—but that doesn't need to mean strenuous hikes, although there are plenty of these. If you have young children, and even if you don't, a drive along Highway 89A and Highway 179 takes you by many of Sedona's well-known mountain beauties. You and your kids will be amazed at what's outside your car window. Seemingly dreamlike, the red rocks streaked with pinks, cream, and purple rise up from the high mountain desert.

From various points on 89A among the formations you see in the distance are Cockscomb, a series of pointed pinnacles followed by a flat topped rock much like a rooster's cockscomb; Chimney Rock, a tall tower, much like a chimney, protruding from a mound; and Coffee Pot Rock whose shape with a cylindrical tower on one side and a short spout-like horizontal ridge suggests (you guessed it) a coffee pot. From Highway 179 you see one of the most photographed of all of Sedona's

---

Sedona and Oak Creek Canyon at a Glance

- Magical landscape of pastel painted bluffs, buttes, and boldly shaped geological formations

- Hiking and jeep tours in the alluring backcountry

- 12th-century cliff dwellings at Montezuma Castle National Monument

- Shopping for artists', craftsmen's, and Native American wares

- Sedona-Oak Creek Chamber of Commerce, (520) 282-7722

---

formations, Cathedral Rock, noted for its tall bluffs and spires flanked by stalwart masses of rock, Bell Rock with its rounded sides like a school bell, and Snoopy Rock, a series of pinnacles and humps that, with imagination somewhat resembles Charles Schultz's beloved beagle.

Sedona boasts two state parks, Slide Rock and Red Rock. **Slide Rock State Park** is 5½ miles north of Sedona on Highway 89A; (520) 282-3034. Along with its steep red rock canyon walls, this 55-acre park is known for its natural water play. The erosion has created a series of smooth rocks surrounded by a creek. Locals call this run a "water slide" because with an inner tube, you can float along the creek. There's more watery fun at the ole' swimming hole, Grasshopper Point, 2.5 miles north of Sedona from the Enchantment Resort. From Memorial Day to Labor Day try your luck fishing for German brown trout.

Red Rock State Park, Lower Red Rock Loop Road, 4 miles south of Highway 89A; (520) 282-6907. This 286-acre park was set aside to preserve the riparian habitat along Oak Creek. More than 160 species of birds, including bald eagles and black hawks nest within the park's boundaries. The Miller Visitor Center educates kids and others about the region's wildlife. Young children like duck, raccoon, fox, and coyote footprints in the center's walkway. Check the schedule for weekly guided nature walks; these include bird watching and moonlit strolls to appreciate the stars. An easy walk is the .4 mile-loop from the Visitor Center to Oak Creek. Longer, but not difficult, is the 1.6-mile roundtrip hike to House of Apache Fire, an adobe-style former vacation home named after the fires lit by the Yavapai-Apache Native Americans who helped build the house.

Hiking

There are dozens of trails in the region aside from those at Slide Rock and Red Rock State parks. Many come to hike and meditate in **Boynton Canyon,** Boynton Pass Road, known for its beauty and its renown as a primary energy spot or power center. Legend has it that this is also the site of Kachina Woman, revered by Native Americans as the Mother of the Earth.

The **West Fork of Oak Creek** also is popular with hikers. **Trail 108** crosses the tributary several times, is easily traversed, and well-marked. **Trail 117** loops the canyon's rim, affording sweeping views. Off Hwy. 89A is the trailhead for **Trail 122,** also known as the **Long Canyon Trail.** Follow the old jeep road through a green gate. Scribbled in the registration book there is a comment, "About one hour ahead, climb up on the rocks to the left of the trail for a great view!" Aptly named, this hike, best suited for hearty preteens and teens, requires uphill climbs and takes at least three hours round-trip.

Another popular hiking area is **Wilson Canyon.** Trails are accessible from the Wilson Mountain National Recreation Area parking lot. Experienced hikers only should attempt Wilson Mountain Trail 10, a 7,000-foot climb to the peak while Wilson Canyon Trail 49 provides an easier, mostly level hike through the canyon.

Tours

A jeep tour not only gives your children a sense of being explorers on a western safari, but also provides an easy way to get into and enjoy the back country. We especially liked our jeep tour to **Tuzigoot National Monument,** (520) 634-5564, with **Pink Jeep Tours,** (520) 282-5000, or (800) 8-SEDONA. Although the jeeps are no longer their trademark pink, the tours are every bit as good as before with knowledgeable guides. Our leader, Clay, told us how the early inhabitants used the landscape as their "bible," seeing legends and stories in the rocks. On the way to the cliff dwellings, we drove along dirt roads where the mountain foothills were laced with juniper trees, Arizona cypress, and scrub oak. We paused to find fossils in the white-bleached sponge coral, a testament to this area's undersea status eons ago. Located west of Sedona between Clarkdale and Cottonwood, Tuzigoot National Monument encompasses the remains of a 13th-century, cliffside village built by the Sinagua Indians. On the short walk to the ruins from the parking area, we found pictographs of flute players and animals created on the mountain walls thousands of years ago by ancient artists. Some of the dwelling's walls and rooms that once housed as many as 77 rooms still stand. In these rocky, sheltered homes of long ago Native Americans, you can imagine the women weaving, the men lugging stones, and the children playing. When you're here be sure just to listen: the silence is magical, especially what the Native Americans call the "footsteps of the wind," the sound the breezes make as they dance through the openings in the rock face.

Many other companies offer this tour and additional ones. Tour offerings and itineraries change frequently. Always call ahead for descriptions, reservations, and to be sure your tour is suitable for your age children. **Sedona Red Rock Jeep Tours,** 270 N. Highway 89-A; (520) 282-0254 or (800) 848-7728, offers a variety of one-two-hour trips as well as combination helicopter and horseback rides. **Sedona Adventures,** P.O. Box 1476; (520) 282-3500 or (800) 888-9494 has scenic, 2½-hour jeep tours to Red Rock, Bear Wallow Canyon, and other sites.

Great Ventures Tours, Box 1330; (520) 282-4451 or (800) 578-2643, has a variety of tours including train rides, white-water rafting, helicopter tours, and historic trips. Their Verde River Train Special is a 40-mile excursion that sweeps through red rock canyons, a ghost town, and Indian ruins and includes a chuckwagon dinner. This outfitter tends to either serve groups or to create personalized and often pricey but exciting custom outings for families. **El Rojo Grande Ranch & Stables,** Highway 89A; (520-282-1898 or 800-36-COW-BOY), operates stagecoach rides.

Kids will love a trip down Slide Rock.
(Courtesy Sedona/Oak Creek Canyon Chamber of Commerce)

Some companies focus on the vortices. Companies that offer tours to these power centers include **Sacred Earth Tours,** (520) 282-6826; (800) 848-7728; and **Sedona Nature Excursions,** (520) 282-6735.

Verde Canyon Railroad, 300 N. Broadway, Clarksdale; (800-293-7245), offers day trips that sweep through the Sycamore Wilderness Area and North Verde River Canyon, one of Arizona's most scenic canyons. The train's panoramic windows and open-air viewing cars provide views of the wildlife, towering cliffs, and Sinagua Indian ruins.

Shopping

Tlaquepaque, P.O. Box 1868; (602) 282-4838, an Indian name meaning "the best of everything," is also the name of a shopping complex modeled in Spanish colonial architecture after a Mexican village. Forty specialty shops and restaurants are housed in these shaded courtyards. Several galleries display and sell artists' and craftsmen's wares. Mediums include porcelain, leather, pewter, copper, and jewelry made with semi-precious stones and beads. It's a nice place for browsing even if it is a bit "hokey" in design.

"Uptown Sedona," on Highway 89A, is one of the area's major retail centers. Stores carry Indian arts, crafts and jewelry, Western wear and clothing. For Native American goods, visit **Garlands Navajo Rugs,** Highway 179; (520) 282-4070. Dan Garland buys directly from Navajo weavers and offers a large selection of Navajo rugs as well as kachina dolls, pottery, baskets, and sand paintings. **Oak Creek Factory Outlets,** Highway 179; (520-284-2150), offers discounts on famous name merchandise such as Anne Klein, Geoffrey Beane, Jones New York, Corning Revere, and other brands.

Arts and Entertainment

The Sedona Chamber Music Society, (520) 204-2415, presents concerts year-round at the Church of the Red Rocks and at St. John Vianney Church. **Sedona Arts Center,** N. Highway 89A; (520) 282-3809, has ongoing exhibits of oils, watercolors, sculpture, ceramics, and weaving. The Center's Community Theater group and Swiftwind Productions stage performing arts shows. Southwest Theater Company offers summer performances "under the stars" at Tlaquepaque.

SPECIAL EVENTS

March: Sedona International Film Festival.
May: Hopi Show—arts, crafts, food, dancers.
September: Sedona Jazz on the Rocks.
October: Sculpture Walk; Sedona Arts Festival.
November: Red Rock Fantasy of Lights.
December: Festival of Lights at Tlaquepaque.

WHERE TO STAY

With Four-Stars and Four-Diamonds, the **Enchantment Resort,** 525 Boynton Canyon Road; (520-282-2900 or 800-826-4180), is northern Arizona's highest rated destination resort. Surrounded by the red rock walls of Boynton Canyon, the resort's location is magical.

Room sizes range from studios to two- and three-bedroom adobe style "casitas" complete with kitchenette, living area with fireplace, and separate bedroom. The rooms are generously sized and a one-bedroom casita easily can accommodate a family of four. The resort sports a 12-court tennis center, four swimming pools, outdoor whirlpools, spa and fitness center, and easy access to Sedona's shopping and restaurants.

Two other things make this resort special: Camp Coyote, the resort's comprehensive children's program for ages four to 12, and Enchantment's commitment to educating guests (children included) about the region's Native American history. At Camp Coyote, kids learn about the region through nature walks, making crafts, and storytelling. The facility, located a short drive from the resort entrance (something of an inconvenience), is a roomy and well-stocked adobe villa. Full-, half-day, and evening programs are available as are babysitters for children younger than four. It's wise to book sitters ahead of time and to always make sure that these people meet your expectations.

The resort's cultural ambassador is Uqualla, a full-blooded Havasupai Indian, a member of the tribe that lives along the river at the base of the Grand Canyon. Uqualla, who has a winsome and sprightly demeanor and a powerful voice, takes guests on complimentary walks around the property, pointing out Native American sites and talking about legends and beliefs. He is readily available, sitting outside the entrance or in the lobby, and likes to chat with guests, especially children. Several evenings a week he dresses in full regalia, and recounts Native American stories.

Los Abrigados, 160 Portal Lane; (520) 282-1777 or (800) 521-3131, is in uptown Sedona on a main street. The units, mostly occupied by guests who are part of a timeshare arrangement, are small, plainly furnished, and serviceable with kitchenettes, and a sitting/dining area and separate bedroom. The property has a swimming pool and tennis courts.

Poco Diablo Resort, 1752 S. Hwy. 179; (520-282-7333 or 800-528-4275), features a par 3, 9-hole golf course, tennis courts, two pools, and three spas. Rooms offer views of Red Rock. There are also a number of chain hotels and motels. Best Western has four locations; **Best Western Arroyo Roble Hotel** (520-282-4001), **Best Western Cliff Castle Lodge** (520-567-6611 or 800-524-6343), **Best Western Cottonwood Inn** (520-634-5575 or 800-350-0025), and **Best Western Inn of Sedona** (520-282-3072 or 800-292-6344).

Five RV and camping areas also exist. **Hawkeye Red Rock RV Park** (520- 282-2222) offers 45 sites for tent camping and a swimming pool. **Lo Lo Mai Springs Camping Resort** (520-634-4700) provides 60 sites for camper or trailer parking as well as tent camping. They also feature a Jacuzzi and pool.

WHERE TO EAT

Joey Bistro, 160 Portal Lane; (520-204-JOEY), an Italian restaurant, is informal and offers good-sized portions of pasta, veal, and other Italian dishes. Preteens and teens keep busy identifying the blown-up photographs of famous "Joeys" (Joey Heatherton, Joe Kennedy, G.I. Joe, etc.). The next room in this establishment is called the **Steaks and Sticks Billiard Room,** which is, as the title suggests, a steak restaurant where after dinner you can enjoy a game of billiards. 'Tweens and teens like this also.

The Cowboy Club, 241 N. Hwy. 89A; (520-282-4200), serves a range of Southwestern classics such as chicken Adobe, pan-seared venison, and campfire barbecue along with hamburgers. **Rainbows End,** 3235 W. Hwy. 89A; (520-282-1593), is another family restaurant. Since 1946 this steakhouse has served chicken, ribs, and steaks in a western atmosphere. For lunches or simply lighter fare, **Wendeli's Delicatessen,** 276 N. Hwy. 89A; (520-282-7313), is open from 10 A.M. to 6 P.M. daily for delivery and take-out.

DAY TRIPS

About a two-hour drive away (110 miles) is the **Grand Canyon's South Rim**. If you haven't seen this wonder, take time to visit, even if it's only briefly. See the chapter "Grand Canyon." Five miles from the park's entrance on US 180 is **Tusayan,** a town featuring an IMAX theater that shows "Grand Canyon—The Hidden Secrets."

There are numerous attractions in **Flagstaff,** about 25 miles north of Sedona on Highway 89A. (See the "Grand Canyon" chapter). At 4,100 feet across and 570 feet deep, **Meteor Crater** is the country's largest crater. The 49,000-year-old crater is one-half hour east of Flagstaff on I-40.

Thirty-five miles south of Sedona is **Montezuma Castle National**

Monument, Highway I-17; (520-567-3322). These 12th century "buildings" are some of the oldest and best preserved cliff dwellings in the southwest. One 20-room complex was built by the Sinaguan Indians into a cliff 100 feet above the valley. A second six-story building of 45 rooms was also carved into the cliff's base, but has not aged as well.

Jerome, 37 miles west of Sedona; (520-634-2900), is Arizona's largest ghost town. Once a thriving copper mining town with 15,000 residents, the town rallied in boom years and survived the fluctuating copper market. A 1918 fire swept through the 88 miles of underground tunnels causing residents to begin open pit mining. This literally changed the geography of the area. In addition to the eye-sore holes it created, dynamite blasts rattled the landscape loosening buildings from their foundations. The town's jail slid 225 feet from its original site. Today the town is a State Historic Park. Guides and placards recount the historical importance of this town set atop Cleopatra Hill.

FOR MORE INFORMATION

Sedona-Oak Creek Chamber of Commerce, P.O. Box 478, Forest Road and Hwy. 89A; (520) 282-7722. Or check out their Web site at http://www.arizonaguide.com/sedona.

Sedona Central Reservations, (520-282-1518 or 800-445-4128).

Arizona Central Reservations, (520-282-1982).

Emergency

For police, fire, and medical assistance use 911.

Sedona Police, (520) 282-3100.

Sedona Fire, (520) 282-6800.

Sedona Ranger Station, (520) 282-4119.

Coconino County Sheriff, (800) 338-7888.

Sedona Medical Center, 3700 W. Highway 89A, Sedona; (520) 204-3000.

Pay Less Drug Store, 2350 W. Hwy. 89A; (520-282-9734).

GRAND CANYON NATIONAL PARK

Indescribable beauty, awesome vistas, fascinating natural and cultural history: The Grand Canyon must be seen to be believed. Created by the uplifting of the Colorado Plateau and the erosion caused by the Colorado River, the canyon stretches 277 miles across northern Arizona and is approximately a mile deep. Most visitors experience the canyon by traveling along its rim, stopping to take in its majesty via different vantage points. The South Rim, which includes Grand Canyon Village and Desert View, receives 90 percent of park visitors and is open year-round. The North Rim, a thousand feet higher in elevation, receives far fewer visitors and closes for winter because of heavy snows. The inner canyon, which can be reached only on foot, by mule, or via the Colorado River, is a favorite with hikers and backpackers.

Yes, your children will find the canyon "awesome"—but first a warning. Be careful near the edge of the canyon and on the trails. Guardrails are intermittent, and accidents, unfortunately, happen. This is one area where it's imperative to keep small children firmly in hand; even where there are barriers, unattended kids have been known to climb over them. Some canyon rims, more than 7,000 feet above sea level, can cause dizziness and shortness of breath. Also, because the North Rim is more than a hundred miles from a fully staffed hospital, we don't recommend it for families (it's briefly described later). Enjoy the scenery, but remember to hold onto small children, and be sure the older ones know the rules.

GETTING THERE

The best connections to the Grand Canyon are through **Sky Harbor International Airport,** Phoenix; (602) 273-3300. Connecting flights leave from here, from Flagstaff's **Pulliam Airport** (520-774-1422), and from Las Vegas's **McCarran International** (702-739-5743) to **Grand Canyon Airport** (520-638-2446) on the South Rim. Free van transportation is available to lodges in Tusayan, 7 miles south of the park and, for a fee, to Grand Canyon Village, on the South Rim, via **Tusayan/Grand Canyon Shuttle;** (520) 638-2475. Taxi service is also available. Those making the 200-mile trip to the North Rim can take a **Trans Canyon Shuttle** (520-638-2820) in season, or rent a car at the Grand Canyon Airport.

Greyhound/Trailways services Flagstaff and Williams, Arizona. **NavaHopi Tours** (602-774-5003 or 800-892-8687) handles scheduled bus connections from Flagstaff (about 80 miles south) and Williams (about 58 miles west) to Grand Canyon Village and Tusayan.

Amtrak (800-USA-RAIL) serves Flagstaff and, from April through October, runs a bus from Flagstaff to Williams. At Williams you may take the historic **Grand Canyon Railway** (602-635-4000 or 800-THE-TRAIN), a two-and-three-quarter-hour trip to the South Rim on a turn-of-the-century steam train. Enjoy on-board entertainment and complimentary snacks. After exploring the canyon, reboard the train at 3:15 P.M. for the ride back to Williams. The 1908 **Williams Depot,** listed with the National Register of Historic Places, is itself an attraction.

By car from Flagstaff's I-40, the best approach to the South Rim is via U.S. 180 (about 80 miles) or try the more scenic Route 64 (107 miles). From I-40 in the west, take Route 64 from Williams. For the North Rim from Flagstaff, take U.S. 89 to Bitter Springs, then U.S. 89A to Route 67, then south to the North Rim, a 210-mile drive.

GETTING AROUND

If you're staying at Grand Canyon Village, a car is a convenience but not a necessity because the village is eminently walkable. There are free shuttles from late May to late September along the South Rim and West Rim Drive. You can also get taxis and bus tours at the Village, as well as in Tusayan and at the North Rim. A car, however, will allow you to drive the scenic East Rim.

You can reach the inner canyon, which includes Phantom Ranch, only

Grand Canyon National Park at a Glance

- Awesome vistas, fascinating natural and cultural history

- Sunrise at Hopi Point and West Rim Drive; sunset at Yaki Point and East Rim Drive

- Prehistoric Pueblo Indian ruins

- Hiking and mule rides (for the hearty) to the inner canyon

- Grand Canyon National Park, (520) 638–7888

by foot, mule, or via the Colorado River from April to October on trips that range from three to twenty-two days. It's advisable to make river reservations one year in advance. Minimum age requirements vary. For a complete listing of bus, horseback, and river tour operators, check the Grand Canyon Chamber of Commerce *Visitor's Guide* (see For More Information).

Transportation Desks providing information on wheelchair accessible vehicles, taxis, coaches, tours, mule and horseback rides, Phantom Ranch facilities, and air tours are located at lodge lobbies.

If you drive your own car, a number of scenic overlooks afford breathtaking views. The East Rim Drive (Highway 64), open to vehicles year-round, follows the canyon rim for 26 miles east of Grand Canyon Village to Desert View (the park's east entrance). The West Rim Drive, closed to private vehicles from late May through September, follows the rim for 8 miles west from Grand Canyon Village to Hermits Rest.

WHAT TO SEE AND DO

The South Rim

If you come to the South Rim in summer, as most tourists do, be prepared for crowds at the more popular spots. Entrance fees at press time were $10.00 for each private vehicle or $5.00 per bus/tour van passenger, pedestrian, or cyclist. The admission is good for seven days and includes both rims.

If you're not on a tour, what you see depends on how much time you allot for your trip. The first view of the canyon is usually from the scenic overlook at Mather Point. Each overlook provides a different perspective of this vast canyon, so take advantage of as many as you can. Ideally, you will come at different times of day. Sunset at the canyon, especially at Yaki Point and East Rim Drive, is a not-to-be-missed treat; if you can rouse the kids, sunrise is also special, particularly at Hopi Point and West Rim Drive.

First stop: the visitor center (520-638-7888), 6 miles north of the park's south entrance station. Hours vary from season to season but typically have been 8:00 A.M. to 5:00 P.M. with extended hours during the peak season. A ranger is stationed here and can dispense information along with maps and brochures. *The Guide,* a free park newspaper, is full of basic tourist information. Also free: *Young Adventurer,* featuring activities and information for kids. The park offers a series of four Junior Ranger patches ($1.50 each) to different age groups, from preschool to thirteen years, who are committed to learning more about the park and protecting its resources. Inquire at the visitor center, Yavapai or Tusayan Museum, or the North Rim information desk.

The visitor center's bookstore offers a good supply of books, slides, and postcards. Its exhibit hall features natural and cultural history displays, including dioramas that the kids will like. At the auditorium, a variety of brief audiovisual presentations are shown throughout the day; check the schedule for times and topics. The lobby's bulletin board lists ranger-led rim walks, talks, and evening events. The courtyard has an interesting display that shows different types of vessels that have run the Colorado River, including the oldest —a 1909 Cataract Boat.

Less than a mile northeast, the recently renovated **Yavapai Observation Station** offers sensational canyon views from its picture windows. Panels identify the buttes, points, and tributary canyons that are visible. The exhibits present the canyon's geologic history in a way that school-age and older kids can appreciate: via rock samples, ancient fossils, and a geologic clock that tells the time (in millions of years) it takes to form the rock layers revealed by the Colorado River. Educational videos and Indian lore about the canyon make this a worthwhile stop. Here you can also buy books, postcards, maps, and slides. From the museum—if your kids are old enough and hardy—consider walking the easy, paved, flat, self-guided 2.7-mile nature trail that travels west leading to Maricopa Point, with vistas of the Colorado River. The trail passes the Hopi House, a well-stocked gift shop, and the grand old log-and-stone El Tovar Hotel. You can buy inexpensive brochures on the trail's biology and geology at the visitor center, Yavapai Observation Station, or at Verkamp's Curios, next to the El Tovar.

East Rim

If you budget enough time—at least one day or more—take a drive along the **East Rim to Desert View.** The 25-mile, one-way drive takes forty-five minutes. We suggest saving the lookouts for the drive back. One exception: **Buggeln Picnic area,** about 1.2 miles east of **Grandview Point.** The scattered picnic tables are shaded by ponderosa pines, and there are some scenic canyon views. As you are rimside, watch the kids carefully.

At the end of East Rim Drive is **Desert View** with its superb overlook and famous 70-foot Watchtower, built in 1932 by the Fred Harvey Company. There's a nominal entrance fee that entitles you to see reproductions of petroglyphs, wall paintings, a Hopi altar, and the tower. Climb the windy stairs for spectacular 360-degree vistas of the canyon and beyond, to the Painted Desert and the San Francisco Peaks. The odd-looking wooden boxes, with slits that are set into the wall at intervals, are reflectoscopes. Look down into the black glass for intensified canyon views. Desert View has a small visitors center as well as a general store, a snack bar, a service station, and a campground.

Three miles west of Desert View, you'll find the **Tusayan Museum and ruin,** constructed by prehistoric Pueblo Indians in approximately A.D. 1185. The small museum has artifacts and models of the Anasazi tribes as well as those of modern day tribes of this region. (Today, the Havasupai people inhabit the inner canyon in a remote village accessible only by foot, pack animals, or from the river. The Navajo live on a reservation to the east of Grand Canyon.)

Inexpensive leaflets describe prehistoric Pueblo farming and foraging methods. Walk along the short paved trail (one-eighth-mile

Hopi Point lookout is a great place to take in a view of the Grand Canyon.
(Courtesy United States Department of the Interior National Park Service)

round-trip) that leads to the ruins where about thirty individuals lived for some twenty years before they moved on. Thirty-minute guided tours are offered several times a day during peak season.

Inner Canyon

If your kids are older, if the whole family is fit, and if time allows, consider hiking a short way into the canyon for a totally different perspective. A number of caveats are in order: Be aware that it takes about twice as long to hike up as it does to go down. Canyon hiking is the reverse of mountain climbing, so save your energy for the return trip. Increase your calorie intake by bringing along plenty of nutritious food. As you descend, you enter a desert environment (except for the river corridor). The temperature at the bottom of the canyon can be as much as 30 degrees Fahrenheit higher than rim temperatures: Summertime highs along the Colorado River can reach 120 degrees. For any trip longer than thirty minutes, take along plenty of water (at least a gallon per person) and drink frequently. Wear a hat and clothing that covers your legs, arms, and body in order to avoid excessive water loss and prevent sunburn. You may encounter wildlife on your hike: Don't feed, touch, or disturb the animals. Day hikers account for 60 percent of the search-and-rescue efforts along Grand Canyon trails: Never, ever, hike farther than your family's stamina (and your supplies) permit. Also, be sure to check with rangers prior to the hike to be certain the trails are open. Finally, don't think you can hike to the Colorado River in one day: It's a two-day trip, and hikers actually have died trying to make it in less time.

Obviously, the message is clear: Inner canyon hiking is not for the neophyte or for younger children. If you have older school-age kids with hiking experience, and if you are a veteran hiker, you may want to consider the **Bright Angel Trail.** A hike down the trails gifts you with an up-close view. The park maintains two trails—**the Bright Angel Trail,** which begins west of the Bright Angel Lodge in the Village, and the **South Kaibab Trail,** which begins near Yaki Point on the East Rim Drive. Try hiking at least a portion, however small. The trail wary should go on the **Bright Angel Trail** since from May to September the rest houses along the way provide water. But still tote your own, as you most certainly on a hot day will want to quench your thirst before the first water fountain at the 1½-mile marker. (Round-trip: 3 miles; time to allow: 2½–4 hours.) Another popular destination is **Indian Garden,** 4.6 miles from the trailhead (allow 6–9 hours round-trip), which features picnic tables and toilets as well as water. Only attempt to trek to **Plateau Point,** 7.1 miles from the rim, and to **Bright Angel Creek,** 9.1 miles from the top and where **Phantom Ranch** offers rustic lodging, if you have older children and teens who are experienced and hearty hikers. Remember, as you descend into the canyon, the temperatures become hotter, as high as 100 degrees plus, and the most difficult part of the trek occurs at the end—going uphill when you are tired. This is not a place to have to carry an exhausted child.

Along the Bright Angel trail, well before the mile-and-a-half rest house, the trail rewards you with marine fossils of branchipods (ancient shelled animals), corals, sharks, and sponges. As you walk through the first tunnel, look for Indian pictographs.

The **South Kaibab Trail,** also park maintained, is another good option. Along the 1¼-mile trip to **Cedar Ridge** you pass different rock layers including Kaibab, Toroweap, Coconino, and Hermit. Enjoy a "treasure hunt" for shell and bird fossils. From Cedar Ridge it's 3 miles to the **Tonto Trail,** a desert region of shrubs, cacti, and, in summer, home to the black-throated sparrow.

To get off the beaten path for backcountry camping, obtain an overnight permit, in advance by mail, from the **Backcountry Office,** Box 129, Grand Canyon 86023.

North Rim

North Rim elevations are higher, the temperatures are lower, and there's much more rainfall (some 60 percent more). Approach this area through the Arizona Strip (the land between the canyon and the Utah border), which leads to a 45-mile drive south on Route 67. The vistas are superb here, along the Kaibab Plateau. If you're staying at the lovely **Grand Canyon Lodge** (see Where to Stay)—even if you're not—go inside, or outside on the viewing deck, for exceptional canyon vistas. On the hotel grounds is the trailhead to Bright Angel Point, a one-half-mile round-trip along the crest of a rock jutting into the canyon. (This is not recommended with young children because of the sheer drop on each side of the trail!)

The North Rim's most popular overlooks include **Point Imperial,** the highest point on either rim at 8,803 feet, 11 miles from Grand Canyon Lodge, with views of the countryside surrounding the canyon. Fifty miles south, **Cape Royal** is another popular stop, with views of Angel's Window, a natural arch. There are rest rooms and a scenic picnic spot near the parking area. Take the nearby **Cliff Springs Trail,** a 1-mile round-trip trail that descends to a forested ravine, past a small Indian ruin, to the creek and spectacular views of the canyon.

Tours

Horseback tours are offered by **Apache Stables,** located at Moqui Lodge. Choose from short rides through Kaibab National Forest to the longer East Rim and other excursions. Call (520) 638–2424.

Mule rides may be easier than hiking but require a good deal of fortitude. You must sit in the saddle for hours, control your mount, and descend into steep terrain. Obviously, this is for older kids only (height requirement is 4 feet 7 inches) and not for heavy parents (weight limit is 200 pounds). You should make reservations at least nine months—preferably a year—before your trip. Call (303) 297-2757.

The following motor coach tours are available from **AMFAC** (303-297-2757): a two-hour trip that travels 8 miles along the rim to Hermit's Rest, a native stone building created in 1914, with stops at viewpoints along the way; Desert View, covering some 52 miles in three and three-quarter hours, venturing east along the rim, stopping at Yavapai Observation Station and Lipan Point—a spectacular overlook; and Desert View and the Sunset Tour, a ninety-minute orientation that heads to the rim for the fading light of sunset. Outbound tours explore surrounding areas, such as Monument Valley and Indian ruins.

You can also float and raft this territory. For day-long adventures try a twelve-hour float trip along the Colorado River, which includes a three-hour ride to the put-in spot and a picnic lunch. While scenic, this journey glides through the Glen Canyon and not the Grand Canyon. Outfitters include **AMFAC** (303-297-2757) and **ARA Wilderness Adventures** (520-645-3279).

The **raft trips,** which last from three days to three weeks, gift you with a bottoms-up view of the canyon and a taste of white water. Remember though, that for many of the shorter trips, you raft into the Phantom Ranch and, alas, must hike back out, a journey of several hours. The park service has a list of more than twenty companies that offer Colorado River raft trips. Family-friendly outfitters include **OARS,** P.O. Box 67, Angels Camp, CA 95222 (800-346-6277; 209-736-4677), which sets a minimum age of twelve; **Canyoneers,** P.O. Box 2997, Flagstaff 86003 (800-525-0924; 520-774-4559), with a minimum age of ten; and **Hatch River Expeditions,** P.O. Box 1200, Vernal, Utah 84078 (800-433-8966; 801-789-3813), which has a minimum age of nine.

Entertainment

There are a variety of ways to keep the kids entertained in the evenings.

Grand Canyon, Hidden Secrets at the IMAX theater, shown daily on a 70-foot-high screen, is a wonderful, larger-than-life film that will keep the whole family enthralled. The theater is located at Highway 64/U.S. 180

at the south entrance to the park; call (520) 638-2203 for show times. **Over the Edge Theatre,** in the village at the community building, presents a multimedia canyon orientation show that uses twelve projectors to create a sensational spectacle. Call (520) 638-2229 for schedules.

Squire Fun Center at the Best Western Grand Canyon Squire Inn, Highway 64 in Tusayan, has a six-lane bowling alley, billiards, a game room, and a big-screen TV. And don't forget the day and evening ranger presentations at the canyon; check at the visitor center for schedules, or call (520) 638-7888.

Shopping

If you're looking for the basics—groceries, camping supplies, clothing, souvenirs, books—check out **Babbitt's General Store** in Grand Canyon Village next to the post office; (520) 638-2262. Fine arts is the specialty at **Gallery Grand Canyon,** Highway 64, Tusayan (520-638-9201), where you'll find top-quality Indian pottery, jewelry, Hopi kachina, Navajo rugs, paintings, and the like.

SPECIAL EVENTS

Contact the Grand Canyon Chamber of Commerce for more information on the following area events.

Easter: Sunrise Services (nondenominational)—Mather Point.
Late April: Moqui Chili Cook-Off.
September weekends: Grand Canyon Chamber Music Festival.
Early October: Arizona Governor's Cup Antique Car Rally.

WHERE TO STAY

Listings of lodgings are available from the Chamber of Commerce and National Park (see For More Information). The hotels and lodges on the South Rim all are open year-round and are within the park, except for Moqui Lodge.

El Tovar, Village Loop Drive, was built in 1905 and is a National Landmark. It has the most deluxe accommodations—and truly breathtaking surroundings, as it's perched on the edge of the canyon. Food is continental.

Bright Angel Lodge, West Rim Drive, is rustic, more affordable, and has two restaurants and a limited number of private cabins by the rim.

Thunderbird and **Kachina,** Village Loop Drive, are both modern, two-story lodges at the rim's edge.

Maswik Lodge, U.S. 180 West, west end of village, in the Canyon Village, has a cafeteria, lounge, and gift shop.

East and West Yavapai Lodge, Mather Center, set in pine and juniper groves minutes from the rim, has a gift shop, cafeteria, and lounge.

Moqui Lodge, Arizona 61, park entrance, is just outside the park in the Kaibab National Forest. It is moderately priced, has a dining room and cocktail lounge, and on-site horseback riding and cooking-out areas.

Trailer Village, near the visitor center, has campsites with full hookups and nearby bath and laundry facilities.

Phantom Ranch, built in 1922, can be reached only by foot, rafting, or by mule. It features western-style cabins and dormitories, a dining hall, beer hall, and fishing and swimming in Bright Angel Creek.

It's important to make reservations as far in advance as possible, either through your travel agent or by calling (303) 297–2757 or contacting **AMFAC Parks & Resorts,** 14001 East Iliffi, Aurora, CO 80014. In addition to Trailer Village (described earlier) the following campgrounds are located in the South Rim area: **Grand Canyon Camper Village** (520–638–2887), 1 mile south of the U.S. 180 park entrance, is considered the best in the area, with 200 RV sites with full hookups, water, and electricity, and sixty tent sites, tipi rentals, flush toilets, coin-operated showers, grills, and picnic tables; reservations are accepted. **Mather Campground,** with 319 RV and tent sites, flush toilets, coin-operated showers, water, laundry, grills, and picnic tables, can be reserved up to eight weeks in advance through DESTINET at (800) 365–2267 or by writing P.O. Box 85705, San Diego, California 92186-5705. **Desert View Campground,** 26 miles east of Grand Canyon Village, operates on a first-come, first-serve basis.

In Tusayan, family choices on Highway 64 include the following: **Best Western Grand Canyon Squire,** with 150 units, dining room, heated pool, and tennis courts (520–638–2681 or 800–622–6966); and the **Quality Inn Grand Canyon** with 185 units, heated pool, dining room, and coffee shop (520–638–2673 or 800–221–2222).

If you can't book lodging in Grand Canyon Village or in Tusayan, try the town of Williams, 60 miles south on Highway 64 (Chamber of Commerce number: 520-635-4061), and Flagstaff, 80 miles south on Highway 180 (520-774-4505 or 800-842-7293).

WHERE TO EAT

The finest (and most expensive) dining in the area is at the **El Tovar Hotel,** although they have a nice children's menu and off-season lunch specials. Elsewhere, area restaurants serve reasonably priced American food. For the most inexpensive meals, head for the cafeterias at **Maswik Lodge** and **Yavapai Lodge** (520-638-2360), in Grand Canyon Village, and **Desert View Trading Post** (520-638-2360). There's a **McDonald's** in town, too.

DAY TRIPS

A good beginning for your Grand Canyon adventure lies 80 miles southwest of the national park in **Flagstaff.** Not only does this city serve as the most accessible airport gateway and the easiest place to pick up your rental car, but the **Museum of Northern Arizona,** Route 4 (520-774-5211), presents a comprehensive exploration of the Colorado plateau, a 130,000-square-mile province of sedimentary rock that, eons ago, forces uplifted a mile or more above sea level. Now encompassing parts of Utah, Arizona, New Mexico, and Colorado, this region sports the Grand Canyon as its crown jewel. If articulating geological phenomena leaves your mouth as dry as the arid areas you're trying to explain, then you'll especially appreciate the museum's colorful charts that trace the earth's changes. The exhibits also describe the region's wildlife and culture. Small by big-city standards, the galleries are just about the right size for grade-schoolers who want to learn but not everything. Even the most blasé child will go wide-eyed at touching the petrified femur of a duck-billed dinosaur, learning rock facts from the computer station, and eying the skeletal model of Dilophosaurus, a dinosaur known only to have inhabited northern Arizona, but who recently gained star status as a creature in *Jurassic Park.*

The **bookstore** presents an admirable collection of adult and children's guides, and the **Museum Shop** offers authentic Native American crafts, including small, flat kachinas suitable for use as Christmas ornaments.

On the one-and-a-half-hour drive from Flagstaff to **Tusayan,** the gateway town for the park's south entrance, the road leads you through ponderosa pine groves and fields dotted with creosote and sagebrush.

Outside the Grand Canyon National Park, State Route 64 intersects with U.S. 89 at Cameron, an interesting historic trading post, hotel, and Indian art gallery. Here, head south for about 20 miles on U.S. 89, and turn left to the ancient Indian ruins at **Wupatki National Monument.** This area was once thriving, full of cosmopolitan villages inhabited by several Native American cultures. By 1300, all that remained were ruins, and today some 2,000 archaeological sites are located within the monument. The better ones have paved roads and are accessible to tourists. The Wupatki Visitor Center (520-556-7040) is 14 miles east of the U.S. 89 turnoff between Flagstaff and Cameron. Here are exhibits of various artifacts of this vanished culture, including pottery, jewelry, and tools. Kids particularly enjoy the Wupatki (Hopi for "Tall House") room, a reconstruction of what living quarters probably looked like. Rangers give lectures and tours of the nearby ruins, or you can take a self-guided trail from behind the visitor center. Archaeologists have reconstructed a ball court; there's also an open-air amphitheater and a series of blowholes, which are thought to have had religious significance. A short drive away are other major ruins. The Lomaki—a small, two-story pueblo some 9 miles northwest of the visitor center—is the best preserved.

If you came to the Grand Canyon expecting to see the **Painted Desert** (as many do), you're in for a disappointment—it's simply too far. But if you are determined, you will have to travel some to see this landscape where trees have turned to stone over eons. Here striations of purple, red, pink, and blue run through large rock mounds that were carved ages ago by the Little Colorado River. It is a display of eerie and breathtaking beauty. The most famous part of the Painted Desert is at Petrified National Park, 190 miles from the canyon's south rim. A more restricted expanse is found at Little Painted Desert County Park, 15 miles north of Winslow (140 miles from South Rim). Closest to the canyon: a narrow band of the Painted Desert along U.S. Highway 89 from about 3 miles north of Cameron to the small village of The Gap. (You could take a detour on your way to the Wupatki ruins. See Petrified Forest chapter.)

After the ruins, you might decide to proceed onto **Flagstaff** (82 miles south of the Grand Canyon National Park entrance). Don't miss the **Lowell Observatory** on Mars Hill (520-774-3358), a mile from downtown. Founded by astronomer Dr. Percival Lowell in 1894, this is the site where Pluto was discovered in 1930 by an observatory worker using Lowell's calculations. See exhibits in the domed visitor center. On selected summer evenings view a slide show, and then gaze through the telescope. Contact the Flagstaff Visitor Center at (520) 774-9541 or (800) 842-7293 for more tourist information.

FOR MORE INFORMATION

Grand Canyon Chamber of Commerce, P.O. Box 3007, Grand Canyon, Arizona 86023 (no phone), will send you an informative visitor's guide. For park information contact **Grand Canyon National Park,** Box 129, Grand Canyon, Arizona 86023, or call (520) 638-7888; or, http://star.ucc.nau.edu/~grandcanyon.

Not all park facilities meet accessibility standards, though the numbers are increasing. Request the *Accessibility Guide* from the visitor center or from the park at the address just given. The National Park Service provides free wheelchairs for park visitors' temporary use. Usually a wheelchair is available at the Yavapai Museum and the visitor center. A temporary permit for wheelchair access to West Rim Drive in summer is available from the visitor center. Inquire at the center or at Yavapai and Tusayan Museums about temporary parking permits for designated parking.

Emergency Numbers

Dial 911 for twenty-four-hour emergency medical service; from hotel rooms, dial 9-911. A twenty-four-hour emergency phone is located to the left of the visitor center. Park rangers patrol the canyon and serve as fire fighters and police officers.

Pharmacy: The South Rim has a clinic and pharmacy open all year; although it's not open twenty-four hours, rangers and clinic staff provide around-the-clock emergency service. Call

(520) 638-2551 or 638-2469 for the clinic, (520) 638-2460 for the pharmacy.

North Rim medical services consist of a clinic staffed by a nurse practitioner from May through October. Rangers perform emergency medical services.

TUCSON

In Tucson, just after a rainfall, the desert smells like creosote and sage. Explore higher in the red rock mountains that ring this city, and the towering saguaros point the way into a landscape where jackrabbits and prairie dogs cool off in the shade of mesquite trees, javelinas leave tracks in the sand, and the wind carries the scent of pine and the buzzing of bees. Here the boulders reveal ancient petroglyphs, the age-old secrets of the Hohokam Indians, "the vanished ones" who disappeared, leaving behind only cliff dwellings, rock designs, and pottery shards.

Tucson's landscape is like that. The subtle shades and variations pull you into its legends and lore. In this town you will learn of cowboys, cactus, Native American culture, and enjoy some special museums.

GETTING THERE

The **Tucson International Airport** (520-573-8100) is 10 miles south of the city and is served by twelve major airlines, including **America West** (800-247-5692), **Delta** (800-221-1212), **Southwest** (800-435-9792), and **Trans World Airlines** (800-221-2000). The **Tucson Airport Information Centers** (520-290-9191), located at the airport, provide tourist information.

For ground transportation, buses come into the **Greyhound/ Trailways** station, 2 South Fourth Avenue; (520) 231-2222. Trains arrive at the **Amtrak Station,** 400 East Toole; (800) 872-7245. The transcontinental route I-10 offers an east-west highway approach to the city; this route joins I-19 and follows the west side of Tucson, offering convenient access to major streets. From San Diego in the west, take I-8, which joins I-10. From the Canadian border, use U.S. 89 to Tucson.

GETTING AROUND

Avis (800-331-1212 or 520-294-1494) and **Hertz** (520-294-7616 or 800-654-3131) are among the car rental agencies. **Sun Tran** (520-792-9222) provides buses throughout Tucson. Some taxi services include **Allstate Cab** (520-624-6611) and **Checker Cab** (520-623-1133), but the locals advise visitors to rent a car. Sites are spread out, and taxis at times are hard to find.

WHAT TO SEE AND DO

Museums and Green Spaces

Start your Southwest tour 14 miles west of town at the **Arizona-Sonora Desert Museum,** 2021 North Kinney Road; (520) 883-2702. Part zoo and part botanical garden, this mostly outdoor facility displays more than 200 live animals and 1,000 species of plants. You find that far from being a boring or barren place, the Sonoran Desert features such diverse habitats as grasslands, riparian (streamside) regions, and mountainous areas.

Highlights to explore include a re-created limestone cave complete with mineral room (kids love the phosphorescent glow-in-the-dark quality of these gems) and a Mexican oak pine woodland thick with hop-brush, mesquite, and mountain yucca, and home to black bear and mountain lions.

Kids love gawking at the ocelots, jaguarundi, and vultures as well as marveling at the myriad shapes of cacti. Allow time to tour the aviary, a soothing place to rest for awhile and spot the birds.

With your eyes and ears sharpened to the desert's variety, enjoy more of the real thing by driving through the **Saguaro National Park** (520-296-8576 or 520-883-6366), whose western section abuts the desert museum. To reach the western section, drive west on Speedway; to reach the eastern section, drive east on the Old Spanish Trail. In each area endless groves of towering saguaro dot the landscape. These cacti serve as the quintessential symbol of the Old West.

Old Tucson Studios, 201 South Kinney Road (520-883-0100), is just a whoop and a holler away from the western section of the

Tucson at a Glance

- Cowboy and Native American culture, plus special museums

- Words kids'll love to learn: jaguarundi, ocelot, hop-brush, mesquite, yucca, and saguaro

- Tombstone, "the town too tough to die"

- Mission San Xavier del Bac, founded in the 1600s

- Tucson Chamber of Commerce, (520) 792-1212

Saguaro National Monument. Since 1939, when Columbia Pictures built this western town as a set for *Arizona,* this red rock and cactus country has served as the backdrop in scores of Hollywood movies and television westerns such as *Gunfight at the O.K. Corral* and *Little House on the Prairie.* Nighttime brings special events such as rodeos, concerts, and musical shows. Call for daily show schedules, filming, and other special events.

The International Wildlife Museum, 4800 West Gates Pass Road; (520) 629-0100. Some people may enjoy this museum of mounted displays and dioramas, but after experiencing the real desert, some people see these exhibits as stilted. There are also films and presentations that show hundreds of species of mammals, birds, and reptiles, as well as an interactive video display of the world's game parks and wildlife refuges. Guided tours offered hourly Wednesday through Sunday, 9:00 A.M. to 5:30 P.M.

For a beautiful display of plants and flowers, visit **The Tucson Botanical Gardens,** 2150 North Alvernon Way; (520) 326-9255. Covering more than five acres of land, the indigenous plants include wildflowers, cactus, and herb gardens. Kids enjoy the interactive Children's Multicultural Garden, and the new Sensory Garden, complete with a sensory treasure hunt. Special events from classes to concerts are frequently scheduled, so be sure to call.

Just outside town, the **Pima Air and Space Museum,** 6000 East Valencia Road (520-574-0462), features more than 180 vintage and contemporary aircraft. Even if you can't tell a Cessna Skymaster from a Lockheed Neptune or a Learjet, all of which are on display, you will be impressed with these flight legends. Particularly interesting are the vintage World War II planes, including gliders and bombers. On the field as well is the *Airforce One* used by Presidents Kennedy and Johnson. You could spend all afternoon here, but count on at least two hours.

Before you head back to town, 9 miles southeast of Tucson is the **Mission San Xavier del Bac,** 1950 West San Xavier Road; (520) 294-2624. The Jesuits founded this mission, which is on the Tohono O'odham Indian Reservation, in the 1600s. Walk around this "White Dove of the Desert," visit the school, and admire the Spanish mission architecture. If you visit during spring, try to catch the San Xavier Pageant and Fiesta.

In town, on the University of Arizona campus, the **John P. Schaefer Center for Creative Photography** (520-621-7968) offers visual treats of a different nature. Aside from the photographers' archives, galleries, library, and research facility, a rare collection of more than 50,000 photographs makes this center a delight. By prior appointment enjoy a private viewing of the original prints of such noted masters as Ansel Adams, Richard Avedon, Linda Connor, Edward Weston, and dozens more.

Stargaze at the **Flandrau Science Center and Planetarium** (520-621-4515), which is also at the university. Check out the star show, laser light show, and 360-degree movie.

Before you leave campus, allow some time to explore **The Arizona State Museum,** Park Avenue and University Boulevard; (520) 621-6302. The museum displays collections of pottery and artifacts used in the daily activities of the Native Americans, including the region's ancient Native Americans.

If you are interested in art, browse through the **Tucson Museum of Art,** 140 North Main Avenue (520-624-2333), and **The University of Arizona Museum of Art** (520-621-7567). Both offer a variety of exhibits from Renaissance and pre-Columbian work to contemporary collections and traveling exhibitions.

Playmaxx/The Yozeum, 2900 North Country Club (520-322-0100), is dedicated to yoyos. The Duncan Family exhibit shows the toy's progression from 1930 to 1990. Visitors can see how yoyos are produced and learn tricks from on site pro-yos. Another family-oriented spot is the **Tucson Children's Museum** (520-884-7511). Ten rooms house hands-on exhibits that spark the imaginations of the young and the young at heart. Included are interactive science exhibits and multimedia presentations. In 1997 **Kartchner Caverns,** the world's largest living cave, opened to the public. To preserve the cave's pristine condition, a limited number of people will be allowed to enter on a daily basis. During certain weeks throughout the year, the caverns will be closed to accommodate the resident bat colony. Call the Convention and Visitor's Bureau for more information.

Parks and Recreation

The **Tohono Chul Park,** 7366 North Paseo del Norte (520-575-8468), is a natural desert park with rabbits, birds, and lizards. On a self-guided tour, discover demonstration gardens that illustrate water conservation, an ethnobotanical garden that recounts some desert history, and a geology wall that re-creates the Catalina Mountain range, which looms nearby. After your stroll, relax with tea or dinner in the Spanish Colonial tearoom. **The Sentinel Peak Park,** off Broadway, west of I-10 on Cuesta, offers a far-reaching view of Tucson and its surrounding area.

For horseback riding and hiking, follow the trails at **Tucson Mountain Park,** 8 miles west on Speedway Boulevard and Kinney Road (520-883-4200), an enclave of 17,000 acres.

When the long days and the Arizona heat begin to make you wilt, cool off at **The Breakers Waterpark,** 9 miles north to exit I-10, then east 1½ miles to 8555 Tangerine Road; (520) 792-1821. Frolic in the water slides, pools, and a playground; volleyball, basketball, horseshoes, picnic facilities, showers, lockers, and food are all available. Call for information about discounts.

Pima County Parks and Recreation (520-740-2690) provides information about local facilities, including swimming pools, tennis and racquetball courts, picnic areas, playgrounds, and ball fields.

A trip to Old Tucson Studios provides something for everyone.
(Photo courtesy Old Tucson Studios/Arizona Office of Tourism)

Sports

Baseball fans will find that the **Colorado Rockies** spend their spring training season at **Hi Corbett Field** (520-327-9467), East Broadway and Randolph Way, beginning in March. In 1998 the Rockies will be joined by the **Arizona Diamondbacks** and the **Chicago White Sox.** Both of these teams will practice in Tucson's new sports complex, due to be completed in late 1997. The **Tucson Toros,** P.O. Box 27045 (520-325-2621), are a championship professional baseball team in the Pacific Coast Conference. Home games are played at Hi Corbett Field April through August. **The University of Arizona** has seasonal football and basketball games at **McKale Center.** Call the University of Arizona ticket office (520-621-2411) for details. **Horse Racing at Rilloto Downs,** 4502 North First Avenue (520-293-5011), begins in November and continues to early May. If you can't stay away from the greens, the **PGA** marks the beginning of its tournament in February with the **Northern Telecom Tucson Open.** Call the **Tucson Activity Line** at (520) 544-4424 for more information.

Theater and Performing Arts

The **Arizona Theater Company,** Brady Court, 40 East Fourteenth Street (520-622-2823), plays during the October-through-May season at the **Temple of Music and Arts,** 330 South Scott Avenue; (520) 884-4875. The **Invisible Theater,** 1400 North First Avenue (520- 882-9721), performs contemporary plays between September and June. The **Gaslight Theater,** 7010 East Broadway (520-886-9428), offers audience-participation theater. During the summer months, the **University of Arizona's** resident company (520-621-1162) hosts a colorful Summer Art Festival.

Classical music fans should get tickets for **The Tucson Symphony Orchestra** (520-792-9155), which performs classical and pop music in the **Tucson Convention Center Music Hall** at 443 South Stone Avenue. In spring and fall, relax outdoors at the **Reid Park Bandshell** and enjoy the sounds of the **Tucson Pops Orchestra;** (520) 791-4873. Tucson also boasts two major opera companies. Supported by a full orchestra, the **Southern Arizona Light Opera Company** (520-323-7888) performs at the **Tucson Community Center's Music Hall** from October through May. From October to March, the **Arizona Opera Company** (520-293-4336) presents four operas at the same location.

Shopping

El Mercado de Boutiques, Broadway and Wilmot, keeps shoppers busy with more than twenty shops offering Native American and Latin folk art, Asian and local arts and crafts. In the Foothills Shopping Center, **The Old Pueblo Museum** offers gems and art for display and for sale. Flea markets, swap meets, antiques and souvenir shopping can be found within **Tucson's shopping district** along Fourth and Seventh streets. Downtown, especially by Congress Street, hosts art galleries, antiques shops, and crafts stores.

SPECIAL EVENTS

February: La Fiesta do los Vaqueros Rodeo, the Rodeo Grounds, has food, horses and cowboys, and a rodeo.

March: Territorial Days is a birthday celebration with 1880s fire-cart races. Wak PowWow, an intertribal celebration.

April: Pioneer Days, historic re-creations of prestatehood Arizona.

August: Fiesta de San Augustin, a celebration of the city's patron saint.

October: Oktoberfest at Mt. Lemmon Ski Valley (520-576-1400) features German food, drinks, dances, and music.

December: Fiesta de Guadalupe, with music, dancing, and food in honor of Mexico's patron saint.

WHERE TO STAY

Resorts

The Westin La Paloma, 3800 East Sunrise Drive, Tucson 85718; (520) 742-6000 or (800) 228-3000. This four-star, four-diamond resort offers golf, a spa with quality treatments, and a year-round children's program. In summer the program expands to become the Kactus Kids Camp, offering swimming, nature walks, and arts and crafts for ages five to twelve from 9:00 A.M. to 3:00 P.M., Monday to Saturday. Other times, the program offers supervised babysitting by the hour at the Children's Lounge for ages six months to twelve years, Sunday through Thursday 8:00 A.M. to 5:00 P.M., Friday and Saturday 8:00 A.M. to 9:00 P.M. Call and ask about seasonal packages. A junior tennis camp is available from June to mid-August. Families can get into the scoring with a family golf clinic for ages five and older.

Tanque Verde Ranch, 14301 East Speedway, Tucson 85748; (520) 296-6275. Guests stay in comfortable casitas and soothe their saddlesore muscles in the hot tub or by swimming laps in the pool. This dude ranch offers a good riding program for adults as well as kids from November to May. Rates include three meals.

For family-friendly lodgings at an inn, call **The Arizona Association of Bed & Breakfast Inns,** 3661 North Campbell, Box 237, Tucson, Arizona, 85719; (520) 277-0775. Listings are offered throughout the state.

La Posada del Valle, 1640 North Campbell, Tucson; (520) 795-3840. This inn offers five guest rooms furnished with antiques and pieces from the twenties and thirties. The inn prefers that children be over twelve.

El Presidio Bed and Breakfast, 297 North Main Avenue; (520) 623-6151. Located in the historic El Presidio district and within walking distance of craft shops and the Tucson Museum of Art, this bed and breakfast offers three suites and a guest house. Children over twelve are welcome only in the guest house, which has a living room and kitchenette.

WHERE TO EAT

Don't leave Tucson without trying some of the city's authentic cuisine. **El Charro Cafe,** 311 North Court Avenue (520-622-1922), has been serving up Mexican food in one location or another for more than seventy years. House specialties, at reasonable prices, include the green corn tamales, caldo de queso (cheese soup), and a variety of enchiladas. **Tony Roma's,** 4620 North Oracle Road (520-887-7662), was judged to have some of the best ribs in America. This barbecue eatery also offers grilled chicken, steaks, seafood, and salads. From late December through April, cowhands will hoot and howl when grub is served at **Triple C Chuckwagon Suppers,** 8900 West Bopp Road; (520) 883-2333. A hearty meal is accompanied by a Western stage show. As this is the West, there are several steakhouses. Check out **O.K. Corral,** 7710 East Wrightstown Road (520-885-2373), **Stuart Anderson's Black Angus,** 5075 North Oracle Road (520-293-7131), or **Ye Olde Lantern,** 1800 North Oracle Road (520-622-6761).

DAY TRIPS

To really understand the fascination with the local flora, fauna, and bold red buttes, get out into the desert with a jeep tour. These trips literally take you off the beaten path, over trails and up boulders into the Santa Catalina Mountains. Your guide leads short walks to observe ancient petroglyphs or examine such finds as "fish hooks" on barrel cactus or the "straw" of the yucca. By reservation **Mountain View Transportation** (800-594-9644) can arrange customized, overnight jeep trips that take you to Tombstone and other nearby attractions.

You won't want to miss **Tombstone,** "the town too tough to die," 70 miles from Tucson; (520) 457-3929. This historic American landmark was the roughest mining town in the West during the 1800s. Take pictures of such famous places as the O.K. Corral, Boothill, Bird

Cage Theater, and the Crystal Palace Saloon, and look for the ghosts of such old regulars as Doc Holliday, Wyatt Earp, and Johnny Ringo. While you're there, explore nearby ghost towns.

For some more history, visit the **Tumacacori National Historical Park,** 48 miles south of Tucson, off I-19; (520) 398-2341. Here the abandoned Mission San Jose de Tumacacori, has been preserved. Its thirty-six acres contain a historical park, a modern museum of the local history, a church, and a patio garden.

Get a glimpse of the future at the famed **Biosphere 2,** 35 miles north of Tucson; (520) 825-6200. Several scientists resided in this glass-enclosed system. Tour the grounds, watch the multi-image slide show, and visit the viewing gallery next to the ocean biome to see the extensive coral exhibit. Call for information and reservations.

Spend another day cooling off in the mountain streams and water-falls of **Sabino Canyon,** 5900 North Sabino Canyon Road, Tucson; (520) 749-2861. You can view this desert oasis in the Catalina National Forest from a guided tram ride that takes you around the canyon to explore, but you will probably want to spend additional time picnick-ing, hiking, and admiring the natural rock walls, pools, and animals that abound nearby.

No visit to Tucson would be complete without a day roaming the trails through the desert on horseback. Try **Pusch Ridge Stables,** 13700 North Oracle Road, Tucson; (520) 297-6908. They offer numer-ous rides designed for visitors of various riding abilities.

FOR MORE INFORMATION

The Arizona Office of Tourism: 1100 West Washington Street, Phoenix, Arizona 85007; (520) 542-TOUR. Website: http://www.arizonaguide.com

The Metropolitan Tucson Convention & Visitors Bureau: 130 South Scott Avenue, Tucson, Arizona 85701; (800) 638-8350 or (520) 624-1817; http//:www.arizonaguide.com/visittucson.

The Tucson Chamber of Commerce: Post Office Box 991, Tuc-son, Arizona, 85702; (520) 792-1212.

OASIS (Older Adult Service and Information System): 3435 East Broadway Boulevard; (520) 882-3114 (offers special events and day trips for people over age fifty-five).

Tucson Activity Line: Post Office Box 35026, Tucson, Arizona, 8574; (520) 544-4424 (provides information about restaurants, attractions, and events).

Road information: (520) 573-7623; **Police** information: (520) 791-4452

Weather: (520) 881-3333.

Emergency Numbers

Ambulance, fire, police: 911

Poison Control: 1501 North Campbell Avenue, Room 1156; (520) 626-6016

Hospitals: El Dorado Hospital, 1400 North Wilmot Road (520-886-6361); **Tucson Medical Center,** 5301 East Grant Road (520-324-1950 or 800-533-4TMC); and **University Medical Center,** 1501 North Campbell Avenue (520-694-0111). All offer twenty-four-hour emergency and trauma services.

LAS VEGAS

It's glitzy, gaudy, and gauche. So why pick Las Vegas for a family vacation? Several good reasons. First, the price. Because gambling pays the bills, most of the hotels charge about half the tab of other cities, making it possible for nongamblers to stay—and eat—in style at bargain rates. This adult playground, minus the gambling, makes a fun-filled family vacation spot that your kids won't soon forget. (You must be twenty-one to gamble in a casino.) A day or two here, amidst the neon and synthetic extravaganzas, balanced with some down-to-earth day trips, can be just the ticket to alleviate those boring vacation blues.

GETTING THERE

McCarran International Airport (702-739-5743) is 5 miles southeast of the city. An inexpensive limousine shuttle service, **Bell Trans** (702-739-7990 or 800-274-7433), operates to the strip hotels; **Gray Line Tours** (702-384-1234) operates airport express service to and from all hotels and motels. Taxis and rental cars are also available.

Amtrak (800-USA-RAIL) serves the city daily. Las Vegas is the only city in the world where the train station is inside a casino resort (Jackie Gaughan's Plaza Hotel, site of the city's original Union Pacific Railroad depot).

The Greyhound Terminal is at 200 South Main Street; (702) 384-8009 or (800) 231-2222. By car, the major artery is I-15 (south to Los Angeles and north to Salt Lake City). U.S. 93 connects Las Vegas to Reno in the north and Phoenix to the south.

GETTING AROUND

You'll find it easy to drive around this compact city. The major hotels and casinos are located in two areas. The downtown area, fondly called Glitter Gulch, includes the 4 blocks of Fremont Street between Main Street and Las Vegas Boulevard. The other area, the Strip, is a 3½-mile section of Las Vegas Boulevard. Every hotel offers free parking.

The **Las Vegas Transit System** (702-384-3540) operates public buses. The **Las Vegas Strip Trolley** (702-382-1404) runs daily every thirty minutes from 9:30 A.M. to 2:00 A.M., stopping at all major hotels along the Strip.

WHAT TO SEE AND DO

Attractions

When is a hotel not a hotel? When it's a Las Vegas mega-theme resort, complete with casino plus much more. Start sightseeing at these spectacular showplaces.

One of the newest Strip hotel casinos, **New York-New York Hotel & Casino,** 3155 Harmon Avenue (702-740-6969), re-creates the very best of New York City in the deserts of Las Vegas. Even the Manhattan skyline is present, created by twelve New York–style skyscrapers that house 2,034 rooms and suites (the buildings are one-third the actual size of those in New York City). Attractions include the likes of the Empire State Building and the Statue of Liberty; a replica of the Brooklyn Bridge and the Soldiers and Sailors Monument; and the Coney Island–style Manhattan Express roller coaster, featuring the ultimate in negative-gravity sensation. The Coney Island Emporium is a family entertainment center featuring the latest in high-tech gadgetry, carnival games, bumper cars, laser tag, an interactive driving simulator, and more. Live street entertainers, including jugglers and a barbershop quartet, perform during peak hours. And no re-creation of New York would be complete without the food of the Big Apple: Italian and Chinese restaurants, as well as New York–style delis, a steakhouse, and even street-vendor hot dogs, satisfy any appetite.

New to the **Rio Suite Hotel & Casino,** on the corner of Valley View Road and Flamingo Road (702-252-7777), is Masquerade Village, transporting visitors into the magical world of Carnivale. Combining entertainment, food, shopping, and gambling, Masquerade Village and *Masquerade Show in the Sky* are the first indoor entertainment

Las Vegas at a Glance

- Bargain-priced, glitzy and gaudy vacationland with new family-oriented attractions

- Fantasy galore: the Manhattan skyline, King Tut's Tomb, booty-and-plunder pirate raids, an erupting volanco, Carnivale parades, and more!

- Daytrips to Lake Mead, Hoover Dam, Red Rock Canyon

- Las Vegas Convention and Visitors Bureau, (702) 892-0711

experience of this kind in Las Vegas. Visitors are invited to take a journey aboard fantasy floats, which suspend from the ceiling, and parade amidst music, dancing, and celebration. Three themed parades—Mardi Gras, Rio, and Venice—complete the show, each with its own music, exotic masks and costumes, and live performances. Participants can even dress up in elaborate, themed costumes before boarding the floats. Show times are on the hour every hour from afternoon to late evening.

Several other Strip hotel casinos also offer spectacular stays.

Luxor, 3900 Las Vegas Boulevard South, (702) 795-8118, for example, is not just another casino. This Egyptian-themed resort comes complete with a River Nile and reproductions of murals and hieroglyphics from such sites as the Valley of the Kings as well as a full-scale model of King Tut's Tomb. While adults game at a 100,000-square-foot casino, kids (or adults) play at Sega VirtuaLand, an 18,000-square-foot area in which Sega, that marvel of computer wizardry, debuts its largest virtual-reality technology. This includes Virtual Formula, an interactive racing game with 3D technology, in which you feel as if you are zooming around the track, competing for the checkered flag.

Treasure Island, 3650 Las Vegas Boulevard South (702- 894-7111), which has appropriated the nickname "the Adventure Resort," is the latest Vegas property of Mirage Resorts Incorporated. There are hourly cannon battles, complete with actors and muskets, between the pirate ship *Hispaniola* and H.M.S. *Sir Francis Drake* at Buccaneer Bay fronting the hotel. (Hint: The pirates win—after all, this is Vegas.) The entertainment continues inside with the French-Canadian troupe, Cirque du Soleil, performing a specially designed show twice nightly. The casino, of course, has a booty-and-plunder decor.

But perhaps even Luxor and Treasure Island might be eclipsed by the city's largest entry, **The MGM Grand Hotel and Theme Park,** 3799 Las Vegas Boulevard South; (702) 891-1111. This hotel not only has 5,005 rooms and a casino but also comes with a thirty-three-acre theme park featuring twelve major attractions, theme streets, four theaters, and a host of rides. This entertainment complex is the largest of its kind, with thirty-story towers, spas, pools, five tennis courts, eight theme restaurants, and a special events arena.

In addition, the Wizard's Midway & Arcade features games of skill plus a video arcade. King Looey's Youth Activity Center, for ages three to sixteen, offers activities from 8:00 A.M. to midnight, including escorted outings to the theme park, behind-the-scenes hotel tours, swimming and tennis lessons, and crafts.

Expected by mid-1997: the world's tallest coke bottle. As part of the Showcase retail and entertainment center next to the MGM Grand Hotel & Theme Park, the **Coca-Cola Oasis** will include the 100-foot-tall bottle, a futuristic soda fountain, and a three-story wall of solid ice. Also in the complex: a United Artist theater, restaurants, and retail shops.

Other family pleasing favorites include the following:

Circus Circus, 2880 Las Vegas Boulevard South (702-734-0410/ 800-634-3450), is cleverly designed to look like a Big Top: Inside is a free carnival midway with food stands and rides plus circus acts. The sight of trapeze artists gliding through the air above the gambling casino is a bit surreal, but most kids (permitted in the observation gallery on the circus level, but not in the casino) love it. A climate-controlled theme park, **Grand Slam Canyon,** is adjacent to the hotel-casino. A takeoff on the Grand Canyon, the park features 140-foot sandstone cliffs, tunnels, grottoes, a waterfall, and a number of rides, including the only indoor double-loop, double-corkscrew roller coaster in the United States.

At the **Mirage,** 3400 Las Vegas Boulevard South (702-791-7111), a computer-driven volcano erupts every fifteen minutes in the evening, starting at dusk. There's also a giant man-made waterfall and a natural habitat that houses rare Royal Siberian white tigers, which can be viewed for free behind a glass safety screen. Five Atlantic bottlenose dolphins frolic in a 1.5-million-gallon pool; they can be viewed both above and below water level (fee).

Caesar Palace, 3750 Las Vegas Boulevard South (702-731-7110/800-634-6661), has a moving walkway that carries visitors through a brief diorama of Ancient Rome. There's also an Omnimax Theatre (702-731-7900), with larger-than-life films that most school-age kids love. At the enormous **Excalibur,** 3850 Las Vegas Boulevard South (702-597-7777/800-937-7777), a first-floor Fantasy Fair features craft booths, medieval games, gypsy carts, and two forty-eight-seat motion simulator adventure rides. The third-floor Medieval Village boasts shops, seven theme restaurants, and strolling costumed singers, jugglers, and musicians.

Planned at press time for mid-1997 at the **Las Vegas Hilton,** 3000 Paradise Road (702-732-5111), is Star Trek: The Experience, including exhibits of authentic Star Trek costumes, props and weaponry, a simulator ride, interactive and virtual reality stations, state-of-the-art computer games, and more. The Cardassian Restaurant and the Starfleet Lounge offer twenty-fourth-century theme dining.

You can't miss the **Las Vegas Fremont Street Experience,** the country's largest urban theater. Providing a facelift to 5 blocks of the Glitter Gulch downtown area, the Fremont Street Experience is a landscaped, palm-tree-lined, decoratively paved, pedestrian mall, lined with restaurants, shops, casinos, and more. Extravagant, multisensory light-and-sound shows light up the night on a 90-foot-tall steel canopy. More than two million computer-operated lights inlaid in the canopy light up in various shapes and patterns, pulsating with blaring music. During the day, the canopy serves as a giant sunscreen, cutting the heat along Fremont Street by as much as 10 degrees.

The 1,149-foot-tall **Stratosphere Tower** on the north end of the Strip is the tallest free-standing observation tower in the country. In addition to serving as a hotel, casino, home to several restaurants (including one at ninety stories up), and wedding chapel, the Stratosphere offers two

The Las Vegas Strip comes alive with superstar entertainment, show spectaculars, and dazzling lights. (Courtesy the Las Vegas News Bureau)

gravity-defying rides: the 895-foot-high High Roller roller coaster, which swings around the top of the tower, and Hot Shot, which takes brave souls 160 feet up in two seconds and then drops them in a near free-fall.

Other Attractions

Wet 'n Wild, 2600 Las Vegas Boulevard South, on the Strip just south of Sahara Avenue; (702) 734-0088. This water park offers everything from the tame—Children's Water Playground with miniature water slides, bouncing Lily Pads, and water cannons—to wild—rides such as Bomb Bay, which drops you feet first from a capsule, creating a free-fall sensation.

In nearby Henderson (about fifteen minutes from the Strip), the following make pleasantly sweet stops on the way to Hoover Dam (see Day Trips).

Ethel M. Chocolates Factory and Cactus Gardens, Mountain Vista and Sunset Road; (702) 433-2500 or (800) 438-4356. Daily free tours show chocolates being made (free sample at the end). Outside, a lovely two-and-a-half-acre Cactus Garden with more than 350 species awaits. Ethel's last name was Mars, and she was the mom of Forest Mars, creator of Mars Bar, M&Ms, and Milky Way.

A free factory tour of **Kidd's Marshmallow Factory,** 8203 Gibson Road (702-564-5400), reveals all you ever wanted to know about how to make these puffy, white confections. You receive a free bag of the goodies at the tour's end.

Museums

Las Vegas is not all "mega" extravaganzas, as evidenced by the following interesting museums (a word used loosely in some cases).

Guinness World of Records Museum, 2780 Las Vegas Boulevard South; (702) 792-3766. This collection of world records covers the biggest, smallest, fastest—stuff that kids love. Browse the videos of world records being set and the life-size replicas. Interactive computers feature a World of Sports data bank, with thousands of sports records brought to the screen at the touch of a button. The World of Arts and Entertainment rocks with a jukebox that plays popular songs. Animal World recounts such oddities as the oldest monkey and the most poisonous jellyfish.

Imperial Palace Auto Collection, fifth floor of Imperial Palace Hotel, 3535 Las Vegas Boulevard South; (702) 731-3311. The more than 200 antique and classic cars on display include many formerly owned by famous personalities—such as a 1939 Mercedes Benz custom built for Adolph Hitler and President Dwight D. Eisenhower's 1952 Chrysler Imperial limousine parade car.

Las Vegas Natural History Museum, 900 Las Vegas Boulevard North; (702) 384-3466. While not huge, this museum is interesting. Three animated dinosaurs, fairly new acquisitions, are popular. The shark room, highlighted by a mounted 14-foot great white shark, has smaller, live versions swimming in a 300-gallon tank. A large hands-on room offers a variety of do-it-yourself activities, such as digging for a fossil or rubbing a dinosaur. Mounted international wildlife (lions, tigers, bears, and cheetahs) and a flight room with mounted birds, such as raptors, geese, and swans, round off the bill of fare. Ask about special programs and workshops.

Liberace Museum, 1775 East Tropicana Avenue; (702) 793-5595. Even kids who haven't the slightest idea who this popular entertainer was enjoy some of the kitschy offerings here. One of the museum's three buildings houses his pianos (including ones once owned by Chopin and George Gershwin) and his spectacular cars. Another building is devoted to the dazzling sequined costumes and jewelry that Mr. Showmanship wore on his worldwide tours. Still another building features the extensive memorabilia collected by Liberace during his lifetime. A sizable part of the admission goes to fund scholarships for deserving students.

Lied Discovery Children's Museum, 833 Las Vegas Boulevard North; (702) 382-KIDS. It was voted "Best Museum" in the *Las Vegas Review Journal*'s annual "Best of Las Vegas" poll. Even before you enter, you know it will be fun: The outside resembles a playhouse, with a tepee-shaped structure on the left. Kids let loose at this hands-on place, where there's a Toddler Towers to crawl and slide through, a Space Shuttle and Gyrochair to maneuver, a Musical Pathway to tap a tune on, a KKID radio station to play disc jockey at, and much more. Traveling exhibits, workshops, performances, and demonstrations happen throughout the year.

Parks and Zoos

Southern Nevada Zoological Park, 1775 North Rancho Drive; (702) 648-5955 or 647-4685. This small zoo appeals most to younger kids. They like the petting zoo and the more than fifty species of reptiles and small animals of the southwestern deserts. Other animals not indigenous to the area—monkeys, a lion, and a tiger among others—also please.

Theater, Music and the Arts

Just about every hotel has some kind of entertainment, though not all is suitable for kids. For listings of current shows and cultural events, check the entertainment pages of the daily *Las Vegas Review Journal* and *Las Vegas Sun,* or call the Chamber of Commerce at (702) 735-2451. **Ticket Time** (702-597-1588 or 800-697-SHOW) specializes in all Las Vegas shows, concerts, golf, and special events.

A note about casinos and shows: Remember that no one under twenty-one is allowed in the casinos. If you want to gamble, choose a hotel with a supervised children's activity center, or take turns being with your kids while the other parent tries his or her luck.

The entertainment in Las Vegas can be relatively inexpensive, and glitzy, but not always appropriate for children. Each show has its own restrictions. Topless shows are obviously not suitable for kids, but some other types of song-and-dance extravaganzas might be delightful. Often individual performers set their own rules about not admitting children younger than a certain age. Check with the box office and the Convention and Visitors Bureau before purchasing tickets.

Sports

The AAA **Las Vegas Stars** baseball team, a farm club for the San Diego Padres, plays at Cashman Field Center from April through September; (702) 386-7201. Championship boxing is also held regularly, as is PGA championship golf.

Shopping

Two malls are located on the Las Vegas Strip: **Fashion Show Mall,** just north of the Mirage, 3200 Las Vegas Boulevard South, has name stores such as Saks, Bullocks, and Neiman Marcus along with 145 specialty shops and eateries—plus a celebrity walk of fame. **Forum Shops at Caesars,** on the ground floor of the hotel-casino, 3570 Las Vegas Boulevard South, is filled with upscale boutiques and restaurants; it recreates ancient Roman streetscapes, with ornate fountains, classic statues, and huge columns and arches.

The Boulevard Mall, a short cab ride from the Strip, 3528 Maryland Parkway, is the largest shopping center in Nevada, with scores of specialty stores and Sears and J.C. Penney as anchors. Bargain hunters may want to try the **Belz Factory Outlet World Mall,** Las Vegas Boulevard South and Warm Springs Road, about 3 miles south of the Hacienda Hotel. This mall, the only nonsmoking facility in Las Vegas, has seventy-two outlets including twenty-five children's stores. **The Las Vegas Factory Outlet Stores of America,** 9115 Las Vegas Boulevard South, offers thirty acres of open-air shopping and fifty outlets.

SPECIAL EVENTS

April: Giant Picnic Land, Lied Discovery Children's Museum, food and fun festival with picnic games and activities, music, and entertainment.
End of May or early June: Helldorado Festival with rodeos, parades, beauty contest.
July: Fourth of July Jamboree, Boulder City.
September: Jaycee State Fair with carnival, entertainment, livestock shows; Art in the Park Fair, Boulder City.
October: Las Vegas Invitational PGA Golf Tournament.
December: National Finals Rodeo.

WHERE TO STAY

With approximately 86,053 surprisingly affordable guest rooms, your family has a large selection of accommodations: everything from inexpensive motels to a penthouse suite on the Strip. It's imperative, however, to reserve well in advance. This is a convention paradise, and sometimes every last room will be booked. **Las Vegas Reservation Systems** (800-233-5594) claims to offer the lowest rates to all Las Vegas hotels. **City Wide Reservations** books rooms as well as hotel packages; call (800) 733-6644. The *Official Visitor's Guide* has a good listing of area accommodations.

If you're prepared for the hustle and bustle of Las Vegas, the megaresort **Circus Circus, Treasure Island, MGM Grand Hotel and Theme Park,** and **Luxor** (described earlier) will do quite nicely. **Harrah's,** on the Strip (702-369-5000), with restaurants, casino space, and a thirty-five-story room tower, and offers 2,699 rooms and 108 suites is a good bet. Not too far from the action is the **Mardi Gras Inn,** a Best Western, at 3500 Paradise Road; (702) 731-2020 or (800) 528-1234. It offers 300 minisuites with separate living area, refrigerator, in-room movies, outdoor pool, and free airport shuttle. **Gold Coast Hotel and Casino,** 4000 West Flamingo Road (702-367-7111 or 800-331-5334), a mile west of center Strip, has a bowling center, two movie theaters, outdoor pool, and free child care until midnight for ages two (potty trained) to eight years.

WHERE TO EAT

The *Las Vegas Official Visitor's Guide* contains a descriptive listing of restaurants. The *Zagat Las Vegas Restaurant Survey,* available by calling (800) 333-3421, provides an alphabetical listing of about 300 Las Vegas restaurants, rated by food, decor, service, and cost. Try at least one of the legendary, lavish hotel buffets—the best bargain going. The Circus Buffet at **Circus Circus Hotel/Casino,** 2880 Las Vegas Boulevard South (702-734-0410 or 800-634-3450), is served at breakfast, brunch, and dinner (the latter two offer a sundae bar, as well). Prices are rock bottom. Don't expect to be alone: There are four serving lines that accommodate between 12,000 and 13,000 persons daily—more than four million a year. Try the Round Table Buffet at the **Excalibur,** 3850 Las Vegas Boulevard South; (702) 597-7777 or (800) 937-7777. Hot and cold entrees are served from 7:00 A.M. to 10:00 P.M. daily while knights in armor add to the atmosphere. Try some of the restaurants at Luxor, MGM Grand, and Treasure Island.

Dining and entertainment can easily go hand in hand in Las Vegas. Try one of the following, both on the Strip. **Dive! Las Vegas,** (702-369-DIVE), serves up submarine sandwiches in a sublike environment. Diners enter the restaurant through a vertical hatch; the two-story hull-shaped interior is complete with portholes, periscopes, sonar screens, and a giant video wall showing films of the sea. Dine with athletes, or at least their sports gear, in booths shaped like giant baseball mitts at the new **All Star Cafe** (702-795-8326), located in the Showcase Mall in front of the MGM Grand Hotel. Memorabilia honoring Andre Agassi, Amanda Beard, Tiger Woods, Wayne Gretzky, and other sports greats, plus sports videos and a huge scoreboard tracking events around the country, offer plenty for diners to gawk at while waiting for their food.

If the kids crave fast food, take them to the **Mardi Gras Food Court,** Riviera Hotel and Casino, 2901 Las Vegas Boulevard South; (702) 734-5110 or (800) 634-6753. The nine quick-serve restaurants here include Burger King, Tico Riko, Forenza Pizza, Orient Express, and Baskin Robbins. For something more substantial away from the slot machines, try the **Bootlegger Ristorante and Lounge,** 5025 South Eastern Avenue; (702) 736-4936. They serve tasty, moderately priced Italian-Continental meals. Pasta, chicken, veal, and other continental fare are on the menu of **Cafe Michelle,** 1350 East Flamingo Road (702-735-8686), a sidewalk café in the Mission Center.

DAY TRIPS

Lake Mead, a welcome blue oasis in the middle of the desert, is about 30 miles southeast of Las Vegas. The largest man-made body of water (by volume) in the United States, created by the construction of Hoover Dam, the lake extends 110 miles when filled to capacity. More than 550 miles of shoreline, and six marinas, mean plenty of boating, water skiing, and fishing. For campers, there are six developed campgrounds. Open daily from 8:30 A.M. to 4:30 P.M., the Lake Mead Visitor's Center (702-293-4041) is 4 miles northeast of Boulder City on Boulder Highway, U.S. 95. Take a tape for a self-guided tour of the lake's Northshore and Lakeshore roads. Come aboard the paddlewheeler *Desert Princess* (702-293-6180), a tour boat that offers a pleasant way to see the dam, especially with young children. Narration, food, and beverages are offered.

Hoover Dam, considered one of the world's great engineering achievements, is a popular tourist destination. Guided, thirty-five-minute tours leave the top of the dam every few minutes and take visitors inside the structure to see its inner workings. The Hoover Dam Visitors Bureau, 1228 Arizona Street, Boulder City (702-294-1988), shows a free movie daily, every half-hour, about the history of the dam's construction.

Red Rock Canyon, 15 miles west of Las Vegas, is a favorite setting for TV and film Westerns. Enjoy the sculptured sandstone outcroppings and the magnificent geological formations. Follow the scenic, 13-mile, one-way loop for splendid vistas of the blazing-red rock formations. Take time to walk some of the several short trails, which afford glimpses of wildlife as well as streams, springs, and seasonal waterfalls. Picnic sites are located at Red Spring and Willow Spring. Call the Visitors Center at (702) 363-1921 for more information.

Nearby, **Bonnie Springs Ranch/Old Nevada,** West Charleston Boulevard (702–875–4191), is a restored pioneer village with gunfights in the street, train rides on weekends, cactus gardens, two museums, a shooting gallery, a restaurant, and an ice-cream parlour. The Ranch has a petting zoo and horseback riding.

From Thanksgiving to Easter, you can ski at **Lee Canyon Ski Area,** Mt. Charleston, Toiyabe National Forest (702–646–0008), about forty minutes northwest of Las Vegas. **Mt. Charleston Recreation Area,** on U.S. 95 (702–873–8800), also offers summer diversions, such as picnic and campground sites, lookout points, and hiking trails.

If you have never visited the **Grand Canyon,** consider taking a one-day or two-day/one-night air tour from Las Vegas, 200 miles from the attraction. **Scenic Airlines** (702–739–1900 or 800–634–6801) offers a number of packages to the area, including a flight without a tour. Ask about their kids' rates for ages two to eleven.

FOR MORE INFORMATION

Las Vegas Convention and Visitors Authority, 3150 Paradise Road, Las Vegas 89101 (702–892–0711), operates a Visitors Information Center on the Main Concourse of the Convention Center seven days a week from 8:00 A.M. to 5:00 P.M. Website: http://www.vegas.com.

Emergency Numbers
Ambulance, fire, police: 911
Poison Information Center: (702) 732–4989
White Cross Drugs, 1700 South Las Vegas Boulevard, is open
    twenty-four hours, although the pharmacy is open from
    7:00 A.M. to 1:00 A.M.; (702) 384–8075.
Twenty-four-hour emergency room at **Humana Hospital
    Sunrise,** 3186 South Maryland Parkway; (702) 731–8000.

LAKE TAHOE

This beautiful alpine body of water, which bisects California and Nevada (two-thirds is in California), lures visitors with winter skiing; summer swimming, boating, and hiking; and year-round casino gambling and headline entertainment on the Nevada side. This distinctively blue lake at the northern end of the Sierra Nevada mountains, 22 miles long and 12 miles wide with 72 miles of shoreline, is the second deepest lake in the United States.

Whether you stay on the north or south shore (the lake's most developed areas) is a matter of personal preference. Both offer access to the great outdoors; however, the north shore is convenient to more ski areas. While both have Nevada casinos, the north shore has less neon. The lake's largest city, South Lake Tahoe, California (population 22,000), is in the midst of a long-range, multimillion-dollar upgrading. Just northeast, the city of Stateline, Nevada, is known for its strip of famous casinos.

GETTING THERE

Reno/Tahoe International Airport (702-328-6400) is served by nine major carriers. Some major hotels offer free shuttles. Ground transportation to the south shore's five major hotels is via **Tahoe Casino Express** (702-785-2424 or 800-446-6128), which has fourteen round-trips daily. The trip takes one hour and twenty minutes. **Aero Trans** (702-786-2376) provides shuttles to the north shore. It's 29 miles to the north shore communities of Incline Village and Crystal Bay, Nevada. Car rentals are available at the airport.

Amtrak (800-USA-RAIL) services the area, with stops at East Commercial Row and Lake Street in Reno, and at 10065 Donner Pass Road in Truckee, California.

Greyhound stations (800-231-2222) are at 155 Stevenson Street, Reno; 10065 Donner Pass Road, Truckee; and in Harrah's, Lake Tahoe. Two major freeways, U.S. 50 and I-80, link Lake Tahoe with the rest of the country. North shore communities are on Highway 28, which connects with California Highway 89 on the west shore and Nevada Highway 50 on the east shore. The point where Highways 89 and 50 connect on the south shore is called the "Y."

GETTING AROUND

A car is helpful, but not imperative. Skiers can take the free shuttles offered by many ski areas (see Winter Pleasures). The roads are often congested, particularly on weekends. Note that Highway 89, which traverses the western shore, is full of zigs, zags, and 10-mph zones—though it is more scenic than the eastern route.

Visitors are encouraged to use public transportation whenever possible. (At press time many hotels were offering free bus passes.) North shore buses are run by **Tahoe Area Regional Transit** (TART); (916) 581-6365 or (800) 736-6365. **South Tahoe Area Ground Express** (STAGE) serves the city of South Lake Tahoe; call (916) 573-2080. Check out their discount transfer coupons to the summer Bus Plus Van (916-541-6368) to south and west shore beaches, as far as Meeks Bay, where TART buses leave for the north shore. **Nifty 50 Trolley** runs from Zephyr Cove Resort on the Nevada side to Camp Richardson Resort (California side) between June and September, daily from 10:00 A.M. to 11:00 P.M. All-day tickets are $2.00.

WHAT TO SEE AND DO

No matter what time of year you visit, the outdoors will be your focus. In summer enjoy the beaches, boating, hiking, and biking; in winter take to the hills for good family skiing. *Lake Tahoe: A Family Guide* by Lisa Gollins Evans (Mountaineer Press) offers detailed information on hiking trails and other outdoor activities.

Beaches

Among nearly thirty beaches ringing the lake, the following have family appeal:

Lake Tahoe at a Glance

- Alluring alpine lake community with bountiful outdoor activities and unusual museums

- In summer: swimming, boating, jet skiing, kayaking, river rafting, biking, hiking, fishing, picknicking

- In winter: downhill and cross-country skiing, snowmobiling

- Comstock silver mining history in nearby Virginia City

- Lake Tahoe Visitors Authority, (916) 544-5050 or (800) AT-TAHOE

Northeast Shore: **Sand Harbor,** in Lake Tahoe Nevada State Park, 8 miles south of Incline Village on Highway 28, features white sand, picnic areas, nature trail, a boat launch, and rest room with showers. There is a parking fee. The amphitheater here is the scene of summer concerts and theatrical productions (see Special Events).

South Shore: **Baldwin Beach,** Baldwin Beach Road, about a mile west of the U.S. Forest Service Visitor's Center, Highway 89, is scenic, quiet, accessible to bikers along the South Shore Bike Trail and has shallow water (see Biking).

West Shore: **D.L. Bliss State Park,** almost 17 miles south of Tahoe City on Highway 89, is considered by many to have the finest beach on the lake, with sparkling white sand and coves for snorkelers. The park is also noted for some of the area's best trails. Arrive early; parking is limited.

North Shore: **Kings Beach State Recreation Area** (916-546-7248), the largest of twenty-one beaches in North Tahoe, boasts four acres of white, sandy beach. A public pier, a boat-launch facility, jet skis, paddleboat rental, and parasailing highlight this downtown gem. There's also a newly built beachfront promenade, plaza, and picnic facility.

Boating, Kayaking, and River Rafting

Boat rentals are available throughout the north and south shore. **Tahoe Paddle & Oar** runs guided kayak tours from the North Tahoe

Beach Center, King's Beach, 7860 North Lake Boulevard (off Highway 89 between Tahoe City and Truckee), weekdays from June to October; call (916) 581-3029 for information.

Sight-seeing boats provide a leisurely way to see the lake. *M.S. Dixie II* paddlewheeler (702-588-3508 or 882-0786) offers narrated scenic cruises daily, year-round, leaving from Zephyr Cove, Nevada, 4 miles north of south shore casinos on Highway 50. Breakfast, brunch, and sunset dinner cruises are possible, as are day trips to glacier-carved Emerald Bay, one of the state's most photographed sites. The Bay is also the destination of the glass-bottomed *Tahoe Queen,* which leaves daily, year-round, from Ski Run Marina, South Lake Tahoe. Call (916) 541-3364 or (800) 23-TAHOE for reservations. At the north shore, take the new *Tahoe Gal* from North Tahoe Cruises from the Lighthouse Center in Tahoe City. Call (916) 583-0141.

Take to the Truckee River by raft. After a six-year drought, a recent abundance of water makes for a swift, but gentle, ride. Try **Fanny Bridge Rafts** or **Truckee River Raft Rental** (916-583-0123); or **Truckee River Rafting/Mountain Air Sports** (916-583-7238).

Nature and Hiking Trails

You don't have to be a survivalist to enjoy hiking around the lake. For the hearty, the **Tahoe Rim Trail,** with 115 miles cleared and maintained by volunteers (it will soon increase to 150 miles and encircle the lake), is a good choice. Spooner Lake, Highway 28 near the intersection of U.S. Highway 50, is one of the most popular accesses.

Squaw Creek Meadow starts at the bridge behind the Olympic Village Inn at Squaw Valley, off Highway 89 between Tahoe City and Truckee. At first the beginners' trail is steep, but soon the terrain levels. (Pick the more gentle left path at the fork.) In summer (mid-July is peak season), meadows bloom with colorful wildflowers.

At the **U.S. Forest Service Visitor's Center,** Highway 89, South Shore (916-573-2674), the National Forest Service offers some interesting self-guided tours, but first go inside to learn about the area's history. In summer, Monday through Friday, a one-hour Woodsy Ranger program for ages five to thirteen features environmental games and a ranger-led nature walk. Families with young children should opt for the short (0.15-mile loop) **Smokey's Trail,** just south of the center, that stresses campfire safety. Kids who remember what they learned receive a patch or comic book. The **Rainbow Trail,** another good bet, travels a half-mile loop through pine forests to meadows, with a stop at the Stream Profile Chamber on Taylor Creek. The building is partly underwater, so you can look out windows to see trout, salmon, and other fish swim by.

The **Tallac Historic Site Trail,** a mile one way, passes the Kiva Beach picnic area and several turn-of-the-century summer estates of some of San Francisco's richest and most famous citizens. Reserve tours of the posh Pope House in advance through the Visitor's Center. There's no admission to enter the **Tallac Museum** (916-541-5227), located inside another grand home where an elegant room has been restored. **Trail of the Washoe,** a 0.75-mile loop, features information about the history and culture of the Washoe tribe, members of which came from the mountains to spend their summers here before white settlers arrived.

The **Tahoe Meadows Handicapped Access Trail** was designed for those in wheelchairs, the blind, and families with small children. The leveled trail, a 1.3-mile loop around the meadow, includes ten bridges over gullies and meadow streams and is marked with signs. The trailhead is about a half mile below the Mt. Rose Highway summit (10 miles from Incline Village on Mt. Rose Highway 431) at the Tahoe Rim Trail trailhead. The **U.S. Forest Service Visitor's Center** and **South Lake Tahoe Bike Path** (described earlier) are also accessible to those in wheelchairs.

Eagle Falls is one of the most photographed places in the world. Hike 1 mile up to the falls and Eagle Lake. Avid hikers can keep going into the Desolation Wilderness, where dozens of snowmelt-fed lakes await. Camping is allowed; self-registration is mandatory at the trailhead. Call Tahoe Trips and Trails (800-581-HIKE) for additional hiking information.

Biking

Biking is big in Tahoe, where there are 5 miles of unpaved biking trails for every mile of paved roads. A number of bike rental concessions are located throughout the area. Call or visit early on weekends to avoid being disappointed.

The South Lake Tahoe Bike Path, a 3.4-mile easy trail that parallels Highway 89, is so lovely that your family won't be alone, but the pedaling is still fun, especially if you have little kids who delight in being pulled in a baby trailer or sitting in a canvas-topped surrey. Most cyclists ride from east to west: The eastern end is about 1.5 miles north of the Highway 89 and 50 intersection. From here, it's about a 1.5-mile ride northwest to the long expanse of Pope Beach. If you're renting a bike, access the trail 0.3 miles west at Camp Richardson Resort and Marina (915-541-1801); baby trailers and four-person surreys are for rent. Pedal a half-mile west to Kiva Beach, a lovely place for a swim. From the pine-shaded picnic area, cyclists link up with trails along the lake to the Tallac Historic Site (described earlier). (Bikes aren't allowed on nature trails.) Push on for 0.7 miles to rest at beautiful Baldwin Beach (see Beaches).

The **North Lake Tahoe Bike Path** is paved and hugs the lake all the way to Sugar Pine Point State Park, 10 miles south of the trailhead. Or, head north and ride along the wild and scenic Truckee River for 5 miles. Stop at the River Ranch Lodge at the end of the river and rest.

Mountain bikers also can have their sport here. The most popular trail, the challenging **Flume Trail,** starts at Spooner Lake, east of Incline Village, and travels up a high ridge affording splendid lake views. Call **Nevada State Park** (702-831-0494) or the **U.S. Forest Service Visitor's Center** at (916) 573-2674 for information.

At **Northstar at Tahoe,** 6 miles southeast of Truckee on California State Highway 267 (916-587-0215 or 800-GO-NORTH), you can rent mountain bikes from the Mountain Adventure Shop in Northstar Village, where you can get trail maps and ask about guided tours. Mountain bike school packages are offered on selected weekends. Chair lifts carry bikers and hikers to midmountain and to the top of Lookout Mountain. Other attractions: a ropes course 50 feet in the trees near the Village lets those age ten and up pursue mentally and physically challenging games and exercises. The course is open Thursdays through Sundays. There's also a climbing wall and an orienteering course (register at Mountain Adventure Shop). Trail and pony rides, tennis, golf, swimming (with lessons), and Minors' Day Camp for ages two (potty trained) to ten round out the summer fun.

Squaw Valley, off Highway 89 between Tahoe City and Truckee; (916) 583-6985 or (800) 545-4350. This self-contained village boasts more than 30 miles of single tracks and roads for all levels. Rent bikes at the mountain bike store and repair center at the base (elevation 6,200 feet). The Cable Car whisks you and your bike up 2,000 vertical feet to the center of the resort's trail network. Choose trails that wind through meadows of wildflowers, or, if your gang is up to it, attempt a more challenging uphill push. **High Camp Bath and Tennis Club** (elevation 8,200 feet) is the center of summer fun and offers numerous activities. Plans for a hotel adjacent to the Bath and Tennis Club are in the works.

Winter Pleasures

Northstar-at-Tahoe and **Squaw Valley USA** are two of two dozen area downhill and cross-country ski areas. Northstar-at-Tahoe (916–587-0215 or 800–GO–NORTH; http://www.aminews.com/northstar), 6 miles from Lake Tahoe's North Shore, was recently ranked sixth in North America for its kids' programs by *Snow Country* readers, and by *Ski* as being a top family ski resort. Lessons are available for all skill levels, with a Magic Carpet lift in the kids' ski school area. Minor's Camp offers full- and half-day child care for ages two to six, plus the option for a learn-to-ski program for ages three to six; call (916) 587–0278 for reservations. Kids ages five to twelve can learn to ski with Starkids or snowboard with the Shred Kids program. Northstar also offers 65 kilometers of groomed and tracked cross-country trails. Lessons, rentals, and snowshoes are available. Accommodations are mostly condominiums and homes spread out over the mountain, with some hotel rooms available in The Village. A free shuttle bus provides transportation to the slopes from several lodging points.

Located on the North Shore, **Squaw Valley USA** (916–583–6955 or 800–545–4350) is off Highway 89 between Tahoe City and Truckee. Children's World houses the kids' ski school, lessons center, and day care. Two- to three-year-olds can join in the Ten Little Indians child care program, while three-year-olds can add on a one-hour ski lesson. Call ahead for reservations. The Junior Mountain and Snow School provides full- and half-day lessons for kids ages four to twelve; snowboard lessons are available for those ages seven to twelve. Take a break from skiing at the Olympic Ice Pavilion (916–587–5437), an Olympic-size outdoor ice rink at the High Camp Bath and Tennis Club; swimming and bungee jumping are also found here.

Nearby **Resort at Squaw Creek** (916-583-6300 or 800- 583-6300), a four-diamond property, is designed to look like a European village, and it offers rooms, suites, and bilevel penthouses. A shuttle bus to the ski area is free.

Alpine Meadows Ski Area (800-441-4423; http://www.com/ alpine), 6 miles northwest of Tahoe City, off Highway 89. The Children's Snow School, has lessons for ages four to six. The Kids Ski Camp offers two-hour group lessons for ages six to twelve. Alpine Meadows doesn't offer any on-mountain or base lodging, but tracking down one of more than 6,000 lodging units in the North Tahoe/ Truckee area shouldn't be a problem. Try **River Ranch Lodge** (916-583-4264 or 800-535-9900), located on the banks of the Truckee River, or call (800) TAHOE-4U for more options. **Diamond Peak,** 1210 Ski Way, Incline Village, Nevada; (702) 832-1177. Kids' highlights include a Pre-Ski program for three-year-olds, Sierra Scouts Adventure learn-to-ski program for ages seven to twelve, and Super Scouts for ages seven to twelve with basic skills. Pete's Play Land acquaints little ones with the snow and features playground slides and climbing equipment. Free shuttles are available from areas throughout the north shore. **Ski Homewood** (916-525-2992), 6 miles south of Tahoe City, offers lake views, ski and snowboard programs for ages four and up, and a combination of preschool and ski school at the Children's Center.

South Shore: **Heavenly,** straddling the state line; (702) 586-7000 or (800) 2-HEAVEN. An aerial tram operated in summer offers scenic vistas of the Sierra Nevadas and Lake Tahoe and access to a 2-mile round-trip hiking trail. Winter ski lessons are offered for ages four to twelve, with most of the children's activities taking place near the California base lodge. Kids in the ski or snowboard school, or those taking a private lesson, ski at the Enchanted Forest, a specially designed beginner area, where the Magic Carpet lift carries young skiers uphill. Also offered at Heavenly is the Ski with a Ranger tour, an opportunity for adults and children alike to enjoy a two-hour ecological ski tour, complete with ranger discussion on the mountain's geology and wildlife; the tours are recommended for intermediate or better skiers. And, look for a new gondola soon, planned to carry 2,800 persons per hour from the stateline casino area to the resort. As for accommodations, Heav-

Children and adults will enjoy a day on the slopes at Squaw Valley.
(Photo by Hank deVre/courtesy Squaw Valley Ski Corporation)

enly's convenient location to Stateside, Nevada, provides plenty of options. Or, try the more homey feel of **Inn by the Lake,** South Lake Tahoe; (916-542-0330 or (800) 877-1466). The inn, which comprises one hundred rooms and suites, some with kitchens, is a good family choice.

Three favorites of locals: Twelve miles west of South Lake Tahoe, **Sierra-at-Tahoe** (916-659-7453 or 800-AT-TAHOE; http://www/aminews.com.SierraTahoe) offers a low-key atmosphere for those families with beginners and youngsters easily intimidated by the hustle and bustle of larger ski bases. A quarter of the terrain (totaling forty-four slopes and trails) is aimed at beginners. First Track offers an innovative learn-to-ski program; new snowboarders and skiers progress at their own pace through a series of instructor-manned teaching stations. The Wild Mountain Children's Center offers full- and half-day lessons for kids ages four to twelve; ski and snowboard lessons are both available. Other highlights: a Magic Carpet lift; Mountain Cubs (ages four to six), Mountain Coyotes (ages seven to nine), and Mountain

Explorers (ages ten to twelve) ski programs; Wild Willie, the resort mascot; and Dyno-Tykes Day Care for ages two to five, with ski lesson add-ons available for three- to five-year-olds. A free shuttle bus stops at thirty-eight nearby accommodations.

Kirkwood (209-258-6000), about forty-five minutes from South Lake Tahoe, has a new Children's Center, featuring the Timber Creek Learn-to-Ski area, just for kids. Mighty Mountain ski school offers lessons for kids ages four to twelve, and day care is available for ages three to six. Eighty kilometers of cross-country trails, rentals, and snowshoes are additional features. There are miles of marked cross-country ski trails and rentals around the lake as well as designated snow-play areas.

About forty-five minutes from South Lake Tahoe is **Sorenson's Resort and Hope Valley Cross Country** (916-694-2230 or 800-423-9949). There are no specific kids' programs, but families remain a large majority of the clientele here. Explore 10 miles of groomed trails and 50 miles of marked trails on your own on a guided Wildlife Ski Tour, available to skiers and snowshoers alike. Troll Tracks is the kids' cross-country ski and learning area; sledding and snowman-making are also part of the fun. The twenty-nine cabins range from studios to three-bedroom units, and most have kitchens. **Lakeview Cross Country** (916-583-9353), two miles northwest of Tahoe City, offers gorgeous lake views on 65 kilometers of groomed trails and skating lanes. Rentals and lessons are also available.

Kids as young as seven can ride along on the guided snowmobile tours, which cover 14 miles of groomed trails offered by **Zephyr Cove Snowmobile Center,** 760 Highway 50, Zephyr Cove, Nevada, 4 miles north of the south shore casinos; (702) 588-3833. In summer, Zephyr Cove opens its marina for boat rentals; it has a nice beach, snack bar, and restaurant, plus volleyball and horseback riding. It also offers lodge rooms, cabins, and a campground with hookups for RVs. The *M.S. Dixie II* paddlewheel boat is docked here.

Museums and Historical Sites

Ehrman Mansion, Sugar Pine Point State Park, 10 miles south of Tahoe City on Highway 89; (916) 525-7982. Tour this elegant 1900 summer home, led by rangers who sometimes don period costumes.

Also on the grounds is an 1860 log cabin built by one of the area's first white settlers. An old water tower adjacent to the mansion houses a nature center with interactive exhibits on plants and animals. Open late summer through Labor Day.

Emigrant Trail Museum, Donner Memorial State Park, just off I-80 at Donner Lake exit west of Truckee; (916) 582-7892. A tribute to the emigrant movement of the mid-1800s, this small museum houses a covered wagon and homestead. Exhibits tell about the natural history of the Sierra Nevada and the construction of the Central Pacific Railroad. Walk along the self-guided nature trail; then enjoy the park's natural wonders, with camping, picnicking, boating, and fishing among the possibilities. The museum is closed Thanksgiving, Christmas, and New Year's Day.

Gatekeepers Log Cabin Museum, south end of Fanny Bridge, Tahoe City; (916) 583-1762. This handcrafted building houses a collection of Native American (Washo) baskets, tools, clothing, pictures, early railroad and logging equipment, and other area memorabilia of the region's nineteenth and early twentieth century. Open summers only.

Vikingsholm (916-525-7277 or 525-7232) is a replica of a hundred-year-old Norse castle constructed in 1929 on Emerald Bay (south shore) as a summer retreat. Costumed rangers give tours from July to September. Arrive by private boats (see Boating) or hike in about a mile from Highway 89. (Although swimming is allowed at Emerald Bay, be forewarned that there's lots of boat traffic.)

Visit the **Sierra Nevada Children's Museum** (916-587-5437) for kid-friendly displays and arts and crafts.

Other Attractions

Ponderosa Ranch, 100 Ponderosa Ranch Road, Highway 28, North Shore at Incline Village; (702) 831-0691. This is where *Bonanza,* the legendary TV show and the TV movie *Bonanza: The Next Generation* were filmed. Although the inside of the Cartwright's home may not mean a thing to your kids, they will still enjoy this re-created town. The fun-filled ranch is open mid-April through October.

The north shore's new **Incline Village Recreation Center,** 980 Incline Way (702-832-1310), includes a pool, gym, dance studio, game room, sport shop, and on-site child-care center. The center plans year-round family-oriented activities, classes, and programs, including special children's nights and teen dances; visitors are welcome.

Theater, Music, and the Arts

The visitor's bureaus listed below are your best sources for what's going on. Don't miss the **Valhalla Festival of Arts and Music** on the south shore, a summer-long cultural celebration featuring outdoor concerts (such as a jazz concert on top of Heavenly Mountain), performances, and events, including children's activities. Tickets are available through **Tahoe Tallac Association** (916-541-4166).

The Reno area is home to a ballet company, the Reno Philharmonic, the Nevada Opera, the Reno Little Theater—plus lots of splashy casino shows. Remember, however, that persons under twenty-one are not welcome in the gaming areas of the casinos. Call ahead to be sure. The Reno/Tahoe Visitor's Information Center can supply dates, times, and locations: (800) FOR-RENO.

Shopping

Many stores have souvenirs of the friendly, green, lake "monster," Tahoe Tessie. At Tahoe Tessie's Museum and Gift Shop, 8612 North Lake Boulevard, Kings Beach, north shore (916-546-TSSI), Tessie herself appears on weekends (summers only). A forty-eight-page adventure book, *The Story of Tahoe Tessie, the Original Lake Tahoe Monster,* includes a history of Lake Tahoe. Tahoe Tessie is also at the boarding site of the *M.S. Dixie II.*

SPECIAL EVENTS

March: Snowfest, ten-day winter carnival, North Lake Tahoe; day and night activities include opening torchlight parade, ski races, snowboarding and snow-sculpturing contests, spaghetti feeds, "crazy" events, street dances, fireworks, and children's theaters.

May: Victorian Square, Cinco de Mayo Celebration, a giant outdoor fiesta with music, dance performances, authentic foods, and arts and crafts.

June: Annual Wagon Train, south shore, featuring parade of authentic wagons, buggies, and riders on horseback; Valhalla Renaissance Festival, Richardson's Resort, south shore. Truckee-Tahoe Air Show, with stunts, displays, and hot-air balloons.

June–September: Valhalla Festival of Arts and Music, south shore, featuring the Wa She She E Deh Fine Arts Festival and Arts Market; Native American culture, crafts, and fine arts; the Tallac Historic Site; and the Lake Tahoe Summer Music Festival.

July: Music at Sand Harbor, Sand Harbor State Park amphitheater (4 miles south of Incline Village); Antique Boat Show; Star Spangled Banner 4th of July, south shore, the largest fireworks display west of the Mississippi; Isuzu Celebrity Golf Championship, Edgewood, south shore.

August: Shakespeare at Sand Harbor, Lake Tahoe Nevada State Park amphitheater; Great Gatsby Weekend, Tallac Museum, including kids' activities; Truckee Championship Rodeo; Concours d'Elegance, Sierra Boat Company.

September: Cool September Days; Chili Cook Off; Great Reno Balloon Race; Reno Grand Prix; National Championship Air Races, Reno.

October: Snow Dance, Preston Park, Incline Village, authentic ceremony by Sierra Nevada Miwok Indians. Weekend activities also feature craft fair, salmon specialties, traditional food; Kokanee Salmon Festival, U.S. Forest Service Center, south shore; Oktoberfest (800–824–6345), Alpine Meadows Ski Area, traditional Bavarian food, drink, dancing, and twenty-piece oom-pah band.

November: Ski resorts open Thanksgiving Day; Autumn Food & Wine Jubilee (800–824–6345), Squaw Valley, thirty local restaurants plus California wineries.

December: Sparks Hometowne Christmas; this Victorian-style celebration includes tree lighting, parade, caroling, theatrical events, crafts, entertainment, and food. Alpenlight Festival (800–824–6348), festive holiday events throughout the north shore.

WHERE TO STAY

North Lake Tahoe Resort Association (800-TAHOE-4-U) has a computerized **Central Reservation Service,** which represents lodging properties in their Travel Planner. Ask about summer and winter packages. On the south shore, the **Lake Tahoe Visitors Authority**'s central reservation number, (800) AT–TAHOE, is to book lodging, shows, attractions, and ski-lift tickets. Ask for a free, all-season travel planner. There's a high concentration of condos and vacation home rentals in the posh **Incline Village** and **Crystal Bay** area, a good bet for families. Call (800) GO-TAHOE for information. All the visitor's bureaus supply campground information (see For More Information). (The wide selection includes three national forests: Tahoe to the north, Toiyabe to the east, and Eldorado to the southwest.)

Besides Northstar, these lodgings in Tahoe and the Squaw Valley areas offer something special for families.

North Shore: **Resort at Squaw Creek,** 400 Squaw Creek Road, Olympic Valley, California; (916) 583-6300 or (800) 327-3353. This pretty property features 405 accommodations, including rooms, suites, and bilevel penthouses with kitchens. Enjoy three pools, tennis, outdoor ice skating, ski-in/ski-out access to Squaw Valley, an equestrian center, hiking and mountain bike trails, and a Mountain Buddies program for ages five to thirteen. Summer day care and year-round babysitting are available for children under five.

Hyatt Lake Tahoe, Incline Village; (702) 832-1234 or (800) 553-3288. Mom and dad can try their luck in the big casino while kids ages three (potty trained) to twelve have fun at Camp Hyatt (daily Memorial to Labor Day; Friday and Saturday year-round).

South Shore: **Embassy Suites Resort,** 4130 Lake Tahoe Boulevard, Highway 50, South Lake Tahoe; (916) 544-5400 or (800) EMBASSY. The 400 suites–each with a refrigerator, microwave, and coffeemaker–include some that are child proofed. Swim in an indoor pool, and enjoy free continental breakfast.

The recently-opened **Embassy Vacation Resort** (800-856-9364), at the Ski Run Marina Hotel, is adjacent to the lake and just 1 mile from the stateline casino area. Two-bedroom, two-bathroom vacation condos with kitchens, living rooms, and several other amenities are available on a time-share basis.

WHERE TO EAT

Lake Tahoe features a number of restaurants (North Lake Tahoe alone has more than one hundred), so your choices are many. Call (800) TAHOE-4-U for north shore restaurant suggestions, and the

South Lake Tahoe Chamber of Commerce (916-541-5255) for recommendations in their area. Here are a few possibilities.

Incline Village/Crystal Bay: Locals like the **24 Hour Coffee Shops** at the Crystal Bay Club and Tahoe Biltmore, Highway 28, Crystal Bay (702-831-0512), and the Hyatt Regency at Incline Village (800-468-2463). The food is good and the prices are reasonable.

Tahoe City/West Shore: **Grazie!**, Roundhouse Mall, 700 North Lake Boulevard; (916) 583-0233. They offer Italian food in a lovely lakeside setting. Lunch is served weekdays; dinners nightly.

South Shore: **Red Hut Waffle Shop,** 2723 Lake Tahoe Boulevard, South Lake Tahoe; (916) 541-9024. (There's also one in Stateline, Nevada.) They serve breakfast and lunch—big helpings at good prices.

DAY TRIPS

Virginia City, about one hour northeast of the north shore, was once a thriving mining town. The silver mined here aided in financing the Union during the Civil War, in building San Francisco, and in bringing statehood to Nevada. Take a thirty-five-minute trip through the historic **Comstock mining district** aboard the **Virginia and Truckee Railroad;** (702) 847-0380. Tour an underground mine and the nearby Victorian mansions. Contact the Virginia City Chamber of Commerce for more information; (702) 847-0311.

The Reno/Tahoe Tourist Information Center (702-827-RENO or 800-FOR-RENO) can tell you what to see and do in and around **Reno,** a fifty-minute ride from Incline Village and an hour-and-ten-minute drive from south Lake Tahoe. The Reno/Sparks Visitors' Centers are located at the Reno/Tahoe International Airport and downtown in the National Bowling Stadium.

Because Tahoe, about 30-40 miles away, offers more of the outdoors plus gambling, with less of Reno's intensity, Tahoe is most likely the place for most of your stay. Because most flights arrive and depart from Reno, however, you might consider staying in town for a night or two. Generally, hotel rooms are less expensive here than in Tahoe. Many of the casinos here have Las Vegas counterparts, including **Circus, Circus,** 500 North Sierra Street; (702) 329-0711 or (800) 648-5010. Decorated to look like a giant circus tent, it, like its sister hotel, offers circus acts.

Wilbur D. May Great Basin Adventure in Rancho San Rafael Park, 1502 Washington Street; (702) 785-5961. This child-oriented theme park features mining exhibits, a discovery room, a petting zoo, and a play area. Reno's **National Bowling Stadium** (702-334-2600), the nation's first, is topped by a geodesic dome housing an IWERKS Theater with "sensor seats" and eighty championship lanes.

Other attractions with family appeal include the **National Automobile Museum,** 10 South Lake Street at Mill Street; (702) 333-9300. It houses more than 200 rare, restored old vehicles, some experimental, others that belonged to presidents and celebrities. **Fleishmann Planetarium,** 1650 North Virginia Street (702-784-4811), is on the University of Nevada-Reno campus and offers star and laser shows and telescope viewing. Reno's cultural offerings are listed under Theater, Music, and the Arts.

The neighboring town of Sparks has **Wild Island** amusement park, I-80 East and Sparks Boulevard; (703) 331-WILD. Enjoy the water slides, wave pool, miniature golf, and grand prix mini-auto racing.

For More Information

North Shore: **North Lake Tahoe Resort Association,** P.O. Box 5578, Tahoe City, California 96145; (916) 583-3494 or (800) TAHOE-4-U.

Incline Village/Crystal Bay Visitor's and Convention Bureau, 969 Tahoe Boulevard, Incline Village, Nevada 89451; (702) 832-1606 or (800) GO-TAHOE.

South Shore: **Lake Tahoe Visitors Authority,** 1156 Ski Run Boulevard, South Lake Tahoe, California 96150; (916) 544-5050 or (800) AT-TAHOE.

Reno/Tahoe, P.O. Box 837, Reno, Nevada 89504; (800) FOR-RENO.

Emergency Numbers

Ambulance, fire, police: 911

North Shore:

Call the hospital for poison control information and for medicine in an emergency after pharmacy hours.

Twenty-four-hour emergency medical services (including pharmacy and poison control): **Tahoe Forest Hospital,** Pine Avenue and Donner Pass Road, Truckee, California; (916) 587-6011

South Shore:

Twenty-four-hour emergency medical services: Barton Memorial Hospital, South Avenue and Fourth Street, South Lake Tahoe, California; (916) 541-3420

9 ❀ California

MONTEREY PENINSULA

The Monterey Peninsula, 125 miles south of San Francisco, is a scenic stretch of coastline, pine forests, and unmistakable California elan. This spit of land is surrounded by Monterey Bay on the north, the Pacific Ocean on the west, and Carmel Bay on the south. Waves crash with a fierce splendor on these rocky shores and colonies of sea lions sunbathe on the flat tops of seaside boulders. A state park makes it easy and affordable for families to savor the views. Golf is revered and there's no shortage of trendy shopping in the upscale boutiques of Carmel-by-the-sea. The region's towns, Monterey, Pacific Grove, Pebble Beach, Carmel-by-the-Sea, and Carmel in the Valley, offer a variety of accommodations and sites.

The first documentation of the area is in 1542 when Don Juan Cabrillo, a Portuguese explorer, came in search of California's riches. Neither he nor his crew set foot on land here, but he is credited with being the first European to anchor in "La Bahia de los Pinos" (the Bay of the Pines). Sixty years passed before Sebastian Vizcaino, in 1602, landed on the Peninsula which he named after the Count de Monte Rey, the Spanish merchant whose orders he was sailing under. By 1777 Monterey was the capital of Alta (upper) and Baja (Lower) California.

When Mexico revolted from Spain about 45 years later in 1822, Monterey became the capital of Mexico. Commodore John Drake Sloat ended years of territorial disputes between Mexico and the United States, when in 1846, he arrived in Monterey and hoisted the American Flag over the Custom house. In 1850 California was admitted to the Union.

Monterey maintained its seafaring routes and grew from a quaint fishing village into a city recognized for its fish processing and canning.

The Monterey canneries became a household name with the publication of John Steinbeck's *Cannery Row*.

GETTING THERE

The **Monterey Peninsula Airport,** 200 Fred Kane Drive; (408-648-7000), four miles east of Monterey, is a small airport currently served by seven airlines. **Alaska Air** (800-426-0333), **American Eagle** (800-433-7300 or 800-624-6262), **Continental** (800-525-0280), **Northwest** (800-225-2525), **Skywest** (800-453-9417), **United/United Express** (800-241-6522), and **USAirways** (800-428-4322) offer regularly scheduled flights.

Five car rental companies are represented at the airport: **Avis** (408-647-7140), **Budget Rent-A-Car** (408-373-1899), **Dollar** (800-800-4000), **Hertz** (800-852-3879), and **National** (408-373-4181). **Alamo Rent-A-Car** (800-327-9633) and **Monterey Rent-A-Roadster** (408-647-1929) have offices in Monterey.

Several companies shuttle passengers to and from the airport. Included are: **49 Express** (408-655-4949), **American International Transportation Service** (408-649-0240), **Monterey-Salinas Airbus** (408-442-BUSS), and **Peninsula Transportation/Airport Limo** (408-372-5555).

Greyhound and feeder buses from **Southern Pacific Railroad** and **Amtrak** are also available.

GETTING AROUND

Monterey Salinas Transit (MST) provides bus service throughout the Peninsula. Call (408) 899-2555 for transit schedules and information.

Catch the **WAVE** (Waterfront Area Visitors Express); (408-899-2555) from Memorial Day through Labor Day. These buses run circular routes from downtown Monterey through popular tourist areas from 9 A.M. to 7 P.M. daily. Tickets ($1.00 for adults, $0.50 for children six to 18, seniors, and disabled) entitle you to unlimited rides all day. A taped history that also points out the area's highlights is played.

WHAT TO SEE AND WHAT TO DO

Monterey Museums and Historical Sites

The **Monterey Bay Aquarium,** 886 Cannery Row, Monterey; (408) 648-4888 or 800-756-3737); (E-Quarium: http://www.mbayaq.org.). This facility, focusing on the marine life and habitats of Monterey Bay and the ocean, is a must-see. Located on the site of a former cannery, the aquarium's setting on the shores of Monterey's Inner Bay is a plus. Not only is this area one of the largest marine sanctuaries in the U.S., but the broad seascape lends the appropriately airy feel of limitless horizons to this attraction. The aquarium displays more than 6,500 fish and marinelife.

In the entranceway to the Outer Bay Wing, one of the facility's highlights, thousands of silver anchovies swim and sparkle like so much magical fairy dust. In another tank pink and purple striped jellyfish pulsate and float like other-worldly balloons. If your kids haven't already become entranced, then the 34-foot-tall, one-million-gallon tank showcasing the region where Monterey Bay meets the Pacific Ocean should cast a wondrous spell. Here kids come eyeball-to-eyeball with big green sea turtles, toothy barracudas, flat ocean sunfish, blue sharks, stingrays, and sunfish.

Not as dramatic, but as much fun is the kids' learning area across the hall. A series of hands-on exhibits let kids learn through play. Press a button and hear the bark of sea lion, the whistle of a humpback whale, and the screechy chatter of a dolphin. Feel blubber, learn how flippers, fins, and flukes help marine life to navigate and find out the answers to kid-friendly questions. A typical query that tweaks a kid's curiosity: If a human baby drinks the equivalent of 6 bottles of milk a day, how much milk does a baby grey whale drink daily? The answer—the equivalent of 2,000 bottles a day.

Three other major exhibits are the Kelp Forest, Monterey Bay Habitats, and Sea Otters along the Rocky Coast. At 28 feet high, the Kelp Forest exhibit is one of the tallest aquarium exhibits in the world, but more importantly, it is the first re-creation of a living kelp forest community. Sardines, leopard sharks, and other fish swim in this exhibit. The Monterey Bay Habitats, where sharks, rays, salmon, and bass swim, re-creates deep reefs, sandy sea floor, shale reefs, and the wharf. The endangered California sea otter, whose population was dec-

Monterey Peninsula at a Glance

- Dramatic coastline and pine forests with unmistakable California elan

- Not-to-be-missed Point Lobos State Reserve and Monterey Bay Aquarium

- Trendy shopping in charming Carmel-by-the-Sea

- Historic houses, including the Royal Presidio Chapel, First Theater, and Robert Louis Stevenson House

- Monterey Peninsula Visitors and Convention Bureau, (408) 649-1770

imated by 18th- and 19th-century fur hunters, is the star of the 55,000-gallon otter exhibit. All of the otters in the aquarium had been separated from their mothers at an early age by rough seas. Daily highlights are the feeding shows at 10:30 A.M., 1:30 P.M., and 3:30 P.M. "Fishing for Solutions: What's the Catch?," opened in 1997, addresses and aims to provide solutions to environmental maritime issues such as over-fishing and human coastline development.

The **Monterey Peninsula Museum of Art,** 559 Pacific Street; (408-372-5477) and 720 Via Mirada Street; (408-372-3689). Often praised as "the best small town museum in the United States," this facility features Monterey regional art, in addition to Californian, Asian, and Pacific Rim art, international folk art and photography.

Steinbeck's Spirit of Monterey Wax Museum, 700 Cannery Row, Suite 11; (408) 375-3770. Wax museums can be tacky, but somehow grade-school kids love them. More than 100 wax life-size figures in dozens of scenes illustrate the 450-year history of Monterey and Cannery Row. The taped voice of John Steinbeck, who made the blue-collar, cannery district famous, narrates the tour.

The **Maritime Museum of Monterey,** 5 Customs House Plaza, Monterey; (408) 373-2469, links Monterey's early years in the 16th century when Spanish galleons sailed into the bay with explorers and missionaries to its 1920s heyday as a major fishing and canning port. On display is an historic Fresnel lens with approximately 1000 prisms from the Point Sur Lighthouse as well as rare chronometers and sextants salvaged from wrecks.

Colton Hall, Pacific Street, (408) 649-5640. In 1849 this building served as the meeting place for 48 delegates from all parts of California who came together to draft the state's constitution. Now a small museum details the city's history. If you take the time to visit, stop by the adjacent old jail built in 1854.

You can discover more of Old Monterey at **Monterey State Historic Park,** 20 Customs House Plaza; (408) 649-7118. This 7-acre park encompasses what's reputed to be Monterey's oldest structure as well as several historic 19th century buildings. You can explore on your own but you'll get more background on one of the three daily walking tours offered for a nominal fee. House and garden tours are also available. Several of the park's buildings are only open Memorial Day through Labor Day and other buildings have restricted hours. Always call ahead for hours.

The two-mile walking tours begin with the **Royal Presidio Chapel,** (also known as the **San Carlos Cathedral**), Church Street; (408) 373-2628. Constructed in 1770, this building is considered by many to be the oldest structure in Monterey. Also on the route is the **Customs House,** Custom House Plaza at Fisherman's Wharf, where Commodore Sloat raised the American flag in 1846, thus commandeering 600,000 square miles of territory for the United States. Built in 1844 as a saloon and boarding house, the **First Theater,** Pacific and Scott streets; (408) 375-4916, hosted California's first paid theater performance. Since the 1930s, Troupers of the Gold Coast have been performing 19th century melodramas at this site. A two-story adobe, the **Pacific House,** Calle Principal and Scott Street, (408) 649-7118, contains the **Monterey Museum of the American Indian** and **Casa Soberanes,** 336 Pacific Street, an 1842 home occupied by the Soberanes family until 1922, is noted for its period antiques. The **Old Whaling Station** has a whalebone sidewalk and **Stevenson House,** 530 Houston St., gained fame as Robert Louis Stevenson's fall abode in 1879, the place where he wrote "Vendetta of the West," and out-

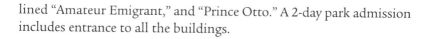

lined "Amateur Emigrant," and "Prince Otto." A 2-day park admission includes entrance to all the buildings.

Parks and Playgrounds

The **Dennis the Menace Playground,** Pearl Street; Monterey, (408) 646-3866. This themed playground is a treat for younger kids. Opened in 1956 with the assistance of Hank Ketcham, the cartoon character's creator, the park has since seen three renovations. Today's park includes Steam Engine No. 1285, donated by the Southern Pacific Company, a favorite for climbing, a Dennis the Menace sculpture, which kids love to pose beside, slides, swings, and other equipment.

Green Spaces, Natural Places

Point Lobos State Reserve, State Route 1, Box 62, Carmel; (408) 624-4909. Don't miss this park as it will be among the highlights of your trip. Three miles south of Carmel on Highway 1, Point Lobos State Reserve offers dramatic rocky shores, easy trails, and frequent sightings of sea lions, otters, and harbor seals. Its underwater acres comprise the nation's first underwater reserve and its above ground trails wind by aromatic stands of California sagebrush, and along paths blooming with apricot-colored monkey flowers. Other trails lead you under canopies of Monterey pines and cypress trees to panoramic views of the sea. Two easy trails lead to Sea Lion Point and to views of Bird Island.

Along the Sea Lion Point Trail look for sea otters in the kelp, for harbor seals basking on low rocks and for barking California sea lions on the offshore rocks. Between December and May, you can spot migrating gray whales here often along the Cypress Grove Trail. Look for the whales' sprays of mist. If you see their tail, relax for five minutes. It means they've taken a deeper dive and will resurface soon. Bird Island Trail leads cuts through woods and above sandy beaches where harbor seals sometimes sun. The sea surges through the crevices in the off-shore cliffs and cormorants, oystercatchers, and brown pelicans circle above.

In the early 1850s a few Chinese fishermen and their families built homes on the Point at Whalers Cove. One of their residences, known as the Whaler's Cabin, still stands. It was built with wooden planks,

Reach out and touch at the Monterey Bay Aquarium.
(Courtesy Monterey Peninsula Visitors' and Convention Bureau)

granite from a nearby quarry, and six whale vertebrae. Today, it houses the Reserve's Whaling Station Museum, a small facility displaying such whaling items as scrimshaw, tools, and pots.

17-Mile Drive, a scenic route stretching from Pacific Grove to Carmel, (408) 625-8426, (408) 624-6669, or (800) 654-9300, is a private drive that leads you along the Monterey Peninsula and through the Del Monte Forest. You drive past California's sea splashed, scenic coast and by manicured golf courses and elaborate mansions. Less dramatic than Point Lobos State Reserve, 17-Mile Drive intrigues. This road began as a carriage path for guests at the posh Hotel Del Monte. In the 1880s horse-drawn carriages carried visiting swells on day trips. Stops were made along the way for picnics on pebbled beaches and to absorb the forest's beauty. There are four entrances to the drive.

Shepherd's Knoll showcases sweeping views of Monterey Bay and the San Gabilan Mountains. Spanish Bay is a great place for picnicking because of its waterfront view. The view from what is now Spyglass Hill Golf Course, as legend has it, inspired Robert Louis

Stevenson in his creation of *Treasure Island*. Cypress Point Lookout is said to offer the best view of the Pacific coast along the drive. On clear days, the Point Sur Lighthouse, 20 miles south, is visible. Perhaps the most familiar landmark on 17-Mile Drive is the Lone Cypress. This tree, seemingly clinging to bare rock, has come to be an unofficial symbol of the area. There is a vehicle use fee of this drive. Bicycles are allowed but cyclists must enter through the Pacific Grove gate. Call for restrictions and fees.

Sports and Outdoor Activities

Golf is of prime interest here and Monterey Peninsula boasts 18 golf courses. **Pebble Beach** is, perhaps, the best known, but Spyglass Hill and Cypress Point are also consistently rated by golf experts as being among the top ten courses in the world. Pebble Beach and Spyglass are two of the 11 courses open to the public. Par 71 **Laguna Seca Golf Club,** York Road, Salinas; (408-373-3701), **Old Del Monte Golf Course** (par 72), 1300 Sylvan Road, Monterey; (408-373-2436), and the two-course **Rancho Canada Golf Club** (par 71 and 72), Carmel Valley Road, Carmel Valley; (408-624-0111) are some others. For tee times at Old Del Monte, Pebble Beach, and Spyglass call The Lodge at Pebble Beach; (408) 624-6611 or (800) 654-9300.

Typically, private clubs have reciprocal privileges at other private clubs. **Monterey Peninsula Country Club,** 17-Mile Drive, Pebble Beach; (408) 373-1556 offers a choice of two courses. **Corral de Tierra Country Club,** Corral de Tierra Road; (408) 484-1325, is about ten miles east of Monterey. For active and retired servicepeople, there is the **U.S. Navy Golf Course,** Garden Road, Monterey; (408) 656-2167.

If with all this water, your family needs to get out on it instead of just looking at it, try kayaking. **Adventures by Sea,** 299 Cannery Row; (408) 372-1807, rents kayaks, bikes, and inline skates, and also offers guided kayak tours. **Monterey Bay Kayaks,** 693 Del Monte Ave.; (408) 373-KELP or (800) 649-5357, is another outfitter renting kayaks and offering guided tours.

The migration of California gray whales from Alaska to Baja California draws hundreds of naturalists from late November through early February. Several companies, both in Monterey and farther south, offer whale watching cruises. **Monterey Sport Fishing,** 96 Fisherman's Wharf #1, Monterey; (800) 200-2203, has seven departures daily from

December through March for its one and one-half to two-hour narrated cruises. In the summer months, June through September, three daily cruises search out blue whales, orcas, humpbacks, and dolphins.

Theater and the Arts
Monterey Peninsula
Carmel's well-known **Shakespeare Festival** is held every fall at the 1910 **Forest Theatre**, (408) 626–1681. A canopy of tree's limbs drapes over the seating area. Audiences are encouraged to come to performances early so they may enjoy picnic suppers prior to the shows. The **Golden Bough Playhouse**, Monte Verde Street, Carmel; (408) 649–6852, offers a variety of productions each season. **Carmel Music Society** (408) 625–9938 performs classical music at the Sunset Cultural Center. Other stages and playhouses on the Peninsula include the **Wharf Theatre** (408) 649–2332 and **California's First Theatre** (408) 375–4916, both in Monterey.

SPECIAL EVENTS

January: AT&T-Pebble Beach Pro-Am Golf Tournament

March: Dixieland Monterey; Carmel Kite Festival

April: Victorian Home Tour (in Pacific Grove); Annual Adobe Tour

June: Films in the Forest at Outdoor Forest Theatre, Carmel

June–September (Friday evenings): Carmel Art Walks

July: Monterey Blues Festival; California Rodeo

August: Monterey Historic Automobile Races, great classics race at Laguna Seca

September: Monterey Jazz Festival; Carmel Shakespeare Festival

October: Butterfly Parade (Pacific Grove), a celebration of the Monarch butterfly migration.

December: Christmas in Adobes

Shopping
Monterey
Since its construction in 1846, **Fisherman's Wharf** has seen many lives. Originally, schooners bringing goods from around Cape Horn

unloaded their cargo at the pier. Less than a decade later, trading vessels were replaced with whaling ships as that industry boomed. A much smaller aquatic creature put Monterey on the map: sardines. Adjacent to the Wharf is Cannery Row where those smelly little fish were processed and canned during the twenties and thirties.

Today, the Wharf is still a fish market, but more prominent are the shops, galleries, and seafood restaurants that line either side of the wood plank stretch. Sport fishing, sight-seeing, and whale watching boats can be chartered from the Wharf as well.

The tinnery that supplied Monterey's sardine plants with cans was converted into California's first outlet center. The **American Tin Cannery Factory Outlets,** 125 Ocean View, Monterey; (408) 372–1442, is comprised of upscale retailers such as Anne Klein, Reebok, Joan and David, and London Fog. Save from 25 to 65 percent on apparel, accessories, shoes, leather goods, housewares, and china at these and 50 other stores.

In the six blocks surrounding **Cannery Row,** between Reeside and David Avenue, (408) 373–1902 is a collection of shops that carry everything from comic books to prints, photographs, gourmet coffee, toys, watches, and much more.

Upscale and charming **Carmel-by-the-Sea** is best known for its art galleries and boutiques. Your best bet is to explore the region bordered by Junipero Street, Monte Verde Avenue, 4th Avenue, and 8th Avenue. Nearby, **Carmel Plaza,** Ocean Avenue, Carmel; (408) 624–0137 offers more than 50 fine shops in a courtyard setting.

DAY TRIPS

Big Sur

One of California's most scenic drives is along a 90-mile stretch of Highway 1, a two-lane route from Carmel south to San Simeon (Hearst Castle). This region is known as **Big Sur,** a name derived from "El Sur Grande," which Spanish sailors dubbed the area when it was still an unexplored wilderness. For much of the route, the Santa Lucia Mountain Range is on one side and on the other is the rocky Pacific coast. Much of the region is part of California's state park system. Restaurants and small hotels dot the highway in places. Camping, hiking, backpacking, and fishing are all popular activities in the area. Some highlights include: the **Point Sur Lighthouse,** situated on a rocky point, (408) 625-4419; the **Bixby Bridge,** (about 13 miles south of Carmel), with its canyon and ocean views; **Andrew Molera State Park** (408) 667-2315 has trails along beaches and bluffs, camping and horseback riding; and **Pfeiffer Big Sur State Park,** (408) 667-2315, a popular and sometimes crowded park with a beach, camping, and a lodge.

At the tail of Big Sur is **Hearst Castle**; (800-444-7275), the former hilltop estate of eccentric millionaire William Randolph Hearst. This State Historical Monument has room upon room filled with European art and antiques. Four different two-hour tours are guided every 10 minutes from 8:30 A.M. to 3:00 P.M. Reservations are required.

WHERE TO STAY

Monterey

Located along Cannery Row, **Monterey Plaza Hotel,** 400 Cannery Row, Monterey; (408) 646-1700 or 800-631-1339), is in the heart of town. Some of the hotel's 285 rooms have views overlooking the ocean, while others overlook Cannery Row. The Wharf, Aquarium, and Maritime Museum are literally steps away. The **Fireside Lodge of Monterey,** 1131 Tenth Street, Monterey; (408-373-4172 or 800-722-2624), is set in a residential neighborhood, a short walk from the attractions. Rooms have refrigerators and cable TV. Continental breakfast is provided and pets are welcome.

Best Western's Monterey Beach Hotel, 2600 Sand Dunes Drive, Monterey; (408) 394-3321 or (800) 242-8627, is beachfront and offers 196 rooms, some with garden views. The **Holiday Inn,** 1000 Aguajito Road, Monterey; (800) 234-5697, offers family amenities and services at reasonable prices. The property has rooms and suites, two tennis courts, and a swimming pool, and is not far from Fisherman's Wharf and the Aquarium.

For families looking for more spacious accommodations, consider renting a cottage, condominium, or home. Three local agencies can help find the property best suited for your needs. **Monterey Bay Vacation Rentals,** 400 Foam Street, Ste. C, Monterey; (408-655-7840), rents a range of properties from modest to elegant. **Pine Cone Property**

Management, P.O. Box 221236, Carmel; (408-626-8163) and **San Carlos Agency,** 26358 Carmel Ranch Lane, Carmel; (408-624-3846), also offer long- and short-term rentals.

Carmel-by-the-Sea and Carmel Valley

If you are looking for a family-friendly resort, try the **Carmel Valley Ranch,** One Old Ranch Road, Carmel, about six miles from Carmel-by-the-Sea. This upscale but casual resort offers 100 suites on 1,700 acres of rolling hills. Clusters of rooms are set in tiers on hillsides shaded by California oaks. It's common to catch sight of deer grazing at twilight. Decorated with traditional California style furniture and beige and green colors, the suites are family-friendly. The living area has its own television, a microwave, coffee-maker and refrigerator as well as a fireplace. The bedroom, which is spacious, also has a fireplace and television. Children would, however, need to go through the parent's bedroom to reach the bathroom.

Along with golf, the ranch offers tennis courts, horseback riding, hiking trails, and swimming pools. Since the tennis club has an active junior program geared to locals, the coaches are sensitive to kids' instructional needs and child-sized equipment is available. Adjacent to the tennis center is a playground with climbing equipment and a grassy area for play. A swimming pool is nearby. If your kids like horses, don't miss the riding outings into the mountains. These come with scenic views and tales of the wild west. Even in the Oaks, the resort's fine dining room noted for its seafood, children can order from an inexpensively priced kids' menu of burgers, chicken strips, and spaghetti and meatballs. (408) 625-9500 or (800) 4-CARMEL.

The Carmel Innkeepers Association has created the "Host of the Day" program to assist travelers who have no reservations but are looking for accommodations. Within walking distance to the beach and close to town is **Dolores Lodge,** Third Street, Carmel-by-the-Sea; (408) 625-3263 or (800) 215-6343. Continental breakfast is included. Since 1929 the **Cypress Inn,** Lincoln and Seventh, Carmel-by-the-Sea; (408-624-3871 or 800-443-7443), has been Carmel's landmark hotel. The **Best Western Townhouse Lodge,** San Carlos and Fifth; Carmel; (408-624-1261), offers 28 units two blocks from the village center. Some two-room units are available. **Hofsas House,** San Carlos between Third and Fourth, Carmel; (408-624-2745), a family-run Tudor-style inn downtown, welcomes families. Along with rooms with television, the facility has a heated pool, on-site parking, a sauna, and provides continental breakfast. The **Carmel Mission Inn,** Highway 1 and Rio Road, Carmel; (408-624-1841 or 800-348-9090), is adjacent to the Carmel Mission.

Just a short drive from the Peninsula, the **Blue Sky Lodge,** Flight Road, Carmel Valley; (408-659-2256 or 800-733-2160), has family units with fireplaces and living rooms as well as a heated pool. Bring Fido or Socks along, as pets are welcome too.

WHERE TO EAT

Monterey

Many of Monterey's eateries can be found near the waterfront, particularly along Cannery Row and Fisherman's Wharf. Enjoy shrimp every way imaginable at the **Bubba Gump Shrimp Co.,** 720 Cannery Row, (408) 373-1884. This chain eatery also offers salmon, crab legs, steaks and pork chops as well as a children's menu. You'll consume the views of Monterey Bay as hungrily as the food at **The Fish Hopper,** 700 Cannery Row; (408) 372-8543. The restaurant serves locally caught seafood as well as steaks, and fresh pasta. There is a children's menu. Patrons of **The Clock Garden,** 565 Abrego; (408) 375-6100, are seated in a fountain garden setting. Terra cotta shaded lamps hang over wooden tables and benches. Homemade soups, salads, burgers, and seafood are served for lunch. Pasta, steaks, and roast chicken are among the selections added to the dinner menu. The casual **Tarpy's Roadhouse,** Hwy. 68; (408) 647-1444, is in a turn-of-the-century building and serves seafood, steaks, rabbit, and duck. For Italian fare, try **Domenico's,** Fisherman's Wharf #1; (408) 372-3655 or **Spardaro's Ristorante,** 650 Cannery Row; (408) 372-8881.

Carmel

Carmel offers a greater choice of restaurants than Monterey. A wide variety of cuisines, from New American to Thai, and numerous establishments are available. For standard American meals of pizza, pasta, and steak, head to **Fabulous Toots Lagoon,** Dolores between

Ocean and Seventh; (408) 625-1915. Toots also boasts the largest selection of ribs on the Peninsula. If the weather is nice, request to sup *al fresco* at the **California Market,** Hwy. One; (408) 622-5450. Pasta, salads, and sandwiches are complemented by spectacular views of the Carmel Highlands Coast. Carmel's Mexican restaurants include **Baja Cantina,** 7166 Carmel Valley Road; (408) 625-2252, **Chevy's** 123 Crossroads; (408) 626-0945, and **Plaza Linda,** 9 Defino Place; (408) 659-4229. However, it is said that if you have only one night to dine in Carmel, go to **California Thai,** San Carlos and Fourth Ave.; (408) 622-1160. As the name implies, California ingredients and influence are coupled with classic Thai recipes.

FOR MORE INFORMATION

The **Monterey Peninsula Visitors & Convention Bureau,** P.O. Box 1770, 380 Alvardo Street, Monterey 93942; (408) 649-1770.

Monterey Visitors Center, 401 Camino El Estero; (408) 649-1770.

VCB InfoCenter Phone Information (24-hour service); (408) 649-1770.

Carmel Business Association, P.O. Box 4444, Carmel 93921; (408) 624-2522; http://www.chamber.carmel.ca.us.

Carmel Valley Chamber of Commerce, (408) 659-4000.

Emergency

For **police, fire, ambulance, and Coast Guard,** dial 911.

Community Hospital of the Monterey Peninsula, (408) 624-5311.

Natividad Medical Center, (408) 755-4111.

Doctors on Duty—Medical Clinic, (408) 372-6700 or (408) 649-0770

ANAHEIM/ORANGE COUNTY

Anaheim/Orange County has been called Southern California's playground—and for good reason. Anaheim's future as a dream vacation destination for families was sealed in 1955 when Walt Disney opened the Magic Kingdom in Disneyland. Ten minutes away, Knott's Berry Farm has attracted families for generations. Orange County also offers families many other reasons for coming, including 42 miles of coastline often dubbed the "American Riviera." Their tourist and convention bureau is quick to point out that Anaheim is *not* a suburb of Los Angeles, which is 28 miles north, but rather a destination unto itself. Still, if you have time, do take in some of the bountiful attractions that Los Angeles offers (highlights follow).

GETTING THERE

The four area airports are served by major airlines. **Los Angeles International** (LAX) (310-646-5252), 31 miles northwest of Anaheim (approximately fifty minutes), is the major international gateway into Southern California. **John Wayne/Orange County Airport** (714-252-5006), 16 miles southeast of Anaheim (about 25 minutes), offers direct nonstop service to nineteen U.S. destinations. **Ontario Airport** (909-983-8282) is 27 miles northeast of Anaheim (about 45 minutes). The smallest airport is at Long Beach (310-421-8293), 20 miles west (about thirty minutes). SuperShuttle is among several companies providing service from hotels to airports twenty-four hours a day; phone (714) 517-6600/(800) 554-6458—outside California.

Greyhound is at 100 West Winton Street, Anaheim; call (714) 999-1256 for information or (800) 231-2222.

Amtrak (800-USA-RAIL) has a station at Anaheim Stadium, a mile from the Anaheim Convention Center, and makes several other Orange County stops.

Two major freeways, I-405 and I-5, run north and south through Orange County.

GETTING AROUND

A car is a necessity in this land of freeways, but if you would rather not drive, many hotels operate shuttle services to popular attractions. The **Orange County Transit District** (OCTD) (714-636-7433) runs buses throughout the county. Several shuttle operators such as **Fullerton Metro Center Shoppers Expedition Express** (714-535-2211) run buses to malls from Disneyland area hotels and motels. **Southern California Rapid Transit District** (RTD) serves Los Angeles County and some areas of Orange County. Call (213) 626-4455.

WHAT TO SEE AND DO

Theme Parks

Let's face it: You didn't come here for culture (although it is available). The following attractions are the reasons families flock to this area.

Disneyland, 1313 Harbor Boulevard; (714) 781-4565 or (714) 999-4565. Before leaving home, purchase a good guidebook, and plan your tour strategy. If you can avoid peak park times, do so. (These include weekends, Memorial through Labor Day, Christmas Day through New Year's Day—the busiest of all—and other school holidays.) Opening hours vary; call in advance. Then arrive as early as possible (about a half hour before opening) to beat the crowds—and the heat. The park is huge—eighty-five acres in all—so don't try to see too much, too soon. If you can, tour the park in portions (one-, two-, and three-day passports are available).

Disneyland has eight theme areas: Adventureland, Critter Country, Fantasyland, Frontierland, Main Street U.S.A., New Orleans Square, Tomorrowland, and Mickey's Toontown. The latter, the newest theme land (the first addition in more than twenty years), is a cartoon character community where Disney stars, including Roger Rabbit, interact with guests.

Anaheim/Orange County at a Glance

- Theme parks plus with 42 miles of coastline equal an ideal family vacationland

- Disneyland, Knott's Berry Farm, Universal Studios, Hollywood, and more

- The presidential: Richard Nixon and Ronald Reagan presidential libraries

- Beaches, boating, and whale watching

- Anaheim/Orange County Visitor and Convention Bureau, (714) 999–8999

Tomorrowland's major renovation should be completed in the spring of 1998. New thrills include a high-speed journey on rocket cars, an interactive pavillion of technology, and Astro Orbitir, the new landmark marking the entrance. You can rent strollers by the main entrance (even small kids beyond stroller age may welcome the ride because touring the park is wearying). There's a Baby Center for preparing formulas, warming bottles, and changing infants. Tomorrowland is undergoing an extensive renovation to be completed in the spring of 1998. New attractions will include a 3D, high-speed journey in futuristic rocket cars and an interactive pavilion. Magic Eye theater's current 3D adventure, *Captain EO*, will be replaced by *Honey, I Shrunk the Audience*. Along the Disney parade route, a new nighttime presentation, "Light Magic," will wow visitors. Fiber-optic light, illustrations, projections, and Disney characters are all part of the "Main Street Electrical Parade." Other changes include a Pocahontas show at Fantasyland Theater and the Indiana Jones Adventure, Disney's biggest ride yet.

Disney is also developing a new theme park, Disney's California Adventure, scheduled to be completed in 2001 along with an expansion of the Disneyland Resort. As the name suggests, the new park "celebrates" California's beaches, natural wonders and movie magic.

Knott's Berry Farm, 8039 Beach Boulevard, Buena Park; (714) 220-5200 or 827-1776. Started in 1940, this nonglitzy park has grown to 150 acres and six theme areas containing more than 165 rides, attractions, live shows, shops, and restaurants (including the still-going-strong Famous Chicken Dinner). A favorite with the younger set: Camp Snoopy, a six-acre wooded area with waterfalls, streams, and lakes. Attractions include the Bear-y Tales Playhouse with slides, giant sawdust-filled punching bags, and a mirror maze; scaled down rides; interactive scientific experiences at Thomas Edison Inventors Workshop; and trained forest animals. Attractions include the world's largest inflated Snoopy figure—a 38-foot-tall structure where kids bounce and bump on air-filled cushions—and a soaring, spinning Camp Bus ride for the entire family. Older kids thrill to Montezuma's Revenge Roller Coaster and the Sky Tower parachute jump. Ghost Town is still here to amuse the younger kids with its jail, blacksmith shop, general store, and stagecoach rides. Some new attractions are the all-senses 3D film, Cyber Sports in 3D at Nu Wave Theater, and Air Hedz, a two-story food, games, and music center. Jaguar is one of California's longest family roller coasters, and Mystery Lodge is a special effects journey in native North America. In 1997 Knott's debuted the Windjammer, a surf-inspired, dual roller-coaster race that thrills visitors with side-by-side loops, 60-foot drops, and twisting turns over water. Stroller rentals and two baby stations, with changing tables and a microwave for bottle heating, are available.

If you still have time or energy, you're close to **Movieland Wax Museum,** 7711 Beach Boulevard (714-522-1155), just east of Knott's. More than 280 costumed wax stars pose in scenes from famous movies—including Macaulay Culkin in *Home Alone.*

Raging Waters, 111 Raging Waters Drive, San Dimas; (909) 592-6453. Located in southeast Los Angeles County, Raging Waters is close to Anaheim and, at forty-four acres, is the largest water park west of the Mississippi. With slides, rides, sandy beaches, a man-made river, and a wave pool, there's something for everyone, including tiny tots. Bring lots of sunscreen, take plenty of shade breaks, and plan on spending the better part of the day.

Universal Studios, 100 Universal City Plaza, Universal City

A hard day at the beach may be just what you need on a vacation to Anaheim.
(Courtesy Anaheim Area Visitor and Convention Bureau)

(between Hollywood and the San Fernando Valley); (818) 508-9600. Families do bring very young kids here, but most attractions are designed for school-age and older kids. Some rides have special effects younger children may find frightening. Two favorites are **Earthquake—The Big One,** which "traps" riders in a subway as an earthquake occurs, complete with collapsing earth, shooting flames, and a huge flood; and in the **King Kong Encounter,** guests sit on the Brooklyn Bridge while a 30-foot Kong comes too close for comfort, breaking suspension cables and power lines in the process. **Back to the Future** is great fun, combining a ride, a Delorean, high-tech video thrills, and the sensation of a super-duper roller coaster.

Fortunately, there are gentler alternatives, including the delightful **E.T. Adventure,** where guests enjoy a ride on a sky-bound bicycle. Stage shows include **The Rocky & Bullwinkle Show; Animal's Actors Stage,** where more than sixty trained animals perform; and the fifteen-minute **Beetlejuice Graveyard Revue,** featuring famous horror figures gyrating to rock 'n' roll hits. **An American Tail: Fievel**

Goes West offers a live stage show and a wonderful interactive playground where everything is oversized, as seen from a mouse's-eye view. There's a 15-foot-high banana peel to slide down and an 11-foot slice of Swiss cheese to crawl through. A new streamlined backlot tram tour takes riders through locations and settings from *Home Alone 2* and *E.T,* as well as television show sets. Come within inches of dinosaurs at **Jurassic Park—The Ride.** Five-story-tall dinosaurs attack guests at speeds up to 25 feet per second as visitors are whisked along the tracks of this coaster, which brags an 84-foot plunge and the steepest water descent ever built.

Six Flags Magic Mountain, 26101 Magic Mountain Parkway, Valencia (Santa Clarita Valley); (805) 255-4111. For preteens and teens who crave excitement, this 260-acre theme park offers plenty. The specialty: roller coasters, with such daunting names as Psyclone, Flashback, Revolution, Ninja, and Colossus, which is rated as one the top ten in America. There's lots more, too: water flume rides; shows; and for the younger set, a petting zoo and Bugs Bunny World, a six-acre area with mini-roller coaster and other scaled down rides. High Sierra Territory, a depiction of the California woods, is a water ride, rock maze, and has the world's tallest artificial walk-through tree. Superman the Escape begins in an ice cavern high atop the park's mountain range. One escape from enemy forces thrusts passengers from 0 to 100 mph in seven seconds. A ride highlight: 6.5 seconds of weightlessness. The park has a baby-care center and stroller rentals.

Adventure City, a.k.a. The Little Theme Park Just for Kids, 1238 Beach Boulevard (714-236-9300), is a two-acre theme park for children ages two to twelve. Opened in 1994 and designed to resemble a small town from the pages of a children's book, Adventure City offers eleven rides and attractions, a snack shop, a game and party area, and entertainment. Educational programs and displays address topics ranging from transportation to crime prevention.

Museums

Orange County is home to **The Richard Nixon Library and Birthplace,** 18001 Yorba Linda Boulevard, Yorba Linda (about 7 miles north of Anaheim); (714) 993-5075. Families with school-age kids, no matter what their political persuasion, may find this place surprisingly interesting. Interactive exhibits allow visitors to summon Nixon's recorded opinions on various issues, listen to the famous "smoking gun" tape from Watergate days, and view life-size statues of world leaders. Across the pond, Nixon's birthplace, a small farm, has been restored and includes original furnishings and family photos. **The Ronald Reagan Presidential Library and Museum,** 40 Presidential Drive, Simi Valley (805-522-8444), which includes a chunk of the Berlin Wall, is 20 miles north of downtown Los Angeles.

George C. Page Museum, 5801 Wilshire Boulevard, Los Angeles; (213) 936-2230. Located in Hancock Park, this twenty-three-acre property is in the midst of the La Brea Tar Pits (overland explorers found the bubbling asphalt pools on this site in 1769). It features Ice Age fossils, discovered in the early 1900s, of mammals, birds, plants, insects, and reptiles. Behind glass windows, workers in the museum's paleontology labs dust and identify fossils from the still-oozing pits. Along with two short films (*Dinosaurs, the Terrible Lizards* and *The La Brea Story*), there are more than one million fossils and reconstructed skeletons of creatures who got stuck in the pits. Try to pull large poles out of sticky asphalt, and you will realize how hard it was to escape.

If you have time, explore the **Los Angeles County Museum of Art,** also in Hancock Park at 5905 Wilshire Boulevard; (213) 857-6111. This large complex includes the Ahmanson Gallery with paintings by Rembrandt and Picasso. The newer Robert O. Anderson Building features traveling exhibits and twentieth-century art. The museum sponsors frequent cultural activities, as well as programs for parents and kids. Stop for lunch at the indoor/outdoor Plaza Cafe, then stroll through the park—a lively place with mimes, street musicians, and vendors.

Los Angeles Children's Museum, 310 North Main Street in the Los Angeles Mall downtown; (213) 687-8800. Aimed at ages two to twelve, this museum's interactive, educational exhibits are guaranteed to please. Highlights include Sticky City, featuring giant foam shapes with Velcro tapes; a storehouse of LEGO blocks for young builders; and a recording studio where kids create music with studio instruments and synthesizers, or radio dramas with sound effects. Weekend performances by mimes, actors, and storytellers and weekday theatrical games and dance workshops are held at the Louis B. Mayer Performance Space, the area's only theater designed exclusively for kids.

Special family events are held throughout the year.

Another primarily-for-kids place is the **Children's Museum,** 301 South Euclid Street, La Habra; (310) 905-9793. Many of the exhibits are in the waiting, baggage, and freight rooms of the historic, renovated Union Pacific Depot. Permanent exhibits include a Touch Table with a rotating collection of birds' nests, feathers, shells, and the like; a Bee Observatory; LEGO city, where kids can build to their heart's content; an indoor carousel; a Preschool Playpark; a Science Station where electricity, images, and reflections are explored; and a Kids on Stage area with costumes, props, sets, lighting, and sound. Call to find out about special workshops, Saturday programs, and preschool storytelling hours.

California Museum of Science and Industry, 700 State Drive, Exposition Park (downtown Los Angeles); (213) 744-7400. It's free, it's fabulous, it's the country's second-largest science/technology museum (the Smithsonian is the first). Unfortunately, at press time there was a dramatic staff cutback and talk of closing this splendid facility completely—call to find out. Hopefully, you will be able to enjoy the wide variety of interactive exhibits.

The Bowers Museum and Kidseum, 2002 North Main Street (714-567-3600), is dedicated to the fine arts of indigenous people, particularly Pre-Columbian, Oceanic, Native American, and Pacific Rim cultures. More than 70,000 objects are in its collection, making it one of California's largest cultural institutions. Kidseum is the hands-on, interactive center of Bowers. Exciting programs for children celebrate culture through storytelling and puppet shows.

Natural History Museum, also in Exposition Park at 900 Exposition Boulevard; (213) 744-3414. Everything you might expect to find at a natural history museum is here (including dinosaurs). The fourth largest of its kind in the country, this vintage museum (circa 1913) has a sparkling Gem and Mineral Hall; a taxidermy exhibit of North American and African mammals in natural surroundings, a Hall of American History that includes old cars; a lively Hall of Birds, with sounds and animation; and—tops with younger kids—the Ralph M. Parsons Discovery Center, a huge room where kids from age two are encouraged to touch fossils and other objects, examine insects through a magnifying glass, listen to the ocean from a seashell, and explore various discovery boxes. This museum is a winner.

Simon Wiesenthal Center's Museum of Tolerance, 9786 West Pico Boulevard; (310) 553–8403. The message this museum conveys is a crucial one for kids: understanding among all people. The Tolerancenter explores the dynamics of racism and prejudice in American life via thirty-five participatory installations. At Understanding the Los Angeles Riots, visitors input personal profiles (age, gender, ethnicity) and are asked questions about social justice and responsible citizenship. A wall-sized computer map pinpoints more than 250 hate groups around the country. At the Holocaust Section, each visitor gets a different photo passport with the story of a child whose life was changed by the Holocaust. As the visitor proceeds through the tour, the passport is updated, and the child's fate is revealed at the end—an extremely moving experience. At the second-floor Multimedia Learning Center, more than thirty workstations give visitors, via touchscreen technology, access to a huge amount of information on World War II and the Holocaust.

Barnsdall Art Park, 4800 Hollywood Boulevard, Los Angeles; (213) 485–4474. Included in this eleven-acre park and arts center is a Junior Arts Center that offers free Open Sunday family art workshops on forty Sundays a year. Some are held at the center; others are at various community service centers around the city. In August, the Center sponsors a Children's Festival of the Arts in the park.

The **Skirball Cultural Center,** 2701 North Sepulveda Boulevard, Los Angeles; (310) 440–4500, is a 125,000-square-foot complex housing exhibits that relate Jewish history. Its main exhibit, Visions and Values: Jewish Life from Antiquity to America, couples objects from the museum's collection and multimedia presentations to share the story of Jews. It concentrates on postbiblical journeys and the successful integration into present-day America. Designed for young people, the Discovery Center livens history and archaeology through hands-on activities and encounters with artifacts.

The Museum of Television and Radio (310–786–1000) is the sister facility to the New York City–based museum. Exhibits and programs continually change, but recent ones included Rock 'n' Roll and Radio, Star Trek: The Tradition Continues, and Hirschfield: Radio and Television Drawings.

Parks and Zoos

Griffith Park, north of Hollywood (213-664-1181), with 4,100 acres of wooded land, is the largest park within the boundaries of any U.S. city. At the Park Ranger Visitors Center, 4730 Crystal Springs Drive (213-665-5188), obtain directions to a miniature open-air train, a simulated roller coaster and plane adventure, pony and wagon rides, and an antique carousel. At Travel Town, on Zoo Drive, a small outdoor museum displays old vehicles: fire engines, a Union Pacific steam engine, and old city streetcars. Hiking trails, tennis courts, golf courses, guided horseback rides, nature trails, and a swimming pool are among the other offerings. The park is also home to **Griffith Observatory,** 2800 East Observatory Road (213-664-1191), with sky shows and astronomy exhibits. Solar telescopes operate by day; at night, view the moon and planets via a Zeiss refractory. Also in the park: **Gene Autry Museum of Western Heritage,** 4700 Western Heritage Way; (213) 667-2000. The museum displays the history of the American West through art and artifacts, such as authentic weapons of Western heroes and costumes and props from radio, movie, and television Westerns. Noteworthy is the museum's famed collection of cowboy boots. Films are shown in the 222-seat theater.

Nearby is the **Los Angeles Zoo,** 5333 Zoo Drive; (213) 666-4090. Spread out over 113 acres, it's home to more than 2,000 mammals, birds, reptiles, and amphibians, grouped into respective geographical areas. (Don't miss the cuddly koalas in the Australia environment.) Adventure Island, the children's zoo, highlights animals of the American Southwest through interactive exhibits. A tram ride circles the zoo, with stops at strategic areas (the hilly terrain can be tiring for young—and old—feet). Treat the kids to an elephant or camel ride.

Beaches

Orange County's 42-mile coastline includes beach communities reached via the Pacific Coast Highway: Seal Beach, Huntington Beach, Newport Beach, Laguna, Corona del Mar, Balboa, Dana Point, San Clemente, and San Juan Capistrano. A popular choice for families is **Balboa,** with its 919-foot fishing pier that ends in a public beach, with rest rooms and showers nearby. Lifeguards keep watch during summer and post flags when the tide is coming in. The waves here are fairly gentle compared with those at the popular surfing beaches, such as Huntington. From January through March, outfitters such as **Whale Watching Excursions** (714-695-9444) offer outings from the Newport Beach area.

Los Angeles County has 72 miles of shoreline, from Malibu in the north to Long Beach (where you can board the *Queen Mary*) in the south. Colorful street performers ply their trade along Venice Beach's Oceanfront Walk. Santa Monica Pier and its famous boardwalk feature carnival games, carousel rides, and free summer concerts.

Theater, Music, and the Arts

Orange County is a cultural hotspot with numerous theaters, including the 3,000-seat **Orange County Performing Arts Center,** which features world-class performers such as the New York City Ballet. The Sunday Calendar in the *Los Angeles Times* features weekly events or call (213) 688-ARTS. *Destination Los Angeles,* published by the LAVCB, lists ticket agencies and addresses for TV show tickets. Many shows don't admit kids under ten years; the *Tonight Show* refuses anyone under eighteen years.

Studio tours: NBC Studios in Burbank offers weekday backstage tours, including a walk through a newsroom and a chance to see the *Tonight Show* crew rehearsing. Call (818) 840-3537. The **Warner Brothers VIP Tour,** 4000 Warner Boulevard, Burbank (818-954-1744), emphasizes the technical and the behind-the-scenes aspects of movie and television production. Limited to those over age ten. **Paramount Studios,** 860 North Gower Street, Hollywood (213-956-5575), gives out free tickets weekdays at 8:00 A.M. for TV show tapings—most require audience members to be sixteen or older. For the Paramount two-hour studio walking tour, visitors should be age ten or older.

Sporting Events

Anaheim has two professional sports teams. The **California Angels** baseball team (714-634-2000) plays their games at Anaheim Stadium, 2000 Gene Autry Way. The **Mighty Ducks** professional hockey team plays at Arrowhead Pond in Anaheim, 2695 East Katella; (714) 704-2428.

Arrowhead is also home to the **Anaheim Splash,** an indoor soccer team, and the **Anaheim Bullfrogs** roller-hockey team. Head to Los Angeles for **Dodgers** baseball at downtown's Dodger Stadium (213-224-1491), basketball with the **Lakers** at the Forum (310-419-3100) and the **Clippers** at the L.A. Sports Arena (213-748-8000), or hockey with the **Kings** at the Forum (310-673-6003).

Shopping

Fashion Island Shopping Center, 600 Newport Center Drive, Newport Beach (714-721-2022), on a hill overlooking the ocean, is Orange County's only open-air regional shopping center. There are movie theaters, summer weekly music concerts, kids' activities—even a koi pond. **The Irvine Ranch Farmer's Market,** on the first level of the Atrium Court, is a wonderful place to buy produce and other culinary delights.

Hobby City, 1238 South Beach Road, Anaheim (714-527-2323), has a doll and toy museum, miniature train ride, and lots more, including a restaurant. It's 2 miles south of Knott's Berry Farm.

For something completely different in greater Los Angeles, head to Beverly Hills to window shop and people watch along the posh Rodeo Drive.

SPECIAL EVENTS

AOCVB can provide a current listing of events and contacts, or call their visitor information line at (714) 999-8999, ext. 9998. For more information on Los Angeles area events, call (213) 689-8822.

January 1: Tournament of Roses Parade and Rose Bowl Game, Pasadena.

February: Festival of Whales, Dana Point, held weekends in late February, features concert series, sporting competition, street fair, and film fest.

March: Fiesta de las Golindrinas (Return of the Swallows), Mission San Juan Capistrano; month-long celebration of the annual arrival of the swallows from Argentina on St. Joseph's Day. Mud-Slinging Festival.

Easter: The Crystal Cathedral in Garden Grove, adjacent to Anaheim, puts on The Glory of Easter.

April: Air Show at El Toro Marine Corps Air Station features several flight demonstration teams. Knott's Berry Farm's Country Fair includes shows and country bands. Imagination Celebration.

May: Cinco de Mayo on Olvera Street, Los Angeles, features mariachis and Spanish dancers. Strawberry Festival, Garden Grove, includes a carnival, arts and crafts, and parade. Anaheim Children's Festival.

June: Surfing Championship, Huntington Beach Pier, the world's largest surfing contest.

July: Orange County Fiesta, Mile Square Park, Fountain Valley, offers carnival rides, sports, music, fireworks, and more. Orange County Fair, Costa Mesa Fairgrounds, with rides and rodeo.

July–August: Laguna Canyon holds its huge Festival of Arts and Pageant of the Masters, with nightly re-creations of artworks featuring live models and a full orchestra.

August: Ringling Brothers Barnum and Bailey Circus, Arrowhead Pond of Anaheim.

September: Sand Castle and Sand Sculpture Contest, Corona del Mar State Beach. Newport Seafest at Newport Beach spans two weekends. Tall Ships Festival.

October: Anaheim Harvest Festival with crafts, foods, and family entertainment.

November: The Glory of Christmas Pageant, Crystal Cathedral, Garden Grove.

December: Christmas festivities include Tree Lighting at Mission San Juan Capistrano and Las Posados candlelight processions on Los Angeles's Olvera Street; Christmas Boat Parade.

WHERE TO STAY

Anaheim/Orange County has 43,000 rooms (18,000 in Anaheim) in everything from budget motels to luxury hotels. Ideally, families should stay as close to Disneyland as possible. For lodging in greater Los Angeles, consult the *Destination Los Angeles* guide available from the LAVCB (see For More Information).

Here are a few choices.

The Disneyland Hotel, 1150 West Cerritos Avenue, Anaheim;

(714) 956-6400. Connected to the park by the monorail, this recently refurbished hotel offers 1,131 rooms, eleven restaurants and lounges, three swimming pools, a tropical beach, marina (with pedal-boats, remote control tugboats, and a miniature *Queen Mary*), Fantasy Waters shows twice weekly, and Disney character meals at breakfast and weekend dinners year-round, and daily during summer and holidays. Expensive, yes—but worth the splurge. One definite perk: Hotel guests receive passes entitling them to enter the park one hour earlier than other visitors. Call to see if the children's program has been revived.

Anaheim Hilton Hotel and Towers, 777 Convention Way; (714) 750-4321. Two minutes from Disneyland, the Hilton has 1,600 rooms and suites, a year-round pool, several Jacuzzis, and a game center. The summer Vacation Station daily kids' program is for ages five to thirteen.

In the budget range, try **Peacock Suites,** 1745 Anaheim Boulevard; (714) 535-8255. This 140-room facility features pool, spa, and fitness center. Room amenities are microwave, refrigerator, satellite TV and VCR, and in-room safe. Included in the low room rate is deluxe continental breakfast and shuttle service to and from Disneyland, just 2 blocks away. A bit more upscale, **Summerfield Suites West Hollywood,** 1000 Westmount Drive, West Hollywood (310-657-7400 or 800-833-4353), offers suite rooms, a complimentary buffet breakfast, and laundry facilities. The property is about twenty minutes from Universal Studios and popular beaches. Ask about their summer family specials. The **Century Plaza Hotel and Tower,** 2025 Avenue of the Stars, Los Angeles (310-277-2000), offers surprise gifts at check-in for children three through twelve. Car seats, changing tables, and bottle warmers are available.

The **Westin South Coast Plaza,** 686 Anton Boulevard, Costa Mesa, California 92626 (714-540-2500 or 800-228-3000), offers the new Westin Kids Club amenities. These include child-friendly rooms and children's sports bottle or tippy cup upon check-in as well as a safety kit with a night-light, Band-Aids, and emergency phone numbers. Rooms feature bath toys and bath products for kids, and parents can request—at no charge—jogging strollers, potty seats, bicycle seats, and step stools. Restaurants and room service also feature children's menus. Just minutes away by car are Disneyland, Knott's Berry Farm, and Newport Beach.

WHERE TO EAT

The AOCVB publishes a *Best Places Guide to Dining, Services and Shopping in Orange County.* The kids will get a kick out of **The Overland Stage Restaurant,** Inn at The Park Hotel, 1855 South Harbor Boulevard, Anaheim; (714) 750-1811. The decor is Old West (complete with stagecoach) and the food is hearty American, with a children's menu available.

Two dinner theater experiences for kids: **Medieval Times Dinner and Tournament,** 7662 Beach Boulevard, Buena Park (800-899-6600), serves a four-course dinner (no utensils allowed) to guests who sit in an arena while knights joust on horseback. **Wild Bill's Western Extravaganza,** 7600 Beach Boulevard, Buena Park (714-522-6414 or 800-883-1546), puts on a two-hour Western show as guests dine on a four-course meal.

DAY TRIPS

Could you really go home without exploring Hollywood? It "ain't what it used to be," but a walk down Hollywood Boulevard is a must. Look for the famous 50-foot Hollywood sign that graces the Hollywood Hills, on the town's northern end. Storefronts along the boulevard showcase movie memorabilia, including Dorothy's ruby red slippers from *The Wizard of Oz.* At **Mann's** (formerly Grauman's) **Chinese Theater,** 6925 Hollywood Boulevard (213-464-8111), celebrities' feet, heads, signatures (and even a nose—Jimmy Durante's) have been immortalized in cement since 1927. As you walk through downtown, you'll tread on the Hollywood Walk of Fame, containing the names of celebrities framed by terrazzo and brass stars, including Marilyn Monroe at 1644 Hollywood Boulevard, Elvis Presley at 6777, and John Lennon at 1750 Vine Street.

Memories of the 1992 riots—and visions of traffic and parking headaches—may result in tourists shying away from downtown L. A. The AOCVB suggests that those staying in Anaheim take an Amtrak ride into downtown. It's easy and convenient: The Children's Museum (described earlier) is across the street from the station. Afterwards, take a stroll on the colorful cobblestoned walkways of Olvera Street in Old Los Angeles. A Mexican-style marketplace sells piñatas, crafts, sombreros, and other gifts and crafts. Restaurants range from fast food to sit-down Mexican eateries. **San Diego,** 90 miles south of Anaheim, makes for a perfect day or two, thanks to Sea World, Balboa Park and its fabulous museums, San Diego Zoo, historic Old Town, beaches, and more.

FOR MORE INFORMATION

The Anaheim/Orange County Visitor and Convention Bureau is located across from Disneyland at the Anaheim Convention Center, 800 West Katella Avenue, Anaheim 92803; (714) 999-8999. A *Kid's Guide to Orange County* is available for a small fee from the AOCVCB. The book highlights attractions that will interest children five to twelve years old and their families. The **Los Angeles Convention and Visitors Bureau** operates two visitor information centers: The Downtown Los Angeles center at 695 South Figueroa Street (213-689-8822) is open Monday through Saturday from 8:00 A.M. to 5:00 P.M., and the Hollywood Visitor Information Center is at The Janes House, Janes Square, 6541 Hollywood Boulevard (213-689-8822), open Monday through Saturday, 9:00 A.M. to 5:00 P.M. Helpful publications include *Destination Los Angeles,* which also has extensive listings for Southern California.

L.A. Parent, Box 3204, Burbank 91504 (818-846-0400), is a monthly newspaper featuring family events and relevant news.

The **Los Angeles County Commission on Disabilities** publishes a free brochure on public and private services. Write or call them at 383 Hall of Administration, 500 West Temple Street, Los Angeles 90012; (213) 974-1053 or 974-1707 (TDD). The Junior League offers *Around the Town with Ease,* listing wheelchair facilities of more than one hundred of the area's destinations. Send $2.00 for postage and handling to them at Farmers Market, Third and Fairfax, Los Angeles 90036, or call (213) 937-5566.

Emergency Numbers
Ambulance, fire, police: 911
Poison Control: (800) 544-4404
Twenty-four-hour pharmacy: Sav-On, 1021 North State College (at La Palma); (714) 991-9161
Twenty-four-hour emergency room: Anaheim Memorial Hospital, 1111 West La Palma; (714) 774-1450

SAN DIEGO

Glorious weather, a beautiful bay, plus green expanses, lively arts, and festivals combine to make San Diego alluring. Free beaches stretch 70 miles, from Oceanside in the North County south to the Mexican border, just 17 miles away.

GETTING THERE

San Diego International Airport—Lindbergh Field (619–231-5221) is 3 miles northwest of downtown. Shuttles (including complimentary hotel shuttles), car rentals, and taxis are available. San Diego Transit Route 2 buses leave every half hour for downtown.

Amtrak (800–USA-RAIL), Santa Fe Depot, C Street and Kettner Boulevard, provides service to and from Los Angeles.

Greyhound/Trailways, 120 West Broadway (800–231-2222), operates daily service to Los Angeles, connecting to cities throughout the United States.

By car, San Diego is about 120 miles south of Los Angeles, two-and-one-half hours via freeway Interstate 5. Interstate 8 leads drivers from Yuma, Arizona, and from the East Coast. Interstate 15 provides access from Riverside County, Nevada, and the west.

GETTING AROUND

Metropolitan Transit Corporation buses (619–233-3004) serve the metro area. **San Diego Trolley** (619–233-3004) services the downtown area, south to the Mexican border at Tijuana, and San Diego's East County. The Transit Store at Broadway and First Avenue downtown has free transit maps and sells MTS tickets, including Day Tripper passes for unlimited rides on all MTS buses, trolleys, and the Bay Ferry to Coronado, and discounts to Sea World.

The **San Diego-Coronado ferry** (619-234-4111) leaves from the Broadway pier off Harbor Drive.

The San Diego metropolitan area stretches 30 miles, from the northern suburb of Del Mar to the Mexican border, so a car is extremely helpful. Main downtown thoroughfares are Harbor Drive, which runs along the waterfront; Broadway, which goes through downtown; and Sixth Avenue to Balboa Park. Stay off the freeways at rush hour.

WHAT TO SEE AND DO

Because San Diego is so spread out, attractions are grouped according to location. Many of the following involve at least one full day.

Balboa Park

Located just north of downtown, this 1,200-acre park is reached by crossing the Cabrillo Bridge (also called the Laurel Street Bridge) toward the California Tower (which has a carillon that chimes the hours) onto El Prado, the park's main pedestrian thoroughfare. The park is adorned with green lawns, fountains, palms, and majestic eucalyptus trees, and it features museums, a huge zoo, sports facilities, restaurants, and a performing arts complex, plus weekend street entertainers. Weekend **Punch and Judy** shows are held at the **Marie Hitchcock Puppet Theater,** the Palisades Building; (619) 685-5045. A free tram makes twelve stops through the central core of the park. The **Balboa Park Visitors Center,** in the House of Hospitality, 1549 El Prado (619-239-0512), provides a free map and sells discounted passports to several museums (which also sell the passports). Many offer free admission on various Tuesdays of the month. There are fourteen museums, so be selective. Here are some top choices.

San Diego Museum of Man, 1350 El Prado; (619) 239-2001. Exhibits at this museum, located just under the California Tower, deal mainly with anthropology and archaeology, centering around Early Man, pre-Columbian Maya, and the Southwest Indians. Costumes and customs of San Diego's widely diverse ethnic communities are part of the Lifestyle and Ceremonies exhibit, which also includes a video on reproduction suitable for most school-age kids (even groups of preschoolers come to watch it). The new Children's Discovery Center

San Diego at a Glance

- Glorious weather, a beautiful bay, green expanses, lively arts and festivals—in short, something for everyone

- Bai Yun and Shi Shi: two giant pandas at the San Diego Zoo

- Free beaches, waterfront boardwalks, harbor cruises

- A taste of Mexico in nearby Tijuana

- San Diego Convention and Visitors Bureau, (619) 232–3101

features Time Travel to Ancient Egypt, a hands-on, interactive exhibit based on an ancient Egyptian eighteenth-dynasty nobleman's home. Elsewhere in the museum is the permanent Egypt Gallery exhibit. (See Special Events for other information.)

Reuben H. Fleet Space Theater and Science Center, 1875 El Prado; (619) 238–1233. Watch exciting films projected on the giant OMNIMAX theater screen, but be sure your kids are prepared for the potentially frightening realism. Everyone seems to like the 3-D laser light shows held Wednesday through Sunday evenings. Sky Show and Star Gazing parties are held the first Wednesday of every month at 7:00 P.M. A Space Theater ticket also buys admission to the hands-on Science Center, where more than fifty exhibits demonstrate the principles of science by allowing kids to do such things as peek through periscopes and listen to heartbeats through stethoscopes.

San Diego Natural History Museum, 1788 El Prado; (619) 232–3821. Your kids will love this venerable institution. (It's more than one hundred years old.) Steer them toward the Desert Discovery Lab, with live reptiles, and the Scripps Hall of Mineralogy, where there's a walk-through mine tunnel and twelve hands-on learning centers. All kids automatically gravitate toward the dinosaur skeletons. Ask about nature walks, films, and other special happenings.

San Diego Zoo, 2920 Zoo Drive; (619) 234-3153; http://www. sandiegozoo.org. This is one of the best. Some 3,900 animals of 800 species, many rare and endangered, live in this hundred-acre, world-renowned facility. Arrive as early as possible, as this place is extremely popular. Two of the newest bioclimatic habitats simulating natural surrounding include Polar Bear Plunge (an arctic animal kingdom) and Hippo Beach—both guaranteed to please all ages.

Recently, the giant panda duo of Bai Yun and Shi Shi joined the animal population at the zoo. The pandas, from the People's Republic of China, reside in the Giant Panda Research Station, where visitors can watch them roam about and play.

Zoo admission includes the Children's Petting Zoo, with its goats, sheep, guinea pigs, bunnies, and an animal nursery, as well as all shows (the aerial tramway and a 3-mile guided bus tour cost extra). The baby monkeys and other cuties behind the glass viewing area delight kids and adults. Strollers, a good idea, are available at the zoo entrance. Southeast of the zoo, behind the Spanish Village Art Center, where arts and crafts are exhibited, a miniature railroad and a carousel await.

If you still have time and energy, consider these other Balboa Park attractions: **San Diego Aerospace Museum,** 2001 Pan American Plaza (619-234-8291), with a collection of aircraft, spacecraft, and related artifacts; **San Diego Automotive Museum,** 1030 Pan American Plaza (619-231-AUTO), featuring more than sixty classic and collectible cars; **San Diego Model Railroad Museum,** 1649 El Prado (619-696-0199), with six giant model railroad exhibits, Lionel toy trains, and working semaphore; **San Diego Museum of Art,** 1450 El Prado (619-232-7931), featuring Egyptian and pre-Columbian through twentieth-century artists—plus a Sculpture Garden cafe; **Timken Museum of Art,** 1500 El Prado (619-239-5548), a free museum displaying European art by such notables as Rembrandt and Cezanne as well as a collection of eighteenth- and nineteenth-century American paintings and Russian icons; and, new in the Park, the **Mingei Museum of International World Folk Art.**

Old Town

Old Town San Diego State Historic Park, a twelve-acre park just north of downtown at Juan Street, and bounded by Wallace, Juan, Twiggs, and Congress streets, is the site of the state's first permanent

Spanish settlement. Historic buildings grace the **Old Town Plaza,** a pleasant place to linger and people watch. The best way to explore this 6-block area is on foot: San Diego Avenue turns into a pedestrian mall. Cars are allowed on Juan and Congress streets, both lined with shops and restaurants. The Visitors Information Center at Robinson Rose House, 4002 Wallace Street, on the south side of the plaza (619-220-5422), has videos, maps for a self-guided tour, and ranger-led tours daily at 2:00 P.M.

Your kids' ages and interests will determine how many places to visit. Some of the more interesting buildings: the one-room **Mason Street School** (on Mason Street) is the city's first schoolhouse, with vintage desks and a pot-bellied stove; *San Diego Union* **Newspaper Historical Building,** San Diego Avenue, is restored to its 1868 appearance, the date of the first issue. The **Seeley Stables,** on Juan Street, the city's stage-coach stop, features Western and Native American memorabilia, including toys, musical instruments, and a collection of horse-drawn vehicles. An hourly slide show features scenes of early California (admission).

The Seaside

The beautiful **San Diego Harbor** bustles with activity: pleasure crafts, commercial and cruise ships, sportfishing and navy ships. A sight-seeing cruise affords one of the best ways to savor the harbor. If your kids won't be bored, consider a one- or two-hour narrated tour offered by San Diego Harbor Excursion, 1050 North Harbor Drive (619-234-4111), and several other companies. For a shorter cruise, board the **San Diego ferry** (at the foot of Broadway) for a fifteen-minute ride to Coronado. At the dock, Ferry Landing Marketplace, consider renting bikes. Quiet and flat **Coronado,** at about 12 square blocks, affords easy family cycling. If you're not staying at the **Hotel del Coronado** (see Where to Stay), stop by this National Historic Landmark. (Trolleys run between the landing and the hotel.)

If your kids are landlubbers, don't fret. Along San Diego's Harbor Drive, the **Embarcadero** waterfront walkway is a lovely place to stroll. It unofficially starts at Ash Street at the **Maritime Museum,** 1306 North Harbor Drive; (619) 234-9153. There you board the 1904 luxury steam yacht *Medea;* the turn-of-the-century ferryboat *Berkeley* (which carried passengers to Oakland during the earthquake of 1906); and the

Paper flowers are always in bloom in San Diego's Old Town section, which is considered California's birthplace. (Photo by Bob Yarbrough/courtesy San Diego Convention and Visitors Bureau)

Star of India, the oldest (over 125 years) active tall ship in the world. Several of the ship's cabins have been restored (including one with an old dollhouse and little high-button shoes). Below deck are interesting displays of knot tying, sail rigging, and other nautical skills. The *Berkeley* has exhibits on oceanography and naval history, including models of several well-known ships.

Less than a mile south is **Seaport Village,** West Harbor Drive at Kettner Boulevard (619-235-4014), a lively shopping, dining, and entertainment complex. Let the kids take a spin on the restored **1890 Looff Carousel,** once a Coney Island fixture, featuring delightful hand-carved animals. Fast-food emporiums and snack bars are plentiful; there are also four sit-down restaurants. A grassy section in the middle of the village attracts skaters, sun bathers, kite fliers, and street performers and hosts frequent celebrations.

If you take Harbor Drive north around the bay, you arrive at **Point Loma,** a large promontory at the end of Catalina Boulevard, which features the **Cabrillo National Monument** (619-557-5450) at the Point's tip. The paths around the monument's visitor center afford spectacular views of San Diego. Take a trail south to the **Old Point Loma Lighthouse,** in service from 1855 to 1891, which has the restored family quarters of the last lighthouse keeper. To the delight of all, from late December to the end of March, Point Loma is a terrific place to watch the annual migration of Pacific gray whales.

San Diego's other bay, **Mission Bay Park** on Mission Boulevard, north of downtown and south of La Jolla, offers lots of activity as well. This man-made 4,600-acre waterfront recreation area is three-fourths public land. Your first stop should be the Visitor Information Center, 2688 East Mission Bay Drive (619-276-8200), directly off the Mission Bay Drive exit off Route 5. Pick up free brochures on the park's facilities.

Cyclers, rollerskaters (rentals available), joggers, and skateboarders take to the **Mission Boulevard boardwalks.** The 2-mile stretch of **Mission Beach,** on the Pacific side of the peninsula, is one of the area's oldest. The water is rougher and the beach narrower in the north end, near **Belmont Park,** 3145 Mission Boulevard (619-491-2988), a shopping and entertainment center along the boardwalk. Once an abandoned amusement park, the Plunge, a 1925 indoor pool, and the Giant Dipper wooden roller coaster have been restored. A new indoor Pirate's Hideaway features soft, modular recreational playground equipment for children ages two to twelve. **Bonita Cove,** southeast of Belmont Park, is a good family bayside beach with calm waters, grassy knolls for picnicking, and a playground.

The highlight of Mission Bay: **Sea World of California,** 1720 South Shores Road; (619) 226-3901. This place is big, so consider a stroller, which you can rent near the entrance. Most kids like Baby Shamu and mom (the Summer Nights performances have particular charm), but chances are the antics of Clyde and Seamore, the sea-lion duo, will appeal even more. In all, five shows, which include the bird, whale, and dolphin and water-ski shows, keep kids busy. In addition, tour the four aquariums for a fascinating glimpse of sea life. Shark Encounter, with a submerged viewing tube, allows visitors to walk through the sharks' habitat. While fascinating, this may frighten the very young who may not realize they are not in danger.

Standouts among the park's more than twenty major educational exhibits include the park's Rocky Point Preserve, a two-part habitat for bottlenose dolphins and Alaska sea otters, and Dolphin Bay, the world's largest interactive habitat for bottlenose dolphins. Buy the trays of fish and squid sold at the park so that your kids can take part in the animals' daily feeding. (Hand-washing stations are nearby for after feeding.) For a touch of magic your kids won't soon forget—reach down and feel the dolphin's smooth skin. Another popular exhibit is the Otter Outlook, with its underwater viewing area. The new Wild Arctic is the largest attraction in the park's history. Visitors board a jet helicopter simulator and are whisked away to Base Station Wild Arctic. Here, children can play in the polar dens, learn about animals on the touch-screen kiosks, and glimpse arctic animals like polar bears, beluga whales, walruses, and harbor seals.

Let the kids loose at Shamu's Happy Harbor, a play area with interactive games for children 37 to 61 inches tall. A 320-foot Skytower offers panoramic views, as does a Skyride in enclosed gondola cars that ascend to a height of 100 feet on the half-mile round-trip over Mission Bay.

Other Attractions

The **Children's Museum of San Diego,** 200 West Island Avenue (619-233-KIDS), is a hands-on museum—in a new, splashy location—geared toward kids ages two through twelve. Afterwards, relax across the street at the **Children's Park** on the Martin Luther King, Jr. Promenade. The 200-foot-diameter pond with spray fountain is quite a sight.

The views from **Cabrillo National Monument** are hailed by locals as the best around. For $4.00 a car, families can take in the views, tour the lighthouse, and hike to the tide pools below.

La Jolla

A posh suburb 12½ miles (about fifteen minutes) north of San Diego, La Jolla offers several attractions.

The Scripps Institution of Oceanography operates the **Stephen Birch Aquarium** at Scripps, 2300 Expedition Way; (619) 534–FISH. It displays more than thirty large tanks of colorful saltwater fish. A 70,000-gallon tank simulates a La Jolla kelp forest, complete with sea anemones, starfish, crabs, and lobsters. This aquarium offers a fabulous view of the La Jolla coastline and easy access by pathways to the popular La Jolla Shores beach. Be sure to come early.

Ellen Browning Scripps Park, at the La Jolla Cove, along Coast Boulevard below Prospect Street, features a children's pool at the south end, where a seawall protects the waters from strong waves and currents. It's a great place to teach the kids snorkeling—though, as you might expect, it's frequently crowded.

North of La Jolla, don't miss **Torrey Pines State Reserve,** North Torrey Pines Road (Old Highway 101) (619-755-2063), a preserve for the world's rarest pine trees, *Pinus torreyana.* Thousands of these unusual, gnarled trees—more than half of the world's total—grow on cliffs 300 feet above the ocean. The Visitors Center (make a left after entering the park's gate and proceed up the hill) has a video presentation and area information.

Theater, Music, and the Arts

San Diego is an important center for regional theater productions that often end up on Broadway or off-Broadway. For half-price day-of-performance or full-price advance sale tickets to theater music, and dance events, call TIMES ARTS TIX at (619) 497-5000, or visit their booth at Horton Plaza, Broadway at Broadway Circle, downtown. The bimonthly *What's Playing on Stage in San Diego,* available around town, lists all current performances of the ninety-member San Diego Theatre League. These include puppet performances and theater for young audiences. Also consult the Thursday "Night Day" section of the *San Diego Union Tribune* or the weekly San Diego *This Week.*

Music offerings: From mid-June to mid-August, the Spreckels Organ Pavilion in Balboa Park (619-239-0512 or 235-1105) features free family twilight concerts on Sunday afternoons year-round.

Sports

For **San Diego Chargers** professional football (619-280-2111) and **San Diego Padres** professional baseball (619-283-4494), head to San Diego Jack Murphy Stadium, 9449 Friars Road. **San Diego Gulls** ice hockey team of the West Coast Hockey League (619-225-GOAL) skate at San Diego Sports Arena, 3500 Sports Arena Boulevard. **San Diego**

Sockers (619-224-GOAL), members of the new Continental Indoor Soccer League, also play at the Sports Arena. **The Aztecs,** the city's major college team, kick off at Jack Murphy Stadium; call (619) 594-4549.

Shopping

Downtown **Horton Plaza,** between Broadway and G Street and First and Fourth avenues (619-239-8180), is a multilevel, postmodern maze of large and small shops, fast-food emporiums, restaurants, a farmers' market, and more. Old Town's **Bazaar del Mundo,** a Mexican-style shopping center at 2754 Calhoun Street, offers colorful, handcrafted wares. The historic **Gaslamp Quarter,** a 16-block downtown historic district, has Victorian buildings and renovated warehouses that house antiques dealers, specialty shops, and art galleries.

Walking tours are available on Saturdays (donation required) from the headquarters at 410 Island Avenue; (619) 233-5227. Audio tours are also available.

SPECIAL EVENTS

Contact the San Diego CVB for more information on the following annual events.

March: Ocean Beach Kite Festival, with kite building, decorating, and flying contests.

April: Fightertown Festival a Miramar Naval Air Station features classic car show, carnival midway, craft fair, military displays, and stages with music, dancing, and martial arts.

Early Spring: Art Alive, floral interpretations of paintings and sculptures from San Diego's Museum of Art.

May: Cinco de Mayo celebrations throughout the area; International Children's Festival, five days of professional music, storytelling, comedy, and puppetry performances plus arts and crafts; American Indian Cultural Days, with singers and dancers, traditional food, exhibitions, and arts and crafts, Balboa Park.

June: Old Town Heritage Festival; Indian Fair, Balboa Park; Threshing Bee and Antique Engine Show, Vista, two consecutive weekends of early American crafts, farming, log sawing, blacksmithing, food, entertainment, and daily antique tractor parade.

July: Ringling Brothers and Barnum and Bailey Circus, San Diego Sports Arena; Sand Castle Days at Imperial Beach Pier includes children's contest, parade, and fireworks at dusk.

September: Street Scene, the state's largest music festival, transforms 18 blocks of the historic Gaslamp Quarter into a music and food festival. American Indian Day features arts and crafts, singers and dancers, food and entertainment, Balboa Park.

October: Haunted Museum of Man, Balboa Park; Escondido Downtown Street Faire, with arts and crafts vendors, bands, international food, and children's rides; Threshing Bee and Antique Engine Show (see June); Underwater Pumpkin Carving Contest, La Jolla.

November: Mother Goose Parade with floats, clowns, bands, and equestrians, El Cajon.

December: Del Mar Holiday of Lights, with light displays, children's rides, entertainment, and Santa; Old Town events include Las Posadas and Holiday Open House; San Diego collegiate Holiday Bowl and downtown parade; Christmas on the Prado events, Balboa Park; San Diego Harbor Parade of Lights.

WHERE TO STAY

The SDCVB has a *Visitors Planning Guide,* which includes an accommodations directory. **San Diego Hotel Reservations** (800–SAVE–CASH) features discounted rates to more than 250 area resorts and hotels. Contact **Bed & Breakfast Directory** for San Diego, P.O. Box 3292, San Diego 92163 (619–297–3130), for referrals and information on the thirty inns and homes throughout the county, or order their complete directory for $3.95. Here are some lodging choices for families in varied locations.

Downtown: **Harbor Hill Guest House,** 2330 Albatross Street (619–233–0638), is an inexpensive bed and breakfast with harbor views and kitchenettes. **Embassy Suites Downtown,** 601 Pacific Highway (619–239–2400 or 800–362–2779), has refrigerators, pool, and some rooms with harbor views.

Mission Bay: **The Hyatt Islandia,** 1441 Quivira Road (619–224–1234 or 800–233–1234), has more than 400 units; some in a seventeen-story tower with bay and ocean views and others in marina suites in a three-story building. The huge pool is a hit with kids. Camp Hyatt activities for ages three to twelve are held weekends from Memorial to Labor Day from 4:00 to 10:00 P.M.

Coronado: The grand **Hotel del Coronado,** 1500 Orange Avenue; (619) 435-6611 or (800) 468-3533. This has long been favored by the rich and famous (and shown in several movies). There's a beach, Olympic-size pool, poolside video arcade, bike rentals, tennis courts, and full spa. In summer, the hotel offers afternoon Camp Oz for ages four to six and Camp Breaker for seven to twelve, an evening kids' program several evenings a week, plus tennis programs for all ages, and organized family activities.

San Diego County North: **Rancho Bernardo Inn,** 17550 Bernardo Oaks Drive; (619) 487-1611, (800) 542-6096—CA, or (800) 854-1065. The inn is a half hour from Sea World, the Zoo, Wild Animal Park, and the airport. This resort has 287 units, with golf, tennis, fitness center, pools, free bikes (and 5 miles of trails), and an activity program for ages five to seventeen in August and during major holidays, from 9 A.M. to 9 P.M.

WHERE TO EAT

A dining guide is available from the International Visitor Information Center, 11 Horton Plaza. Much of the time, you'll grab a bite by the bay or give in to fast-food convenience. "Cool" preteens and older siblings can check out the **Hard Rock Cafe** in La Jolla, 909 Prospect Street; (619) 454-5101. Go to **Hob Nob Hill,** 2271 First Avenue (619-239-8176), for inexpensive but satisfying meals; try the Canadian blueberry pancakes for breakfast. **The Old Spaghetti Factory,** 275 Fifth Avenue (619-233-4323), serves ample portions of pasta in a real trolley car.

DAY TRIPS

If the San Diego Zoo hasn't satisfied your craving to see animals, head to Escondido, 30 miles northeast of downtown, to **San Diego Wild Animal Park,** 15500 San Pasqual Valley Road; (619) 675-7900 or (800) 628-3066. At this 2,100-acre preserve, endangered and rare animals roam freely in areas that replicate their native habitats. Heart of Africa, the newest exhibit, opened in May 1997, lets families trek through simulated forests, savanna, and wetlands. Keep your eyes out for warthogs, bat-eared foxes, wattled cranes, and okapi, plus endangered animals including cheetahs and bontebok. From the park's research station, located on an island lagoon, you can spot flamingos, shoebill storks, and Kikuyu colobus monkeys swinging in the California sun.

Hidden Jungle, re-creates an 8,500-square-foot Central American rain forest with sloths, turtles, tropical hummingbirds, spiders, ants, and—most fascinating—2,000 butterflies. Board the fifty-minute guided monorail tour, free with admission, for an easy view of the park. Young children like the Petting Kraal, with its gentle deer, sheep, and goats. Check the park's schedule for the animal shows, and don't miss the bird show at the amphitheater.

With the border city of **Tijuana** only 17 miles south of downtown, why not pay a brief visit to Mexico? Although you can drive, and many visitors park on the U.S. side and walk into Tijuana, consider using the San Diego trolley. There are several tourist information booths after you cross the border. **The Tijuana Cultural Center,** Paseo de los Heroes y Mina, has an OMNIMAX theater and museum of Mexican History and Art. No passport or visa is required for a stay of less than seventy-two hours within 75 miles of the border.

Note: When only one parent (whether that parent is married or divorced) is entering Mexico with a child or children, Mexico requires a notarized statement from the other, nontraveling parent indicating that the traveling parent has permission to take the child into Mexico for a specified amount of time. This rule is designed to cut down on child kidnappings by disgruntled noncustodial parents. Obtain a similar letter when you are traveling with children who have a different last name from yours.

FOR MORE INFORMATION

San Diego Convention and Visitors Bureau: Wells Fargo, 401 B Street, Suite 1400, San Diego 92101; (619) 232–3101
International Visitor Information Center: Horton Plaza, First

Avenue and F Street; (619) 236-1212, or find San Diego on the Web at http://www.sandiego.org.

Information center on East Mission Drive (off Route 5): (619) 276-8200

San Diego Family Press (619-685-6970), a monthly publication containing events, is free at museums, supermarkets, and libraries, or send $2.50 to cover postage and handling to Box 23960, San Diego 92123.

Emergency Numbers

Ambulance, fire, police: 911

Poison Control: (619) 543-6000

Twenty-four-hour pharmacy: Savon Escondido, 318 West El Norte Parkway; (619-489-1505)

Hospital: UCSD Medical Center, 225 Dickinson Street; (619) 543-6400

SAN FRANCISCO

It's easy to fall in love with San Francisco: Surrounded on three sides by shimmering water, the city has rolling hills, a lively waterfront, charming Victorian homes, as well as lofty skyscrapers, great restaurants, loads of entertainment—and, of course, those fabled cable cars. The weather can be superb. Summer foggy mornings are frequent, but when the sun is bright and the sky clear, the year-round temperate climate is appealing. (Summer daytime temperatures average 54 to 65 degrees. Bring along long pants, light jackets, and sweaters because the winds frequently whip up, both on the ocean and bay sides.)

GETTING THERE

San Francisco International Airport (415–761–0800), 14 miles south of the city off U.S. 101, is served by more than fifty-five major scheduled carriers. A $2.4 billion expansion project has been completed. Shuttle services to town, taxi service, and car rentals are available. Some passengers prefer the convenience of the smaller **Oakland International Airport** (510–577–4000) across the bay.

Greyhound Bus Lines is at Transbay Terminal, 425 Mission Street at First; (800) 231–2222. Interstate lines headquarters at Transbay Terminal include **AC Transit** (510–839–2882), which goes to the East Bay via the Oakland Bay Bridge; **Golden Gate Transit** (415–332–6600), which goes to Marin and Sonoma counties; and **SAM-TRANS** (San Mateo County Transit), which heads to San Mateo and the San Francisco International Airport; (800) 660–4287.

Rail service is provided by **Amtrak** (800–USA–RAIL) to the Oakland depot at Sixteenth and Wood streets, with shuttle service to the San Francisco Transbay Terminal. **Caltrain,** Fourth and Townsend streets (800–660–4287–northern California), operates daily trains to San Jose. Shuttle buses transport passengers to and from the Transbay Terminal.

San Francisco at a Glance

- Kid-pleasing sights and attractions in a charming, scenic city

- A ride on those fabled cable cars

- Hands-on activities at the Exploratorium

- 24 blocks of exotic sights and smells in Chinatown

- "The Rock"—Alcatraz Island

- San Francisco Convention and Visitor Bureau, (415) 391-2000

By car, most travelers from the east enter via I-80, which ends at the Bay Bridge, linking Oakland to San Francisco. Scenic U.S. 101 runs north-south through the state and enters the city via the Golden Gate Bridge. The faster north-south route, I-5, runs east of the city, connecting to the Bay Bridge via I-580 and I-80 from both the north and south.

GETTING AROUND

With a good city map in hand, walking is the best way to see the 46-square-mile city—although the hills can be tough on youngsters. **San Francisco Municipal Railway** (Muni) runs the city's cable cars, buses, and five metro lines, which go underground downtown and on the streets in the outer neighborhoods; (415) 673-6864. One-, three-, or seven-day Muni Passports are good on every regularly scheduled Muni vehicle, including cable cars, and are valid for reduced fares to ball games at Candlestick Park and discounted admission to two dozen museums and attractions. Passports are sold at the San Francisco Visitor Information (see For More Information) and other outlets; call (415) 673-6864 for specific locations.

A ride on a cable car is a must. Purchase tickets before boarding at self-service ticket machines at all terminals and major stops. There are three lines. Twenty-six cars begin at Powell and Market streets: The Powell-Hyde Line (No. 60), considered the most scenic, terminates at Victorian Park near the Maritime Museum and Aquatic Park; the Powell-Mason Line (No. 59), ends near Fisherman's Wharf. The eleven California Street Line cars (No. 61) start at the foot of Market Street and run through Chinatown to Van Ness Avenue.

BART (Bay Area Rapid Transit) runs speedy aluminum trains that connect eight San Francisco stations with Daly City to the south and with twenty-five East Bay stations; call (415) 788-BART.

Golden Gate Ferry (415-332-6600) travels between the San Francisco Ferry Building, at the foot of Market Street, and downtown Sausalito and Larkspur.

WHAT TO SEE AND DO

Museums and Zoos

The Exploratorium, 3601 Lyon Street (415-563-7337), is in the Marina district, within the walls of the Palace of Fine Arts, the only remaining structure from the 1915 Panama Pacific Exposition. This hands-on museum is frequently hailed as the best science museum in the world. Others have borrowed ideas and exhibits from the Exploratorium, which was founded in 1969 by physicist Dr. Frank Oppenheimer.

More than 700 displays encourage all ages (some 60 percent of visitors are adults) to push, pull, talk, look through, feel, and listen to exhibits that are based on light, sound, vision, hearing, touch, motion, waves, animal behavior, heat, and temperature. You and the kids will learn about phenomena that exist everywhere in nature. Step inside the Distorted Room, where nothing is exactly as it appears. Stand in front of the Anti-Gravity Mirror, where you take flight without leaving the ground. Move a 400-pound pendulum with a tiny magnet. Freeze water with a vacuum. Outside, enjoy views of San Francisco's skyline across the bay, and, at the Wave Organ exhibit, listen to the wave-activated "liquid" music emanating from twenty pipes that extend into the bay.

When it's time to reenergize, there's a cafe for sandwiches and light snacks. Inquire about special activities and workshops. You must

The sights, sounds, and excitement of San Francisco lie on the other side of the famous Golden Gate Bridge. (Photo by Carl Wilmington/courtesy San Francisco Convention and Visitors Bureau)

reserve in advance and pay extra to enter the Tactile Dome, a pitch-black, crawl-through experience recommended for adults and kids over seven; call (415) 561-0362 to reserve.

Several worthwhile museums for families are located in the eastern section of the Golden Gate Park (a must-see, must-do stop that is described further under Parks and Zoos). The **M.H. de Young Memorial Museum,** near Tenth Avenue and Fulton Street (415-750-3600), has twenty-two galleries of American art, from the seventeenth to nineteenth century, by such artists as Whistler, Cassat, Homer, Copley, and Sargent. The large gallery of landscapes, *trompe l'oeil,* and still-life pieces from the turn of the century is a fine place to introduce youngsters to American art. Colorful and dramatic tribal art from Africa and Oceania is also visually appealing to kids. Frequent traveling exhibitions require extra admission and advance tickets. Studio workshops for ages seven to thirteen are offered by artist-teachers. There are tours of current exhibits every Saturday. Admission also allows entry to the adjacent **Asian Art Museum,** Tea Garden Drive, a facility with more than 10,000 pieces of Asian sculpture, paintings, and ceramics from various periods. Call (415) 668-8921 or 688-7855 for information on daily tours and on films and storytelling hours for children.

California Academy of Sciences (415-221-5100 or 750-7145—tape), directly across from the de Young Museum, includes both an aquarium and planetarium. At the Steinhart Aquarium, kids can touch creatures from the deep in a hands-on tidal pool, then gaze wide-eyed at the schools of fast-swimming fish darting about the 100,000-gallon Fish Roundabout Tank. There's also a living coral reef tank and lots of other marine creatures—14,000 to be exact—to delight the kids. Feeding times for dolphins, seals, and penguins are especially popular with youngsters. The Morrison Planetarium presents daily sky shows and, on selected evenings, Laserium light shows (415-750-7141; 750-7138 for Laserium).

The museum itself has lots to appeal to kids: the glimmering Gem and Mineral Gallery (with a giant quartz stone); the Wild California hall, which shows the state's diverse habitats; The Far Side of Science Gallery, featuring more than 160 cartoons by Gary Larson (a big hit with the preteen and teen set); Life Through Time, a three-and-one-half-billion-year exploration of the evidence for evolution; and The Space and Earth Hall, with its simulated "earthquake floor." Call ahead to check hours for the Discovery Room, where kids are welcome to touch and explore such objects as birds' nests and shark teeth.

Bay Area Discovery Museum, 557 East Fort Baker, Sausalito; (415) 487-4398. Located beneath the Golden Gate Bridge at East Fort Baker, just south of Sausalito, this vibrant hands-on museum is geared to ages two to twelve, but even older kids will be intrigued by many of the exhibits. A transportation exhibit in a renovated 1930s gas station delights kids. The exhibit includes a computer command center where kids try to solve traffic problems; an Interactive Media Center, with a broadcast studio and computer work stations; an Interactive Science Laboratory; and an ever-changing Maze of Illusions. In addition to special workshops, arts and science programs, and festivals, the museum runs a number of field trips, including family camping and hiking trips.

If you have time, a visit to one the following will be entertaining. **The Mexican Museum,** Fort Mason Center, Building D,

Laguna Street and Marina Boulevard South (415-441-0445), offers special free art activities, music, theater, dance, and exhibition tours one Sunday each month. **Josephine D. Randall Junior Museum,** 199 Museum Way off Roosevelt Way (415-554-9600), includes a petting corral, a working seismograph, mineral and fossil displays, and special classes most Saturdays. The **Cartoon Art Museum,** 814 Mission Street (415-227-8666), houses exhibits by local and nationally known cartoonists, including art from comic books and animated movies. Works date from the 1730s to the present; there's also a children's gallery. **San Francisco Cable Car Museum,** Washington and Mason streets (415-474-1887), shows a film about how these vehicles work. There are also scale models of cable cars and vintage photos. But the real attraction is watching the exposed machinery pull the cables under the city's streets. This facility is the working powerhouse and repair shop of the entire motorless cable car system. Visitors can watch the fascinating cable-winding process from a mezzanine gallery and visit a room where the cable can be observed under ground.

Parks and Zoos

Along with the two museums above, **Golden Gate Park** (415-666-7200) offers 1,017 acres full of family fun: playgrounds, several lakes, twenty-one tennis courts, a polo field (where you can watch matches), a nine-hole golf course, horse stables for riding (lessons offered—415-668-7360), and, at the park's southeast corner, off Kezar Drive, a charming 1912 carousel and children's playground. There's even a small herd of bison that grazes just off Kennedy Drive. **The Conservatory of Flowers,** John F. Kennedy Drive; (415) 666-7017. In the northeast corner, the conservatory is the oldest building in the park. (Shipped in pieces from England, it was completed in 1879.) It's home to rare orchids, a tropical garden, and seasonal flower displays. **Huntington Falls,** on Strawberry Hill, a small island surrounded by Stow Lake in the eastern end, is the tallest artificial falls in the West. You can rent motorboats, paddleboats, and rowboats by the hour at the boathouse on Stow Lake Drive; (415) 752-0347. A city map with an overview of the Golden Gate Park is available from the Convention Bureau or from park headquarters in McLaren Lodge, corner of Stanyan and Fell.

Families congregate around the **Music Concourse,** the heart of the park (right around the de Young Museum), where the Golden Gate Park Band performs on Sundays. In this area, you'll find the **Japanese Tea Garden,** Tea Garden Drive; (415) 752-1171. This serene five-acre area, constructed for the 1894 Midwinter International Exposition, features ponds, Japanese greenery, a pagoda, an arched moon bridge, Buddha, and, in the spring, fragrant Japanese cherry blossoms. Women in kimonos serve tea and cookies at the Tea House.

Because the park is so vast, a car is helpful, although parking can be a problem. On Saturdays and Sundays, roads are closed to all vehicular traffic to accommodate bicycle riders and skaters. (You can rent roller skates throughout the park.) You may opt to take a Muni bus (call 415-673-MUNI), or you can take a shuttle from the UCSF Medical Center on Irving and Second. The shuttle runs every ten minutes and drops off at various locations in the park. Friends of Recreation and Parks (415-221-1311) conduct walking tours of the park on weekends from May to October. At press time, a discounted adult pass to five of the park's attractions (three museums, Tea Garden, and Conservatory of Flowers) was available. Call the SFCVB for information at (415) 391-2000.

The San Francisco Zoological Gardens and Children's Zoo, Sloat Boulevard and Forty-fifth Avenue (415-753-7061 or 753-7083 for tape), is ranked among the country's top city zoos. It's home to more than 1,000 animals and birds who live in attractive landscaped enclosures. Along with the expected, more unusual inhabitants include pygmy hippos, snow leopards, and a rare white tiger named Prince Charles. The $2 million Gorilla World is the world's largest gorilla habitat. There's also a Koala Crossing and, adjacent to the main zoo, near the carousel, a Children's Zoo (separate admission) where your kids can pet and feed gentle barnyard animals. At the Insect Zoo, the scorpions, ants, honeybees, and other creepy crawlies, including the world's largest centipede, wow the kids. A weekend afternoon insect show is sure to please.

On the Waterfront

You and your family will probably spend much of your time on San Francisco's vibrant waterfront. **Golden Gate National Recreation Area** (GGNRA) comprises approximately 28 miles of California coastline and is the largest urban park in the world. It's also the most popular U.S. National Park, attracting some seventeen million visitors a year. The park stretches from San Mateo in the south through parts of the San Francisco waterfront to the Cliff House and Fort Point, to Alcatraz, and across Golden Gate Bridge north to a portion of Marin County.

Fort Point, a brick formation completed in 1861 at the base of the Golden Gate Bridge, affords scenic views of the city. (Yes, you can walk across the 2-mile stretch. The walkway is free, but bundle up—it can be chilly.)

If your kids are up to it, walk along the shoreline for nearly 4 miles by following the **Golden Gate Promenade** footpath. This stroll, which begins at Fort Point, provides scenic views as you wind by bocce ball courts, the yacht harbor, and Fort Mason Center. GGNRA park headquarters are at the Fort Mason Center, Bay and Franklin streets; (415) 979-3010 or 556-0560. Obtain maps and park information at the center, formerly a surplus military property, now a lively arts and recreation complex offering more than 1,000 activities monthly—and superb picnic facilities.

The footpath terminates at Aquatic Park, the lagoon adjacent to the Hyde Street Pier, at the foot of Polk Street, the location of the **National Maritime Museum;** (415) 556-3002. This museum features ship models, painted figureheads, shipwreck photos, and other artifacts. Admission is free.

Near **Fisherman's Wharf,** which includes Piers 43-47 at Taylor and Jefferson streets, several historic ships are open to the public—including the *Balclutha,* a steel-hulled, square-rig vessel built in 1886 in Scotland and the last of the Cape Horn fleet; the 1895 lumber schooner *C.A. Thayer;* and the 1890 ferryboat *Eureka.* Only U.S. ranger-guided tours are allowed to board the scow schooner *Alma;* call (415) 556-3002. On the third Saturday of every month, kids can take afternoon tours of the historic ships at Hyde Street Pier. Reservations are required; (415) 556-1871.

Fisherman's Wharf, Piers 43-47 at Taylor and Jefferson streets—and the northern waterfront, off Jefferson Street (at the end of the Powell-Hyde cable car line from Union Square)—is one of the city's top tourist attractions. Here you'll find dozens of seafood restaurants and sidewalk stands, vendors selling souvenirs, street performers, fishing vessels, and nearby attractions such as **Ripley's Believe it or Not!**

Museum, 175 Jefferson Street; (415) 771-6188. Recently remodeled, it contains such oddities as a cable car made from 275,000 matchsticks, a walk-through kaleidoscope, rotating tunnels, and more. The **Wax Museum at Fisherman's Wharf,** 145 Jefferson Street (800-439-4305– CA), features four floors of more than 270 celebrities from Eddie Murphy to a re-creation of King Tut's treasure-filled tomb. The **Guiness Book of World Records,** 235 Jefferson Street (415-771-9890), records the biggest, the smallest, and most bizarre, plus videos of world's records being set and fun hands-on exhibits.

Sight-seeing cruises of the bay by the **Red & White Fleet** (415-546-BOAT or 800-BAY-CRUISE–CA) are available at Piers 41 and 43½. Along with forty-five-minute cruises under the Golden Gate Bridge and around Alcatraz, the line offers a number of other cruises. One option is a fifty-five-minute trip to **Marine World Africa USA,** Marine World Parkway, 30 miles northeast of San Francisco in Vallejo (707-643–ORCA), an exciting oceanarium and wildlife park. The **Blue and Gold Fleet** (415-705-5444) leaves from **Pier 39** (Embarcadero and Beach Street) for a seventy-five-minute cruise, sailing under both the Golden Gate and Bay Bridges and offering close-up views of both sides of Alcatraz (see Other Attractions).

Pier 39—a two-level complex featuring loads of shops, restaurants, and video arcades—is a real hit with kids. On the second level, the **San Francisco Experience** (415-982-7550), a half-hour multimedia spectacular, tells about the city's past and present in an entertaining way. The lobby houses an interesting earthquake exhibit and antique amusement devices.

Another Pier 39 hit is the **Marine Mammal Interpretive Center,** J on level 2 for docents (415-289-7339), established after a herd of California sea lions took a fancy to the locale. Depending on the season and weather, up to several hundred of these blubbery, barking sea denizens may be sunning themselves near K dock, level 1. At Pier 39 is **Underwater World** (415-623-5300), a 707,000-gallon marine, research, and education facility. The attraction simulates an underwater dive and offers visitors a 400-foot-long journey through a transparent tunnel, from which they can glimpse marine life indigenous to local rivers, coastal wetlands, and ocean waters—even sharks and stingrays.

On the GGNRA's western (Pacific) shoreline, **Cliff House** and **Seal Rocks,** 1090 Point Lobosa (415-386-3330), offer spectacular views. The house, the third on the spot, is on the site of the elaborate estate of inventor Adolph Sutro. Today the building combines an eatery, a pub, and a gift shop. The lower restaurant is a great place to watch the sea lions and shorebirds that usually congregate at Seal Rocks, 400 feet offshore. (If you have binoculars, bring them along.) If the day is clear, you may also be able to see the Farallon Islands, about 30 miles away. You can also see the remains of the historic Sutro baths, an enormous swimming and restaurant complex that burned down in 1966. Below Cliff House is **Ocean Beach,** a 4-mile stretch of sandy shoreline, great for walking or jogging (though it's windy here), but not swimming because the current is dangerous. One of the few swimming beaches in the city is **China Beach,** at Twenty-eighth Avenue and Sea Cliff, on the city's northern edge, where lifeguards are on duty during the summer. Be prepared for the bay's chilly water.

Other Attractions

Alcatraz Island, 1½ miles from shore, is an extremely popular attraction that most kids enjoy. "The Rock," a maximum security federal prison phased out in 1963, was once home to such famous criminals as Al Capone and Machine Gun Kelly. Red and White boats leave from Pier 41 (415-546-BOAT) daily every half hour starting at 9:30 A.M. Tickets are available daily beginning at 8:00 A.M.; it's a good idea to buy them at least one day in advance in summer. Dress warmly and wear comfortable shoes. On the island, you can take self-guided trail walks (the terrain here is steep), audiocassette tours narrated by former inmates and guards through the main cell block, and ranger-led programs.

One of America's newest national parks is the **Presidio of San Francisco** (415-556-0865), a military post with a history of Spanish, Mexican, and American rule. Strategically located next to the Golden Gate Bridge and the Bay, the Presidio grounds offer great views, as well as historic cannons and barracks, military ruins, and more. Walking tours are available. The Presidio Museum chronicles the role of the military in San Francisco's history and development.

Among the city's diverse neighborhoods, **Chinatown,** with its gateway at Grant and Bush, is a favorite with kids. Stroll through the gateway, bedecked with dragons and stone lions, and meander 24 blocks crowded with people and exotic sights and smells—restaurants, food markets, temples, and small museums. The **Chinese Culture Center,** 750 Kearney, on the third floor of the Holiday Inn (415-986-1822), offers rotating exhibits of arts and crafts along with educational and cultural programs.

Several blocks to the north of Chinatown in the Russian Hill neighborhood, take a slow (very slow) drive down Lombard Street, called the "world's crookedest." There are nine (count them) hairpin turns as the street descends Russian Hill on the block between Hyde and Leavenworth. The view from Hyde Hill is superb. It's also possible to walk the street, up and down staircases—if your kids (and you) have the energy.

Tours and Walks

The **Barbary Coast Trail** captures the spirit of the Gold Rush, the Comstock Lode, and the 1903 earthquake, taking strollers past fifty historic sites and landmarks, including seven museums. The 3.8-mile trail begins downtown at the Old Mint and goes to the Maritime National Historic Park, right across from Ghirardelli Square. From here, take a twenty-minute cable ride back to the beginning. Maps are available at the San Francisco Visitor Information Center in Hallidie Plaza, Powell at Market Street.

The **Herb Caen Promenade** (formerly the Embarcadero Promenade) stretches a mile and a half from Pier 39 to the San Francisco–Oakland Bay Bridge. This palm-lined concrete walkway affords walkers views of Treasure Island, the East Bay, boats, and the city's skyline.

Free **City Guide Walking Tours** are available seven days a week, year-round, rain or shine. The walks, ranging from ninety minutes to two hours, are sponsored by the San Francisco Friends of the Library. More than one hundred volunteer-led tours cover a variety of themes. Schedules are available at the San Francisco Visitor Information Center in Hallidie Plaza, Powell at Market Street, or by calling (415) 557-4266.

Shopping

Visiting one of the city's lively retail and restaurant complexes is an experience in itself. A family favorite is **Ghirardelli Square,** 900 North Point Street; (415) 775-5500. Bordered by North Point, Polk, Beach, and Larkin streets, it has more than seventy shops and restaurants. The oldest building, the Woolen Mill, dates back to 1854. From 1893 to the early 1960s, the Domingo Ghirardelli family produced chocolate here. Some of the original vats and ovens are in operation at the Ghirardelli Chocolate Manufactory on the plaza level of the Clock Tower.

Japan Center, Post and Buchanan Square (415-922-6776), occupies 3 square blocks just south of the city's small Japanese quarter. The complex houses restaurants and sushi bars, Japanese baths, theaters, and various shops. In spring, the center and the surrounding Japantown area are the site of the Cherry Blossom Festival.

The Cannery, ½ block from the Hyde Street cable car turnaround at 2801 Leavenworth and Beach (415-775-7104), was once a Del Monte peach cannery. The 1906 buildings were renovated into a three-level complex with shops, galleries, restaurants, a comedy club, and street performers. **The Anchorage,** 2800 Leavenworth (415-775-6000), a 2.6-acre site in the heart of Fisherman's Wharf, has specialty shops, restaurants, and a courtyard where street performers entertain.

Theater, Music, and the Arts

The Visitor Information Center's twenty-four-hour phone hotlines have updates on arts events; call (415) 391-2001. BASS/Ticketmaster centers can be found in several locations, or you can charge tickets by phone. Call (510) 762-2277 for information. TIX Bay Area, on the Stockton side of Union Square (415-533-7827), has selected day-of-performance tickets for theater, dance, and music events. Cash only; no reservations or phone orders accepted. Call for opening hours (closed Sunday and Monday). They also sell full-price tickets to many events in the neighborhoods and outlying areas through BASS tickets.

Kidshows offers a variety of musical, theatrical, and storytelling performances during the school year. They're located in the Cowell Theatre, Landmark Building A, Fort Mason, Marina Boulevard and Buchanan Street. Call (415) 392-4400 for information.

Sporting Events

Baseball fans can watch the **San Francisco Giants** play at Candlestick Park, 8 miles south of San Francisco; call (415) 467-8000 or (415) 674-MUNI for Ballpark Express bus information. **The Oakland Athletics** play at the Oakland Coliseum, off I-880; call (510) 762-BASS for ticket information. The **San Francisco 49ers** football team plays at Candlestick Park. Games are usually sold out well in advance; call (415) 468-2249 for ticket information. **San Francisco Bay Blackhawks** pro soccer team plays at Spartan Stadium in San Jose, about forty minutes from San Francisco. Call (408) 295-4295 or (800) 677-HAWK for information. The **Golden State Warriors** play NBA basketball at the Oakland Coliseum; call (510) 638-6300.

SPECIAL EVENTS

The Datebook, a pink insert in Sunday's *San Francisco Examiner,* is an excellent source of weekly events, including fairs and festivals. For a detailed quarterly events SFCVB calendar, request the *San Francisco Book,* $2.00. (See For More Information.) Among the highlights are these events.

January–February: Chinese New Year Celebration includes Miss Chinatown USA pageant, outdoor festivities, cultural programs, and Golden Dragon parade on final Saturday night. (Be prepared for noise!)

April: Cherry Blossom Parade: More than 2,000 Californians of Japanese descent and performers from Japan participate in an elaborate offering of Japanese culture and customs.

May: Cinco de Mayo Parade/Celebration, includes two days of outdoor cultural festivities and live entertainment; Carnaval, in the Mission District, is a Mardi Gras–like celebration that includes a parade, street festival, and costume contest.

June: North Beach Festival (415-403-0666), the country's oldest urban street fair, offers arts and crafts, live entertainment, and more.

June–September: Make*A*Circus Summer Festival Days (415-776-8470) feature a circus performance followed by a Circus Skills workshop for the audience.

July: Fourth of July Celebration, Crissy Field in the Presidio, features family festivities and fireworks display.

September–October: Renaissance Pleasure Faire, weekends, in Blackpoint Forest, features thousands of costumed participants who stage an Elizabethan harvest festival.

October–November: Grand National Rodeo, Horse and Stock Show, Cow Palace.

December: Pickle Family Circus Holiday Show, Palace of Fine Arts.

WHERE TO STAY

A lodging guide is available from the SFCVB. Bed-and-breakfast reservation services include **Bed and Breakfast International** (415-696-1690 or 800-872-4500), for stays in private homes throughout the state; and **Bed and Breakfast San Francisco** (415-479-1913 or 800-452-8249), for inns, home stays, apartments, houseboats, and yachts in San Francisco and beyond. Hotel reservation services include **Golden Gate Reservations** (415-252-1107 or 800-423-7846) and **San Francisco Reservations** (415-227-1500 or 800-677-1550).

Other lodging possibilities include the following.

Four Seasons Clift, 495 Geary Street; (415) 775-1700 or (800) 332-3442. This stately hotel in the Union Square area is "grand" in every sense of the word. Expensive, yes—but if you're going to splurge, this is the place to do it. The hotel is kid friendly, with toys for toddlers, pint-size terry robes, magazines for teens, bedtime snacks of milk and cookies, and, if you need them, high chairs, diapers, and strollers. There's a pediatrician on call twenty-four hours—and a kids' menu available on twenty-four-hour room service. You'll also get a list of child-friendly attractions. A family plan offers two rooms (connecting whenever possible) at a single-room rate.

The **Westin St. Francis,** 335 Powell at Union Square, San Francisco, California 94102 (415-397-7000 or 800-228-3000), offers the new Westin Kids Club amenities. These include child-friendly rooms, children's sports bottle or tippy cup upon check-in, as well as a safety kit with a night-light, Band-Aids, and emergency phone numbers. Rooms feature bath toys and bath products for kids, and parents can request—at no charge—jogging strollers, potty seats, bicycle seats, and step stools. Restaurants and room service also feature children's menus.

Also in the Union Square area, **The Savoy,** 580 Geary Street (415-441-2700 or 800-227-4223), is a smaller property with eighty-three rooms, and moderately priced. Families are welcome, and cribs, and children under fourteen are free.

The **Hyatt Fisherman's Wharf,** 555 North Point Street (415-563-1234 or 800-233-1234), is conveniently located and offers Hyatt's family-friendly amenities of kid's menus and room service plus a heated pool.

Columbus Motor Inn, 1075 Columbus Avenue (415-885-1492), is several blocks from Fisherman's Wharf. It's comfortable enough, with color TV, air conditioning, and in-room coffee—and works well for a family on a budget. Ask about their family units: two adjoining rooms with shared bath.

Hyde Park Suites, 2635 Hyde Street; (415) 771-0200 or (800) 227-3608. This attractive facility is 6 blocks from the Wharf, with small suites that include fully equipped kitchens.

About 4 miles from San Francisco's International Airport and about twenty minutes from downtown, **Summerfield Suites San Francisco,** 1350 Huntington Avenue, San Bruno (415-588-0770 or 800-833-4353), offers two-bedroom suites, a bonus for families.

WHERE TO EAT

The San Francisco Book (see For More Information) contains a comprehensive listing of restaurants. In many cases, you'll find yourself grabbing a bite while on the go. There are a number of fine fast-food places in Pier 39: **Apple Annies** (415-397-0473), for pizza and sandwiches; **Boudin Sourdough Bakery and Cafe** (415-421-0185), serving sandwiches made with the city's famous French sourdough bread. Boudin also has branches in Ghirardelli Square, Fisherman's Wharf, and several other locations citywide. For a casual sit-down meal, **Charley Brown's** in The Cannery, 2801 Leavenworth (415-776-3838), is a good, moderately priced choice because of their bountiful children's burger platters. (Parents can indulge in the prime ribs.) The preteen and teen set will be happy at the **Hard Rock Cafe,** 1699 Van Ness Avenue at Sacramento Street; (415) 885-1699. For burgers, ribs, chicken, and sandwiches, the **Alcatraz Bar and Grill,** Pier 39 (415-434-1818), is a hoot. The decor is "early prison"—and there are related exhibits, artifacts, and a jail cell. The back room has spectacular bay views.

DAY TRIPS

The Greater Bay Area offers loads of kid-pleasing sights. Don't miss a trip to **Muir Woods National Monument** in Mill Valley, 17 miles north via U.S. 101; (415) 388-2595. This 550-acre preserve is home to majestic redwoods, some as high as 252 feet and up to 1,000 years old. At the new visitor center, kids can get a Junior Ranger Pack with a variety of activities they can complete to earn a patch. The majority of the main trails are fairly level and paved for easy walking.

On the East Bay, the city of **Berkeley** is home campus for the University of California. Strolling around this city of 100,000 is an experience your preteens and teens will enjoy: The counterculture of the 1960s is still very much in evidence. Street performers, shops, cafes, and vendors abound on Telegraph Hill, just south of the campus. Take a self-guided walk around the campus: The Visitors Center, in University Hall, University Avenue and Oxford Street, is open weekdays; call (510) 642-5215. Maps and brochures are available.

FOR MORE INFORMATION

San Francisco Convention and Visitor Bureau, P.O. Box 429097, San Francisco 94142-9097, will send you the comprehensive guide *The San Francisco Book* and lodging information for a nominal fee. Their Visitor Information Center is in Benjamin Swig Pavilion on the lower level of Hallidie Plaza at Market and Powell streets; (415) 391-2000. A twenty-four-hour recorded message lists daily events and activities: (415) 391-2001. Website: http://www.sfgate.com

San Francisco Peninsula Parent Newsmagazine, P.O. Box 1280, Millbrae, California 94030 (415-342-9203), includes area events for families. Disabled visitors may obtain information from the Disability Coordinator in the Mayor's Office of Community Development (415-554-8926) or from The Easter Seal Society (415-752-4888). For public transportation information, request the *Muni Access Guide,* Muni Elderly and Handicapped Programs, 949 Presidio Avenue, San Francisco 94115; (415) 923-6142—weekdays.

Emergency Numbers
  Ambulance, fire, police: 911
  Poison Control: (800) 523-2222
  Twenty-four-hour pharmacy: Walgreens,
    3201 Divisadero Street at Lombard; (415) 931-6415
  Hospital with twenty-four-hour emergency rooms:
    San Francisco General Hospital Medical Center,
    1001 Potrero Avenue; (415) 206-8000 or 206-8111 for
    emergencies. **The Medical Center at the University of**
    California, 505 Parnassus Avenue at Third Avenue;
    (405) 476-1000.

13 ✦ California

YOSEMITE NATIONAL PARK

Yosemite National Park, on the eastern border of central California, comprises 1,169 square miles that include towering sequoias, huge granite boulders, toppling waterfalls, hidden lakes, and unspoiled forest. This area affords families truly breathtaking scenery and myriad ways to enjoy it. Although the park is open all year, summer attracts the most tourists: some three million. If you visit then, expect crowds, traffic, and difficulty in finding lodging (unless you've booked well in advance). The 7-mile stretch of the **Yosemite Valley,** the most frequented section of the park, is eye-catching any time of the year. If possible, visit in the off-season; however, summer is the only time you can be guaranteed passage into the eastern high country, which is often snowed in from late autumn until late spring.

Yosemite experienced the largest flood in its history on January 1 and 2, 1997. Sustaining the most damage were the areas surrounding the Merced River in Yosemite Valley and along route 140 to El Portal. Visitors will find many changes in available facilities and much reconstruction for the next several years.

GETTING THERE

Fresno Air Terminal, 97 miles south (209-498-4095), is the closest airport; it is served by **Delta, United, USAir,** and **American.** Many Yosemite-bound tourists also arrive at **San Francisco International,** 13 miles south of San Francisco (415-876-7809), a four- to five-hour drive; or **Los Angeles International,** Century and Sepulveda (310-646-5252), six hours away. Rental cars are available at all three airports.

Yosemite Gray Line (209-443-5240 or 800-640-6306—California) offers daily bus service to and from Yosemite and the Fresno airport, the Merced and Fresno **Amtrak** stations (800-USA-RAIL), and Merced and Fresno **Greyhound** stations (800-231-2222). Connections are also possible via Amtrak and express bus from Oakland to Merced and from San Diego and Los Angeles to Fresno; call Amtrak for information. **Via Bus Lines** (209-384-1315) also goes to Yosemite from Merced, connecting with Amtrak, Greyhound, and Trailways.

Three highways come to Yosemite, all intersecting with Highway 99, which runs north-south through the Central Valley. There are four entrances to the park. West: The **Big Oak Flat** entrance is 98 miles east of Manteca via Route 120, the most direct route from San Francisco (however, this area can be snowy in winter). The **Arch Rock** entrance is 75 miles northeast of Merced via Route 140, and is considered the major route. (Due to flood damage, Route 140 will be under construction. Delays should be expected, especially in the fall, winter, and spring months.) South: **Wawona,** 64 miles north of Fresno, is accessed by Route 41, the shortest route from Los Angeles. East: **Tioga Pass,** open Memorial Day through October, is 10 miles west of Lee Vining, off Route 120. Winter visitors are advised to take Route 140 through Mariposa, the least mountainous route, which may not require chains, although it's wise to carry them when traveling through the Sierra Nevada.

GETTING AROUND

Yosemite National Park has about 250 miles of roads and 840 miles of hiking trails. Almost 95 percent of the park is undeveloped. Consult the map on the back of the *Yosemite Guide,* a newspaper detailing current park events, available from any entrance station or visitor center.

Free shuttle buses service the more populated sections of the park, making a car unnecessary for getting around. With children, however, a car is undoubtedly more convenient. Bus routes covered include eastern **Yosemite Valley** (all year), **Mariposa Grove** and **Tuolumne Meadows** (summer only), and **Badger Pass Ski Area** (winter only). The shuttle stops at museums, natural areas, historical sites, shops, and lodges.

Bike rentals are available in the Valley at **Yosemite Lodge** (209-

372–1208) all year and at **Curry Village** during the summer (209–372–1200—summer). Although children's bikes (and helmets, required for all riders) are available, child carriers are not, and only one rider per bike is allowed. Rental bikes are not permitted outside Yosemite Valley and are prohibited from pedestrian and hiking trails and the last ⅓-mile section of the Mirror Lake Road.

Saddle trips for ages seven and older, ranging from two hours to a full day, are available from Yosemite Valley, Easter to mid-October, and during summer in Wawona, White Wolf, and Tuolumne Meadows. Reservations recommended; call (209) 372-8348 for information. Helmets, available free at the stables, are required.

River rafts can be rented, along with life jackets and paddles, in early summer at Curry Village for rafting on the Merced River. If the previous winter is severe, causing fallen trees, rafting might be suspended. Rafting is not allowed on Merced River above Yosemite Valley Stables or below El Capitan Bridge because of hazardous rapids and park regulations.

A variety of sight-seeing tours, most by bus, are also offered by the park's new concessionaire, **Yosemite Lodge Tour Desk.** Reserve by calling (209) 372-1240. Information is available at hotel tour desks or next to the **Village Store** in Yosemite Village. If you're staying in the park, you can order pack lunches the night before from either your hotel or from one of the park shops.

WHAT TO SEE AND DO

The Yosemite Valley, 7 miles long and 1 mile wide, includes **Yosemite Village,** the center of the park's activities, offering lodgings, shops, and restaurants. Come here to get oriented, particularly if you are entering from the west. You may want to stop at some of the notable vistas you'll pass *before* arriving at the **Yosemite Valley Visitor Center** (209-372-0299) because the circle road around the valley is one-way.

At the visitor center, the auditorium behind the center has a multimedia presentation that will familiarize you with the park's offerings. There's also a short slide show in the center entitled "One Day in Yosemite," showing visitors how to make the most out of a brief stay.

Yosemite National Park at a Glance

- Breathtaking scenery and myriad ways for families to enjoy it

- An 1870s Ahwahneechee Indian village

- Bridalveil Fall, El Capitan, Half Dome, Tuolumne Meadows

- Biking, saddle trips, river rafting, hiking, mountaineering, skiing

- Valley Visitor Center, (209) 372-0200

Chat with park rangers, who will suggest hiking trails and touring routes, and explore natural history displays. Behind the center, an authentic re-creation of an **1870s Ahwahneechee Indian village** offers a short, self-guided trail.

Next door, the **Yosemite Museum's Indian Cultural Exhibit** (209-372-0291) features a **Fine Arts Gallery** with rotating exhibits of historical paintings, photos, and resident artist interpretations, as well as the Indian Cultural Exhibit, and displays of the park's first inhabitants, the Miwok and Paiute people, from 1850 to the present. Kids like the displays of leather clothing and handwoven baskets, augmented with demonstrations of basket weaving, bead work, and traditional games.

Here are some of the park's most famous landmarks that your family won't want to miss.

Bridalveil Fall is off Southside Drive (the Valley Road). Park your car; then follow a paved 0.25-mile trail (there's a small, 100-foot rise) to the base of the 7,569-foot cascade.

El Capitan, a gigantic, granite mass—the largest single granite rock on Earth—towers nearly 4,000 feet in the air. The rock is on your left as you drive farther into the valley. There are several turnouts where you can stop for fabulous views: You may even see daring rock climbers inching up the stone walls. (Don't do this unless you are an experienced rock climber.)

At the east end are two of Yosemite's ten waterfalls: **Vernal Fall** and **Nevada Fall.** Families with older children accustomed to hiking may follow a moderately steep trail that starts from Streneon's Trail at Happy Isles and goes to the footbridge overlooking 300-foot **Vernal Fall** (it's 3 miles round-trip). If you're really hale and hardy, it's another 2 miles to **Nevada Fall,** then on to the top of another park landmark, **Half Dome,** a famous 8,842-foot-tall rock.

A much easier way to sightsee, especially with younger kids, is to sign up for a park tour. The park service offers a free shuttle (parking can be a real hassle in summer). If you decide to drive, you get an excellent view of the Dome by taking a left across Sentinel Bridge, parking your car, and walking to the center of the bridge. Eighty-seven million years old in plutonic rock years, this huge domed, sliced-in-half beauty is the symbol of Yosemite.

Yosemite Falls, a short walk from the visitor center, is the highest waterfall in North America. It comprises three cascades: **Upper Fall** drops 1,430 feet; **Cascades** (Middle Fall) goes another 675 feet, pouring into **Lower Fall,** with a 320-foot drop. View the falls from the parking lot, or, for a closer perspective, walk along the 0.25-mile path that begins near Yosemite Lodge and leads to the base.

An easy trail with kids is the self-guided nature trail that starts in front of the visitor center. Pick up the pamphlet *A Changing Yosemite* at the trailhead. The 2-mile paved loop circles through Cook's Meadow. As you proceed up Highway 41 leaving the valley, don't miss **Tunnel View** (park just before the Wawona Tunnel), where you can look below into the valley for an unforgettable panorama of **El Capitan, Half Dome, Sentinel Rock,** and **Bridalveil Fall.** As you continue on Highway 41, you'll come to the turnoff road to **Glacier Point,** with more spectacular vistas. This road, however, is closed in winter.

Wawona

Highway 41 heads through the mountains south to **Wawona** (a Native American word for evening primrose). Here you'll find **Wawona Pioneer History Center** (209-375-6514), with historic Yosemite buildings from the 1800s and early 1900s. Rangers conduct tours, and volunteers wear period costumes from late spring until midfall. The **Wawona Stables,** next door, offer a variety of scenic rides through this corner of the park. Younger children can be strapped on a friendly lead pony. Call (209) 375-6502 for information. **The Wawona Hotel** is on State Route 41, 27 miles from Yosemite Valley; (209) 252-4848. This National Historic Landmark, built in 1879, is a good stop for breakfast, lunch, or dinner; try a Sunday brunch or summer Saturday western barbecue. Reservations are a good idea. The *Yosemite Guide* lists the interpretive programs held in this park section.

Nine miles south of Wawona is the **Mariposa Grove of Big Trees.** While you can view a number of giant sequoias from the parking lot, get an up-close view by following the 0.8-mile self-guided nature trail to the huge **Grizzly Giant,** thought to be 2,700 years old. You can take a narrated **Big Trees Tram Tour** that departs right from the grove several times daily, spring through fall. Reservations are not required.

Tuolumne Meadows

The alpine **Tuolumne Meadows,** on the park's eastern side, offers a high-country experience. This pristine area is filled with sparkling lakes, granite domes, and rolling meadows where wildflowers bloom in spring and summer. **The Tuolumne Meadows Visitor Center,** open summers only, is a little more than an hour and a half drive from the valley on Route 120 East, (209) 372-0263. It features geological exhibits, wildflower species, and displays on John Muir, the naturalist who founded Yosemite in the late 1800s.

In summer, spend an awesome day on the **Tuolumne Meadows Tour.** Photo opportunities range from **Tioga Road** (the highest auto pass in the Sierra) to the overlook at **Mono Lake** (nesting grounds for 90 percent of the California gull population and notable for the **tufa towers**—calcium carbonate formations that line its shores) to the summit of **Lee Vining Canyon.** Horseback tours are also available.

Note: The high elevations may cause some people to experience altitude sickness, particularly young children or persons who have heart and lung diseases. Altitude sickness frequently affects people at elevations above 8,000 feet. Although the valley's elevation is 4,000 feet, Tioga Pass is 9,945. The sickness is characterized by headache, nausea, irritability, insomnia, shortness of breath, general malaise, and fatigue. Acclimate yourself, if possible, by attempting higher elevations gradually over a period of two or more days; and avoid alcohol, sugar, and high-fat meals. Drink plenty of water. Those who develop altitude sickness should descend to a lower elevation as soon as possible and, if symptoms persist, go to the Yosemite Medical Clinic, in Yosemite Valley, which specializes in treating this illness.

Family Fare

Kids love the **Happy Isles Nature Center,** 1 mile southeast of Curry Village (209-372-0287), open daily from late spring until October. This museum and exhibit area include numerous dioramas, interactive exhibits, wildlife displays, a display of Yosemite at night, and books for kids. Films are also shown periodically.

Junior (ages eight to ten) and **Senior Rangers** (ages eleven to twelve) spring into action from June through August. Park rangers lead programs several days a week, including exploring "secret" places in Yosemite Valley and Tuolumne Meadows. A child earns a certificate for Snow Rangers in winter. A $3.00 fee is required to cover expenses. Sign up one day ahead of time at **Happy Isles Nature Center** (see later listing).

Families with older kids may want to take advantage of what many consider some of the world's best rock climbing and the best rock-climbing school: **Yosemite Mountaineering School and Guide Service,** headquartered at Tuolumne Meadows from June to October and at Curry Village from October to May. Participants, who don't have to be especially athletic, must be fourteen for a regular class; kids under fourteen can arrange group lessons in advance; call (209) 372-8444 (in winter); (209) 372-8435 (in summer). Free art classes for all ages are offered at the **Art Activity Center** next to the post office at Yosemite Village every day from spring through fall; sign up at the center.

The **Yosemite Theater,** Valley Visitor Center, holds several musical shows perfect for families, including **Yosemite by Song and Stories.** Older children enjoy actor Lee Stetson's interpretations of **John Muir** one-man shows (no babies allowed). Tickets may be purchased at the visitor center.

Free evening programs feature interpretive talks, slides, and movies at campgrounds and hotel amphitheaters; consult the *Yosemite Guide* for schedules.

Le Conte Memorial Lodge, shuttle stop #12, on the way to Curry

Village (209-372-4542), offers a children's center with special programs for ages five to twelve led by the Sierra Club on Wednesdays and Thursdays in July to the first week of August.

Family campfires with songs and stories take place several times a week in all major areas from late June to early September.

Winter Activities

Snow season usually begins in November and lasts through March, with an average snowfall of 180 inches, making Yosemite a skier's haven—yet, at 4,000 feet, Yosemite Valley's temperatures remain mild. More winter perks: It's easier to spot wildlife—coyotes, raccoons, mule deer, and perhaps even a bear—when the trees are barren of leaves. (Never feed the park's animals in any season.) Moreover, the dramatic winter light offers a different perspective of the mountains. And, naturally, the crowds are thinner. Winter offers many possibilities.

Family skiing is popular at the **Badger Pass Ski Area,** 20 miles from Yosemite Valley on Highway 41; (209) 372-1333. Families have been coming here for generations, attracted to the relatively small mountain, with one triple chair, three doubles, one surface lift, and nine ski runs. The **Yosemite Ski School,** the first in California, has an excellent reputation. Babysitting for ages three (toilet trained) to nine is available in the Badger Pup Den. From January to March, bargain midweek ski packages are available. The park also has 350 miles of cross-country ski trails, many in the Badger Pass area.

The outdoor ice skating rink in Curry Village, on the valley's southeastern edge, provides a perfect view of Half Dome behind the trees. The rink and concessions are typically open from late November to March. Rentals are available, and there's a warming hut and snack bar, where you can buy hot cocoa. Call (209) 372-8341 (winter).

Take a family-oriented daytime naturalist program on Wednesdays. Rangers point out animal tracks, identify trees, and explain how humans and animals differ in the way they adapt to the cold. Tours depart from the Yosemite Lodge lobby; call (209) 372-1274 for more information.

See the **Sierra Nevada** from a vantage point unreachable by mechanized means on a winter snowshoe walk. You can rent snowshoes for kids ten years and older. Rangers lead the two-hour journey from the Badger Pass Ski Area to Clark Range. Call the **Badger Pass Ranger sta-**

The Badger Pups ski program will delight kids during a winter vacation to Yellowstone's Badger Pass. (Courtesy Yosemite Concession Services, Yosemite National Park)

tion, at (209) 372–0409. Tours take groups of about thirty-five five days a week when the downhill ski area at Badger Pass is open.

Children who participate in any winter outdoor National Park program may ask a ranger for a Junior Snow Ranger certificate. Two certificates enable him or her to purchase a Junior Snow Ranger patch for a nominal fee.

SPECIAL EVENTS

While the park has some annual events, most of the fairs and festivals take place in the communities surrounding Yosemite. See Day Trips for other activities in these areas, and call the local visitors bureaus.

January: Chefs' Holidays, a month-long festival of free daytime cooking demonstrations and evening banquets by America's best chefs, Ahwahnee Hotel.

March: Western Artists Art Show, Ahwahnee.

April: The Great American Chili Cook-Off, Madera, with special events, food, and entertainment; Family Day Parade, Raymond, includes children's carnival and craft fair; Yosemite Winterfest, Badger Pass, costume contests, races, barbecue, and torchlight parade ends the ski season.

Easter Holidays: Special activities for adults and kids at Badger Pass include Easter egg hunt on the slopes.

May: Fishing Derby, Bass Lake; Chowchilla-Madera County Fair.

July: Boat parade and fireworks, Bass Lake.

August: Three-day Warbird Airshow displays former military aircraft from North America and abroad, Madera; Sierra Mono Indian Fair Days, North Fork, with foods, traditional dances, and games.

September: Madera County Fair, Madera; Sierra Mountaineer Days, Oakhurst, with parade, carnival, barbecue, and dance.

October: Mountain Apple Fest and Craft Fair, Oakhurst, with orchard samples, cider, and handmade artwork incorporating apples!

November: Yosemite Western Artist Christmas Boutique, Oakhurst, arts and crafts sale.

December: Yosemite Pioneer Christmas, caroling, candlelight tours, and stagecoach rides, Wawona; holiday events at Badger Pass include Santa Skis, movies, crafts, caroling; Christmas at Fresno Flats, Oakhurst, nineteenth-century open house.

WHERE TO STAY

In-park lodging can range from a rustic campground to the gracious **Ahwahnee Hotel.** It's nearly impossible to get a reservation inside the park on short notice. Plan ahead. Bookings for rooms can be made at all park hotels exactly 366 days in advance. Call Central Reservations (209–252–4848) in the morning, 366 days before your arrival, and have a flexible schedule. You may also mail reservation requests to **Yosemite Reservations,** 5410 East Home Avenue, Fresno, California 93727; (209) 252–4848. For last-minute reservations, try calling thirty, fifteen, or seven days in advance of your arrival, common times when room reservations are canceled.

Right in the center of it all, the **Yosemite Lodge,** a mile west of Yosemite Village, near the base of Yosemite Falls in the heart of the val-

ley, offers cabins, cottages, or lodge rooms plus a pool and restaurant.
The **Ahwahnee Hotel,** set in the woods 1 mile east of Yosemite
Village Park Headquarters; (209) 252-4848. The 1927 lodge has a
granite-and-concrete-beam facade, stained to look like redwood, and
123 recently redecorated rooms. Public rooms are decorated with
handwoven Indian baskets and Persian rugs. An incredible view
includes Glacier Point and Half Dome. This is the only park lodging
offering color TV and room service. A restaurant, a pool, tennis, gift
shops, and a cocktail lounge round out the offerings.

Curry Village is on the eastern edge of Yosemite Valley across the
Merced River from park headquarters; (209) 252-4848. It offers eighteen standard rooms, 103 cabins with private bath and eighty without, and 427 tent cabins with central bath. All are within reach of the
skating rink, shops, and restaurants of Curry Village. Not fancy, but
you'll find the most reasonable rates here. Sometimes, tent cabins
may be the only accommodations available on short notice (as little as
two weeks in advance); the park suggests booking one, with the
chance of upgrading once you arrive.

Hotel accommodations near the Mariposa Grove can be found
at the **Wawona Hotel,** 27 miles from Yosemite Valley on Highway
41; (209) 252-4848. About half of the 105 rooms in this Victorian
lodging have private baths. Other pluses: a pool, a tennis court, stables, an adjacent golf course, and dining services from April to
November.

The Redwoods, Highway 41, 6 miles inside the south entrance,
P.O. Box 2085, Wawona 95381 (209-375-6666), offers everything from
rustic cabins to more modern homes with one to five bedrooms.

Tuolumne Meadows Lodge, open in summer, offers sixty-nine
tent cabins, mostly to persons heading to the High Sierra Camps or
for day hikes in the area. The area has a store, a restaurant, stables,
and a service station.

There are fifteen campgrounds in the park. Some accept campers on
a first-come, first-serve basis; most require reservations through DES-
TINET (800-436-7275). Space fills quickly, so call early. Reservations are
accepted four months prior to arrival. Campground reservation centers
managed by DESTINET are located in the day-use parking area at Curry
Village and in Tuolumne Meadows during summer. A permit for back-

country camping can be obtained from the Wilderness Center; call (209) 372-0200. For additional campground information, call the **Public Information Office of the National Park Service;** (209) 372-0200.

For accommodations outside the park, call **Yosemite's Gateway Reservations** at (209) 454-2030. Keep in mind the distance of the gateway cities, via curvy mountain roads: **El Portal,** the closest, is 14 miles from the Valley Visitor Center; **Midpines,** the next closest town, is 36 miles. The most lodging options can be found in Mariposa, 43 miles away. Obtain a free brochure of all lodging in the county from the **Mariposa County Chamber of Commerce,** Box 425, Mariposa 95338; (209) 966-2456. *The Madera County Visitors Guide* contains a lodging guide to the Oakhurst/Bass Lake/Fish Camp/Madera area, including a list of bed and breakfasts (see Day Trips for contact name and phone).

Some good choices for families include the following.

Marriott's Tenaya Lodge, 1122 Highway 41, Fish Camp 93623; (209) 683-6555 or (800) 635-5807 (41 miles from Yosemite Valley, 2 miles from the park's south entrance). The lodge offers morning, afternoon, and evening programs for ages five to twelve from Memorial to Labor Day. Clay making, nature walks, pool play, volleyball, and Indian lore storytelling are part of the fun. This luxury resort has some suites, nonsmoking rooms, an indoor/outdoor pool, activities, and three dining options.

In Oakhurst, about 15 miles south of Yosemite, you'll find the **Best Western Yosemite Gateway Inn,** 40530 Highway 41, Oakhurst 93644; (209) 683-2378 or (800) 528-1234. The two-bedroom units, many with microwaves and refrigerators, are perfect for families. Indoor/outdoor pools keep the kids happy. Families may cook out at the barbecue area.

The Pines Resort, at Bass Lake, 14 miles from Yosemite's southern entrance, P.O. Box 329, Bass Lake 93604 (800-350-7463), offers chalets with kitchens.

WHERE TO EAT

There are a number of places in the park for snacks and meals. For complete listings, contact the **Yosemite Concessions Services Corporation** (see For More Information).

In Yosemite Village, **the Yosemite Village Store** (209-372-1000) is a year-round operation that sells everything from camping gear to meat, fresh veggies, and granola bars for the trail. **Degnan's Delicatessen,** a stone's throw to the north (209-372-1000), sells sandwiches, salads, candy, and cold drinks. Right next door, **Degnan's Fast Food** (209-372-1000) features fried chicken, frozen yogurt, and pizza.

Restaurants

For the most reasonable prices, try **The Yosemite Lodge Cafeteria,** Yosemite Village (209-372-1000), operating year-round, or the **Curry Village Cafeteria,** Curry Village (209-372-1000), open summers only.

The Four Seasons Restaurant at Yosemite Lodge (209- 372-1000) offers a family setting, children's menu, and dishes such as trout, steaks, enchiladas, and hamburgers. It's open for breakfast and dinner year-round. The dinner line can be long, so sign up early.

The Tuolumne Meadows Lodge, beside the Tuolumne River, is a tent that serves breakfast and dinner during the summer.

The Curry Village Pizza Patio, Curry Village, is open from spring to fall, featuring a nice outdoor area for sunny days.

For a fine dining experience, **The Ahwahnee Hotel Dining room** (209-372-1489), which some say is the most beautiful restaurant in the country, serves breakfast, Sunday brunch, lunch, afternoon snacks, and dinner. Reservations are required for dinner only, when preferred attire for men is coats and ties, dresses or evening pant suits for women.

DAY TRIPS

If you're en route to or lodging outside the park, you may consider attractions found in communities just south of the park, including Oakhurst, Fish Camp, Bats Lake, and North Fork. Contact the Southern Yosemite Visitor's Bureau, P.O. Box 1404, Oakhurst 93644 (209-683-INFO), for details on the following.

Fish Camp. Hop aboard The Logger Steam Train, a 4-mile, forty-five-minute railroad excursion through Sierra National Forest's most spectacular scenery, or try Jenny Railcars, quaint "Model A" powered railcars, offering a thirty-minute narrated trip. The trains are operated by the Yosemite Mt. Sugar Pine Railroad, 56001 Highway 41; (209) 683-7273. The station complex houses the Thornberry Museum (call the railroad at 209-683-7273), filled with logging company equipment, gift store, picnic area, and sandwich shop, with an inn and a restaurant next door. The trains run year-round, weather permitting.

Oakhurst. Take the kids to see Oakhurst's mascot at the corner of Highway 41 and Road 426. The talking fiberglass bear tells about the now extinct California Grizzly and about respect for nature. Fresno Flats Historical Park, Road 427 (209-683-6570), lets you imagine life here in the late nineteenth and early twentieth centuries when the town (formerly Fresno Flats) was a stopover for travelers on their way to Yosemite. Visit restored buildings, a log barn, two jails, two schoolhouses, and a cabin in which President Theodore Roosevelt is said to have slept. Oakhurst Community Park, just off Highway 41, is a pleasant respite for a picnic and has a playground.

Bass Lake. Bass Lake is a popular vacation spot surrounded by miles of rolling, pine-covered hills and expansive meadows. Take a narrated tour of the lake aboard *Bass Lake Queen II,* daily during summers and on spring and fall weekends. The bargelike boat docks in front of Ducey's on the Lake on the North Shore; (209) 642-3121.

North Fork. At the **Sierra Mono Museum,** at the intersection of Malum Ridge Road (274) and Mammoth Pool Road (225), between North Fork and South Fork (209-877-2115), see elaborately woven Native American baskets, artifacts, and other crafts. The museum was built and is run by members of the Mono Indian tribe. Early August brings a two-day **Indian Fair and Powwow** at the North Fork Recreation Center. Visit the **Mono Wind Nature Trail and Flower Garden,** Road 209, off Road 233, 2 miles east of North Fork; (209) 877-2710. It has cedar bark houses, a semi-underground sweat lodge, and a granary where acorns were stored for winter use. A self-guided, mile-long trail winds past twenty-three stations identifying plants used by the Monos for healing, utensils, and food. Flower gardens bloom with more than one hundred varieties of perennial and annual plants, and fresh flowers can be cut for a small fee. The Mono Indian family who run this facility give occasional workshops, teaching Indian sewing, food-gathering techniques, and other Mono Indian skills.

Grounds are open year-round on weekdays and by prearrangement weekends and holidays.

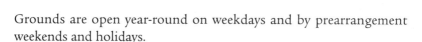

FOR MORE INFORMATION

The National Park Service Information Office, P.O. Box 577, Yosemite National Park, California 95389; (209) 372-0200—recording with general information. **The Valley Visitor Center,** P.O. Box 577, Yosemite National Park, California 95389; (209) 372-0200. For information on the park's hotels, tours, and eateries, contact **Yosemite Concession Services Corp.,** 5410 East Home Avenue, Fresno, California 93727; (209) 252-4848. Website: http://www.nps.gov

A free list of services and facilities for visitors with disabilities is available at visitor centers.

Emergency Numbers

Ambulance, police, fire, and emergency medical care: 911 from public phones or 9-911 from hotel rooms

Twenty-four-hour medical assistance, including poison control and pharmacy: Contact the **Yosemite Medical Clinic** in Yosemite Village; (209) 372-4637. The clinic and an independent dental office (209-372-4200) are located in Yosemite Valley.

CRATER LAKE NATIONAL PARK

Crater Lake, Oregon's only national park, is in a remote area 80 miles northeast of Medford, the nearest major city. While not a national park "superstar" (and fortunately lacking the crowds that this status brings), this park does have enough majestic, placid beauty to be considered an "undiscovered gem." The highlight is Crater Lake—the deepest lake in the United States at 1,932 feet—created by the fiery eruption of Mt. Mazama more than 7,700 years ago. The eruption buried Indian communities as far as 70 miles away. As the mountain collapsed inward, it formed a caldera that filled with rain and snowmelt until it became the pure, deep blue it is today. The lake, along with the somewhat eerie, volcano-created landscape around it, makes for fascinating sight-seeing. Since the Cascade Mountains rise above 7,000 feet, summer is short, with snows often arriving in October.

GETTING THERE

The nearest airport of any significant size is **Jackson County Airport** (541-772-8068) in Medford, about 80 miles southwest of the park, with daily service from United and Horizon airlines. Major car rental companies are at the airport.

Amtrak (800-USA-RAIL) stops at South Spring Street Station, in the town of Klamath Falls, 64 miles southeast, where car rentals are also available.

Greyhound (541-779-2103 or 800-231-2222) has a station at 1200 Klamath Avenue, Klamath Falls, and at 212 North Bartlett, Medford (541-779-2103).

I–5, the state's main north-south route, is about 70 miles west of the park's west entrance (take the Crater Lake/Highway 62 exit in Medford). State Route 62 also connects with points south and the park's southern entrance. State Route 138 leads to the park's northern entrance, open summers only. Note: It's a good idea to tank up before entering the park. Once in the park, gas is available at Mazama Village, during summers only.

GETTING AROUND

A car is a necessity. Because of heavy snow (common as late as May and June), most roads in the park are open only in July, August, and September. At other times, when chains or traction devices may be required, the only access is the road from the western and southern entrances to park headquarters and Rim Village.

WHAT TO SEE AND DO

Start your visit at the main park visitor center, **Steel Center,** in the headquarter's area southwest of the lake, 3 miles below Rim Village. Open year-round from 9:00 A.M. to 5:00 P.M., the center shows an eighteen-minute video about the lake. The film retells the eruption of Mt. Mazama from the eyes of the local Native Americans of that time, the Maklaks. **The Rim Visitor Center,** Rim Village, is open June through September. At the **Sinnot Memorial Overlook,** near Rim Village, rangers hold fifteen-minute talks on the lake's formation from July 4th through Labor Day. The overlook offers a magnificent panoramic view of Crater Lake.

Scenic Drives

In summer, the 33-mile drive around **Crater Lake** provides access to more than a dozen scenic viewpoints, most along the side of the road. Start driving clockwise at either of the visitor centers. A drive all the way around the meandering road without stopping takes about an hour, but plan to get out of the car and sightsee, so allow several hours to enjoy this scenic route. Take along snacks or lunch, as there are several nice picnic areas.

Crater Lake National Park at a Glance

- Majestic, placid beauty with no crowds
- Pinnacles: an eerie landscape of volcanic spires
- Day hikes; boat tours, bicycling, fishing, skiing, Junior Ranger programs
- Daytrip to Oregon Caves National Monument
- Crater Lake National Park, (541) 594-2211

It's worth the drive out to the **Pinnacles,** a rather eerie landscape of fascinating volcanic spires, accessible by a 7-mile dead-end road off Rim Drive near Kerr Notch. Reached via a ¾-mile paved spur road, **Cloudcap,** another "must see" on the east rim, treats you to the highest viewpoint accessible by car.

Note: Stay away from the edge of the caldera, and keep behind rock walls at all points along the caldera rim. Keep a tight grip on young children at all times. Footing can be difficult on the steep and unstable volcanic rock and soil of the rim and inner caldera walls. Bring jackets and warm clothing, as the winds sweeping through here can make it quite chilly.

Hiking

A number of day hikes are well-suited to families. With younger kids, try one—or both—of the following easier and shorter treks. **Castle Crest Wildflower Trail** is a 0.4-mile loop from the trailhead on East Rim Drive, a half mile from park headquarters, or a 1-mile loop from across the headquarters' parking lot. The trails are usually covered with snow from early October to early July. The easy hike (watch out for patches of uneven ground and rocks) takes from thirty to forty-five minutes and leads to a small brook, lush vegetation, and, in the summer months, clusters of wildflowers. Another easy thirty-minute hike is **Godfrey Glen,** a 1-mile stretch, 2.4 miles south of headquarters, that travels through ancient forests and affords views of **Annie Creek Canyon,** wildflowers in season, and, with luck, some deer. Park rules prohibit visitors from feeding animals.

An easy but longer hike of about one hour starts west of Rim Village parking area and leads to **Discovery Point.** This 1.3-mile, one-way trek affords great lake views; at the point a plaque commemorates John Wesley Hillman's 1853 discovery of Crater Lake.

With older children accustomed to hiking, try the moderately strenuous 1.6-mile round-trip trek to **Watchman Peak,** a 8,035-foot-high precipice with a lookout tower that provides a spectacular lake view. The hike leaves from the parking lot between Watchman and Hillman peaks on West Rim Drive. Good news: There are chemical toilets here.

Boat Touring

In summer don't miss the one-hour-and-forty-five-minute ranger-narrated boat tour of Crater Lake; call (541) 594–2511. During peak season, boats leave nine times a day from the Cleetwood Cove dock, which is at least a one-hour drive and hike from Rim Village. Be forewarned: It's necessary to hike from the parking area down a very steep 1-mile trail, which climbs 700 feet. This trail, the only access to the shore and boat docks, is recommended only for those in good physical condition and *not* for anyone with heart, respiratory, or leg problems. Visitors are advised to take along jackets (the temperature on the lake may be considerably colder than that on land), water, snacks, sunglasses, sunscreen, sturdy hiking shoes—plus cameras and binoculars. A composting toilet is available near the docks.

The boats, which carry up to sixty passengers, cruise around the lake along towering cliffs and by the **Phantom Ship,** a rather odd-looking basalt island that, in certain light, looks like an early battleship. There's a stop at **Wizard Island,** a cinder cone that rises 760 feet above the lake's surface. If you want to stay and explore, hike the 1-mile trail to the cone's top and picnic. Some hardy souls swim in the lagoon (temperatures usually range from 45°F to 50°F and seldom get higher than 60°F). Those who stay can take a later boat back, but the return

The awe-inspiring beauty of Crater Lake will stay with you and your family for a long time. (Courtesy Oregon Tourism Division)

will depend upon available space on subsequent boats; you're not guaranteed a ride back until the final tour of the day, which arrives at the dock after 5:00 P.M. (Don't forget the return requires you and the kids to have enough energy to hike back up the trail.)

Programs

The Junior Ranger programs, usually one hour long, offer enjoyable ways for ages six to twelve to learn about the park. These are often held at **Mazama Campground Amphitheater;** check at the visitor center. At the end of the program, each child receives a Junior Ranger book. After completing four exercises, plus attending another interpretive program, your child receives a Junior Ranger badge.

Evening campfire programs at Mazama Village Campground Amphitheater, 4 miles south of the Steel Center, feature a different ranger talk each night. In the winter season, ranger-led interpretive snowshoe walks usually are offered on weekends.

Biking

Bicycles, including mountain bikes, are allowed only on paved roads and the Grayback motor nature trail.

Fishing

Although fish are not native to Crater Lake, as a result of stocking in past years, Kokanee salmon and rainbow trout await anglers. Fishing is allowed at Cleetwood Cove (see Boat Touring) and Wizard Island.

Skiing

Cross-country skiing, a winter draw for the park, is allowed on trails and roads that aren't plowed during the winter. These include Rim Drive, but not on the 3-mile stretch of road from Park Headquarters to Rim Village. The closest downhill skiing to Crater Lake National Park is at Williamette Pass, 50 miles north on Highway 58 (541-484-5030), and Mt. Ashland, 18 miles west of Ashland (follow signs from I-5); (541) 482-2897 or (800) 547-8052—Southern Oregon Reservations.

SPECIAL EVENTS

August: The Rim Run, with some 500 runners following the 33 miles around Rim Drive, takes place the second Saturday in August. This special event is popular enough to strain lodging and eating facilities. Beware. Either book early for the fun, or avoid the crowds by visiting another time.

Area events include the Oregon Shakespeare Festival in Ashland (see Day Trips) and Horse and Buggy Days, July 4th, downtown Klamath Falls.

WHERE TO STAY

Accommodations in the park are at **Crater Lake Lodge** and the **Mazama Village Motor Inn** (541-830-8700), open from late May to October, weather permitting. Each of the Motor Inn's forty rooms has two queen beds and private baths in motel-type cabins. Crater Lake Lodge has seventy-one guest rooms and a dining room.

Crater Lake National Park has two campgrounds: **Mazama Campground** has 198 wooded sites, flush toilets, potable water, pay showers, laundry facilities, and telephones. It is operated on a first-come basis, generally closing for the season in mid-October, weather permitting. **Lost Creek Campground,** off the East Rim Drive on Pinnacles Road, is a small, sixteen-site, tent-only campground that usually closes for the season in mid-September. Reservations are not available. Arrive early in the day, as campsites fill quickly. If these campgrounds are filled, try the National Forest campgrounds to the west of the park.

Lodging options within a 25-mile radius of the park are limited as well, though there are a handful of inexpensive motels. The visitor center can supply you with a listing of nearby lodging, including **Fort Klamath Lodge Motel,** Highway 62, Fort Klamath (541-381-2234), 6 miles from the southern entrance to the park. Fort Klamath also sports a grocery store and a coffee shop. **Diamond Lake Resort** (541-793-3333 or 800-733-7593) is on a mountain lake 13 miles northwest of the park's northern rim. It has forty plain but modern motel rooms, ten housekeeping studios with kitchens, and forty-three rustic cabins, plus three restaurants, as well as fishing and boat rentals. The **Ashland** area, 89 miles southwest, has the highest number of bed-and-breakfast inns in the state, approximately four dozen. Contact the **Ashland Bed and Breakfast Reservation Network,** P.O. Box 1051, Ashland 97520; (541) 482-2337. Also try **Southern Oregon Reservations** (800-547-8052), which books accommodations and packages. The *Oregon B&B Directory,* 230 Red Spur Drive, Grant Pass 97527 (800-841-5448), lists bed-and-breakfast homes throughout the state, including some in the Crater Lake area.

WHERE TO EAT

At Rim Village, the **cafeteria** adjacent to the gift shop serves breakfast, lunch, and dinner, plus snacks, desserts, and deli sandwiches year-round. Winter service includes prepackaged sandwiches, soups, beverages, and snacks. Upstairs, the **Watchman Deli Lounge** has burgers, sandwiches, pizza, snacks, beer, wine, and spirits (families welcome) in summer only. Also, the **camper services building,** at Mazama Village, near the Annie Springs entrance station, 4 miles south of park headquarters, is open during summer. It sells convenience store items and also has a coin laundry, shower facilities, and unleaded gas.

Dining options near the park are limited. The Medford/Ashland area has the highest concentration of restaurants. In Ashland, try **Omar's,** at the intersection of Siskiyou Boulevard and Highway 66; (541) 482-1281. In business for almost fifty years, this local favorite gains praise for steak and fresh seafood and has a children's menu.

DAY TRIPS

Ashland, 89 miles southwest, is worth a visit, especially because its the home of the **Oregon Shakespeare Festival;** (541) 482-4331. The festival, which runs from mid-February through the end of October, is among the oldest and largest in the country. From mid-June through September, period English dances precede outdoor performances of the Bard's classics. The theater offers work by other playwrights as well. Kids also enjoy the two-hour backstage tour of dressing rooms, costumes, props, and stagehands at work, plus a visit to the Shakespeare Festival Exhibit Center, where costumes can be tried on. The festival's Elizabethan Theatre overlooks charming **Lithia Park** in the town center, which has a duck pond, playground, band shell, nature trail, and creek. In June, the park hosts a Renaissance dinner, Feast of Will, that serves up food, period music, and dancing. (Reserve through the festival number above, or through Southern Oregon Reservations, 800-547-8052, which has festival packages including tickets and accommodations.)

Ashland also has its share of art galleries and antiques shops, as does its neighbor, **Medford,** where the **Main Antique Mall,** 30 North Riverside (541-779-9490), is the largest in southern Oregon.

The Oregon Caves National Monument is worth a stop, particularly if you are continuing on to the Pacific Coast. It's two hours west of Medford, at the end of Highway 46, 20 miles east of Cave Junction; (541) 592-2100. The marble cave high in the Siskiyou Mountains is the state's largest—perhaps the largest on the West Coast—and is filled with stalactites, stalagmites, flowstone, and other formations. The seventy-five-minute guided tours operate frequently, year-round, though on busy summer days you may have a wait of an hour or more. Because exploring the caves involves a certain amount of coordination (there are 200 steps to climb), small children must meet a height requirement before being allowed on the tours. Above ground, explore the area's scenic trails. The Oregon Caves Château offers lodgings and meals from June to September.

Closer to the national park, the town of **Klamath Falls** offers a forty-five-minute historical trip in a restored 1906 trolley. Board the trolley at the **Baldwin Hotel Museum** (summer only), 31 Main Street (541-883-5207), or at the **Klamath County Museum,** 1451 Main Street; (541) 883-4208. Both feature historical and archaeological exhibits. One more museum stop: The **Favrell Museum,** 125 West Main Street (541-882-9996), has an extensive arrowhead collection that fascinates some kids.

Although there is no river rafting in the park, the nearby Rogue River is famous for its white water and scenery. Among the river runners who offer family-friendly and/or just-for-family trips: **OARS** (Outdoor Adventure River Specialists), Box 67, Angels Camp, California 95222 (209-736-4677 or 800-346-6277), features four-and five-day Rogue River trips for kids seven and older. For a list of additional outfitters, contact **Oregon Guides and Packers,** Box 10841, Eugene, Oregon 97440; (541) 683-9552.

FOR MORE INFORMATION

Crater Lake National Park: Box 7, Crater Lake, Oregon 97604; (541) 594-2211. Website: http://www.nps.gov

Ashland Chamber of Commerce and Visitor Center: 110 East Main Street, Ashland, Oregon 97520; (541) 482-3486.

Handicapped information: Most viewpoints are wheelchair accessible. There are ramps at Rim Village Visitor Center and at its cafeteria/gift store. Mazama Village campground amphitheater has paved walkways. Also accessible are the rest rooms at Mazama Village, Steel Information Center, and Rim Village.

Emergency Numbers

Ambulance; fire, police: 911 from public phones in the park or from concession phones.

First aid stations: Steel Information Center and Rim Village Visitors Center, or any patrol ranger in a park service vehicle. For serious injuries, the park dispatcher will summon an ambulance to a hospital in Medford.

Hospitals: Medford's Rogue Valley Medical Center, 2825 East Barnett Road (541-770-4144), with twenty-four-hour emergency room and trauma center. **Klamath Urgent Care Center,** 2655 Shasta Way, Klamath Falls (541-882-2118), open 9:00 A.M. to 7:00 P.M., Monday through Saturday; 11:00 A.M. to 4:00 P.M. Sunday.

Pharmacies: Phoenix Pharmacy, 700 North Main Street, Phoenix (541-535-1561), open 9:00 A.M. to 6:00 P.M. weekdays, until 5:00 P.M. Saturday

Poison Control: (800) 452-7165

PORTLAND

Portland seems to have it all: clean air (thanks to strict legislation); a cheerful, uncongested downtown with fountains, statues, shops, and places for pedestrians to linger; a lively cultural life; good restaurants; a fine selection of museums; plus a superb location, with ocean beaches to the west and some of the Northwest's most spectacular scenery to the east. All of this combines to deliver a postcard-perfect family vacation.

GETTING THERE

Portland International Airport (PDX) is 10 miles northeast of downtown (503-335-1234) and served by some twenty airlines. Car rentals, cabs, shuttle service, and public bus transportation are available. **Amtrak** (800-USA-RAIL) is at 800 Northwest Sixth Avenue. **Greyhound** (800-231-2222) is at 550 Northwest Sixth Avenue.

By car. The main north-south route to Portland, I-5, originates in southern California, extending through Seattle. I-405 may also be used for north-south travel. Most traffic from the east comes from I-84, which becomes Banfield Expressway before intersecting with I-5 and Burnside Street, a main downtown artery. East-west thoroughfares are U.S. 26 and U.S. 30.

GETTING AROUND

Tri-Met, 701 Southwest Sixth Avenue (503-238-7433), provides excellent bus and trolley transportation. An extensive part of downtown, Fareless Square, is a fareless ride zone. Nearly all of the sixty bus lines run through the downtown transit mall along Southwest Fifth and Sixth avenues. Tickets and information are available at **Tri-Met's Customer Assistance** Office in Pioneer Courthouse Square, on

Southwest Sixth between Morrison and Yamhill. **Metropolitan Area Express** (MAX) light rail line travels a 15-mile route from downtown east to Gresham, gateway to Mount Hood. Construction is currently underway to expand service west to the communities of Beaverton and Hillsboro, with completion expected by fall of 1998.

The Willamette River divides the compact city in two, with downtown on the west bank and a mostly residential area on the east bank. The Lloyd District, also on the east bank, comprises retail stores, hotels, and restaurants. Much sight-seeing can be done on foot in the downtown area. Burnside Street divides the city north and south.

WHAT TO SEE AND DO

Museums

American Advertising Museum, 50 Southwest Second Avenue; (503) 226-0000. This small museum is best appreciated by middle-school and older kids because it's "text heavy"—though it does have a monitor playing an hour's worth of 1980s commercials that invariably appeal to the younger set. Kids also can join their parents in watching early television commercials, including looking at the Burma Shave signs and watching Arthur Godfrey sell Lipton Soup.

Other permanent exhibits include the original California Raisins and an antique figurine collection featuring Campbell Soup kids, as well as Snap, Crackle, and Pop, the Rice Krispie Kids, and more.

Oregon Museum of Science and Industry, OMSI, 1945 Southeast Water Avenue; (503) 797-4000 or (800) 955-6674 (advance tickets and taped schedule of events). This fabulous facility, the nation's fifth largest science museum, shows kids that science is fun. Six halls of wonder feature computer games, tornado and earthquake simulators, space adventures, sailboats, and more. Tours of the U.S.S. *Blueback* submarine, featured in the movie *The Hunt for Red October,* are available. At the futuristic-looking Hello World station, kids send signals into outer space. Check out the exhibits, which have included a look at Leonardo da Vinci's futuristic concepts, as well as the annual Reptile and Amphibian Show, every Labor Day weekend. Sit back and enjoy the OMNIMAX Theater, with its five-story dome, and the Murdock Sky Theater, with its laser and astronomy shows. Combination tickets are

---

Portland at a Glance

- A postcard-perfect family vaction spot

- Cheerful, uncongested, and pedestrian-friendly downtown

- Good restaurants and a fine selection of museums, parks, zoos

- Spectacular scenery in nearby Columbia River Gorge and along the Oregon coast

- Portland Oregon Visitors Association, (503) 222-2223; (800) 345-3214

---

available. The Family Memorial Day Marine Science Weekend offers an in-depth look at Oregon's northern coast.

Portland Art Museum, 1219 Southwest Park Avenue at Jefferson Street; (503) 226-2811. This comprehensive museum covers thirty-five centuries of art—European, Asian, African, and Native American. The baskets, masks, canoes, and totem poles of the Northwest Coast Indians particularly please younger kids. Family Days, which occur five or six times a year, usually are linked to a special exhibit. On these days, children enjoy discounted admission, hands-on activities, and entertainment.

The **Children's Museum,** 3037 Southwest Second Avenue (503-823-2227), presents hands-on exhibits designed for children from tots to age ten. Kids make a splash with water play, cook in a bistro, or weigh and ring up food at the Kid City Grocery Store. Long recognized as a leader in ceramic education, this museum's Clayshop, free with museum admission, allows kids to pound, pull, and roll out clay into something artistic or functional (a nominal fee to fire items). Through 1997, the Children's Cultural Center features Living Legends: American Indians Today. Kids can beat the powwow drums, fish the Columbia River, and explore a "tipi" to learn about Indian culture.

If your kids grow wide-eyed at a big house, visit **Pittock Mansion, 3229** Northwest Pittock Drive; (503) 823-3623. This huge manor house, built between 1909 and 1914 by the founder of *The Oregonian* newspaper, has tours. Allow time to stroll among the five acres of gardens—great for picnics—and the additional forty-one acres of trails in adjacent Forest Park. The **Oregon Maritime Center & Museum,** 113 Southwest Naito Parkway (503-224-7724), features the sternwheeler *Steamer Portland,* seen in the movie *Maverick,* as well as ship models, photos, and navigational instruments.

Parks, Zoos, and Gardens

Washington Park, encompassing 332 acres on the west end of downtown (entrance at the head of Park Place), offers picnic areas, forested hiking trails, and tennis courts. (Note: The park was designed by the Olmsted brothers, who also created New York's Central Park and San Francisco's Golden Gate Park.) The excellent **Metro Washington Park Zoo,** 4001 Southwest Canyon Road (503-226-1561), is here. Dedicated to the conservation of rare, threatened, and endangered species, the zoo has more than one thousand animals representing 192 species. Highlights include the Cascade Exhibit, featuring the fish and wildlife that inhabit this region. The zoo is also known for its Asian Elephant Breeding Program, with more than two dozen born thus far. Recent additions are a one-and-a-half-acre Elk Meadow exhibit, featuring four native Roosevelt elk; and a Maasai goat kraal where kids can hug cute pygmy goats. The zoo also maintains a Penguinarium, a rain forest, and more. Check the special activities for the frequent keeper talks, birds of prey and reptile shows, summer family concerts, family overnights, and one-day family programs and excursions. Be sure to ask about the summer kids promotion.

Washington Park and Zoo Railway (fee additional) not only gets you off your feet for a bit, it takes you to the noted **International Rose Test Garden,** Southwest Kingston in the park, Washington Park Station. See just some of the man hundreds of roses that earned Portland the nickname "City of Roses." Just uphill on Southwest Kingston, the peaceful **Japanese Garden** (503-223-4070) charms with an Oriental Tea Garden, complete with an authentic Tea House. Still further uphill is the **Hoyt Arboretum,** 4000 Southwest Fairview Boulevard;

(503) 823-3655/3654. It contains the largest collection of conifers in the United States, spread out on 200 acres with 10 miles of trails. For kids who like to walk, this is a scenic delight.

Next to the zoo is the **World Forestry Center,** 4033 Southwest Canyon Road; (503) 228-1367. The center's forestry exhibits include a tropical rainforest exhibit, an old-growth forest, a 70-foot talking tree, and the multimedia presentation "Forests of the World." Just north of the Center is the **Oregon Vietnam Veterans Living Memorial,** where simple black granite slabs mark each year's losses.

Downtown's **Tom McCall Waterfront Park** is a 2-mile greenway, formerly an expressway, on the west bank of the Willamette River, Front Avenue between the Steel Bridge and the Riverplace Marina, (503) 823-2223. It is popular with joggers, walkers, and cyclists. In summer kids frolic in the **Salmon Street Springs,** Naito Avenue and Salmon Street, where there are one hundred jet sprays to keep them cool.

Also worth visiting: **The Grotto,** Northeast Eighty-fifth Avenue and Sandy Boulevard (503-254-7371), with panoramic views of the Columbia River, Cascade Mountains, and Mount St. Helens; **Crystal Springs Rhododendron Garden,** Southeast Twenty-eighth Avenue (503-771-8386), a seven-acre garden with a spring-fed lake and almost 1,500 varieties of rhododendrons and azaleas.

Other Attractions

Check out **Pioneer Courthouse Square,** a single-block public plaza in the heart of Portland. Among the public art works appealing to the younger set is the *Weather Machine,* a 25-foot mechanical sculpture that tells the atmospheric conditions via lights, symbols, and figurines. Be there for the daily noon forecast, when lights flash, plumes of steam billow, and trumpets herald the hour. On clear days, Helia, a sun, shines; in stormy weather a dragon appears; and when there's mist or drizzle, you'll see a blue heron (chances are he'll appear at least once during your stay, as it rains often in Portland). Pioneer Courthouse Square also hosts concerts, festivals, special events, and floral displays (Another bonus: public rest rooms are nearby.)

Ira Keller Memorial Fountain, Third Avenue and Southwest Clay Street, directly across from the Civic Auditorium, entertains

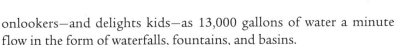

onlookers—and delights kids—as 13,000 gallons of water a minute flow in the form of waterfalls, fountains, and basins.

Oaks Amusement Park (503-233-5777), on the banks of the Willamette River, offers thrilling rides, roller skating, and picnic facilities.

Tours

The sternwheeler *Columbia Gorge* departs from Waterfront Park at Southwest Front and Stark streets for two-hour narrated cruises of the harbor area on weekends from early October to mid-June. The boat also departs from Cascade Locks. During summer, the boat cruises the Columbia Gorge (see Day Trips). Call (503) 223-3928 for schedules. Other touring boats include the *Portland Spirit* (800-224-3901 or 503-224-3900) and the *Queen of the West.*

Theater, Music, and the Arts

To find out what's happening, see the Friday Arts & Entertainment insert of *The Oregonian* daily newspaper or the free weekly tabloid, *Willamette Week.* Ticketmaster (503-224-4400) has tickets to most major entertainment events. Tickets are available by phone, at Ticketmaster outlets, and at all G.I. Joe's stores.

The **Portland Center for the Performing Arts** complex is the focus of the city's cultural life. The jewel of the complex is **Arlene Schnitzer Concert Hall,** a renovated vaudeville house of the 1920s, 1037 Southwest Broadway, where the Oregon Symphony performs classical, pops, family, and kids' concerts. Across the brick plaza is the **New Theatre,** with two performance spaces for plays. A few blocks away, at 222 Southwest Clay Street, the **Civic Auditorium** hosts performances by the Portland Opera, the Oregon Ballet Theater, and the Oregon Children's Theatre Company. For ticket and schedule information for the complete complex, phone (503) 248-4335.

Ladybug Theater, Oaks Park, at the foot of Southeast Spokane Street (503-232-2346), features improvisational children's theater for ages three to ten (but it's also appreciated by older kids and adults). Performances are weekends during the school year and weekdays during summer.

Shopping

Portland's retail core is located downtown. Just off Pioneer Courthouse Square, you'll find **Meier & Frank,** 621 Southwest Fifth (503-223-0512), the city's oldest department store; and **Nordstrom,** 701 Southwest Broadway (503-224-6666). Just to the east, **Pioneer Place,** 700 Southwest Fifth Avenue (503-228-5800), an eighty-store pavilion, includes the only **Saks Fifth Avenue** in the Northwest. Preteens and teens love **NikeTown,** corner of Sixth and Salmon streets: (503) 221-6453. The store "museum" displays Michael Jordan's Wheaties box, Scottie Pippen's shoes, and other sports memorabilia. The younger set will adore the multi-video screens in the floor and the fish tanks in the walls.

The outdoor **Portland Saturday Market** in downtown's Skidmore District, at the west end of the Burnside Bridge, is a lively place where artists, craftspeople, entertainers, farmers, and cooks sell locally produced goods from open-air booths. It's open Saturday and Sunday, March through Christmas.

The **Lloyd Center,** on the east bank between Ninth and Fifteenth and Multnomah and Halsey (508-282-2511), has glass-enclosed walkways between 180 shops, restaurants, and an indoor ice skating rink.

Also worth investigating are **Powell's City of Books** (503-228-4651, ext. 249); the **Nob Hill Neighborhood** (503-297-3454)—try Northwest Twenty-first and Twenty-third avenues); **Northeast Broadway;** and **Southeast Hawthorne Boulevard** (503-233-7633).

Sports

The popular NBA **Portland Trail Blazers** basketball team plays in the new state-of-the-art Rose Garden arena; (503) 231-8000. **Portland Winter Hawks Hockey,** part of the Western Hockey League, plays at the Rose Garden arena and the Memorial Coliseum, 1401 North Wheeler Street. **Portland Pride,** indoor soccer, and the area's new professional women's basketball team, **The Portland Power,** also play at the Coliseum. Call the Coliseum's ticket office (503-235-8771) for information. The **Portland Rockies** baseball team can be seen at the historic Civic Stadium from June through September. Call (503) 223-2837.

SPECIAL EVENTS

For exact dates of the following events, contact the Portland/Oregon Visitors Association. For twenty-four-hour events information, call (503) 222-2223, or the audio calendar of events, (503) 225-5555, code 3608.

April: Oregon Trails Blossom Festival; entertainment, food, and historical tours and demonstrations, Hood River.

May: Mother's Day Weekend Annual Rhododendron Show, Crystal Springs Rhododendron Gardens. Cinco De Mayo Festival, honoring Portland's sister city, Guadalajara, Mexico, features ethnic food, entertainment, and arts and crafts.

June: Portland Rose Festival/Grand Floral Parade, a three-week festival of more than seventy events, including a carnival, air show, rose parade, boat races, and more.

July: Waterfront Blues Festival.

August: The Bite: A Taste of Portland features Northwest bands and food from Portland's restaurants.

September: Portland Marathon includes a kids' run.

October: ZooBoo, at the Metro Washington Park zoo, features haunted train rides, a not-too-haunted house, face painting, games, and more.

December: Festival of Trees, Memorial Coliseum; Zoolights Festival at Metro Washington Park Zoo; Portland Parade of Christmas Ships.

WHERE TO STAY

Portland, Oregon: The Official Visitor's Guide contains lodging information. **Northwest Bed & Breakfast,** 1067 Hanover Court South, Salem (503-243-7616), has hundreds of listings in cities, on mountains, and along the coast. Another agency, **Oregon Bed & Breakfast Guild** (800-944-6196), will send a free directory of participating properties.

There's also the **Oregon Bed and Breakfast Directory,** 230 Red Spur Drive, Grants Pass 97527 (800-841-5448), which has descriptions of 150 lodgings in the state. To receive a copy, call.

The **Heathman Hotel,** Southwest Broadway at Salmon (503-

241-4100 or 800-551-0011), another first-class hotel, is a registered Historic Place. This renovated first-class 1920s Beaux Arts hotel charms with tastefully decorated rooms and suites, a complimentary video movie library, and top-notch restaurant, all just steps from the Performing Arts Center.

Though a bit on the pricey side, the **Marriott Hotel—Downtown Portland,** 1401 Southwest Naito Parkway (503-226-7600 or 800-228-9290), is the only downtown hotel with a free indoor pool (which, to some traveling families, is a necessity). This is a large hotel with more than 500 rooms, some with refrigerators (upon request); a kid's menu is available at the restaurant.

The more moderately priced **Mark Spencer Hotel,** 409 Southwest Eleventh Avenue, is also downtown; (503) 224-3293 or (800) 548-3934. It offers standard and one-bedroom suites with kitchens. Though the clientele is predominantly businesspeople, this hotel works well for families, too. The **Holiday Inn Portland—Downtown,** 1021 Northeast Grand Avenue, is another moderate choice; (503) 235-8433 or (800) HOLIDAY. You might also try the **Comfort Inn-Lloyd Center,** 431 Northeast Multnomah; (503) 233-7933 or (800) 4-CHOICE.

Rose Manor Inn, 4546 Southeast McLoughlin Boulevard (503-236-4175 or 800-252-8333), is in the city's Southeast neighborhood. It has an outdoor pool, seventy-six motel-style rooms, some with kitchenette, and some adjoining two-bedroom duplex townhouses.

For suite space, try **Shilo Inn Suites-Airport,** 11707 Northeast Airport Way (503-252-7500 or 800-222-2244), or **Embassy Suites,** 9000 Southwest Washington Square Road (about 8 miles from downtown); (503) 644-4000 or (800) 772-3897. For additional choices and reservations, contact Portland's 24-hour reservation service, (888) 606-6363.

WHERE TO EAT

The city's official visitor's guide, *Portland, Oregon: The Official Visitor's Guide,* contains a listing of restaurants, as does the Friday Arts & Entertainment insert of *The Oregonian.* Fresh Oregon-grown produce highlights many restaurant dishes. For some kid-pleasing options, try the following.

Old Wives' Tales, 1300 East Burnside (503-238-0470), is a trendy place for a tasty bite. The menu ranges from vegetarian to Italian to Middle Eastern. Kids romp in the playroom while parents linger over coffee. **Original Pancake House,** 8601 Southwest Barbur Boulevard (503-246-9007), is a Portland institution (particularly on weekends, when the crowds are thick). They serve pancakes plain and simple or embellished with an endless variety of toppings. For something a little different, head to **Greek Cusina,** 404 Southwest Washington; (503) 224-2288. Evenings include tasty dinners, folk music, belly dancing—even plate breaking (a Greek tradition your kids will like)! The restaurant also serves breakfast and lunch. If you don't mind being serenaded by an accordion player, go to **Der Rheinlander,** 5035 Northeast Sandy Boulevard (503-249-0507), for large portions of hearty German food at reasonable prices.

DAY TRIPS

Mount Hood National Forest and the Columbia River Gorge

The great outdoors is an easy day trip away from Portland. With more than 1,200 miles of trails, a river, and mountains, **The Mount Hood National Forest Office** offers excellent recreational opportunities. For specifics about winter sports such as skiing, snowshoeing, and hiking, contact the Forest Office a 2955 Northwest Division Street, Gresham 97030; (503) 666-0771.

About 30 miles east of Portland, on Oregon's northern border, the spectacular **Columbia River Gorge** carves its way through the steep Cascade Mountains. Don't miss driving the **Columbia River Scenic Highway,** which offers some of the most beautiful scenery in the Northwest. From Portland, access the gorge via I-84, or take the more scenic U.S. 30. Thirty miles of this road—from Troutdale east to Dodson—is a designated scenic highway. After this stretch, the narrow, two-lane highway, which passes along trails, picnic spots, and seven major waterfalls, merges back and forth into I-84. Off exit 31 is the spectacular **Multnomah Falls,** the state's top tourist attraction and the country's second highest falls, cascading 620 feet to the gorge. Take a paved trail to the viewing platform for fabulous views. The base area has a visitor center and a restaurant (503-695-2376).

For water wonders of a different sort, visit the huge hydroelectric **Bonneville Dam;** (541) 374-8820. The Bradford Island Visitor Center, off exit 40 of I-84, features an underwater observatory where you can watch salmon make their way upstream on the dam's ladder. Walk along the canal side to watch the boats and barges. Tour the large fishery on your own. In the neighboring town of Cascade Locks, the beautiful **Cascade Locks Marine Park** (541-374-8619) has picnic grounds, a playground, and camping; it's also the launching site for the sternwheeler *Columbia Gorge* (see Tours), which cruises the gorge in the summer and heads to Portland in the late fall.

The next town is **Hood River,** known as the "sailboarding capital of the world" (events held at the Waterfront Center Event Site), and also noted for the region's many apple orchards.

Besides admiring the smooth gliding of the sailboarders, and the scenery from your car, from May to September you can board the **Mt. Hood Railroad,** 110 Railroad Avenue; (541) 386-3556 or (800) 872-4661. It employs vintage 1906 railcars to travel through the gorge and the foothills of Mt. Hood. Sometimes these splendid views are enhanced by reenactments of old-fashioned western train robberies. Another stop of interest might be **Children's Park,** Ninth and Eugene streets (541-386-5153), an adventure park for all ages, designed with input from local kids.

Phil Zoller's Guide Service, 1244 Highway 141 (at what is known locally as B.Z. Comer), White Salmon, Washington (509-493-2641), 14 miles north of the town of Hood River, runs white-water rafting trips through the gorge on the White Salmon River year-round, although the recommended season is from April through September. The spring-fed river's temperature remains at 45 degrees throughout the year; wet suits are available, including kids' sizes. While there is no minimum age for children, use common sense and ask the guides about appropriateness. The half-day trip includes a narration of the gorge's history, wildlife, and folklore.

In season, be sure to get some fresh fruit at the roadside stands. **Rasmussen Farms Pumpkin Funland** (541-386-4622), Hood River, has storybook characters and animals created from pumpkins, gourds, and vegetables, plus a Halloween Hut decorative maze. For more infor-

A day at the Oregon Coast Aquarium is a day well spent.
(Photo by Kent Kerr/courtesy Oregon Tourism Division)

mation on the gorge area, call the **Columbia River Gorge Visitors Association** at (541) 296-2231 or (800) 255-3385.

From Hood River, you can head south on Route 35 to **Mt. Hood** (about 40 miles) over **Barlow Pass,** where you can hike parts of the last portion of the Oregon Trail, then loop west to Portland on U.S. 26. However, covering the gorge *and* the mountain—particularly with kids— is a very full day, almost too full; consider staying overnight or visiting on separate days.

Mt. Hood, the tallest of the Oregon Cascades at 11,239 feet, and one hour southeast of Portland, offers skiing (three major ski areas twist down the mountain) as well as a summer alpine slide at **Mt. Hood Skibowl** (503-222-BOWL) near the quaint village of Government Camp. **Timberline Ski Area,** the summer training ground of the U.S. Ski Team (800-547-1406—lodge reservations, or 231-7979 from Portland), has winter and summer skiing. The U.S. Forest Service has free daily tours of the huge wooden lodge built in the 1930s as a VPA project, and now a National Historic Landmark. The **Mount Hood**

Visitors Information Center, 65000 East Highway 26, Welches (503-622-4822), is open daily.

The Oregon Coast

Another refreshing day-trip possibility is the Oregon Coast, with its rugged scenery and sandy beaches for strolling and picnicking. The **North Coast** stretches from Astoria, 95 miles northwest of Portland, where the Columbia River meets the Pacific Ocean, to Newport, 135 miles south. **Astoria,** the first American settlement west of the Rockies, sports Victorian homes, historic landmarks, and interesting sights. Murals depicting the area's settlement adorn the **Astor Column;** (503) 325-6311. From atop the 125-foot column on Coxcomb Hill, enjoy vistas of the Columbia River and surrounding countryside. **Fort Clatsop National Memorial,** Route 3, 5 miles southwest of Astoria (503-861-2471), is a reproduction of the fort where the Lewis and Clark Expedition passed the winter of 1805. In summer, rangers in period clothing demonstrate frontier skills. Year-round at the visitor center is an audiovisual presentation.

Seaside, the Pacific Northwest's largest beach-resort community, sports a 2-mile promenade for strolling, which features an antique carousel and the **Seaside Aquarium,** Second Avenue at the Promenade; (503) 738-6211. If you're planning on continuing south to Newport, one of the largest Oregon Coast ports, skip the small Seaside Aquarium and instead visit the newer, bigger, and better twenty-three-acre **Oregon Coast Aquarium,** 2820 Southeast Ferry Slip Road, Newport; (503) 867-3123. This winner's aquarium's pools, cliffs, caves, and dunes replicate those of coastal Oregon and feature a number of animals, including seals, sea lions, and three sea otters rescued from Exxon's *Valdez* Alaska oil spill. Keiko, the killer whale featured in the movie *Free Willy,* now calls this aquarium home. At the Touch Pool, kids hold starfish and other little creatures. Many of the animals here play with toys—from Frisbees to plastic balls referred to as "environmental enrichment devices." These "toys" are part of a new movement —with this aquarium at the forefront—that maintains that such play challenges animals and promotes curiosity and dexterity.

Newport's flat, wide beaches are a perfect place to explore tide pools during low tide. **Ona Beach State Park,** 7 miles south of Yaquina Bay Bridge, is a favorite sandy spot.

The 47-mile stretch of the **Oregon Dunes National Recreation Area** is between Florence and North Bend, with plenty of opportunities for hiking and camping.

FOR MORE INFORMATION

The **Portland Oregon Visitors Association,** 26 Southwest Salmon, can provide you with helpful tourist information; (503) 222-2223 or (800) 345-3214. Website: http://www.pova.com

Emergency Numbers

Ambulance, fire, police: 911

Hospital: Twenty-four-hour emergency room, pharmacy, and pediatrics care: **Emanuel Hospital & Health Center,** 2801 North Gantenbein Avenue (503-280-3200); **Providence St. Vincent's Hospital** (503-291-2115); **Providence Portland Medical Center** (503-215-1111); and **Legacy Good Samaritan Hospital and Medical Center** (503-229-7711)

Pharmacy: Safeway Pharmacy, 1025 Southwest Jefferson Street, is open until 8:00 P.M. on weekdays, and until 4:00 P.M. on weekends; (503) 223-3709.

Poison Control: (503) 494-8968

SPOKANE

In 1996 Washington made the top ten list of most visited states in the United States Spokespeople attribute this to the state's easy blend of cities juxtaposed to wilderness and country settings. Spokane fits that profile. Although Spokane lacks Seattle's "sizzle," Spokane offers families a friendly, manageable, and interesting city that serves as a gateway to northern Idaho's green spaces; Idaho's border is just 18 miles away. The regions, while spanning two states, are marketed together. Spokane provides the urban charm while Idaho's Couer d'Alene, Kellogg, Wallace, Harrison, and the surrounding countryside of lakes and mountains ringed with fir trees offer the great outdoors.

GETTING THERE

The **Spokane International Airport,** (509) 455-6455, is served by several major carriers as well as some smaller, regional airlines. Alaska Airlines (800-426-0333), Air Canada (800-776-3000), Delta Airlines (800-221-1212), Horizon Air (800-547-9308), Northwest Airlines (800-225-2525), Southwest Air (800-435-9792), and United Airlines (800-241-6522) all offer regular flight schedules. Amtrak (800-872-7245) services the Passenger Station (509-624-5144). And bus service is provided by Greyhound (509-624-5251) and Northern Trailways (509-838-5262).

GETTING AROUND

Rental car companies include Avis (509-747-8081), Budget (509-838-1434), Dollar (509-458-2619), and Thrifty (509-924-9111). Airport Shuttle Service (509-535-6979) or Spokane Cab (509-535-2535) provides service from the airport to downtown. For bus schedules and other information, call the Spokane Transit Authority at (509) 328-7433.

WHAT TO SEE AND DO

Parks and Green Spaces

Many consider **Riverfront Park,** off I-90 along the Spokane River, (509) 456-4FUN, or (800) 336-PARK; a 100-acre tract of green cut through by the Spokane River, to be the city's centerpiece. This oasis has lawns, ponds laced by weeping willow trees and play areas. A landmark is the big red wagon, Division and Stevens streets. Kids love to climb up the ladder, peer over the rim of the giant-sized wagon, take a deep breath, and slide down the front. About a block away is one of the park's treasures, the **Looff Carousel,** a 1909 antique carousel complete with 54 hand-carved horses and a calliope. To help preserve this gem, it's housed in a former natatorium. Little kids love to ride the horses, lions, and other whimsically carved critters.

This is a great park for biking as cars are only allowed in certain peripheral areas. Bring your own or rent one of the four-wheeled biking creations, good for families of 4 or more. Some have benchers and others have special kids' seats as well as places for two pedalers. When the river isn't dammed, you can enjoy the site of cascading waterfalls (February through June) as you pedal about. Try the gondola ride, (509) 625-6600, for a trip over the falls and under the Monroe Street Bridge. Riverfront Park also features amusement rides, mini-golf, and an ice rink.

Manito Park & Gardens, 4 West Twenty-First Avenue; (509) 625-6622, creates an enchanting urban landscape comprised of five major gardens. Duncan Garden is a formal garden with roots dating back to ancient Egypt, Persia, and Rome. Annual plantings begin in May and peak from mid-July through early October. Rose Hill blooms with 1,500 roses in more than 150 varieties. The Joel E. Ferris Perennial Garden displays native Northwest perennials, the Spokane/Nishinomiya Japanese Garden is a place of serenity, and the Gaiser Conservatory couples tropical foliage with floral displays.

North of Spokane on Highway 20 is **Gardner Cave,** part of Crawford State Park; (509) 446-4065 or (800) 562-0990. The second largest limestone cave in the state, Gardner's chambers were created about 70 million years ago. Rangers lead you through tours of the stalagmites and stalactites.

Spokane at a Glance

- Friendly, manageable, and interesting—with access to the backcountry

- Bobcats, leopards, panthers, and lions at Cat Tales Zoological Training Center

- Historic sites: Campbell House, Cheney Cowles Museum, Broadview Dairy Museum

- Daytrips to Lake Coeur d'Alene, Kellogg, and Wallace in northern Idaho

- Spokane Convention and Visitors Bureau, (509) 624–1341

Also north of Spokane is **Cat Tales Zoological Training Center,** N. 17020 Newport Hwy., Mead; (509) 238–4126 or http://www.spokane.net/cattales) is a four-acre preserve north of Spokane dedicated to the conservation of big cats and to the education of the public. All of the four-legged inhabitants arrived here after being abandoned or abused. When an animal's history is known, a plaque provides the details. Some tigers were rescued from difficult lives in traveling circuses and others arrived after owners discovered that the cute wild kitten they purchased was not so manageable or friendly when it reached 200 or so pounds. What's amazing about the place is that you can get close to, about 10 feet from a safely caged big cat. That's a rare treat.

Cat Tales' residents include bobcats, Bengal tigers, leopards, panthers, and mountain lions and "lbs," aka "pound dog," a mutt who long ago befriended Jambo, the male African lion and continues to boss Jambo around. The best time to visit, especially in summer, is about an hour before closing. During the day, especially if it's hot, the animals laze about lethargically. But between 4:00 P.M. and 5:30 P.M., the animals start to get active. It's time for an educational encounter led by an expert followed by feeding time. When we were there we watched a black leopard display his amazing ability to leap by gracefully jumping more than 7 feet in easy glides from tabletop to tabletop. Just prior to feeding time, the cats become restless and pace, making it easy to see just how big a 600-pound tiger "kitty" really is.

Museums and Historical Attractions

Cheney Cowles Museum and Historic Campbell House, 2316 West First Ave.; (509-456-3931), displays exhibits concerning the development of the Northwest region and local Indian cultures. Changing shows include traditional and contemporary arts and historical and current issues exhibitions. Adjacent to the museum is the 1898 **Campbell House,** a National Register Historic landmark. At this restored house, you sense the lifestyle of a mining tycoon during Spokane's turn-of-the-century "Age of Elegance." The museum is open Tuesday through Saturday.

Learn about milk production at the **Broadview Dairy Museum,** 411 West Cataldo; (509) 324-0910. The museum, housed in the original Broadview Dairy Building, provides visitors with an overview of the dairy industry and its history. The facility is closed on Wednesdays and Sundays.

More Attractions

Wonderland Golf & Games, North 10515 Division St.; (509) 468- 4FUN. This indoor and outdoor amusement center features more than 80 video games, nine batting cages, pool tables, go carts, and bumper cars. Pizza and other old standbys are served at Wonderland's Rock-a-Fire Explosion Pizza Theater where Fatz, Mitzi, and Billybob perform skits and sing famous songs.

Bumpers Fun Centers has three locations, the Northtown Mall (509) 489-4000, Riverfront Park (509) 624-6678, and U-City (509) 928-8445. The centers feature gamerooms with arcade games, miniature golf, an IMAX theater, and ice skating. Combine the fun of tag and hide and seek at **Laser Quest Spokane,** West 202 Second Ave.; (509-624-7700). This multi-level maze provides music, a fog machine, and hours of fun.

Arts and Entertainment

The **Opera House** shows the best of Broadway's productions. **The Metropolitan Performing Arts Center,** 901 West Sprague; (509-

455–6500), or the Met, hosts musicals concerts such as the classical jazz of Wynton Marsalis to the cutting edge rock of Pearl Jam as well as ballets. The classical music front is also upheld by the **Spokane Symphony,** 601 West Riverside; (509–624–1200). The oldest, continually performing in-residence jazz orchestra in the country is Spokane's **Jazz Orchestra.** They perform as many as 12 concerts each year. The region's only resident professional theater troupe is **the Interplayer's Ensemble,** 174 South Howard; (509–455–7529). Their seven-play season runs from October through June with shows on Tuesdays through Saturdays. The **Uptown Opera** (509–489–9828) produces two to four operas each season. Three amateur community theaters include the **Spokane Civic Theater,** 1020 North Howard; (509–325–2507), which puts on a variety of musicals, dramas, and comedies, the **Valley Repertory Theater,** and the **Artistic Community Theatre.**

Sports

Spokane claims two sports teams. The **Spokane Indians,** a minor league baseball club, play their season at the Fairgrounds. In the winter months, the **Spokane Chiefs** skate in the arena.

SPECIAL EVENTS

May: Annual Bloomsday 12K; Lilac Festival; Artfest.

June: Hoopfest—one of the largest basketball tournaments in the country; National Street Rod Association.

July: Cheney Rodeo; Cherry Pickers Trot and Pit Spit.

September: Spokane Interstate Fair.

October: Green Bluff Apple Festival (weekends).

December: Victorian-style Christmas.

Shopping

Two major shopping development projects are underway as of press time. Washington Water Power and Wells & Co. have joined to renovate the old **Steam Plant** in Spokane. They intend to open a shopping and eating gallery on the site in 1998. Also being redeveloped is **River Park Square.** A new mall anchored by Nordstrom and a 24-screen cinema is scheduled to open in 1999.

WHERE TO STAY

Spokane boasts as many as one dozen bed and breakfasts. For referrals, call the **Spokane Bed and Breakfast Association** (509) 624-3776. **Fotheringham House,** 2128 West 2nd Avenue; (509) 838-1891, a restored Victorian with an inviting walkway blooming with lavender and roses, accepts well-behaved children. Of the four guest rooms, one has a private bath and the other three share two bathrooms. Rates include a full country breakfast. This bed and breakfast is located in a quiet neighborhood across the street from Patsy Clark's restaurant. (See "Where to Eat.")

Cavanaugh's Inn at the Park, 303 West North River Drive; (509) 326-8000 or (800) THE-INNS, is situated adjacent to Riverfront and provides a resort-like atmosphere with its grounds and indoor and outdoor pools. The **Red Lion City Center,** 322 North Spokane Falls Court; (509) 455-9600 or (800) 848-9600, is conveniently located about two blocks from Riverfront park's big red wagon.

WHERE TO EAT

Patsy Clark's Mansion, 2208 West 2nd Avenue; (509) 838-8300, is worth a visit simply to savor its grandeur and good, Continental cuisine. Not inexpensive and not suitable for young kids, Patsy's will please well-behaved gradeschoolers and teens. Patrick, "Patsy" Clark, an Irish immigrant, married into a wealthy mining family and added his own fortune to theirs. This house was his "show-off" palace with many of the original touches still remaining. The second floor landing is adorned with the tallest Tiffany-designed stained glass windows in a private residence. Be sure to see the small dining room now called the "President Bush Room" after George Bush's visit here. This Oriental themed intimate eating area has etched glass wall sconces, intricate stained glass, fringesd lamps, and dragon shaped fire irons. Evidently Patsy was a womanizer who made his wife unhappy. Ask the waiters at closing to tell you about her ghost who reputedly still roams these halls.

Spokane has many other less grand and moderately priced restaurants. **The Rockin' B Ranch,** 3912 North Idaho Road; (509-891-9016), serves chuckwagon-style barbecue in a 7,000-square-foot barn. Accompanying the meal, the Riders of the Rockin' B sing old cowboy songs and perform quick shows. **McDonalds, Kentucky Fried Chicken,** and **Wendy's Old Fashioned Hamburgers** have dozens of locations in the area.

DAY TRIPS

Northern Idaho, or Idaho's "panhandle," is a region of dense forests, lakes, meadows, and mountains covered with huge cedar and fir trees—a green, pristine slice of "God's country." Coeur D'Alene in the southern part of the panhandle, about 16 miles from the Washington state border, is a major resort area. Coeur d'Alene today names a lake, a river, a mountain range, a mining district, a forest, and a city, and the area is regarded as the "Playground of the Northwest." Sixty lakes can be found within a sixty-mile radius of the city, making the region a popular summer destination. Winter brings snowmobiling, skiing, and hundreds of miles of cross-country trails.

The major attraction is **Lake Coeur d'Alene,** a big, blue expanse stretching for 25 miles, covering 25,100 acres and featuring 135 miles of shoreline. The **Coeur d'Alene Resort,** Second and Front; (208–765-4000 or 800–826-2390), is the town's premier resort property. (See Where to Stay.) Kids like walking on the resort's 3,300 foot floating boardwalk, reputedly the world's longest. The path leads by the dock, restaurants and boat, canoe, and kayak rental shops. A kid-pleaser is a tour of the lake. **Lake Coeur d'Alene Cruises,** Independence Road; (208–765-4000), offers narrated one-hour tours of the lake.

If your family would rather be in the water than on it, canoes, kayaks, paddleboats, and jet skis can be rented from the **City Dock** on Independence Point. **Coeur d'Alene City Park,** Lakeside Drive and First Street, has a public beach. This sandy area stretches west, joining the **North Idaho College Beach,** which offers views of the lake and the Spokane River. Along these sandy shores the Coeur d'Alene Native Americans used to camp and enjoy salmon bakes.

Tubbs Hill, Third Street and the Lake, adjacent to the City Dock, provides a scenic look-out. A 135-acre city park on land homesteaded

Big smiles on the antique Looff Carrousel in Spokane's Riverfront Park.
(Courtesy Spokane Area Convention and Visitors' Bureau)

in 1882 by German immigrant Tony Tubbs, this undeveloped bit of shoreline in Coeur d'Alene has the **Tubbs Hill Historical Nature Walk,** a two-mile loop that affords scenic views of the lake. A trail guide is available from the Coeur d'Alene Parks Department, 221 South Fifth Street; (208) 769-2252.

Fourteen miles north of Coeur d'Alene is the **Silverwood Theme Park,** North 26225 Hwy. 95; (208-772-0515). Themed as a Victorian-era mining town, Silverwood offers train rides, carnival rides, an air show at selected times and days, and the Grizzly, the park's wooden roller coaster. Silverwood Theme Park is open daily June through September.

East of Coeur d'Alene on 1-90 are Kellogg and Wallace. **Kellogg** is best known for the **Silver Mountain** ski area; (208) 783-1111. With a 3.1-mile gondola trip, Silver Mountain bills itself as "the world's longest single cable ride." The area's two peaks, Kellogg and Wardner, reach 6,300 and 6,200 feet respectively. In summer and fall the gondola ride offers scenic vistas. On a clear day you can see Montana to the east and Canada in the north. Have little ones and others unnerved by the incline ride in the seats facing the mountain.

In winter Silver Mountain offers SKIwee classes for ages 5–12. MINIrider is a program for seven- to twelve-year-olds who want to learn how to snowboard. Ages two through six can either play in day care, receive lessons, or combine both in the Minor's Camp.

About 50 miles from Coeur d'Alene, **Wallace**, the "Silver Capital of the World," is listed on the National Historic Register because some of its buildings are more than 100 years old. Many feature their original cast iron cornices, pilasters, and decorative glass. Just such features as well as its mountain background made Wallace the place where the movie "Dante's Peak" was shot. Remember the main street that is blasted apart by the volcano's force? That scene was shot in downtown Wallace.

During the 19th century Wallace served as a Panhandle hub of mining and railroading. **The Wallace District Mining Museum,** 509 Bank Street; (208-753-7151), is housed in an old bakery. Displayed are mine lighting devices ranging from stearic candles and oil lamps, to more modern electric lamps as well as other tools and artifacts. A 20-minute video, "North Idaho's Silver Legacy," screened in the 40-person theater shows the toil of mining. One-half block west is the ticket office for the **Sierra Silver Mine Tour,** 420 Fifth Street; (208-752-5151). If you've never been underground in a mine, don a hard hat for this one-hour guided walking tour through a mine tunnel. The guide points out such early 20th century equipment as the Diamond Drill machine which drills for a core sample and the "slusher" which brings the rock out and dumps it. The best demonstration is of the blasting board. The guide explains how the five hole burn method was employed to ignite the dynamite that blasted through these rock walls, and special effects create the flash and boom of the blast. Buy your tickets in town and take the trolley to and from the mine. A taped narration during the trips highlights mining history and points out historic sites in town.

The **Northern Pacific Railroad Museum,** Sixth and Pine Street, Wallace; (208) 752-0111, focuses on the importance of railroads to this region. Most kids will find the static displays boring. The first floor re-creates the interior of a train station complete with ticket window, a telegrapher's desk, and heavy oak waiting benches. Upstairs exhibits depict the route of the North Coast Limited. The museum has a rare,

13-foot glass map of the Northern Pacific Railroad. Kids giggle at the early 1900s high tank flush toilet.

For those interested in horses, sample a stay at **Hidden Creek Ranch,** 7600 East Blue Lake Road, Harrison; (208) 689-3209, or (800) 446-DUDE. Bookings are also available through American Wilderness Experience, (800) 444-DUDE. The aroma of sage, cedar, and mint from the pipe ceremony made the night air smell sweet outside the tipi set-up in a grassy meadow by a pond. A steady stream of whirling smoke spun skyward as the stars began to pop and glow in the northern Idaho night sky. Inside, the heated lava rocks took on the reds and oranges of a fiery sunset and the drummer beat an ancient pattern as we called upon the four directions to carry our prayers and thoughts outward into the corners of our planet.

This sweat lodge is just part of what makes **Hidden Creek Ranch** special. In its brochure, Hidden Creek indicates the ranch's commitment " to being one with nature…. In the spirit of this Native American philosophy, we help our guests to reconnect themselves with the earth and also to awaken their awareness for a means to save Mother Earth." There are also medicine trail hikes, sacred circle dances, yoga, and massages as well as trap shooting, fishing, and pontoon boat rides.

To an overlay of Native American philosophy and a core program of good riding instruction, Hidden Creek adds such cushy vacation accouterments as maid service, comfortable lodge rooms in modern log cabins, waiters, and an evening cocktail hour. This place is no rough n' rustic, down and dirty ranch for wanna-be wranglers who think mud, dust, and discomfort get them closer to the real west. This dude ranch appeals to die-hard riders, sometime saddle bosses, absolute greenhorns, as well as those who want nothing more physically challenging than a rocking chair and a good book.

Hidden Creek is also a place for families. From mid-June through August a kids' program operates for ages three through early teens. Preschoolers keep busy with storytelling, nature awareness walks, arts and crafts, visits to the petting coral, and pony rides. Ages 6 and older go out on kids' trail rides and families play together at afternoon ropin' sessions, evening campfires, and hay wagon rides. The six-day has a kids' overnight in Native American tipis. There are always cookies in the lodge cookie jar along with juice, tea, coffee, hot chocolate, and milk.

With a capacity of 40 to 50 guests, including children, Hidden Creek is large enough to hire experienced wranglers and small enough to pay particular attention to its guests. But the key to fitting in here is to make sure your family feels at ease with the ranch rhythms, which sometimes require strict adherence to a predetermined schedule. Rules are emphasized, and that's good for maintaining safety requirements and smooth ranch operations, but sometimes the frequent reminders made us feel uncomfortable, as if somehow we were fifth graders who needed a hall pass and a mini-lecture instead of a family on vacation— and we're not a rowdy bunch. But all in all, we had a good time and learned about horsemanship, Native American ways, and about ourselves.

FOR MORE INFORMATION

Spokane Convention and Visitors Bureau, 926 West Sprague, Ste.
   180, Spokane, 99204: (509) 624-1341;
   http://www.spokane-areacvb.org.
Spokane Visitor Information Center, 201 W. Main.

Emergency
For police, fire, and medical emergencies, dial 911.
Poison information center, (800) 572-0638.
Deaconess Medical Center, 800 West Fifth Avenue;
   (509) 458-5800.
Holy Family Hospital, 5633 North Lidgerwood; (509) 482-0111.
Sacred Heart Medical Center, 101 West Eighth Avenue;
   (509) 455-3131.
Valley Hospital, 12606 East Mission; (509) 924-6650.

OLYMPIC NATIONAL PARK

Snowcapped mountains, ocean shores, and temperate rain forests await visitors to **Olympic National Park,** encompassing some 900,000 acres in the center of the Olympic Peninsula in northwest Washington State. The sharp contrast in surroundings, unusual wildlife, and overall lack of commercialization make for a down-to-earth, back-to-basics vacation. Your family can venture into the misty rain forest, where Sitka spruce and Douglas fir loom over mossy footpaths; view majestic Mt. Olympus; explore tide pools on Pacific beaches; and see some outstanding scenery, including wildlife. (However, you probably won't see the Roosevelt Elk, whose protection was one of the main reasons the park was created. The species is shier than elk found farther east.)

GETTING THERE

Port Angeles, some 75 miles west of Seattle, is the main entry point for **Olympic National Park. William Fairchild International Airport** is 1 mile west of Port Angeles, off Highway 101; (360) 452-5095. It's served by **Horizon Airlines** (800-547-9308), with daily flights from Seattle, Victoria, and Portland. Rental cars are available. The closest major airport is **Seattle-Tacoma International Airport,** 120 miles away.

Amtrak and Greyhound do not service the Olympic Peninsula.

Because the Olympic Peninsula is connected on the east by the Kitsap Peninsula, which projects north between Hood Canal and Puget Sound, you may have to travel on a ferry or cross a bridge to arrive here. Coho Ferry, at the foot of Laurel Street, Port Angeles (360-457-4491), provides daily, year-round passenger and auto services to and from

Victoria, British Columbia. **Victoria Express,** 115 East Railroad Avenue at Landing Mall on the waterfront, provides passenger service in summer only; call (360) 452-8088, (800) 633-1589—Washington, or (604) 361-9144—Canada. **Washington State Ferries,** based in Seattle (800-84-FERRY), has year-round service across Puget Sound and between Port Townsend and Whidbey Island, Edmonds and Kingston, and Seattle and Bainbridge Island.

The bus system is **Clallam Transit,** 217 West Nineteenth, Port Angeles; (360) 452-4511. It provides limited service to Lake Crescent, Forks, and other nearby areas, as well as winter weekend trips to Hurricane Ridge.

By car, all three areas of the park (mountains, forest, and coast) are accessible by Highway 101, with spur roads leading to many areas inside the park.

GETTING AROUND

A car and good hiking boots are necessary. An option to driving is one of the sight-seeing tours offered by **Olympic Van Tours;** (360) 452-3858. Journeys to **Hurricane Ridge** and the **Hoh Rain Forest** can be made by reservation only.

Port Angeles is the site of the **Olympic Visitors Center,** the largest in the park. From here, **Heart o' the Hills Road,** an 18-mile paved road, begins its ascent to Hurricane Ridge Visitors Center (not always reachable in winter). No roads pass through the rugged heart of the rain forest. The few secondary roads that do penetrate the interior are mainly trailheads for the vast network of trails.

A number of the trails in the park are handicapped accessible. Contact any visitor center for information.

WHAT TO SEE AND DO

First, come prepared. Summer months bring less rainfall, but rain gear is essential for the occasional downpours. Much of the backcountry here remains snowed in until the end of June. Carry your own water supply, and never drink any untreated backcountry water, no matter how clear it may appear! The visitor center sells water purification tablets.

Olympic National Park at a Glance

- An uncommercialized vacation area rich with wildlife and beauty

- Tide pools, "sea stacks," and ancient petroglyphs along the Pacific coast

- The Hall of Mosses in the Hoh Rain Forest

- Summer hikes and winter snowshoeing in the subalpine meadows at Hurricane Ridge

- Olympic Park Visitor Center, (360) 452-0330

Because the park is so vast, we've divided it into sections. Some of the visitor centers and ranger stations listed have naturalist programs that the entire family will enjoy. Because of budget cuts, however, programs have been curtailed. The children's section of the park's newspaper contains a list of activities (including ranger-led walks, talks, or campfire programs) that, when completed, entitle a child to a Junior Ranger Badge.

It takes at least two days to sample the park's major sites: ocean beaches, rain forest, and Hurricane Ridge. Here are some of the highlights.

Northern Rim

Start at the major entrance, **Olympic Park Visitor Center,** 3002 Mt. Angeles Road (off Race Street); (360) 452-0330. Pick up free maps, and tour the **Pioneer Memorial Museum,** which displays aspects of the early loggers' lives, as well as exhibits on the park's flora.

Highway 101 west of Port Angeles skirts the southern shore of 8½-mile-long, glacier-carved **Lake Crescent.** This scenic drive offers fjord-like views. Self-guided hikes are possible around Lake Crescent, on the park's northwest boundaries. Obtain trail booklets, such as *Ever Changing, Ever Green,* at trailheads at **Storm King Ranger Station** (360-928-3380), where there's an information booth and interpretive programs; at **Lake Crescent Lodge,** also on the south shore; and at the Fairholm Ranger Station, on the north shore. From these points, embark on trails rated easy to moderate that visit such sights as the 90-foot-high **Marymere Falls** (where the last part of the trail is fairly steep). **The Fairholm Station** features an easy 0.75-mile nature trail perfect for youngsters. Experienced hikers may want to tackle the difficult **Mt. Storm King Trail,** which covers 4.2 miles and climbs 1,700 feet. The trail can be accessed from either Lake Crescent Lodge or the Storm King Ranger Station.

If you've brought your bikes, the **Spruce Railroad Trail** on the northeast shore of Lake Crescent offers the best opportunity for a bike tour. The trailheads are located at the North Shore and Lyre River, and the 4-mile trail follows the World War I era Spruce Railway Bed.

From Lake Crescent, it's about a 13-mile ride (west, along Highway 101 then south via a spur road) to **Sol Duc Hot Springs Resort,** U.S. 101, 40 miles west of Port Angeles; (360) 327-3583. Here you can soak in hot tubs (fee), if you so desire; the tubs are located about 12 miles south of Highway 101. After kids get accustomed to the sulfur smell, they may like the soothing waters. **Salmon Cascades,** 6 miles along Sol Duc Road, can be reached by a short trail. From a viewing platform, autumn visitors watch the annual migration of salmon returning from the sea to spawn. **The Ancient Groves Nature Trail,** a 0.5-mile loop, is another good, short trail, and is located 8.3 miles along Sol Duc Road.

Hurricane Ridge, 17 miles south of the Olympic Visitors Center in the subalpine meadows of Olympic high country, is the northern rim's most popular area. Hurricane Ridge affords splendid views of Mt. Olympus, the park's southern interior, and, to the north, the Strait of Juan de Fuca and British Columbia (on a clear day). Naturalist programs and guided walks, exhibits, hiking trails, and picnic areas are available. **Obstruction Point Road,** a steep 8.4-mile dirt road leading east from Ridge, offers the best views of Mt. Olympus.

A good hike for families: the **Meadow Loop Trail,** beginning at the visitor center and weaving for 2 miles through flower-filled meadows and mountain vistas. Deer and bear populate the woods and alpine meadows around here. Some of the deer have become bold enough to graze in the frequently crowded parking lot. As with any wildlife you may encounter, keep your distance, and never feed any animals in the park.

The beauty of Olympic National Park will captivate every member of the family.
(National Park Service photo)

In winter, **guided snowshoe walks** (snowshoes provided free of charge) take place every weekend from late December through March. In the heart of ski season, this area offers two rope tows and one Poma lift for downhill skiers. Rentals are available. **Cross-country skiers** make good use of the snow-covered nature trails. Dress warmly. Winter storms are common along Hurricane Ridge, which is often subjected to high winds and low temperatures. Rangers warn that hypothermia is the leading cause of death in the park.

Northwest Area

If you approach the park from the northwest along the spur road leading from Route 112, you arrive at **Lake Ozette,** the most westerly lake in the contiguous United States. Two trails leave from the Ranger Station for the ocean beaches. The northernmost, **Cape Alava Trail,** 3.3 miles, leads through lowland coastal forest to the beach; a second trail stretches 3 miles to **Sand Point.** You can take the Cape Alava Trail, hike for 3 miles on the beach, and then return via the Sand Point trail—if your kids can walk 9.3 miles. Many kids enjoy both the challenge and the scenery. Cedar walkways on the trails make footing easier for smaller feet, but hiking shoes, tennis, or soft-soled shoes are recommended because the wood is slippery when wet or frosty. Besides exploring tide pools for marine life, hikers can see unusual sea stacks, those eerie eroded remains of coastal cliffs that rise from the water, and pass by Indian Petroglyphs.

Western Area

The Hoh Rain Forest, the only temperate rain forest in North America, is 91 miles from Port Angeles (turn off 12 miles south of Forks). Each year this forest receives 150 inches of rainfall, creating a beautiful, lush landscape (including some of the world's largest trees) that you won't find anywhere else in this country. At the **Hoh Ranger Station Visitor Center** (360-374-6925), Highway 101, check the bulletin board for notices, campground activities, and guided walks.

Trailheads for two nonstrenuous trails kids enjoy begin right behind the visitor center. **The Hall of Mosses,** a 0.75-mile trail, passes through moss-draped maples, while the **Spruce Nature Trail,** 1.5-miles, ventures along the Hoh River. You may forget that you are actually in Washington and not in the Amazon as you wander through humid air, under towering trees, past lush greenery, and over fern-covered floors. Don't forget your camera.

A number of trails wind down to deserted beaches along the more than 57 miles of wild, rugged coastline in the western area. Before hiking to or on any of the beaches, obtain the "Strip of Wilderness" folder at any ranger station, as there are certain precautions you should take. Either write down or carry a tide table (available at visitor centers) to avoid being trapped by high tides: People have lost their lives thinking they could beat incoming waters as they hiked around a point or headland. Always use overland trails where they exist. Moreover, be careful, as sudden high waves can pick up and hurl beach logs.

If you're driving to the coast from the Hoh Rain Forest, you'll first come to Ruby Beach, with scenic views, deep red sand made of tiny garnet crystals, spectacular sunsets. Certain points of the beach trail can be passed only at low tide.

From Ruby Beach, only the south 14 miles of 101 (known as the **Kalaloch-Ruby Beach Highway**) are accessible by car. The six beaches along this stretch can be reached by paved roads that lead to trails that range from 0.25 to 3.5 miles long. Exploring tide pools at low tide is a wonderful way to teach children about the ecology of this area.

At the end of this stretch, on the park's southwest boundary, is the **Kalaloch Information Station.** This area serves as a center for beach vacationers, with a general store, lodge, gas station, ranger station, and campground. Enjoy several beach and coastal walks here, as well as nightly campfire programs at the Campground Amphitheater from late June to early August.

Southern Area

Quinault, on the park's south central boundaries, is the home of the Quinault Indians. Wander onto the **Maple Glade Rain Forest Trail,** which runs for 0.5 mile, beginning across from the Quinault Ranger Station; (360) 288-2444. Yet another rain forest adventure awaits along the nearby 1-mile **Graves Creek Nature Trail.** These lesser known areas are less crowded alternatives to the Hoh Rain Forest trails.

Adventure

Active families enjoy the park to the fullest with the help of outfitters.

Try **Olympic Raft and Guide Service,** 464 Highway 101 West, Port Angeles; (360) 457-7011 or 452-1443. They offer river-rafting trips in the Olympic National Park that are recommended for all ages, including a Class II, half-day beginner's trip down the Elwha River and two Class I trips—one through the Queets Corridor, the other down the Hoh River.

Olympic Park Institute, 111 Barnes Point Road, Port Angeles, has family field seminars exploring the wonders of the park. Call (360) 928-3720 or (800) 775-3720 for a free catalog.

Uncle Dave's Guide Service, near milepost 178 on Highway 101 (360-374-2577), offers guided float trips and fishing excursions along the Hoh River.

Other delightful day adventures, depending on the age of your child, include llama treks, guided berry-picking tours (a popular summer pastime), sea kayak tours around Port Townsend, scenic flights, and mountain-bike trips. For details on travel to the North Olympic Peninsula, contact the **North Olympic Peninsula Visitor and Convention Bureau;** (800) 942-4042. The bureau has a free visitor's guide. Also check out their Web site: http://www.northolympic.com.

Olympic National Forest

Much of the Olympic National Forest that borders the eastern edge of the park is more accessible and more developed than much of the park's interior. Pick up information on forest trails at one of the two ranger stations: **Hoodsport** (360-877-5554) and **Quilcene** (360-765-3368), U.S. 101 south.

SPECIAL EVENTS

Neighboring communities liven things up on the Olympic Peninsula with a variety of events.

January: Polar Bear Dip, Port Angeles; Centrum's Chamber Music Festival, Port Townsend.

February: Discovery Bay Salmon Derby; Hot Jazz, Port Townsend.

March: Clallam Bay/Sekiu's Spring Fling.

April: Rain Fest, Forks; Audubon Society's Bird-A-Thon, Sequim.

May: Irrigation Festival, Parade and Music Festival, Sequim; Juan de Fuca Festival of the Arts, Port Angeles.

June: Community Clambake and International Days, Port Townsend.

July: Fork's Old Fashioned Fourth Celebration, with frog pulls, arm wrestling, and fireworks; Wine and Food Festival, downtown Port Angeles; Clambake, Sequim; Jazz, Port Townsend.

August: Jefferson County Fair, Port Townsend; Clallam County Fair, Port Angeles; Derby Days and Kiddie Parade, Port Angeles; Makah Days, Neah Bay.

November: Festival of Trees, Port Angeles.

December: Christmas Fair Arts and Crafts and BazArt, fine art sale, Port Angeles.

WHERE TO STAY

There are a number of lodging choices within the park, including sixteen campgrounds operating on a strictly first-come, first-serve basis. Most are relatively primitive, with only two having hookups and showers. These are **Sports Center & RV Park,** near milepost 178 on Highway 101 (360-374-9288); and the **Hoh River Resort & RV Park,** between milepost 175 and 176 on Highway 101 (360–374–5566). Year-round campgrounds with summer naturalist programs are located at **Heart O' the Hills, Hoh, Kalacoch,** and **Mora.**

Accommodations within the park range from beachside cabins to historic lodges. Be sure to reserve well in advance for the summer season.

Kalaloch Lodge, U.S. 101, 36 miles south of Forks (360–962–2271), is open year-round. Accommodations range from forty modern cabins with kitchenettes (fifteen on a coastal bluff overlooking the ocean), plus eight lodge rooms or ten motel units. While there is no TV or phone in rooms, there is a coffee shop and cocktail lounge as well as a grocery store and service station.

Lake Crescent Lodge, U.S. 101, 21 miles west of Port Angeles (360–928–3211), is open late April to late October. Choose from five rooms in the main lodge (none have private baths), thirty modern guest rooms, and several cottages (four with fireplaces). Roll-away beds and cribs are provided for a small fee. Services include a dining room, cocktail lounge and rowboat rentals.

Lake Quinault Lodge, on the shore of Lake Quinault (360–288–2571 in Washington State or 800–562–6672), is a rustic timber lodge built in 1926. F.D.R. stayed here in the 1930s and so liked the area and a particular type of elk that he took steps that eventually resulted in the creation of the park. Lake Quinault's main lodge has thirty-two rooms, two suites, and thirty-six lakeside rooms, all with private baths.

Log Cabin Resort is at 6540 East Beach Road on the northeast end of Lake Crescent; (360) 928–3245. It is open year-round and offers lodging ranging from rustic one-room log cabins to lodge rooms, most with private baths, except for the four rustic cabins that share a bathhouse. The "resort" also has a forty-site RV campground.

Sol Duc Hot Springs Resort, U.S. 101, 40 miles west of Port Angeles (360–327–3583), is open mid-May to late September. There are thirty-two cabins, all with private bath and six with full kitchens, plus a swimming pool and three hot-springs pools. The lodging features a dining room, snack bar, and grocery store, but no TV or phones in the room.

Nearby communities have a variety of hotels, motels, and bed and breakfasts. For information, write the **North Olympic Peninsula Visitor and Convention Bureau,** P.O. Box 670, Port Angeles, WA 98362; (800) 942–4042.

Port Townsend

Diamond Point Inn, 241 Sunshine Road, Port Townsend (360-797-7720), is a bed and breakfast that welcomes kids to stay in one of their six rooms (suites available). **Anapurna Inn,** 538 Adams (360-385-2909), accepts children of all ages (and pets). They feature suites with kitchen facilities.

The **Bishop Victorian Guest Suites,** Washington and Quincy streets (360-385-6122), has some two-bedroom suites. **The Harborside Inn,** 330 Benedict Street (360-385-7909 or 800-942-5960), offers comfortable waterfront rooms. A few feature kitchen facilities.

Port Angeles

Red Lion Bayshore Inn, 221 North Lincoln (360-452-9215 or 800-547-8010), is right on the waterfront. It has 185 rooms on two levels, an outdoor pool and Jacuzzi, and an adjacent coffee shop.

The **Best Western Olympia Lodge,** 140 Del Guzzi Drive (360-452-2993), is another good choice; as is the **Uptown Motel,** 101 East Second (360-457-9434 or 800-858-3812), which has a great view, and suites and rooms with refrigerators and microwaves.

WHERE TO EAT

All the lodges and resorts within the park have on-site restaurants, which serve breakfast, lunch, and dinner, except at Sol Duc, where breakfast and dinner are served in the main dining room, with lunch at the Poolside Deli. Buy sandwiches, snack foods, and supplies from the **Fairhold General Store** (360-928-3020) on the western end of Lake Crescent; it's open April 1 through October 1 (except Memorial and Labor days). The **Hurricane Lodge Visitors Center** serves sandwiches and light meals.

Port Angeles has a fair share of family-friendly restaurants. At the **Bushwhacker Restaurant,** 1527 East First Street (360-457-4113), the menu includes prime rib, clam chowder, shrimp, and a salad bar. For Italian food, stop in at **Gordy's Pizza and Pasta,** 1123 East First Street; (360) 457-5056. Choose from an array of salads, pastas, pizzas, and sandwiches. Homemade cheesecake is their dessert specialty.

DAY TRIPS

Convenient to the Lake Ozette area of the park is a day trip to Neah Bay, a small fishing village off Route 112, where the **Makah Cultural and Research Center,** 8 miles south of Makah Reservation on the Pacific Ocean near Cape Alava (360-645-2711), is well worth a visit. The driving time to cover the 72 miles from Port Angeles to the cultural center is about two hours. Along the way near the coast, you might catch sight of trumpeter swans and bald eagles that frequent this region. A mud slide in the coastal village of Ozette, 15 miles south, uncovered a site containing hundreds of perfectly preserved Makah Indian artifacts more than 500 years old. The subsequent archaeological dig was one of the largest in North America, and many of the finest objects are on display here, including trinkets, tools, ceremonial pieces, and whaling and sealing instruments of these ocean-dependent Indians. A longhouse replica features soft voices speaking the Makah language.

Returning east from Neah Bay, take Highway 112 to Pysht to visit the **Merrill & Ring Pysht Tree Farm,** Highway 112; (360) 963-2382 or (800) 998-2382. This "managed tree farm" offers guests a slide show, forestry trails that teach harvest cycles, and weekly guided tours (call for schedules).

You can also take a ferry ride to the attractions of charming Victoria, British Columbia. (See the chapter Victoria.)

Although the town of Port Angeles is a convenient gateway to the park, some may find it rather dreary. A more appealing option: **Port Townsend,** on the Puget Sound, has lots of Victorian charm and an active cultural life, including a number of summer music festivals (see Special Events), art galleries, historical sights, and a scenic coastline. Contact the Port Townsend Chamber of Commerce, 2437 Sims Way (360-385-2722), for visitor information.

West of **Port Townsend** are several worthwhile attractions in the **Sequim** area. **The Dungeness Spit National Wildlife Refuge,** 3 miles north of Highway 101 near Sequim (360-683-5847), is home to 150 species of wildlife and approximately 250 different bird species. This 6-mile arc is the longest natural sand spit in the world, growing 34 feet in length a year. From here you are treated to fabulous views of the **Strait of Juan de Fuca, Mount Baker,** the **San Juans, Vancouver**

Island, and the **Olympic Mountains.** Frolic in the sand at the pit's base, or if your kids are energetic, take a 5.5-mile hike to the coast guard lighthouse, open to visitors Thursday through Monday. Remember, though, that the hike requires about two hours one-way. Look for harbor seals on your journey. Bring plenty of water, a lunch, and jackets because the weather changes suddenly.

Also in the Sequim area is the **Olympic Game Farm,** 1423 Ward Road (follow the signs from Sequim); (360) 683–4295. You can drive through or take a summer guided walking tour to see a wide assortment of animals including jaguar, rhino, timber wolves, cougar, and buffalo. An extra summer treat: a stocked pond (poles and bait supplied). A map and more information are available from the **Sequim/Dungeness Chamber of Commerce;** (360) 683–6197 or (800) 737–8464.

FOR MORE INFORMATION

Park Information: Olympic National Park, Office of the Superintendent, 600 East Park Avenue; (360) 452–0330. **The Olympic Park Visitor Center,** 3002 Mt. Angeles Road, Port Angeles (360–452–0330), is the park's largest. Website: http://www.nps.gov

Area information: North Olympic Peninsula Visitor and Convention Bureau; (360) 452–8552 or (800) 942–4042.

Emergency Numbers

Park emergencies or to report a crime: 911 or (360) 452–4501, 7:00 A.M. to midnight during the summer, until 5:30 P.M. off-season. After hours, in Clallam County (northern peninsula from Forts to Port Angeles and Sequim), dial 911. In other areas, call (360) 452–4545. You may also contact a park ranger at the **Hoh Ranger Station;** (360) 374–6925.

Hospital: Olympic Memorial Hospital, 939 Caroline, Port Angeles, has twenty-four-hour emergency services; (360) 457–8513.

Twenty-four-hour pharmacies: Jim's Pharmacy, 424 East Second Street, Port Angeles (360–452–4200); **Sequim Plaza Pharmacy,** 933 North Fifth Avenue, Sequim (360–683–1122)

Poison Control: (800) 542–6319

SEATTLE

Seattle ranks prominently on most top ten lists of splendid U.S. vacation destinations. The city is in a superb location, surrounded by mountains (the Cascades to the east and the Olympics to the west), by evergreen forests, salt water (Puget Sound, an arm of the Pacific), and by fresh water (Lake Washington). Sight-seeing and recreational opportunities abound.

Originally built on seven hills (one has since been leveled), the city sports a lively waterfront and a multitude of family-friendly attractions. Yes, the mild climate is also moist (bring rain gear), but the locals have adapted to the inclement weather (which one resident says is more like a steady drizzle than real downpours).

GETTING THERE

Seattle-Tacoma (Sea-Tac to the locals) **International Airport** (206-433-4645 or 800-544-1965), about 16 miles from downtown, is served by more than forty airlines. Airport shuttles include a motor coach and a van service; taxi service and car rentals also are available.

Amtrak (800-USA-RAIL) is at Third and Jackson.

The **Greyhound** bus station is at Eighth Avenue and Stewart Street; call (206) 624-3456, (800) 231-2222, or (206) 628-5523.

By car, persons coming from the north or south enter Seattle from I-5; those from the east via I-90.

GETTING AROUND

Although some of downtown Seattle's hills are steep, walking is a good way to see the city (wear comfortable shoes). You will want a car if you plan to explore Metropolitan Seattle's attractions.

Metro buses (206-553-3000) are free between 6:00 A.M. and 7:00

P.M. in the city's core area between Battery and South Jackson streets and Sixth Avenue and Alaskan Way.

The elevated Monorail travels a mile from downtown Seattle to Seattle Center.

Vintage trolleys run frequently along the waterfront to Pioneer Square and the International District; call (206) 553-3000.

WHAT TO SEE AND DO

Museums and Attractions

Seattle Center, 305 Harrison; (206) 684-8582 or 684-7200. This seventy-four-acre park built for the 1962 Seattle World's Fair includes landscaped grounds with fountains and trees, theaters, an amusement park called Fun Forest, and, next door, The Center House with a variety of shops and restaurants—as well as **The Seattle Children's Museum,** 305 Harrison; (206) 441-1768. Tykes "work" and play in a mini-neighborhood, with kid-size doctor's office, grocery store, public buses, and fire engines. In the Little Lagoon, toddlers play with a giant busy board, crawl through a friendly whale, and watch colorful fish swim in the aquarium. Frequently changing cultural exhibits feature costumes, games, and musical instruments from around the world. A professional artist at the Imagination Station helps kids and adults create masterpieces in paper, textiles, and clay. Ask about special events and workshops.

Another kid pleaser located within the Seattle Center is the **Pacific Science Center,** 200 Second Avenue North; (206) 443-2001. This modern structure, also called "The Cathedral of Science," boasts pools and fountains and more than 200 hands-on exhibits, plus dinosaurs, a planetarium with sky and laser shows, and an IMAX Theater. Kids especially like the giant fiberglass moon and the Native American longhouse.

Seattle Center surrounds **The Space Needle,** Fifth Avenue North and Broad Street; (206) 443-2100. From the top level observation deck of the city's 605-foot landmark, you have a superb view of the city, Puget Sound, and—if the weather is clear—Mt. Rainier, Mt. Baker, and the Cascade and Olympic ranges. Save this for a sunny day. The obser-

Seattle at a Glance

- A misty, waterfront city sizzling with family-friendly attractions

- Kid-pleasing museums and science centers, plus zoos and aquariums

- Pike Place Market—a colorful smorgasboard of shops and restaurants

- Ferry rides to the San Juan Islands

- Seattle-King County Convention and Visitors Bureau, (206) 461-5840

---

vation deck is open from 8:00 A.M. to midnight.

Museum of Flight, 9404 East Marginal Way South (on Boeing Field); (206) 764-5720. Located within "The Red Barn," the original Boeing air plane factory, this museum retells the history of night, from Leonardo da Vinci to the Wright Brothers to today's space age. Most kids are fascinated by aircraft; kids will be intrigued by the more than forty aircraft on display, including a flying ambulance (C-45 Mercy Plane), Boeing B-47 Bomber, and barnstorming *Curtiss Jenny.* Perhaps the most famous exhibit features *Airforce One,* the presidential jet that served Presidents Eisenhower, Kennedy, and Johnson. Visitors are encouraged to walk through the exhibit, which highlights the presidential suite, conference room, Kennedy's pipe rack, Johnson's ten-gallon hat rack, and more. Plans are in the works to open the Air Traffic Control Tower Exhibit. This mock control tower will face a working runway and feature authentic control-tower equipment and recordings.

The **Museum of History and Industry (MOHAI),** 2700 Twenty-fourth Avenue East; (206) 324-1126. This museum features exhibits about Native Americans and immigrants from Europe, Asia, and Africa who have made unique contributions to Seattle since the city's inception in the 1800s. Among the 70,000 artifacts are many that children relate to:

a large costume collection, hundreds of dolls and toys, plus the carpenter's glue pot that started the great Seattle fire of 1899 and many artifacts of the fire's destruction. At the Hands-on History section, kids play with puzzles, games, and toys, and try on period clothes. There's even a video produced just for kids about the heritage of the Pacific Northwest. Special programs for kids and families coincide with current exhibitions. Each summer, Super Wednesdays! workshops present special programs.

The **Seattle Aquarium,** Pier 59, Waterfront Park, 1483 Alaskan Way; (206) 386-4300 or 386-4320—tape. Head to the underwater viewing area and be transfixed by creatures—including sharks and octopus—gliding through the enormous tank. A new tide pool exhibit re-creates the sealife of the Washington State Coast. Kids enjoy handling the starfish and anemones in the touch tanks. Helpful staff members answer questions.

Next door to the aquarium is the **Omnidome Film Experience,** Alaskan Way, Pier 59, Waterfront Park; (206) 622-1868. The theater has been featuring a film about the eruption of Mount St. Helens, shown on their 180-degree dome screen. (Warning: Very young children are sometimes frightened by the "you are there" realism.)

The **Hiram M. Chittenden Locks** (more commonly called The Ballard Locks), 3015 North West Fifty-eighth Street; (206) 783-7059. Another popular attraction is on this 8-mile canal that connects saltwater Puget Sound with freshwater Lake Washington. Depending on the tide, boats are raised or lowered from 6 to 26 feet. Hour-long tours take place twice daily. Another kid pleaser is the fish ladder on the south side of the locks. Here watch salmon or trout (depending on the season) jump over twenty-one concrete steps from the sea to fresh water. The locks and grounds, which include the seven-acre Carl English Gardens, are open to the public daily from 7:00 A.M. to 9:00 P.M.

Parks and Zoos

Seattle boasts an extensive park system. Across from Pike Place Market, First Avenue at Pike Street, **Victor Steinbrueck Park** is a nice place to watch ferries sail across Puget Sound and to listen to the street musicians. The waters of the sound are chilly, but if a beach is on your mind, the sandiest and largest is at **Alki Beach Park,** Alki Avenue Southwest, in west Seattle. There's a popular bicycle/jogging trail (nearby shops rent

Seattle's landmark Space Needle dominates the downtown skyline.
(Photo by Jim Bell/courtesy Seattle-King County News Bureau)

bikes) and great views of passing ferries and the Olympic Mountains.

Woodland Park Zoo, 5500 Phinney Avenue North, 10 miles north of downtown; (206) 684-4800. Considered one of the ten best in the United States, the zoo is particularly known for its natural habitats. Kids' favorites include the five-acre African Savanna, where hippos, zebras, lions, and giraffes roam, separated from viewers by hidden natural barriers. In addition to elephants, the huge Elephant Forest also has a tropical forest, a Thai temple, and a working Thai logging camp. Tropical Rain Forest is complete with lush trees and vegetation, orchids, and waterfalls. The Trail of Vines replicates the jungles of India and Southeast Asia; as visitors walk along an elevated boardwalk, they can glimpse orangutans residing in treetops.

The **Point Defiance Zoo & Aquarium,** 5400 North Pearl Street, Tacoma (206-591-5227), is one of the Northwest's best. More than 5,000 animals reside here in a setting that overlooks Puget Sound.

Special Tours

Four water sight-seeing companies offer tours from the waterfront, including **Argosy Cruises,** which departs daily from Pier 55 for one-hour cruises in the harbor; (206) 623-1445. That's just about right for younger kids, who tend to get antsy on tour boats. With older kids, you might consider the two-and-one-half-hour tour of Seattle's Elliot Bay and Lake Washington Ship Canal via the Ballard Locks, which is offered by **Gray Line Water Sightseeing;** (206) 623-4252. **The Spirit of Puget Sound** has lunch, dinner, and midnight cruises that include a live Broadway Review. These cruises depart from Pier 70; call (206) 443-1442 to reserve. **Tillicum Village and Tours** has a cruise from Pier 56 to Blake Island State Park for a salmon-bake dinner cooked over an open-pit alder fire in a North Coast Indian cedar longhouse. The meal is followed by costumed tribal dancing. Call (206) 443-1244 for information.

Shopping

Shopping in Seattle is a many splendored thing. Have your pick of colorful wares, admire the scenery, and munch on tasty bits of food at the **Pike Place Market,** First Avenue at Pike Street (206-682-7453), one of the city's top tourist attractions. This colorful market, begun in 1907, is a great place to buy produce, cheese, fresh seafood (packed in dry ice for transport home), crafts, flowers, baked goods, coffee, spices in bulk, and even "junk." Stairs or an elevator lead to the harbor.

The waterfront stretches from Pier 51 on the south to Pier 70 on the north, where there is a complex of shops and restaurants in a restored wharf. Pioneer Square (which adjoins the Kingdome sports arena, 201 South King Street) spans some 18 blocks and includes a variety of art galleries (more per square foot than in any other U.S. city), shops, restaurants, and the **Klondike Gold Rush National Historical Park,** 117 South Main Street; (206) 553-7220. This national park inside a storefront offers five free films on the Gold Rush of 1897.

In the International District, east of the Kingdome, are exotic Asian shops and restaurants, including **Uwajimaya,** 519 Sixth Avenue South, (206-624-6248), a large Japanese supermarket, bazaar, and delicatessen.

NikeTown has set up shop in downtown Seattle and carries a full line of sports gear, as well as exhibits of athlete memorabilia. For the teens in your clan who like grunge and retro-fashion, check the stores along First and Second Avenues. A local favorite is **Retro Viva,** 1511 First Avenue, (206) 624-2529.

Theater, Music, and the Arts

Seattle Weekly, on newsstands every Wednesday, offers extensive listings of cultural events. **Ticketmaster Northwest** has tickets to concerts, sports, and fine arts events. Call (206) 628-0888 to charge or to find out their locations about town. For half-price day-of-performance tickets for theater, music, and dance events, head to **Ticket/Ticket's** two locations: at the Broadway Market, 401 Broadway East; or at Pike Place Market Information Booth, First and Pike streets (206-324-2744). Seattle has more equity theaters than any U.S. city outside New York, including **Seattle Children's Theatre;** (206) 441-3322.

Sports

The **Seattle Mariners** American League baseball team plays at the Kingdome from April through early October; call (206) 628-3555. The **Seattle SuperSonics** basketball team shoots hoops at the Key Arena from October through April; call (206) 283-DUNK. The **NFL Seahawks** are at the Kingdome from August through December; (206) 827-9766. And the **Seattle Thunderbirds** play hockey at the Key Arena; call (206) 448-PUCK. University of Washington football is also a popular fall attraction; call (206) 543-2200.

SPECIAL EVENTS

Contact the Seattle Convention and Visitors Bureau for more information on the following:

February: Northwest Flower and Garden Show, featuring more than thirty-five gardens, including children's gardens.

May: Seattle International Children's Festival, a six-day event featuring more than one hundred performances by professional companies from six continents.

Memorial Day weekend: Northwest Folklife Festival features scores of musicians and artists performing on twenty stages.

Mid-July: Bite of Seattle, a large food fair offering culinary specialties from some of the city's best restaurants.

Late July–early August: Seafair, the city's largest festival, includes a variety of community celebrations culminating in hydroplane races, a giant parade, and "crazy events," such as milk-carton boat derbies.

Labor Day Weekend: Bumbershoot, an arts festival ranked among the top five festivals nationwide, offers kids' activities, music, dance, theater, comedy, visual and literary arts.

WHERE TO STAY

Seattle has a wide variety of lodging in different price ranges. Information on bed and breakfasts can be obtained from **Pacific Bed and Breakfast Agency,** 701 North West Sixtieth Street, Seattle 98107 (206-784-0539), or the **Washington State Bed-and-Breakfast Guild,** 242 North West Market Street, Seattle 98107 (800-647-2918).

Families may prefer staying in the Seattle Center area because it's more economical than downtown (and within easy reach via the Monorail). Some modest but perfectly acceptable choices are **Sixth Avenue Inn,** 200 Sixth Avenue (206-441-8300); **Park Inn,** 225 Aurora Avenue (206-728-7666), which has an indoor pool; and **Quality Inn City Center,** 2224 Eighth Avenue (206-624-6820 or 800-4-CHOICE), which features some family suites with kitchenettes.

For the big splurge, try the elegant **Four Seasons Olympic Hotel,** 411 University Street (206-621-1700 or 800-223-8772), with an indoor pool, a health club, and several restaurants, or the **Mayflower Park Hotel** (206-623-8700).

The Westin Hotel, 1900 Fifth Avenue, (206-728-1000 or 800-228-3000), which sports great city views, a fitness center, an indoor heated pool, and the Westin Kids Club. Rooms, if requested, can be child safe and child friendly (already equipped with necessary cribs, etc.). Upon registration parents receive a safety kit complete with night-light, Band-Aids, and identity bracelets. Kids get their own amenity—a soft-drink cup or laundry bag with crayons. You can request such niceties as a jogging stroller, emergency diapers, potty seats, bicycle seats, refrigerators, and step stools.

WHERE TO EAT

The *Seattle Visitors Guide* has a listing of restaurants. Visit the **Pike Place Market,** where goodies range from warm sourdough bread to crisp Washington State apples.

Fresh seafood is a specialty of this area. **Ivar's Acres of Clams,** Pier 54 (206-624-6852), is an informal place that serves much more than clams.

Red Bobin, 1100 Fourth Avenue (206-447-1909), is known for their gourmet burgers, but there's also other kid-pleasing fare.

Planet Hollywood, Sixth Avenue (next to NikeTown), is decorated with celebrity memorabilia.

Parents shouldn't miss a stop at one of the city's ubiquitous coffee bars for espresso. Ask for hot chocolate for the kids.

DAY TRIPS

Puget Sound has hundreds of islands, and exploring at least one makes an ideal day trip. **Washington State Ferries,** 801 Alaskan Way, (206-464-6400 or 800-843-3779—WA), offers ten routes with twenty-five vessels. From the Seattle Waterfront, among the most popular, short scenic day trips for families are the car ferries to Bainbridge Island. Take your bike and a picnic lunch aboard the ferry and pedal around this scenic island.

The beautiful **San Juan Islands**—with their small towns, rolling countryside, and tiny harbors—are the state's most popular offshore destination. Automobile ferries, which leave from Anacortes, some 90 miles north of Seattle, serve four of the islands. If you have time only to visit one, the best family island is **San Juan,** where there are a variety of restaurants, small resorts, motels and bed and breakfasts, beaches, a whale-watching museum, bald eagles, and Friday Harbor— the largest town in the San Juan chain.

Note: These islands are very popular in summer. Call to see how early you should arrive at the ferry. If you're planning on overnighting, reserve in advance. For more information on the islands, call the **State of Washington Tourism;** (206) 753-5600 or (800) 544-1800.

Mt. Rainier, at 14,411 feet, has a National Park that's 98 miles southeast of Seattle. You might opt to stay overnight at Paradise Inn in Ashford (360-569-2275), 20 miles east of the Nisqually entrance. The park and surrounding Cascades offer hiking trails, lakes and rivers for fishing, horseback tours, and miles of scenic beauty. The Henry M. Jackson Visitor's Center, located at Paradise (206-569-2212), features exhibits, films, and splendid wraparound views.

If your kids need a theme park in their lives, **Enchanted Village,** 36201 Enchanted Parkway, Federal Way (206-661-8000), 27 miles from Seattle, will do. This amusement park has roller coasters, carousels, musical shows, and other rides, and, next door, Wild Waves Water Park has the things you'd expect—from giant slides to artificial surf.

In winter, skiers will find four ski areas on **Snoqualmie Pass,** 54 miles from downtown.

FOR MORE INFORMATION

Seattle-King County Convention & Visitors Bureau, 520 Pike Street, Suite 1300, Seattle, WA 98101; (206) 461-5840. There is a Visitor Information Center at Washington State Convention and Trade Center, ground level, 800 Convention Place; (206) 461-5840. Website: http://www.seeseattle.org

Seattle's Child is a parent's publication listing events and other information of interest to families. Call (206) 441-0191.

Emergency Numbers
Ambulance, fire, police: 911
Poison Control: (206) 526-2121
There is no twenty-four-hour pharmacy; some of the larger
    Pay Less Drug Stores, with locations around town, are open
    until 9:00 P.M.; call (206) 223-1128.
Hospitals with twenty-four-hour emergency rooms include:
    Northwest Hospital, 1550 North 115th Street
    (206-364-0500) and **Virginia Mason Hospital,** 925 Seneca
    Street (206-583-6433). Call the hospitals to inquire about
    prescriptions when the pharmacies are closed.

VANCOUVER

Vancouver, the largest city in western Canada, with more than 1.8 million residents, is surrounded by inlets of the Pacific Ocean on three sides. To the north rise the majestic Coast Mountains; the fertile farmlands of the Fraser Valley nestle in the east. Along with spectacular natural beauty, this cosmopolitan city also offers temperate climate (the mildest in Canada), a friendly, ethnically diverse populace, and enough activities to ensure a fun family vacation.

GETTING THERE

Vancouver International Airport (604-276-6101), on an island some 9 miles south of downtown, is served by nineteen major airlines. Bus, limousine service, and taxis provide transportation to major downtown hotels. Website: http://www.yur.ca

Greyhound Lines of Canada, 1150 Station Street (604-662-3222), is the largest bus line serving Vancouver from points across Canada and North America. **Quick Shuttle** (604-244-3744 or 800-665-2122— United States) has frequent bus service between Vancouver's downtown Sandman Inn, 180 West Georgia, and Seattle, either downtown or to Sea-Tac Airport.

VIA Rail Canada, #215, 1150 Station Street, offers service through the Rockies to Banff; call (604) 640-3741 or (800) 561-8630 in Canada and (800) 561-3949 in the United States. **BC Rail,** 1311 West First Street, North Vancouver, has trains to Whistler and the interior of the province; (604) 631-3500.

Vancouver is the major departure point for more than ten major cruise ship lines heading to Alaska.

By car, Vancouver is a three-and-one-half-hour trip from Seattle via I–5, which becomes Highway 99 at the U.S.-Canadian border. Highway 1, the TransCanada Highway, enters Vancouver from the east.

GETTING AROUND

B.C. Transit (604-521-0400) operates city buses, the SkyTrain light rapid transit system, which runs between downtown Vancouver and Surrey, about fifty minutes southeast, and the SeaBus, a 400-passenger commuter ferry between downtown and the foot of Lonsdale in North Vancouver—a scenic, twelve-minute ride across Burrard Inlet. Day passes are available. Transit literature, including a free *Discover Vancouver on Transit* guidebook, are available from the Vancouver Tourist Info Centre, public libraries, and BC Transit Lost Property at SkyTrain Stadium Station.

Most of major attractions are located in the city's heart, a peninsula surrounded by English Bay, First Narrows, and Burrard Inlet.

WHAT TO SEE AND DO

Museums and Historical Sites

Science World British Columbia, Quebec Street and Terminal Avenue at the Science World/Main Street Skytrain station; (604) 268-6363. Hands-on fun is the name of the game at this delightful place (formerly the Expo 86 Centre) where all ages find activities that are fun, fascinating—and, yes, educational. Walk inside a camera, or through a distorted room where nothing is exactly as it seems; talk through a tube that echoes back; have a close-up look at an ant farm; play with giant bubbles; compose a tune on an electric piano. The attractions include everything from eye-boggling "scientific show biz" demonstrations to The Bubble Show. In the Search Gallery, younger visitors explore by crawling through a beaver lodge or walking inside a hollow tree. Check the weekend and holiday special events, as well as the OMNIMAX theater schedule; call (604) 875-OMNI for show schedules. For snacks, try the Bytes Cafeteria.

The Vancouver Museum (604-736-4431) is on the main level at 1100 Chestnut Street (in Vanier Park), a building that also houses the **H.R. MacMillan Planetarium** (604-738-7827) on the top floor. The planetarium's programs include astronomy shows, laser/rock concerts, and family and children's matinees. At the **Gordon Southam Observatory,** next to the main building, visitors are welcome to gaze

Vancouver at a Glance

- Temperate climate, majestic scenery, and friendly people

- UBC Museum of Anthropology, Vancouver's most spectacular museum

- Spring, row, climb, and throw in the Participation Gallery at the B.C. Sports Hall of Fame

- Kids Only Market—200 shops, services, and play areas just for families

- Walk the Capilano Suspension Bridge, the longest and highest in the world

- Vancouver Touristinfo Centre, (604) 683-2000

through a telescope to view far-off wonders on clear days. Admission is free, but call first to see if it's open: (604) 738-2855.

After the planetarium, head downstairs to the Vancouver Museum, the largest civic museum in Canada, which houses thousands of impressive artifacts from Greater Vancouver and around the world. Kids enjoy the eclectic objects, which run the gamut from a dugout canoe to a collection of vintage police badges to elegant European evening dresses. The museum also houses crafts, carved sculptures, masks, and other ceremonial objects from the First Nations people of the Pacific Northwest Coast.

Ask about the frequent children's programs, which involve creative ways to appreciate the museum's displays; preregistration is often required. Special temporary exhibits are always on view.

Vancouver Maritime Museum, 1905 Ogden Avenue; (604) 257-8300. Just west of the Vancouver Museum, this museum brings to life the maritime heritage of this thriving port city, as well as the history of the British Columbia coast. At the entrance to the museum, the huge Kwakiutl totem pole out front sets the tone. Inside the majority of the exhibits are temporary, frequently incorporating hands-on activities. The model ship displays are particularly intriguing to kids. Admission includes a guided tour of the Royal Canadian Mounted Police Arctic schooner *t. Roch,* one of the first vessels to transit and circumnavigate the Northwest Passage. The harbor behind the museum also includes a floating display of privately owned historical and modern vessels.

Considered Vancouver's most spectacular museum, the **UBC Museum of Anthropology** (MOA), 6393 Northwest Marine Drive, on the campus of the University of British Columbia (604-822-3825 —recording), is worth a stop. Some label it one of the finest small museums anywhere. Devoted to collections from cultures around the world, this museum is particularly acclaimed for both its holdings from the First Nations of British Columbia and its setting. Located in an award-winning glass-and-concrete building on the Point Grey Cliffs, the museum is surrounded by Haida houses that overlook the mountains and the ocean. Although this is not a hands-on place, the museum has several "touchables," including the *Bear* sculpture in the hallway at the base of the ramp and the hanging drums (kentongans) in the Research Collection. Don't miss the contemporary Northwest Coast sculpture *The Raven and the First Men;* carved from a huge block of laminated yellow cedar, it portrays the moment in a Haida story when a raven discovers the first Haidas emerging from a clamshell. Programs include Sunday afternoon concerts and storytellers for both adults and children.

Later, consider a relaxing stroll in **UBC Botanical Gardens,** 6804 Southwest Marine Drive; (604) 822-3928. This pleasant retreat includes a Physick Garden, with medicinal plants used throughout history; a shaded Arbor Garden, particularly inviting in summer (though its vines thrive year-round); and an Asian Garden, with exotic kiwi fruit vines.

The **Vancouver Art Gallery,** City Centre at Hornby Street and Robson Square (604-682-5621—recorded information), is located in the heart of downtown, inside a renovated landmark, nineteenth-century building. Regularly changing exhibits are displayed in an attractive fashion. There's also a permanent display of what's considered the most important collection of works by Emily Carr, one of Canada's greatest artists. Ask about the regularly scheduled family workshops. The Gallery Cafe is open daily.

See where sports began at the **B.C. Sports Hall of Fame and Museum,** B.C. Place Stadium, 777 Pacific Boulevard South; (604) 687-5520. The Participation Gallery encourages visitors to spring, row, climb, and throw. The museum is open Wednesday through Sunday, 10:00 A.M. to 5:00 P.M.

Special Tours

In Vancouver you must get out on the water. Take a narrated tour of Vancouver harbor aboard the paddlewheeler M.P.V. *Constitution,* which departs twice daily from the north end of Denman Street. If you have time, we recommend the boat-train day trip, which features a cruise up the spectacular fjord of Howe South to the logging port of Squamish aboard the motor vessel *Britannia,* followed by a return on the *Royal Hudson* steam train, with 1940s vintage coaches. Bunker C. Bear, the train's mascot, makes frequent appearances to the delight of the kids. Call 1st Tours, a division of Harbour Ferries, for information and reservations; (604) 688-7246 or (800) 663-1500—United States. Or, opt to take the *Royal Hudson* to and from Squamish. Trains leave Wednesdays through Sundays and holiday Mondays from early June to late September.

Parks, Gardens, and Beaches

Stanley Park, at the northwest end of Georgia Street and within walking distance of the downtown core, is a terrific place for family fun, with tennis courts, lawn-bowling greens, a jogging oval, three restaurants, snack bars, a miniature golf course, beaches, and more. The thousand-acre park (800 acres of coniferous forest and the rest developed for recreation) sits on a peninsula with a 5½-mile seawall, or pathway, perfect for strolling or bicycling. Rent bikes from Stanley Park Rentals, 1798 West Georgia (604-681-5581), near the park entrance. Horse-drawn tram tours are available. Website: http://www.worldtel.com/vancouver/stanley.html

More impressive: the **Vancouver Public Aquarium** (604-682-1118), with more than 8,000 deep-sea denizens, including beluga whales, sea otters, killer whales, and reef sharks. The aquarium features a walk-through Amazon rain forest, complete with tropical birds, lush vegetation, and piranhas. A five-minute walk northwest of the aquarium leads to the miniature steam train. Website: http://www.vanaqua.org

Part of Stanley Park, **Prospect Point** is at the northern end of the peninsula, at about the halfway point of the seawall. West is the English Bay side, where several sandy family beaches can be found along **Beach Avenue. Second Beach,** west of Lost Lagoon, has a large saltwater children's pool with lifeguards, concession stands, and washrooms.

In all, the city has 11 miles of beaches, but the water is generally brisk, so be prepared. **Kitsilano Beach,** not part of Stanley Park, is over the Burrard Bridge, west of the Vancouver Museum/Planetarium. This is the liveliest beach in town, with concession stands, an adjacent park with a playground, and a busy public swimming pool.

Queen Elizabeth Park, Thirty-third Avenue and Cambie, is home to the **Bloedel Floral Conservatory;** (604) 872-5513. Under its huge glass geodesic dome (which offers a sweeping view of the city and its surroundings) bloom some 500 varieties of tropical and subtropical plants from around the world. Tropical birds fly overhead, and Japanese koi swim in pools—a tranquil, delightful place any time of year. Elsewhere in the park, enjoy tennis courts, lawn bowling, pitch and putt golf, and grassy picnic spots.

The first authentic Chinese garden to be built outside of China is the **Dr. Sun Yat-Sen Classical Chinese Garden,** 578 Carrall Street; (604) 662-3207.

Other Attractions

Take your kids and walk over the **Capilano Suspension Bridge,** part of the CSB&P Park, 3735 Capilano Road, North Vancouver; (604) 985-7474. This gently swaying suspension bridge—the longest and highest in the world—spans 450 feet across and 230 feet above the Capilano River. On the west side, a nature park provides trails through a lush forest where a waterfall flows to the river below.

CN IMAX Theatre, #201-999 Canada Place, on the waterfront at Canada Place, the cruise ship terminal; (604) 682-2384. Canada's only IMAX 3-D theater is open daily from noon to 11:00 P.M. Check the schedule of films projected on a giant screen five stories high.

At **Grouse Mountain,** 6400 Nancy Greene Way, North Vancouver (604-984-0661), take a scenic ride up an aerial tramway to 3,700 feet. Besides the scenic vistas, enjoy a multimedia Theatre in the Sky that features hourly shows on how Vancouver evolved from a frontier out-

Heli-hiking above Howe Sound near Vancouver is an experience like no other.
(Courtesy Vancouver Ministry of Tourism)

post into a thriving city (admission included with Skyride). Horse-drawn carriage rides are available, and there's a children's adventure playground. From the end of November to end of March, Grouse Mountain is a downhill ski area.

Lookout! at Harbour Centre, 555 West Hastings Street (604–689–0421), offers a glass elevator that ascends 550 feet for a sweeping panorama of the city, mountains, and ocean. A twelve-minute multi-image presentation, "Once in a World, Vancouver," displays historical settings and describes the city. A coffee bar serves light snacks. When you come down to earth, browse through the Harbour Mall's specialty shops, or grab a bite at one of its numerous eateries.

Maplewood Farm, 405 Seymour River Place, North Vancouver; (604) 929–5610. This municipal park has domestic farm animals to feed; a petting zoo with rabbits, guinea pigs, and ponies; milking demonstrations daily at 1:15 P.M.; and special events, such as a May Sheep Fair. It's open daily year-round, except Monday.

Playland Family Fun Park, Hastings at Cassian; (604) 255–5161. The park keeps big and little kids happy with more than forty rides and attractions (including the largest wooden roller coaster in Canada), a petting zoo, two live rock 'n' roll revues, and more. It's open spring through Labor Day.

Parents and kids alike can clown around at **Bonkers—The Great Canadian Indoor Playground,** 1620-1185 West Georgia Street; (604) 669-9230. The **Pacific Space Centre,** 100 Chestnut Street (604-738-7827), offers an interactive journey through space and time. Check out the working model of the Space Arm and satellite images of Earth. The **Seymour Demonstration Forest** is touted as one of the best-kept secrets on Vancouver's North Shore, designed to educate visitors on the delicate relationship between logging and forest management. Pack a lunch and hit the 13.7-mile round-trip route to the massive Seymour Dam. Worth checking out along the way are the fish hatchery and Forest Ecology Loop Trail around Rice Lake.

Theater, Music, and the Arts

Check the *Vancouver Sun*'s entertainment section and Thursday "What's On" column for current happenings, or call the Arts Hotline at (604) 684-ARTS. The *Georgia Strait* weekly newspaper also carries club and concert listings.

Ticketmaster (604-280-4444) has tickets to all major events, including those at the **Vancouver Civic Theatres,** 649 Cambie Street. This downtown complex features three major theaters: **Queen Elizabeth, Orpheum,** and **Vancouver Playhouse**) where performances include Broadway shows, Ballet British Columbia, Vancouver Opera, and the Vancouver Symphony Orchestra. Every Sunday from September to June, the **Festival Concert Society** (604-736-3737) presents Sunday Coffee Concerts from 11:00 A.M. to noon at the **Vancouver Playhouse.** Performances range from classical music to ballet to modern dance and jazz. Free in-theater babysitting is available for children (all ages).

From mid-July to mid-August, take your family to the Broadway-style musical at the Malkin Bowl in Stanley Park. Call TicketMaster for information.

Saturday Afternoon Live, a kids' series, is presented at Vancouver East Cultural Center, 1895 Venables Street at Victoria (604-254-9578), from late fall to early spring.

Sports

See **B.C. Lions** football (604-669-2300) a B.C. Place Stadium, 777 Pacific Boulevard, June through November. **Vancouver Canadians,** the top farm team of the Chicago White Sox, go to bat at Nat Bailey Stadium, 4601 Ontario Street; (604) 872-5232. The top-ranked **Vancouver Canucks** NHL hockey team plays at General Motors Place, 800 Griffiths Way (604-899-7400), from autumn through spring. The **Vancouver Grizzlies,** the area's NBA team, play there as well. For tickets, call (604) 280-4444. **Vancouver 86ers** soccer kicks off from mid-May to September at Swanguard Stadium in Central Park, Kingsway and Boundary, Burnaby. For game information, call (604) 299-0086.

Shopping

Vancouver's underground network of malls makes shopping fun and easy, even when the weather isn't cooperating. **Pacific Centre Mall** (604-688-7236), with some 200 stores, is the largest. The three-level complex spans 3 city blocks connecting two major department stores, Eaton's and The Bay, at opposite corners of Georgia and Granville streets. The city's liveliest thoroughfare, **Robson Street,** which stretches from Burrard to Bute streets, is full of small, trendy shops and cafes.

For something different, head to the **Lonsdale Quay Market,** 123 Carrie Cates Court, North Vancouver (604-985-2191), an indoor, waterfront public market next to the North SeaBus terminal. Fresh fruits and vegetables are sold on the first level. The second level is filled with shops, boutiques, and Kids Alley—several stores catering to kids, featuring clothing, games, and toys. There's an unsupervised "ball room" where kids can play while parents shop. The Lonsdale Quay Hotel (604-986-6111) is on the third level.

Be sure to spend some time browsing **Granville Island,** 1496 Cartwright Street (604-666-5784), located between the Granville and Burrard bridges. It's a rejuvenated industrial island turned recreation center, with art galleries, bookstores, theaters, a houseboat community, loads of take-out food and restaurants, and **Kids Only Market** (604-689-8447)—a two-floor complex housing 200 specialty shops, services, and play areas just for families. This large and airy market often features storytellers, musicians, face painters, and crafts workshops. There's a crawl wall for kids and strollers and bike rentals, too, for touring the scenic waterfront. Nearby, at 1328 Cartwright, is a small water park open from June to August (604-689-8447) that offers fun for young ones, with wading pool and sprinklers. The island is accessible by taxi (parking is very limited), bus (about a twenty-minute trip from downtown, involving one transfer), or by Granville Island Ferry (604-684-7781), which is the most fun. The ferry leaves from a dock behind the Vancouver Aquatic Center and makes the short trip across False Creek to the Granville Island Public Market, a mostly enclosed area with everything from summer produce to quick snacks. Kitty-corner to the market is an Information Centre, 1592 Johnson Street (604-666-5784), where you can pick up maps and view a slide show detailing the island's history. If the weather is warm and you have the time, you might want to rent a kayak (children allowed with an experienced adult) from Ecomarine Ocean Kayak Center, 1668 Duranleau Street; (604) 689-7575.

SPECIAL EVENTS

For more details on the following, contact the Vancouver Tourist Info Center; (604) 683-2000.

May: Vancouver International Children's Festival, Vanier Park, with theater, dance, music, and storytelling; Cloverdale Rodeo, Cloverdale (one hour east), one of North America's biggest.

July: Gastown Grand Prix Bicycle Race; Vancouver Sea Festival, English Bay, ten days of festivities featuring a parade, fireworks, salmon barbecues, and boat races.

Late July–early August: Vancouver Chamber Music Festival features six nights of performances by young, internationally acclaimed musicians; Vancouver International Comedy Festival, Granville Island, includes ten days of informal, daytime performances and ticketed evening shows that include everything from standup to mime to puppeteers; Powell Street Festival, celebrating Japanese culture.

August: International Air Show, Abbotsford Airport.

September: Vancouver Fringe Festival brings some hundred Canadian and international performance troupes for eleven days of drama, comedy, dance music, and clowning in ten theaters.

October–April: Vancouver's Entertainment Season, focusing on sports and cultural events. For information, visit http://www.van-entertainment.com.

December: Christmas Carol Ship Parade, Vancouver Harbour.

WHERE TO STAY

Tourism Vancouver has a helpful accommodations directory, which includes maps. Call Discover British Columbia at (800) 663-6000 for bed-and-breakfast, lodging, and travel information.

Here are some other "best bets" for families.

On the luxury end, **Westin Bayshore,** 1601 West George Street (604-682-3377 or 800-228-3000), couldn't be at a nicer location for families—right at the entrance to Stanley Park. With the ocean and mountains in the background, it has a resort feel, yet downtown is just a short walk away. No doubt, kids will be thrilled by the circular, outdoor pool. It also offers the new Westin Kids Club amenities. These include child-friendly rooms, children's sports bottle or tippy cup upon check-in, as well as a safety kit with a night-light, Band-Aids, and emergency phone numbers. Rooms feature bath toys and bath products for kids, and parents can request—at no charge—jogging strollers, potty seats, bicycle seats, and step stools. Restaurants and room service also feature children's menus. **The Four Seasons,** 791 West Georgia Street (604-689-9333 or 800-332-3442), features large rooms, a heated pool, and free cribs. Ask about their special weekend rates, which makes this first-class hotel much more affordable. Downtown a good choice is the **Hyatt Regency,** 655 Burrard Street; (604) 683-1234 or (800) 233-1234. It offers the Hyatt family-friendly features of children's menus, including room service. The Regency Club floor rooms, while pricier, include breakfast and snacks that might very well prove time and cost effective for your clan. Ask about their babysitting services.

The more moderately priced **Riviera Motor Inn,** 1431 Robson Street (604-686-1301), is an apartment hotel with forty studio and one-bed-room units, each with fully equipped kitchens and large, cheerful bedrooms. Great location, too—and most of the rooms have views of the North Shore mountains.

Bosman's Motor Hotel, 1060 Howe Street (604-682-3171 or 800-663-1333), offers a convenient location just on the edge of downtown. They have a hundred modern, quiet rooms, a pool, and—a rare commodity in these parts—free parking.

About 8 miles south of Vancouver, in Richmond, the **Delta Pacific Resort and Conference Center,** 10251 St. Edwards Drive (604-278-9611), features several pools, a playground, and a supervised children's center. Here for two-hour stretches (no longer at one time, but you can take your child out and then bring him or her back later) children ages three through eight can enjoy crafts and games. The center is open from 9:00 A.M. to 8:00 P.M. This center is convenient if you want a quiet adult dinner or some pool time by yourself, but this is not day-long children's program.

WHERE TO EAT

The *Vancouver Book* offers a comprehensive listing of restaurants. Try the local seafood: oysters, clams, mussels, crab, and Pacific salmon. If your kids aren't into fish, there are lots of other food that reflects Vancouver's ethnic diversity.

Gastown, the charming, cobblestoned area that surrounds Maple Tree Square—the city's original core—at the end of Water Street, is a fun place to stroll and shop. **The Old Spaghetti Factory,** 53 Water Street (604-879-9000), is crammed with antiques and kid-pleasing decorations. They offer generous portions of pasta, veal, chicken, or steak in the ambience of a 1910 streetcar.

A block away from Gastown, **Chinatown**—second largest on the continent (only San Francisco's is larger)—has a wide variety of eateries, which serve primarily Cantonese cuisine. Try the **Fish Pond,** 122 Powell Street (604-683-9196), which has vintage Chinatown artifacts and features a fascinating fish pond. Lunch is served Monday through Friday; dinner is served daily.

And for good old burgers, stop by **White Spot** hamburgers, a city tradition since 1928. Their two downtown eateries are at 1012 Robson Street (604-681-4180) and 580 West Georgia Street (604-662-3066).

DAY TRIPS

There are a number of interesting day trips from Vancouver, including Victoria.

Step back in time at **Fort Langley National Historic Park** (604-888-4424), at the corner of Mavis and Royal streets in the historic town of Fort Langley, 25 miles east of Vancouver. Inside the restored fort, established in 1827 as a Hudson Bay Company fur trading post and later a provisioning point for the 1858 gold rush, costumed interpreters practice barrel making and blacksmithing, trade beaver pelts, and present talks. During the summer, daily programs include nineteenth-century cooking and demonstrations by artisans. Across the street, at the **Langley Centennial Museum and National Exhibition Centre** (604-888-3922), exhibits include wood carvings, stone sculptures, and basketry, as well as the Coast Salish Indians' hunting, fishing, and war implements. Other exhibits highlight the life of early settlers and include a homesteader's kitchen, a Victorian parlor, and an early general store. A short ride southeast on Highway 1 leads to the **Vancouver Game Farm,** 5048 264 Street, Aldergrove (604-856-6825), where young ones see some one hundred wildlife species and enjoy a miniature train ride, play park, and picnic area.

Take another historical journey to **Burnaby Village Museum,** 6501 Deer Lake Avenue, Burnaby, twenty minutes east of downtown Vancouver; (604) 293-6500 or 6501. Costumed blacksmiths, pharmacists, and other townsfolk make this village of pioneer life between 1890 and 1925 come alive.

Whistler/Blackcomb, rated the number one ski resort in North America, is 75 miles north of Vancouver via the scenic Sea to Sky Highway. The twin summits offer some 200 trails and the highest lift-serviced verticals in North America. (Be forewarned: Whistler is also acquiring the reputation of being expensive.) Central reservations can tell you about special seasonal hotel and golf packages; (604) 932-4222, 685-3650 in British Columbia, or (800) WHISTLER.

Kids' Camp at Blackcomb includes a Child Minding program for ages eighteen months to three years; a Wee Wizards skiing fundamentals for ages two and three; and various ski programs for ages four to thirteen. Kids Night Out for ages six and older includes dinner and entertainment. Whistler's Ski Scamps ski schools offer fundamentals for ages two to four and five to twelve as well as the more advanced Mountain Scamps classes. Club Free, for skiers or snowboarders ages twelve to sixteen, offers teens challenges and fun with peers.

In summer, when prices are considerably more affordable, there's lots to do, including swimming at one of five nearby lakes and traveling to the top of Whistler Mountain via a fully enclosed express gondola, or to Blackcomb's summit via express chairs. (Both accommodate mountain bikes; rentals are available at various locations, including Whistler Village.) Summer glacier skiing is offered on Blackcomb from mid-June to August.

If there's a tennis hopeful in your bunch, try **The Chateau Whistler Resort,** 4599 Chateau Boulevard; (604) 938-2044, (800) 268-9411—Canada, or (800) 828-7447—United States. They offer a summer Tennis Tigers program for kids ages five to twelve, ranging from half-day to weekend and week-long camps for ages seven to twelve, with morning tennis and afternoon hiking, in-line skating, and swimming. Two- and three-day Adventure Camps for adults are also open to teens. Twice weekly Kids' Night Out for five years and older includes dinner and entertainment from 5:30 P.M. to 8:00 P.M. The Canadian Pacific resort, at the base of Blackcomb Mountain, also boasts indoor/outdoor pools and hot tubs, golf, and two restaurants.

FOR MORE INFORMATION

The Vancouver Touristinfo Centre, Waterfront Centre, Plaza Level, 200 Burrard Street (604-683-2000), provides tourist information and literature. The **Downtown Vancouver Business Improvement Association** operates a kiosk at the corner of Georgia and Granville. Wheelchair travelers can obtain information about serves from **Canadian Paraplegic Association,** 780 Southwest Marine Drive, Vancouver; (604) 324-3611. Website: http://www.tourism-vancouver.org

Emergency numbers
Ambulance, fire, police: 911
Twenty-four-hour emergency care: St. Paul's Hospital, 1081 Burrard Street (604-682-2344), is a major downtown hospital. Also: **Children's Hospital,** 4480 Oak Street; (604) 875-2345.

There are no twenty-four-hour pharmacies in Vancouver. **Shopper's Drug Mart,** 1125 Davie Street, is open until midnight every night except Sunday and holidays, when it closes at 9:00 P.M.; (604) 865-5752.

Poison Control: (604) 682-5050 or 682-2344

THE BIG ISLAND

No tour of Hawaii is complete without a visit to the island of Hawaii, known also as the Big Island. This is the largest of Hawaii's islands, with 4,038 square miles. This is the Hawaii of legendary volcanoes and landscapes of lava-striped earth, complete with the active volcano Kilauea, which still shoots red-hot lava, steaming into the Pacific or oozing over a roadside. And on this island you'll also enjoy good snorkeling, lush gardens, and languid waterfalls.

GETTING THERE

Hilo International Airport (808-934-5801), on the eastern side of the island, is the largest airport. Rental cars and taxis are available. The **Keahole Airport** (808-329-2484) services Kona on the west coast with interisland carriers, and local flights. The **Waimea-Kohala Airport,** Kamuela (808-885-4520), is a small airport offering service to the Waimea area in the north.

GETTING AROUND

If you want to do much sight-seeing, rent a car. If you want to rent a car in Hilo, and then drop it off in Kona, ask ahead of time about the dropoff charges. Rental car companies available at the Hilo Airport include **Alamo Rent-A-Car** (808-961 or 800-327-9633), **Avis** (808-935-1290 or 800-331-1212), **Dollar** (808-935-1497), **Hertz** (808-935-2896), and **National Car Rental** (808-935-0891 or 800-227-3876). Most of the same companies are represented in Kona; **Avis** (808-327-3000 or 800-331-1212), **Dollar** (808-329-2744 or 800- 800-4000), **Hertz** (808-329-3566 or 800-654-3131), and **National Car Rental** (808-329-1675 or 800-227-7368).

The **Mass Transportation System** (MTS), 25 Aupuni Street, Hilo (808-935-8241), operates the **Hele-On Bus.** Taxi service is available in Hilo through **Hilo Harry's** (808-935-7091) and **Bob's Taxi** (808-959-4800). In Kona, call **Paradise Taxi** (808-329-1234) or **Marina Taxi** (808-329-2481).

Bicycles offer a chance to travel at a more leisurely pace, but the roads are rough and sometimes dangerous. Families with teens who are skilled cyclists may want to rent bikes.

WHAT TO SEE AND DO

The Eastern Side: Hawaii Volcanoes National Park

If you only have one day on the eastern side of the island (cruise ships dock in Hilo just for the day), head straight to **Hawaii Volcanoes National Park,** about 30 miles (forty-five minutes) southwest of Hilo. (Follow Route 11 south and the signs that say TO VOLCANO.)

At the **Hawaii Volcanoes National Park Visitor Center,** P.O. Box 52 (808-967-7311), watch a twelve-minute volcano film and pick up the *Road Guide To Hawaii Volcanoes National Park,* an indispensable book with clear explanations and mile markers that make a self-driven tour easy and informative. There are two places to eat nearby. If hungry, walk across the street to **Volcano House,** Box 53, Hawaii Volcanoes National Park, perched at the edge of the Kilauea Crater; (808) 967-7321 or (800) 325-3535. A buffet lunch is served from 11:30 to 1:30, and dinner is from 5:30 to 8:00 P.M. Be careful: Tourists arrive by the busload—mostly for lunch—and the place is often crowded. A snack bar also serves a small selection of sandwiches, cookies, and fruit salad.

An alternative is to have breakfast, or lunch on pastas and good burgers, at the **Volcano Golf and Country Club.** Two miles south of the park entrance, take the turnoff near the Kilauea Military Camp; (808) 967-7331.

To explore **Hawaii Volcanoes National Park,** wear good sneakers or hiking boots because you'll want to wander along the numerous trails, many of which are short and easily negotiated by small children. Dress in layers, as the weather is changeable, and bring along some rain gear. In addition to the 150 miles of hiking trails, there are also several scenic driving routes.

Hawaii at a Glance

- An unforgettable vacationland, with lush gardens, lanquid waterfalls, and other delights

- Hawaii Volcanoes National Park: pure drama

- Ancient Hawaiian history amidst the giant carved idols and temple ruins at Pu'uhonua o Honaunau

- Hawaiian cowboy life at Parker Ranch

- Hawaii Visitors Bureau, (808) 961-5797

Tour **Crater Rim Drive,** which makes an 11-mile circuit around Kilauea caldera, taking you through steaming **sulphur banks,** a rain forest of ohio trees, and roadsides full of ferns, to scenic stops at the **Kilauea Iki Crater,** a crusted lava lake 3,000 feet wide, where steam vents form clouds. Other highlights: **the Thurston Lava Tube and Devastation Trail.** At the lava tube, visitors walk through the .3-mile tunnel of a cooled down lava flow. Along **Devastation Trail,** a .4-mile boardwalk through the swath of 1959 lava destruction that felled an ohio tree forest, the contrast of the white gray limbs against the blackish brown ground gives kids a sense of volcanic force.

At the **Keanakako'i Crater,** a great pit, the fissures in the ground and the black lava fingers that flowed into rifts impart an eerie sense of drama. Steam vents dot the road from here to the **Halemaumau Crater,** where sulfur escapes into the air. (Those with asthma or respiratory problems should roll up their windows and drive by. Don't stop.) Hawaiians say that Halemaumau is the home of Pele, the goddess of volcanoes.

Visit the **Thomas A. Jaggar Museum,** adjacent to the Hawaiian Volcanoes Observatory; (808) 967-7643. Kids love the clever exhibits of seismographs and scientific explanations for volcanic eruptions that are coupled with dioramas of the Hawaiian legends of Pele. This is a true natural history museum, featuring historical documentaries of volcanic eruptions and self-guided tours.

The **Chain of Craters** road takes you 25 miles past more rift zones and crater overlooks. Check with the visitors center or one of the park rangers to see if you may drive right up to some of Kilauea's most recent lava flows.

Hilo

Hilo, the capital, curls around the harbor on the island's east side. The city, with its frequent "liquid sunshine" is a fishing and flower center. Start early by catching the outdoor fish auction with its pungent smells at the **Suisan Fish Market,** Lihiwai Street at the Wailoa River (daily except Sunday).

Gardens and Green Spaces. The frequent rain and sun keeps Hilo lush; it's home to several flower nurseries and gardens. The colorful **Liliuokalani Gardens,** Lihawai Street and Banyan Drive, exhibit Hilo's Japanese influence, with arched bridges and pagodas adorning its thirty acres. With picnic tables and rest rooms, this is a good run-off-some-energy stop. For more flowers stop by **Orchids of Hawaii,** 2801 Kilauea Street (808-959-3581); and **Hilo Tropical Gardens,** 1477 Kalanianaole Avenue (808-935-4957).

For more extensive gardens, tour **Hawaii Tropical Botanical Gardens,** a nature preserve and sanctuary at Onomea Bay, about 7 miles north of Hilo, RR 143-A, Papaikou 96781; (808) 964-5233. Wear pants and long sleeves, carry an umbrella or bring a rain slicker, and use bug spray—but all this is worth it if you like gardens. From Highway 19 north take a right turn where the sign says SCENIC ROUTE 4 MILES LONG. Continue for about 1 mile to the Old Yellow Church, which marks the garden's parking area. Purchase tickets here, grab a trail map for a self-guided tour, and board the van that takes you the a short distance to the gardens. (If you've forgotten your bug spray or your umbrella, these are available for your tour at the small shelter near the van pick-up and drop-off point.)

Go slowly to savor these forty-five acres, which currently include twenty acres of gardens with more than 1,800 species of plants. Allow at least an hour or more. The trail winds you past such niceties as Turtle Point, where the sea spray shoots in the air, and sometimes you see turtles; Lily Lake, filled with koi; Cook Pine Trail, which ends in an amazingly tall tree; and bird aviaries where Hama and Kua, two blue-and-yellow macaws sometimes say "hello" after some coaxing. (Don't feed them.) Other trails take you by bunches of palm trees, a waterfall, orchids, brightly colored ginger plants, cascades of heliconias, and much more. Kids need to walk here as some paths won't accommodate strollers, but most children will enjoy the peaceful, flowering scenery.

Visit **Rainbow Falls,** about 2 miles from Hilo's harbor in Wailuku River Park, for an easy look at this staple of Hawaiian legend. In the morning sun, the splashing waters create a colorful rainbow as it tumbles 125 feet. For another view, try the walkway behind the tumbling water.

Beaches. Locals recommend three beaches most often: **Coconut Island Park,** near the Liliuokalani Gardens, has shade, picnic tables, a view, and a natural shallow area good for kids. **Onekahakaha Beach Park,** off Machida Lane, has a beach, lifeguards, and an area protected by a breakwater. (Swim only within the breakwater, outside of it the waves and undertow are too rough for safety.) While not hard to get to, the directions sound complicated. Ask the locals for the specifics. **Richardson's Ocean Park,** 2349 Kalanianaole Avenue (808-935-3830), offers good snorkeling and swimming.

Mauna Kea

Mauna Kea, sometimes called the "White Mountain" because of its snow-topped summits, reaches a height of 13,796 feet. To get here the hearty take Route 200 northwest from Hilo, which is isolated, and rough in spots, but affords nice views. Route 200 cuts across the Big Island, intersecting Route 190 near Waimea.

Heading up here is advised *only* for those who have four-wheel-drive vehicles and are expert at mountain driving in bad weather. A typical rental car won't make the trek on this extremely rough and steep road with its frequent wind, rain, and even snow near the top. For those few who are confident and meet all the conditions for this journey, including breathing comfortably at 13,000 feet, the reward is the top-ranked **Mauna Kea Observatory Complex,** located at the mountain's peak. (Don't forget to bundle up, as it's cold at the summit.) On selected weekends from May to September, visitors who reserve well in advance can see, and take a peek through, the various world-class telescopes. Exciting as this sounds, remember that the trip up is demanding and not to be undertaken lightly. Always check ahead, and book in advance with the Observatory; call (808) 935-3371.

Hamakua Coast to Waimea and the Waipio Valley

The Hamakua Coast stretches northward for about 50 miles, from Hilo to Waipio. **Akaka Falls State Park,** Akaka Falls Road, Route 220 (808-933-4200), is about 13½ miles north of Hilo on Route 19, then 5 miles west on Akaha Falls Road. It offers hikes, some uphill, to pretty waterfalls. A circular forty-minute path through ferns, bamboo, and other greenery leads you to **Kahuna Falls,** which tumbles and crashes 100 feet below, and to **Akaka Falls,** which plunges even further to more than 400 feet.

Kolekole Beach Park, just a bit north of Honomu, is a popular spot for locals, but *don't* swim here as the ocean is dangerous and rough. Continue along Route 19 until it branches off to Highway 240. (If you continue west on Route 19 you'll reach Waimea.) Highway 240 ends at the **Waipio Valley,** a scenic swath of greenery with taro fields that stretch out below. Locals recommend you *do not* drive the steep road from here that leads to Waipio. Instead go with those who have been doing this for awhile. The **Waipio Valley Shuttle** (808-775-7121) can lead you in their stalwart vehicles through the Waipio Valley, or try a mule-drawn wagon tour with **Waipio Valley Wagon Tours,** P.O. Box 1340, Honokaa 96727; (808) 775-9518. Purchase tickets for these two-hour tours (bring your own food) at the company's ticket office in Kukuihaele.

Waimea (Kamuela)

To reach Waimea, sometimes called Kamuela to distinguish it from Kauai's Waimea, continue northwest from Akaka Falls on Route 19 to where it branches off to Highway 240 (also called 24). Continue west on Route 19 to Waimea. If you are arriving from the Saddle Road, Highway 200 near the Mauna Kea Recreation Area, continue on Highway 200 to Route 190 to Waimea.

In Waimea be sure to visit the **Parker Ranch,** one of the largest privately owned spreads in the U.S. with 225,000 acres. This ranch gives you a view of cowboy life Hawaiian style. First browse the **Parker Ranch Visitor Center and Museum,** Parker Ranch Shopping Center,

Routes 19 and 190, Waimea; (808) 885-7655. The **John Palmer Parker Museum** displays photographs and relates the history of the generations of the Parker family who made this land prosper.

You can also visit the **Historic Parker Ranch Homes** on Mamalahoa Highway, the site of the Parker family's 1800s ranch house and museumlike home. After touring the Parker Ranch area, stop at the **Lapakahi State Historical Park,** (808) 889-5566, a small fishing village settled some 600 years ago. Visitors can see how people lived, worked, worshipped, and played in those ancient times.

Special Tours

Swoop high above Kilauea's lava in a helicopter. Although expensive, a look into the mouth of a steaming volcano may be a once-in-a-lifetime perspective. Try **Kenai Helicopters—Kona,** P.O. Box 4118, Kailua-Kona; (808) 885-5833 or (800) 622-3144.

The Western Side: The Kailua-Kona Area

In **Kona** there's a small beach in town if your kids must swim and can't wait for a better, and perhaps, cleaner bit of sand and surf. **Kamakahonu Beach** is in front of the King Kamehameha Hotel adjacent to the Kailua Pier, where the water doesn't seem the clearest, but there are no waves.

The Kailua-Kona area on the west coast is the home of much impressive Hawaiian history. In Kailua, the **Hulihee Palace,** 75-5718 Alii Drive (808-329-1877), dates back to 1837. The palace features fine koa wood furnishings, Hawaiian quilts, and tapas.

Even more interesting for learning ancient Hawaiian history is **Pu'uhonua o Honaunau,** formerly called the City of Refuge National Historical Park, off Route 160 about 19 miles south of Kailua-Kona. This sanctuary, established in the fifteenth century, gave refuge to defeated warriors, women, and children in wartime, and to breakers of religious taboos seeking purification by priests. Wander among displays of giant carved idols, ruins of a temple, carved wooden images, historic campsites, and displays of koa wood canoes. Try your hand at an ancient game of *konane* (checkers). A simple peace pervades this 180-acre park, a pleasant place to spend an hour or so imagining the Hawaii of ancient kings and priests, and enjoying a picnic lunch.

Green Spaces, Beaches, and Marine Parks. For a respite, stroll the more than fourteen oceanfront acres of gardens at **Kona Surf Resort and Country Club,** 78-128 Ekukai Street; (808) 322-3411. Located about 6½ miles from Kailua-Kona along Alii Drive, the hotel welcomes drop-ins. **Keauhou Bay,** about a half-mile farther south, is the sailing point of the *Fair Winds,* 78-7128 Kaleiopapa Street; (808) 322-2788. (Purchase tickets at the small *Fair Winds* shop across the street from the harbor.)

During the one-hour sail to the snorkel spot at **Kealakekua Bay,** a Marine Life Conservation District, the guides fit you with snorkel gear and teach you how to snorkel. While child's sizes, including fins, masks, and flotation vests are on board, it's always a good idea to bring your own just to be sure. The snorkeling here during the day can be more relaxed as this area is not as crowded as Molikini off of Maui. The hard corals and the schools of brightly colored fish—including yellow tangs, surgeon fish, rainbow-hued parrot fish, and ornate butterfly fish—charm kids and adults. From the snorkel area you can see a monument to Captain James Cook, who was killed here in 1778 in a dispute with natives.

Hapuna Beach State Park, north of Kailua-Kona off Route 19 (808-933-4200), offers good snorkeling with schools of tropical fish, but *only* for excellent swimmers who can handle the frequent big waves. A favorite among Kona tourists is **Magic Sands Beach** (or Disappearing White Sands Beach), named after the winter storms that periodically wash away the sand and expose the rocky beach, only to deposit more sand later. The feisty surf may be intimidating for small children and new swimmers.

A short drive east of Kona is the 1,300-acre **Kaloko-Honokohau National Historical Park,** (808) 329-6881. The park contains more than 200 historical artifacts, including Hawaiian grave sites, fishing shrines, and petroglyphs.

Special Tours. The **Atlantis Submarine** plunges into the ocean off Kona. Young passengers should be at least 36 inches tall and unafraid of tight quarters. The reward: a diver's-eye view of coral and schools of fish without the work of diving. Reserve ahead at the Atlantis Submarine's desk at the King Kamehameha Kona Beach Hotel, Alii Drive; (808) 329-6626 or (800) 548-6262.

Try your hand at an ancient game of konane (checkers) at Pu'uhonua o Honaunau.
(Photo by the author)

Hawaii Forest and Trail (808-329-1993) offers eco-adventures on untouched private lands. The hikes in these remote areas range from easy to difficult, and focus on the surrounding environment and local history. **Hawaiian Walkways** (808-885-7759) also offers ecologically-focused day hikes, including packs and food. **Kenai Helicopters—Kona,** P.O. Box 4118, Kailua-Kona; (808) 885-5833 or (800) 622-3144 offers flight tours.

More Sports: Bicycling, Snorkeling, Golf. We suggest biking for experienced mountain bikers only—older teens and fit adults. Bike rental shops include **Chris' Bike Adventure** (808-326-4600), **Mauna Kea Mountain Bikes** (808-885-2091), and **Kona Bike Tours,** inside Hawaiian Pedals, on the boardwalk, Kona Inn Shopping Village, 75-5744 Alii Drive (808-329-2294). Ask about tours down the slopes of Mauna Kea (difficult), through a lush forest, or try a leisurely ride to Kona's historic and tourist spots with Kona Bike Tours.

Snorkel Bob's, near the Kona Hilton's parking lot (808-329-0770), offers snorkel gear and boogie boards, including a selection of prescription-lens masks that make it easy for those who normally wear glasses or contact lenses to see the fish clearly. **King Kamehameha Divers,** in the King Kamehameha Hotel (808-329-5662), offers dives for beginners as well as those who are certified, and some snorkel equipment.

Golf in Hawaii most always comes with a view. Among the courses on the Kona side: **Makalei Hawaii Country Club,** 72-3890 Hawaii Belt Road (Mamalahoa Highway); (808) 325-6625 or (800) 606-9606. Check the free island and rental car guides for discount coupons, sometimes for as much as 30 percent off greens fees. The **Keauhou-Kona Golf Course,** 78-7000 Alii Drive, Kailua-Kona (808-322-2595), is another good bet. Pricier, but with a spectacular view, is the course at **Mauna Kea Beach Golf Course,** One Mauna Kea Beach Drive, Golf Course, P.O. Box 218, Kamuela, 96743; (808) 882-5888 or (800) 882-6060. One hole tests your skill by having you hit over the Pacific. The **Waikoloa Hilton,** Waikoloa Beach Resort, offers good golfing as well; (808) 885-1234 or (800) 233-1234.

SPECIAL EVENTS

January: In Hilo, see the Hilo to Volcano 31-Mile Ultra Marathon, which takes place midmonth. Also, the Senior Skins Golf Tournament features golf legends.

February: Hilo Mardi Gras.

April: The Merrie Monarch Festival in Hilo features Hawaii's renowned hula competition, festivals, and a parade in celebration of Hawaii's last king, David Kalakaua. The Big Island Bounty Festival features Hawaiian cuisine.

May: Lei Day, the first of the month. Don't miss the Kailua-Kona Triathalon in Kona, which tests athletes with cycling, running, and swimming on a "path."

June: In Hilo, Kohala, and Kona, experience the festivals during the King Kamehameha Celebrations. A prime event for golfing fans is the Mauna Kea Beach Hotel's Pro Am Golf Tournament.

July: The International Festival of the Pacific, Hilo, celebrates the diverse ethnic groups inhabiting Hawaii. On the Fourth of July, see real Hawaiian cowboys strut their stuff at the Parker Ranch Rodeo and

Horse Races. Also on Independence Day, witness Turtle Independence Day, the Mauna Lani Bay Hotel and Resort, a day that sees turtles raised in captivity released into the ocean.

August: Hawaiian International Billfish Tournament, Kailua-Kona, the world's largest billfish tournament.

September: The Queen Liliuokalani World Championship Long Distance Canoe Racing Champs, in Kona, is one of the major canoe races in Hawaii with men's and women's teams from several countries.

September/October: Aloha Week Festivals take place throughout the Big Island, showcasing Hawaii's history with dance and community celebrations.

October: The Ironman World Triathalon Championship, in Kailua-Kona, tests athletes with a 2.4-mile Waikiki Rough Water Swim, a 112-mile Around-Oahu Bike Race, and a 26.2-mile marathon.

November: The Kona Coffee Festival in Kailua and Keauhou has tours of coffee plantations and ethnic foods.

December: Hawaii International Film Festival, Hilo, Kona, Volcano, and Waimea.

WHERE TO STAY

Hawaiian hotels have a reputation for being accommodating and costly. Not all lodging in Hawaii is expensive, but you may need to reserve up to a year in advance to reserve a place at some of the state parks, or many months in advance for prime weeks at some of the poshest places. Many establishments offer programs especially for children. As these programs differ, check with individual hotels for details.

Best Buys

Best Budget Lodging. At **Hapuna Beach State Park,** (808-329-3560) rustic cabins cost a nominal rate. No baths, but there is a comfort station on property. You must book these more than a year in advance. Call (808-974-6200). Volcanoes National Park has cabins at the **Namakani Paio Campground** (808-967-7321), about 3 miles up from Volcano House, that are equipped with beds and towels for four. Cabins share a bathhouse.

Camping. Volcanoes National Park has campgrounds. Obtain a brochure from **Park Headquarters,** Hawaii Volcanoes National Park (808-967-7311); or from the **National Park Service,** 300 Ala Moana Boulevard, Honolulu 96850 (808-541-2693). Remember that the supply of firewood in Hawaii is sparse, and fire building is dangerous; therefore, tote along a small stove.

Condominiums. Condos offer families welcome breathing space, the convenience of kitchens, and often more room for less money than hotels. Condos are a good buy and come with all the civilized amenities (though make sure that the unit you've rented has air conditioning; not all units in a building do). The **Aston Shores at Waikoloa,** on the Kohala Coast, Route 19, 26 miles north of Kailua-Kona (808-885-5001 or 800-92-ASTON), offers one- and two-bedroom condos, and may by the summer of 1994 offer a limited children's program. The deluxe resort condominium complex of **Kanaloa at Kona** overlooks Keahou Bay and offers one- and two-bedroom suites. Call (800) OUTRIGGER for reservations.

Resorts. **The Royal Waikoloan,** P.O. Box 5300 (808-885-6789 or 800-537-9800), with twenty cabanas and more than 500 rooms, is less pricey than its posh neighbors. The Royal Waikoloan, an older property, offers a beautiful wide beach on the Kohala Coast; family-friendly rooms, many with refrigerators, plus a limited program of children's activities, which could turn into a full-scale program by the summer of 1994. Ask about their special packages, often combined with stays at Outrigger Hotels on another island.

The Big Island offers many **Bed-and-Breakfast** homes. Most of the time these are less expensive than a stay at a comparable resort. Even when priced comparably, bed-and-breakfast inns offer families a personal, neighborly sense of Hawaii with accommodations in a community or on an estate. Not all bed and breakfasts welcome families. Check ahead, and be honest about your family's needs. Reservation services include **Bed & Breakfast Hawaii,** P.O. Box 449 Kapaa (808-822-7771 or 800-733-1632), which services all the Hawaiian Islands. For $12.95 you can order their directory, *Bed and Breakfast Goes Hawaiian,* a thick listing of inns on all the Hawaiian islands, plus tips on local restaurants.

Some family-friendly listings include "H-4C," a guest cottage on nine tropical acres, 4 miles south of Hilo's airport, and about thirty minutes to Volcanoes National Park. "H-43" offers two rooms in an eighty-nine-year-old house in Waimea. A two-bedroom apartment, "H-62," about fifteen minutes from Hapuna Beach, has views of Mauna Kea, and comes with a kitchen. H-38" offers two guest rooms in a large home overlooking Kealakekua Bay.

Hawaii's Best Bed and Breakfast, P.O. Box 563, Kamuela 96746 (808-885-4550 or 800-262-9912), specializes in upscale properties, some of which may be suites for families.

Resorts with Kids' Programs

The Mauna Kea Beach Hotel, One Mauna Kea Beach Drive, Kamuela, 96743; (808-882-7222 or 800-882-6060). Located on one of the area's most beautiful beaches, the hotel also has a world-class art collection. Jewel-colored parrots chatter in the lobby, and museum-quality art—from seventh-century Buddhas to Japanese screens—graces garden walkways. The resort offers a comprehensive, free kids' program for six- to twelve-year-olds that runs summer, Christmas, and Easter from 8:30 A.M. to 4:30 P.M. (with lunch), and again from about 6:00 P.M. to 9:00 P.M. for dinner and movies.

Kona Village Resort, 13 miles north of Kailua-Kona on Route 19, P.O. Box 1299, Kailua-Kona 96745; (808) 325-5555 or (800) 367-5290. This resort creates a Hawaiian village feel by having guests stay in thatched (but plush) *hales* (cottages). This resort has a free, year-round children's program for ages six to twelve from approximately 8:00 A.M. to 5:30 P.M. Early dinner for children at 5:30 P.M. is followed by games and movies. Programs for kids five and under, as well as teenagers, are also available.

The posh **Hilton Waikoloa Village,** 17 miles north of the Kona Airport (808-885-1234 or 800-233-1234), proffers a Hawaiian "fantasy experience" with its great pool (lots of slides) and dolphin education program. Camp Menehune operates daily, all year long, for five to twelve year olds, from 9:00 A.M. to 4:00 P.M. and from 6:00 P.M. to 10:00 P.M. (fee). For teens thirteen to seventeen, there's the Coconut Club. Chill out in the lounge ($10 cover charge) to listen to favorite music and play air hockey or ping pong, or join in complimentary sports activities. Excursions to nearby attractions are also available.

Treat yourself to the top-rated **Mauna Lani Bay Hotel and Bunga-**

lows, One Mauna Lani Drive, 25 miles north of Kailua-Kona; (808) 885-6622, (800) 367-2323, or (800) 992-7987 in Hawaii. It offers a complimentary Camp Mauna Lani Bay for ages five to twelve during summer, Christmas, and Easter from about 9:00 A.M. to 3:00 P.M., and 5:00 to 11:00 P.M. Included are Hawaiian arts and crafts, pole fishing, and water sports.

The new **Four Seasons Resort Hualalai,** P.O. Box 269, Kailua-Kona 96745 (808-325-8000 or 800-332-3442), is on the Kona Coast, overlooking the sea and the mountain for which it is named. Huge Polynesian-style rooms are spread out in bungalows amid swimming pools and fish ponds. Kids For All Seasons is available daily, free of charge, from 9:00 A.M. to 5:00 P.M., for children ages five to twelve; there is a fee for lunch. Activities emphasize Hawaii, sea life, arts-and-crafts, and outdoor fun. The Sheraton's **Orchid at Mauna Lani,** 1 North Kaniku Drive, Kohala Coast 96743 (800-885-2000), about an hour north of Kona, offers 539 rooms in a setting very much in tune with the environment. A 10,000-square-foot lagoon winds among palm trees and lava rocks, while waterfalls, rocky cliffs, and fish ponds complete the lush surroundings. Kids ages five to twelve can explore the tide pools, learn Hawaiian games and songs, feed turtles, and more at the Keiki Aloha children's program. The Teen Adventure Program offers a variety of watersports and eco-adventures.

WHERE TO EAT

Family dining can be inexpensive in Hawaii if you choose wisely, and follow the locals.

In the Hilo Area

For pizza, head for the **Cafe Pesto,** on the east coast of the island at South Hata Boulevard, Hilo; (808) 969-6640. The moderately priced **Pescatore Italian Restaurant,** 235 Keawe Street, Hilo (808-969-9090), has a good marinated tuna, as well as other entrees. The **Queen's Court,** in the Hilo Hawaiian Hotel, 71 Banyan Drive (808-935-9361), is noted for its Friday night seafood buffet. For breakfast, try **Ken's House of Pancakes,** 1730 Kamehameha Avenue (808-935-8711); or **Don's Family Deli,** 485 Hinano Street (808-935-9099), offers ribs, chicken, homemade chili, and fish for reasonable prices.

On the West Side of the Big Island

On the west side of the island, near Kona and Kealakekua, restaurants of choice include the **Ocean View Inn,** in the heart of Kailua on Alii Drive (808-329-9998), with a variety of culinary choices.

At the **Kona Ranch House,** Kuakini and Palani highways (808-329-7061), locals especially recommend the breakfasts. Breakfast, lunch, and dinner are served at the inexpensive **Lanai Coffee Shop** in the Kona Hilton Hotel, 75-5852 Alii Drive; (808) 329-3111.

Fine dining is available at many of the luxury resorts, particularly at the **Mauna Lani,** the **Mauna Kea,** and the **Hilton Waikoloa Village** (see Where to Stay). These resorts also offer poolside snacks, which sometimes are a good deal, and sometimes are too pricey.

Specialty Foods

Be sure to taste some of the Big Island's special treats. Among the best bites: macadamia nuts, mouth-watering papaya, hearty Kona coffee beans, and real sugarcane. Pick up free samples of Kona coffees and macadamia nuts south of Captain Cook at **Kona Plantation Coffee Co.,** Highway 11, Kona Coast; (808) 328-8424.

Downtown Kona—and other places on the island—features **Lappert's Ice Cream,** Alii Drive, Kailua Kona; (808) 326-2290. The popular flavors include papaya, lychee, and coconut macadamia nut fudge.

FOR MORE INFORMATION

Hawaii Visitors Bureau: Hilo, 250 Keawe Street, 96720 (808-961-5797); Kona, 75-5719 West Alii Drive, Kailua-Kona 96740 (808-329-7787). Pick up a copy of their *Accommodation and Car Rental Guide.* Website: http://www.gohawaii.com

Division of State Parks: (808) 933-4200; **National Park Service,** 300 Ala Moana Boulevard, Honolulu 96850; (808) 967-7311; **Volcanic activity hotline:** (808) 967-7977.

Emergency Numbers
   Ambulance, fire, police (island-wide): 911
   Poison Control: (800) 362-3585

In Hilo
   Hospital: Hilo Hospital, 1190 Waianvenue Street;
   (808) 964-4111
   Pharmacy: Long's Drugs, 555 Kileau Avenue, Hilo;
   (808) 935-3357

In Kona
   Hospital: Kona Hospital, Kealakekua Avenue; (808) 322-9311
   Pharmacy: Kona Coast Drugs, Kailua; (808) 329-8886;
   Long's Drugs, 75-5595 Palani Road, Kailua-Kona;
   (808) 329-8477

KAUAI

After Hurricane Iniki devastated Kauai, the bougainvillea is back and so are the sugarcane fields, the fragrant hibiscus, and the ferns feathering the roadsides. On Kauai the famed eucalyptus tunnel that signals the turn-off from Highway 50 toward Poipu still impresses. Magically, none of the aged, towering trees were felled by the winds, a sign many locals interpret as confirming the special spirit of Kauai, known as the Garden Isle.

Back as well are all of Kauai's golf courses, many businesses, and about 30 percent of the accommodations, including several major hotels. The island is almost but not quite as green as before, and it offers tourists two big pluses: fewer crowds and frequent discount packages on lodging, golf, and attractions.

Always less developed than Maui, and more verdent, Kauai presents the languid and less populated Hawaii of long ago. On the sands, the fairways, and the hiking trails, you're likely to savor some space. The island is lush, with green fluted mountains and dense vegetation.

Kauai also lends itself to camping and to hiking. These budget-minded alternatives put you in close proximity to the island's natural beauty. But plan ahead, as most spaces book a year in advance.

A word of caution: The isolated beaches that look ideal can be dangerous. Rip tides and strong undertows claim many lives in Hawaii. Read the signs, observe the cautions, and when in doubt, look, but don't swim. When camping, always be prepared for sudden inclement weather, register at park headquarters, and keep to the trails.

GETTING THERE

There are two airports in Kauai. **Lihue,** the larger airport, offers flights from Honolulu through **Aloha Airlines** (800-367-5250 from U.S., 800-235-0936 from Canada), **Hawaiian Airlines** (800-367-5320), or **Mahalo Airlines** (800-277-8338). **Princeville Airport,** on the beautiful north shore, is serviced by **Aloha Island Air** (800-323-3345 or 800-367-5250).

Getting Around

The airport has shuttle buses, taxis, and rental cars. **Robert's Hawaii Tours** (808-245-9558), and **Kauai Island Tours** (808-245-4777) offer airport-to-hotel transfers. Taxi companies include **City Cab** (808-245-3227) and **Kauai Cab Service** (808-246-9554).

The most convenient place to rent cars (book ahead) is at the airport. (While one spouse or older teen waits for the luggage, have the other spouse get in the rental car line as these can be long.) Companies include **Alamo** (800-327-9633), **Avis** (800-831-8000), **Budget** (800-527-0700 or 808-245-1901), **Dollar** (800-800-4000 or 808-245-3651), **National** (800-227-7368 or 808-245-5636), and **Hertz** (800-654-3011 or 808-245-3356). **Pedal and Paddle** (808-826-9069) rents mountain bikes, helmets, and locks, so you and your teens can enjoy a free-wheeling Kauai tour.

WHAT TO SEE AND DO

Because Kauai's roads circle the island, the best way to discuss sites is by grouping them according to region.

The North Shore: Great Drives, Hikes, and Beaches

The 40-mile, seventy-five-minute drive north from Lihue along Route 56 through **Hanalei** to **Haena State Park,** to **Ke'e Beach** (808-241-3444) at the northwestern end of Kuhio Highway, Route 56, is a scenic delight. Subtle shades of green and sunlight dapple the road to Hanalei, and beautiful beaches and valleys mark the landscape. In Kauai even a main road such as Route 56 blooms with vegetation. For the drive wear (or take along) your bathing suits and your hiking shoes as you may want to pause awhile to sun on the sand, or to hike. But don't be tempted to swim at unknown beaches as the surf and tides can be rough. Swim only where you know it to be safe.

Near the town of Kapaa, take a small detour from Route 56 and

Kauai at a Glance

- A lush, beautiful island, less crowded than the other islands

- Waimea Canyon State Park, the Grand Canyon of the Pacific

- Quilts, koa wood furniture, drums, and even a bamboo nose flute at the fascinating Kauai Museum

- Flight-seeing tours over sugar cane fields, canyon gorges, waterfalls, and cliff burial caves of ancient kings

- Kauai Updates, (800) 262-1400

travel about 3 miles along Route 583 (Maalo Road) to **Wailua Falls** where twin waterfalls cascade 80 feet over the cliffs.

If you need a beach break, push on to just past **Kilauea** (and before Princeville) to **Kalihiwai Beach.** To get here from Route 56, detour onto Kalihiwai Road, but don't cross the river. Locals recommend this beach for strong swimmers (ask around, and be sure to check conditions). For a calmer beach, continue along Kalihiwai Road to **Anini Beach County Park,** known for its good snorkeling and windsurfing.

You can take Route 56 back to **Princeville,** a north shore resort area that offers options for lunch, golf, and good swimming at the Princeville Resort. Nearby the **Hanalei Valley Lookout** conveys a sense of Old Hawaii with its expanse of taro, and sugar fields cut by the Hanalei River. Although not overly disturbed by tourists or trinket shops, Hanalei, a picture-perfect small coast town, harbors a few nice boutiques for T-shirts and sportswear, plus a few informal eateries. On the main street the 1841 Waiol Mission sparkles, a jewel of stained glass and simple lines.

From Hanalei continue west on Route 56 to **Lumaha'i Beach,** site of some backdrops for the movie *South Pacific,* but DON'T SWIM HERE as the undertow can be deadly. Continue a bit further west to **Haena State Park,** Kuhio Highway, Route 56 (808-241-3444), whose three caves intrigue kids. The **Maniniholo Dry Cave** comes at the end of a lava tube. The **Waikapalae** and **Waikanaloa caves,** both created by the goddess Pele according to legend, impart a sense of ancient Hawaiian power with their crashing waves. At **Ke'e Beach,** about 8 miles west of Hanalei, near the beginning of the Kalalau Trail, many locals like to swim and snorkel when the conditions are right, but be careful of the sometimes rough surf and the undertow. Use good judgment; a safe bet would be to check conditions by calling the authorities or enjoy sunning, sand castle building, and tossing a Frisbee with new-found Hawaiian friends.

The **Kalalau Trail,** the land route that stretches for 11 miles one way across the Na Pali cliffs, part of the **Na Pali Coast State Park,** can only be reached by hiking or by boat. These cliffs, once home to ancient Hawaiian kings, impress with their fluted green ridges, secluded caves, and dramatic sea views. The sometimes arduous path starts near Ke'e Beach, dips into deserted beaches (don't swim), and passes slivers of cascading waterfalls. For an easy sampling of these scenic vistas without the work, try a helicopter, raft, or kayak trip (see Special Tours). A doable climb for sure-footed grade-schoolers is the first half-mile (yes, it's uphill) to the first lookout point for **Ke'e Beach,** a windswept swath of sand and sea. From the trailhead to this lookout, wild orchid and kukui trees dot the path. Hold young ones' hands so they won't slip on the rocks and roots. With older children or teens, continue for another 1½ miles to **Hanakapiai Beach.** (Be sure to bring water and a nutritious snack such as trail mix.) However tempting it is, swimming is not recommended here.

As the trail cuts through the **Na Pali Coast State Park,** it becomes more arduous. Hiking the entire Kalalau Trail gifts you with incredible views, plus a sense of the solitary majesty of these cliffs. Only hearty, healthy, experienced hikers should attempt the entire trek (11 miles each way). We don't recommend it unless you can deal with backpacks, boots, narrow trails, and sudden weather changes, and lots of climbs. And always check with the park rangers first.

The South Shore: Poipu Area, Great Beaches, Green Spaces, and Golf

The drive from Lihue to the popular **Poipu beach** area is about 14 miles (thirty minutes). Take Route 50 West to the turn-off to Route 520 South. (Some road signs label this as Route 52; but don't worry, you're on the right path.) In **Old Koloa Town** on the way to Poipu, many but not all the stores have reopened. You can still buy your T-shirts from **Crazy Shirts,** grill your own kebabs at the **Koloa Broiler,** and snack on **Lappert's Ice Cream.**

The Poipu beach area, devastated by Iniki, still offers swimming, and great golf packages. Try the **Kiahuna Golf Club,** 2545 Kiahuna Plantation Drive (808-742-9595).

Poipu's Lawai shore road leads to **Spouting Horn,** a public park where black lava blowholes shoot spray ten to twenty feet in the air. Here you can easily sense Iniki's force. Scraggly and denuded palms still dot the roadsides, and some houses still lurch off their foundations. But the spirit of rebuilding predominates, and new lumber seems to sprout almost everywhere.

On the way back from Koloa, take a pleasant detour on Route 530 West (again, also called Route 53) to the Hailima Road to the **National Tropical Botanical Garden,** P.O. Box 340, Lawaii 96765; (808) 332-7361. This little-known island wonder is spread on 186 acres of the Limahuli Valley. Be sure to reserve ahead—before you arrive in Hawaii—as the small tour groups fill quickly and to find out about the Garden's status since Hurricane Iniki.

Kids, especially, appreciate the convenience of the van that transports you to various locales for a leisurely, nonstrenuous walk and talk led by a knowledgeable guide. Here thousands of fragrant orchids, towering palm trees, glistening ferns, and flowers line pathways that stretch to the sea on property once home to Queen Emma. This is the place to teach your kids about plumeria, monkeypod trees, orchids, heliconia, banana plants, as well as the myriad types of palms.

The Waimea Canyon and Kokee State Park

Allow at least a half-day to explore one of Kauai's great wonders: **Waimea Canyon State Park.** Dubbed the "Grand Canyon of the

Be sure to take in the breathtaking view of Waimea Canyon, the "Grand Canyon of the Pacific." (Photo by author)

Pacific," it's 1 mile wide and 10 miles long. The entrance is about 36 miles (seventy-five minutes) from Lihue. Along the way to the **Waimea Canyon Lookout,** at 3,400 feet, several easy hikes yield views of the pink-and-gray striated rock formations. For preschoolers, stroll the Iliau Nature Loop, a flat .3 mile, which gives little ones a chance to "hike," hear birds, and view a dreamscape vista of red cliffs shrouded in mist. At the Waimea Lookout the canyon appears as a dramatic sweep of pink-and-gray striations sporadically marked with small ridges of green, and the silvery streams of waterfalls. **Outfitters Kauai** (808-742-9667) offers biking tours from the canyon to the coast.

Adjacent to the Waimea Canyon is **Kokee State Park,** Division of State Parks, P.O. Box 1671, Lihue, Hawaii 96766; (808) 241-3444. (The entrance is about 8 miles further along the road.) It features camping facilities and sweeping canyon and mountain views. Maps of the hiking trails can be found at the Kokee Museum of the Kokee Lodge, which serves breakfast, lunch, and dinner.

If you've packed a picnic lunch, a good spot several miles away is **Puu Ka Pele.** Waipoo Falls (if there's been enough rain) beckons, and the covered benches have a canyon view. The **Kalalau Valley Lookout,** at 4,000 feet, offers another spectacular view. Arrive early (before 10:00 A.M.) so you have a better chance of a view unobstructed by clouds.

Other Attractions

You are likely to be driving through Lihue, so take some time to visit the small, but interesting **Kauai Museum,** 4428 Rice Street, Lihue; (808) 245-6931. Inside, you'll enjoy the patina of the fine koa wood tables and calabashes, and the kids will like the items of Hawaiian culture such as quilts, bowls, *ipu* (drums made from gourds), and decorated *tapas* (cloth). A bamboo *ohe hano ihui* (nose flute) gets some giggles. The large 1920s canoe and the photographs of old Hawaii evoke the era before tour buses and big hotels. An adjacent building features scenic photographs of the Na Pali Coast and Waimea Canyon. For a sight-seeing pause, bring sandwiches and plan to use the covered courtyard for a picnic. The gift shop offers a nice selection of books about Hawaii for children, as well as the usual assortment of fish magnets and T-shirts.

Although the **Grove Farm Homestead,** P.O. Box 1631, Lihue 96766 (808-245-3202), is difficult to find—the small sign on Nawiliwili Road is easily missed—it may interest older children. The docent-led tours of this former eighty-one-acre sugarcane plantation started by George Wilcox in 1864 may drag on, but you do learn about that era's Hawaiian life-style. Listen for a bit, then ask if you may stroll the grounds by yourself. The barracks built for the workers provide insight into their lives, plus the sense of the rigors and regulations of plantation life.

Convenient to the Lihue airport, the **Kalapaki Beach,** near Route 51 and the Nawiliwili Harbor, at the Kauai Marriott Resort & Beach Club, offers a nice, but not overwhelming swath of sand, but lots of calm surf, great for kids. There is also shopping, dining, and tours at the Kauai Lagoons.

Snorkeling is popular in Kauai; try **Makua Beach,** or Tunnels Beach, on the North Shore, or **Koloa Landing** and **Prince Kuhio Park** on the South Shore. Windsurfers can head to the steady breezes and protected lagoon waters of **Anini Beach,** North Shore (good for beginners and intermediates); those with more advanced skills might opt for Makua Beach. Surfing lessons and equipment rentals are available at the **Margo Oberg Surfing School,** 2253 Poipu Road, Koloa 96756 (808-742-6411), outside the Kiahna Plantation Resort on Hanalei Bay, South Shore. Seven-time world champion surfer Margo Oberg runs the school.

Golf

Golf is a great island draw, especially because the golf courses are open even if the hotels are not. Kauai sports four of the top ten courses in Hawaii, as rated by *Golf Digest,* including the Prince Course on the North Shore, rated number one. Aficionados say that the courses, restored and reopened before the hotels, entice duffers with discounts and uncrowded greens. Locals, in fact, have been swinging in a golf heaven complete with low fees and no waits.

Among the choices: **The Princeville Makai Golf Course,** highly rated (808-826-3580) and the **Prince Golf Course** (808-826-5000). While the Kauai Marriott, on the southeast coast not far from the airport, has yet to set a date for its second debut, golfers get to play the adjoining **Lagoons Course** at Kauai Lagoons (808-241-6000) at a preferred rate when staying at a participating hotel. Their signature, the Kiele course, is also open.

Special Tours

Flight-seeing. Besides hiking, enjoy Kauai's coast by air and by sea. A **flight-seeing** view of the canyon, while costly, is memorable. Soar above the Alakai swamp, through the Waimea Canyon, and along the Na Pali coast. Float over taro and cane fields, across canyon gorges, next to waterfalls, and landscapes made famous by *Jurassic Park,* and beside the cliff burial caves of ancient kings. Surprisingly, this bird's-eye view gives you a sense of Kauai's impressive greenery. The island is lush after all those winds, but not quite as verdant as before. The fluted Na Pali cliffs still loom majestic, but seem a bit browner, and in places the trunks of uprooted trees litter the hillsides like so many dried white bones.

Among the island's best operators are **South Sea Helicopters,** P.O. Box 1445, Lihue 96766 (808-245-2222 or 800-367-2914). In

Lihue both operators depart from the heliport at the airport. In Princeville, Papillon flies from an airport.

Kayaking. Paddle along the snakelike Hanalei River with **Kayak Kauai Outfitters,** P.O. Box 508, Hanalei 96714, on the main street; (808) 826-9844. This easy ride, perfect for small children, glides past banks lined with java plum trees and yellow-flowered hau bushes, and it ends with some snorkel time at a nearby beach.

Rafting. For a water view of the majestic Na Pali coast, book a **Captain Zodiac** (or **Na Pali Zodiac**), P.O. Box 456, Hanalei 96714 (808-826-9371 or 800-422-7824). Turtles and spinner dolphins often surface on your way to the sea caves. If possible, book the early morning raft trip as often after about noon the ocean gets rough, precluding the exploration of caves, and often proving too bouncy a ride for some tummies. If you or your children are prone to seasickness, be sure to take the appropriate medication before rafting. (Check with your physician.)

Horseback Riding. **Pooku Stables,** P.O. Box 888, Hanalei 96714 (808-826-6777), offers three types of scenic group rides. See the Hanalei valley, enjoy a longer country ride, or (the most fun) take a three-hour picnic ride to a waterfall. Swimming is allowed. The stable encourages you to bring a bathing suit and hiking shoes.

The following stables offer trails along the beach: **CJM Stables,** 1731 Kelaukia Street, Koloa 96796 (808-742-6096) and **Garden Island Ranch,** 9250 Kaumualii Highway, Waimea 96796 (808-338-0052).

Whale Watching. **Na Pali Adventures** (800-659-6804) offers daily sightseeing tours of Kauai, emphasizing whale-watching tours from December to April, when the North Pacific Humpback Whale migrates through Hawaii's warm waters.

SPECIAL EVENTS

February: The Captain Cook Festival features food, rides, games, parade, and races.

May: All across the island, May Day is Lei Day in Hawaii, with celebrations and lei-making competitions.

July: Each year, Na Hula Ka'Ohikukapulani displays the traditional dances of Hawaii and Polynesia. Koloa Plantation Days remembers the Hawaiian sugar plantations with week-long celebrations.

August: The island's largest rodeo, the Hanalei Stampede, Pooku Stables.

October: At Kalapaki Bay, it's the Kauai Loves You Triathalon, featuring a 10K run, 40K bike race, and a 1.5K swim.

WHERE TO STAY

Poipu

Most Poipu hotels and condominium properties have reopened with the exception of Waiohai Beach Resort, Poipu Beach Resort, and the Sheraton Kauai, which is scheduled to reopen in late 1997.

The **Hyatt Regency Kauai,** 1571 Poipu Road, Koloa 96756 (808-742-1234 or 800-233-1234), Poipu, was the first luxury resort to reopen (March 30, 1993) after Iniki. This resort actually gained 30 more feet in the width of its beach after Iniki's waters. As a result, the resort's formerly small swath of sand now seems acceptable. After the winds, this relatively new hotel, which first opened November 15, 1990, required a $30 million renovation that included retiling the roofs, recarpeting, redecorating the lower-level rooms, and landscaping anew. But the tall palms once again sway in the sea breezes, the koi ponds are lively with fish, and the open-air pagodas add grandeur without too much glitz. At **Camp Hyatt Kauai,** children between three and twelve years are entertained from 9:00 A.M. to 4:00 P.M. with Hawaiian stories, crafts, hikes, field trips, and snorkeling. If you request an evening program twenty-four hours in advance, Hyatt will keep your child occupied from 6:00 to 10:00 P.M. with games, movies, and outdoor activities. The Family Fun Theater features complimentary movies on Tuesday nights. All movies shown, including *Jurassic Park* and *Raiders of the Lost Ark,* were partly filmed in Kauai. The Keiki Buffet is especially for kids, offering a daily rotating menu of favorite foods. When there are enough teens in house (check ahead), the hotel offers **Rock Hyatt,** a series of intermittent outings and activities for ages thirteen to seventeen. Be sure to check with reservations for the frequent packages.

Poipu Kai Resort, RR 1, Koloa, Kauai 96756 (808-742-6464 or 800-777-1700), set on 110 acres, offers one- and two-bedroom units with kitchens as well as several three-bedroom houses.

The **Poipu Bed and Breakfast Inn,** 2720 Hoonani Road, Koloa, Kauai 96756, welcomes well-behaved children. Pick the large Plumeria Room, or the two-bedroom, two-bath suite. The inn also has available a playpen, high chair, and crib on a first-come basis. Call (808) 742-1146 (Hawaii), (408) 688-8800 (mainland), or (800) 552-0095.

The **Embassy Vacation Resort Poipu Point,** 1613 Pe'e Road, Koloa 96756 (808-742-1888) offers 210 one- and two-bedroom units. Amenities at this plantation-designed resort include a toddler's pool, health club, and activities desk. Adventure packages are available at **Poipu Kapili,** 2221 Kapili Road, Koloa 96756 (808-742-6449 or 800-443-7714), a luxury condominium resort on the South Shore. Try Hike, Bike, and Snorkel; Paddle and Waterfalls; or Bicycling Canyon to Coast.

Kiahuna Plantation Outrigger, 2253 Poipu Road, Koloa; (800-OUTRIGGER), has beachfront condos with one- and two-bedroom units. Facilities include a swimming pool, tennis courts, and two championship golf courses nearby. A children's program runs from June through September.

North Shore

The **Princeville Hotel,** Princeville, on the north shore not far from the famed Na Pali cliffs and coast, reopened October 1994. The noted Makai and Prince golf courses reopened in the spring of 1993. Call the hotel (800-826-4400) or Sheraton Worldwide Reservations (800-STAY-ITT). The hotel offers the Keiki (child) Aloha, offered free in summer to ages five to twelve. Scheduled activities throughout the day include shell collecting, kite flying, and pole fishing. Evening programs run on certain nights and feature movies, storytelling, and arts and crafts. Call ahead to be sure these programs will be in operation. Scheduled to open in mid-summer, the Hanalii Bay Resort, 5380 Honoiki Road, Princeville 96722, (800) 367-5004, will have one-, two-, and three-bedroom suites as well as a children's program.

Snug between the mountains and the beach, **The Hanalei Colony Resort,** P.O. Box 206, Hanalei 96714 (808-826-6235 or 800-628-3004), offers 52 two-bedroom condominiums in a secluded North Shore location. Nearby is the Na Pali coastline, world-famous for its hiking trails. Guests are encouraged to try their hand at Hawaiian arts-and-crafts, enjoy North Shore windsurfing, and visit the Limahuli Garden, the ancient setting of many of Hawaii's rare plant species.

Waimea

Try the rustic cabins at **Kokee Lodge,** P.O. Box 819, Waimea, Kauai, Hawaii 96796; (808) 335-6061. They feature family-friendly amenities at budget prices. Accommodating three to seven people, the cabins come complete with a stove, refrigerator, bathroom, basic dishes, and linens at budget rates. As always with a bargain, book a year in advance, but check for cancellations. Another bonus: cheap eats at the Kokee Lodge restaurant, which serves breakfast and lunch daily. Try the thick Portuguese bean soup called "local soul food" by the natives.

Waimea Plantation Cottages, 9400 Kaumualii Highway, Waimea; (808-338-1625 or 800-9-WAIMEA), offers restored plantation homes with one, two, and three bedrooms. Amenities include ceiling fans, period furniture, and *lanais* (porches). There is a swimming pool, tennis court, and grass courtyard, but despite being oceanfront, you can't swim here. This may irritate many kids and parents.

Lihue and Kapa'a

The **Outrigger Kauai Beach,** 4331 Kauai Beach Drive, Lihue 96766 (800-462-6262), features a swimming pool, and a limited children's program in summer. **Plantation Hale,** 484 Kuhio Highway, Kapaa, operated by Outrigger Hotels, and across the street from Waipouli Beach, features one-bedroom condominiums with kitchenettes; (808) 822-4941, (800) 688-7444 or (800) 775-4253.

The **Aston Kauai Beach Villas,** 4330 Kauai Beach Drive, Lihue 96766, offer oceanfront condominium rentals. This property apparently does not offer a kids' program, although that may change. Call (808) 245-7711 or (800) 922-7866.

The **Kaua'i Marriott Resort & Beach Club,** 3610 Rice Street, Kalapaki Beach, Lihue 96766 (808-245-5050), is situated on a quarter mile of white sand beach on Nawiliwill Bay. Guest rooms and suites are available. For children ages five to twelve, the Kalapaki Kids Club offers daytime entertainment, emphasizing Kauai's culture and environment. Reservations are required one day in advance and can be made through the hotel concierge; the program is available Tuesday through Saturday from 9:00 A.M. to 3:00 P.M.

Guests at the **Lae Nani Condominiums** in Wailua on the Coconut Coast can meander on self-guided tours to visit the ancient birth site of the islands' kings, see Hawaiian petroglyphs, and walk by the historic landing ports of canoe voyagers of days past. The complex offers one- and two-bedroom condos with kitchens and expansive lanais. Call (800) 367-7052 or (800) 822-4938, or visit them on the Web at http://ten-io.com/vri/.

Other Accommodations

Camping. **Kokee State Park,** Division of State Parks, P.O. Box 1671, Lihue, Hawaii 96766; (808) 241-3444. Adjacent to the Waimea Canyon, this state park offers camping facilities and views of the Kalalau Valley.

To reserve a spot at one of Kauai's state parks, send a letter stating when and where you want to camp, along with a copy of the driver's licenses for each adult in your group. Remember that there is a five-night maximum at Kokee State Park.

Some locals suggest avoiding **Polihale State Park** as in years past campers have been robbed.

The **Great Molokai Ranch Trail,** Hawaii's second largest ranch, is dedicated to the preservation of the region's natural environment and cultural history. **Paniolo Camp** (808-552-2741 or 800-254-8871), the first of four camps planned for the Trail, offers 40 one- and two-unit tents mounted on wooden platforms. Activities include swimming, horseback riding, volleyball, and safari tours.

Kauai also offers **beach camping** at seven parks. Family favorites include **Anini Beach Park** on the north shore and **Salt Pond** on the west, both with broad sands and usually manageable undertow. (Check with officials.) Permits are required per-adult per-night (children under eighteen are free), and the limit is four days in one park and twelve days total at all the parks. For beach camping applications and information, contact the county office. Write the **Department of Parks and Recreation,** 4193 Hardy Street, Lihue, Hawaii 96766; (808) 241-6660.

More Bed-and-Breakfast Lodging. For additional **Bed-and-Breakfast** lodging, contact **Hawaii's Best Bed and Breakfast,** P.O. Box 563, Kamuela, Hawaii 96743. They represent about one hundred accommodations throughout Hawaii. Many are cottages on farms, or private estates. For brochures, call (808) 885-4550, for reservations only, (800) 262-9912.

Bed and Breakfast of Hawaii, P.O. Box 449, Kapaa, Kauai, Hawaii 96746, represents about two hundred places throughout the islands, with about seventy on Kauai. Ask for their guide *Bed and Breakfast Goes Hawaiian* (fee); call (800) 733-1632. For example, on Kauai's south shore, this registry offers "Kalaheo K29," a one-bedroom apartment complete with kitchen, minutes from Poipu Beach; "K24" in Poipu, which can accommodate twenty people in nine units, several of which have kitchens, and some have two bedrooms; and "K39A," a suite on a three-acre estate (appropriate for children over twelve).

WHERE TO EAT

Grab a skewer and grill yourself some mahi mahi, chicken, or steak at the **Koloa Broiler,** Koloa Road, in Old Koloa Town not far from Poipu; (808) 742-9122. The do-it-yourself approach keeps entree costs down.

The **Bull Shed,** 796 Kuhio Highway, half-way between Waipouli and Wailua, in the Harbor Village, features an extensive salad bar and prime rib; (808) 822-3791. **Chuck's Steakhouse,** at the Princeville Center (808-826-6211), attracts locals as well as tourists. The **Aloha Diner,** 971 F Kuhio Highway, Waupouli (808-822-3851), is another local favorite.

The **House of Seafood,** on Lawai Beach at the Poipu Kai Resort (808-742-6433), features good Hawaiian seafood, but the price is a bit more than the usual family fare. The specials may include fish with macadamia-nut sauce or ginger-baked fish. The **Kapaa Fish and Chowder House,** 4-1639 Kuhio Highway (808-822-7488), offers entrees such as coconut shrimp, seafood fettucini, and sautéed clams.

For island cuisine with an *au naturel flair,* suitable for families, try the **Ilima Terrace,** Hyatt Regency Kauai; (808) 742-1234. Children are sure to find something on the varied menu they like, and if not, the view of Keoneloa Bay and the beach is sure to please.

DAY TRIPS

Take a day excursion by raft, kayak, horseback, or helicopter (see Special Tours). Visit the other islands (see Island Hopping in the introductory chapter).

FOR MORE INFORMATION

Order a Kauai Vacation Planner by calling (800) AH-KAUAI. Website: http://www.gohawaii.com

Emergency Numbers

The **Chamber of Commerce,** 2970 Kele Street; (808) 245-7363

The **Hawaii Visitors Bureau,** 3016 Umi Street; (808) 245-3971

Ambulance, fire, police: 911

Fire Department: nonemergency, 4223 Rice Street; (808) 241-6500.

Police Headquarters: nonemergency, 3060 Umi Street; (808) 241-6711.

Wilcox Hospital, 3420 Kuhio Highway; (808) 245-1100

Longs Drug Store, Kukui Grove Center; (808) 245-7771

MAUI

Maui, nicknamed the "Valley Isle," offers some of the islands' plushest resorts and best golf courses. It's a popular island, especially for first-timers to Hawaii, and for families with teens as there's plenty to see and do both during the day and at night. Magical Maui moments include bike riding down mountain slopes, snorkeling at a semisubmerged volcanic cone, and driving a scenic highway dotted with waterfalls.

The major resort areas are the Kihei/Wailea region, Kaanapali and north to Kapalua, and the less populated and more-difficult-to-reach Hana, on the island's far eastern tip.

GETTING THERE

Maui has three airports. **Kahului Airport** (808-872-3830), the island's main airport, is the only one that operates at night. **United Airlines** (800-241-6522), **Delta Airlines** (800-221-1212), and **American** fly directly to Maui's Kahului Airport from various mainland gateways. **Aloha Airlines** (800-367-5250) and **Hawaiian Airlines** (800-367-5320) fly to Kahului Airport from Oahu. The small airport at **Hana** (808-248-8208) is limited to propeller planes that take the work out of the long drive to this lovely and less populated spot. The airport at **Kapalua-West Maui** (808-669-0228), convenient to this resort area, accommodates commuter planes and Aloha Airlines planes.

GETTING AROUND

Rental cars make exploring Maui's diversity easy. Book well in advance. You can rent cars at Kahului and Kapalua-West, but not at the Hana airport. For Hana, arrange to have your hotel meet you, or call **Dollar Car Rental** (808-248-2837); they will send a van for you.

Avis (800-331-1212 or 808-871-7575), **Budget** (800-527-0700 or 808-871-8811), **Hertz** (800-654-3131 or 808-877-5167), **National Car Rental** (800-227-7368), **V.I.P. Car Rentals** (808-877-2054 or 800-367-6080), and **Rainbow** (808-661-8734) are all regulars, along with about thirty other competing rental agencies.

A & B Moped Rental, 3481 Lower Honoapiilani Highway (808-669-0027), rents mopeds to licensed drivers 18 years and older for about $28 per day. Bicycling about the island is also popular, especially for bicycling down Haleakala (which you should do only under the guidance of a reputable tour operator). Companies include **Maui Downhill** (808-871-2155) and **Maui Mountain Cruisers** (808-871-6014).

Maui has no real public transportation system. Those staying in Kaanapali can get a lift with the **Kaanapali Resort Trolley Car,** which stops at major resorts; with the **Lahaina Express** (808-661-8748), a free bus that operates between Lahaina and the Kaanapali resorts from about 9:00 A.M. to 10:00 P.M.; and with the **Kaanapali Shuttle** that transports visitors for free every hour between hotels and condos. Little ones might like a ride on the **Lahaina Kaanapali and Pacific Railroad,** a restored sugarcane train pulled by a steam locomotive; call (808) 661-0089.

Taxis are available. **Red and White Cabs** (808-661-3684) and **Wailea Taxi** (808-879-1059) are two of the island companies.

WHAT TO SEE AND DO

Your kids will never be bored in Maui. Besides miles of beaches for swimming, sunning, and snorkeling, Maui offers good golf, tennis, spas, kids' programs, shopping, and great resorts.

Beaches

Maui boasts more miles of beaches safe for swimming and watersports than any other Hawaiian island. Try **Wailea**—its mile and a half of shoreline is divided into five crescent beaches. The popular snorkeling spot, **Molokini Crater,** is nearby. Other good snorkeling beaches include **Honolua Bay** and **Kapalua Bay.** Budding windsurfers may want to visit **Dig Me Beach** in Kaanapali (popular with teens) or **Hookipa Beach Park.**

Haleakala National Park

Spend at least one day exploring **Haleakala National Park,** Haleakala National Park Headquarters, Crater Road; (808) 572-9306. You can drive, bike, or hike down this dormant volcano, which dominates the island.

In Hawaiian *Haleakala* means house of the sun, aptly named as this mountain looms formidably at 10,000 feet. If you want to catch the sunrise at the mountain's peak, a spectacular sight, start your drive to the summit early, and dress warmly. It can be cold at the higher elevations. At the top the mountain is a "moonscape" of brown-and-red craters. White wisps of clouds hang suspended against the gray peaks of lava cones, and the earth inside is a trail of black ashen pebbles and thin quietness.

But even if you arrive after dawn (allow about two hours for the drive up), the trip is worth the trouble. The scenery changes from sugar fields, to farms, ranches, eucalyptus groves, koa trees—and near the summit—to an eerie stretch of craters and black earth.

Stop at the **Visitors' Center** for some informative books. From here it's about another 10 miles to the summit. Look for nene geese, Hawaii's state bird, and Silverswords, a plant with spindly shooting tendrils that only grow in the high dry lava beds of volcanic peaks. This trip is popular with kids ages five to twelve, who can complete a series of activities in a free booklet, like learning about an endangered species or a few easy Hawaiian words, and then be sworn in as Junior Rangers. The program lasts about two hours.

On your way up or down, take the kids for breakfast or lunch (11:30-3:00) on Haleakala's slopes at the **Kula Lodge,** Highway 377; (808) 878-2517. The inexpensive entrées include omelettes, bean soup, and burgers.

A popular Haleakala adventure is a bicycle tour down this mountain. The trip, from the van ride up, to the bike ride down with a stop for lunch, can take four hours. It's best to go in the morning before the mist obscures some views. Because the mountain features twenty-nine hairpin turns, this exhilarating outing is recommended only for agile parents and children twelve and over who follow directions. The precipice of a mountain is no place for daredevil kids. Some reputable companies include **Maui Downhill,** 199 Dairy Road, Kahului

Maui at a Glance

- Sophisticated and popular, with plenty to do for families with teens

- Miles of safe beaches for swimming and snorkling

- Eerie craters and black earth at the mountaintop of Haleakala National Park

- Great drives: the road to Hana, with surprises around every turn

- Maui Visitors Bureau, (800) 224-3530

(808-871-2155); and **Maui Mountain Cruisers,** 353 Hanamau, Kahului 96732 (808-871-6014). Bike trails extend from the east end of the island at the Wailea Resort to Kapalua on the west end.

Biking lets you savor the scenery, but a car trip gets you the same views. As you descend, the scenery changes from the earth browns and reds to the greens of koa trees. The wind ripples through the pili grass that covers the hillsides. When you pass the eucalyptus grove, the air is pungent with its aroma. For the last 1,500 feet, you'll see cows grazing in meadows and sugarcane fields.

On Haleakala's slopes be a *paniolo*, a Hawaiian cowboy. Sign up for a horseback ride with **Pony Express,** P.O. Box 535, Kula, Maui; (808) 667-2200. Located at about 4,200 feet, this "up-country" ranch offers two-hour guided rides (minimum age is ten). While the horses keep an easy walking pace, you enjoy the sweeping vistas of sugarcane fields far down the slopes that reach to the blue Pacific. The rustle of the horses' hooves in the calf-high reedy grass creates a tranquil aura. For those who can sit in the saddle for seven hours, Pony Express offers horseback trips into the crater, an exciting venture. **Thompson Ranch,** Thompson Road, Kula (808-878-1910), also offers ranch trail rides as well as trips into Haleakala's crater.

Just a few miles from Pony Express, **Makawao,** a simple town, sports local craft shops and galleries along Baldwin Avenue. For some of the best *saimin,* a native soup of noodles and pork, stop at **Kitada's Kau Kau Korner,** Baldwin Avenue (808-572-7241), a one-room cafe, where you squeeze in with others at the faded formica tables. For a bargain price, you get a steamy bowl big enough for two. For the ride back to the hotel, grab some pastries from **Komoda's Bakery,** 3674 Baldwin Avenue; (808) 572-7261. This shop is noted for its cream puffs, but most everything looks good.

Also worth a stop on Haleakala's slopes is the **Upcountry Protea Farm,** Kula (808-878-2544), where exotic flowers are grown. The farm has a half-acre walk-through garden, and a picnic area where you can lunch on sandwiches from the farm store. **Kula Botanical Gardens,** on Highway 377 past the turnoff to Haleakala Crater (808-878-1715), offers more tropical plants. (Admission; open daily 9:00 A.M.–4:00 P.M.)

On the Hana side of the park, hike on marked trails past the **Seven pools at Kipahula,** a series of waterfalls. The trail to Waimoku Falls passes through a bamboo forest.

Another popular hiking spot is **Iao Valley**—look for the unique rock formation, the Iao Needle. On the drive there, stop by Heritage Gardens at Kepaniwai Park, where you'll find plenty of picnic space among replicas of Japanese, Chinese, and Portuguese dwellings and gardens. Pick up information on Iao State Park's nature and petroglyph art at the Hawaii Nature Center (808-244-6500).

Great Drives: The Road to Heavenly Hana

The road to Hana is one of America's great drives. From Kahului for 52 miles—about three hours—the route presents a panorama of Hawaii's best: pineapple fields, windsurfers, black-sand beaches, cascading waterfalls, grotto-like swimming holes, and lush vegetation. Cabbage-sized yellow and red hibiscus, sprays of purple Queen Emma blossoms, African tulip trees, arcing banana stalks, wispy palm trees, delicately fingered ferns, and white-and-yellow ginger blossoms line the blacktop.

Here are sweeping vistas of coast, cliffs, and clouds; no hotels, billboards, or condos mar the view as you commune with nature. The least expensive and most enjoyable way to experience this scenic but serpentine route (with more than six hundred curves and fifty-six one-lane bridges) is to drive it yourself. Remember to book your rental car well in advance. But like everything in paradise, there's a "price." Don't plan on driving to Hana and back again in one day. The drive is too exhausting, especially for little kids, who may not take to the winding roads. Bring along some anti-motion sickness medicine for your kids just in case.

Ideally, allow at least two days for this drive; stay overnight in Hana (book well in advance). And wear your bathing suit under your clothes, for along this road are wonderful places to pause—sensuous waterfalls and superb beaches are just some of the delights. If you insist on driving the round-trip in one day, be sure to leave Kahului by 8:00 A.M. in order to allow enough time for a rejuvenating swim at Hamoa Beach, as well as a daylight return trip. Be sure to get gas for the car in **Paia** (a small town of funky shops flanked by sugarcane fields and the sea) because the next gasoline awaits in Hana. The **Shell Service Station,** Route 380 before Route 36 (which is the Hana Highway), and 1 mile before the airport (808-572-0550), rents a narrated tape describing the scenic points on the road to Hana.

The road surprises at every turn. Hau tree branches canopy the path allowing thin slants of light, but around the next bend the road breaks into bright sun as feathery hillsides of wild eucalyptus, mango, guava, and papaya trees billow toward the sea. The rustle of 30-foot-tall bamboo stands sounds like soft rain, and the rush of waterfalls lures you across the many one-lane bridges.

With frequent ascents, descents, and narrow lanes, the road can be demanding as it winds along Maui's northeastern coastline to Hana, a tiny town well worth a visit for its twin jewels: the **Hotel Hana-Maui,** offering good food and comfortably elegant rooms, and nearby **Hamoa Bay Beach,** which James Michener dubbed the most beautiful in Hawaii.

Contrary to what many guidebooks state, the road to Hana is reasonably well maintained, if always narrow and windy. But the 10 miles beyond Hana to **Ohe'o Gulch** (frequently misnamed the **Seven Sacred Pools**) will try your soul. Locals say they like the pothole-and-gravel-packed path to the Kipahulu district, the southeastern-most sector of Haleakala National Park, just as it is to keep the crowds from the pristine serenity of these volcanic-carved pools. But for seekers of lush Hawaii before the tourist floods and glitzy hotels, the Hana drive is heaven.

The first must-see on this adventure comes within 2 miles. Pull over at **Hookipa Beach,** one of Maui's best windsurfing spots. While you can't rent a board here, you can watch as many as fifty yellow, white, orange, and red sails of local aficionados glide the perfect wave.

Sixteen miles later, after the pineapple fields have yielded to high ridges of mist-topped hillsides, the **Waianu Fruit Stand,** announced by its HALFWAY TO HANA SIGN, blooms like an oasis. Let the kids out here for cheap eats—cokes, chips, fruit, shaved iced—and leg stretching.

About 7 miles from the fruit stand, look for cars parked by the roadside (this is a clue to **Puohokamoa Falls**). A short path from the highway leads you to the falls. Cool and clear, these waters deliver a quintessential Hawaiian fantasy: splashing in a waterfall.

Next pull-over: the **Wailua Lookout.** Walk up the stairs almost concealed by a tunnel of hau branches for a picturesque view of this sea-coast village complete with the white steeple of St. Gabriel's Church.

With waterfalls and bathrooms, **Puaa Kaa State Park,** about 5 miles further along (14 more miles until Hana) draws picnickers, especially those with preschoolers. Tarry here, or try **Waianapanapa State Park,** further along, but just ½ mile beyond the Hana airport, near the town. This is the perfect pastiche of black-sand beach, trails, and underwater caves shallow enough in places for supervised swimming by children. An ancient legend attributes the red cast of the cave waters not to the tiny shrimp but to the memory of a fleeing princess murdered by her jealous husband.

Hana itself, low-key and inviting, curls around the harbor, then stretches for several blocks before fading into grass-covered mountains and fields. Refresh yourself with lunch. For down-home informality, try the ribs and sweet-and-sour chicken buffet at the **Hana Ranch Restaurant** (808–248–8255), or wash up in the park, and head for luncheon at the **Hotel Hana-Maui** (808–248–8211, 800–325–3535, or 800–STAY–ITT), Highway 36, a hideaway of about ninety-six rooms now operated by Aman Resorts in the heart of town. The open-air dining room with views of frog ponds, sweeping lawns, and manicured gardens lends the place the feel of an oasis.

Sated, head for **Hamoa Bay Beach,** 1½ miles from Hana. The broad row of kamani trees provides shade, and the sand stretches in a wide arc against the blue sea.

Linger here for awhile—or the entire day and the one after. Rest up because the next 10 miles of road to **Ohe'o Gulch** take at least one hour; bumps and potholes prevail. The reward: the shimmering row of twenty volcanic pools. If limited for time, hike the .2 mile to the lower pools.

The path takes you back to ancient Hawaii. On this wind-blown promontory, white water crashes on the black lava rocks below as you pass the ruins of a thousand-year-old Hawaiian village. Just beyond, the gray lava pools, carved by the Ohe'o stream coming down Mt. Haleakala, offer secluded swimming—though the spot is becoming more and more popular.

Further along this road (ask the locals how to get there) is **Charles Lindbergh's grave,** on the site chosen by the aviator who was buried on August 26, 1974. Read his epitaph, which states in part, "If I take the wings of morning and dwell in the uttermost parts of the sea...."

An important warning about the drive to Hana: Many tour groups cart vanloads of tourists along the Hana road, departing from Kahalui about 7:30 A.M. and returning about 6:00 P.M. Some continue to Ohe'o Gulch; others stop at Hamoa Bay Beach. There's no time for swimming, but Hana is a lunch stop. If you are vulnerable to car sickness, be careful. Seven hours in the back of a van may be hard on the stomach, especially for kids. Our advice—avoid these one-day trips; but if you must, operators include **Robert's Hawaii, Inc.** (808-871-6226), **Ekahi Tours** (808-877-9775), and **Trans Hawaiian** (808-877-7308).

More Hikes and Tours

South Pacific Kayaks and Outfitters (800-77-OCEAN) offers a kayak trip along the Makena coast, a Streams and Waterfalls hike, and a Bamboo Forest hike. Organized hikes, ranging from easy to difficult, are also offered by **Hike Maui** (808-876-0308), **Hawaii Nature Center** (808-244-6500), and the **Nature Conservancy of Hawaii** (808-572-7849).

Special Tours by Sea

Whale watching. More excitement abounds in Maui's seas. From November through April, boats cruise by schools of whales, and the horizon jumps with pods of humpbacks cresting the waters. February and March are the most exciting months as often you can see whales

The surf is always up at Hanoa Bay beach. (Photo by the author)

tail slapping, spy hopping, and fin waving. Shoreline sites with great whale-watching views include the beaches at Wailea and Kaanapali, harborside in Lahaina, and Makena Beach.

In season many of the snorkeling and sailing companies offer whale-watching cruises. The **Pacific Whale Foundation,** 101 North Kihei Road, Suite 25, Kihei (808–879–8811), offers whale information and eco-adventures. Often hotels offer whale-watching packages. Each January the **Four Seasons Resort Wailea** (800–334–6284) hosts the Celebration of Whales, a three-day event combining lectures, whale-watching cruises, art, and a Hawaii Humpback Whale workshop for kids five and older.

Snorkeling. Some of the best snorkeling can be found at **Molokini,** a volcanic crater whose conelike crescent breaches the Pacific about an hour's launch from **Maalaea Harbor.** Because Molokini is a preserve, the tame fish eat from your hands. Even the most blasé video tyke will yell "Wow" when tiers of rainbow-colored parrot fish, yellow tangs, and blue-and-green wrasse nibble bread from his fingers. Many boats have some "seeboards" equipped with built-in masks so that little kids and nonswimmers can still get eyeball to eyeball with the fish. These rent quickly, so reserve yours as soon as you get on deck. Most companies include lunch. *Four Winds* (808- 879-8188) is one of the few that offer a hot barbecue lunch of burgers, chicken, or mahi mahi. Another good choice is the *Wailea Kai,* booked by the **Ocean Activities Center,** 1325 Kihei Road, Wailea, Hawaii; (808) 879-4485. En route to Molokini the crew talks about safety, instructing those who need to learn the techniques of snorkeling. A light breakfast is served, and at the site, the crew prepares lunch.

Other snorkeling cruises leave from Lahaina's harbor to Lanai. Ask your concierge or check with the **Ocean Activities Center. Blue Water Rafting,** P.O. Box 10172, Lahaina (808-879-7238), offers a variety of snorkeling expeditions as well as whale-watching excursions. Free snorkeling, as well as scuba and windsurfing, instructional clinics are available at the Ocean Activities Center at the Renaissance Wailea Beach Resort (808-879-4485).

For a diver's view of sealife without having to be certified for SCUBA, try the **Atlantis Submarine;** (800) 548-6262 or (808) 667-2224. In Maui, a boat leaves from the Lahaina harbor for the dive site where you board this recreational submarine outfitted for forty-six passengers. Two each share a porthole for the hour viewing, a wonderful window on the wonders of sea life. (The entire trip lasts about one hour and forty-five minutes.) Kids love seeing schools of fish float by, especially those tots who have not mastered snorkeling. Maui offers the deepest dive of the Atlantis's three locations in Hawaii. Going down to 150 feet it's the only one that shows black coral. While there is no minimum age for a dive, the minimum height for a passenger is 3 feet, so most kids four years and older can experience this. Be aware: If you tend toward claustrophobia skip this. Atlantis Submarines also dive off Kona, the Big Island, and Waikiki, Oahu.

Combination tours, combining a dive and helicopter tour of Hana or west Maui, are also available. For all 2:00 P.M. dives, passengers receive one free admission pass for a child under twelve when purchasing one full-price ticket.

Flight-seeing

Various companies offer helicopter tours of Maui. While exciting, these flight-seeing forays are pricey. If you want to splurge on one of these, we recommend saving the bird's-eye view for a helicopter ride over Kauai. However, here are some of Maui's helicopter tour opera-tors: **Blue Hawaiian Helicopters** (800–745–BLUE), **Hawaii Heli-copters** (808–877–3900 or 800–346–2403), and **Sunshine Helicopters** (808) 871–0722.

Shopping and Green Spaces: Lahaina

Lahaina is the place for souvenir shopping. For the grandparents back home, pose for a **Bud the Birdman** postcard. You can't miss him with his nine macaws and parrots perched in front of the Pioneer Inn. He'll drape six or more of these fine feathered friends on your arms, shoulders, and head. (Ask about Rainbow who likes to pose with sun-glasses.) The next day pick up your five postcards with your picture and the ditty "We're on Maui and you're not! Na na na na na."

Lahaina is the place to stock up on **taro chips,** something like a tortilla chip but made from the taro plant, and **Maui chips,** ultra-crispy potato chips.

Fortified, browse for T-shirts in the many shops. Try **The Art Tee Gallery,** Pioneer Inn Arcade, 665 Front Street; (808) 661–6116. It offers some unusual and arty designs with bold graphics, or nostalgic scenes such as "Baseball is Forever." Keep walking along Front Street, and browse the **Lahaina Hat Company,** 705 Front Street, for that per-fect sunhat-in-paradise; nearby **Sergeant Leisure** offers good quality shirts, shorts, and sweats.

Cool off with some of **Lappert's Aloha Ice Cream,** 808 Front Street, at the corner of Front and Marketplace; (808) 661–3310. A great place to pause and enjoy your cone is under the giant banyan tree in the park on Front Street, bordered by Hotel and Canal streets. Kids love this shady, sprawling tree whose limbs and roots seem to take over the entire block. Before leaving here browse the local crafts at the **Banyan Tree Gallery,** Front Street, located in the park; (808) 661–0111.

Historic Museums and Attractions

Admission is free at the **Maui Tropical Plantation** (808–244–7643) near Waliku. Take a guided tour, or narrated Tropical Tram ride (for a fee), amidst sugar cane, pineapple, papaya, bananas, coffee, macadamia nuts, and tropical flowers. Open 9:00 A.M. to 5:00 P.M. The history of Maui's plantation past and sugar industry is chronicled at the **Alexander & Baldwin Sugar Museum** (808–871–8058) in Kahului. Open daily except Sunday from 9:30 A.M. to 4:30 P.M. Join the singing conductor aboard the **Lahaina-Kaanapali & Pacific Railroad** (808-661-0089), or the Sugar Cane Train, a replica of the 1890 Hawaiian railroad. The musically-inclined conductor conveys information on the mountains and history of Maui's western shore. **Whalers Village** (808-661-5992) in Kaanapali and the **Whale Center of the Pacific** (808-661-5992) tell the story of Hawaii's whaling industry. The former has hands-on exhibits for kids and free admission.

For arts and cultural entertainment, contact the **Maui Arts and Cultural Center** (808-244-SHOW) for a schedule of shows and exhibits.

SPECIAL EVENTS

March: Wake up bright and early for the Maui Marathon, which leaves at 5:30 A.M. from the Kaahumanu Shopping Center, Kahului to Whalers Village, Kaanapali. The Na Mele O Maui Festival celebrates Hawaii with a children's song contest in the Hawaiian language and a hula festival.

April: Pay homage to the whale during Whale Day at Kalama Park. Admission is free, and there is music and food all day long.

July: Makawao Fourth of July parade and rodeo. The Annual Pineapple Festival features a cooking contest, free tastings, games, and entertainment.

August: Watch the long boats skim over the surface of the water at the Hawaiian Canoe Racing Association State Championships at Hanakaoo Beach. The Haleakala Run to the Sun gets its name because the marathon runners begin the race at sea level and run 36.2 miles to an elevation of 10,000 feet. The Maui Onion Festival takes place at Whalers Village.

October: Aloha Festivals, cultural celebrations of music, dance, and history.

WHERE TO STAY

Kihei/Wailea

We like the **Kihei/Wailea** area best. Not as building-to-building dense as Kaanapali, or as isolated as Hana, both Wailea and Kihei (just a holler down the road from Wailea) are near enough to Maalaea harbor for day trips, close to Haleakala for hiking, and near Lahaina for shopping. Kihei, a town, sports a neighborhood feel and is less pricey than the resort-laden Wailea. A nice treat: The drive from Kihei/Wailea to West Maui. After a soft rain shower, make a game of counting the frequent rainbows that arc over the road.

Condominiums. Condominiums are a great buy for families, offering more space for your money and the convenience of cooking in.

In Kihei the **Aston Kamaole Sands,** 2695 South Kihei Road, Kihei, Hawaii 96753 (800-922-7866), is across the street from Kamaole Beach with its lifeguard, sandy shores, and sweeping lawn. Often travelers fifty-five and over receive a 20 percent discount plus a free rental car, and some members of airline frequent flyer clubs get one free night for every three-night stay. In addition, a year-round kids program for ages four to twelve is offered free to guests, Monday to Friday, usually from 9 A.M. to noon, and 1:00 P.M. to 3:30 P.M.

Another good condo pick is **Destination Resorts** (800-367-5246), with six condominium communities in Wailea, an upscale area home to the resorts of Four Seasons, Renaissance, and Aston Wailea. These condominiums share the same beach as the Wailea resorts. Golf fairways and clever land use convey a sense of greenery and open space. The condominiums **Ekolu** and **Grand Champions,** a short drive to the beach, are the least expensive but the **Ekahi** property offers beachfront convenience for not too much more. Ask about packages.

Another plus: With a Destination Resorts booking, your kids may use Aston Wailea Resort's well-run children's program (808-879-1922), or sign on for a spot at the Renaissance Wailea's children's program.

Resorts: Wailea

The **Grand Wailea Resort and Spa** (800-888-6100 or 808-875-1234), formerly the Grand Hyatt, is a great place for families and among the most elegant (casually elegant, of course) resorts in Hawaii. At Camp Grande choose from six different programs for kids ages three to twelve, which include environmental and wildlife exploration activities, field trips such as a ride on a glass-bottom boat, a trip on the

Sugar Cane Train, and educational activities such as a day devoted to learning about whales. Activities are offered daily, year-round, from 8:00 A.M. to 4:30 P.M., with an extra charge for evening and dinner activities from 5:00 P.M. to 10:00 P.M. Rock Grande is a teen program for ages thirteen to nineteen, offering intermittent activities such as sailing trips, shopping excursions, and beach parties, when enough teens are in residence. The elaborate swimming pools are a plus for families.

The **Four Seasons Resort Wailea,** 3900 Wailea Alanui (800-334-MAUI or 808-874-8000), has 380 rooms and looks out over the ocean. Families with infants are relieved to know that the hotel supplies all kinds of baby equipment, from strollers to bottle warmers. The year-round, complimentary Kids For All Seasons program entertains ages five to twelve from 9:00 A.M. to 5:00 P.M. with Hawaiian songs and legends, hula dancing, and traditional Hawaiian craft making. Day passes, which are relatively costly, are available to guests so that they may enjoy the elaborate pool at the adjacent **The Grand Wailea Resort and Spa.**

The **Renaissance Wailea Beach Resort,** 3550 Wailea Alanui Drive, Wailea (808-879-4900 or 800-HOTELS 1), has two swimming pools, two golf courses, and fourteen tennis courts. All year a kids' program called Camp Wailea runs for ages five to twelve. Counselors keep the young ones active from morning until afternoon.

The **Aston Wailea Beach Resort,** 3700 Wailea Alanui (800-367-2960 or 808-879-1922), spreads out over twenty-two acres of Maui's south shore. The resort's special features include nightly live entertainment, golf courses, grass tennis courts, and the **Keiki's Club Gecko** children's program, which translates to something like "The Kid's Good Luck Lizard Club." The activities include Nintendo games, finger painting, hula lessons, and tide pool discovery sessions. Lunch and a T-shirt are included in the fee, and the program is offered Tuesdays, Thursdays, and Saturdays for ages five to 13 from 9:00 A.M. to 3:00 P.M.

The **Kea Lani Hotel and Villas,** 4100 Wailea Alanui, Wailea 96753 (808-875-4100 or 800-882-4100), is an all-suite and -villa property in Wailea. It offers families extra room and a relatively inexpensive children's program for ages five to twelve, year-round, Monday to Saturday from 9:00 A.M. to 3:00 P.M. The fee includes a Keiki Lani T-shirt, lunch, and snacks. The program seems to have good counselors and creative crafts. Kids paint coconuts, create volcanoes, play beach games, and go swimming. The catch: You must sign up by 6:00 P.M. the night before. Each room features a sitting area with television, stereo and VCR, plus a microwave, refrigerator, and coffeemaker, as well as pull-out couches that can accommodate grade-school kids with no problems. (Teens may feel crowded, so inquire about their villas or larger suites.) For increased privacy, the bathroom opens to both the sitting area and the master bedroom.

The **Aston Kamaole Sands,** 2695 South Kihei Road, Kihei 96753 (808-931-1400 or 800-922-7866), on Maui, operates Kamp Kamaole, a free, year-round children's program for ages four to twelve from 9:00 A.M. to noon, and 1:00 P.M. to 3:00 P.M. Kids go on beach walks, fish, and learn how to make their own leis. Call Aston Hotels and Resorts; (800) 922-7866.

Kaanapali

The **Westin Maui** is off State Route 30, 2365 Kaanapali Highway, Kaanapali 96761; (808) 667-2525 or (800) WESTN-1. It features Keiki Kamp from June through August, and on major holidays, for ages five to twelve year-round. The program is from 9:00 A.M. to 3:00 P.M. and in the evening from 6:00 P.M. to 9:00 P.M. Also in Kaanapali, the **Hyatt Regency Maui,** 200 Nohea Kai Drive, Kaanapali Beach (800-233-1234 or 808-661-1234), offers Camp Hyatt year-round for ages three to twelve from 9:00 A.M. to 3:00 P.M., and 9:00 A.M. to 12:30 P.M. or 12:00 P.M. to 3:00 P.M. An evening program for a separate fee is available Fridays and Saturdays from 6:00 P.M. to 10:00 P.M. With enough teens in house, the hotel offers Rock Hyatt, intermittent activities and day trips for teens.

The **Whaler at Kaanapali Beach,** 2481 Kaanapali Parkway, Kaanapali 96761 (800-367-7052 or 808-661-4861), offers the complimentary Ohana Summer Activities Program for ages five to twelve from mid-June through Labor Day. Some special outings require a fee. **The Sheraton Maui,** 2605 Kaanapali Parkway (800-325-3535 or 808-661-0031), offers a free Keiki Aloha children's program from mid-June through August for ages five to twelve. Intermittent activities include arts and crafts and pole fishing; on some evenings, movies and Hawaiian storytelling keep kids occupied so parents can enjoy a romantic dinner. Sheraton's new 142-yard fresh water swimming lagoon, complete with lava-rock waterways, is a hit with kids. When available, families can book a second room for their kids at a 50 percent discount. Or families can opt for a junior suite, designed specifically for families. They feature two double beds, a pull-down wall bed, refrigerator, microwave oven, and 665 square feet of space.

For the most space, try the **Embassy Suites Resort Maui,** 104 Kaanapali Shores Place; (800) GO-2-MAUI or (808) 661-2000. The Embassy Suites offers a complimentary full breakfast, plus a year-round children's program. Hours and activities vary, so check ahead. **The Aston Kaanapali Shores,** 3445 Lower Honoapiilani Highway (808-931-1400 or 800-367-5124), is a condo property that offers a year-round kids' program for ages three to ten from 8:30 A.M. to 3:30 P.M. Monday through Friday. Lunch is extra.

For reservations and information about any of Aston's twenty-nine Hawaii properties, call (800) 922-7866. But shop smart by comparing Aston's prices and packages with those offered by tour wholesalers, and by **Hideaways International** (800-843-4433), and companies that also book Aston properties.

Hana

The **Hotel Hana-Maui,** P.O. Box 9, Hana 96713 (808-248-8211 or 800-321-HANA), offers ninety-six units in the heart of Hana, and not on the beach. The free Keiki Aloha Sunshine Club for ages five through twelve operates from the middle of June to the end of August each year. The intermittent activities include arts and crafts, snorkeling, dancing, mini-excursions, a photo contest, boogie boarding, and more. Kids will like the nearby Hamoa Bay Beach most of all. Very active kids or teens may be bored here as this property is laid-back, quiet, and secluded, all of which delights parents and plagues teens.

Aloha Cottages, 73 Keawa Place, P.O. Box 205, Hana, Maui, Hawaii, 96713; (808) 248-8420. This place has about seven units, including two family cottages that can sleep five. The **Hana Bay Vacation Rental,** P.O. Box 318, Hana, Maui, Hawaii 96713 (800-657-7970), offers some condominiums as well as homes. **Hana Plantation Houses,** P.O. Box 489, Hana, Maui 96713, offers twelve rental units near Hamoa Bay Beach; toll-free on Maui (808) 248-7248, toll-free elsewhere (800) 657-7723.

Primitive camping is available near **Ohe'o Gulch** in Haleakala National Park. Rustic cabins are available (book well in advance) at **Waianapanapa State Park.** Contact the Division of State Parks, 54 South High Street, Wailuku, Hawaii 96793, or phone the Maui office at (808) 243-5354.

Kapalua

The **Kapalua Bay Hotel & Villas,** 1 Bay Drive, Kapalua (808-669-5656), offers Kamp Kapalua for kids ages five to twelve. Activities include sand castle contests, Hawaiian crafts, hula lessons, and eco-adventures. The beach here was rated America's Best Beach in 1991. Also in Kapalua, the **Ritz-Carlton,** 1 Ritz-Carlton Drive, Kapalua (808-669-6200), keeps young ones entertained with The Ritz Kids. Full- and half-day programs are provided year-round for ages five to twelve. A different environmental theme is featured each day. And for those thirteen and up, full- and half-day Eco-Tours are available, taking teens into the West Maui Mountains.

WHERE TO EAT

On Haleakala's slopes. Near Crater Road, tour **Sunrise Protea Farm's** quarter-acre garden while you picnic on their inexpensive sandwiches. Another good bet for lunch, dinner, or even breakfast is **Kula Lodge Restaurant,** Highway 377 (808-878-2517), where the menu features inexpensive teriyaki burgers, and pasta.

In Paia. Locals swear by **Mama's Fish House,** 799 Poho Place (808-579-8488), which offers fresh fish prepared several ways. A children's menu is available.

In Lahaina. Lahaina offers lots of inexpensive eateries. Try **Take Home Maui,** on Dickenson Street. Even though the store looks like a convenience store and shipping warehouse (which it is), go inside. The deli sandwiches are fresh, and if you're lucky, you'll get a spot at one of the few tables on their porch. The **Hard Rock Cafe,** 900 Front Street (808-667-7400), offers those famous burgers, as well as lime chicken, and ribs. The **Lahaina Broiler,** 889 Front Street (808-661-3111), offers sea breezes with its moderately priced breakfasts, lunch, and dinners. The sandwiches are good at the **Old Lahaina Cafe and Luau,** 505 Front Street; (808) 667-1998.

In Kaanapali. **Leilani's on the Beach,** in Whalers Village (808-661-4495), has good seafood and steaks. Also in Whalers Village, the **Rusty Harpoon** (808-661-3123) offers early-bird specials, as well as fresh fish, pasta, and chicken dishes. To treat yourself to some fine dining at upscale prices, try some of the luxury hotels' restaurants, particularly the **Swan Court** at the Hyatt Regency; (808) 661-1234.

The hotels in Wailea offer some fine dining. For inexpensive lunches, head for the poolside bars for burgers. **Cafe Kula,** The Grand Wailea Resort and Spa, offers healthy food at reasonable (for a hotel) prices. The pastas and salads are wonderful, and save room for the banana split—served with homemade sherbet and fruit. The food here is good-for-you healthy stuff, and it tastes great.

When you want to celebrate by enjoying a pricey meal, the Wailea hotels have lots to offer. Among the finds: **Raffle's Restaurant,** Renaissance Wailea Beach Resort (808) 879-4900. This restaurant is also known for its elaborate Sunday brunch. **Seasons,** at the Four Seasons Resort Wailea, offers great food, and half-portions for children; (808) 874-8000.

DAY TRIPS

In addition to the scenic drives, exploration of Haleakala, and snorkeling and whale-watching cruises, try **island hopping.** From Maui, it's easy to visit the other islands, especially **Lanai** and **Molokai.** Lanai's south coast is known for its dive sites. **Hulopoe Bay** offers easy snorkeling and lots of fish.

FOR MORE INFORMATION

Maui Visitors Bureau, P.O. Box 580, Wailuku, Maui, Hawaii 96793 (800-244-3530); the **Chamber of Commerce,** 250 Alomaha Street; and **Consumer Complaints** (808-243-5381).

For the **County Department of Parks and Recreation,** Wailuku, call (808) 243-7230, for permits dial (808) 243-7389, and for weather (808) 877-5111.

A free booklet, *"Maui, The Magic Isles,"* showcases the tri-isles of

Maui—Maui, Lana'i, and Moloka'i—and is available by calling (800) 525-MAUI, or writing the Maui Visitors Bureau, P.O. Box 580, Wailuku, Maui, Hawaii 96793. Website: http://www.gohawaii.com

Emergency Numbers

Ambulance, fire, police: 911

Hospital: Maui Memorial Hospital, Kaahumanu Avenue, Kahului; (808) 244-9056

Pharmacy: There are no twenty-four-hour pharmacies. For extended hours: Call **Long's Drugs** in Kahului, 100 East Kaahumanu Avenue, (808) 877-0041; In Kihei, call **Long's Drugs,** 1215 South Kihei Road, (808) 879-2259. In Lahaina, try **Craft's,** Lahaina Shopping Center, (808) 667-4384.

23 ⚲ Hawaii

OAHU

Oahu will surprise you. The most populated of Hawaii's islands, with about 860,000 people, Oahu has 599 square miles and is the third largest of the Hawaiian islands. The beat changes from the bustle of the blanket-to-blanket bodies of Waikiki to the sweeping curl of sunlit waves on north shore beaches that made surfing into a world-class sport. As the name suggests, Oahu, the gathering place, pulls together a sampler of Hawaii from the legends of old Polynesia, the lushness of botanical gardens, to the modern skyline of Honolulu.

GETTING THERE

The **Honolulu International Airport,** one of the busiest airports in the country, has an international terminal and an interisland terminal. Among the major carriers that fly into Honolulu are **United** (800-241-6522), **Continental** (800-525-0280), **American Airlines** (800-433-7300), and **Northwest** (800-225-2525). Especially with such long-haul destinations, always check out special, promotional fares, and packages, including airline packages. Often these offer airfare and lodging for much less than if you booked them individually.

GETTING AROUND

Taxis, which are readily available, include **Aloha State Cab** (808-847-3566) and **Charley's** (808-531-1333), both well-known. **The-Bus** (808-848-5555), the city's bus system, can get you around most of the island. When you board ask for transfers and check with the driver (if not beforehand) about the quickest and least expensive way to get to your destination.

Car rentals are popular. Check for the best rates, and book well in advance. Rental companies include **Avis** (808-834-5536 or 800-

331-1212), **Budget** (808-537-3600 or 800-527-0700), **Dollar** (808-831-2330 or 800-800-4000), **Hertz** (808-831-3500 or 800-654-3131), and **National** (808-831-3800 or 800-227-7368).

WHAT TO SEE AND DO

Waikiki Area Attractions

Diamond Head State Monument, off Diamond Head Road between Makapuu and Eighteenth avenues (808-587-0300), is probably Oahu's most noted landmark. Allow two hours for the round-trip hike to the 760-foot summit of **Diamond Head,** a volcanic crater that curves close to Waikiki's shoreline. Bring flashlights (a nice touch for little kids) to assist you through the darker tunnels. The wind in the grass and the quiet let you imagine this landmark as King Kamehameha saw it when he worshipped at a *heiau,* an ancient Hawaiian temple, on Diamond Head's slopes.

Beaches. The best family beaches are on the **South Shore,** where swimming, snorkeling, and wandering among the tide pools are popular. Use caution when swimming during the summer, when there's a high, strong surf. **Waikiki** is located here, as well as **Hanauma Bay** and **Sandy Beach. Waikiki's** sands are famous, and very crowded. Some hotels tend to stake out small areas where they offer such helpful beach gear as chairs and umbrellas; some of the less expensive hotels don't offer these items. Vendors sell inexpensive grass mats, which make easily transportable beach "blankets." The mats can also be purchased at local drugstores and sundry shops. If you want the shade, or a choice spot, arrive early. Another option: Tour the town in the morning, and come back to your hotel for some afternoon sun and fun. Check the local conditions, but Waikiki's beaches generally offer safe swimming.

Locals like the **Ala Moana Beach on the South Shore** at **Ala Moana Park,** Ala Moana Boulevard, complete with reef for snorkeling, and the **Kapiolani Park Beach Center,** Kapiolani Park (described next), is also another good bet.

Parks and Zoos. Even in Waikiki authentic Hawaii lives. Especially on Sunday, a stroll through **Kapiolani Park,** between Waikiki's beach and Diamond Head, at the end of Kalakaua Avenue. Locals relax here on this 170-acre expanse of lawns and picnic and play areas. Pack a ball and a kite, and soon you and your kids will be sharing a game of catch and a breeze with a local *keiki* (child).

Visit the **Waikiki Aquarium,** 2777 Kalakaua Avenue; (808) 923-9741. This is the place to introduce your children, especially those too young for snorkeling, to underwater wonders. Rare monk seals sun and swim here. Kids look wide-eyed at such strangely striped, spotted, and rainbow-hued Hawaiian reef dwellers as lion, butterfly, and squirrel fish, as well as lazy, green sea turtles, and yellow-hued coral that sprouts like wildflowers. The gift shop offers many allowance affordables, including fish magnets, stickers, pencils, and puzzles.

At the **Honolulu Zoo,** 151 Kapahulu Avenue (808-971-7171), Mari and Vaigai, two Asian pachyderms, steal the show. During Elephant Encounters, these tame behemoths bow, sit, carry handlers in their trunks, and place leis on giggling children. Check the zoo schedule. Admire the giant **banyan tree,** a fantastical conglomeration of limbs just outside the zoo's entrance.

The **U.S. Army Museum,** Fort DeRussy, (808) 438-2821, is located on Battery Randolph, formerly one of Oahu's coastal defense forts. Fifteen exhibits document Hawaii's military history, several focusing on World War II. Admission is free and the museum is open Tuesday through Sunday, 10:00 A.M. to 4:30 P.M.

Special Waikiki Tours. The **Atlantis Submarine** (808-973-9811 or 800-548-6262) offers a diver's-eye view of the deep without the work (and skill) of SCUBA. This recreational submarine, which also hosts tourist "dives" near the Big Island and Maui, has a shuttle vessel that departs from the Hilton Hawaiian Village, Waikiki. To board these subs (one holds 48 passengers; the other 64), kids must be at least 3 feet tall. Don't go if you're prone to claustrophobia, but do go if you want to get a new perspective on underwater life. To enhance the reef for the Waikiki dive, the Atlantis Submarine sank a ship, a vintage prop plane, and a man-made reef. From your portholes watch schools of parrot fish, angel fish, and yellow tangs cruise by.

Free events: The **Royal Hawaiian Band** plays on Friday nights at the Iolani Palace, Saturday evenings at Kapiolani Park. Tuesday through Thursday, head to the **Kodak Hula Show** at the Waikiki Shell

---

Oahu at a Glance

- Tropical paradise with places for those who like bustle and well as those who like solitude

- The classics: Diamond Head, Waikiki, the U.S.S. *Arizona* Memorial

- Lessons in island lore, swimming, and hula in Waimea Falls Park

- Advanced surfing at Banzai Pipeline and Sunset Beach

- Hawaii Visitors and Convention Bureau, (808) 923-1811

---

in Kapiolani Park. Check out an arts-and-crafts fair in Thomas Square, Kapiolani Park and Ala Moana Beach Park, learn the hula at the Royal Hawaiian Shopping Center, or take in spectacular Waikiki night views from the Hanohano Room at the Sheraton Waikiki Hotel.

Greater Honolulu Area Attractions

There's more sea life at the **Hawaii Maritime Center,** Pier 7, Ala Moana Boulevard and Bishop Street, Honolulu Harbor; (808) 523-6151. View whaling harpoons, koa wood canoes, and the *Falls of Clyde,* the only four-masted full-rigged ship. Open daily from 8:30 A.M. to 5:00 P.M.

The Bishop Museum, 1525 Bernice Street (808-847-3511), details the islands' natural history and cultural heritage. Make a game of searching for treasures amid the somewhat stodgy and static displays, many of which may bore this generation of high-tech video kids. Among the finds: vivid yellow and orange feather capes worn by the royals, Polynesian masks with dramatic swirls, and native carvings. Kids may also enjoy the traveling exhibits, the occasional hula dances performed by area schoolchildren, and the Planetarium shows, which light up the Polynesian skies. Open seven days a week, from 9:00 A.M.

to 5:00 P.M. The **Royal Hawaiian Mint** (808-949-6468) opened in 1995 and displays rare Hawaiian coins, the minting process, and more.

Hanauma Bay State Underwater Park, on the southeastern tip of Oahu, is a good snorkel spot, but often crowded. Tour operators who provide transportation from your hotel and back and rental of snorkel gear include **Paradise Snorkel Adventures** (808-923-7766).

The **Honouliuli Preserve** is located on the summit of Oahu's Waianae Range and protects many of the region's endangered flora and fauna species. Take a hike with **Nature Conservancy Hikes** (808-537-4508) and catch a glimpse of 48 rare plant species, found nowhere else in the world; an endangered species of tree snail; the native scarlet honeycreeper; and the Hawaiian owl. **Hawaii Nature Center Hike** (808-955-0100), in upper Makiki Valley, also offers hikes for adults and kids.

Horseback riding is another option for exploring Oahu's natural beauty. Try the 145-year-old **Kualoa Ranch** (808-237-7321) for a variety of trail options.

Other Not-too-Far From Honolulu Attractions

The most famous metropolitan Honolulu must-see is the **U.S.S. *Arizona* Memorial,** Pearl Harbor Naval Base, Pearl City; (808) 422-2771. Arrive before 9:00 A.M. (the visitor center opens around 8:00 A.M.) to be sure to obtain a free ticket to the floating memorial that marks the spot of the sunken *Arizona,* the grave of 1,177 sailors who died in the surprise Japanese attack. Each person must pick up his or her own ticket; this prevents tour groups from totally booking the monument.

While you wait for your timed entrance, browse the small museum, which personalizes the war by presenting some of the "ordinary" heroes and fighters. The gift shop offers a wide selection of books for all age levels. Particularly interesting is *Pearl Harbor, A Child's View of Pearl Harbor from Attack to Peace* (Kansas City, MO: Woodson House Publishers, 1993). Written by Dorinda Makana Onalini Nicholson, who was a child during the attack, this book presents the war from her viewpoint, including trying to escape the bombs and searching for her dog who was left behind in the initial hurry to flee.

Before heading out by boat to the floating memorial, you see a film, which explains the basics of the surprise attack on the U.S. fleet

You can see authentic hula dances at Waimea Falls Park. (Photo by the author)

and the devastations the Japanese inflicted. From the memorial itself you can see part of the rusty hull of the ship below. Depending on your child, this may or may not have an impact.

Next to the Arizona Memorial Visitor Center is the **USS *Bowfin* Submarine Museum and Park,** (808) 423-1341. The highlight is the USS *Bowfin,* a World War II submarine. Kids four and older can squeeze along its narrow passageways for a below-decks look at life alongside big torpedo tubes. At the museum learn about submarine design, and view a Japanese submarine torpedo—manned by one person, bound for glory and suicide.

About a twenty-minute drive from Waikiki, **Sea Life Park,** 41202 Kalapianaole Hwy., Waimanalo 96795 (808-259-6476 or 800-767-8046), combines science and showmanship. Watch the sea life in reef tanks, and learn about Humboldt penguins at their Hawaiian Ocean Theater, whales and dolphins at the Whaler's Cove Show, endangered Hawaiian Monk Seals at the Hawaiian Monk Seal Cave Center, and green sea turtles at the Turtle Lagoon. Inquire about workshops that provide an up-close look at sea turtles, dolphins, sharks, and whales; and special Behind-the-Scenes tours, which show how the handlers train sea turtles, whales, and dolphins.

Save this one for just before you fly home. For a last bit of island lore, visit the **Pacific Aerospace Museum,** in the departure terminal of the Honolulu International Airport, near the cafeteria and shops; (808) 839-0777. The modest fee is well worth it because this hands-on museum, while small, is fun, and certainly a welcome break from the bleakness of sitting around the gate. The Great Sky Quest Theatre presents a three-theater multimedia show composed of film, slides, and dioramas that detail the development of trans-Pacific flight.

Learn about the first flights, including one in 1925 in which the pilot ran out of fuel 365 miles from Hawaii's shores, so he stripped the fabric from his plane, created sails, and "blew" into shore. A diorama carefully explains the Pearl Harbor battle, at a level that even early grade-school children can understand.

The main gallery, outside the theater, offers an array of hands-on fun. Test your flying skills by "landing a plane," design your own aircraft via computer, and plot the best route across the Pacific Rim.

(Be sure to see the Day Trips for the many wonderful attractions on the North Shore.)

Tours

Paradise Cruises (800-334-6191) offers daily, narrated cruises from Kewalo Basin to Pearl Harbor on the *Star of Honolulu.* **Top Gun Tours** (808-396-8112) offers the area's only historic tour of Oahu's military bases, stopping at the Pearl Harbor Memorial, Hickham Air Force Base, and the Wheeler Army Air Base and Schofield Barracks (no tours on weekends). **Glide** above the island and see all the way to Kaena Point on Oahu's western tip. Call (808) 677-3404 for glider plane reservations.

SPECIAL EVENTS

January: Professional golfers take part in the PGA Hawaii Open Golf Tournament, and the Hula Bowl hosts college football all-stars each year.

February: Humpback Whale Awareness Month, with a wealth of lectures, and arts on display at the Sea Life Park. View demonstrations and displays of the year's new products at the Family Expo in Honolulu. Oahu hosts the Buffalo's Big Board Surfing Classic, the NFL Pro Bowl, and, just for kids twelve and under, a race of their own—the Keiki Great Aloha Run. Hawaii Mardi Gras is always lots of fun because area restaurants serve Creole and Cajun food, and the parade comes alive with colorfully masked dancers and steel drums. Oahu celebrates Japanese culture with games, entertainment, and various demonstrations at the Cherry Blossom Festival Culture and Craft Fair.

March: Watch the skies or take part in the Oahu Kite Festival, Queen Kapiolani Park. The fifth day of the month is the International Day of the Seal, celebrated at Sea Life Park with prize drawings, games, and crafts for the whole family. Have you ever seen 20,000 yellow rubber ducks race down a canal? Now's your chance, at the Great Hawaiian Rubber Duckie Race, in Honolulu.

April: The Hawaiian Festival of Music takes place all around Oahu, including choir and band concerts. At the Ala Moana Beach State Park, the Tin Man Biathlon features a 2.7-mile run and an 800-meter swim. On Easter, Sea Life Park hosts an Easter Egg Hunt.

June: June 11th is a state holiday, King Kamehameha Day. Events and activities vary yearly, but usually include the King Kamehameha Celebration Floral Parade, and Hawaiian arts and crafts. The King Kamehameha Hula Competition brings contenders to Honolulu from all corners of the world.

August: Witness the qualifying rounds for the Ironman Triathlon, at the Windward Triathlon, consisting of a 10-mile run, 50-mile bike ride, and mile swim.

September: The Outrigger Hotels Hawaiian Oceanfest includes women's professional windsurfing competition, run-and-swim races, paddle boarding, outrigger canoe paddling, and ocean medley relay. Attend the fund-raising Kamokila Hula Festival and Concert, a celebration of the music and dance of Hawaii.

November and December: At the Sunset Beach Park, men and women compete at the Triple Crown of Surfing: Event #3—World Cup of Surfing. Football fans won't want to miss the Aloha Bowl, and on New Year's Eve celebrate with the rest of Honolulu at First Night

Honolulu, an alcohol-free evening festival, featuring more than 200 events, including magicians, jugglers, and dancers.

WHERE TO STAY

Although Waikiki long ago turned its palm trees into high rises, this famed strip offers easy access to city attractions as well as inexpensive accommodations. A good lodging bet is the **Outrigger Reef Hotel,** 2169 Kalia Road; (808) 923-3111. Call **Outrigger Hotels,** (800) 688-7444. Unlike many of the twenty other Outrigger hotels in Waikiki, which seem to hunker among the town's noisy blocks, and cater to college kids on the loose, the **Outrigger Reef** sits surfside in a slightly quieter location along Kalia Road. The family-friendly amenities include a pool, rooms with two double beds, plus a pull-out couch, refrigerator, balconies, and no charge for children seventeen and under who share with parents. Ask about the frequent packages that often include free rental cars or deals for staying at the **Royal Waikoloan,** Outrigger's flagship hotel on the Big Island.

Older parents and grandparents should book the 50-plus Program for a 20 percent discount, or receive a 25 percent discount if you're a member of the American Association of Retired Persons.

The **Hyatt Regency Waikiki,** 2424 Kalakaua Avenue (808-923-1234 or 800-233-1234), offers optional packages for families as well as honeymooners. Ask about their often-available package with rental car, welcome gifts, Hawaiian leis, and discounts on local activities. At Camp Hyatt Waikiki, children between the ages of three and twelve enjoy movies, games, arts and crafts, and Hawaiian stories. Behind the waterfall on the second floor is a mini-museum. Aunty Malia awaits to share Hawaiian stories, crafts, and games. On Fridays at 5:00 P.M., stop by the Great Hall Atrium for Aunty Malia's Pau Hana Show, a Hawaiian song and dance presentation. Directly behind the hotel, watch the changing of the guards each evening at 6:15 P.M. at King's Guards on Koa Avenue.

The **Hilton Hawaiian Village,** 2005 Kalia Road (808-949-4321 or 800-445-8667), is a huge complex with twenty acres of gardens, three swimming pools, and a good-sized beach. In addition to the regular hotel rooms, there is also the upscale and quieter (but pricier) Ali'i

Tower accommodations. The hotel offers the Rainbow Express Young Explorers Club, a year-round children's activity program for ages five to twelve from 8:30 A.M. to 3:00 P.M. or a half-day program from 12:30 P.M. to 3:00 P.M. Kids enjoy photo safaris, beach expeditions, and field trips. New activities include a wildlife and ecology tour, cooking class, parade, and hike.

Four **Sheraton Hotels** in Waikiki offer the Keiki Aloha Sunshine Club, free activities for ages five to twelve year-round. The toll-free reservations number for all Sheraton properties is (800) 782-9488. Hotels participating in the kids' program in Waikiki are the **Sheraton Waikiki,** 2255 Kalakaua Avenue (808-922-4422); the **Sheraton Moana Surf,** 2365 Kalakaua Avenue (808-922-3111); and the flagship of Sheraton's Oahu hotels, **The Royal Hawaiian,** 2259 Kalakaua Avenue (808-923-7311). The latter, the "Pink Palace," once catered to the elite famous when only the wealthy could afford Hawaii. The graciousness is still there, as are the hand-carved wooden doors in the original hotel, whose rooms have been modernized. There's also a newer wing.

All of these Sheratons are beachfront and offer morning free Keiki Aloha sessions (9:00 A.M. to noon), supervised lunch (noon to 1:00 P.M.), afternoon sessions (1:00 P.M. to 5:00 P.M.), and evening sessions in the summer (6:30 P.M. to 9:00 P.M.). Activities include movies, dances, crafts, beach and watersports, and excursions to popular attractions.

The newly restored **Kahala Mandarin Oriental,** 5000 Kahala Avenue, Honolulu 96816 (808-739-8888), has its very own resident dolphins. A permanent lagoon houses the dolphins and visitors can watch three daily feedings and educational programs. The hotel's Keiki Club is available for kids ages five to twelve. Activities include lei making, puppet shows, Hawaiian folk tales, shoreline exploring, and more. Reservations are required by 6:00 P.M. the previous day. Half-day programs run from 9:00 A.M. to 12:00 P.M. and 1:00 P.M. to 4:00 P.M.; full-day from 9:00 A.M. to 4:00 P.M., with lunch.

The five-star **Halekulani** is beachfront in Waikiki, 2199 Kalia Road 96815; (808) 923-2311 or (800) 367-2343. It features a complimentary children's program (lunch and admission fees to attractions are extra) for ages six to eleven. The program operates mid-June through about August 20, and also for two weeks at Christmas. Children visit the Hawaii Maritime Museum, go on catamaran rides, swim in the pool, and try their hand at arts and crafts.

North Shore

The **Turtle Bay Hilton Golf and Tennis Resort,** P.O. Box 187, Kahuku, 96731 (808-293-8811 or 800-HILTONS), offers horseback riding, ocean-viewing pools (the surf can be rough here), and an eighteen-hole golf course. The **Turtle Bay Hilton**'s program offers activities for ages five to twelve. Check ahead to be sure the program is operating.

WHERE TO EAT

First a word about **luaus.** Most big hotels on every island offer these. Some are more "authentic" than others, but to accommodate tourists many have become less traditional, offering tourists lots of food, little authenticity, and some Hawaiiana. These can also be costly for a family. Check with your hotel concierge or new-found island friends to see which ones are worth the expense. Among the better luaus are the ones at The Royal Hawaiian (808-923-7311) and Paradise Cove (808-973-5828). Most of the luaus require reservations, and many offer children's prices.

Waikiki Area

Waikiki blooms with inexpensive eateries. Try breakfast at **McDonald's, Denny's,** or at any of the numerous coffee shops. At **Perry's Smorgy Restaurant,** 2380 Kuhio Avenue (808-926-0184) in the **Outrigger Coral Seas Hotel.** The food is just average, but the prices are low for heap-your-plate buffets. With southern fried chicken, mahi mahi, turkey, roast beef, and spaghetti on the unlimited buffet, even the finickiest tot will find something of interest.

On Kalakaua Avenue in Waikiki, try **Duke's Canoe Club** (808-923-0711), for local fish, steak, and chicken dishes, or the recently-opened **Planet Hollywood** (808-924-7877).

Check out the new **Texas Rock 'n Roll Sushi Bar** (808-923-ROLL) at the Hyatt Regency Waikiki, featuring a combination of Hawaiian favorites with Honolulu's creative sushi. Livening things up are kimono-clad hostesses, wait staff in western garb, country western and rock and roll music, and karaoke.

The **Waiahole Poi Factory,** Kamehameha Highway and Waiahole Valley Road, open only Friday afternoons, features a lunchtime feast of genuine home-cooked Hawaiian delicacies at a low price. **Monterey Bay Canners,** 2335 Kalakaua Avenue (808-971-3595), features a variety of seafood dishes, a children's menu, and a relaxed environment. They are also located at the Pearlridge Center (808-483-3555).

When you dine at the **Lewers Street Fish Company,** Lewers Street (808-971-1000), or the **Waikiki Seafood and Pasta Company** (808-923-5949), you receive half-price coupons for future meals at either restaurant. The **California Pizza Kitchen,** 4211 Waialae Avenue (808-737-9446), is a chain of gourmet pizzerias whose menu also includes salads and pastas. They have several locations throughout Oahu. The **Wailana Coffee House,** 1860 Ala Moana Boulevard (808-955-1764), across from the Hilton Hawaiian Village, is an inexpensive eatery. For a good breakfast buffet, try the **Parc Cafe,** in the Waikiki Parc Hotel, 2233 Helumoa Road; (808) 921-7272. Kids prices are reduced.

While dining out during your visit, ask about kids' prices and use the early bird specials, which can reduce a full meal to $7.00 to $8.00 if you arrive before 6:00 or 6:30 P.M., a convenient family dining time. Also check the free tourist guides, such as *Spotlight Oahu Gold,* for discount coupons to restaurants and attractions.

Ala Moana Center Area

The **Makai Food Court** at the Ala Moana Center, 1450 Ala Moana Boulevard, offers a range of ethnic choices, from Thai to Italian to Hawaiian. The **China House,** 1349 Kapiolani Boulevard (808-949-6622), near the Ala Moana Center, features Oriental cuisine and welcomes families. The **California Pizza Kitchen,** 1910 Ala Moana Boulevard (808-955-5161), offers good pizza and pasta. **Restaurant Row,** 500 Ala Moana Blvd. (808) 538-1441, offers more than ten restaurants, including Burger King and Sunset Grill. At the Ward Warehouse, the **Old Spaghetti Factory** (808-591-2513) specializes in pasta with a variety of sauces.

Other Places Around Oahu

At **Stuart Anderson's,** 1050 Ala Moana Boulevard (808-591-9292), adults savor the steaks, while kids usually opt for the barbecued ribs, french fries, and crispy shrimp. For Mexican fare, choose from chimichangas, tacos, and burritos at **Compadres,** 1200 Ala Moana Boulevard; (808) 591-8307. The **Hee Hing Restaurant,** 449 Kapahulu Avenue (808-735-5544), promises fresh fish, delicious noodles, and a large selection of dishes to choose from.

DAY TRIPS

A must-do day trip takes you across the island to the north shore through sugarcane and pineapple fields bounded by blue sea and green cliffs. Helpful hint: Wear your bathing suit.

Visit **Waimea Falls Park,** 59-864 Kamehameha Highway at Wei Mei; (808) 638-8511 or (808) 942-5700. This 1,800-acre botanical garden about 40 miles from Waikiki features lush vegetation and lessons in island lore. Take the tram, or stroll, through the gardens of red and purple bougainvillea, hibiscus, past trees draped with Spanish moss, and clusters of ginger plants, to the waterfall. Cliff divers, announced by the call of a conch shell, tumble effortlessly from as high as 60 feet. Swim here, then follow the crowd to a performance of a traditional hula, where costumed dancers relate tales of stalwart warriors and stoical princesses. Also visit the ancient temple known as Hale Iwi.

For teens, Waimea Falls Park offers adventure tours, which let you ride through the park's North Valley. To take the three-hour guided ATV (all-terrain vehicle) trek (book only if you know how to handle these sometimes-tricky-to-operate vehicles), you must be sixteen and weigh at least ninety pounds.

The park also offers guided mountain tours and kayak rides along the Waimea River.

After Waimea Falls Park, continue north for several miles, but pull over when you see the surfboards. Watch the experts catch a wave at such legendary beaches as **Banzai Pipeline** and **Sunset Beach.** Look, but don't swim as the undertow and often 30-foot-high waves make these shores dangerous for even the most accomplished swimmers.

The **Polynesian Cultural Center,** 55-370 Kamehameha Highway, Laie, 96762 (808-293-3333 or 800-367-7060), entertains with lively hands-on history. Allow several hours to explore this forty-two-acre living history park, or even stay for the dinner luau and the elaborate evening review. (Reserve ahead of time.) At the re-created villages of Samoa, New Zealand, Tahiti, Fiji, Old Hawaii, the Marquesas, and Tonga, the costumed interpreters—some sporting elaborate tattoos and dried leaf and feather skirts present facts with quick vaudeville pacing. As you learn how to play the nose flute, twirl poi balls, weave baskets, carve tikis, and blow conch shells, these interpreters crack jokes and deliver deadpan looks. The Samoan villager, for example, was irresistible with his wide-eyed, worried stare as he playfully instructed us in the arduous task of splitting a coconut for its juice and milk.

Don't miss the IMAX film *Polynesian Odyssey* whose montage of canyons, cliffs, and ocean scenes evokes the bravery of the first voyagers who used their starry-eyed wonder and instinctive skills to cross an unknown sea. As always, be aware that the larger-than-life IMAX images may scare some younger children.

FOR MORE INFORMATION

For general information contact the **Chamber of Commerce of Hawaii,** 1132 Bishop Street (808-545-4300), and the **Hawaii Visitors and Convention Bureau,** 2270 Kalakaua Avenue, Suite 801 (808-923-1811), or the **Waikiki/Oahu Visitors Association,** c/o The Kiely Company, Pauahi Tower, 1001 Bishop, Suite 881, Honolulu 96813. For **Camping/State Park** information, call (808) 587-0300. For **weather** information, call 973-4380. **Handicabs of the Pacific,** P.O. Box 22428, Honolulu, Hawaii 96823 (808-524-3866), provides special transportation, tours, and cruises for people with disabilities. Website: http://www.gohawaii.com

The Hyatt Regency Waikiki offers the **Children's Guide to Fun Under the Sun,** a booklet containing exciting things to see and do in the area, which is available for a nominal fee.

Emergency Numbers
    Ambulance, fire, police: 911
    Twenty-four-hour emergency care: The **Queens Medical Center,** 1301 Punchbowl Street; (808) 547-4311.
    CALL-A-NURSE, (808) 225-6877, is a free health care information referral line, Monday through Saturday 8:00 A.M. to 4:30 P.M. For the hearing-impaired, ASK-2000 (275-2000).
    Kuhio Pharmacy, 2330 Kuhio Ave; (808) 923-4466.

THE INSIDE PASSAGE— HAINES, SKAGWAY, SITKA, AND GLACIER BAY

HAINES

Along the Inside Passage on the northern end of the Lynn Canal, Haines is on a narrow peninsula between the Chilkoot and Chilkat inlets. John Muir first visited Haines in 1879, and in 1903 the U.S. Army selected Haines for its first outpost in the Alaskan Territory. The city is known for its scenic setting and for its fall gathering of bald eagles. Another plus: In fall, winter, and spring, the Northern Lights, the Aurora Borealis, are visible from Haines.

The average July temperature hovers around 66 degrees Fahrenheit; the average January temperature is 17 degrees, but can go as low as –15 degrees. Dress appropriately. Remember that in fall and winter daylight is limited. While mid-October has about ten hours of daylight, mid-November has about seven and a half hours, and by December there are only six hours of daylight, with sunrise about 10:00 A.M. and sunset as early as 2:30 P.M.

GETTING THERE

The closest major airport to **Haines** is 80 miles away in Juneau. **Alaska** Airlines (800–426–0333) offers flights into Juneau. For the thirty-five-minute flight from Juneau to Haines there are four air taxi firms: **Haines Airways** (907–766–2646), **L.A.B. Flying Service** (907–766–2222 or 800–426–0333), **Skagway Air Service** (907–983–2218), and **Wings of Alaska** (907–766–2030 or 800–478–9464 in Alaska only). The airlines provide shuttle service into town.

The **Alaska Marine Highway** has ferries to the Haines-area local terminal (907–766–2111) on a year-round schedule. From Juneau, the ferry ride takes about four and a half hours. From Skagway, the ferry takes about one hour. During the summer, the ferries run more frequently than in the winter. Contact the Alaska Marine Highway System, P.O. Box 25535, Juneau 99802–5535; (800) 642–0066 in the United States and (800) 665–6414 in Canada. **B.C. Ferries,** 1112 Fort Street Victoria, B.C. V8V 4V2 Canada (604–669–1211), offers service to Prince Rupert, B.C., where you can catch the Alaska Marine Highway System.

The **Haines-Skagway Water Taxi and Scenic Cruise,** P.O. Box 246, Haines 99827 (907–766–3395), which operates mid-May to mid-September, connects these two cities, which are only 15 miles apart by water, but 360 miles by road. By taking an early water-taxi shuttle service, you could see either town as a day trip from the other.

Haines is also accessible by land. The scenic **Haines Highway** connects with the Alaskan Highway at Haines Junction. The 155-mile drive south from Haines Junction to Haines along the Haines Highway, which takes about three and a half hours, passes through the Chilkat Bald Eagle Preserve and climbs the summit of Chilkat Pass.

Several bus companies travel to Haines. Contact **Alaska Denali Transit** (907–273–3331), **Alaska Sightseeing Tours** (800–426–7702), and the **Alaskon Express** (800–544–2206).

GETTING AROUND

The **Haines ferry terminal** (907–766–2111) is 4 miles out of town. To get into town, try the **Haines Shuttle and Tour** (907–

766-2819) or a taxicab. **The New Other Guy's Taxi & Tours** (907-766-3257) offers sight-seeing tours and taxi service. In town, **Sockeye Cycles** (907-766-2869) rents bikes and, in high season, arranges tours. Call ahead to be sure.

Car rentals in town include **Affordable Cars,** Captain's Choice Hotel, P.O. Box 392, Haines 99827 (907-766-3111); **Avis,** Halsingland Hotel, P.O. Box 1589, Haines 99827 (907-766-2733); **Hertz,** the Thunderbird Motel, P.O. Box 589, Haines 99827 (907-766-2131); and **Independent Car Rental,** the Eagle's Nest Motel, P.O. Box 250, Haines 99827 (907-766-2891).

Be sure to stop at the **Haines Visitor Center,** Second Avenue and Willard Street; (907) 766-2234. They offer a walking tour of town and information about the Eagle Preserve, lodgings, and restaurants.

WHAT TO SEE AND DO

Attractions

Even though the main tourist draw for Haines is its scenic setting and site as gateway to more of Alaska's glorious outdoors and wildlife, the town has a few things worth a brief visit.

Throughout the year, families can learn about Native Americans at the **Sheldon Museum and Cultural Center,** P.O. Box 629; (907) 766-2366. Exhibits focus on the Tlingit Indians and the pioneers who inhabited the upper Lynn Canal. From May to September, the museum is open at least from 1:00 to 5:00 P.M., often longer in summer. But in winter the facility is open generally Sundays, Mondays, Wednesdays from 1:00 to 4:00 P.M., and by appointment. To keep order in the Haines area during the gold rush era and in times of territorial disputes with Canada, the U.S. Army in 1903 established **Fort William H. Seward** (west side of town at the south end of Haines Highway), named for the U.S. secretary of state who arranged the purchase of Alaska from Russia. Take the self-guided walking tour of the fort, which was decommissioned after World War II. Maps are available from the **Haines Visitor Bureau,** P.O. Box 530, Haines 99827; (907) 766-2234 or (800) 458-3579.

Some buildings are more interesting than others. Outside the **Fort's Headquarters,** #7 on the walking tour, now a private residence,

---

Haines, Skagway, Sitka, and Glacier Bay at a Glance

- Native American culture, gold rush history, and Alaska's wildlife in a scenic setting

- In Haines each fall, the world's largest gathering of American bald eagles

- In Skagway, narrow-gauge train rides, hiking, and Klondike gold history

- In Sitka, Tlingit Indian culture and Russian heritage, plus sea kayaking

- Glacier Bay National Park and Preserve: simply stunning

- Alaska State Chamber of Commerce, (907) 586-2323

---

note the cannon, cast in 1861, one of the first breech-loading naval guns designed to use shell casings and to be loaded from the rear. Notice, also, the totem pole, carved by Alaska Indian Artists, featuring representations of the eagle and the bear. The **Post Exchange, #16** on the walking tour, was a multipurpose recreational center that housed a gymnasium, movie theater, store, and bowling alley. Here the military men kept a pet bear nicknamed "Three Per," short for three percent bear, who, legend has it, would prefer beer, but if no one was buying him any, he begged for ice-cream cones.

On site at the fort now is a replica of a **Chilkat Tribal House, #8** on the parade grounds, part of the **Chilkat Center for the Arts;** (907) 766-2160. Here local artists can be seen carving totem poles and making jewelry. In summer, the **Chilkat Indian Dancers** perform in their native costumes. Inquire ahead about schedules and performances.

Dalton City, P.O. Box 385, Haines 99827 (907-766-2476), on the Southeast Alaska State Fairgrounds, is a re-creation of an 1890s gold rush town. In summertime, the area features sled-dog demonstrations, arts and crafts, gold panning, plus restaurants and shops. Dalton City was the set location for the movie *White Fang.*

Nature: The Eagles

In Fall: Each fall from mid-October through January, hundreds of bird-watchers from around the world travel to Haines for the world's largest gathering of American bald eagles. Twenty miles outside of town on the Haines Highway, between mile marker 10 and mile marker 28 (when driving into town from HainesJunction, you pass this way), is the 48,000-acre **Alaska Chilkat Bald Eagle Preserve,** Southeast Regional Office, Division of Parks and Outdoor Recreation, 400 Willoughby, Juneau 99801. More than 4,000 bald eagles congregate here, with the prime viewing area between mile marker 18 and mile marker 24. This 6-mile stretch along the river flats of the Chilkat River are known as the "Eagle Council Grounds." Thousands of eagles congregate here from early October through February. Some are drawn from their homes hundreds of miles away to this specific area because of the natural phenomenon, called the "alluvial fan reservoir," responsible for 5 miles of nonfrozen water on the Chilkat River during freezing months. Because warm water percolates into the flats and keeps the waters from freezing, salmon, who die shortly after spawning, come here. The eagles feast on the abundant salmon carcasses.

When eagle viewing, for safety, be careful to pull off the main road into an eagle-viewing area so as not to block the road or be susceptible to accidents. Also, don't walk on the river flats, as this disturbs the eagles, who prefer being viewed from afar. Bring binoculars and, for photography, zoom lenses. Remember that in the heart of winter daylight is only from about 10:00 A.M. to 2:00 P.M., and it rains or snows frequently.

In Spring and Summer: Although many fewer eagles congregate in Haines in spring—April through May—the weather is much kinder, and warmer. April also brings nesting season for the eagles, who begin with courtship rituals, such as diving eagles locking their talons and somersaulting through the air.

In spring you also can view migrating trumpeter swans, sandhill cranes, arctic terns, and shorebirds. You may also get a glimpse of graz-

An exciting train ride through the White Pass reveals the rugged beauty of Alaska's mountains. (Courtesy Southeast Alaska Tourism Council)

ing moose, or brown and black bear. A highlight of the first two weeks of May: migration of sea lions, which may be accompanied by humpback and orca (killer) whales.

About 200 resident eagles stay in the preserve in summer. Even though there may be less wildlife, you can still catch sight of eagles diving for fish and perching in treetops.

Alaska Nature Tours (described next) offers guided trips year-round.

Special Tours

For a day tour of the area, bring your camera along on **Alaska Nature Tours,** P.O. Box 491, Haines 99827; (907) 766–2876. Experts on the natural history of Alaska lead a variety of bus tours. Some include guided walks and hikes, as well as birding treks, into the heart of the **Valley of the Eagles,** the **Chilkat Wildlife Preserve.** The excursions take place year-round. In summer Alaska Nature Tours offers a three-hour trip and an all-day tour with a guided hike. Summer is the busy season, so book far in advance. In fall and winter, their Complete Chilkat Bald Eagle Preserve package includes a guided tour, meals, and lodging at the Captain's Choice Motel.

Since 1978, Al Gilliam of **Alaska Cross Country Guiding and Rafting,** Box 124, Haines 99827 (907-767-5522), has been operating many personalized trips into the heart of Alaska's pristine wilderness, including the **Chilkat Bald Eagle Preserve** and **Kluane National Park.** Most of his trips are based out of his backcountry cabins (new ones overlook the eagle preserve). Gilliam offers an interesting combination of fly-in, raft-out river trips and day hikes. Your takeout point is 3 miles from the cabin.

On Gilliam's three-day, six-person **Tsirku Valley Glacier Camp Fly In–Raft Out** trip, offered from July 1 through September, enjoy a scenic bush-plane flight up the Takhin Valley to the base camp cabin located at the foot of DeBlondeau Glacier. Each night you come back to this cabin, where meals are provided. To keep costs down, guests help with the preparation of meals.

Hike around the base of the glacier, and on the last day raft down the swift, yet flat Tsirku River through the Chilkat Bald Eagle Reserve. As you float silently down the river, bald eagles feed, right, and take flight. Groups range from two to six. There's a slight discount for ages twelve to fourteen; the trip is not recommended for kids under twelve, but discuss the maturity and swimming ability of your children with Gilliam.

Gilliam also offers raft trips on the wild Alsek River, a class IV white-water river that cuts through Kluane National Park, Yukon Territory; and another rafting trip on the Tatshenshini River, a class III white-water river. This ten-day trip starts in the Dalton Post, Canadian Yukon, and ends in Glacier Bay National Park.

Chilkoot Sled Dog Adventures, Dept. SATC5, P.O. Box 826, Haines, 99827 (907-767-5566), has authentic sled-dog demonstrations, as well as trips to the Valley of the Eagles on motor coaches.

SPECIAL EVENTS

Festivals

January: Alcan 200 Road Rally, a 200-mile snow-machine race from the American-Canadian border to Dezadeash Lake on the Haines Highway and back.

July: Haines Rodeo, includes dancing, barbecues, and beauty pageants.

August: Southeast Alaska State Fair, with lots of entertainment —from horse shows to miniature train rides—for all ages.

October: Alaska Day Celebration celebrates the purchase of Alaska and pioneer days.

Sportfishing

March and April: Trout fishing, from the banks of the Chilkat River.

Mid-September to mid-November: Coho salmon, sportfishing from the banks of the Chilkat River; no boat necessary. Average size coho is ten to twelve pounds.

Mid-December through February: Dolly Varden Trout Sportfishing, ice fishing at Mosquito Lake.

WHERE TO STAY

Condominiums are available even in Haines. The **Fort Seward Condos,** the historic Fort Seward building, P.O. Box 75, Haines 99827 (907-766-2425), offers furnished apartments with cooking facilities. Also in the historic Fort Seward building is the **Fort Seward Lodge,** P.O. Box 307, Haines 99827; (907) 766-2009 or (800) 478-7772. It has ten rooms, some with shared and some with private baths, and two with kitchenettes.

The Captain's Choice Motel, Second and Dalton streets; (907) 766-3111, (800) 247-7153 in continental United States, (800) 478-2345 in Alaska and Canada. It overlooks Portage Cove and has forty rooms. The thirteen-room **Eagle's Nest Motel** is at 1183 Haines Highway, P.O. Box 250, Haines 99827; (907) 766-2891 or (800) 354-6009 in Alaska. Located at the foot of the Chilkat Mountains, it offers basic accommodations and some rooms with kitchenettes. **The Thunderbird Motel,** downtown, P.O. Box 589, Haines 99827 (907-766-2131 or 800-327-2556), has twenty rooms, six of which have kitchenettes.

The Bear Creek Camp and Hostel, 2 miles from Haines on Small Tract Road (907-766-2259), offers basic cabins that sleep up to four at an inexpensive price. In addition, bunks are available in the hostel. Upon request, the owners will meet you at the ferry terminal. Several bed-and-breakfast accommodations are available. Ask about the preferred age of children the facility welcomes. Bed and breakfasts include **Officer's Inn Bed & Breakfast,** Historic Fort Seward, P.O. Box 1589, Haines 99827; (907) 766–2000, (800) 542–6363 in continental United States, (800) 478–2525 in Canada. **Chilkat State Park** is about 7 miles south of downtown, and **Chilkoot Lake** is about 11 miles north of downtown, but 4 miles from the ferry; each has thirty-two sites for tents or recreational vehicles.

WHERE TO EAT

The **Haines Visitors Bureau** (800–458–3579 in the United States and 800–478–2268 in Canada) has a list of restaurants (see For More Information). Here are some choices. **The Bamboo Room,** Second Avenue near Main Street (907–766–2800), offers seafood, steak, and burgers. **The Chilkat Restaurant and Bakery,** Fifth Avenue (907–766–2920), serves all of the above plus fresh-baked breads and pastries. **Mountain Market** (907–766–3390), downtown on the corner of Third Street and Haines Highway, features sandwiches, fresh juice, baked goodies, and an espresso bar. **Porcupine Pete's,** Main and Second Avenue (907–766–9999), besides sandwiches, adds sourdough pizza, homemade soup, a soda fountain, and ice cream. At **33 Mile Roadhouse,** Haines Highway, located near the eagle preserve (907–767–5510), hamburgers are the specialty. For something a bit more upscale, try the **Fort Seward Lodge,** in Fort Seward; (907) 766–2009. Offering dinner only, the restaurant specializes in crab, seafood, and stew.

DAY TRIPS

Among the most exciting day trips are the adventure tours available from Haines (see Special Tours). The other towns along the Inside Passage, depending on their location, offer attractive day trips such as Skagway, by way of the Haines Skagway Water Taxi and Scenic Cruise (see Getting There). From Haines, plan to spend a few days in the Glacier Bay and Juneau (see Ketchikan/Juneau chapter).

FOR MORE INFORMATION

Haines Convention and Visitors Bureau, P.O. Box 530, Haines 99827; (907) 766-2234, (800) 458-3579 in the United States, (800) 478-2268 in Canada. Alaska Internet Travel Guide: http://www.Alaska-Online.com/travel/alaska.htm

Emergency Numbers
Ambulance, fire, police: 911
Hospital: **The Lynn Canal Medical Clinic,** Second and Willard streets (907-766-2521), is open from 9:00 A.M. to 5:00 P.M. and provides pharmaceutical needs. After hours, follow the instructions on their recording for both medical and pharmaceutical services, as there is no twenty-four-hour pharmacy.
Poison Control: Call Anchorage: (800) 478-3193.

SKAGWAY

Skagway, in Tlingit, means "home of the north wind." Skagway, situated at the northern end of the Inside Passage at the head of the Lynn Canal and surrounded by the Coast Mountains, is about 80 air miles northeast of Juneau. Skagway surged as a boomtown during the 1897 to 1898 gold rush days, growing from a handful of residents to about 20,000. Now the town's 750 residents cater to the curious. Skagway can be cool even in summer; in July, temperatures range from 55 to 75 degrees Fahrenheit; in January, temperatures range from 15 to 32 degrees Fahrenheit.

GETTING THERE

The **Alaska Marine Highway** ferries travel the one-hour route from Haines to Skagway. You can pick up the ferry in Juneau as well. The Skagway ferry terminal is located at the south end of well-traveled Broadway Street; (907) 983-2941 or (800) 642-0066 for general information. Skagway is the northernmost port for the Alaska Marine

Highway System, with connections to all the other communities in Southeast Alaska and Bellingham, Washington. In addition, many major cruise ships dock in Skagway for the day. Check the itinerary. The **Haines-Skagway Water Taxi and Scenic Cruise,** P.O. Box 246, Haines 99827 (907-766-3395), operates mid-May to mid-September; it connects these two cities, which are only 15 miles apart by water, but 360 miles by road. By taking an early water-taxi shuttle service, you could see either town as a day trip from the other.

By car from the Yukon, take the **Klondike Highway,** which joins the Alaska Highway at Whitehorse, capital of the Yukon, and connects with Skagway 113 miles away. Tour buses take visitors to Skagway from the Yukon as well as from Alaska's interior. Among the motor-coach companies: **Alaska Direct** (907-277-6652), **Alaskon Express** (800-544-2206 or 907-983-2241), and **Sourdough Shuttle and Tours** (800-478-2529 or 907-983-2523).

Airlines that fly into Skagway: **Haines Airways** (907-766-2646) provides daily scheduled flights. Other carriers are **L.A.B. Flying Service** (907-983-2471), **Skagway Air Service** (907-983-2218), and **Wings of Alaska** (907-983-2442).

Skagway offers several railroad excursions. The scenic **White Pass and Yukon Railroad** (described later) can take you between Skagway and Whitehorse. There are also day excursions from Juneau to Skagway, and rail/motor-coach tours from Skagway to the Yukon and to Alaska's interior. The train station is located at Second Avenue; (907) 983-2217, (800) 343-7373, or (800) 478-7373.

GETTING AROUND

The downtown area of **Skagway,** only about 6 blocks long, is easily toured by walking. If you must hire a car or cab, call the following. Among the car rental companies in Skagway: **Avis** (907-983-2550 or 800-331-1212), **Sourdough Shuttle Car and Van Rental** (800-478-2529 or 907-983-2523), and **ABC Motorhome Rental**s (800-421-7456 or 907-279-2000). Skagway has several taxicab companies as well: **Frontier Excursions** (907-983-2512), **Sourdough Shuttle** and Tours (907-983-2523), **Pioneer Taxi and Tours** (907-983-2623), and **Southeast Tours** (907-983-2990).

WHAT TO SEE AND DO

The **Skagway Convention and Visitors Bureau,** between Second and Third avenues and Broadway in the AB Hall (907-983-2854), offers a variety of pamphlets and walking-tour brochures.

White Pass and Yukon Railroad

With limited time in Skagway, save town for last, and be sure to head for the hills first, a more interesting tour if you must choose. Sign on for a full- or half-day trip that follows the arduous path of the Klondike fortune seekers up to Fraser in great comfort with a day trip on the **White Pass and Yukon Railroad,** P.O. Box 435, Skagway; (907) 983-2217, (800) 343-7373, or, in Canada, (800) 478-7373. This scenic three-hour ride, offered mid-May to mid-September, is especially good for persons with limited stamina for walking, such as young tots and some grandparents with limited mobility.

The White Pass and Yukon Railroad, a narrow-gauge train, takes you along one of America's great history trails, climbing almost 3,000 feet in 20 miles. You pass canyons, gorges, waterfalls, rushing streams, mountains laced with clouds, gold rush graveyards, and Dead Horse Gulch, named for the 3,000 animals that died in the struggle over this pass. The narrow footpaths and difficult climb testify to the compulsion of those struck with gold fever. A trip originating in Canada in Bennett and traveling to Fraser and into Skagway incorporates time for a short hike before arriving in Skagway at 6:30 P.M.

Klondike Gold Rush National Historical Park

Skagway's business district is the centerpiece of the **Klondike Gold Rush National Historical Park** visitor center, White Pass and Yukon Route depot building, Second Avenue and Broadway; (907) 983-2921. The wooden facades here look like turn-of-the-century stores. Park brochures relate that in 1976 this park was created to preserve the physical and emotional history of the gold rush. The way to tour this downtown area of the park, which is about 6 blocks long, is to walk. Park rangers offer walking tours and interpretive programs from June through Labor Day.

The visitor center offers some black-and-white photos of prospectors. *Days of Adventure—Dreams of Gold,* a thirty-minute film, is shown hourly from 11:00 A.M. to 3:00 P.M., May through October. Also offered are walking tours of the Historic District guided by a ranger. On your tour of the town, make a stop at the **Arctic Brotherhood Hall,** Broadway Street, whose exterior walls are covered with more than 20,000 pieces of flat driftwood. Once the place of a private fraternal order, it now houses the visitor center. If your kids aren't spooked by cemeteries, you may want to walk a bit out of town to the **Gold Rush Cemetery** to see the graves of such Skagway legends as Soapy Smith and Frank Reid.

Not officially part of the National Park, the small **Corrington Museum of Alaskan History** is at Fifth Avenue and Broadway; (907) 983-2580. With its photos of Klondike legends such as Soapy Smith and his gang, and Dawson Charlie, the museum is worth a visit. It also has a scrimshaw collection, plus a small display of Tlingit totems and masks, and trade beads.

The **Skagway Streetcar Company** also puts on a show called *The Days of '98.* This musical centers on Skagway's historical past, when gold drew them in from all around and when outlaw Soapy Smith created his legend. Kids may like this combination of old-fashioned attire and easy-to-digest history.

Hiking: The Chilkoot and White Pass Trails

This is the real McCoy, the Gold Rush trail that caused many to die. The 33-mile arduous **Chilkoot Trail** is accessible only by foot (unless you want to see part of it from the comfort of your train window aboard the White Pass and Yukon Railroad). The trail, open late May through September, begins near the Dyea town site, 9 miles from Skagway, and travels over the Chilkoot Pass to Lake Bennett. From Skagway, shuttle service and taxis go to the trailhead.

Rangers estimate the hike to take between three and five days one way. Obviously, this trek is suitable for only a few experienced hikers, adults, and older teens who are well versed in difficult climbs in changeable weather. Proper equipment includes warm clothes— even in summer, as temperatures drop near the summit—rain gear, waterproof tent, campstove and fuel (no wood is available), hiking

The outpost town of Skagway is a great place to visit.
(Photo by Clark Mishler/Courtsey Alaska Tourism Marketing Coucil)

boots, food, and extra rations. Before attempting this hike, talk with the rangers about weather conditions. This is bear country, so know what to do about food storage, and take other precautions (wear bear bells).

Most people should not hike this trail, simply because of its difficulty. Although arduous, this trail is not a wilderness hike. The park service estimates that in July and August thirty to eighty hikers begin the hike each day. In 1992, more than 2,800 hikers climbed through the Chilkoot Pass. Ask the rangers for reliable, licensed outfitters who offer guided hikes.

Obtain a hiking permit from the visitor center in town, Second Avenue. If you plan to start in Dyea, you must clear Canada Customs before leaving Skagway, as part of the trail goes through Canadian territory. Call **Fraser Customs** (403-821-4111) or sign the required forms at the Park Service Visitor Center, Skagway.

Most families should not attempt to hike this famous trail. For most, the scenic view from the train window will suffice.

SPECIAL EVENTS

March: Buckwheat Ski Classic; Windfest, a winter celebration.

July: Soapy Smith's Wake—enjoy the local culture and toast the infamous con man Jefferson "Soapy" Smith with complimentary champagne; Fourth of July Celebration.

August: Dyea Dash.

September: Klondike Trail of '98 Road Relay.

December: F.O. Eagles Christmas Party.

WHERE TO STAY

The largest hotel in town is the **Westmark Inn,** Third Avenue and Spring Street, P.O. Box 515, 99840; (907) 983-6000 or (800) 544-0970. It is operated by Holland America Line/Westours, to accommodate the many people who disembark cruise ships and spend the night in Skagway. Other guests are welcome; check for availability.

The **Gold Rush Lodge,** P.O. Box 514 SE, Skagway 99840 (907-983-2831), offers modern rooms. Although the **Golden North Hotel,** P.O. Box 431, Skagway 99840 (907-983-2451), is among Alaska's oldest hotels, it offers comfortable rooms and a restaurant.

The Historic Skagway Inn Bed and Breakfast, P.O. Box 500, Skagway 99840 (907-983-2289 or, in Alaska, 800-478-2290), is open year-round. Once a woman's boardinghouse, it now has twelve rooms with Victorian decor, five of which are family size.

The Dyea Campground, operated by the National Park Service, offers twenty-two free sites. Contact the rangers, **Klondike Gold Rush National Historical Park,** P.O. Box 517, Skagway 99840; (907) 983-2921.

WHERE TO EAT

The Northern Lights Cafe, Broadway between Fourth and Fifth avenues (907-983-2225), offers light meals of Greek, Mexican, Italian, and American origins. Breakfasts and dinners are also served daily.

While in town, enjoy a night out at the **Prospector's Sourdough,** Broadway between Third and Fourth avenues; (907) 983-2865. It has a coffee-house decor and a menu of fresh salmon, soups, and salads. The old **Red Onion Saloon,** Second Avenue and Broadway (907-982-2222), is considered Skagway's best bar; it features live music, tasty Alaska amber beer on tap, and great pizza.

For a slightly more upscale meal, try the **Chilkoot Dining Room,** the Westmark Inn (907-983-6000), or the restaurant at the **Golden North Hotel,** Third and Broadway (907-983-2451).

DAY TRIPS

From Skagway, take a day trip to Haines using the water taxi (see Getting There) or fly to Juneau for a day or an extended tour. A popular driving route is the Golden Circle Route, which connects Skagway to Whitehorse via the Klondike Highway, Whitehorse to Haines Junction and Kluane National Park on the Alaska Highway, to Haines on the Haines Cutoff and then to Skagway via the Alaska Marine Highway System. For a brochure, contact information centers (see For More Information).

FOR MORE INFORMATION

Contact the **Klondike Gold Rush National Historical Park Visitor Center,** White Pass and Yukon Route railroad depot, Second Avenue and Broadway; (907) 983-2921. The **Skagway Convention and Visitors Bureau** is at Seventh and Spring streets, P.O. Box 415, Skagway, Alaska 99840; (907) 983-2854. For the **Skagway Chamber of Commerce,** write to P.O. Box 194, Skagway, Alaska 99840; (907) 983-2297.

For Golden Circle Route information: The **Whitehorse Information Center,** 302 Steele Street, Whitehorse, Yukon; (403) 667-2915. The **Haines Junction Information Centre** is at **Kluane Park Headquarters,** Haines Junction, Yukon; (403) 634-2345. Contact the **Haines Information Centre** at Second and Willard streets, Haines; (907) 766-2234.

Emergency Numbers
Ambulance, fire: 911. Firehouse located at Fifth and State streets; (907) 983-2300.

Police: 911. The police station is in City Hall, Seventh and Spring streets; (907) 983-2301.

Medical assistance and Poison Control: A medical clinic, Eleventh and Broadway streets, provides services Monday to Friday from 9:00 A.M. to 5:00 P.M.; (907) 983-2255. For after-hours medical emergencies, call 911. The **Physicians Assistant** offers after-hours medical referrals; (907) 983-2418.
Poison Control: (800) 478-3193

SITKA

Sitka boasts remnants of native Tlingit Indian culture, as well as traces of its Russian heritage, which dates back to the 1799 arrival of fur trader Alexander Baranov. Despite the relatively small size of its downtown area, Sitka, in terms of landmass, is the largest city in North America, with 4,710 square miles.

GETTING THERE

Sitka Airport is served by **Alaska Airlines** (907-966-2266, 907-966-2261), which connects Sitka with Seattle, Ketchikan, Juneau, Anchorage, Fairbanks, and Glacier Bay. The **Alaska Marine Highway** ferries (800-642-0066) stop in Sitka. Several cruise lines visit Sitka as well. Because of Sitka's location on the west coast of Baranof Island, no roads connect Sitka with other towns, although there are roads within Sitka.

GETTING AROUND

Sitka Ferry Terminal Buses, Prewitt Enterprises, P.O. Box 1001, Sitka 99835 (907-747-8443), meet the ferries in season and transport passengers the 7 miles into town. Prewitt Enterprises also operates **Sitka Airport Service,** P.O. Box 1001, Sitka 99835; (907) 747-8443. These buses meet planes and make regularly scheduled stops at the major downtown hotels. Among the taxicab companies: **Arrowhead Taxi** (907-747-8888) and **Sitka Taxi** (907-747-5001).

A car is not really necessary for visiting Sitka, as the downtown area is reasonably compact. Among the car rental companies available: **All-star Rent-A-Car,** 600 Airport Road (907-966-2552 or 800-722-6972);

Avis, 600 Airport Drive, Sitka 99835 (907-966-2404); and **AAA Auto Rental,** 2033 Halibut Point Road, Sitka 99835 (907-747-8228).

WHAT TO SEE AND DO

Attractions

This is an easy town to visit on your own, so if you're visiting from a cruise ship, forget the group tours. Again, as with most Inside Passage towns, the real delights lie just beyond the towns' borders in the wilderness areas. Pick up a map at the visitors bureau in the Centennial Building near the dock, and walk to all the attractions. Also, ask about performances of the **New Archangel Russian Dancers,** P.O. Box 1687, Sitka, Alaska 99835; (907) 747-5940. This troupe performs authentic dances in Russian costumes.

Favorite sites include **St. Michael's Russian Cathedral,** Lincoln Street (907-747-8120), with its onion-shaped domes. Built from 1844 to 1848, but burned in 1966, the church was rebuilt by the townspeople, who saved its valuable collection of icons.

A highlight of Sitka is the 107-acre **Sitka National Historical Park,** P.O. Box 738, Sitka, Alaska 99835; (907) 747-6281. A half-mile from town, follow the self-guided trail, lined with fifteen totem poles, to the site of the Tlingit fort, burned by the Russians after their decisive 1804 battle against Tlingit warriors. The visitor center displays Indian and Russian artifacts. Bring the kids to the Tlingit arts program, and watch the talent of the Native Indian carvers.

A few other local sites are the **Sheldon Jackson Museum,** 104 College Drive, Sheldon Jackson College, which has Eskimo and Indian sleds, kayaks, masks, and other artifacts; plus the **Isabel Miller Museum,** Centennial Building (907-747-6455), which houses an extensive collection of Sitka's history in photographs, antiques, paintings, and a diorama of Sitka as it was in 1867.

The **Alaska Raptor Rehabilitation Center,** 1115 Sawmill Creek Road, P.O. Box 2984, Sitka 99835 (907-747-8662), rehabilitates wounded or ill birds of prey and then releases them back into the wild. Kids love seeing these eagles, hawks, and other majestic birds up close. In summer, hours are extended to follow cruise-ship schedules.

Special Tours

Enjoy an invigorating journey with **Sitka Sea Kayaking Adventure,** 9085 Glacier Highway, Suite 204, Juneau 99801; (907) 789-0052. On a motorized zodiac, this outfitter leads you to a wilderness base camp where you are taught safe oceangoing kayak techniques. Once you've mastered these, explore the natural beauty of the surrounding protected waters and, with the help of a guide, search for various wildlife. Minimum age is eight. The season runs from May to September. Ask about dates when you may catch sight of migrating whales.

Persons who would rather let others do the driving should contact **C-Jo Charters,** 204 Cascade Creek Road, Sitka 99835; (907) 747-8862. They will take you aboard their 43-foot boat to explore secluded beaches and waters. Fishing is available.

Some cruise lines offer marine tours that last almost four hours. Be careful. These tours are almost always costly, and depending on the outfitter, the weather, luck, and the locale you're visiting, you may or may not see significant amounts of wildlife. Inquire ahead of time. You travel into the maze of waterways that surround Sitka. Motoring around the many tiny islands conveys a sense of the intricacy and abundance of the sea, but sometimes the lack of wildlife can be disappointing. One trip revealed only a cluster of starfish, desperately being videotaped by a participant, and a lone eagle sitting quietly in the high branches of a spruce.

Alaska Adventures Unlimited, P.O. Box 6244, Sitka 99835 (907-747-5576), offers year-round full- and half-day sportfishing, natural history, and photography tours, and welcomes families.

For a native's view of the area, book a guided day tour with **Sitka Tribe of Alaska,** 456 Katlian Street, Sitka 99835; (907) 747-7290. As you tour the area, guides recount Tlingit history, myths, and legends.

For sportfishing, contact **Alaska Dream Charters,** 713 Katlian Street, Sitka 99835; (907) 747-8612 or, in the United States, (800) 354-6017. From April to September, this outfitter takes you out on the Sitka Sound and lets you try your luck at catching such Alaskan specialties as king salmon, silver salmon, and halibut.

Wilderness adventures abound in Alaska.
(Courtesy Chilkat Guides, Ltd.)

SPECIAL EVENTS

January: Russian Christmas and Starring—enjoy Russian food and the lively performances of the New Archangel Dancers.

March: Summer Biathlon.

May: Sitka Salmon Derby.

June: Sitka Summer Music Festival.

October: Alaska Day Festival—join in the celebration on the 18th, when Sitka residents wear period costumes and reenact the ceremonies that, in 1867, marked the transfer of Russian America to the United States.

December: Christmas Holiday Festival.

WHERE TO STAY

Sitka offers several bed-and-breakfast accommodations that offer a variety of attractions. Enjoy peace and tranquillity, with a view of

Sitka Sound and Mt. Edgecumbe, at the **Creek's Edge Guest House,** P.O. Box 2941, Sitka 99835; (907) 747-6484. For a cottagelike atmosphere, **Helga's Bed and Breakfast,** P.O. Box 1885, Sitka 99835 (907-747-5497), has beachside accommodations, fresh Alaskan breakfasts, and fishing charters available. The **Annahootz Bed and Breakfast,** P.O. Box 2870, Sitka 99835 (907-747-6498), has bedroom suites, with private baths and minikitchens. **The Westmark Shee Atika,** 330 Seward Street, P.O. Box 78, Sitka 99835 (907-747-6241), offers upscale accommodations for southeast Alaska and is open year-round. Interior walls are decorated with native murals, and rooms have views of the harbor and surrounding mountains. **The Potlatch Motel,** 713 Katlian Street, P.O. Box 58, Sitka 99835 (907-747-8611), is a moderate hotel, open year-round, whose suites offer cooking facilities.

WHERE TO EAT

Channel Club, 2908 Halibut Point Road (907-747-9916), offers dinners only and specializes in salmon and king crab. Reserve ahead in high season. For Italian cuisine, try the **Marina Restaurant,** 205 Harbor Drive (907-747-8840); or, for Mexican, try **El Dorado,** 714 Katlian Street (907-747-5070). **Bayview Restaurant,** 407 Lincoln Street (907-747-5440), serves hamburgers and Russian specialties.

FOR MORE INFORMATION

Sitka Convention and Visitors Bureau, P.O. Box 1226, Sitka 99835 (907-747-5940); Greater Sitka-Chamber of Commerce, P.O. Box 638, Sitka 99835 (907-747-8604).

Ferries: **Alaska Marine Highway System,** P.O. Box 25535, Juneau 99802-5535; (907) 465-3959 or (800) 642-0066. Write to the **Alaska Division of Tourism,** Department 401, P.O. Box 110801, Juneau 99811-0801 (907-465-2010), for *The Official State Vacation Planner.* For disabled visitor services, call Access Alaska (907-248-4777).

Emergency Numbers
Ambulance, fire, and police: 911

Hospital: Sitka Community Hospital, 209 Moller Drive;
(907) 747–3241

Twenty-four-hour pharmacy: There is no twenty-four-hour
pharmacy. **White's Pharmacy,** 705 Halibut Point Road, is
usually open until 7:00 P.M. For emergencies, call Sitka
Community Hospital.

Poison Control: (800) 478–3193

GLACIER BAY NATIONAL PARK

Encompassing more than 3.3 million acres of mountains, glaciers,
and pristine waters, **Glacier Bay National Park and Preserve,** about
90 miles northwest of Juneau, is a highlight of any Inside Passage tour.
Established as a National Monument in 1925, enlarged and reclassi-
fied as a Park and Preserve in 1980, and declared a World Heritage Site
in 1993, Glacier Bay National Park presents the vistas of Alaska you've
imagined: fluted glaciers, blue-white sweeps of ice, and dramatic
mountain peaks. **Glacier Bay,** the "gem of the Inside Passage," flows
within the park, winding for 65 miles at widths varying from
2 1/2 miles to 10 miles.

GETTING THERE

The only access to **Glacier Bay** is by boat or plane, both of which
land in the nearby small town of Gustavus, a twenty-minute flight or a
three-hour boat ride from Juneau. Even with limited time, try to
squeeze in a day trip to Juneau. **Alaska Airlines** (800–426–0333) offers
flights between Juneau and Gustavus.

GETTING AROUND

In **Glacier Bay National Park and Preserve,** getting around is a
form of recreation in itself because the primary way to experience this
area is by being on the water. Other ways: Fly above the bay or hike the
mountains.

To help preserve the spectacular beauty and to protect the wildlife,
the Park Service limits access to this area. If you wish to tour these

waters on your own, contact the Superintendent, **Glacier Bay National Park and Preserve,** Gustavus 99826; (907) 697-2230. For information about which private vessels may enter the bay, and for regulations, call (907) 697-2268 from May through September.

WHAT TO SEE AND DO

Watch for Whales

The best way to see these behemoths of the deep is to be out on the water with them during the summer migration—June through August. But landlubbers can also catch a glimpse of these majestic mammals. A choice spot for observing these giants is from **Point Adolphus,** which is across the Icy Strait from Gustavus. Because the tidal flows from Cross Sound, Icy Strait, and Glacier Bay mingle here, bringing with them large supplies of plankton, shrimp, and small fish, the hungry whales hang out here. There's something magical, almost eternal, about hearing "There she blows!" and watching a whale breach the sea, his body slicing cleanly through the waters.

Be Dazzled by the Glaciers

Thick mountainous ridges of ice-blue, or white, or pink—depending on the light and the hour—rise up from the water, structures so creviced, fluted, massive, and odd that they seem to be from a distant age and an alien world. Quiet pervades the scene, casting an almost primordial spell. Then the glacier "calves," and a huge chunk of ice breaks and tumbles into the sea, throwing up white mists of spray. As the thunderous crash breaks the calm and the deep vibrations bounce off the peaks and echo down the channel, you sense the changing force and face of nature. This is a sight and sound you and your family won't soon forget. Among the most "popular" of Glacier Bay icy wonders are Muir, Riggs, and Margerie glaciers because they are relatively easy to reach.

One of the nicest things about touring Glacier Bay is the ease with which all ages can share this experience. Whether your family catches these sites from a comfy deck chair of a pampering cruise ship, or snuggled together on a rolling raft, this will be one trip you'll talk about for a long time.

Enjoy the Wildlife

What looks like a shadow on a floating chunk of ice could be cream-and-brown-spotted harbor seals and their pups or sea lions out sunning for the afternoon. Search the horizon for pods of humpback, minke, and orca (killer) whales.

Then there are the birds. More than 200 species hover, nest, and feed on these rocky shores. Be sure to bring your binoculars to see up close the colonies of such brightly colored birds as the black oyster-catchers, unmistakable with long, red bills; the tufted and horned puffins, seeming somewhat comical with white faces, rounded bodies, and thick yellow-orange beaks; and the white-bellied arctic terns crowned with black. In the presence of whales, colossal mounds of ice, fish-catching birds, and barking seals, even the most blasé of kids will say, "Wow!"

By water. Some cruise ships have access to **Glacier Bay National Park and Preserve,** and some don't. To protect the park and the wildlife, the National Park Service limits the number of motorized vessels. If this much-heralded attraction is on your must-see list, and you are planning to visit by cruise ship, book a vessel that has the privilege to be here.

Smaller ships have an advantage. They offer more time in Glacier Bay, as much as twenty hours on a small ship, compared with the five or six hours on a large cruise ship. Smaller vessels can navigate the narrower inlets in search of pods of whales and the more abundant wildlife. But smaller ships also have fewer entertainment facilities—no nightclubs, dance floors, video arcade, or children's program. As a result, these are better for adult children, or teens who want to see the most without making the scene. Among the smaller vessels: **Alaska Sightseeing/Cruise West,** Fourth and Battery Building, Suite 700, Seattle, WA 98121 (800-426-7702); **Clipper Cruise Lines,** 7711 Bonhomme Avenue, St. Louis, MO 63105 (800-325-0010); **Glacier Bay Park Concessions, Inc.** (described later); **Special Expeditions Marine,** 1415 Western Avenue, Suite 505, Seattle, WA 98101 (800-527-6298); and **World Explorer Cruises,** 555 Montgomery Street, San Francisco, CA 94111-2544 (415-391-9262 or 800-854-3835). The latter offers fourteen-day cruises with an emphasis on learning about culture and wildlife.

The larger cruise ships, however, still put on a good show. This is a time to be out on deck looking at the icy-blue cliffs and listening to the thunderous roar as the glacier calves.

From **Glacier Bay Lodge,** Bartlett Cove, a tour boat departs daily for a nine-hour cruise of Glacier Bay. Inquire at the lodge. During the season, call (800) 451-5952. At other times, contact Glacier Bay Lodge, Inc., 520 Pike Street, Suite 1400, Seattle, WA 98101; (206) 623-2417 or (800) 451-5952.

By air. A glide above Glacier Bay presents a unique view of the sweeping expanse of ice and sea. This is a good (if pricey) option if your time is limited. Among the companies offering flight-seeing: **Air Excursions,** P.O. Box 16, Gustavus, 99826 (907-697-2375); **L.A.B. Flying Service, Inc.,** P.O. Box 272, Haines 99827 (907-766-2222); or **Haines Airways Inc.,** P.O. Box 470, Haines 99827 (907-766-2646).

By land. Only two official trails cut through the park from the headquarters at Bartlett Cove. Check with the rangers about naturalist-led tours. The **Beach and Forest Loop** may be the easier of the two, with its mile path through the woods to the shore. Some scrambling on rocks may be required. The 1.5-mile **Bartlett River Trail** winds through the woods to the river.

Even though the glacier allures, like some unknown and enchantingly different country, don't leave the formal trails of Glacier Bay National Park and Preserve unless you and your group are experienced hikers who understand the terrain, as well as the wildlife and the weather. Always consult with the park rangers first. Rain, rising tides, and slippery slopes make backcountry hikes suitable only for aficionados who know this park's topography and potential dangers.

Special Tours

Glacier Bay Park Concessions, Inc., 520 Pike Street, Suite 1400, Seattle, WA 98101 (800-451-5952 or 206-623-2417), offers both air and small cruise ship packages. See the bay for one to three days with departures from Juneau, Haines, or Skagway. This company also offers seven-day, six-night tours. **Glacier Bay—Your Way,** P.O. Box 5, Gustavus 99826 (907-697-2288 or 800-628-0912), creates sportfishing, kayaking, and whale-watching tours for a day or overnight from May through September. What would it feel like to paddle alongside a

Don't miss the breathtaking beauty of Glacier Bay.
(Courtesy Southeast Alaska Tourism Council)

whale? Find out with **Spirit Walker Expeditions,** P.O. Box 240, Gustavus 99826; (800) KAYAKER or (907) 697-2266.

WHERE TO STAY

In the Park

Glacier Bay Lodge provides accommodations from May through mid-September within the park. In season contact the lodge, at Bartlett Cove, P.O. Box 199, Gustavus 99826; (800) 451-5952. At other times, call or write Glacier Bay Lodge, Inc., 520 Pike Street, Suite 1610, Seattle, WA 98101; (206) 623-2417 or (800) 451-5952. These park rooms, the only under-roof lodging within the park, frequently come with wonderful vistas, and always have a private bath (request a room with a view). Be sure to book as far in advance as possible.

Camping

Camping is available at Bartlett Cove and, for boaters, at Sandy

Cove. Camp at the park only if your clan is composed of seasoned campers, hearty backpackers, and, generally, teens or adult children. As supplies are not available within the park and are only available in limited quantities in Gustavus, you must plan to tote in your gear and much of your food. Contact the park service (907-697-2230) about sites, weather conditions, permits, availability, and bear-resistant canisters for food storage.

Condominiums and Bed-and-Breakfast Inns

Even the hamlet of Gustavus has condos. Try the **Whalesong Lodge,** P.O. Box 5, Gustavus 99826; (907) 697-2288 or (800) 628-0912. They offer three-bedroom condominiums or bed-and-breakfast accommodations. Whatever you book, you can add such packages as boat tours, sport fishing, whale watching, and kayaking. Another option, created from an original homesteader farmhouse, is the **Gustavus Inn at Glacier Bay,** P.O. Box 60, Gustavus 99826; (907) 697-2254 (September to April) or (913) 649-5220. It overlooks Icy Strait and welcomes children. Rates can include three meals daily, and locals highly recommend the food, especially the seafood. Guests have access to bicycles and are encouraged to fish in the river. The inn also arranges Glacier Bay boat tours.

Puffin's Bed and Breakfast, P.O. Box 3, Gustavus 99826; (800) 478-2258 in Alaska or (907) 697-2260. From May through September, the inn provides private cottages, bicycles, whale-watching tours, fishing and kayaking outings, and local transportation. Another seasonal choice, open May through September, is the **Glacier Bay Country Inn,** P.O. Box 5, Gustavus 99826; (907) 697-2288, fax (907) 697-2289. This comfortable country inn offers big breakfasts, nature walks, fishing, overnight trips into Glacier Bay, and whale watching. Ask about the preferred age of children.

Cabins

If your budget is tight, but your spirit is willing to explore the wilds, try **Salmon River Rentals,** P.O. Box 13, Gustavus 99826; (907) 697-2245. They offer rustic, housekeeping cabins—oil heat, microwave, refrigerator, bathroom, and cooking facilities.

WHERE TO EAT

Most of the area's lodges have restaurants that accommodate overnight guests and others as well. **The Glacier Bay Lodge,** within the park, serves breakfast, lunch, and dinner from about June through the end of September; (907) 697–2225. The locals recommend the seafood, especially the salmon. For many, the **Gustavus Inn** (see Where to Stay) offers the best food in the area; (907) 697–2254.

DAY TRIPS

Continue your Inside Passage tour by visiting other classic stops: Juneau, Ketchikan, Sitka, Skagway, Vancouver, and Victoria. (See the appropriate chapters for each of these cities.) In addition, for more wildlife, continue your journey farther west along Alaska's southern coast (not part of the Inside Passage) to **Kenai Fjords National Park,** Headquarters and Visitors Center, P.O. Box 1727, Seward 99664; (907) 224–3175. This national park, comprising 580,000 acres that stretch for 50 miles along part of the southern shores of the Kenai Mountains, boasts scores of sea lions, seals, sea otters, and whales as well as porpoises, puffins, and gulls. You can drive to **Exit Glacier,** about 12 miles from Seward. Inquire about summer naturalist programs and ranger-led hikes. A hiking trail allows you close access to this glacier, but be careful of falling ice because pieces break off unpredictably. Hardy teens and good hikers might want to attempt at least part of the 3-mile (one-way) steep hike to the **Harding Icefield.**

Seward, the gateway city for this national park, is reachable via the Alaska Marine Highway System (the state ferry) and, in summer, via the Alaska Railroad (800–544–0552 or 907–265–2494), which travels from Seward, past Mt. McKinley, and on to Fairbanks. Seward is also reachable by highways.

FOR MORE INFORMATION

Gustavus Visitors Association, P.O. Box 167, Gustavus 99826;

(907) 697-2358. **Glacier Bay Information,** Superintendent, Glacier Bay National Park, Gustavus 99826; (907) 697-2230. **Alaska Airlines Vacations** (800-468-2248) offers tour packages.

Anchorage Visitor Information Center, Fourth Avenue and F Street, Anchorage 99501; (907) 274-3533. **Alaska State Chamber of Commerce,** 217 Second Avenue, Juneau 99801; (907) 586-2323. **Southeast Alaska Tourism Council,** P.O. Box 20710, Juneau 99802; (800) 423-0568 or (907) 586-5758. **Alaska Bed and Breakfast Association,** 369 South Franklin, Suite 2000, Juneau 99802; (907) 586-2959.

For information on tour operators, outfitters, and accommodations, obtain copies of both *Alaska, the Official State Guide Vacation Planner,* Alaska Division of Tourism, P.O. Box 110801, Juneau 99811 (907-465-2010); and *The Inside Passage Alaska Trip Planning Guide,* P.O. Box 20710, Juneau 99802, available from the Southeast Alaska Tourism Council; (907) 586-5758 or (800) 423-0568. Check the Alaska Internet Travel Guide: http://www.alaska-online.com/travel/alaska.htm

Emergency Numbers

First-aid: For all emergencies, including medical emergencies, contact Park Headquarters; (907) 697-2230.

Hospital: Juneau-Bardett Memorial Hospital; (907) 586-2611
Poison Control: (800) 478-3193

KETCHIKAN AND JUNEAU

KETCHIKAN

Ketchikan is Alaska's southernmost major city and is reputedly the wettest spot in Alaska, with an average 165 inches of rain each year. Totem poles, salmon, and nearby Misty Fjords National Monument make it famous. Ketchikan, the fourth-largest city in Alaska, is one of the centers of the salmon industry.

GETTING THERE

Ketchikan, situated on the lower tip of Alaska's panhandle on the southwestern shore of Revillagigedo Island, is just ninety minutes by air (660 air miles) from Seattle. **Ketchikan's Alaska Marine Highway** ferry terminal is 1 mile northwest of the town, on the North Tongass Highway; (907) 225-6182 or (800) 642-0066. Ferries travel to Ketchikan from Seattle (a forty-hour trip), from Prince Rupert, B.C. (six hours), and from southeast Alaskan communities. **Alaska Airlines** flies from Seattle, landing on Gravina Island, which is just a five-minute ferry ride across the Tongass Narrows into town.

GETTING AROUND

Ketchikan has limited city bus service, although some buses meet the ferries. Match schedules by consulting with the Alaska Marine Highways office. For getting around downtown by cab, call **Alaska Cab** (907-225-2133), **Yellow Taxi** (907-225-5555), or **Sourdough**

Cab (907-225-6651). **Allstar Rent-a-Car,** 2842 Tongass Avenue, Ketchikan 99901 (907-225-5123), rents used cars at very good rates.

WHAT TO SEE AND DO

Start off on the right foot by picking up a map. Sign up for a walking tour with guides from the **Visitor Center,** 131 Front Street (907-225-6166), or, because Ketchikan, like most Alaska towns, is small, browse on your own. On your walking tour, venture over to **Thomas Basin,** one of the three major harbors in Ketchikan, and watch the fishermen pull up their nets after a day's catch.

Stroll by infamous **Creek Street Historic District,** a row of painted wooden houses on stilts, which in gold rush days, as legend has it, was known as "The Line," and housed Dolly Copeland Arthur's ladies of the night. These shops now sell jewelry, books, and cards. Legend has it that the reason Dolly owned so many frame houses is that the law, such as it was, specified that if you had more than two unmarried women in a home, the property could be labeled a whorehouse and was therefore illegal. To get around this, Dolly bought up a row of houses and put two "working girls" in each. Only the most ardent of gold rush nostalgia buffs will enjoy **Dolly's House Museum,** 24 Creek Street (907-225-6329), this madam's former home filled with some of her memorabilia. A better bet might be to use the time perusing the boutiques.

A small museum, but worth a stop, especially in bad weather, is the **Tongass Historical Museum,** Ketchikan Centennial Building, 629 Dock Street; (907) 225-5600. It displays Alaskan Indian artifacts, art, and has research facilities. If you're short on time, skip this and head for the totem poles and cultural and historical objects at the **Totem Heritage Center, Saxman Totem Park,** and **Bight State Site** (see Totem Poles, below).

Some kids love fish hatcheries, whereas others hate the thought of them, let alone the fishy smell. Depending on your brood, you might also stop at the **Deer Mountain Fish Hatchery,** 1158 Salmon Road (907-225-6760), near the Totem Heritage Center.

For more Indian culture, you may want to stop at the **Shotridge Studios Cultural Center,** 407 Stedman Street; (907) 225-0407 or (800) 770-0407. Not only will you find a museum display and gift

---

Ketchikan and Juneau at a Glance

- Outdoor adventures and historic city sites
- Totem poles at Totem Heritage Center and Saxman Totem Park in Ketchikan
- Authentic Alaska king salmon bakes in Juneau
- Misty Fjords National Monument, Mendenhall Glacier
- Flight-seeing, canoeing, kayaking, and backcountry tours
- Alaska State Chamber of Commerce, (907) 586-2323

---

shop, but sometimes in summer you can see performances of the **Tongrass Tribe Dancers,** a Tlingit dance group whose families are descendants of Ketchikan's original people. Also, Monday through Saturday between 9:00 A.M. and 5:00 P.M., watch Isreal Shotridge, a Tlingit master carver, at work carving totem poles.

Totem Poles

For nearby totem poles, walk the 6 blocks from the dock, or take an inexpensive cab ride to the **Totem Heritage Center,** 601 Deermount Street; (907) 225-5900. This small museum houses the largest collection of unaltered totem poles in Alaska. The thirty-three poles on display were retrieved from nearby abandoned Tlingit and Haida Indian villages. Up close, these massive, unpainted, cedar forms convey a powerful presence with their intricate carvings of teeth and combinations of human, whale, and beaver features.

Head south of town for about 3 miles to **Saxman Totem Park** where, displayed in a parklike, outdoor setting, is reputedly the world's largest collection of totem poles. Kids like deciphering the carvings and hiding behind these massive structures. Associated with the park is the **Saxman Native Village,** P.O. Box 8558, Ketchikan 99901; (907)

225–5163. It features totem carvers and an opportunity to buy native arts and crafts. Head north of town for about 10 miles along North Tongass Highway to the **Totem Bight State Park,** which features a dozen or so poles and a tribal house.

Nature and Green Spaces

Ketchikan provides easy access to two of Alaska's many wonders: the **Tongass National Forest** and, located within it, the **Misty Fjords National Monument,** 3031 Tongass, Ketchikan 99901 (907–225–2148), a twenty-minute float-plane ride from Ketchikan. This 2.3-million-acre wilderness serves up pristine Alaska, with cascading waterfalls, emerald rain forests, rivers, fjords, and rugged granite cliffs rising 4,000 feet.

With close to 17 million acres, the Tongass National Forest is the largest national forest in the United States. In this expanse of islands, inlets, greenery, glacier channels, and ice fields, you might catch sight of bald eagles, grizzly bears, and trumpeter swans.

An exciting, easy, but somewhat pricey way to see both a part of the Tongass National Forest and the Misty Fjords National Monument is to book a float plane from Ketchikan. An hour's flight-seeing tour gifts you with an aerial view of this wilderness, accessible only by boat or float. As your ten-seater plane heads north, an expanse of water, granite cliffs, spruce-tree forests, glacial-carved fjords, and snowcapped mountains appears. Below you stretches a vast, still expanse, which you enter by landing on a blue-gray lake, surrounded by cliffs and forests. Several companies offer day-long guided boat and plane tours. Ask at the visitor center. Companies include **Alaska Cruises, Inc.,** 215 Main Street, Ketchikan (907–225–6044), which has boat and float-plane trips; **Misty Fjords National Monument Cruises,** Dept. 1994, P.O. Box 7814, Ketchikan 99901 (907–225–6044 or 907–225–3498); **Ketchikan Air Service,** 1600 Airport Terminal, Ketchikan 99901 (907–225–6608), which also has access for the disabled; and **Taquan Air,** 1007 Water Street, Ketchikan 99901 (800–770–8800 or 907–225–8800).

The sturdy, the stalwart, and the experienced can hike more than fifteen trails within the monument from easy 0.25-mile walks to **Hugh Smith Lake** to longer and more demanding treks. (As always, wear your bear bells, bring provisions, and only go if you know what you're doing.)

Special Tours

In addition to flight-seeing, save some time for fishing. Anglers should sign up for half-day fishing expeditions to catch Alaska king or silver salmon. Fees for these half-day expeditions generally include a fishing license (required for all nonresidents sixteen years and older). Teens especially enjoy these excursions. Check with the visitor center for a complete list of outfitters. Among them: **Ketchikan Sportfishing,** P.O. Box 3212, Ketchikan 99901; (800) 488-8254 or (907) 225-7526.

Ketchikan Mountain Lake Canoe Adventure, 9085 Glacier Highway, Suite 204, Juneau 99801 (907-789-0052), offers canoe tours through the Tongass National Forest from May to September.

Southeast Exposure, Box 9143, Ketchikan, Alaska 99901 (907-225-8829), offers guided sea kayaking trips April through October through Misty Fjords National Monument. Rentals and instruction are available, as well as handicap access.

For a tour that includes wildlife and Native American culture of Alaska's backcountry and rain forest by canoe with an experienced guide, call **Alaska Travel Adventures,** 9085 Glacier Highway South, Suite 204, Juneau 99801; (907) 789-0052.

SPECIAL EVENTS

February: Festival of the North, a month-long exhibition of the fine arts.

April: First City Folk Festival; local musicians and guest artists perform free concerts.

Mid-May through mid-July: Little League Salmon Derby, King of Kings Salmon Derby, Killer Whale Halibut Derby. Pick up your fishing rod and join the fun.

July: Independence Day Celebration, fireworks.

December: Christmas Festival of Lights and Holiday Ball, holiday celebration.

WHERE TO STAY

Cedar Lodge, 1471 Tongass Avenue, P.O. Box 8331, Ketchikan 99901 (907-225-1900), is a small, comfortable hotel about ¾ of a mile

The striking features of this mask lend insight into the lives of native Alaskans.
(Courtesy Alaska Tourism Marketing Council)

from downtown, near the ferry. Rooms include kitchens, living areas, and Jacuzzi baths. Ask at the front desk about charter fishing excursions and courtesy car shuttles to town.

The Westmark Cape Fox Lodge, in downtown Ketchikan, open all year, offers all the modern conveniences, including private baths, room service, suites, a restaurant, access to a downtown tram, and handicap access. Call (800) 544-0970 in the United States, (800) 999-2570 in Canada, or (907) 225-8001. **The Ingersoll Hotel** is also in downtown Ketchikan; (800) 478-2124 or (907) 225-2124. Open all year, this is an older property whose moderately priced rooms feature televisions and private baths.

Directly across the street from the ferry, and near the airport, is the **Best Western Landing,** 3434 Tongass Avenue, Ketchikan 99901; (800) 428-8304 or (907) 225-5166. They offer reasonable rates and a cafe for convenience. Another moderately priced lodging is **Super 8 Motel,** Ketchikan; (800) 800-8000 or (907) 226-9088.

For a comfortable stay near the Behm Canal, try the **Salmon Falls Resort,** Mile 17 North Tongass Highway, P.O. Box 5700, Ketchikan

99901; (907) 225-2752 or (800) 247-9059. This comfortable fishing resort features all-inclusive fishing packages that cover meals. **The Waterfall Resort,** P.O. Box 6440, Ketchikan 99901 (800-544-5125 or 907-225-9461), offers packages from May to September that combine accommodations on a remote island and sportfishing.

Several bed-and-breakfast homes welcome families. **The Great Alaska Cedar Works Bed and Breakfast,** 1527 Pond Reef Road, Ketchikan 99901 (907-247-8287), is 11 miles from Ketchikan's airport; it offers private cottages with featherbeds and welcomes well-behaved children. For additional bed-and-breakfast homes, contact the registries listed above.

Within the Misty Fjords National Monument and the Tongass National Forest, rustic cabins are available for rental. These can be reserved up to 180 days in advance. Contact the supervisor, **Misty Fjords National Monument,** Tongass National Forest, 3031 Tongass, Ketchikan 99901 (907-225-2148); and the Forest Service Information Center, 101 Egan Drive, Juneau 99801.

For additional listings, see *Alaska's Inside Passage,* the vacation planner available from the Southeast Alaska Tourism Council, P.O. Box 20710, Juneau 99802; (800) 423-0568.

WHERE TO EAT

Annabelle's Keg & Chowder House, Gilmore Hotel, 326 Front Street (907-225-6009), serves a large variety of entrées for breakfast, lunch, and dinner. On Sundays they feature a champagne brunch. Another popular spot is **Rose's Caboose,** 35 North Tongass Avenue Highway; (907) 225-8377. This renovated caboose features counter service, and it has the best milkshakes and burgers in town.

Visitors must try the fresh Alaskan seafood. For the best halibut in Ketchikan, try a favorite of the locals, **Roller Bay Cafe,** 1287 Tongass Avenue; (907) 225-0696. For pizza, try **The Pizza Mill,** 808 Water Street; (907) 225-6646. For some ethnic fare, try **Chico's,** 435 Dock Street; (907) 225-2833. For pizza as well as Mexican food, try **The Diaz Cafe,** 335 Stedman Street (907-225-2257), which serves dishes from the Philippines as well as American fare.

FOR MORE INFORMATION

Ketchikan Visitors Bureau, 131 Front Street, Ketchikan 99901; (907) 225-6166. For a free visitors guide, call (800) 770-2200.

Emergency Numbers
Ambulance, fire, police: 911
Ketchikan General Hospital, 3100 Tongass Avenue; (907) 225-5171. Contact them about twenty-four-hour pharmacy needs.
Poison Control: (800) 478-3193

JUNEAU

In October 1880, Joe Juneau and Richard Harris made a startling find: They discovered gold in Alaska. And so began sixty years of migration and mining in the future Alaskan capital city of Juneau. At present, the boroughs of Juneau stretch far, encompassing several small communities. This gateway city for Glacier Bay offers abundant choices for getting up close to elemental Alaska, with its spectacular ice fields and imposing glaciers.

GETTING THERE

Planes arrive at the **Juneau International Airport** (907-789-7821) from Seattle and Anchorage. **Alaska Airlines** has ticket offices at the Baranof Hotel downtown and the Nugget Mall in the valley, as well as at the airport. Call (800) 426-0333 (for vacation packages) or (800) 468-2248. **Delta Airlines** also flies to Alaska; (800) 221-1212 (for vacation packages) or (800) 872-7786.

Holland America Line–Westours, Inc., 2815 Second Avenue, #400, Seattle, WA 98121 (800-835-8907 or 206-728-4202), offers a variety of cruise and land packages. The **Alaska Marine Highway** (ferry) serves Juneau. The ferry terminal (907-789-7453 or 800-642-0066) is 14 miles northwest of downtown Juneau in Auke Bay, so be sure to time your arrival to meet one of the buses or the **Mendenhall Glacier Transport Ltd.** (MGT) (907-789-5460). Taxi service is available from Capital Cab, Inc., 106 Peoples Wharf, Juneau 99801 (907-586-2772); and **Taku Glacier Cab Company,** 102 North Franklin Street, Juneau 99801 (907-586-2121). Both companies can provide personalized tours—a boon if you have only a short time in town and need to get around quickly.

GETTING AROUND

Juneau has taxicabs and some bus service. Contact MGT (see Getting There) or the **City Bus** (907-789-6901). Negotiate your own taxi tour, or book a city and surrounding area day tour with **Gray Line of Alaska,** 3241 Hospital Drive (summer desk at the Baranof Hotel); (907) 586-3773. Cab companies include **Capitol Cab, Inc.** (907-586-2773) and Taku Glacier Cab (907-586-2121). Both of these companies will customize personal tours as well.

But the best way to see the sights is to combine some sight-seeing on your own with an outdoor adventure, whether a day trip or an extended tour (see Outdoor Adventures). To go at your own pace, rent a car. Among the rental companies: **Allstar/Practical Rent-A-Car,** P.O. Box 34457, Juneau 99803 (800-722-0741 or 907-790-2414); **Hertz,** 1873 Shell Simmons Drive, Juneau 99801 (800-654-8200 or 907-789-9494); **National Car Rental,** 8602 Teal Street, Juneau 99801 (800-227-7368 or 907-789-9894); and **Rent-A-Wreck,** 9099 Glacier Highway, Juneau 99801 (907-789-4111).

WHAT TO SEE AND DO

In Town

Downtown Juneau features some attractions, but if your visit is limited, start by going on an outdoor adventure and then tour the city in your remaining time.

For information on city sites, a walking-tour brochure is available at several information centers and kiosks in the area: **Marine Park Visitor Information kiosk** on the waterfront along Marine Way, the airport, ferry terminal, cruise ship terminal, and at the visitor information center at the **Davis Log Cabin,** 134 Third Street, Juneau 99801; (907) 586-2201. For a hotline of events, call (907) 586-JUNO.

Start from the Visitor Information Center, Davis Log Cabin, and walk a block left along Third Street to Main Street. Turn right up Main Street to see local artist Skip Wallen's life-size bronze bear sculpture, a perfect wildlife specimen for kids to finger and admire.

Continue uphill to the **State Capitol Building,** Main and Fourth streets (free summer tours), constructed in 1930 as the Territorial Federal Building. For more kid appeal, stop nearby at the **Juneau-Douglas City Museum,** Fourth and Main streets (907-586-3572), with its mining memorabilia and gold rush days lore and legends.

Don't miss the **45-foot totem pole** on Main Street, outside the city museum on the corner of Fourth and Main. There's something special about seeing a totem pole tall and strong in the sunlight. For a "token" of another culture, visit **St. Nicholas Russian Orthodox Church,** Fifth and Gold streets. Constructed in 1894 by the Russians, it has a striking onion-shaped golden dome, and inside are beautiful eighteenth-century icons. Nearby, the playground facilities and running space at **Cathedral Park,** Franklin Street between Fifth and Sixth streets, make a good spot for a rest or an impromptu picnic.

Another town attraction: the **Alaska State Museum,** 395 Whittier Street; (907) 465-2901. It offers a good collection of Native American and Aleut artifacts, as well as presentations on the state's Russian heritage. Stop at the **Centennial Hall Forest Service Information Center,** 101 Egan Drive; (907) 586-8751. Besides portraying Alaska's natural history, it offers information about cabin reservations and park conditions. For a splendid view of the **Gastineau Channel,** the **State Office Building,** Main Street near Fourth Street, has an observation deck.

Cruise and tour directors tout the **Red Dog Saloon** on South Franklin Street, up the street from the cruise ship terminal. Don't be fooled by this ersatz, sawdust-on-the-floor, swinging-door replica of what a gold rush era saloon might have been. But the beer is good, and kids like the gift shop's colorful T-shirts and suspenders.

For kids interested in fish, the **Gastineau Salmon Hatchery,** 2697 Channel Drive (907-463-5114), is a big catch, with its saltwater aquarium and tanks. This facility turns more than 160 million salmon eggs into seafood each year.

When visiting Juneau, you and your family won't want to pass up a trip to the Mendenhall Glacier. (Courtesy Alaska Tourism Marketing Council)

Outdoor Adventures

Glaciers, Ice Fields, Fjords, and Flight-seeing. From Juneau it's an easy drive, about twenty minutes, to a real Alaskan glacier. To reach the **Mendenhall Glacier,** 13 miles from town, head northwest along Egan Drive, which turns into Route 7, and then turn right on Mendenhall Loop Road. Once you see the Mendenhall Glacier (907-789-0097), a 12-mile "river" of white-blue ice, you'll be surprised at how close it comes to the city. Make a quick stop at the glacier's visitor center (907-798-0097 or 586-8800) for the exhibits detailing glacial history.

The Mendenhall Glacier, which had been advancing prior to 1750, now recedes, mostly due to warmer temperatures. Although the glacier moves forward slowly, it wastes away at a slightly faster rate. You might hear the thunderous sound of the glacier "calving" as huge chunks of ice break off and float in Mendenhall Lake.

Often the best time to visit is late in the afternoon, when both the crowds and the light are less intense. Bright sun tends to whitewash the glacial colors, but the softer afternoon rays, or a cloudy day, bring out flashing aquamarine hues.

Walk—at least for a little while—on the trails alongside the glacier. **Photo Point Trail,** a 0.3-mile scenic path adjacent to the visitor center, is handicapped accessible and also good for strollers. Along the 0.5-mile self-guided **Interpretive Trail,** learn about glaciers. A park service brochure details several other trails. For further information, contact the **U.S.D.A. Forest Service,** Juneau Ranger District, 8465 Old Dairy Road, Juneau 99801; (907) 586-8800.

Mendenhall Glacier Transport (MGT), P.O. Box 21594, Juneau 99802 (907-789-5460), offers affordable daily excursions from downtown to the glacier from May to September. To get an aerial view and a "foothold" on this ice wonder, contact **Temsco Helicopters,** 1650 Maplesden Way, Juneau 99801 (907-789-9501). The tour combines flight-seeing with a brief stop on the ice. Other aerial tours swoop over the immense **Juneau Icefield,** a 1,500-square-mile icecap in the mountains, the source of the Mendenhall Glacier.

Additional flight-seeing companies include **Alaska Coastal Airlines, Inc.**, 1873 Shell Simmons Drive, Juneau 99801 (907-789-7818); **ERA Aviation,** P.O. Box 21468, Juneau 99802 (907-586-2030); and **Wings of Alaska,** 1873 Shell Simmons Drive, Juneau 99801 (907-789-0790 or 907-586-3442).

The **Taku Glacier** is another must-see. Wings of Alaska offers a flight-seeing trip to **Taku Glacier Lodge Salmon Bake,** 8991 Yandukin Drive, Juneau 99801; (907) 586-8258. It combines some of Alaska's best-known wonders: a flight over Juneau's ice fields and a hearty salmon bake at the isolated lodge, decorated with bear rugs and raccoon skins, and beautifully situated across from Taku Glacier. During the half-hour flight to and from the lodge in a five-passenger Cessna, you look down on the 1,500-square-mile ice fields, whose soft ridges of white change to deep blue crevices when pierced by sunlight. Book well ahead, as cruise ships often reserve many of the tables. Call the lodge (907) 789-0790 or Wings of Alaska.

Fjords. Along **Tracy Arm Fjord,** 50 miles southeast of Juneau, view jagged cliffs rising to 7,000 feet, and see such frequent wildlife as seals and, in season, humpback whales. **Alaska Rainforest Tours,** 369 South Franklin Street (907-463-3466), provides a six-hour catamaran cruise of this region. **Tracy Arm Fjord Glacier Cruises,** 76 Egan Drive (800-451-5952 or 907-463-5570), offers full-day cruises or a half-day cruise and flight-seeing package.

Skiing. **Eaglecrest Ski Area,** 12 miles from downtown Juneau (write: 155 South Seward Street, Juneau 99801); (907) 586-5284. Eaglecrest sports thirty downhill trails and 10K of nordic (cross-country) trails, plus two chair lifts and a ski school. Among the family-friendly features is a toddler-and-parent program that teaches adults how to ski with tots ages three to five. Rental equipment and a cafeteria are on site. In summer, come here to use these trails for scenic hikes.

Gold Panning. Find out about Juneau's gold rush roots with the **Gold Panning and Gold History Tour,** 9085 Glacier Highway, Suite 204, Juneau 99801; (907) 789-0052. Elementary-age children especially like panning for these special nuggets.

Shopping

Of all the U.S. Inside Passage ports, Juneau offers the best place to buy your souvenirs. The shops along **South Franklin** present an interesting array of T-shirts and trinkets. **Taku Smokeries,** 230 South Franklin Street, Juneau 99801 (800-582-5122 or 907-463-3474), is a fine catch for sending something fishy to the folks back home. The smoked sockeye salmon—a Juneau specialty—is very good.

For another strictly Alaskan souvenir, try the gold nugget jewelry at the **Jewel Box,** 248 Front Street (907-586-2604); or browse **Dockside Jewelers,** 145 South Franklin Street (907-586-3910). For Alaskan native arts and crafts, head for the **Mt. Juneau Trading Post,** 151 South Franklin Street (907-586-3246); and **Raven's Journey,** 2 Marine Way, #124 (907-463-4686), which specializes in masks, totems, and jewelry.

SPECIAL EVENTS

April: Sea-to-Ski Relay, a gathering of more than 700 athletes for the annual relay that combines skiing, running, and biking; Alaska Folk Festival, a state celebration usually held the second week in April.

May: Juneau Jazz & Classics, a ten-day music festival with renowned jazz musicians.

June: Gold Rush Days, mining and logging competitions and demonstrations. Friday Concerts in the Park (June through August).
August: Golden North Salmon Derby.
December: Torchlight Parade at nearby Eaglecrest Ski Area, the only developed downhill ski facility in southeast Alaska.

DAY TRIPS

Admiralty Island National Monument, Information Center, 8461 Old Dairy Road, Juneau 99801; (907) 586-8751. You can reach Admiralty Island, part of the Tongass National Forest, by seaplane from Juneau or Sitka or by ferry. With beaches, meadows, trees, and an abundance of wild berries, this island supports a large population of brown bears. Also, a significant number of bald eagles nest along the coast. To fish and cruise in the waters surrounding Admiralty Island National Monument, contact **Ocean Ranger Charters,** 6744 Gray Street, Juneau 99801; (800) 233-2033. These outings also take you ashore to natural hot springs and secluded coves. Even though Admiralty Island has a few cabins and campsites, we do not recommend bedding down in the middle of bear country. Contact the **U.S. Forest Service,** 101 Egan Drive, Juneau 99801 (907-586-8751), for conditions and more information.

Alaska Travel Adventures, 9085 Glacier Highway, Suite 204, Juneau 99801; (907) 789-0052. They offer a three-hour float trip (calm water, beautiful scenery) down Mendenhall River past icebergs and forests; the trip includes a smoked-salmon snack.

Alaska Discovery Expeditions, 234 Gold Street, P.O. Box 20669, Juneau (907-586-2332), offers kayak day trips, heli-hiking, and a daylong tour of a bear sanctuary on Admiralty Island. A charter plane drops you off, and a guide leads you to Pack Creek for a glimpse of the bears and bald eagles. *Be sure to follow the guided directions.* Bears, alas, are not at all like Winnie-the-Pooh; they are wild and dangerous.

Several outfitters get you paddling Juneau's waters in a kayak. Besides Alaska Discovery Expeditions, try **Custom Kayak Adventures,** 2215 Meadow Lane, Juneau 99801 (907-789-0326); and **Kayak Express,** 4107 Blackerby Street, Juneau 99801 (907-780-4591).

WHERE TO STAY

For comfortable accommodations, try the **Westmark Juneau,** 51 West Egan Drive, Juneau 99801; (800) 544-0970 or (907) 586-6900. It's conveniently located across from the waterfront and close to the convention center. **The Baranof Hotel,** 127 North Franklin Street, Juneau 99801 (800-544-0970 or 907-586-2660), is a historic 194-room property. Some rooms come with kitchenettes. **The Prospector Hotel,** 375 Whittier Street, Juneau 99801 (800-331-2711 or 907-586-3737), is near the State Museum and has some rooms with kitchenettes.

Two bed-and-breakfast homes that welcome families: **Blueberry Lodge Bed and Breakfast,** 9436 North Douglas Highway, Juneau 99801 (907-463-5886), is a handcrafted log lodge overlooking a wildlife refuge and is near an eagle's nest. **Jan's View Bed and Breakfast,** P.O. Box 32254, Juneau 99803 (907-463-5897), at the base of Mt. Juneau 1.5 miles from downtown, welcomes well-behaved children. More a temporary home than an actual home stay, the **Cashen Quarters Bed and Breakfast,** 315 Gold Street-j93, Juneau 99801 (907-586-9863), features five apartments equipped with kitchen facilities, television, and telephones. For additional bed-and-breakfast options, contact the **Alaska Bed and Breakfast Association** (907-586-2959).

For persons looking for a rough-it-back-to-basics Alaskan retreat, a U.S. Forest Service cabin in the Tongass Forest comes with a wood stove and plywood bunks. Contact the **Forest Service at Juneau's Centennial Hall** (907-586-8751), and reserve in advance.

WHERE TO EAT

What's an Alaskan tour without a salmon bake, many of which are offered in and around Juneau? Some options: **The Gold Creek Salmon Bake,** 1061 Salmon Creek Lane, Juneau 99801 (907-789-0052), has an authentic Alaskan menu of king salmon. After this meal, try your luck at panning for gold in the creek. The **Thane Ore House Halibut Salmon Bake,** 4400 Thane Road, (907- 586-3442), serves salmon and has, on-site, a small mining museum and a fish hatchery. Don't forget about the food and the flight at the **Taku Glacier Lodge Salmon Bake** (described earlier), 8991 Yandukin Drive, Juneau 99801; (907) 586-8258.

After a full day of sight-seeing, take a break in town at the **Heritage Coffee Company,** 174 South Franklin (907-586-1752 or 800-478-JAVA), where the cappuccino is excellent, and, at lunchtime, the soups and sandwiches are good. For some evening entertainment with dinner, try **The Fiddlehead Restaurant and Bakery,** 429 West Willoughby Avenue; (907) 586-3150. The live jazz and classical piano music is as much a treat as their homemade desserts. For more dining options, obtain *Juneau Alaska Attractions and Services* from the Juneau Convention and Visitors Bureau.

FOR MORE INFORMATION

Juneau Convention and Visitors Bureau, 369 South Franklin, #201, Juneau 99801; (907) 586-1737 or fax (907) 463-4961. **Juneau Visitor Information,** Davis Lodge Cabin, 134 Third Street, Juneau 99801; (907) 586-2201, fax (907) 463-6304, or events hotline at (907) 586-JUNO. Check the Alaska Internet Travel Guide: http://www.alaska-online.com/travel/alaska.htm

For a marine forecast, call (907) 586-3997. The **Alaska State Troopers,** 1014 Mile Glacier Highway (907-789-2161), offer information on road conditions. (Don't lose their number in winter.)

Emergency Numbers
    Ambulance, fire, police: 911
    Bartlett Regional Hospital, 3260 Hospital Drive, 3'h Mile
        Glacier Highway; (907) 586-2611. Contact them about
        twenty-four-hour emergency pharmaceutical needs.
    Pharmacy: Juneau Drug Company, Front and Seward streets;
        (907) 586-1233.
    Poison Control: (800) 478-3193

INDEX

PRAISE FOR THE BUCKET LIST MYSTERIES

Murder at the Male Revue
"Mirth and murder make for a winning combination in this cozy whose sleuths are as quirky as the suspects." —*Kirkus Reviews*

Murder Under the Covered Bridge
"Perona crafts another clever adventure ... with a magical ending, and the feisty and smart seniors are an engaging lot and will appeal to Agatha Raisin fans." —*Booklist*

"Cozy fans will enjoy spending time with Francine and friends."
—*Publishers Weekly*

"A wonderful cozy ... This is one group that no matter what your age, you will want to join up with and have a whole lot of fun."
—*Suspense Magazine*

"The second in this series spices up Perona's usual recipe with a little fantasy." —*Kirkus Reviews*

"Plenty of fun ... After reading *Murder Under the Covered Bridge*, you'll have a new appreciation for these seniors who have plenty of rev left under the hood." —*Mystery Scene*

"If you miss getting new episodes of *Murder, She Wrote* every week, you should definitely check out the Bucket List mystery series. Thank goodness Perona has given these senior sleuths long bucket lists, so we can hope for many more adventures with them."
—Donna Andrews, author of
the Meg Langslow series

"Perona kept on building the case for the final result, and did it professionally and with great pacing as well as timing."
—*Reviewing the Evidence*

Murder at the Male Revue

DEDICATION

To Debbie, with all my love. I look forward to waking up with you each and every day and to the adventures life brings us.

—Tony

To Tim, I'm so thankful that we get to do life together. I love you!

—Liz

Murder
at the Male
Revue

Elizabeth Perona

MIDNIGHT INK
WOODBURY, MINNESOTA

First Edition
First Printing, 2017

Book format by Cassie Kanzenbach
Cover design by Lisa Novak
Cover illustrations by Greg Newbold/Bold Strokes Illustration, Inc.
Editing by Nicole Nugent

Midnight Ink, an imprint of Llewellyn Worldwide Ltd.

Library of Congress Cataloging-in-Publication Data
Names: Perona, Elizabeth, author.
Title: Murder at the male revue / Elizabeth Perona.
Description: First edition. | Woodbury, Minnesota : Midnight Ink, [2017] |
  Series: A bucket list mystery ; 3
Identifiers: LCCN 2017004321 (print) | LCCN 2017010849 (ebook) | ISBN
  9780738750644 (softcover : acid-free paper) | ISBN 9780738751849
Subjects: LCSH: Murder—Investigation—Fiction. | GSAFD: Mystery fiction.
Classification: LCC PS3616.E74975 M86 2017 (print) | LCC PS3616.E74975
  (ebook) | DDC 813/.6—dc23
LC record available at https://lccn.loc.gov/2017004321

Midnight Ink
Llewellyn Worldwide Ltd.
2143 Wooddale Drive
Woodbury, MN 55125-2989
www.midnightinkbooks.com

Printed in the United States of America

ACKNOWLEDGMENTS

First and foremost, I thank God, as always, for the opportunities He has put in front of me. As a love gift to Him, I try to put joy and fun and purpose into these stories, in the hopes that they will lift others up. I continue to be amazed at His blessings.

Next, I thank my coauthor and "Elizabeth Perona" partner, my daughter Liz Dombrosky. It is a joy to work with you. Thank you for making this series and this book possible.

So many people contribute to a book, both deliberately and otherwise. I will try to thank all those who have contributed deliberately. Thank you to the Plainfield Police Department staff, especially Det. Scott Arndt, Capt. Jill Lees, Lt. Gary Tanner, and Asst. Chief Carri Weber, for their advice and suggestions. Any errors in police procedure are mine, not theirs. I also appreciate Brownsburg Town Manager Grant Kleinhenz and Assistant Town Manager Brian Hartsell for their help in details about the Town. I should mention that none of the Brownsburg Town Council members are anything like the ones in this book. Nor, for that matter, are any of the Plainfield Town Council members. (My day job is in town government in the neighboring community of Plainfield.) And while Brownsburg is working on the Ronald Reagan Parkway interchange with I-74, there are no land deals going on like the ones I have pictured in the book. At least, none that I know of.

My aunt Nancee Margison has contributed in many ways to this book, and I thank her for that. Thanks also to reader Joy McQueen for lending us her name. She won the right to have a character named after her in a contest. I hope she continues to enjoy this series.

This book would not be possible without the support and help of an incredible writers group, the Indiana Writers Workshop, of which I am privileged to be a member. This manuscript has benefited from their critiques, advice, and sharpened red pencils. Thank you to Teri Barnett, Pete Cava, John and June Clair, Steve Heininger, Sylvia Hyde, Cheryl Shore, Steve Wynalda, and Jeff Stanger. I also want to acknowledge IWW member David Ballard, who passed away during the writing of this manuscript. David was a gifted writer and actor. The group misses him tremendously. His stamp is definitely on this story. Thank you also to the local Speed City Chapter of Sisters in Crime, of which I am a member (a Mister Sister), for their support.

We appreciate being able to work with the Midnight Ink staff once again! Special thanks to our editors, Terri Bischoff and Nicole Nugent, and to our publicist, Katie Mickschl. They make it a pleasure to be part of the Midnight Ink family.

Last, but certainly not least, I want to thank my wife, Debbie, for her love and support in this endeavor. She puts up with my crazy compulsion to tell stories despite the odds of success. None of this would be possible without her. And I also want to recognize my daughter and son-in-law Katy and Taylor Jenkins as well as Liz's husband, Tim, who allow Liz and me to keep on dreaming. How blessed we are!   —Tony

Once again, I'd like to thank God for this opportunity. I'm so glad that my dad and I got to do this whole adventure again.

Next, thanks to my dad for asking me to do this with him. It's been fun—an unexpected adventure that I'm thankful for. I'm looking forward to the future!

Finally, I'm thankful that my kids have become better sleepers/playmates, so that Mommy can get a little bit more work done during the day. ;)   —Liz

ONE

Francine McNamara looked over the decorations that festooned the usually staid Crown Room on the second floor of the Schrier building in Brownsburg, Indiana. She and Mary Ruth Burrows stood at the back of the room preparing for a benefit Mary Ruth would cater that night. The Crown Room was all about dark wood, crown molding, and appointed features. The organizers had installed neon signs, however, flashing messages reading, Do Not Touch the Entertainers and No Grabbing Allowed. While the signs purported to regulate behavior, Francine couldn't help but feel they somehow encouraged audience *mis*behavior.

The stage contained brass dance poles, folding chairs, and toward the back of the stage, a table of props. Francine observed a riding crop, a fake gun, a large knife, arm bands, a feathered boa, a tambourine, two sets of handcuffs, and a jar of crunchy peanut butter, among others. *I don't want to imagine how those props will be used*, she thought.

"Has it really come to this," she said aloud, "that the Crown Room is hosting the Royal Buckingham Male Dance Revue?"

"Not surprising," Mary Ruth answered without looking up from the case of tablecloths she was unloading. "This building may have a Federalist exterior and a two-story glass atrium inside, but it's located next to a Shell station and down the street from a Taco Bell. It's no wonder it went out of business as an upscale event center. The new owners may not have the same high-end vision, but at least they're getting steady bookings. And I appreciate that they're letting renters pick their own caterer."

Francine glanced over at her, a little startled her friend had answered a question Francine didn't realize she'd asked out loud. Mary Ruth was dressed in her standard catering outfit of black pants, black polo shirt with *Mary Ruth's Catering* stitched in pink, and a pink apron tied around her waist. The pants were a little baggy. At one time she'd been borderline obese, but thanks to a personal trainer she'd been steadily losing weight for over eight months.

"What size are those pants?" Francine asked.

"Fourteen. Do you think they're too tight?"

"Quite the opposite. I think you need to invest in a size twelve."

Mary Ruth beamed. She self-consciously primped her auburn hair. The auburn wasn't natural, not anymore. Most of the women in the Summer Ridge Bridge Club dyed their hair. Francine had struggled to match the brown hair she'd had in her thirties, though she could barely remember the exact shade these forty years later. She looked over the bifocal line in her owlishly large glasses and engaged her friend's brown eyes.

"Have you had any backlash since you got hired to do this job? I know there are some people who aren't too happy to see male strippers coming to Brownsburg."

Mary Ruth chuckled. "Mostly from St. Alice." She rolled her eyes. Alice Jeffords was a fellow Bridge Club member. Alice was also Mary Ruth's partner in her business. "I dearly love her, and her financial backing has made all the difference since I've been able to take advantage of the great publicity we've gotten. But sometimes she can get hung up on certain … issues."

Francine thought of the large crucifix Alice wore around her neck. The only time in recent memory Alice had removed it, they'd been able to spy a reference to a Bible passage that revealed her hidden number-one bucket list item was to become a mother. Being in their seventies, it was a nearly impossible wish. And yet, due to a crazy set of circumstances, she'd managed to become a stepmother to NASCAR race driver Jake Maehler, who had turned out to be her husband's secret love child. "Are she and Larry off seeing one of Jake's races this weekend?"

Mary Ruth draped a white cloth over a long rectangular table, nodding. "She couldn't get out of town fast enough. I almost wondered if she was afraid she would lose control if she were here, being around all this male flesh."

"Like Charlotte probably will?" They both glanced toward Charlotte Reinhardt, another Bridge Club member, who had been perusing the props on stage. Charlotte was barely five feet tall and all spit and fire. She had thin hair and wore a wig of silvery curls that never quite sat right on her head. Francine thought Charlotte's mind operated like the wig—always slightly off kilter. But that was one of things she loved about her best friend. Charlotte made every day an adventure, and the way she was juggling the peanut butter and the handcuffs, tonight held promise.

"At least the catering assignment allows us a good cover for being here. I'm not sure how keen I would have been on an expedition to fulfill this particular Sixty List item." Their "bucket lists" were named for the fact they contained sixty items each and were written when the women were in their sixties. Joy McQueen, the unofficial President of their club and a reporter for the Indianapolis

ABC affiliate, had the following on her list: #57 Go to a Male Strip Club.

"I don't know which is harder to believe," Mary Ruth said. "That Joy has never been to one of these, or that she put it on her Sixty List."

"How'd you get this gig again?"

She sighed. "Friends I don't necessarily brag about."

As if on cue, Eric Dehoney swaggered into the room from the back of the stage. Eric was thirty-four but could easily have passed for his twenties. He was Brownsburg's gift to the Royal Buckingham troupe. Six foot three and carved like a Michelangelo statue, he oozed sexiness, from his hazel eyes to his large feet with long toes that Charlotte said were indicative of something "that would send Alice from the room screaming." Behind him came another of the Royal Buckingham dancers, a blond Nordic type who looked barely legal.

"Hello, everyone!" Eric called as he entered. "Has anyone seen Aunt Camille?" His voice was husky and he wore a white undershirt that clung to his body like a second skin. His shorts, dark gray with a red horizontal stripe, were baggy and hung below his knees. His companion wore the same outfit.

"She left about five minutes ago," Francine called. Eric spotted them in the back and headed for the stairs that lead offstage.

Charlotte scooped the knife off the prop table and blocked their way. The blade was about six inches long and, from Francine's perspective, looked as though it could have been real.

"Where're you going so fast?" Charlotte said, aiming it at Eric's midsection.

"Mrs. Reinhardt," he said, slowly crossing his arms over his chest. "Stieg and I just came in to check on the preparation for tonight's auction."

"That's my good fortune," she answered.

"And our misfortune," he said wryly. "What'll it take for you to let us pass?"

"Nothing from you—you're a former student and I do have my standards. But your friend needs to lift up his shirt."

Eric seemed a bit shaken by her remark, but Stieg smirked like he expected this. He lifted the undershirt with one hand and readied the other as though he might need to stop her fingers from wandering. *He might just,* Francine thought.

Charlotte dropped the knife hand to her side, but she was more interested in observing than touching. "Ooooo weee!" she said. "I remember when Philip had a flat stomach, but I don't know that I've ever been so close to muscles like these."

Francine had known Charlotte's late husband, and she couldn't remember him ever having a flat stomach. "That's enough, Charlotte!" she called. "We'll be back later tonight, and maybe you can show your appreciation by tucking a tip in his G-string or thong or whatever the right term is."

Stieg lowered the shirt and backed away from Charlotte. He winked. "I'll look forward to seeing you tonight."

Charlotte returned the knife to the prop table. "I don't know what they're auctioning off, but I'm looking for a trip to the pool on a hunk's arm. I could stare at a sight like that all day." She sighed dramatically.

"There's a list of the auction items back here," Mary Ruth said. She pointed to a bulletin board encased in a glass display near the French entry doors. "But I don't remember seeing anything like that."

Eric and Stieg bounded off the stage and headed for the back of the room. "I guess that would have been a natural item to auction off since the fund-raiser's for an indoor aquatic center. I didn't think of it," Eric said.

"It's not too late to put it in the auction," Charlotte said. "I'd bid on it."

Mary Ruth made a tsking noise. "It's a good thing she didn't behave like that when she was a teacher."

Charlotte stood at the top of the steps leading down from the stage. She stepped both feet onto a stair before moving on to the next one while clutching the railing.

"Go ahead and try it one foot at a time instead of two," Francine said. Years after a botched knee replacement surgery, Charlotte was finally doing better. Francine had been encouraging her to work on her mobility.

Eric turned back to the staircase and extended a hand to Charlotte. She came smoothly down the few steps.

"That was all the encouragement I needed," she told him. "That and seeing you down here."

He laughed again. "You never change."

"I still love life, if that's what you mean. I remember when I had you as a freshman in high school English." Charlotte had served as an English teacher in Brownsburg for many years after Philip had passed away. Eventually she decided she didn't value the money over the aggravation, and reverted to being a substitute until retirement.

"You would have made a better detective than a teacher, I think," he said.

"You didn't like me."

"I didn't like English. But even you didn't like English, not as much as you liked mysteries."

"It was just those required texts," she answered. "*The Scarlet Letter* feels dry and outdated when the girl in the front row is pregnant as a freshman and still wins homecoming princess. It's sad, but hardly scandalous anymore." She sniffed. "I wish they'd have let me teach more Edgar Allan Poe. I might have been okay with that." She trailed Eric back to where Mary Ruth now prepped a second table for food items. Stieg went over and checked the DJ station that had been set up near the buffet tables.

"Eric," Mary Ruth said, "has your aunt told you how she envisions the evening going? She organized this soiree around your appearance."

"Not mine. The Royal Buckinghams'. But I do know what she's looking for." He swept an arm toward the front of the room. "Everyone will pass by here to get their food. We'll have the tables with all the auction items along the walls, and the bar will be next to the DJ station. The bar is important. We want our patrons to loosen up a bit so the bids will be higher. But we don't want them drunk."

Charlotte wandered over to the DJ station, where Stieg had put on headphones. She goosed him.

"Ouch," Stieg said. He looked to Eric as if asking what to do.

"Don't touch the merchandise," Eric called. When Charlotte recoiled, he quickly switched to a more playful tone. "Are you going to be a wild one tonight?"

"That depends. How many articles of clothing is he going to take off?"

"You'll have to stick around to find out. We might go past your bedtime."

"Are you kidding? I'm one of the Skinny-Dipping Grandmas. We stay up till at least nine thirty on a regular basis."

"You'll need to stay up later than that. We've got some surprises planned."

Charlotte pretended to shiver in delight. "What kind of surprises?" She gripped Stieg's considerable bicep and squeezed it. "Is this a clue?"

Stieg laughed and flexed his muscles for her.

"Yes," Eric answered. "That's a clue. But no more touching. It's a mystery. Channel your inner Sherlock Holmes."

"Hot dog! A mystery *and* a strip show. This could be the best evening I've had in a long time."

TWO

"TEN MINUTES UNTIL THE auction closes," Joy announced to the crowd. "Now's the time to start making your final bids. Then we'll start the program."

Her voice is as sparkly as her dress, Francine thought. On the stage with spotlights catching the sequins in her floor-length white gown, Joy looked like an older version of Vanna White. The dress was appropriate for mistress-of-ceremonies duties, befitting Joy's role at the benefit, but Francine would never have felt comfortable in something that attracted so much attention. She was more than happy to be in a Mary Ruth's Catering outfit and blending into the background.

In Alice's absence and with Joy hosting, Mary Ruth had leaned heavily on her grandson Toby and on Francine and Charlotte for catering help, although Charlotte was not always much assistance. Tonight she seemed more fascinated by the allure of nearly naked men than by the delicious food.

The crowd in the Crown Room milled about the auction tables, sipping wine from etched souvenir glasses and cocktails from stemmed glassware. Francine could hear snippets of conversation as women queued up to top any late bids on auction items they really wanted. Those that relished the opportunity to look like they belonged at a fund-raiser were dressed to kill; others, particularly the younger women, were garbed in ripped jeans and Royal Buckingham Male Revue sweatshirts. They looked prepared for the party atmosphere that would ensue after the silent auction was over and the revue started. The men who'd accompanied their spouses laughed and joked uneasily and seemed ready to bolt as soon as dinner and the auction were over.

Eric Dehoney and five additional Royal Buckingham dancers worked the crowd. They were clad in dark chinos and brown polo shirts from the Brownsburg Parks Department. One of them must have been a licensed bartender because he assisted a Crown Room employee in serving local craft beers and wine from behind a portable bar. The others used their considerable physical charms to engage the women.

Francine watched from behind the buffet table she was servicing. To her they looked like well-built employees rather than male strippers. They were sexier fully dressed, she decided.

Mary Ruth snuck up behind her. "Stop staring at them," she whispered. She carried a tray of vegetarian spinach lasagna with white sauce. "Would you please remove the old tray and take it back to the kitchen?"

"I didn't know I was staring." Francine picked up the pot holders she'd used to carry in the first of the dessert trays, a warm cherry cobbler that looked delicious. Mary Ruth never failed to amaze Francine with her food. She seemed to know exactly what would hit the mark with whatever crowd she catered to, and on this cold February night, the warm cobbler was getting a lot of attention. Though Francine had just carried it out, patrons had flocked to the dessert table and carved out almost half of it. She was certain some of them were eating dessert before supper.

"Not that I blame you for staring," Mary Ruth said, sighing. "We just don't have time for it." As Francine removed a nearly empty tray, Mary Ruth nestled its replacement in the holder over the flame keeping the lasagna warm.

"What do you need me to do next?" Francine asked.

Mary Ruth looked over the two buffet tables. At one end, Toby carved roast beef to order from a huge slab. Toby looked pretty handsome himself, slimmed down thanks to Mary Ruth's personal trainer. He sported a neatly trimmed beard and wore a large chef's hat on his head and a white chef's jacket over his catering uniform. He carved the meat to guests' tastes and deftly transferred the slices to their plates. Some of the women flirted with him.

Next to Toby were several baskets of breads—small seeded rye rolls for making the beef into a small sandwich, chewy ciabatta rolls that went with the vegetarian lasagna, and slices of rosemary focaccia bread.

Mary Ruth assessed the situation. "We could use more of the focaccia. I have it in one of the warming ovens. Would you please slice it up and bring it in?"

"Could I have your attention, please?" Joy chirped into the microphone at the front of the room. "The live auction will begin in five minutes. That's plenty of time for you to get your main courses and get settled. The delicious buffet will remain open during the auction, so if you haven't gotten your fill yet or haven't gotten to dessert, not to worry. The food won't go away."

"Fine for her to say that," Mary Ruth murmured. "No matter how much she eats, she stays thin as a rail."

Francine watched Joy come off the stage with unbounded energy. Earlier she had sampled nearly everything Mary Ruth had created, including both desserts, and suffered no ill effects. Even in her seventies, the sequined dress looked perfect on Joy's slim frame.

Joy greeted people on her way back, encouraging them to bid heartily for the auction items. "It's for a good cause!" she repeated to each group of attendees who stopped her.

She trailed Francine to the kitchen. She dropped her smile. "I don't know if I can do this," she said under her breath.

Francine glanced around to make sure there was no one near them. "It'll be okay. Try not to think about your…problem. Just enjoy each moment as it comes."

"I've left a couple of gowns in the room backstage. I can pull a Vanna White and slip out to change into a different one if I need to escape. I don't want to hyperventilate and pass out in front of all these people. Or worse." She narrowed her eyes and glanced from side to side as if warning people to stay away from her.

Joy's "problem," as she'd confessed to Francine, was that her divorce from her husband Bruno had left her scarred. Bruno had left her for a man, and now at the mere suggestion of sex, she either hyperventilated or her stomach cramped like she was going to throw up. Both were embarrassing. She'd given up on men a long time ago, but now that she was dating Roy Stockton, a retired sheriff from Rockville, she wanted desperately to overcome her problem. It was for her that they were checking "go to a male strip show" off the bucket list. At #57, it wasn't very high, but it had become an integral part of her therapy. She hoped that the atmosphere of craziness would offset her negative reaction to nearly naked men, and she would get over her phobia once and for all.

Francine removed a pan of focaccia bread from the oven and proceeded to slice it into pieces with a bread knife. "You're setting yourself up for failure if you plan to fail. Why don't you spend your time visualizing your success?"

Joy's normally high-pitched voice got even higher. "If I visualize those young men gyrating anywhere near me, I get nervous."

"Listen to yourself. You said you're nervous, not repulsed. That's a totally different reaction than you've been having."

"That's right! I did say that!" She started to stand up straighter, but then her face fell. "I still feel repulsed, though. And a little nauseated."

Charlotte burst through the doors into the kitchen. She carried a dinner plate full of sweets from the buffet table: cherry cobbler, the sandwich cookie cake, and scalloped apples, which had been on the table with the sides, but was tasty and gooey enough for dessert. "What are we talking about here?"

"Shoes," Joy said, covering. "These things are killing me. How did we ever wear high heels to work every day?"

"I never did," Francine admitted. "Nurses can wear sensible shoes. But I know what you mean. They used to wreak havoc on my ankles when I wore them."

"Yep, now we're liberated women," Charlotte said, savoring a bite of the cherry cobbler. "We can show up at big events like this and wear sneakers and no one cares a whit about it." She was indeed wearing Converse Chuck Taylor high-tops no one could miss. They were bright orange. She'd paired this with a floral patterned dress in pink that screamed senility next to the orange tennis shoes.

Francine finished piling a pink gingham cloth-lined basket with cut focaccia bread and whisked it out to the dining area. She blinked and let her eyes adjust to the dimmer light in the Crown Room. She replaced the empty basket on the table. Hungry guests coming through Toby's carving station snapped up the bread almost as soon as she set it down. Francine noticed that the seeded rolls for the roast beef were nearly gone. She wondered if Mary Ruth was tending to that or if she should go back and do it herself.

"Francine." Toby used a stage whisper to get her attention. "Could you come over here? I need you to cover for me."

"Ummm." Francine looked around, hoping to see Mary Ruth. "I'm not really very good at carving the roast beef. Maybe I should go get your grandmother."

Meanwhile, Joy made her way back up to the front and pounded a gavel on the lectern to get everyone's attention. The DJ in the back lowered the volume of the background music. "Please don't stop eating and drinking," Joy said. "Though, from the looks of it, I didn't need to remind you of either." That got a laugh. "I hope you've all had time to finish bidding on the silent auction items, because that part of the evening is now closed. We're going to start the live auction here in a minute, but first I want to introduce Camille Ledfelter, whom I sure you will all recognize as our Town Council President. She and her nephew, Eric Dehoney, are responsible for putting together this event to raise money for the new indoor aquatic center. Camille?"

Francine edged closer to Toby. He handed her the large meat fork and the carving knife he was using on the roast beef. "I'd rather you took over right now before my grandmother comes back into the room."

Francine took the knife and fork, but hesitantly. "Why?"

He put his tall white chef's hat on her head. "Because I have to leave."

He must really have to use the bathroom, she thought.

Camille Ledfelter had already situated herself behind Joy at the lectern, so she was able to slide up to the microphone. Camille was in her early sixties and believed in heavy makeup to try to disguise her age. She wore eyeshadow that was lake water blue and long fake eyelashes Francine likened to seaweed growing out of the lake. Camille sported a black evening dress with a beaded bodice. The audience applauded loudly for her. She was the first woman to head the Town of Brownsburg.

"Thank you, thank you for that." Camille applauded the audience. Francine wasn't sure why she was applauding the audience for applauding her, but Camille had a way with crowds. The audience applauded even louder.

Toby took off his white jacket and offered it to Francine.

She shook her head. "Much as I don't want to get my outfit dirty, that jacket's never going to fit me."

He grabbed a white apron from a package of spares under the table. He helped Francine slip it over her head and tied the drawstrings tightly behind her waist. He seemed to be in quite a hurry.

"I hope you're all having a good time getting to know the men who'll be entertaining us shortly," Camille continued as the applause faded. "I know you are as committed as I am to seeing this vision come true for Brownsburg. All the surveys indicate that the number-one attraction residents would like to have is a recreation and indoor aquatic center that is second to none in the area."

The applause swelled and subsided again. "I'd like to thank my nephew Eric for his help in coming up with a unique fundraising opportunity to get us started toward our goal in raising half the funds to build the facility. Could we have a round of applause for the men who are sharing their, uh, talents with us this evening?"

The women applauded loudly and whooped and hollered. The men were more reserved. Francine couldn't blame them. This was a no-win situation for them.

Toby steered her over to the roast beef. No one in line was paying any attention right then to the carving, so Francine had a moment to think about how she would carve the meat. She turned to ask Toby a question but found he'd vanished.

"Eric, could you come up here?" Camille asked. Eric rose from the Council table and bounded up on stage. He took the microphone from her.

"Thank you, Aunt Camille. Let's get this auction started, shall we? I'm going to bring back our official MC, Joy McQueen, in a moment." Applause started to form, but Eric cut it short by holding up his hand. "I'm sure you all love her fun and inspiring reports on senior life for *Good Morning America*, but first, I want to introduce a few live auction items you *didn't* see on the official list."

He paused for dramatic effect, and the room grew quiet quickly. Francine stopped fumbling with the fork and carving knife and concentrated on what was happening on stage. No one was paying any attention to her and the roast beef anyway.

Joy, standing upstage, arms fixed at her side, tried to be inconspicuous. She looked like she was either waiting for her next task or getting ready to bolt. With easy access to the backstage area from where she stood, bolting was a likely option. Francine worried what Joy would do. Camille, meanwhile, had vanished backstage.

Eric continued. "We're going to auction off dates with the single members of our dance troupe." A couple of younger women who had tables close to the front stood and applauded appreciatively, causing Eric to laugh. He singled them out by coming closer to the edge of the stage and pointing to them. "We like that attitude. Let's make sure that translates into money for Brownsburg Parks!"

Eric snapped his fingers and the DJ in the back brought the room lights down to nothing. He switched to pole mounted spotlights that made Eric the only lit figure in the room.

"And our first dancer up for auction tonight ... he's back behind the bar. He's as smooth as the drinks he's poured out for you. Shout out your bids for Isaac Washington!" A new spotlight shown on Isaac.

Francine had to laugh at the name, clearly an alias. Isaac Washington was the name of the bartender Ted Lange played on "The Love Boat."

The music, which heretofore had been soft jazz music suitable for dinner, now pumped up with a heavy drumbeat and pulsating techno rhythm. Isaac stripped off his shirt in time to the music revealing a well-defined torso with broad shoulders and a washboard stomach. Eric took two bids for him, but then a woman Francine recognized as Cass Carter, ex-wife of Council member Fuzzy Carter, made a preemptive bid for him at $600. From the area near the bar she held her wineglass aloft in triumph when no one moved to outbid her.

"Well, there's a woman who knows how to get what she wants," Eric said, throwing in the towel on Isaac as he couldn't draw anyone to go higher. "But there are more to come, ladies, like our next single dancer. He's served you already once tonight by carving up some roast beef for you. Now he'll be carving out a place in your heart. He's our newest recruit for the Buckingham Revue. Ladies, say hello to Toby Burrows!"

Francine nearly dropped her knife. *Toby Burrows? That's why he needed to get away so fast?* He had certainly become a lot sexier with the weight loss and the neatly trimmed haircut, but she wasn't sure about this. Or maybe she was used to thinking of him as Mary Ruth's grandson and couldn't contemplate his changing physique and how that had affected his personality. She stared in shock as Toby Burrows came out from behind the stage curtain and joined Eric.

The room rocked with clapping and whistling. Music blared a pounding beat throughout the room. Toby's hands shook, and he fumbled with the buttons on his Mary Ruth's Catering polo shirt. He began gyrating his hips, moving to the sounds. The two women who'd made the first bids on Isaac stood up again and whooped along with the music. They were joined by women at other tables.

Toby untucked his shirt from his pants as he danced. He reached a hand over his shoulder and grabbed the back of his shirt and slowly yanked it up over his head, revealing a tanned, toned torso. *When did he get ripped like that?* Francine wondered. While his muscles were nowhere near as sharp and defined as Eric's, his body fat percentage had to be in the single digits.

"Let's start the bidding," Eric said, glee in his voice. "Do I hear a hundred dollars?"

"Two hundred," shouted the two women standing together at one of the front tables. They laughed at each other when they realized they'd declared the same bid at the same time.

Joy bolted backstage. Francine sighed, but there was nothing she could do.

Mary Ruth came out of the kitchen carrying a tray of cherry cobbler. It was heavy, and she moved quickly to get it to the dessert station. She spotted Francine holding the carving knife and frowned like this was completely unexpected and she was having a hard time realizing what was going on.

She looked up toward the stage where Toby was now unbuckling his pants. She gasped and the tray wobbled in her arms. *Don't lose it, don't lose it*, Francine willed. Despite her force of thought, the tray slipped from Mary Ruth's arms. It dropped onto the dessert table with a thud and bounced in the direction of a table of patrons. Globs of red gooey cobbler flew everywhere, smacking attendees indiscriminately. Cherries rolled down their clothes leaving smear marks.

The collision of the full dessert tray with the table unsettled the warming container. It rocked underneath the mostly empty pan of cherry cobbler. Mary Ruth tipped toward the table and tried to brace her fall. She sought something to grab. Her arms flailed about.

"Oh! Oh! Oh!" she shrieked. She reached for Francine and almost touched the roast beef. But not quite. Her hands windmilled as she fell into the table and took it down.

The spill-resistant warming container under the near-empty cherry cobbler pan failed to live up to its promise. Fuel spilled onto the floor where paper napkins had settled, setting them on fire. Those who hadn't been hit by the cobbler were quick to realize they needed to put out the flames. They stomped on the fiery napkins.

Unfortunately they also stomped on cherry cobbler. More cherry filling squirted into the audience.

"Just a little accident, folks," Eric said. His voice sounded reassuring, but his eyes were wide with alarm. "Keep the bidding going!"

"Two-fifty!" shouted an older woman.

Those trying to stomp out the flames kept bumping into the roast beef station. Francine dropped the knife and fork and held onto the table with all her might. It rocked but didn't go down. The lamp stand warming the beef began to teeter. She reached for it and almost lost the roast beef in the process. She watched the lamp go and clutched the beef in a bear hug. She felt warm juices running down her arms.

Someone with poor aim ran out of the kitchen with a fire extinguisher, blasting away at anything that looked like it might catch on fire. He managed to put out the flames and coat everyone in range with a white spray at the same time.

Toby, meanwhile, had bounded down the stairs at the sight of his grandmother's collapse. By the time he reached the back of the room, he was going full speed. He slipped on cherry cobbler and skidded toward the roast beef station. "Watch out!" he yelled. He grabbed at the air, trying to find someone or something to halt his advance. He found nothing. His feet slipped out from under him. He fell onto his back and kept sliding.

Toby streaked toward Francine feet-first like a missile honing in on its target. Francine stared wide-eyed at the oncoming disaster. She tried to side step as Toby barreled into the carving station. His first point of impact were the table legs. They collapsed like potato chips hit by a steam roller. Francine was re-securing her bear hug on the roast beef when the Toby juggernaut knocked her feet out from under her.

Still clinging to the roast, she landed backside first onto his chest. Toby had his hands out and braced her fall. As they came to a final halt, Toby sat up. Except for the slab of roast beef, they looked like they were a couple posing for an Olan Mills portrait.

"I have a bid of two-fifty for the male half of the co-ed bobsled team," Eric cracked. "Do I hear three hundred?"

"Three hundred!" shouted a woman with a husky voice.

The bidding continued while the people around the wrecked buffet station helped Toby and Francine to their feet. Someone took the beef from Francine and toted it back to the kitchen.

"Are you all right?" Toby asked Francine as they got to their feet. "I am so sorry."

"A little banged up, but I'll be all right." She brushed herself off and looked away while Toby straightened the only thing he was wearing, his pants.

Mary Ruth also rose to her feet, albeit with help. Her face was slimed with cherry filling and dotted with pieces of fruit, looking like a contestant in a pie-throwing contest. She wiped the filling from her eyes with her apron.

"Sorry," she said, trying to speak over the pulsating music that was still playing. She turned to the two young women covered in cobbler who had braced her under the armpits. "I must have hallucinated. I thought I saw my grandson ..."

It was then that Toby, who had been facing the opposite direction, turned and made eye contact with his grandmother. Mary Ruth blinked. She looked down from his face to his bare torso and then down to his unzipped black chinos.

Thank heavens he's still wearing the chinos, Francine thought.

Mary Ruth collapsed again. The women seemed to anticipate her fall and gripped her tighter. She remained upright but her head hung like she had passed out.

"Grandma?" Toby said. He started toward her but slipped on the cherry cobbler again. He tilted backwards and fell into the only upright buffet table left. It went down with him, raking along the wall and dislodging every electrical power strip plugged into the wall. The music stopped, the lights went out completely, and the room was in darkness.

"Four hundred!" shouted a woman Francine recognized as the neighborhood cougar. "I want him to take me luging!"

The laughter was cut short by the sound of a blood-curdling scream. It sounded like it came from backstage. Worse yet, it sounded like it had come from Joy. Then someone else yelled, "Fire!" and the alarm went off.

THREE

THE NOISE OF THE fire alarm was deafening. Francine felt like the air had been sucked out of the room. She looked for Charlotte. *When did I last see her?* She thought she'd gotten a glimpse of Charlotte's curly wig at the head table offering desserts to the Town Council members. *How long ago was that?* She wasn't there now.

Attendees began launching themselves toward the exit at the back of the room. A bottleneck formed near the downed buffet tables. The frantic unease in the room grew to a fevered pitch. Someone noticed the exit sign at the front of the room and shouted, "Up here!" A small group ran after him toward the exit to the left of the stage.

People screamed as they fled, releasing pent-up emotions.

The two women who'd been holding the unconscious Mary Ruth were losing their grip. Francine saw it coming and grabbed on as well. There was no way they could get her out into the hall and down the stairs until the room cleared. She heaved her friend toward the kitchen. The women were uncertain but didn't let go. Together, they dragged her to the kitchen in safety. They settled her on a stool by the prep table, her arms and head on the tabletop. Then the women fled.

Francine assessed her friend's condition and decided she would be all right for the moment. She wanted to find Joy and Charlotte. She cracked open the door to the kitchen and looked out. She wasn't sure where the fire was, but it couldn't be close. She didn't smell smoke, didn't feel the heat, and saw no sources of flames when she looked out into the room. All she could hear was the pounding of the fire alarm in her ears and the thunder of frantic footsteps on the staircase adjacent to the kitchen wall.

Francine spotted Joy coming down the steps from the stage awkwardly in her long white dress and high heels. Her eyes had a wild look in them. Charlotte was right behind her. They noticed Francine peering out from the kitchen door and hurried toward her. Joy lurched at Francine when she got close and nearly tackled her.

"It's Camille," Joy said, shouting to be heard above the alarm. "She's been stabbed."

"Where?"

Joy gripped Francine's shoulder so tightly Francine felt the nails digging in. "I don't know where!" Joy yelled at her. "Maybe in her back, maybe in her side."

"No, I mean, where is she?"

"Backstage," said Charlotte. "She needs your help. Eric's back there too."

"Oh my God! Oh my God!" Joy covered her forehead like she was shielding her eyes from something unbearable.

"It's the dressing room. It's on the right," Charlotte said. "Call 911. Neither of us has a phone."

"I dropped mine somewhere," Joy said, her hands waving toward an indeterminate place. "I'd taken a few photos during the auction but when Toby started taking off his shirt..." Her voice trailed off.

"We know," Charlotte said, sounding firm. "It's okay."

"I'm sure the Fire Department is on its way, what with that alarm going off," Francine shouted.

She dashed into the now-vacant banquet room. It now looked like cattle had stampeded through it. Banquet tables were tossed aside, their elegant tablecloths smeared with overturned food. Broken glass from trampled wine goblets and beer glasses littered the floor.

Francine was glad to be wearing sneakers, not heels. She hurried across the floor and up the stairs, threw back the stage curtain, and searched for the dressing room. A table with costume changes laid out in orderly fashion led her to the door. She heard Eric's shaky voice coming from inside. "Aunt Camille! Please get up! Please don't leave me!"

She steeled herself, then stepped into the room.

Eric was kneeling on the floor beside his aunt. Tears streamed down his face. His fingers fumbled around her neck trying to find a pulse. He seemed incapable of figuring out how to do it. He looked at Francine as she approached. "I don't know what to do," he said.

Camille's body was twisted away from Francine, Eric's broad back blocking her view. The closer she got, the more she could see of Camille. Blood puddled on the floor beside her. Francine's eyes traced it to the source: a knife protruding from her right side under her rib cage. Just as Charlotte said. She wanted to avert her eyes, but her nursing skills wouldn't let her. *Airway, breathing, circulation.* The ABCs of emergency situations. She made a second assessment to see what could be done. It was tough to concentrate with the fire alarm screaming at them, but she tried.

Assessing Camille's airways and breathing was tough to do with Eric in the way. The knife looked like it had deflated a lung. The size of the instrument struck Francine. She was only used to kitchen knives. The hilt on this one made it look like a hunting knife. The wound would be deep. As she studied what she could see, she noticed the grip was unusual. *I bet that's not a normal hunting knife.* She forced her thoughts back to saving Camille. There did not seem to be multiple stab wounds. The knife appeared to have been thrust under the rib cage, perhaps aimed for the lung.

Was that happenstance on the murderer's part or had the move been practiced? Had it been driven in with force and purpose to puncture the lung? The idea made her squirm.

She steeled herself one more time to the task at hand. She moved to sit next to Camille.

Eric moved out of the way. "Save her," he pleaded.

The fire alarm went quiet with a final, strangled squawk. *I guess that means there wasn't a fire,* Francine thought. *Thank heavens.*

But her next thought was that the alarm had been a distraction. The dead silence now seemed eerie.

She pushed it from her mind. She focused on Camille. *Was she even alive?* Now that Francine had a clearer view, she tried to detect movement in Camille's chest cavity. The movement was slight, but she was still breathing.

"Eric, listen to me." She tried to keep her voice steady. She needed him to hear confidence and just obey. "This is an emergency. Your aunt needs immediate medical attention. The best thing you can do is find the firemen when they arrive and send the paramedics up here as quickly as you can. Can you do that?" She wanted Eric out of the room. She would do what she could, but having to deal with him at the same time would limit her. "I'll stay here and try to keep her alive. I was a nurse for over thirty years. One thing I can say for sure, the sooner the paramedics arrive, the more likely she is to survive."

Whether Eric understood or not, he got up and ran out of the room.

Francine took a deep breath and steadied herself. She turned back to Camille. The woman lay on her right side, the same side the knife protruded from. If the knife punctured only the right lung, her left lung would still be able to function. That was likely what was keeping her alive. Fortunately, being on her right side allowed the left to breathe normally and not have pressure on it.

Pressure! She needed to put pressure on the wound to stem the bleeding. Or try, anyway. She stood and stripped off the white apron Toby had given her at the carving station. The top of the apron was soaked with meat juices, but the bottom was dry. She wrapped it around the wound and pressed.

Camille's eyes popped open as though the rescue effort hurt, but then they closed again.

Should Camille be conscious? Francine wondered. Her body should be gasping for breath with only one lung operational. While keeping pressure on the wound, she looked for evidence of blows to the head. If she'd been knocked out before being knifed, that would account for the unconsciousness.

Francine couldn't see anything obvious, but Camille's thick black hair covered most of her face and neck. Blood dripped from her nose. The only good sign was its bright red color. *Oxygen must be getting to her heart.*

When will the paramedics get here?

She heard movement outside the door and Police Chief Bart Cannon stepped in. Bart was in his mid-fifties with a shaved head that needed to be shaved again soon. He saw her administering first aid and assessed the situation. "The paramedics are on their way," he said. His voice was gruff. "They should be here any minute."

"She's alive, but if she doesn't get to the hospital soon, I'm not sure how long she'll last."

He didn't answer, but scouted the room. Francine continued pressing the wound. Not wanting to look at the blood loss, she studied Cannon's movements. His steps were plodding. He was thick in the midsection. *Heavier than a policeman should be*, she thought. He ran his hand nervously over his head. She could see that his hairline had receded to the sides and back.

Francine didn't have a good impression of him. Jonathan said Cannon was more connected to the good ole boys' network than he was to the current town government. But at the moment, none of that mattered.

"Tell me what happened," he said.

But you were there! She wanted to say. She knew he'd been at one of the front tables. She'd seen him go through the buffet line at some point. But she followed his direction. "I was helping serve dinner. I'm with Mary Ruth's Catering. There was an accident out front and it took out the lights and the music. We heard a scream from backstage, then someone yelled 'Fire,' and the alarm went off. After everyone left, I found Camille in this condition." Francine deliberately left out Joy, Charlotte, and Eric. She would let them tell the chief their stories.

"You look like you know what you're doing."

"I was a nurse for thirty-six years. Retired now."

He nodded absently. He wasn't looking at her. He was taking in the room's contents.

Francine heard the clomping of hurried footsteps on the stage floor. *Hopefully the paramedics have arrived.*

The chief stepped out and hailed them in. There were four paramedics, two men and two women. Eric was with them. The younger of the men wheeled in a cot. The older of the women seemed to be in charge.

"I'm a nurse," Francine told her. "She has a pulse, but it's thready. She's breathing, but not talking. The stab wound looks deep." She scooted away, and the woman took over, issuing orders to the others. They carried a cot and laid it next to Camille's body. Francine saw them ready an IV. She was pretty sure Camille would have to be intubated too.

Cannon was quick to get Francine out of the room. He indicated for her to follow him onto the stage. He allowed Eric to remain.

Charlotte was now at the prop table and hunting through it. "I don't see the knife I had earlier," she said.

Before Francine could answer, Cannon heard her. "What knife?" he asked.

"A prop," she said, clearing her throat. "I'm looking for the prop I was playing with earlier."

He looked at her suspiciously. "I'll want to hear about that later. Are you with Mary Ruth's Catering too?" He sounded less than pleased. Francine surmised he recognized Charlotte. She had a bad reputation for meddling in police business.

Charlotte bristled at his attitude. She matched it with one of her own. "Yes, I'm with Mary Ruth's. Who's going to be the detective on this case? Jud? Because I've got some observations, and I want someone who appreciates my expertise."

Francine could see Cannon counting to ten before responding. "Detective Judson will be here shortly. I'll make certain *he's* the one to question you. Who else is here?"

Charlotte nodded. "There's Mary Ruth, Joy, me, Francine, and Toby."

"I'm surprised you're still here. Didn't you hear the fire alarm?"

Francine answered. "Mary Ruth was in no shape to leave with the crowd. She needed a little time to recover."

"Recover from what?"

Charlotte answered him. "The shock of learning her grandson had become a male stripper."

Francine thought she detected the corners of Cannon's mouth turning up into a smile, but if so, he dropped it quickly. "This way," he ordered.

He led them toward the stairs at the front of the stage. Before they had a chance to step down, the paramedics came out of the backstage room bearing a cot. It held Camille. She was on her back, the IV was attached, and she was being bag-ventilated. She looked to be hanging on to life. The three of them parted to let the hurrying paramedics get past. They whisked her out the back exit, past where the catering tables lay in a heap. Eric trailed closely behind them.

It seemed like the catered event happened hours ago, even though Francine knew it had been less than fifteen minutes.

Detective Brent "Jud" Judson and two police officers entered shortly after the paramedics left.

Charlotte brightened at the sight of the boyishly handsome detective. "Jud! I—"

He held up a hand to stop her talking. "I'm sure you have a lot to tell me," he said, "but I need for you to wait. Can you do that?"

"Well, sure," she said, tapping her foot on the floor. "But—"

Jud cut her off. "That's good."

"But I—"

"Hold that thought."

Jud and Cannon stepped away and conferred in low tones. Francine couldn't hear a thing. Every once in a while Jud would glance over at her.

Jud returned to the two woman as Cannon left via the back exit.

"Where's he going?" Charlotte asked.

"Outside. We're interviewing attendees in the parking lot. It's a traffic jam out there with so many people scrambling to leave.

Which is fortunate for us. Saves us from having to assemble them later."

Jud looked from Francine to Charlotte and back again. "The chief tells me the rest of the catering crew is in the kitchen. True?"

"Five minutes ago it was," Charlotte blurted out. Francine knew Charlotte was desperate to tell what she knew, so she kept quiet.

"Let's go see."

They walked through the kitchen door. Mary Ruth, now conscious, sat on a stool, her back propped up against a stainless steel prep table. Her shirtless grandson, a towel wrapped around his shoulders, sat next to her. They were not talking. Mary Ruth's hair, which was cut short and cropped close to her face, was damp with perspiration. Francine could see beads of sweat on her forehead. Joy was leaned over a counter tapping on her iPad. She looked to be in reporter mode. *Probably sending a story to Channel Six.*

Jud got on his radio. "Anyone out there have the witness forms yet?" There was a response but it sounded garbled to Francine. "Ten-four," Jud answered. "Bring some up."

"Not the forms," Charlotte groaned. "I'd rather tell you what I know."

"In time," Jud said. "In time." Less than a minute later a uniformed officer brought in a stack of forms. Jud passed a couple out to each of them. He made them sit away from each other and gave them pens and brief instructions. "No talking," he reminded them.

After they started, Jud tapped Francine on the shoulder and indicated he wanted to see her out in the banquet room. She stopped filling out the witness form and followed him.

"I'm sorry to see you've witnessed an attempted murder, Mrs. McNamara," he said, once they were out of earshot.

"Not witnessed," she said. "Not in the sense that I saw the attack. And please call me Francine." She appreciated that he held her in respect, but she'd known him since he was a youngster. He'd played football with her sons, especially her youngest son Chad, who was the same age. And Eric Dehoney, she reminded herself. Eric had joined them on the Brownsburg High School team when he was a freshman.

"Noted." He smiled. "If you didn't see her being assaulted, then what did you see? The chief said you were giving Camille first aid."

She skipped the details of Toby bobsledding into the food tables. Charlotte would cover those in excruciating detail when she got her turn. She told of the lights going out, of Joy screaming and of someone yelling, "Fire," and then the alarm going off. She ended with learning from Joy and Charlotte about Camille needing help, and rushing back to the dressing room to find Camille stabbed in the side.

"Did you see anyone leave the dressing room? Anyone running out the back?" Francine tried to remember how the backstage area was set up. Behind the stage curtain was a dressing room recessed into the right side. Opposite the dressing room was a door that led offstage so performers had an exit that would allow them to leave without disrupting the action onstage. The door also led to a nearby exit that opened onto a stairwell. The steps led to the roof one way and to the first floor the other.

"I didn't see anyone. Joy or Eric or Charlotte might have."

"I'll check with them." He jotted notes in a writing pad. "What did you observe about the crime scene? I know you were mostly worried about Ms. Ledfelter, but I trust your powers of observation."

"Because I've become a local expert?" She was sorry the way it came out. "That was uncalled for, wasn't it? I've seen too much death the past year." She tried to remember what the dressing room looked like. It'd been a mess, but had that been a result of the men changing into costumes or the attempted murder? "I remember the knife more

31

than the scene," she answered. "It seemed long to me, maybe nine inches or so, based on the size of the hilt. That's the blade and the hilt."

"How could you tell that?"

"Charlotte picked it up earlier in the day off the prop table. It registered with me because it looked real. I think it must have been."

"Anything special about the knife?"

"I thought … sorry, this sounds gruesome … but I wondered if this were a premeditated act or if it were just happenstance. I thought for the knife to have punctured her lung, which I think it did, it had to have been stabbed with force and direction."

"Meaning the person knew what they were doing?"

"I don't like to think of that, but yes."

"Anything else?"

She rubbed her finger and her thumb together as she stared off, trying to recall any other details. "The hilt of the knife. It protruded from her side. It seemed worn."

This time Jud looked up from his notebook. "Worn? Like it had been well used?"

"Hopefully not as a weapon, but yes. I tried to avoid touching it."

"Distinguishing marks?"

"I can't pinpoint any, but I have this impression it was military issue."

"What makes you say that?"

She shook her head. "It just struck me that way. It seems like a blur."

He grimaced. "I hate to think it would be a vet. Too many stories about vets having psychological issues."

"Won't you be able to retrieve it? I'm sure they sent Camille to Hendricks Regional."

"Sure. But if you remember anything now, that could help us. We won't have to wait."

She blew out a breath. "Sorry. It's just a vague impression I have."

He stopped writing and paced around the room, pausing by the upended catering tables. He stared at the floor where cherry cobbler filling had been smeared across a wide swath. "Is that blood?" He knelt down for a closer look.

In spite of the circumstances, Francine laughed. "No, it's cherry cobbler."

Accepting that for fact, he swiped a finger through it. He lifted it to his nose. "You're right. It smells like cherry. With a bit of almond in it, I think."

"Good detection."

He stood up, wiped his hands, and put his fists on his hips. "I'm just glad to have an explanation for the red footprints on the staircase."

FOUR

Toby, Mary Ruth, Joy, Charlotte, and Francine had all been questioned by Jud, then dispatched to leave. It was late. Jud wanted the room left as it was until the detectives and evidence tech could go through everything, and that included all of Mary Ruth's catering equipment. She hadn't put up much of a fuss. She said she didn't have another catering job for three days, and Jud assured her she could return the next day to retrieve everything. He walked them to the parking lot. Francine pulled the hood on her winter coat over her head in hopes she wouldn't be recognized.

Five police cars with red and blue lights flashing in the darkness blocked the entrances and exits to the lot. Reporters wielding microphones stood near news vans just outside the yellow crime scene tape. They crowded the boundary line when they saw the group appear. Francine had been through this before, way more times than she wished. They all had. Joy walked to the Channel Six van and struck up a conversation with the reporter.

"No talking, Joy," Jud said firmly.

Joy turned and put a hand on one hip. "He's a friend and colleague. You can't stop us from talking. We're not talking about the incident, anyway."

"Mrs. McNamara," a female reporter called. If the other reporters hadn't recognized her on sight, they knew her name now. They all clamored for her attention.

Jud waved them away. "Mrs. McNamara will not be making any statements. Nor will any of the others."

Francine shrugged at them like there was nothing she could do about Jud's decision. She unlocked her Prius and got in. Charlotte got in the other side.

Jud stood waiting for Francine to finish buckling up. "I don't know how you and your friends always seem to be at the wrong place at the wrong time."

Charlotte stuck her head across Francine's lap. "Be glad for it. Otherwise you wouldn't have us to help you. It's hard to get good volunteer help these days."

"I wouldn't know what that looked like," he said under his breath, so Francine would hear. Then, to Charlotte, he said, "I don't have to tell you to leave the investigating to us."

"If you don't have to, then don't."

Chief Cannon, it seemed, was not the only one she had counting to ten before speaking.

At Jud's silence, Charlotte continued. "We don't need to be lectured. We've been through this before."

He finished composing himself. "That's exactly what I mean. Think about it." Then he backed away and closed Francine's door.

Francine drove off, Charlotte muttering about how ticked she was that Jud actually accused them of meddling in official police investigations when all they were doing was helping.

The last thing Francine remembered before she fell asleep was lying on the couch, leaned up against Jonathan, spilling her heart out about the disaster the fund-raiser at the Crown Room had become—how someone had stabbed Camille Ledfelter, how helpless she felt seeing her lying there bleeding, and how she feared for Camille's life. Jonathan just listened and didn't offer any advice. That was what she had hoped for. She was grateful to talk it out.

She couldn't remember how she got to bed, but the next thing she remembered was a ringing noise disturbing her sleep. It was irritating, like a fly buzzing around her, and she tried to ignore it until she realized what it was. But by then the call on her cell was gone. She wiped the sleep out of her eyes and checked the time. It was 8:34. A short night. She checked the phone. She didn't recognize the number. Maybe another reporter. She wondered how Camille was doing, and said a prayer that she was doing well.

Francine slipped on a green flannel robe and fuzzy slippers. She found Jonathan in the breakfast nook eating.

"Glad you're up," he said, putting down his fork. "Feeling any better this morning?"

She shrugged. "I slept okay. But it doesn't change what happened last night. Any word on Camille?"

Jonathan's mouth turned grim. "Joy was on the air about fifteen minutes ago doing a live report from Hendricks Regional. It doesn't look good."

"I was afraid of that last night when I saw how deep the knife had gone into her side."

He lifted his mug. "I made coffee."

"Sounds good." She poured a cup, set it on the table, and slumped into a chair. "Camille had her issues, but she was popular enough to get elected to the Brownsburg Town Council, and then get elected President by the other Council members. Who would want to kill her?"

"I think you're mistaking 'newsworthy' for 'popular.' She was revered for helping the police track down that child pornographer who'd been operating out of the Bulldog Coffee House several years ago, but I'm not sure that made her popular. Before that, she was kind of eccentric. She wasn't popular with Charlotte, not after that run-in. Don't the two of them hate each other?"

"They did have a row. It was over that irrigation system Charlotte had installed. But they patched up their differences. While they aren't exactly friends, they're at least friendly."

Jonathan looked over the two kinds of jam on the table and selected black raspberry. "If you say so." He spread a spoonful over a piece of toast. "At a homeowners' association meeting last summer, Camille referred to it as Charlotte's *irritation* system."

The row between the two occurred at a time when Camille was a Council member but not yet become President. The two lived next door to each other on the far side of the Summer Ridge subdivision. Their properties shared a meter pit. During a hot, dry summer, Charlotte had an irrigation system installed. Immediately after, Camille claimed her pipes started rattling when the irrigation system was on. She blamed it on the workmanship of the contractors. Charlotte countered that the Town had installed the meter pit incorrectly. Camille used her considerable pull at the Town to force Charlotte to disconnect the system.

"I'll check with Charlotte. I thought it was still disconnected."

"Charlotte makes me nuts sometimes," Jonathan said. "And I don't live next door. Although sometimes I think she lives here."

Francine added a little cream and a little sugar to her coffee. "I appreciate that you put up with her not having much of a filter anymore."

"She had a filter at one time?"

"Not nice."

"Well, I dispute the fact that the two of them made up. That little vein on the side of Charlotte's neck starts to throb whenever Camille's name is mentioned."

"You noticed that?"

"Hard to miss on Charlotte. She doesn't get that way very often. She's usually the one doing the aggravating, not the one being aggravated."

His comment made her choke back a swallow of coffee. She changed the subject. "The eggs look good." She started to get up.

"Stay seated," Jonathan ordered. "I'll make you some. There're hash browns left in the skillet I can warm up for you. I sliced up the cranberry walnut bread you made yesterday."

"That would be nice, but finish your breakfast first."

Jonathan finished his toast and took his plate to the kitchen, busying himself with her breakfast. She considered how fortunate they were to have the life they enjoyed. Not that they hadn't worked hard for it; she'd spent decades working at a hospital after taking time off to raise their three boys to school age. Jonathan had built his own accounting firm and still worked part-time at it.

And they'd been fortunate to sustain such good health. Though, again, they'd worked hard at it, she also knew others in their early seventies who suffered from cancer, had heart problems, or took handfuls of medicine each morning. So she was grateful.

Jonathan's tall, lean body moved gracefully around the kitchen, still in sleep clothes. He wore blue-checkered flannel pants with a loose-fitting white long-sleeve t-shirt. His nod to the cold weather was a red fleece pullover over the t-shirt. She would have been cold with only a fleece for added warmth, but Jonathan was typically warm-natured, even in February in Indiana.

The next thing she knew, Jonathan placed a plate of scrambled eggs, hash browns, and cranberry walnut toast in front of her. "Warm up your coffee?"

It was as if she came out of a trance. She tested the coffee and found it to be lukewarm. "I can't believe I forgot to drink it! I must still be half asleep."

"You didn't get home until late. I was surprised you came down as early as you did. Go ahead and eat. I'll take care of it."

Jonathan brought the coffee back hot and headed upstairs to shower.

Francine had barely started her breakfast when she heard the rumble of a car pull up in the driveway. Only one of their friends drove a big old vehicle whose engine had the right frequency to penetrate the walls of the house. *That sounds like Charlotte's car.*

The rumbling stopped. Only a short time later the doorbell rang. Francine smiled. Charlotte must have navigated the walk between the driveway and the front step easily, yet another sign her knee had improved. She answered the door.

Charlotte stepped in, stripped off the neon orange down coat she wore in cold weather, and handed it to Francine. "Thanks." She sniffed the air. "Bacon and eggs, yes? Smells delicious."

"Let me finish mine before they get cold and I'll make you some." Francine led the way through the swinging door to the breakfast nook and Charlotte followed.

"Have you heard anything about Camille?" Charlotte asked. "Eric stopped by their house this morning, but I wasn't dressed yet so I didn't go over. I'm guessing he spent the night at the hospital. I called while he was in, but he didn't answer the phone." She plopped herself in Jonathan's chair. She checked out the toast, which Francine hadn't touched. "Are you going to eat that?" she asked, picking it up and taking a bite.

Francine was annoyed but found it easier to pretend everything was fine. "You seem hungry."

"I'm just stressed, and I eat when I'm stressed. You know that." She took a second bite of the toast and stopped to savor it. "This is delicious."

"Thanks. It's a new recipe I'm testing out for Mary Ruth. Since she's going to be on the Cooking Channel again, she wanted a home cook to try making it before she does the program." Mary Ruth had done several things with the Food Network, competing on *Chopped* and being spotlighted on a couple of other shows. Now she was sharing segments with a group of other senior chefs on a home cooking show called *Senior Cooks on Home Cooking.* It wasn't on until eleven thirty at night, but still, it was fun to think of the national exposure she was getting. *As long as it's her and not me,* Francine thought.

Jonathan came downstairs in his robe. His hair was wet, and he smelled of sandalwood. He was carrying Francine's phone.

"Joy," he said. "It was ringing when I got out of the shower."

She put the phone to her ear. "Hello?"

"I've got some bad news," Joy said. "Camille just died."

Francine's shoulders fell. "That's so sad."

"I know how you feel. I've been monitoring this since the station sent me over early this morning. I saw it coming, though. The hospital had a news conference a half hour ago. When it happened, though..." Her voice trailed off.

Francine relayed the news to Charlotte.

"What should we do now?" Charlotte asked.

"I don't know," Francine said. "Express our condolences to Eric? See if he needs anything?"

Joy overheard them talking. "Finding Eric might be tough," she said. "The hospital's been trying to get hold of him, and Jud's been trying to locate him. He's disappeared."

FIVE

Joy said she had to do a final report for the station and hung up. Jonathan went upstairs to finish getting ready for the day. The news about Camille depressed Francine. Since she lost her appetite, Charlotte finished her breakfast.

"I bet Eric's holed up in his house," Charlotte said, readying a forkful of hash browns to put in her mouth. "He was there when I left."

"Are you sure he was there? You said he didn't answer the phone."

"I heard his Mustang pull in the garage."

Francine knew all about Charlotte's hearing. "You didn't actually see him pull in, though?"

"I know what you're thinking. But it's the high tones I have trouble with, not the low tones."

Francine had to admit that was true. And Charlotte was nosy. She had a way of hearing things when she really wanted to. "Let's assume it's true that Eric's in the house. What would be the purpose of not answering phone calls? He must have left the hospital before he knew Camille had died."

"Listen to yourself, Francine. She was in really bad shape last night. We all knew it was likely. Maybe he didn't want to face it. Maybe he still doesn't want to. You know they had a very close relationship."

Eric's parents had died when he was fifteen, victims of a mass shooting at the post office where they worked. Camille, who was his mother's sister, took him in. Though she hadn't married and had no children, she'd turned out to be a good parent. She'd worked with counselors and school administrators to help him get through the traumatic experience of losing his parents. They'd also had to navigate the tough issues of transferring to a new high school, losing old friends, and experiencing adolescence.

Camille had come to love Eric as a son. Though she never took the place of his mother, she held a very special place in his heart too.

Whether Eric was in the house or not, Francine had to be practical. "We can't very well force our way in."

"I think we should try. He knows you and trusts you."

Camille had appealed to Francine's son Chad to get him involved in the freshman football program since Eric had been in football at his old high school. It helped that he and Chad were the same age. In easing the transition for Eric, Chad became good friends with him.

"I suppose I could at least knock on the door and try to talk my way in."

"Good. Can I get some ketchup for these hash browns? Or maybe a little steak seasoning to sprinkle on them? They need something. Then we can stop by Camille's house on the way to the police station."

Francine was taken aback. "The police station?"

Charlotte used the toast to corner the last bite of scrambled eggs and get it onto her fork. "Did I forget to mention that? Jud wants to see me. He wants to question me about my past with Camille. That's why I'm ready to go so early this morning."

"I wondered."

"I asked if you could come with me. That's just in case he tries to accuse me of killing her. You know I couldn't have done it. He said that was fine, that he wants to talk to you too." She scooped the eggs into her mouth.

Francine checked her cell phone for messages. "He never called to ask."

"Probably just an oversight. I'm sure he's going to. So you'll come with me?"

"That wasn't on my schedule this morning."

"Obviously. You're still in your robe."

Francine huffed, but she made a quick decision. "I'll go get ready. You can find the ketchup in the refrigerator."

Charlotte eased back her chair. "Thanks. And maybe I'll toast up another slice of that cranberry walnut bread. Mary Ruth outdid herself with that recipe. As did you, in following it."

Since Charlotte's car was already over at Francine's, it was natural for the women to take it. If they hadn't been going just a short distance, Francine might have insisted on driving, since Charlotte had a tendency to talk a lot and not pay attention to the road. As it was, she let Charlotte swerve her way to Eric and Camille's.

Charlotte jerked to a stop in the driveway next to a black Lincoln Town Car. "That wasn't here before."

"Whose behemoth is that?" Francine asked.

Charlotte peered at it narrow-eyed. "You don't seriously have to ask, do you? It belongs to Vince Papadopoulos, her nemesis on the Town Council." Vince owned the Papadopoulos Funeral Home along Main Street.

Francine didn't want to get out until she better assessed why he was there. It couldn't be to collect Camille's body—that'd still be at the hospital. She wasn't sure Camille would have wanted to use the services of his funeral home anyway, given their difficult relationship.

Charlotte didn't seem to be in a hurry to get out of the car, either. They saw someone come around the side of the house.

"It's Vince, all right," Francine confirmed.

Vince was a short, swarthy man with a perpetual five o'clock shadow. He was wearing a dark suit, an Indianapolis Colts scarf around his thick neck, and a pair of black driving gloves on his hands. Vince's family had been in Brownsburg since the 1930s. He was one of the last of the "old guard" on the Council who still believed they ran the Town, though Camille's ascension to the Council presidency said otherwise. Vince was frequently out-voted in the five-member Council.

When he saw another car in the driveway, he slowed down and approached them cautiously.

Charlotte rolled down the window. "Hi, Vince," she said. "Come to see the lay of the land now that Camille's gone?"

Vince blanched like she'd read his thoughts. "That's a terrible thing to say," he answered. "I came to express my condolences to Eric. See if there was anything I could do for him."

Like sell him a casket and a funeral service, Francine thought.

"Does he appear to be home?" Charlotte asked.

"If he is, he isn't answering the door. I went around back to see if he was just avoiding company, but the blinds and drapes are closed."

"We came to see if he was home too."

"My advice is, don't waste your time." He got in his Lincoln and backed out of the driveway.

Francine watched him go. "That was pretty rude of you, to imply he would be glad to see Camille is gone."

"You know he has to be. Whenever Camille said A, he said B. There was a lot of animosity there. Let's get out."

45

"Why? He's not home."

"If I were Eric, I wouldn't answer the door for Vince, either."

Camille's house, located next to Charlotte's, was not all that different from hers. Both houses were single-story, three-bedroom, custom-built homes with basically the same floor plan. Charlotte's exterior was brick that had been painted light gray to update it; Camille's retained the traditional red brick color. They walked up to the front step. Charlotte rang the doorbell and waited.

"See? There's no one home," Francine said after half a minute.

"Nonsense." Charlotte went around the side of the house to where the attached garage was located. She peered in the window. "There's a car in there," she called. "Camille's."

"But not Eric's? How did Camille's car get back from the Crown Room?"

"Don't know. I only know it's there. Ring the doorbell again."

Francine pressed the button and listened for the chime.

Charlotte returned. "Any action yet?"

"I could hear the bell, but no response."

She pounded on the front door. "We know you're in there, Eric. Open up!"

Francine grabbed Charlotte's fist to stop her. "Quit it! We're here to sympathize, not break down the door. He may not even know she's passed on."

Charlotte put her fist back in her pocket. "I suppose you're right. I'm just a little nervous about what Camille might have told Eric about that stupid irrigation system. Not that there was anything to it. I was hoping to talk to him before we see Jud."

"So what about the irrigation system? I thought that was behind you."

"We probably ought to go see Jud."

46

Typical Charlotte, stalling to avoid telling me the truth. I'll get it out of her later.

They motored over to Brownsburg Town Hall to meet with Jud.

The Police Department was in the southernmost of two buildings in the Town Hall complex, located at the corner of Green Street and Main Street. The area used to be a part of the old downtown area, but when the buildings were declared too expensive to rehab, the Town purchased the area, tore down the buildings, and redeveloped it. The complex was built linearly like a strip mall but the exterior was bricked to look more like individual buildings with peaked roofs and residential front doors. Jud's office was on the second floor.

The parking lot was crowded, so Francine dropped Charlotte off at the door and then went to park Charlotte's Buick.

"I'm not a credible suspect," Charlotte announced once they were admitted and seated. "Ask Francine. She'll tell you."

Jud frowned. He wore a blue dress shirt, khakis, and a striped tie. He straightened the tie like he needed to look professional, which he might have, considering both of his guests had known him since middle school. He turned to Francine. "Why is she not a credible suspect?"

"Uh," Francine said, taken by surprise. "Because she has an alibi?"

"Right. I have an alibi," Charlotte said.

Jud folded his arms against his chest. "What is it?"

Charlotte shifted in her seat. "Stop looking at me like that, Jud. You know I didn't do it."

"Maybe. But I want to hear your alibi."

"Joy can testify I didn't do it. Joy would have seen me leave the dressing room. And besides, I don't have the strength to stab Camille up under the rib cage like that."

Jud leaned back in his chair. He had a half smile on his face. "That's not an alibi. You're just trying to reason with me."

"But it's a good reason! I'm weak. I couldn't have done it."

"How about you?" Jud asked Francine. "Chief Cannon found you alone in the room with Camille. You were supposedly trying to save her, but that could have been a ruse. You're strong enough to have stabbed her."

Francine was aghast. "I'm a former nurse. I save people! And you've known me half your life! You know—" She stopped when she saw him grinning from ear to ear.

At that moment, Jud's secretary showed Joy into his office. Francine presumed she had come from live reporting because she had make-up on and wore an outfit she'd seen Joy wear on-air before. "I didn't know you were going to be here," Joy said to the other women.

"We didn't know we were going to be accused of murdering Camille," Charlotte said. "You too?"

Jud leaned forward. "For the moment, just in here, we are going to act like you're not suspects. That will not be the case to the outside world. I asked you to be here together because you've already been interviewed separately, and because I know you well enough to know it will be easier to question you this way."

Jud only had two guest chairs in his small office. Since Charlotte and Francine had already taken the two, he pulled in a third for Joy. Francine and Charlotte moved their chairs as close as possible so hers wouldn't have to be half outside the door.

Jud got serious. "First, I want your word that everything we talk about in here is confidential. Especially you, Joy. As a member of the press, I need your assurance you won't report or discuss with anyone anything you learn in here."

Joy nodded. "I'll tell them that since I was a witness, I need to recuse myself of any reporting duties on the case. But I can't do anything about what I've already reported."

"Understood." He turned to Charlotte and Francine. "What about the two of you?"

Charlotte's head bobbed up and down in agreement. Francine tried to look reassuring when she simply said, "Absolutely."

He seemed satisfied. "Joy, let's start with you. I want you to repeat exactly what you saw up to and including when Charlotte joined you in the room. And if either of you," he indicated Francine and Charlotte with a wave of his hand, "have anything to add, I want you to do so."

Joy began with Camille bringing Eric up to start the auction. She went through what she remembered, then said, "Camille went backstage after introducing Eric."

"When did you go back? Right after her?" Jud asked.

"No, I was watching what Eric was doing. I'm not sure why Camille went back. Maybe to use the bathroom or something."

"But there's no bathroom back there."

"No, but she could have used the backstage door. It opens into the Crown Room. Then she could have circled around to find the restrooms. In fact, I thought she had. I heard that door open and close."

"It did," Charlotte said. "I could see the door from where I was sitting at the head table. Someone came out. All the lights were focused on Eric, so it was dark back there. I couldn't see who it was."

Jud scanned his notebook. He looked up at Charlotte. "You were seated at the head table?"

"I brought a bunch of desserts up so they wouldn't have to go get them. Mary Ruth insisted that we do everything we could to make the crowd feel pampered. It was all for charity, you know. Camille had left her seat open to go up on stage, so I took it."

Francine noted that Camille, being Town Council President, had been given the best seat in the house, up front facing the stage.

Charlotte's taking it had put her close to where the first bachelor had done his little strip tease act to hype the bidding for a date.

Jud flipped to a clean sheet in his notebook and made a rough sketch of the floor plan of the Crown Room. He penciled in the door Joy and Charlotte mentioned.

"And why did you go backstage?" he asked Joy. "Was it because you heard Camille?"

Joy got the deer-in-the-headlights look. Francine knew she was trying to come up with a reason to avoid telling the truth, that she was having a "problem" with male nudity. "I, uh, brought several outfits to change into during the evening. Kind of like Vanna White on *Wheel of Fortune*. I thought it would be a good idea to change then, while the bachelors were being auctioned off."

Jud nodded. "Go on."

Joy breathed a little more easily.

"But then you didn't go out the back door, did you?" he asked, leading her to finish her story.

"No. I went to the dressing room door. I felt someone brush by me and run out. Then I heard something fall in the dressing room, so I went in. I turned on the light and saw Camille lying on the floor. I screamed."

"Then someone yelled 'Fire,'" Charlotte interrupted, "and pulled the fire alarm."

Jud examined his sketch. He circled where the fire alarm was located. It was close to the stairwell. "Charlotte, when did you go backstage?"

"After I saw Joy head back. It was before she screamed. Before the lights went out."

"But you didn't go up on stage?"

"No. I used the back entrance, the one we've been talking about." She pointed to the door that was to the left of the backstage area. It was near the fire alarm and the stairwell. "If I'd have gone up the steps to the stage, I'd have been in the spotlight."

"Why did you go back?"

Now it was Charlotte who was sputtering. "I, uh, was concerned about Joy."

Jud gave her an inquisitive look. "Why?"

"She . . . hadn't been feeling well earlier in the evening. She complained of nausea. I wanted to make sure she was all right."

Joy nodded vigorously. "I had complained about that, hadn't I, Francine?"

Francine agreed. "True. She had."

From the suspicious look on his face, Francine guessed Jud wasn't quite buying this explanation. But to her relief, he moved on. "So Charlotte, there must have been a little light if you could see to go back. Did you notice the killer exit the back door, pull the fire alarm, and leave?"

"No. Until the door opened, the only lights in the room were the spots, and they were focused on Eric and Toby."

"But when the door opened . . ."

"There was light for just a brief second or two. The killer shut the door behind him or her. The light was dim, and then it was gone. I really didn't see much of anything."

"Last night you said it could have been a man or woman. Now that you've had a chance to think about it, do you have any better sense of which it might have been?"

She shook her head. "The person was bigger than me for sure, but that only disqualifies ten percent of the population of Brownsburg. Could have been either sex."

Jud tapped his pen on the sketch, thinking. "What about when they screamed, 'Fire'? No clue from the pitch of the voice?"

She shrugged. "Maybe male, but I wouldn't swear to it. It was only one word. After it was yelled, I was more worried about finding Joy and getting out of the room. When she screamed again and when I saw why, I screamed too."

"Eric was there. Could he have done it?"

Charlotte answered matter-of-factly. "Yes, of course he could have. Theoretically, of course."

"Did you try to help Camille?" Jud asked.

Charlotte shook her head. "I wasn't sure she was alive. I had no idea how to treat a stab wound like that. And with the fire alarm going off, I figured the paramedics would be coming and that we just needed to get out of there. Joy looked shell-shocked."

Joy shuddered. "I still think of that knife in her side and it gives me the shakes. I don't know how paramedics do it, day after day."

"Fatal stabbings don't happen very often," he said.

Charlotte looked pensive when Joy mentioned the knife. "Were you able to track down anything about that knife, Jud? It was some kind of specialty knife, I'm sure."

"Tell me what you remember about picking up the knife. Your fingerprints were the only ones we could find on it."

She folded her hands like she was in prayer. "At least you know how they got there."

Her voice had a pleading quality Francine wasn't used to hearing. *I hadn't thought about the fingerprints. No wonder Charlotte was worried about being a credible suspect. Good thing Jud realizes it couldn't have been her.*

"Tell me what you remember."

"Swear you're not going to arrest me."

"Not unless you did it. You're not going to confess, are you? Give me time to set my iPhone to record."

She loosened her shoulders. "No, of course not." The joke seemed to have put her in a better frame of mind. "I remember the handle had some give to it." She held out her hand like she had when she'd held the knife on Eric. "I think it was made of leather. I hadn't expected that, so I remember it distinctly." She thrust her hand forward, like she was really going to stab someone with it.

"Did you pull the knife out of the sheath at all?"

"No." She thought a moment. "It'd been a split-second decision to grab it. The sheath was unusual. Now that I know how sharp the knife was underneath, I'm glad I didn't uncover it. I only wanted to tease Eric's friend into pulling up his wife-beater so I could see those abs of his." She grimaced at the thought of what might have happened.

"What do you mean when you say the sheath was unusual?"

"It was textured. Kind of rough, like the plastic molding machine that made it wasn't very good. I guess maybe that's another reason I thought it was a prop and not real." She returned her hands to prayer position.

Jud didn't show any sign of pulling out handcuffs. "We did find it later. It was buried under some clothes on the changing table. We think the sheath was made using a 3-D printer."

Francine leaned forward. She'd heard her sons discuss those kinds of printers. They sounded exotic. "How do you know that? I'd like to see one of those gadgets."

Jud laughed. "Too expensive for our department to have one."

"What's a 3-D printer?" Charlotte asked.

"It's a machine that re-creates a three-dimensional object," Jud answered. "They generally resemble an open box with an arm that goes up and down and back and forth. It 'weaves' an object with a bead of plastic molding. The machine re-creates an object based on a 3-D computer drawing of it."

"I did a report on one a few months back." Joy looked off in the distance as if she was trying to remember the details. "A senior citizen was making spiders and snakes and leaving them around the nursing home where he lived. Kind of like the old 'Creepy Crawlers' makers we had when we were kids. Anyway, his adult children had to step in and take the printer away from him because he was scaring the heck out of the residents."

Charlotte cocked her head. "So someone designed a sheath for the knife and had this 'printer' make it? And the knife fit right in it? Boy, I'd like to see that."

"I think we all would," Jud said, musing.

"I'd like to get a good look at the knife itself," Francine said. "Can we see it?"

"No, it's in the evidence room."

"Do you have a picture?"

Jud picked up an iPad on his desk. He held it in his hands a few seconds before opening it. "I guess this won't hurt any. And it might help, if you or Joy recognize it."

He called up an image on the iPad and handed it to Francine. She tilted it so Charlotte and Joy could get a look too. It was a close-up photo. Every feature of the actual murder weapon could be seen in full color. *It's a wicked-looking knife*, Francine thought, *with that long, curved cutting blade and that sawtooth serrated edge on top.*

Joy worked her mouth like she'd just eaten something unpleasant. "No wonder Camille died. Look at the blade on that thing. It must have caused a lot of damage."

"Why do people own knives like that?" Francine asked. "Who needs it?"

Jud held up a hand. "It had a particular purpose. It's a Camillus pilot's knife. It was issued by the United States government in the 1960s. Despite its name, its use was more widespread than just pilots. A lot of troops in Vietnam were issued this knife or bought one themselves."

The news stopped Francine. Jonathan had been in the Vietnam War. So had several of their friends. Could that knife have come from someone she knew?

SIX

FRANCINE HAD RESERVATIONS ABOUT people collecting knives and guns. If everyone had the mindset of a true collector, she would feel more at ease with it. But not everyone was like that. And not every collector kept them safe enough to ensure they wouldn't be used improperly. "Still, who needs a knife like that now? And especially in our little town."

"It's not illegal to own a knife like this, even in our 'little town'."

She ignored Jud's sarcasm. She knew the town had over 20,000 people in it and was growing by leaps and bounds. But it still had that small-town feel to her. "Is it authentic?"

"We believe so, although we'd like to know whether it's a recent purchase or been around for a while."

Joy seemed to be in reporter mode as she moved in for a closer look at the iPad. "This is a pretty specific knife. Do any Indianapolis stores carry it? Are you checking with online merchants to see if any were sold to people in this area? I can't imagine there are too many dealers that have a knife like this in inventory."

Jud nodded. "Actually, since there were so many made, these are sold regularly on eBay. We've requested cooperation from the military-oriented sellers that handle the knife, and we're checking out Indianapolis shops, but this incident only happened last night. It hasn't even been twenty-four hours."

"I'm sure there are a dozen ways the killer could have got hold of this knife that are legal and untraceable," Charlotte said. "We just have to hope it's not one of them."

"What about 3-D printers?" Francine asked. "If they're as expensive as you say they are, could we track down who owns one in this area?"

"I said the department couldn't afford one, not that they're expensive. 3-D printers retail for a few thousand dollars. They're not cheap, but not cost prohibitive, either. People have paid more to buy a big-screen television with the latest technology to watch the Super Bowl."

"So I guess that would be difficult to track?"

Jud yawned and leaned back to stretch. "Especially when you consider that Indianapolis is so close. I understand some high-tech companies own them just so their techies can have a new toy to play with."

Joy latched onto Jud's comment. "Wouldn't a business have to claim that as personal property on their taxes? Would the assessor's office have that information?"

"If we could show just cause for a particular business and obtain a search warrant, then we could go through the Assessor's records. Privacy laws prevent it otherwise. It may not be at a business, either. There's no reason an individual couldn't have purchased it."

Charlotte had swiped on the iPad and come up with a photo of the sheath created by the printer. Francine asked her to swipe back to the knife again. The cutting edge of the blade looked sharp, but there were notches and scratches elsewhere that would indicate it had been used. That gave Francine an idea. "If we assume the knife belonged to a Vietnam War veteran, we ought to be able to get a list of those vets who live around here."

Jud held out his hand to take the iPad back. "It's not our purpose to accuse a veteran of doing this."

"I didn't say that. Maybe it was stolen from one. There's an American Legion post in Brownsburg that might have records of who in the area is a veteran. Or what about a VFW post? Do we have any of those in Hendricks County?"

"We don't have a VFW post. Nearest one is in Marion County. We have officers on the Brownsburg police force who are veterans and connected with the Brownsburg American Legion. They're going through those channels to explore any possibility, but again, privacy laws come into play. And not everyone who's a vet registers with those groups. Plus, back then they wouldn't have been able to keep their weapons. The government was touchy about that."

"Where would a vet have gotten one, then?" Joy asked.

Jud gave them a wry smile. "Today? Lots of ways. I mentioned eBay. Also government surplus. The Internet. Stores that specialize in knife collecting. I want to caution against jumping to the conclusion that it was a vet, though. Any knife collector might have an interest in this."

He tired of waiting for Charlotte to put the iPad in his outstretched hand and took it from her. "Let's get back on track. How much do you remember about where everyone was seated? Let's try to figure out who might have been missing when Joy screamed." He tore a blank sheet of paper out of the notebook he was using and handed it to Charlotte. He gave her a pen from a mug on his desk that served as a pen holder. "Please draw me a sketch of what you can remember about last night, where everyone was seated or standing at the time Joy screamed."

Charlotte looked to Francine for help. "I'd been at the head table passing out desserts, but I was kind of distracted by the male dancer and then Toby crashing into the buffet."

"Don't look at me," Francine responded. "I was clutching a giant slab of roast beef at the time."

Jud pressed the pen into Charlotte's hand. "Do your best."

"Okay." Charlotte took the pen and gamely made a child-like top-down sketch of the scene. "Here's what I remember. This is the head table." She pointed to a circle she'd made. "And here's the stage." It was more of a rectangular shape. "Camille's chair was here. She sat facing the stage. That's the seat I took. The rest of the table was mostly Town Council members or their guests." She pointed to the seat to the left of Camille. "Vince Papadopoulos sat here."

"That's right!" Francine poked a finger toward Vince's seat. "He was there, wasn't he? I have to say I was a little surprised. The only time he and Myra show up for fund-raisers is if it's for an anti-abortion activity. But this being for Brownsburg Parks and his being on the Council, he probably didn't have a choice."

"Don't forget that when we stopped by Camille's house on the way here, he was outside trying to find Eric."

Joy perked up. "Vince was at Camille's house today? Did he look suspicious?"

"Vince always looks suspicious," Charlotte said. "It's his swarthy, mob-like features."

"He might be suspicious-looking, but if he was in the chair at the time of the murder, he didn't do it, at least himself," Jud said. "And let's not forget he's a respected business owner. The Papadopoulos Funeral Home has been in Brownsburg for eons."

"I don't remember if he was in the chair or not," Charlotte said. "I was looking in the opposite direction at the time. Toward Francine and her roast beef."

"It's okay. Please continue."

Charlotte tilted her head to the ceiling in thought for a moment. "Next to him was his wife, Myra. And next to her was Fuzzy Carter."

That was an awkward seating arrangement, thought Francine. Myra was the sister of Fuzzy's ex-wife, Cass. She never got along with him after the divorce, and hadn't been too keen on him before. After the divorce, Fuzzy and Vince's relationship had become estranged as well, even though they'd been classmates in high school. Myra and Cass, who'd grown up in a poor rural community in nearby Putnam County, had a sisterhood bond that remained as strong as ever.

"Next to Myra was Tricky Dicky Raden's wife, Glenda, and Tricky Dicky was next to her."

Dick Raden was a member of the Council. He was younger than Fuzzy and Vince, though by how much Francine wasn't sure. She shuddered to think of the buildings Dick's construction firm had built. They were generally the result of short-sighted thinking and resulted in awkward, unattractive buildings shoehorned into key locations that stunted better developments later. He'd only been on the Council for one term, but during that time he'd sided with Vince on almost every issue. As a result, the Council was often bitterly split 3–2. Francine could only be grateful that Vince and Dick were on the losing end.

Charlotte drew in four small squares around the left side of the table to represent the people she'd just talked about. Francine offered to label them, and Charlotte handed her the pen.

"Greg and Janet Tarpen were next to them, Janet in the seat next to Glenda," Charlotte said. Francine added the labels. "I remember that Janet was so excited about the event starting she forgot to enter the calories she consumed into the food tracker app on her phone. And she never forgets that." Janet was a fitness fanatic. She was notorious for keeping track of everything, which was her nature. She was a financial analyst now, but before that she'd worked for one of the big accounting firms in downtown Indianapolis. Jonathan knew her from the accounting world, and he had good things to say about her. Her husband, Greg, was a firefighter with the Brownsburg Fire Territory. Francine thought he could have been a male stripper himself when he was younger. He was good-looking and still kept himself in top shape, but there was no mistaking that he was in his forties now. *Time takes its toll.*

Jud pointed to the crude drawing that Charlotte and Francine had drawn. "Where were the tables that surrounded this one? Did you happen to see who was at those?"

Charlotte's upper brow wrinkled. "There were tables here, here, and here," she said, pointing out their locations. "But I don't remember seeing anyone I know except Chief Cannon. He was at this table with his wife." She pointed to a table behind the head table at a forty-five degree angle. "I remember that they shared their table with the school superintendent from Avon. I can't think of her name, but I remember her because she's a woman. The others with her were mostly women as well."

Jud got up and stretched. "School teachers from Avon, the chief said." He put his hands behind his back and stared at the walls, thinking.

The walls were crowded with frames—Jud and his family, Jud with important state officials, Jud's degree from Indiana University. There were also several art projects made by his kids. Glitter had come off of one of them and sat in a pile on the floor. *Wonder if that's fresh or if the cleaning service is not so good*, Francine thought.

"You have a list of attendees, I imagine?" Joy asked.

Jud answered but continued to look blankly at the wall. "There were over a hundred and fifty guests at the dinner, but some bought tickets at the door, so we don't have all the names. Plus Mary Ruth's staff, plus the Royal Buckingham dancers and their crew. I have my detectives trying to find everyone and get their statements, but it's going to take weeks to do that." He paused and came back to check the diagram. "We're starting with those closest to the stage, plus people like you who were with the catering, and the entertainers. We figure the backstage people were most likely to see anything out of the ordinary."

"Those strippers were out of the ordinary," Charlotte cracked. "I remember every detail of that."

Jud smiled weakly. "You can spare me those details."

Charlotte waggled her eyebrows. "You ever think about being a male dancer, Jud?"

He brushed her comment aside. "I think this interview may be over."

But he meant it only as a joke. He continued asking questions until he was certain he had everything they could remember about who was in the room and where they were at the approximate time of the stabbing. Then he let them go after extracting another promise that they would keep his confidence. Francine was glad when it was over.

The three of them exited into the parking lot. Francine and Charlotte went in search of Charlotte's Buick while Joy walked directly to her car. She'd found a closer spot that was visible from the door. She tooted a goodbye as she left.

"I hate this," Francine said, walking among the cars while keeping an eye out for traffic cruising for a parking space. "I don't remember losing cars this often even ten years ago. Now it happens twice a week."

She thought Town Hall was busy for not being lunchtime yet, but then she remembered it was mid-month. People were hurrying in to pay their utility bills. She could never understand why they didn't pay online or schedule it through the bank, but then not all seniors were comfortable with computers handling their money. At the very least they could mail the payment in.

Charlotte walked slowly but maneuvered around the parking spaces gracefully without a cane. She was using it less and less now, even leaving it at home sometimes. "My knee feels so much better I almost feel guilty using my handicapped parking tag, but at least I make sure I remember where the car is when I come out."

Francine could recall plenty of times they'd searched for Charlotte's car after she forgot where she'd parked but didn't think it was worth the argument. Then she spotted it. "The car's over there," she said, pointing.

They made their way over. But when they looked in, they found an unmoving Eric Dehoney lying on the back seat in a fetal position.

SEVEN

Francine backed away from the car. "I know I locked it," she whispered.

Charlotte nodded reassuringly. "You never fail to click the lock button until the car horn beeps, so I believe you." She strained her neck from where she was standing to see into the back seat. "I don't think he looks injured."

"Don't get so close!"

"For heaven's sake, even if he is injured, he's not going to attack us. Or certainly not you. He practically lived at your house when he wasn't at Camille's."

"That was when he was in high school. It was a long time ago."

"And he's shown lots of hostility toward you in the last year since he's been back in Brownsburg? I say we open the door or knock on the window."

Francine motioned Charlotte to step back where she was. They conferred. Knocking on the window seemed to make the most sense. "You do it," Charlotte said. "He knows you better."

Francine crept up to the back passenger window. She tapped lightly on the pane, peering in to watch for a reaction. Then she stepped backwards.

"No response," she said in a low tone. "I'm going to open the door."

Francine moved in slow motion. After the horror of Camille's stabbing, it was unnerving to find Eric in the back seat of a car that should have been locked. This time she lifted the door handle. At the click of the door becoming unlatched, Eric sat up. He had a look of terror in his eyes.

When he saw who it was, he put a hand on his chest in relief. "Thank God it's you," he said.

"Who did you think it would be?" Francine asked.

"The police," he said. "Or worse."

"Scoot over," Charlotte said. "It's cold out here." She slid in the seat next to him, forcing him to move fully into the seat behind the driver. "Why would you be hiding in my car in the police parking lot if you were afraid of the police finding you? And who would be worse?"

"It's not just the police's parking lot. The parking lot is for the whole complex. And I thought this is the last place they'd expect me to hide. They think I did it. But whoever killed Aunt Camille would be worse."

Francine climbed in the driver's seat and closed the door. She turned around so she could face him and Charlotte. "We just came from talking to Jud, and he says they don't have a suspect. What makes you think they're after you?"

"I don't trust the Brownsburg Police Department. They acted like they suspected me from the start. They were waiting for me outside the hospital room even before Aunt Camille died. I slipped away by pretending I was going to the bathroom but instead took the stairs down to the first floor. I could see a policeman standing by the elevator door when I looked back."

"Maybe they were protecting Camille from whoever tried to kill her."

"Maybe." But Eric did not sound convinced.

They sat for a few seconds with no one saying anything. The car had a stale smell, like it had been closed up a long time. Francine checked to see how long they'd been in Jud's office. Then she checked Eric's clothes. He had a navy wool pea coat on, but it was unbuttoned. She could see that he hadn't changed since the night before and his facial hair showed at least a day's growth. If he'd gone home to Camille's house, he hadn't been there long. Maybe it wasn't staleness she smelled as much as it was Eric.

She started the car to get some warmth going. "I still can't imagine who would have wanted your aunt dead."

Charlotte raised her hands to stop the comments. "Much as I want to hear this, I think we need to take Eric somewhere safe and get to the bottom of this. There's no sense in doing it in the parking lot where people could see."

"I'd like that," Eric said.

Francine buckled her seat belt and checked the rearview mirror. Eric had a nervous look on his face. He was slouching in the back seat so as to not be noticed. He pulled the knit ski cap he was wearing a little farther down on his face. "I'd also like to know how you got into the locked car, Eric."

He gave her a guilty grin. "I had a series of part-time jobs when I was in college in Texas. One of them was with a locksmith." He said it as though that was sufficient to explain his technique. It wasn't, but neither she nor Charlotte questioned him further about it.

They pulled out of the parking lot. Francine turned east on Main Street and headed for Hornaday Drive and the Summer Ridge subdivision.

When they had picked up speed and were away from Town Hall and the police, Charlotte began interrogating him. "So, Eric, can you tell us what happened that night? You were auctioning off Toby, and then you left the stage."

Eric stared out the window. "It was the scream. I turned around and saw that Aunt Camille wasn't there anymore, and I ran to see who screamed."

Francine glanced in the rearview. Eric looked like the emotions had been wrung out of him. "You sound like you had been worried about her before this."

"The last few weeks she never left the house unless I would go with her or if she was meeting someone somewhere," he said, his voice flat. "It was like she never wanted to be alone."

Charlotte's eyes, magnified through her thick, white-framed glasses, loomed large. "Sounds like she was afraid of something."

"I'm pretty sure she was. But she denied it."

Francine tried to concentrate on both the traffic and the conversation, which was difficult. Main Street in Brownsburg was US 136. As a national highway, it was always busy. "So you have no idea what or who it might have been?"

He shrugged, or at least tried to, given that his shoulders were jammed between the back seat and the door. He was still trying to shrink into the seat. "I don't."

Charlotte latched onto Eric's arm and pulled him away from the corner until he was sitting fully in the seat. "We're out of the parking lot and away from the building. You don't have to scrunch down like that. Makes me feel like we're trying to smuggle human contraband out of the country."

Eric gave a nervous laugh but didn't relax.

"It would make no sense to suspect you," Francine said. "Joy screamed before you left the stage. Her account of the events would show it happened before you got there."

"I dunno. Maybe they think I arranged for it to happen."

Charlotte put a hand under her chin, contemplating the situation. "It's true that in these kinds of cases, it's usually someone close to the victim."

"You're not helping," Francine said.

"I'm only trying to account for what the police might be thinking. I didn't say he was guilty." She turned back to Eric. "But since you brought it up, why would they think you arranged it? What do they think you have to gain?"

Eric hesitated. "My life is good. I loved Aunt Camille."

Francine passed the line of cars turning into the Marsh Supermarket parking lot. Once in the right lane to turn onto Hornaday, she glanced back. "Neither of us doubts that."

Charlotte didn't buy the non-answer. "It's money, isn't it?"

His resolve wavered, and he nodded.

"How much?"

He held up two fingers.

"Two … million?"

He nodded again.

There was silence in the car. Charlotte finally broke it. "Did she win the lottery and not tell me about it? That wouldn't be very neighborly. And I even disconnected the irrigation system for her."

Eric said, "She brought me in as a junior partner in her business when I moved back to Brownsburg. I wouldn't know otherwise."

Francine was still a little in shock at the number. "Did she have a big life insurance policy or something?"

"Not that big in the scheme of things," Eric answered. "Two hundred fifty thousand. But she had accumulated a lot of money."

Francine was mentally doing the arithmetic. Charlotte looked to be doing the same. Francine spoke first. "So she had one and three quarter million dollars in the bank?"

"I didn't include the life insurance policy in the first number. And it wasn't in the bank. It's in investments. She worked with a financial advisor."

"Let me guess," Charlotte said. "Janet Tarpen."

Eric gave her a puzzled look. "How did you know?"

"She's on the Town Council."

"Right."

Charlotte raised an eyebrow. "Janet must be pretty good."

Eric crossed his arms over his chest and frowned at her. "Or Aunt Camille was good at her job and made a lot of money. Which she was."

Camille had worked for the local office of the giant conglomerate CableFirm. She had started out as a supervisor in the call center, but then became more and more interested in the technical aspects of Internet connections and WiFi. The company trained her to be a technical expert, and she became so good they made her a manager over the technicians who installed equipment. Then she began doing consulting.

Eric and Charlotte seemed to be at loggerheads, so Francine changed the subject. She'd just pulled into the Summer Ridge subdivision, so she wanted to end this on a better note. "Camille's death has to be quite a shock. Is your family working on the funeral arrangements?"

"We didn't have any other family." His voice registered disappointment that Francine didn't know. "That's why I moved here from Texas after my parents died."

Francine hadn't remembered much about his family situation. "I didn't know if you had grandparents who were still alive or if your dad had any other siblings."

"I guess you wouldn't. It was just Aunt Camille and me."

A few memories flashed in Francine's brain. She remembered how protective Camille had been of Eric those first few years. Not so much of him playing sports, but of activities outside of athletics. She had even gone so far as to make sure Jonathan and Francine knew she didn't approve of Chad and Eric being driven anywhere by Chad's two older brothers, not unless she approved of where they were going. Not Dairy Queen, not the coffee shop, not anywhere. If Eric were a freshman now, Francine was confident the woman would have placed an app on his cell phone to track his every move. Eric hadn't been a stellar student, but to the best of her knowledge he hadn't been in danger of joining a gang, either. He'd seemed to pour his energies into sports. From football season to wrestling to track, he was never out of organized sports.

"Do you need any help making the arrangements?" Francine offered. "If there's anything we can do …" She let the sentence trail off.

"Thank you," he said. "I hid in Charlotte's car because I know you two have a lot of experience solving murders. But I could use help with the funeral too. I don't know what to do." His voice nearly broke into a cry, but he held it together.

"Of course we'd be glad to help," Francine said.

She turned east onto the street where Charlotte and Camille lived. She slowed as they approached Camille's house. This time there was a forest green Jeep Liberty in the driveway.

"Fuzzy Carter is here now," she said.

Eric's head shot up in alarm. He checked the scene, saw the Jeep, and ducked low in the seat. "Let's go somewhere else. I don't want him to see me."

"Okay." Francine's heart beat faster at the fear in Eric's voice. She cruised past the driveway. "Where should we go?"

"How about your house?"

Francine drove the three of them to her house. Eric seemed to be in a hurry to get inside. He was the first one out of the car and to the front porch. It was cold, to be sure, but she didn't think that was it.

What had she and Charlotte gotten themselves into this time?

EIGHT

THE SLEEVE OF FRANCINE'S nylon winter coat made a swish when she pulled her keys from her pocket. The wind whistled past the evergreens near the porch and dusted them with a bit of snow. She shook it off. Since she'd been driving Charlotte's car, she didn't have the garage door opener to let them in through the back. She unlocked the door and let herself, Eric, and Charlotte into the house. She stood over the air register just inside the door and let the warmth engulf her. It felt good. Eric was the last one in. He stopped, closed his eyes, and inhaled deeply as if he could smell food cooking. "I remember some very fine meals here," he said.

Francine looked at her watch. It was coming up on eleven, a little too early for lunch for her tastes, but she had no idea if Eric had even had breakfast. "Why don't we sit around the bar and I'll get some snacks for us. Maybe it will tide us over to lunch."

Eric brightened. "That would be great!"

Francine took their coats and hung them in the closet. Charlotte trailed Eric into the kitchen. She nabbed a stool at the bar and he sat next to her. "Tell me why you don't want Fuzzy Carter to see you."

"He's been really creepy the last few months, always coming over to see Aunt Camille. Several times she had me lie to him about her not being there when she was."

"What did he want to see her about?"

"It had to do with her consulting business. He has her on retainer. It wasn't clear to me what he wanted done, but he was unhappy about something."

Francine wasn't far behind and could hear the exchange. "I thought they were always on the same side when the Council voted."

"Maybe. But that was about Town business. This was about his farming business. At least I think. But it's my guess he wants me to fix whatever problem he was bugging Aunt Camille about."

Francine pulled out a container of party mix and set it on the bar. "Are you working for her consulting business now?"

Eric grabbed a handful. "A little. As her junior partner, I needed to be. I know enough to be dangerous."

That's an interesting way to put it, Francine thought.

Eric munched on the party mix. "I appreciate this. I haven't had much to eat today, but I don't mean to impose."

"You're not imposing," Francine assured him. "Let me fix you something." She fished around in the refrigerator. "Weren't you the one who loved grilled cheese sandwiches?"

"I still do. I just don't allow myself to have them too often."

"How about one now? You could use some comfort food." She said it with the implication that she wouldn't take no for an answer. He didn't object. She got out cheese and bread, buttered the top and bottom, and proceeded to grill the sandwich.

Charlotte poured some party mix on a plate and began to pick pretzel sticks out of it. She ate them one by one. "What will you do now? Do you think you know enough to take over the consulting business? You aren't planning to give up stripping, are you?"

Francine chuckled. "You're not trying to influence him one way or the other, are you, Charlotte?"

She realized what she said. "I guess that didn't come out right, did it? Not that I don't think you're smart enough to do consulting."

Eric grinned. "It's okay. I wasn't the best student, I admit. My forte was phys ed and chorus."

"Cass Carter was your gym teacher, wasn't she?" Charlotte asked, in between munching. "That was before the divorce from Fuzzy."

Eric stiffened a bit at the mention of Cass's name. "She was. I remember hearing she got divorced, but that was a year or two after I was out of high school." He changed the subject. "Back then I wasn't motivated to learn. But when you grow up, your priorities change. I'm a lot more interested in business than you'd think. I bought the Royal Buckingham dance troupe. Did you know that?"

Both expressed surprise. "I had no idea," Francine said. "Although I wondered how you got them to do the fund-raiser here in Brownsburg."

"It's a lot easier when you're the boss."

Charlotte examined the pretzel-less mix and started extracting the peanuts. "Next thing you know, you'll be joining the Chamber of Commerce."

"I have," he said sheepishly. "I was already going with Aunt Camille as a part of her company. But now I'm going as a business owner."

In more than one way, Francine thought, *now that you own her business too.* She hated that she thought it. She told herself she didn't mean anything by it. Eric wasn't capable of doing anything so heinous, was he?

The grilled cheese was perfectly toasted, and she served it to him on a plate.

"Bet you're the first male dancer ever to join the Brownsburg Chamber," Charlotte said.

"Pretty safe bet," Eric replied. "But without Aunt Camille's influence, I'm not sure they'll let me operate a business here."

Francine watched as Eric devoured a quarter of the sandwich in a single bite. Then he refilled his plate with party mix. "I don't think Brownsburg is your target market," she said. "There's probably a place in Indianapolis that would be a better location."

He grew melancholy. "Like I said, it probably won't happen anyway now that Aunt Camille's gone." He closed his eyes.

The two women looked at each other. *Change the subject*, Francine mouthed to Charlotte.

"Speaking of Camille, what made her decide to run for the Council seat?" Charlotte asked.

Francine frowned at her.

Charlotte shrugged. *First thing I thought of*, she mouthed back.

Eric opened his eyes. "She thought she could make a difference."

"I think she's done that," Charlotte said.

Eric took a ragged breath. Francine thought he seemed to be pulling it together. He appraised Charlotte. "I know you and Aunt Camille didn't always see eye to eye, especially about your irrigation system. But she didn't think of you as a bad neighbor, just so you know. It was just the circumstances."

"Despite our differences, I supported her campaign. She's made a difference just stopping Tricky Dicky and Vince's shenanigans, like when they tried to block some critical annexations or repeal the no-smoking ordinance."

"I was proud of her."

"How do Council members get replaced?" Francine wondered aloud. "Is it a vote of the Council, or do precinct committee chairs get involved?"

"It's a caucus of the precinct committeemen," Charlotte said. "You should throw your hat in the ring, Eric."

Eric's eyes widened. "I'm not ready to step into politics. I'm not even ready to see the police yet."

"Would it help if one of us were there? You said you hid in our car because we've had some experience solving murders. It's our advice that you go to the police."

"Not right now," he said. "I need to think about it. I need to find some place to stay that's not at my house."

Francine did not want to volunteer. She was willing to feed him, but until he went to the police, she didn't want it to appear that she was harboring a suspect. Charlotte didn't volunteer either. Francine wasn't sure if it was because he was a former student and the situation would have been too creepy, or if it was because there wasn't a lot of sense to be made in hiding at the house next door to your own. Either way, Eric seemed dismayed at the silence.

"May I use your restroom?" he asked.

She nodded. "You remember where it is?"

"It looks like you've remodeled."

"We have, but the bathroom's still in the same spot."

He left the kitchen through the swinging door and disappeared into the living room.

Charlotte ate the last few peanuts she'd taken out of the party mix. "That boy needs to see the police."

"That's something we agree on. But how do we get him to do it?"

"It's getting close to lunch, isn't it? We need to get him loosened up to the idea. Maybe a beer with lunch?"

"We could try, but his abs don't look like they've seen too many beers."

"That's good. Maybe it'll only take one beer!"

"I meant, he may not choose to drink it."

76

"I knew that. How about one of your caramel cashew brownie sundaes? Put him in a sugar stupor. I bet his body hasn't seen that much sugar and fat at once in a long time."

Francine pulled a mug down from the cabinet. "He's eating grilled cheese. He might go for the sundae."

She made tea while Charlotte rooted through the pretzel- and nut-less party mix selecting rice and corn cereal pieces. She sat down at the bar with the mug. Charlotte pushed the plate toward her. "You can have the wheat cereal. You like it better than I do."

"Which is to say, not at all."

"Either way, they're all yours."

Francine nibbled a few pieces. The two women had a sudden realization. "He's been gone a long time," Charlotte said.

"I bet he's run," she answered.

They got up and went through the kitchen door looking for him. The closet door was open where Francine had hung up his coat. The coat was missing. The front door was slightly open. Francine guessed he hadn't wanted to make any noise, so he pulled it as close to shut as he dared.

"We can still track him," Charlotte said, throwing open the door. "He couldn't have gotten far."

They looked out. He was nowhere to be seen. "No," Francine said firmly. "We are not going to track him. He'll show up when he's had a chance to weigh his options. We've given him the best advice we can." She shut the front door.

"We still need to help him," Charlotte said.

"How?"

"By investigating Camille's death! He came to us for help. As he said, we do have experience in these kinds of things."

Francine crossed her arms over her chest. She'd heard those words before. Not that their group didn't have a good track record, but they always landed themselves in trouble first. She wasn't convinced she wanted to go through that again. "Where would we even start?"

"In this case, I think we should start with motive. Who wanted Camille dead?"

"Seriously, Charlotte? No one wanted her dead. Even if she was worth two million dollars, the only person who stood to benefit would be Eric, and I don't believe for a moment he's guilty of it."

"Don't give me that. *Someone* wanted her dead, or Joy wouldn't have found her with a knife in her side. Think outside the obvious. For example, we've been assuming she left it all to Eric. What if she didn't?"

Francine opened her mouth in surprise and then closed it. Charlotte had a point. If there were an alternate beneficiary, who would that person be? Or, what if Eric found out that he *wasn't* the beneficiary? Would that make him angry enough at Camille to lash out at her? No. She still couldn't picture it being Eric. "Let's go back to the kitchen. We need to explore this some more."

Francine settled them down with tea, paper, and pencil. Charlotte said she'd keep the list. She put Eric at the top.

"He had motive and he had access," Charlotte insisted. "Neither of us really think he did it, but we have to be realistic. The police usually suspect a close family member, and with good reason."

She listed herself second. "My fingerprints are on the murder weapon. We can account for how they got there, but I could have gotten backstage ahead of Joy, stabbed Camille, left the room, then re-entered after Joy."

"You would have had to move awfully fast."

"I'm moving better these days."

"Motive?"

"I've never told you this, but a long time ago Camille blackmailed me."

Francine narrowed her eyes at Charlotte. "She what?"

Charlotte got up and began to wander around the kitchen as she explained. Francine interpreted it as a way to avoid eye contact while she said it. "I loved Philip, you know that. But like most couples, we went through some troubled times. Mercifully it was brief, but he and I were angry with each other for a while and he moved out. It only turned out to be a few weeks, but during that time I was unfaithful. It was wrong, I knew that. I was stupid. But Camille took photographs of the gentleman I had the tryst with coming and going from the house. I have no idea how she knew what was going on."

Francine was aghast. She and Jonathan had argued, but he'd never left and she'd never considered doing what Charlotte had done. "I'm not sure I want to know any more of this."

Charlotte plunged ahead as though she couldn't stop, despite what Francine had said. "All I knew was, after I'd broken it off and Philip and I reconciled, she told me what she had. I didn't know if that was a threat or what, but I offered her some money to lose the photographs. She never bothered me again about it, mostly I think because Philip had the heart attack and died several months later."

Francine took all that in and didn't say anything for a while. "But you and Philip took each other back, and what's done is done. He's been gone a long time now. What could she possibly have over you as far as that goes?"

"I don't know. It's just that between that and the stupid irrigation system we fought about, we haven't had the easiest of relationships."

"But Eric said …"

"Just because Eric doesn't know about the past, doesn't mean he or the police won't uncover some things Camille might have saved. I have to be prepared for the worst."

Part of her wanted to ask questions, like who she'd had the affair with and how much she'd paid Camille, but the other part felt she had no right to know. And besides, surely Camille had gotten rid of the photos by now.

Hadn't she?

NINE

Francine was anxious to move on to a different suspect. "Who would be number three on your list?"

"I don't have a specific person, but I would put members of the Town Council up there." Charlotte returned to her seat and picked up the pencil. "Let's start with Janet Turpen. Apparently she's Camille's financial advisor. I've heard of financial advisors doing all kinds of bad things."

"Generally the bad things they do aren't deadly. More likely she would have embezzled Camille's funds than killed her."

Charlotte didn't disagree but she didn't agree either. "I wish I could remember where she was at the time of the murder. It was dark and Toby was doing his luging act and everyone was distracted. She could have gotten backstage ahead of me." She wrote Janet's name down and went on.

"Vince Papadopoulos is next. He and Camille locked horns over almost every Council matter. Vince perpetually loses. He could be very angry with her. Although, he's just an angry person in general.

I've heard rumors that he's struggling, that the Papadopoulos Funeral Home is for sale."

Francine hadn't heard those rumors, not that they would change her analysis. She found him to be a more likely suspect than Janet, but the evidence was circumstantial in any event. "What about Fuzzy? He was hanging around her house today, and Eric seemed to be afraid of him. But I don't know much about him. We obviously don't travel in the same circles."

"I knew him when I was a schoolteacher. I was there at the time he and Cass went through the divorce. It was ugly. We never did figure out why she kept his last name. Probably spite, especially after she nabbed his family's homestead in the divorce settlement."

"She was quite a bit younger, wasn't she? Is she still teaching?"

"She is. She moved over to Avon schools sometime after the divorce. Fuzzy is in his mid-fifties now, so I guess Cass is in her mid-forties." Charlotte doodled on the page.

"For some reason I think she was at the show," Francine said. "Didn't she bid on the bartender stripper? I feel like she made a shut-out bid."

"We used to call her the Cass-trator. She was a real ball-buster!"

Francine burst out laughing. Cass had been the boys' phys ed teacher, and Francine remembered her as beautiful and strong, an athlete in the mode of Serena Williams. "I think my boys were a little afraid of her."

"Hell, we were all afraid of her," Charlotte said, snickering. "That's what made her a good phys ed teacher, though. She could take command. I think that might have been what caused the break-up between her and Fuzzy. He got tired of being told what to do."

"So then he moves on to the Council, where he lets Camille make all the decisions?" Francine mused about it as she said it. How could that have had anything to do with why Camille was killed?

"Camille did it in a much nicer way," Charlotte said. She looked at the name she'd written below Fuzzy's. "Tricky Dicky Raden is my next choice, though I'm giving him the same rank as Vince. They were always together on the losing end of votes."

Raden had gotten the nickname "Tricky Dicky" because he looked so much like former President Richard Nixon. His head had the same backward slant and the same receding hairline. Then there were the paranoid psychological similarities. Tricky Dicky had a *hunker down, don't trust anyone* mentality that had driven Camille, Janet, and Fuzzy Carter nuts.

"How he convinced people to vote for him is beyond me. He always believed the rest of the Town Council was against him, which was why he ran."

"They *were* against him, all except Vince. It wasn't his imagination. His developments were stupid. Why would you try to stick a Dollar Tree in the retail space for a grocery store in a high-end housing development? But as for how he got elected, his district is mostly rural people who resent the fact the Town annexed them against their will."

Francine propped a hand under her chin. "Let's go back to Vince Papadopoulos for a moment. Wasn't he the Council President before Camille?"

"Yep, another reason he's high on my list. Camille beat him out just barely, three to two. She and Fuzzy became tight after that. For whatever reason."

"It'll probably remain a mystery now," Francine said. "Unless it all comes out when the police solve her murder."

"When we solve it, Francine. When we solve it."

"So you keep telling me."

————

Francine was in the middle of vacuuming the upstairs bedrooms later in the afternoon when she received a phone call from her youngest son, Chad. She had changed into jeans and a blue Indianapolis Colts sweatshirt, even though Indianapolis was in basketball season and the talk had turned to the Pacers. The Colts sweatshirt was one of the warmest she owned. She felt the phone buzz in her pocket and turned off the vacuum.

"You didn't think to call or at least text me that you were involved in another murder investigation?" he asked without saying hello. "This may be getting to be a routine occurrence for you, but it's not for any of us kids. I checked with Craig and Adam, and they hadn't heard from you, either. How were we supposed to know you were okay?"

"I was going to call you later. Your father and I didn't want to worry you."

"It worries me when I see Joy reporting on the national news about another event that has your Sixty Lists written all over it, but then it turns into a story about a murder in Brownsburg!"

Drat that Joy and her reporting, Francine thought, feeling a little guilty. *What's the world coming to when you can't even keep your son who lives in Kansas City from sounding like a Jewish mother?* "No one else was hurt. It was a targeted attack."

"I was sorry to see that it was Camille Ledfelter who died. How is Eric holding up? Do you know? I heard he was doing a benefit for the Parks Department when it happened. That had to be awful."

Francine wiped her brow with the sleeve of her sweatshirt. "It was. I was helping Mary Ruth cater the event. The lights went out, and when they came up, Camille had been stabbed. She died later at the hospital. Eric was there for the whole thing."

"Do you know anything about the funeral arrangements? I can't come, but I want to send a sympathy card and donate to a charity in her memory."

Francine wondered how much she should tell Chad about their offer to help with the funeral arrangements. Eric had said he would take them up on it, but then he disappeared and they still hadn't heard from him. But full disclosure was probably the best course of action. Or, at least almost full disclosure. "Eric was just here this morning." She tried to sound as casual as she could. "Charlotte and I have offered to help him make the arrangements. He didn't know where else to turn."

She could practically see Chad smiling over the phone. "In some ways, I'm not surprised," he said. "You and Dad were surrogate parents to half the kids on the football team."

For a moment Francine was swept into the past. She remembered the excitement and the hoopla that surrounded each game. She and Jonathan hosted breakfasts for the offensive linemen before they went to school on those mornings. By the time Chad began playing for the varsity team, Francine and Jonathan were fairly well entrenched in the group of parents who provided support.

"It's a long time since then," she said, "but I'm glad he felt comfortable coming to us. I don't know when the funeral will be, though."

"I think I'll give Eric a call, see if there's anything I can do."

She hoped Eric would at least answer the phone. She wasn't confident he would. "Let me ask you a question. Has Eric always been single? I understand for a male stripper that's probably a good thing, but I don't remember him having this kind of loner personality in high school."

"He changed during senior year. There were rumors it had to do with a girl, but he was very secretive about it. I think he carried a torch for her for a long time afterwards."

"Who was she?"

"We never found out. Not sure why he was so guarded about it, but he must have done it for a good reason." He paused. "Mom, I think it's great that you're helping Eric with the funeral arrangements, but please don't get involved in Camille's murder."

"Why would you even think that?"

He snorted with laughter on the other end. "Two reasons. Number one, Aunt Charlotte will drag you into it." The boys always called her "Aunt Charlotte," even though she wasn't actually a member of the family. "And number two, you can't resist a mystery."

"That's not true! Charlotte is the one who can't resist a mystery."

"Okay, then. You can't resist a *puzzle*. But it's the same difference here."

Francine could see how he might have that perspective. "I'm not going to argue with you. But I am not getting involved."

She added *much* under her breath.

Chad filled her in on the latest about Laura and the twin girls. Chad and Laura lived in Overland Park, Kansas, where he was the comptroller for a Fortune 500 company. He'd followed in his dad's footsteps and gone into accounting, but where Jonathan was content to start his own firm and be his own boss, Chad had sought the corporate life. Laura had been a practicing speech pathologist with a school corporation until kids had come along. Then they'd made the decision for her to stay home. Francine thought they were almost throwbacks to the era she'd grown up in.

After hanging up the phone with Chad, she had her hand on the switch to start the vacuum up again when Joy called. "Can you come over?" she asked.

Ordinarily this wouldn't have sent shivers up Francine's spine, but she was already primed from having made a list of suspects with Charlotte and then being asked by Chad not to get involved. "Sure." She tried to keep suspicion out of her voice. "What's up?"

"I need help trying to salvage as much as I can from the auction. This was Camille's baby, so I wasn't totally involved, but now it's fallen to me to try to piece the results together."

Francine was relieved it wasn't more than that. "When do you need me?"

"Are you busy now?"

Francine wheeled the sweeper down the hall and into the hall closet. *That's what friends are for*, she thought. "I'll be right over."

She bundled up for the walk over to Joy's house with her winter down coat, fuzzy earmuffs, and knitted scarf. The air was crisp and cold. Like most days in Indiana in February, it was overcast and gray. The wind seemed to come out of all directions and batted at her cheeks like a cat playing with a ball. Joy lived on Bridge Trail Road, the main entrance to the Summer Ridge subdivision. As the birds fly, it was a very short distance to Joy's house, but in practicality she would have to jump two fences and cross a yard with dogs to get there. So she walked the long way: down Overlook Court, across the Summer Ridge Drive East, and up Bridge Trail Road. By the time she got there, her cheeks were red.

"You look downright frosty," Joy said. "C'mon in. Can I get you coffee or tea to thaw you out?"

"Tea would be great. I'd love it just to stop my hands from shaking." She tried to unzip her coat but her fingers were frozen, despite the woolen mittens she'd worn.

"Let me get that," Joy said. She pulled on the zipper and unfastened the coat. Francine slipped out of it, placed the earmuffs and scarf in the side pocket, and handed it to Joy.

"I've got everything laid out on the kitchen table. Go on in while I hang this up."

Francine didn't need a second invitation. She could smell some kind of apple cinnamon spice emanating from the kitchen and knew the oven would be warming the whole room.

Joy's house was a three-bedroom, two-bath ranch with one outstanding feature—a large sun room that faced south. When the sun shone in the winter, it was exceptionally warm and toasty, but that was not the case today. The oven was a better choice.

"What are you baking?" Francine asked. "Smells delicious."

"It's an apple cinnamon coffee cake. I got it frozen from Mary Ruth, so I can't take credit for actually making it. I'm having it at Bridge Club this evening."

Francine had totally forgotten about bridge in the craziness. "I wasn't sure if we'd be having it after last night's..." She wanted to say *murder*, but the word didn't want to come out. "Problems."

"I've done enough reporting for the television station for one twenty-four-hour period. I'm off until tomorrow, and I don't want to even think about it. Bridge will be a good distraction for all of us."

Francine wasn't sure much bridge would be played, but she knew Joy would go into the evening hoping it would, as good a bridge player as she was. "Heaven knows we need a distraction."

"I'm glad you agree." Joy led the way into the kitchen. She pointed to the boxes, baskets, and stacks of paper that were piled on her kitchen table. Even expanded with two leaves, the table couldn't contain everything without some of it being stacked. "There's the mess," she said. "After I wrapped up my reporting duties outside the Crown

Room this morning, the police let me gather it up and bring it back. I threw it on the table and haven't had the heart to dig in by myself."

Francine saw that the coffee cake was out of the oven and on a cooling tray. She cracked open the door to the stove and basked in the warm air coming out of it. She let her fingers dangle, flexing them to get them moving normally. "What's in the boxes?"

"The auction items." Joy picked up a piece of paper. "Each page has an auction item listed at the top, a note on how much it's worth, and lines so people can write down their bids. Didn't you look at any of this last night?"

"I didn't have time. I was going to take a look later, but you know how that went."

Joy shuddered. "I keep going over it in my head. I can't believe it happened."

"It'll keep you on the air for weeks."

"You know I promised Jud I'd recuse myself. I can't go back on it."

Francine's fingers seemed to have loosened up. After a couple of minutes of thawing, she closed the oven and perused the table. She found a summary sheet of the items to be bid on. An idea came to her. "Are all of the items here? Did any of them get stolen?"

"The bigger ones are back in the second bedroom. I still need to match up the bid document with the actual donation to make sure we have them, but I think they're all accounted for. Theft didn't appear to be the motive."

A teakettle whistled, and Joy filled two mugs with boiling water. They each selected a tea bag. "How can I help?" Francine asked.

Joy indicated a pad of green pre-printed spreadsheet paper. "I've made a spreadsheet with all the items. I need you to go through this stack of bid sheets and put the highest bid on the Winner line along with the name, address, and contact information. I'm going to try to reconcile the list with the physical item. Of course, not all items were there. Some are made to order, like Mary Ruth's Fabulous Flourless Chocolate Cake."

"I wonder how much it went for." Francine paged through the bid sheets until she found it. "Eighty dollars." She scrunched up her nose. "That's low."

"I think a lot of people were saving their money to throw at the dancers. I'm hoping we'll tally enough to justify not having a follow-up fund-raiser anytime soon."

Joy started laying out some of the prizes in an orderly line across the sunroom floor. She placed a sticky note on each one identifying it and checked it off her list. Francine tried to locate the bid sheet for each one to identify the winner.

"I'm sorry the evening didn't work out for you. I know you were hoping to get your problem resolved before you had to see Roy next."

Joy shrugged. "He won't be expecting me to be in the mood, not for a while. I probably have another two weeks before he suggests it again."

Francine still felt bad about Joy's fear of intimacy with Roy. She wondered how they would be able to discreetly hire a male dancer now to test out Joy's reaction to mostly naked men.

The doorbell rang. Before they could get to it, they heard the door swing open.

"Sorry, I'm late," a woman's voice called. The door slammed shut. The person tromped into the kitchen, thoroughly covered in warm outwear. The knee-length coat was red, and the attached hood had an inner white down that almost covered her face. On her feet were black leather boots made for style and not for snow. The figure flipped back the hood, but by then Francine already knew who it was. Marcy Rosenblatt, publicist.

"It's colder than Donald Trump's welcome to a Mexican immigrant out there," Marcy said. She shivered as she took off the coat.

She dropped it on a chair before Joy could reach out to take it. "Hi, Francine. Joy didn't say you were going to be here."

"It was a last-minute thing."

"Well, it's good you're here. I have some terrific ideas how we can get additional exposure from this latest fiasco you've gotten yourselves into, and I can't wait to tell you about them."

TEN

MARCY WAS SHORT BY Francine's standards, about five foot four. Though in her forties, Marcy's long hair hung straight and was so thoroughly black there was no question it was dyed. Her nose was large on her face and slightly hooked. She spoke with a vague New York accent that had crept into her delivery recently. Francine was aware it was new because, like it or not, Marcy had been in their lives since Friederich Guttmann's death, and she showed no signs of going away.

"It's a tragedy, not a fiasco," Francine said. The coldest thing in the room was the woman's apparent attitude toward Camille Ledfelter's gruesome death.

"Call it what you will, it's still an amazing opportunity for one and all. How you always find yourselves in these situations is beyond me, but it's why I love hanging around you. Whose Sixty List item were we trying to accomplish here?"

Francine shot a worried look at Joy. "We were volunteering our time to help a worthy cause, Marcy. We were participating in a fund-raiser for a recreation and indoor aquatic center in Brownsburg." She hoped Marcy wouldn't find out Joy's secret. Even though Joy was one of her best clients, Marcy believed that any publicity was good publicity. Visions of Dr. Phil analyzing Joy's reaction to nearly naked men on nationally syndicated television while an audience smirked at her was a nightmarish possibility.

"Did I say you weren't?" Marcy responded. "I'm just saying sometimes with your Bridge Club, you do the obvious to hide the real reason for doing something." Marcy tugged at the tips of her leather gloves and pulled them off her hands. "What's that smell? It's divine."

"Cinnamon apple coffee cake," Joy said. "One of Mary Ruth's recipes. I just finished baking it. I'd offer you some but I'm saving it for Bridge Club tonight."

"Speaking of Mary Ruth, will she be here?"

"Tonight, but not before." Joy finished checking off a wood-framed painting that was one of the auction items. "Turns out she sprained her ankle when she fell at the fund-raiser. Toby took her to the doctor today."

Francine was sorry to hear about the ankle. She would have to give Mary Ruth a call.

Marcy scooted an auction item off a chair and settled in. She pulled an iPad out of her purse and turned it on. "Let's get down to business. Joy, you've already done several segments for the local news about Camille's murder. Any for *GMA*?" Marcy often used initials now instead of *Good Morning America*.

Like it's become routine already, Francine thought. There was something amazing and something sad about that, all at the same time.

"I can't do any more reports on it since I'm a witness."

Marcy must have already written notes on her iPad, because it looked like she was updating entries as they talked. "Really? Because for the next day or two, you can probably do on-the-scene reports, even if all you're doing is reporting the same stuff over and over again. All the stations do that kind of thing, yours included. I could see you doing this from the hospital, the Crown Room, the Police Department ..."

"I gave my word to the police," Joy said, without looking up. She continued to focus on auction items in front of her. "And anyway, another story will push it aside at any moment, given the number of shootings that come out of Indianapolis on a daily basis."

"How about personal pieces? I can think of at least half a dozen angles to keep it in the news and you on the air." Marcy poked at her screen. "The best one is this: the strippers themselves. I could see you doing a piece about them, how this has affected their *body* of work." She laughed at her own joke.

Joy rolled her eyes. "I can't sell it as a part of my regular feature on senior life, and I have no real reason to pitch something like that as a new story."

"You might be able to sell it if the Bridge Club tried to help some of them through this 'tragedy,' to use Francine's word. Have any of them shown signs of stress or need? What about the lead fellow? It was his aunt who died, wasn't it?"

Anger was Francine's immediate reaction. She bit the inside of her cheek to give herself time to think of a response. She didn't like to use the type of language that came to mind. She spoke as emphatically as she could. "We are *not* going to exploit his tragedy for our gain. Camille had been like a mother to Eric."

Marcy waved her hand dismissively. "Consider *his* gain for a moment. Maybe he *needs* the exposure. Maybe this will help take his career as a stripper to the next level."

Francine knew more than Marcy did about Eric owning the dance troupe, his plans for the business, and the money he stood to inherit. She still didn't think the exposure was what he needed right then.

"As a stripper," Joy cracked, "exposure is his life. How much more does he need?"

She said it off-hand with a grin, but it took Francine by surprise. Instead of behaving like the person who had found Camille nearly dead, Joy was skirting the boundaries of good taste. *Bad influence*, she thought.

Marcy made a little gun with her hand and pulled the trigger in delight. "Depends on how much he wants his career to rise. I hear the competition is stiff."

"That's enough of that," Francine said.

"Sometimes you have to laugh," Marcy said, "even in a dark situation." She scrolled down the screen looking at other ideas. "So let's focus on you for a moment. Do you have any connection to Brownburg Parks and Recreation?"

Francine set aside the papers she was working on and planted her fists firmly on her hips. "I was there helping Mary Ruth cater the event. Alice is on vacation, so she really needed me. And not everything has to boost a career. Not Mary Ruth's, not Joy's, not yours."

Marcy looked right through her like she hadn't heard a word. "Speaking of exposure, you usually end up soaking wet on camera when things like this occur. Wasn't there any water around when Toby Burrows took out the whole buffet line?"

"She was clutching a big slab of roast beef at the time," Joy said, "though we don't have a photo of that."

"Too bad. But wasn't the roast beef juicy? Didn't it soak the front of her shirt?"

"I was wearing a heavy-duty apron at the time," Francine said, her voice neutral. She hoped she was giving off an aura of being annoyed because she was certainly peeved. She needed Marcy to leave. Either that or she needed to leave.

"Perhaps Mary Ruth will be more cooperative," Marcy said. "She knows how good exposure can lead to a stint on Food Network."

Joy's face brightened. "Could we do something with Toby Burrows becoming a stripper? Like, 'stripping chef cooks naked burritos,' or something like that?"

In spite of her best efforts to block ideas like that, Francine had to choke back a laugh. The concept was hilarious. "You'd never get Mary Ruth on board. She's already struggling with Toby becoming a stripper. We saw that Friday night. For all we know, Toby did it for just one night. I'm not sure he really wants to be a stripper."

Marcy continued to ignore Francine's nay-saying. "The potential for conflict makes great drama. This is like Paula Deen bringing her boys into the Food Network fold, only they weren't as rebellious." She called up a keyboard on the screen and typed in a couple of notes. "How do I get in touch with him without going through Mary Ruth?"

"Good luck with that," Joy said. "He lives in the basement at Mary Ruth's house. I don't see him moving out until he finishes culinary school. Unless he becomes successful as a stripper."

"We'll assume he will. Do you have his cell number?"

Joy shook her head. Marcy looked at Francine hopefully. Francine could feel a smug smile coming on. Finally she had something that could block Marcy from pursuing the ludicrous notion that they all needed more public attention.

But then Marcy got a bemused look on her face. "What about Charlotte? She's a publicity hound. She even did that commercial for the local spa specializing in enemas. She was there, wasn't she?"

"She was," Joy said. "She was really looking forward to it."

Francine was becoming exasperated with Joy. She tried to counter the information Joy was feeding Marcy. "But there wasn't much to see. The dancers were saving their best for later, and only one dancer got auctioned off anyway before Toby took out the lights and the fire alarm got pulled. And do I need to remind you that Camille was murdered?"

Marcy stared off toward the ceiling like she was formulating a strategy. "I bet Charlotte was disappointed. I bet she'd love to be surprised by a personal performance."

"No," Francine said. "I forbid it. That is not a good plan."

"Joy mentioned that the Bridge Club would be here tonight." Marcy turned to Joy. "You did, didn't you?" Her tone was halfway between teasing and asking innocently.

"You're not invited," Francine said.

"It's my house," Joy said. "You can't forbid her to come."

Francine pointed accusingly at Marcy. "She doesn't even play bridge."

"I'm hurt," Marcy said as though wounded. "You've never seen me play. What's number one on your bucket list, Francine? Maybe I should focus on helping you accomplish that."

Francine doubted Marcy could make anything of it. "To save a life, all by myself. No help from EMTs or medics." She thought back to when she found Camille. She had been relieved to see the emergency squad show up. Could she have done more than they did? "Not that I hope to be in critical circumstances like that ever again."

Marcy gave her a blank look. "Commendable. I could see it as a one-note story, but nothing with legs."

"Good."

"Well, I know when I'm not welcome," Marcy said. She turned her iPad off and slipped it into her purse. "I have a lot of work to do so I need to be off. Sorry I can't stay to help." She picked up her coat and put it on as she made her way to the front door. Joy followed to see her out. Francine went along, though she wasn't certain if Marcy was offended or not.

Marcy paused at the door and wrapped a scarf around her neck. "Oh. Did I mention I have an appointment this afternoon with a couple of dancers from the Royal Buckingham troupe?" She winked at Francine. "Maybe I'll mention Charlotte to them. See you all soon."

She opened the door and exited, closing the door behind her without a look back.

Joy leaned against the wall and faced Francine. "I don't know why you two have to be at odds. She's been a big help to my career, one I never thought I'd have. Here I am late in life, and I'm doing something that's fun and meaningful to me. Why can't you appreciate that?"

"I do appreciate what she's done for you, Joy. But for the rest of us, it's been a mixed bag, even for Mary Ruth. She's trying to balance her catering work, her on-again/off-again relationship with Food Network, and being a mentor to Toby. What I resent is that Marcy keeps trying to help where she's not needed or wanted."

"We're all interconnected." Joy straightened up and returned to the kitchen. "She's mentioned that before. When one of us rises, the others do too. If you show up on *Dr. Oz*, by association, my stock goes up at *GMA* since you and the others appear occasionally in my reports."

"That doesn't mean I should have to be on *Dr. Oz*. And do you really need any more exposure? Really?"

"No, I'm happy. But Marcy knows more than we do about this stuff. Maybe it's her way of keeping me on the air. Or Mary Ruth's company fully booked."

"Should I worry that she knows about Bridge Club tonight?"

Joy shrugged. "I doubt it. I think she just said it to get your goat. And anyway, the strippers are fully booked, at least the ones I talked to."

They got back to work, but Francine couldn't let go of Marcy's parting comments. She had mentioned Charlotte, the Bridge Club, and the male strippers before she left. Although they were separate issues, Francine's mind kept linking them together.

What if Marcy followed through on the threat? If it was just the four of them at Bridge Club tonight, and if Joy saw a male stripper in person and was okay with it, then all the better. Or if Joy did get sick at the sight of the stripper, wouldn't it still be okay because at least they could eliminate that as a way of "curing" her? They could move on and try another solution. *As long as it's just us.*

But she also knew it wasn't in Marcy's nature to let this go.

ELEVEN

FRANCINE SAT AT AN antique secretary's desk she'd dug out of the ancient greenhouse that stood on the property she'd inherited from her great-grandfather, Doc Wheat. In front of her was the leather-bound journal containing Doc Wheat's homemade remedies, which had been world famous until the advent of modern pharmaceuticals. A sign she'd created this morning was attached to a nameplate she'd had as the head nurse at the cancer care center, her last job before retirement. The sign read, "Could I have saved Camille?"

Jonathan walked into the upstairs guest room that served as her study. He stood behind her and considered the sign. "You can't beat yourself up about Camille's death. She was probably too far gone. Doc Wheat's formulas can only do so much."

She put her finger on the place where she stopped reading to answer him. "I could have tried. I have the ampule of number 58. It's one of the few samples that were left in the greenhouse. It's labeled 'for emergencies only.' Number 58 was designed for difficult-to-treat wounds that were bleeding badly."

She held it up to him. The ampule was tiny and contained a liquid with just the palest blue tinge to it.

"But you've never tried it," he said. "It could be the same formula he gave Dolly, the one that led to a lot of deaths. I still find it ironic that he came to view death as a necessary evil when the waters prolonged life."

Francine had already worried about a possible connection to Dolly. "It's not the same formula. This one has a blue-ish cast. The other one was clear."

He massaged her neck. "Have you had any luck deciphering his handwriting?"

She let him knead his hands into a part of her neck that felt tense. "It's not the handwriting. He had excellent penmanship. It's his abbreviations. This is the one I can't be sure of." She pointed to a notation on the yellowing page. "It almost has to be 'second spring,' but I can't find a reference anywhere to where the second spring is."

"We've been over all three hundred acres of the property," Jonathan answered. "I don't recall seeing another spring."

"What else could this be?"

He leaned over the desktop and squinted at the writing. "You're right. I don't know what else '2d sprng' could mean." He straightened up.

Francine got a whiff of sautéed onions and peppers when Jonathan leaned over. "You've been making dinner, haven't you?" She checked her watch. "I'm sorry. I got so preoccupied with this I didn't realize the time."

"I made chicken fajitas with rice and beans. You ready to take a break?"

She stood. "I'd better be. It's six o'clock, and we have Bridge Club tonight at seven."

"It's not here, is it? We'll have to scramble if it is."

"It's at Joy's, but still, we need to eat so I can help with dishes before I leave."

———

By the time Francine walked over to Joy's house, she was five minutes late. Charlotte's big Buick and Mary Ruth's catering van were parked in the driveway.

Joy answered the door and pulled her in. "I can't believe you walked over here. It's nighttime and the temperature is dropping."

"It's not that far." She removed the scarf from around her neck. Joy took her down coat and scarf and hung them in the closet.

"C'mon in. Mary Ruth's already shuffling the cards."

"I can't do anything else," Mary Ruth called from the dining room. "I sprained my ankle last night and now I need to keep my foot up."

Francine and Joy entered the dining room. It was old-fashioned and formal, the type no one used much anymore. Mary Ruth sat at the corner of Joy's highly polished dining table, her right foot elevated on an adjacent chair with an ice pack on it. Charlotte sat to her left. Joy's reading glasses were across from Mary Ruth so Francine took the spot across from Charlotte.

Mary Ruth dealt the cards. "It feels like it's been forever since we played bridge." She was very deliberate when she handled cards, snapping down each card as she went.

"It's been a full month," Joy said. "Last time I think Alice was the big winner."

The Summer Ridge Bridge Club was comprised of five women, and usually one of them wasn't able to play, so they rarely had to draw from the deck to determine who would sit out. "I think Jonathan and I were in Rockville that weekend," Francine said.

Charlotte glared at her. "You spend so much time there I'd guess you were incarcerated at the Rockville women's prison, except Jonathan goes with you."

Francine examined her cards. A couple of aces and a diverse hand. She hoped Charlotte had something good and it was no-trump. "It's nothing like that," she said. "We want to build a cabin there this spring, but there's a lot of mess to clean up first from the explosion and the fire." She hated to think about how all that had gone down. The only thing that made it easier was knowing Zed's fate.

"Where do you stay when you're there?" Mary Ruth asked. "I don't think there are any Holiday Inns in Rockville."

"At a bed-and-breakfast on the main drag through Town. It's a very nice place."

Mary Ruth passed first. Charlotte passed and Joy bid a club. Francine had to pass and Mary Ruth tried to find a fit with hearts. They ended up at two hearts, not a difficult way to begin. Francine was grateful to have the aces. If the suits were reasonably split, she could hope to pick up a couple of tricks.

"Did I tell you Eric was back at their house for a short time this afternoon?" Charlotte looked like she was dying to share a secret.

"He was?" Francine asked. "Were you able to talk to him?"

"I scooted over there as fast as I could."

Francine could well imagine that Charlotte had been watching that house like a birder waiting for some exotic fowl to come into view. She snorted. "I'll bet you did!"

If Charlotte noticed any criticism in Francine's response, she ignored it. "He let me in when he saw it was me, though I had to follow him around while he gathered up his clothes. The house was in a bit of a mess."

"He didn't stay?"

"I said he was only there for a short while." She paused.

"Well?" Joy asked, since Mary Ruth was playing the hand. "What did you learn? Spit it out. You know you're dying to tell us."

"Only that he was staying with a friend tonight, and that he was taking some of Camille's financial records with him. There were some things he said he wanted to go over."

"Did you encourage him to go to the police like we talked about?" Francine asked.

"He said he would go in the morning, after he had time to think everything through. I do wonder where he's staying, though."

Mary Ruth scooped up a trick. She'd easily made the two hearts, but now she was going for more. "I *know* where he's staying," she said without looking up.

All three of the others stopped. "What?" they asked, almost in unison. "Where?"

"In my basement. He's staying the night with us." She said it very matter-of-factly.

Francine stopped in mid-action removing a card from her hand. "Don't you find that scary? Someone might be trying to kill him."

"I hardly think so."

"Said the person who didn't see the knife sticking out of Camille's side," Joy said.

Charlotte nodded. "And let me tell you, that was a wicked-looking knife."

Mary Ruth still seemed unconcerned. She finished taking in the tricks. Between Francine and Charlotte, they'd only received two, both from Francine's aces. Mary Ruth had trumped everything else.

"Jud said it was a Vietnam-era knife," Charlotte added, going back to their conversation.

Mary Ruth recorded the score while Charlotte gathered the cards and began shuffling.

"Do you think it was a Vietnam vet?" Francine asked.

"Here's a better question: do we know any Vietnam vets who hated Camille?" Charlotte said, countering Francine's question.

Joy gave a quick response. "I don't know any. But I know someone who had a brother who died in Vietnam who doesn't like Camille. Vince Papadopoulos."

"Really? He had a brother?" Francine asked.

Joy nodded. "I went to a candidate forum he was at. He must have mentioned it every chance he got. He talked about how his brother's death influenced him."

Francine was intrigued. "He was at the head table with Camille. He might have seen her go backstage. Was he doing anything odd or unusual that night?"

Charlotte began dealing. "Earlier he was at the bar laughing and talking with his sister-in-law, Cass." Cass and Vince were famous for barely tolerating each other, even though Cass and Vince's wife Myra were sisters.

Francine regarded her with surprise. "How many years ago did she and Fuzzy divorce? Fifteen?"

"Sixteen," answered Charlotte. "It was several years before I retired. She had taken a sabbatical for a semester, and when she came back, they divorced. We teachers were supportive of her rather than him, though I have no idea what caused the divorce."

Mary Ruth shifted the cold pack on her leg. "Surely there were rumors."

"Believe me, I tried to get it out of her," Charlotte said with a wink. "But she knows how to keep a secret."

"Francine picked up her cards. Overall, it was a much better hand. She had six spades, ace-king high. The rest was on the weak side. She hoped Charlotte had something that would help.

Charlotte passed. "Sorry, Francine, it looks like it might be a long night. I'm not getting any cards."

Joy bid one heart. Francine bid one spade. Mary Ruth bid two clubs and Charlotte passed again. Joy bid two hearts.

Francine passed with a sigh on her second turn, as did Mary Ruth, and it was another two-heart game.

Mary Ruth spread her cards out on the table. "I didn't think we needed to go any higher, and hearts works reasonably well with my hand."

Joy made the hand easily. "So if it turns out not to be Vince," she said, shuffling for the next hand, "who else might have or want a knife like that? How do we find a list of Vietnam vets in the county?"

"The Brownsburg American Legion post would be a good place to try," Mary Ruth suggested. "Though with all those privacy laws, they might not be able to release them."

Charlotte leaned in conspiratorially. "Then we'll just have to engage a Vietnam vet in conversation," she said. She had a mischievous smile on her face. "There's a special Sunday night bingo tomorrow night. Anyone want to go?"

"I haven't been to the bingo in ages!" Joy said in her chirpy voice, the one that annoyed Francine when she used it for long periods of time. "I'm free tomorrow night too."

"I don't have any catering events coming up," Mary Ruth said. Her voice cracked with emotion. "My events for the rest of the month have fallen through. Apparently our group comes across too many dead bodies. I've been advised that people don't like dead bodies turning up at parties." She sighed.

Joy stopped shuffling the cards and started dealing them. "I'm sure it's just a knee-jerk reaction. You're not only the best caterer in Brownsburg, you're the best on the west side of Indianapolis. Probably the entire metro area. They'll be back."

Francine gathered her cards into her hand as Joy dealt them. "I don't see anyone else in Indianapolis on Food Network."

"You know what this calls for?" Charlotte asked. "Intervention. Joy, where's that coffee cake you made for tonight? We need to get it out now."

Joy finished dealing and stood up. "I'll put it in the oven to heat up. For once, Charlotte is right." She left to go into the kitchen.

"What do you mean, for once?" Charlotte called after her.

They heard Joy puttering around in the kitchen.

"I would feel bad for Toby, since he needs the experience for his cooking classes," Mary Ruth said, "but all of a sudden he's getting booked as a stripper." Her head sunk onto the table. "Dear God, please don't let this last."

"So it's true, then?" Francine asked. "Marcy Rosenblatt was over here this afternoon and she said the strippers were getting lots of attention. She implied that their dance cards were getting full."

She lifted her head and nodded. "His cell phone has been going off all afternoon between bookings and the press calling. I've noticed Eric's phone's been going off since he arrived this afternoon, but he's declining press interviews. Thank heavens for that."

Joy returned and took her place at the table.

Francine looked at the three of them. "Does anyone think Eric really needs protection? Or does he just think he does?"

Mary Ruth and Joy shrugged. Charlotte answered. "That same kind of fear is what he told us Camille was going through before her death. He seems to be going out of his way to avoid being alone.

Maybe he feels safer with others around. Though we all know how that turned out for Camille."

Mary Ruth groaned. "I'd just be glad to get him out of the basement and away from Toby, now that I know Eric's encouraging him to be a stripper. I guess I'd feel safer too if he moved back into his own house."

Charlotte gave Mary Ruth a thumbs-up sign. "We can help you out there, can't we, Francine? Tomorrow we'll come talk to him now that we know where he is."

And just like that, Francine found herself back in the fray.

TWELVE

FRANCINE AND JONATHAN ATTENDED church the next morning at Calvary United Methodist Church. Since she was an early-to-bed, early-to-rise kind of person, Francine preferred to go to the early service at nine o'clock. It was also a more traditional service, and that suited her just fine. Contemporary services felt more like a performance to her than a worship service.

But this Sunday, even the nine o'clock service didn't feel right. There was a pall hanging over the congregation. Camille Ledfelter hadn't been a member of Calvary, but so many people knew her that it was still a shock. Several people had come up to Francine to talk about it, knowing she had been there. After deflecting questions for what felt like an hour, she took a worship folder from an usher and found a seat next to Jonathan in their usual pew. It had only been ten minutes.

He leaned into her and whispered in her ear, "Lots of curiosity, I would say."

"Why are people so fascinated by dead bodies?"

"Why do they keep turning up when you're around?"

She elbowed him in the gut. "You're not helping."

He grinned from ear to ear. "Sorry."

The head pastor no sooner started the service when Francine heard her cell phone buzz in her bag. Fortunately, she had remembered to set it to silent.

Charlotte had sent her a text. Charlotte was technology-challenged and didn't often send texts, but when she got up the will to figure it out, she made up for her infrequency with length.

Police showed up at Camille's house. Carried out documents, a computer, and sacks of stuff I couldn't determine. Eric was not there. I'm pretty sure Jud had a search warrant, but no one to serve it on so they just went in. I laid low. I didn't want to be there if he found something Camille might have had on me. Why make myself readily available for questioning?

It was a rhetorical question, and didn't need an answer. She slipped the cell phone back in her purse. A few minutes later, during the first song, it buzzed again.

Francine, did you get my text? This is Francine, isn't it? I'm never sure if I'm doing this right. It has your name on the conversation, though.

Am in church, she texted back.

I figured that. I'm going to the later service.

Are the police gone now?

Yes, took them about an hour.

You sat there for an entire hour and didn't text me anything about it until they were gone? Francine marveled at Charlotte's restraint.

Would it have mattered? You were getting ready for church.

Francine didn't want to get into a text conversation with Charlotte. She was already missing the Call to Worship while texting and would soon miss the Scripture Reading if she didn't end this thing with Charlotte quickly. ANYTHING NEW?

No.

SINCE YOU'LL BE AT THE LATER SERVICE, I'LL GO BY ON MY WAY HOME TO SEE IF ANYTHING HAS CHANGED. OVER AND OUT.

She didn't wait for Charlotte to respond. She turned off her cell phone. The liturgist asked them to be seated and read a passage from Isaiah 55, verses 8 and 9.

For my thoughts are not your thoughts,
Nor are your ways my ways, says the Lord.
For as the heavens are higher than the earth,
So are my ways higher than your ways,
And my thoughts than your thoughts.

Francine found the passage comforting. She often wondered what to make of the extraordinary things that had come into their lives: the notoriety, the inheritance from Zed, the spring in Parke County, her amazing friends. And yet they had been too often surrounded by death. The one thing she knew for sure was that there was a sense of joy and of grace in their lives that she could only account for through God. She found reassurance that the divine Mind had so much greater capacity than hers, that a greater Wisdom was in control.

Charlotte appeared at the end of the service. She was waiting in the lobby for everyone to file out of church. She made her way toward Francine and Jonathan through the exiting crowd like a salmon swimming upstream during spawning season. Francine was pleased to see her doing it without her cane, which she tended to use in crowds.

"Eric's back," she said, a bit breathless. "At least I think so. Toby turned his car into the driveway of Camille's house just as I was leaving. He opened the garage door and pulled in. Eric couldn't be seen, but then, he crouched in the back seat of your car yesterday when he didn't want to be seen. I stopped and knocked on the door—pounded actually—but no one would answer."

Francine didn't like that they were discussing this openly. She took Charlotte's arm and steered her over to a nook that had only a few people in it. Jonathan took the opportunity to find someone else to talk to. "Maybe Eric sent Toby over to pick up some items," she told Charlotte. "Maybe Eric still isn't there."

"Trust me, my intuition tells me he's there. You should go by and try to see him."

"I will, after Sunday School."

"But he might be gone by then!"

"And if he isn't, we know he's staying at Mary Ruth's house. I can try over there."

Charlotte was exasperated. "But don't you want to see Camille's house now that it's been searched by the police? Aren't you curious to see what they took?"

"You texted me a list! And besides, I haven't been in Camille's house for so long I wouldn't know what they took versus what they didn't. The long and short of it is, *you* want to get in there."

Charlotte tapped her foot. "I suppose I do."

"I can't make that happen. But I promise I'll go over there after Sunday School and see what's going on."

———

After Sunday School, she and Jonathan bid farewell to Charlotte, who stayed behind for the later service. They drove back to their house so Francine could change clothes before she headed over to Camille's in hopes of finding Eric at home and being allowed to come in. If nothing else, she wanted to check to make sure he did go to the police.

It was a frosty morning. She zipped up her winter down coat, wrapped the scarf around her neck, and turned up the coat collar so it rode close to her ears. Reaching the sidewalk, she faced the cold wind and sped walked over to Camille's house.

Camille lived on North Ridge Court, which was an afterthought to the subdivision of Summer Ridge Estates. The court wasn't internally connected to the main drag, so Francine had to use the sidewalk that ran along Hornaday Road to get to North Ridge. Traffic buzzed by her as she hurried.

How easy it would be for someone to breach the right-of-way and hit me, she thought. It wasn't a pleasant thought, but Camille's gruesome stabbing and knowing from Charlotte that the police had searched Camille's house had her thinking of conspiracies and cover-ups and other things one found in a Vince Flynn novel.

Camille's death was grisly, and yes, it had been done at a public venue. No mistaking that. But it may well have been a singular thing. Someone wanted to get her out of the way. That reason could be related to the fact she was President of a contentious Town Council. It might have nothing to do with Eric or his presumed inheritance. Unless Eric knew something he wasn't telling.

She reached the stoop of Camille's single-story house and rang the doorbell. The house was closed up tight and the curtains were drawn, but she knew Eric wasn't interested in announcing his presence in the house. She heard the clump, clump, clump of footsteps approaching the door as she pulled her coat tighter around her. She saw Toby peer out of the front window. He hurriedly unlocked the front door and then held it open for her. "Come in, come in. It's cold out there."

She stepped into the house. It may have been cold outside, but it was warm inside. Or at least Toby was warm. His black hair was matted to his head with perspiration, and he wore a damp, off-white hand towel draped over his shoulder like a stole. He used it to mop up sweat that poured off him. Dressed in a black short sleeve compression shirt, his tattoos were on full display and the tight fit showed off the results of his hard work in becoming a male stripper.

"Thanks, Toby. Is Eric here?" She tried looking past Toby but he was too bulky. "He asked me yesterday if I could help with the funeral arrangements since he'd never done that before. I thought I'd stop by."

She didn't know what she was looking for, maybe Eric, maybe a clue as to what Camille had done to get someone mad enough to stab her, but she took in everything she could.

"Eric's downstairs doing cardio work. I was too, but then I heard the doorbell ring when the music stopped."

Whatever had caused the music to stop resolved itself because Francine jumped when it suddenly came back on at full blast. "What is that?"

"That's the Killers," he said. "We're almost done. Maybe ten minutes. Can you wait?"

He didn't wait for an answer, but dashed around a corner and disappeared. She heard his first footfalls on the steps to the downstairs but they were quickly muffled by the overpowering noise of whoever was singing at full volume. *The Killers*, she reminded herself. *Creepy name for a rock band, especially with what's going on.*

Ten minutes. She slipped off her scarf, stuffed it into her pocket, and unzipped her coat. She took it off and looked for a closet. The house plan was almost identical to Charlotte's. There was a door to her immediate left and she was certain it was a coat closet. She extracted a coat hanger and hung hers up.

Ten minutes, she thought again. *Charlotte could get herself in a lot of trouble in a deceased person's house in ten minutes.*

The hallway leading to the bedrooms was on the opposite side of the room. Francine stared at it. The floor was wood, not carpet, and she worried that maybe someone would hear her if she crossed to the hallway and peered into the bedrooms. What if the floor creaked? Then she laughed at herself. The music was loud enough to cover a herd of elephants migrating across the Indian subcontinent.

She told herself she wouldn't actually walk into the bedrooms. She was only looking for any obvious clues she could detect while simply looking for a restroom. Yes, that was it. She was looking for a restroom. Still, she tiptoed across the room and down the hall.

The first door she came to was the bathroom. *Great*, she thought. *Now what will I say I'm looking for if Eric or Toby finds me down by the bedrooms?* But it wasn't enough to stop her. She kept walking.

The second door was closed. Closed meant she wouldn't look in it, she told herself. She moved on to the next door and peered in. It was a nondescript beige room with matted photos of fall scenes that looked like they'd been taken at McCloud Nature Park, a park tucked away in the northwest corner of the county. She recognized the restored iron truss bridge that was over a century old, moved in from Pulaski County. It was clearly a guest bedroom, but it looked like a guest had just moved in, and she was fairly certain that someone was Toby.

There were two more doors. The next one was likely occupied by Eric, and the farthest bedroom would have been Camille's.

How long had she been in the hall? Couldn't have been more than a couple of minutes. She surely had at least five minutes left. With the music still pounding out of the downstairs session, she advanced to the second doorway. It was Eric's, as expected. Lots of clothes strewn around the room. She moved onto the last doorway. Its door was closed. She turned the knob and pushed on it, expecting it to open. It didn't. She rattled the knob. It was locked.

Locked? Why was it locked?

On the face of it, the door was locked to keep people out. Like her. She took a step back and studied the situation. Probably had four minutes. Did she really want to go forward? She wasn't sure how to get into locked rooms anyway.

No, she thought. *I am not going in there.* She'd only have three, maybe four minutes. That was if Toby was accurate with his time estimate.

She headed back down the hall toward the living room where she'd entered the house.

The first closed door she'd come to was right ahead of her. If it was a three-bedroom house, then what was behind that other door?

She put her hand on the handle and turned it like she had Camille's bedroom, but this one gave way. She opened the door wide.

Inside was a treasure trove of information. This was Camille's study, and file folders were stacked all over a desk on the far side of the room.

I can't go in, she thought. *I have only two minutes at the most.*

The music stopped. Her head snapped toward the basement like she might get caught. But then the Killers started pounding out the same song.

Three more minutes, at least.

She advanced on the file-packed desk.

THIRTEEN

THE SMELL IN THE room was slightly stale, like the air didn't circulate much. But then, the room didn't encourage one to linger. There were no cozy touches; this was a business kind of space. The walls were a utilitarian grayish-white, the window treatments were mini-blinds, and the floor was carpeted in a gray berber. Camille's framed high school diploma was hung on the wall over the desk. Francine studied it for a moment as she approached. *Brownsburg High School.* She knew Camille had lived in Brownsburg for a long time, but didn't know she'd graduated from the high school. Francine saw no other diplomas.

Her attention shifted to the desk itself. There was space where it looked like a computer should have been. *Probably in Jud's hands,* Francine thought. She wouldn't have had time to fool with it anyway.

She picked up a stack of tabbed manila folders and sorted through them. The tabs had subjects written on them. There seemed to be no particular themes. Some had names, some had what she guessed were projects. How else to explain *I-74/RRP TIF infrastructure,* which Francine interpreted to mean sewer and water improvements the town had extended to the Ronald Reagan Parkway interchange at Interstate 74.

Why did Jud not take these? She could come up with two reasons. First, his men had photographed the contents, intending to come back later if there was a need to get them. The second was more intriguing: these were the files that Eric had gathered up last night and taken with him to Mary Ruth's house. That would mean he had judged them to be most important. She surveyed the stack. There were maybe twenty or so thick files, plus a handful of thinner ones. Any of them could contain valuable information, but how would she know in two, maybe three, minutes?

The top folders have to be the most recent ones looked at, she reasoned. The top four bore the names of other Council members: Dick, Vince, Fuzzy, and Janet.

She opened the one for Dick first, hoping to find some dirt. She had never liked Tricky Dicky much and if Camille had been collecting anything negative about him, she would have been happy to come across it. But inside she found a spreadsheet. It had *Lizton State Bank* written across the top, a couple of account numbers on the side, and deposit amounts written under the months, which covered from January of the previous year to the current February. The amount was the same each time, $916.67.

It wasn't an extraordinary amount of money, and she wasn't even sure what it meant. What did Council members make per month, less taxes? She guessed it could be in that range. She wasn't sure why Camille would be tracking that kind of information anyway. After all, wouldn't that be part of the Town's payroll? Wouldn't that be in the purview of the Clerk-Treasurer?

She moved on to Vince's folder next. Like Dick's, it was a slim folder and it too had a spreadsheet. Dick's bank was listed as Old National and it had the same amount written under the months,

$916.67. Ditto for the folder for Fuzzy Carter, whose bank was Chase.

She focused on the sounds in the house. The Killers didn't seem to be winding down, but how long had she been in the room? She'd lost track of time. She felt her face flush hot as she contemplated what would happen if she got caught rummaging through the files in a room that had been closed off. She opened Janet's file hurriedly.

Janet's file was thicker and contained a number of reports written memo style. The "To" line in the first was to Camille alone. Janet was heavily involved in negotiations with a big-name developer to bring a major outlet mall to the new I-74 interchange. With hotels, multi-family housing, restaurants, and other supporting retail, several hundred acres were involved. But there was one problem, and that problem was an uncooperative landowner that stood between two farmers more than willing to sell off big chunks of land for a tidy profit. The landowner: Fuzzy Carter's ex-wife, Cass. She had wrested control of Fuzzy's former homestead in a contested divorce settlement. The piece of land was critical. On the map, it was a seventy-acre island in the middle of a sea of potential Nordstrom Racks and Filene's Basements.

Interesting, but hardly a reason for Camille's death. She was just about to move on to the next file when she noticed the name of one of the other landowners. It was a limited liability corporation, Jacqueline Roberts Craig and Charles LLC. The name Jacqueline jumped out at her.

The music stopped. It took a couple of seconds for the silence to register. When it did, she closed the file, dropped all the files on the desk, turned and rushed out of the room. She heard footsteps coming up the stairs as she closed the door behind her. She ducked into the bathroom next to it and closed that door. She held her breath a few seconds. Eric called her name. She let out a breath. He surely hadn't seen her. She flushed the toilet and checked herself in the mirror. Did she have a guilty look on her face? She faked a smile at herself, noting that it only increased the number of lines in her already wrinkled face. *I've earned every one of those wrinkles*, she thought, *especially today*. She cleared her throat and opened the door.

"In here," she said, stepping out into the hall.

Eric appeared at the entryway to the living room. He wore his perspiration like a shirt, which was noticeable because he had none on. His abs couldn't have been any more visible if he'd carried around a sign pointing them out. *It's a pity Joy isn't with me*, she thought. *We'd know right now if she'd be okay.*

"Thanks for coming over," Eric said. He had a bath towel in his hands and was drying himself off with it. But the sweat kept coming. "Toby and I needed to finish practicing a routine."

Francine was close enough she could smell the pungent odor of male sweat, tinged with a bit of Old Spice that was working overtime and not cutting it. "Sorry I didn't call ahead, but you've been on my mind. I wanted to know how you were getting along, especially with the funeral details. You said you needed help."

"You're fine. I appreciate your concern. If you can stand the smell of me, I have some questions I hope you can answer. I'd take a shower, but until my body cools off, taking a shower would be pointless."

"Sure," she said. "What do you need to know?" She found she was talking to his torso instead of his face. Was this how men end up talking to a woman's breasts? She forced herself to look up. She wondered if her face were getting red again.

"Maybe I should go take a cold shower to cool off. Let me make myself presentable and I'll be out in a minute."

He can either read minds or he's seen this kind of reaction before. She was still embarrassed by her mindless staring. "Okay," she said. It was all she could think of saying.

"Why don't you wait out in the living room and make yourself comfortable?" he offered.

"Yes, thank you. I will."

They passed each other in the hall. He went into the room she'd thought was his and closed the door.

Out in the living room Toby was stepping out a pattern she guessed was the dance routine he and Eric had been working on. He was staring at the floor watching his feet as she went by on the way to the sofa.

He looked up as she went by. "Don't mind me. I'm just trying to get this down." Unlike Eric, Toby was still in a shirt, though it was even more soaked than when she'd first arrived. *Don't those shirts shed water?*

"How many routines do you have to know?" she asked.

"I'm working on three. Two group numbers and one I'm doing on my own. This is my solo. Do you want to see it?"

"No," she said decisively. She did not need to see one of her best friend's grandsons stripping down to his skivvies.

His face registered shock.

Oh no! I've offended him! "Not that I wouldn't want to see it under the right circumstances," she said. "This is just awkward." She pasted the fake smile on her face she'd practiced earlier. *I probably look cheesy*, she thought.

He laughed. "Right," he said as though he understood. "I think I'll go cool off and then change." He danced back to the guest room with the same steps he'd been using and closed the door.

Lots of closed doors around here, Francine thought. She looked for a place to sit. Camille's living room looked like it was torn out of the pages of a Pottery Barn catalog—teak wood furniture holding knickknacks, lamps in antique bronze, and chairs and a sofa in impractical white leather. She wondered if things ever got dirty here. They would in her house. Perhaps two million dollars allows one to avoid dirt. If so, it wasn't foolproof, because apparently there had been one dirty thing she couldn't fix, and it had gotten her killed.

Francine snagged a spot on the sofa. She sank into the plush cushions and hoped she'd be able to get out without help. She rifled through the magazines on the end table next to the couch. *Midwest Living, Indianapolis Monthly, AARP the Magazine*—exactly the sorts of things she expected to see, although *Indianapolis Monthly* skewed a lot younger than she and Camille were. *Nothing here*, she thought, after reading a few articles.

Underneath those she found a copy of the front section of the *Hendricks County Flyer* from two weeks ago. It was folded back to a page three article about the American Legion Post having an event honoring Vietnam-era veterans. The event was several days away at the Legion.

The knife found in Camille's back was from the Vietnam War. *Coincidence?* She contemplated mentioning it to Charlotte and was aghast at the slippery slope she was sliding down. So far she'd rummaged through Camille's private files, perused the magazines on her end table looking for clues, and shortly would question her nephew with the pretense of helping him with funeral arrangements. *I'm actually going to be helpful*, she reminded herself. *And if he reveals any information that helps solve the crime, all the better.*

She was going to the Legion tonight with the Bridge Club to play bingo. Maybe they would find out more about the event for Vietnam veterans when they were there.

She heard a door open from down the hall and Eric soon entered the living room. His hair had been toweled dry, but beads of sweat still formed on his forehead. He wiped his brow with a hand towel before they rolled down his face. He wore a *Star Wars Rogue One* t-shirt, and while it was damp, it wasn't completely soaked like his body had been earlier. "Thanks for waiting for me," he said.

"How can I help with the funeral?" she asked.

"I've set it for Tuesday, and I need to put together something for people to look at. I want it to say what a good person she was and show how much she's accomplished in her life. She's lived in the neighborhood for a long time. I figured you and Charlotte and some of the other women would have photos and could put together a slide show or some kind of tribute to her life."

Details ran through Francine's head. While Camille had lived next to Charlotte for a long time, none of them would have kept newspaper clippings about Camille. Charlotte might have some about the meter pit incident, but if she did, they wouldn't provide the kind of story he was looking for. And yet, this offer had potential.

"Tell you what, Eric. It would take a long time to hunt through our photographs looking for her specifically. Plus, we're not going to know what was important to her during her life. The best source for that would be her files. Could we look through those and see what we can come up with?"

Eric weighed her response. "I guess you're right. You really aren't going to have that kind of information, are you? Maybe this is something I'm going to have to do. I just don't know when I'm going to find the time. And I'm so bad at creating poster board presentations."

"You don't have to go it alone," she answered quickly. "We can do it for you. We just need to pull the information from your house."

His forehead creased and relaxed as he went through mental gyrations contemplating his options. Francine thought of the files she'd discovered in Camille's office. She wondered if Eric was hesitant to let them have access.

He seemed to make a decision. "The police went through the house this morning and took a number of things. Plus, Aunt Camille wasn't a very neat housekeeper. Let me clean up her office and her bedroom and sort through what I can find. Otherwise it might be looking for a needle in a haystack."

"If you need help, I've seen messier bedrooms." She tried to flash a winning smile. "Remember, I had three boys."

He chuckled at that but shook his head. "I appreciate it, but let me do some cleanup first."

They made arrangements for her to come back tomorrow about the same time, and she said she'd bring Charlotte with her. If he shared any of the bad blood with Charlotte that Camille had, she didn't sense it. He found her coat for her while she stared longingly down the hall at the closed door to Camille's office.

Should have gone in there first, she thought.

FOURTEEN

THE FIRST THING FRANCINE did when he closed the door was check the time. It was twelve thirty. Charlotte ought to be home from church. She headed next door.

Her knock was rapid, frantic. "Charlotte! It's me, Francine." She was cold, but mostly she wanted to get inside to share what just happened. Had she gone too far? Why was she doing this? She was sincere in wanting to help Eric with the funeral arrangements for Camille, but she had definitely crossed over into sleuth territory again.

Charlotte swung the door open as though she'd been waiting for her, which Francine gathered she had. She held a large pair of Army green binoculars in one hand. "Come in, Francine. I thought you'd never get here."

Charlotte was dressed in a zippered red knit sweater with a snowflake design on it. Her wig of silver curls wasn't quite straight, as usual. Francine eyed the binoculars.

"Where did you get those?" she asked. She stepped in and felt the temperature difference immediately. The warmth was wonderful.

Charlotte tended to keep her house a little toastier than most of the group.

"They were on sale at the Gander Mountain in Avon," she said. "These babies'll let you zoom in on a target half a mile away. Deer hunters use them."

"Must have cost you a pretty penny." Francine took off her coat and hung it on a coat stand in the hallway.

"Black Friday sale, but it would have been worth every cent even at the regular price. I can see into the Plums' front room once the sun goes behind their rooftop, which happens about five thirty this time of year. You know they're smoking marijuana."

"You have proof?"

"I've watched them. If I could figure out how to rig a camera to the lenses, I'd take pictures to prove it."

In many ways, Francine was relieved Charlotte was mostly technology-challenged. "Have you been spying on the Ledfelter house next door?"

Charlotte shut the front door. "Naturally. Though I can't see into any of the bedrooms. Camille always kept the blinds closed and the drapes drawn, which takes out the two bedrooms on this side. I think Eric moved into one of them."

Francine mentally reviewed her brief tour of the Ledfelter home. Eric's bedroom did face Charlotte's house. "You're right, from what I saw when I was in there."

"Let's talk about what you saw." Charlotte scooted behind Francine and gave her a push toward the library room down the hall. "How about a little nip while we do that? It's cold out, and nothing takes the chill out like a little brandy."

Francine cringed. She wasn't fond of Charlotte's rotgut brandy, but she could stomach the cheap liquor if she had to. "How nice," she said.

The room Charlotte had converted into a library was the twin of the room Camille had turned into an office. But where Camille's office had been a barren, utilitarian space, Charlotte's was filled with her character. Solid wooden bookcases were filled with her eclectic choices in books. They went from floor to ceiling. There was even a feeling of antiquity to the room as light streamed in the window revealing dust motes floating through the air. That was one area Charlotte and Camille were similar: they weren't housekeepers. "The only problem with this room," Charlotte said, pouring each of them a finger of brandy in a crystal sherry glass, "is that it faces the wrong direction. I can't snoop very well."

"You can see next door to Father William's house." Francine looked out the window. "Especially this time of year with the barren trees. You can see right through the branches." An Episcopal priest and his wife lived on the other side of Charlotte.

"I suppose you're right, but what good is it? He and Betty are so well-behaved they could give purity lessons to Ivory soap." She handed one of the sherry glasses to Francine. "Here. Drink up!"

Francine examined at the syrupy amber liquid in the glass. She swirled it for a second, put her nose to the glass and breathed in. While she was no connoisseur when it came to spirits, she knew the type of brandy Charlotte usually bought, and this was not it. This was lighter, more transparent, and had a smooth viscosity to it. It smelled of apple and vanilla. "Is this your usual brandy?" she asked. She took a sip. "It seems more refined." It still burned on her throat but had a caramel finish to it that the fruit-based brandy never had.

"You're good, you know that?" Charlotte picked up the bottle and handed it to her. "It's not brandy. It's cognac."

Cognac, the stuff of William Churchill and Dr. Dre, Francine thought. She checked the label. "Charlotte! This is a Prunier Cognac!"

"That explains why it spoke to me in a French accent," Charlotte cracked. "I thought maybe it was because I had too much of it when I opened it yesterday."

Francine studied the bottle. It was a VSOP, which the label said meant "Very Superior Old Pale." While she wasn't sure how much it cost, she knew it was much pricier than what Charlotte usually bought. "Where did you get this?"

"Camille gave it to me on New Year's Day. At first I thought it might be a gift, but then she put her house on the market the next day, so I took it to be a bribe instead. Sort of like, 'please don't interfere with my sales attempt.' As though I would start up my irrigation system when a buyer was in the house." She rolled her eyes. "Like I would do that in the winter."

Implying you would do it if it were summer? Francine thought. She hoped not, but you could never be sure.

"And anyway," Charlotte continued, "my system never did produce the racket in her house that she claimed it did. The guys from DPW told me that privately, but since she was President of the Town Council they knew better than to contradict her. They just kept quiet and didn't say one way or the other."

Francine took another sip. She was beginning to appreciate the burn in her throat. She'd have to visit Charlotte more often in the afternoon, at least until the cognac ran out. "This doesn't strike me as the kind of thing Camille would buy though, especially not as a gift. I wonder how much it cost."

"You could look it up on that phone of yours." Charlotte eased herself in her favorite chair, an apricot-colored recliner that also rocked. She leaned back in it. "This stuff makes me feel all warm and tingly inside." She put the glass to her lips. "I don't need my blanket when I drink it."

"Promise me you won't make a hot toddy out of it. It's too good for that."

"Not even tempted. Now tell me what you learned from Eric. He's in there, isn't he?" She began rocking in the chair.

Francine took her usual chair across from Charlotte, a wooden rocking chair. It had a multicolored crocheted blanket draped over it that provided a bit of padding against the hard back. "Eric wants me to come back tomorrow. He wants you and me to go through Camille's photos and press clippings and whatever else we can find to put together something visual for her funeral. He wanted time to clean up her office, though, before he let us in."

Charlotte rubbed her chin in thought. "Why? What's in her office?"

"Financial records, for one thing," she said. It slipped out before she had really thought about it. She didn't want to admit to Charlotte that she'd been snooping. It might come back to bite her sometime if she tried to discourage Charlotte from doing the same.

Charlotte pounced on the gaffe. "You sound like you've seen them." Her rocking picked up speed.

"I may have gone into the room by mistake when I was looking for the restroom."

Charlotte practically snorted. "I've been in her house. There's no mistaking the restroom. Besides, it's the first room on the left down the hall. Just like mine. For you to have gone past it, you'd ..."

"... have to have been trolling for information. Okay, I admit it."

"So, what financial information?"

"I didn't know what to make of it, really. Bank account information for Tricky Dick, Vince, Fuzzy, and Janet. Might have been related to pay for being on the Council, but I'm not certain. I didn't have much chance to examine it before Eric and Toby came upstairs from working out in the basement."

Charlotte's rocking continued at the faster pace. "That's probably something Eric will clean up. We may not see that again."

"She had a big stack of files on her desk. Those were the top files. I figured she must have been looking at them recently."

"Or Eric was looking at them."

"I hadn't thought of that." Francine sipped the cognac again and contemplated the records she'd seen. "I wonder how much access Eric had to Camille's finances. He said she made him a partner. He lived with her for what, a year?"

"He moved back to Brownsburg before Christmas, so it's actually been a year and a few months. I could check my calendar."

Francine frowned at her. "You keep track of stuff like that?"

"I record little things that go on in the neighborhood. You violate the privacy of dead women by rifling through their financial records when their next of kin isn't looking. I don't see that you have any moral superiority here."

Francine could trot out a litany of Charlotte's violations of privacy over the years, but that wouldn't be productive. "Let's get back to Eric and Camille. Eric seemed surprised earlier when he admitted that Camille had banked two million dollars. He obviously knew about it, but he said it with a kind of amazement like he'd just discovered it or still hadn't quite grasped it."

"You think he didn't know where it came from or you think he was surprised at the amount?"

"I hadn't given it any thought until now. I had guessed it was just the amount. If he knew where it came from, would he have been surprised?"

"Maybe so, if he just discovered it." Charlotte slowed her rocking and picked up her glass of cognac. She used it to gesture at Francine as she talked, like Sherlock Holmes using his pipe to gesture at

Watson. "Do you think there might have been something illegal as to how she obtained the money?" Charlotte asked.

Well, in the last couple of days I've learned she essentially black-mailed you and also attempted to bribe you. She did it subtly, but neither reveals what I'd consider a trustworthy person. Francine leaned forward. "It's possible. Though we are talking about a respected Council member here. Council President, in fact. Would she chance that?"

"She's dead, Francine. Someone killed her. She did something someone didn't like. Of course it could have been illegal. When have politicians ever *not* been susceptible to temptation?" Charlotte thought a moment. "Or I suppose it's possible the person who killed her did something illegal and she discovered it."

And tried to use it to her advantage. That may be more like it, Francine thought. "Camille was not the sort of person who got along with everyone."

"Exactly. Look at her and me. We were neighbors for a long time, and then I had this irrigation system installed and suddenly I'm a pariah. She fabricated a story about the noises she was hearing and tried to get everyone against me."

"And yet she gave you this bottle of cognac." Francine mused about that as she took another sip.

"And now we have the chance to put together a retrospective of her life for her funeral." Charlotte stopped rocking and looked Francine in the eye. "We're helping out her nephew and at the same time helping ourselves to information that may solve the mystery of her death. What could be better? We're being helpful! How could Jud object to that? If he knew. Which we'll probably tell him once we have the information that will help him solve this case."

Francine wished she could be as optimistic. "What other motives could there be besides money? Maybe we're focusing too much on the money aspect because we're surprised she had more than we thought. It might have nothing to do with her death."

"Stabbing her and deflating her lung is dramatic. I can't think of many reasons to do that if we exclude money."

The image of Camille crumpled on the floor with the hilt of a knife sticking out of the side of her dress surged into Francine's mind. *Such a horrible thing.* She belted down the remaining drab of cognac in her glass.

Charlotte stood as though she could read Francine's mind. "Makes one want to drink, doesn't it? Let's have another finger." She took the glass from Francine and shuffled over to the wet bar, passing by the window as she went. "That looks like Jud's car that just went by. I think it pulled in at Camille's."

"Where?" Francine used her arms to push herself out of the rocking chair she'd sunk into, propelling herself toward the window. The view of the street from the side window wasn't good, and if a car had gone by, it wasn't visible now.

"Let's go to the front window. When they come out, we'll be able to see what happens."

The women watched for five long minutes. At the end of that time, Jud came out carrying the stack of files Francine had seen on the desk. He also had a computer Francine hadn't seen before.

Charlotte pointed. "I saw them take one computer out yesterday. Wonder how they missed this one."

"I didn't see it in the office. But those look like the files that were stacked on the desk. Not sure we'll get much information now."

"Dang that Jud. He's one step ahead of us."

Francine felt the same disappointment, but had to remind herself Jud was doing his job. "Maybe it's for the best. Now we can really focus on doing what Eric asked, putting together a retrospective of Camille's life."

"I hope she's got other files to pull from. With her two computers gone and that stack of files, there may not be much left."

"I guess we'll know tomorrow."

Charlotte headed back to fill their glasses.

"I don't think I need any more cognac," Francine said, "In fact, I need to be getting home to get supper started."

"Don't forget bingo tonight. You're going, aren't you?"

"What time is the bingo?"

"Warm-up games start at six. The regular games begin at seven."

Francine almost laughed. "You have to warm up to play bingo?"

Charlotte set the bottle of cognac down. She flared her elbows out at her side, working her arms. "Exactly. You have to get the eye-hand coordination going. Those numbers come fast, you know."

"I won't be there for the warm-ups," she said, knowing she would prefer to enjoy dinner with Jonathan. They'd planned an early dinner. "But I should be able to make the regular bingo."

Charlotte put the bottle away. "I could bring the cognac over to Eric's tomorrow. Maybe a little afternoon warmth will help our creativity."

"Camille's life was interesting enough. I'm not sure we need creativity to do it justice. But if you want to bring it, please do."

"We'll toast Camille, since I got the bottle from her. A salute to her philanthropy, even if it didn't show up much during her lifetime."

Francine left Charlotte's house contemplating Charlotte's last words. What had caused Camille's change of heart in recent months? Not that she'd been evil or anything, but she hadn't been known for her charitable work. Yet in her last months, she'd given Charlotte a bottle of relatively expensive cognac and spearheaded the fund-raiser for the Parks Department.

Curious.

FIFTEEN

FRANCINE WAS PACKAGING UP the leftovers from dinner when her cell phone rang. She glanced at the screen. It was Mary Ruth. She answered it.

"I've got a job! A catering job. Well, it's not a paying job. I'm doing the bereavement dinner Tuesday after the funeral. We had a lot of leftover food from the benefit because everyone ran out before the show got started. It was Toby's idea to repurpose it for the bereavement dinner, and Eric agreed. But I'll need help reworking what we have into something new. Can you help me Monday morning? Alice is due back the day of the funeral, and she says she'll help serve, but I need prep help."

Francine glanced at the calendar she kept in the kitchen. It hung on the end cabinet facing the dining table. It was a holdover habit she had from when the boys were all home and their schedules were unmanageable without a visual representation of time. Though their schedule was far less hectic now, she continued to use it.

"I can help Monday morning, but I need to be out by noon. Charlotte and I are working on some kind of presentation about Camille for the funeral."

"That's okay. Do you want a ride over to the bingo?"

"I was going to drive Charlotte over. That is, unless she's left early to hit the warm-up games. Why don't we come pick you up?"

There was a pause before Mary Ruth answered. "I guess it's okay. It's not too far to the Legion. I go nuts if I'm in the car with Charlotte too long. Especially now that the scent of a killer in is her nostrils. She won't talk about anything else."

Francine had to grant that Mary Ruth was probably right. "It was her idea to go to the bingo too. Trying to find out who's a Vietnam vet. There are probably hundred in Hendricks County alone, if not more."

"Well, find out if she's left early. If she hasn't I still don't mind driving you."

"I'll let you know." Francine disconnected.

Even if they had a complete list of the Vietnam veterans, she wondered just how much they would learn from the information. She reminded herself that Jud cautioned them against jumping to that conclusion. Still, there had to be some kind of rhyme or reason as to why that particular knife had been used.

———

The Brownsburg American Legion Post 331 was located on Main Street in a one-story red brick building across the street from Flap Jacks, one of Charlotte's favorite breakfast places. But Charlotte had indeed gone early to hit the warm-up games, so Mary Ruth picked up Francine and drove her over. The two turned into the driveway leading back to the parking lot.

"It's full," Mary Ruth said.

The Legion parking lot indeed was full of cars. There was not a single space available. "What about the overflow lot next door?" Francine pointed to the signs that directed to the adjacent lot.

Mary Ruth followed them and eased the catering van into the last slot left. "I hope Charlotte has saved us a seat. It looks like a lot of people are here."

"It's a big hall," Francine said. She'd been to the Legion post before. Jonathan was a member, though not a very active one. "Let's hope there's room."

They hurried through the door labeled BINGO ENTRANCE. Mary Ruth led Francine past the display case of memorabilia from various wars and down the hall toward the large meeting room where the bingo games were held. She could hear general activity but no numbers being called. It sounded like they had gotten there in time.

The room was full but not crowded. Charlotte had scoped out a table toward the back of the room near the kitchen and reserved a few spots. Chairs were tilted up against the table, a universal warning that those spaces were taken. She stood and waved to Mary Ruth and Francine. "Over here."

Francine gave the thumbs up to Charlotte to let her know she'd heard, but Mary Ruth tugged at her arm and steered her over to where they purchase bingo cards. "We need to get these before they start the first game. The caller is getting ready to go." Francine looked toward the front of the room and saw the bingo balls swirling about in an enclosed box, ready to be selected.

"How do we buy cards?" Francine asked, mystified by the procedure. She knew how to play bingo but this was a major operation. Packs of disposable bingo cards sat near several cash register stations, which were located just beyond the kitchen window where you could order and pick up dinner. Francine could smell fried food as they passed. Looking inside, she saw lots of unhealthy stuff like cheeseburgers frying on a grill, French fries bubbling in a deep fat fryer, and nachos being smothered with thick, gooey yellow cheese. She wasn't even hungry, but she had to admit, it beckoned like a siren's song. She forced herself to look away.

"That'll be twenty dollars," a cashier told Mary Ruth, who pulled cash out of her purse.

"I'll buy the special games too," Mary Ruth added, after taking possession of the thick oblong packet of paper the cashier handed her. Francine could see that the top sheet in the packet had twelve separate bingo cards detailed on it. She wasn't sure she'd have enough time in between calls to check even half that many for numbers, but there didn't seem to be a smaller option.

Mary Ruth turned to Francine. "Do you have a dobber?"

Francine wrinkled her nose. "What's a dobber?"

Mary Ruth pulled one out of her purse and showed it to her. It was a tube-like cylinder filled with fluorescent pink highlighter fluid that could be "dobbed" onto the disposable card. "You use it to keep track of the numbers that have been called."

Francine shook her head. "No. Does that mean I can't play?"

"Of course not, silly. You could buy one here. But I have an extra one." She handed Francine a dobber that inked in neon green.

"You play often?" Francine asked in surprise.

"Not all that often, not compared to some of these gals. I play once a month."

Francine paid for the regular games but skipped buying the special games, like coverall bingos. She and Mary Ruth carried their cards over to the table where Charlotte had reserved seats. They sat side by side across from Charlotte and a fellow who looked to be about their age with dirty blond hair pulled back in a long ponytail and a fuzzy Willie Nelson beard.

"It's about time you got here," Charlotte said. "The caller's about to start."

"How long have you been here?" Mary Ruth asked.

"Since six. I started with the warm-up games."

Francine and Mary Ruth sat at the chairs which had been tilted against the table. There was one left. "Where's Joy?" Francine asked.

"Over there." Charlotte pointed across the room to the last table at the far wall, about midway down the table. "Either it's my imagination or I was followed all the way over here by that weedy-looking guy. She's trying to make conversation with him to find out which it is."

"You were followed?" Francine practically shouted it.

"Shhh," Mary Ruth said. "The caller is getting ready to announce the first number. It's a regular bingo—five numbers up and down, straight across, or diagonally."

Francine took off her glasses. The glasses helped with mostly nearsighted issues. By taking them off she hoped to see more clearly across the room to where Joy sat. But even then, the only thing she could determine was that he appeared to be tall, gangly, and young, with a small head and large ears. He looked harmless enough.

Joy had bingo cards spread out in front of her, getting ready to mark the first number, but kept talking to him at the same time.

Francine turned her attention back to their table. Mary Ruth pulled a Beanie Baby out of her purse. It was a white cat. She set it at the upper left hand edge of her bingo packet. Francine watched this in curiosity.

"Good luck charm," Mary Ruth said. "Her name is Flip." She dobbed the area around Flip, checking to see if the dobber worked. It did.

"You better get set up if you expect to play the first round," Charlotte advised Francine.

Mary Ruth rushed to help Francine get the packet laid out and the dobber ready. She no sooner had her hand poised over the card than the caller said, "B-12."

Just before she said it, the B-12 lit up on a backlit screen across the room. Francine started at the beginning and had only checked her sixth card when the caller announced the next number, O-69. Francine looked up in panic. "I'm not finished marking B-12 yet," she whispered to Charlotte.

"Then only play the first six," she said.

"Don't be silly," Mary Ruth hissed back. "I've got plenty of time. I'll cover the rest of the card for her."

"You have that kind of time?" Francine asked.

"I could play two sets of these cards if it didn't cost forty bucks. Hate to pay that much money for one evening, even if it lasts three hours."

"We're going to be here three hours?" Francine said, incredulous. "I don't want to be here three hours."

"They take smoke breaks," Charlotte said. "About one every hour."

That explained why the guy next to Charlotte smelled like cigarette smoke but wasn't actually smoking. Francine was pretty sure they didn't allow smoking in the hall. She wouldn't have come otherwise, no matter how many veterans they could talk to. "When do we talk to the veterans?" she asked, looking around.

"Only during the breaks," Mary Ruth advised. "No distracting other people while they're playing."

Francine wanted to look up and across the room to see if Joy had stopped talking to the young man who might have followed Charlotte to the bingo, but she didn't dare turn her attention from the card. She was having difficulties keeping up, and she figured Mary Ruth was counting on her to cover the six cards on her end.

It wasn't long before two people shouted "Bingo!" They held up little flags to stake their claim to the money. Everyone around Francine groaned. "I had casers on two of the cards," Mary Ruth said. "And you had one here, Francine." She showed her where Francine had only needed a B-2 to win.

Francine was excited she'd almost won, but not as excited as she was by the news that Charlotte might have been followed. "Why do you think he was following you?"

"I spotted his car when I was leaving Summer Ridge. It was kind of beat up and about twenty years old, which you see every once in a while in our subdivision but usually with a Domino's light on top delivering pizzas. He didn't have the light. He let a car get between us, but he followed me down Hornaday Road and turned left onto Main. By then he was right behind me. I had only mildly supposed it was a tail until he pulled into the parking lot behind me. Then I began to worry."

Francine eyed him again from across the room. "He doesn't look the type to follow older women around."

"I know. Joy was waiting for me. When I told her what had happened, she seemed intrigued. She said to leave it to her."

Both bingo players with their flags in the air were declared to have valid bingos, and a new game started. This time it was for an L-shaped bingo. Francine tried to wrap her mind around that one. "It's like a bishop's move in chess," Mary Ruth explained, "only four up and two over instead of two up and one over."

Charlotte, who didn't play chess, said, "You're only confusing her. It's the letter L. She held her thumb and forefinger against her forehead. "Like in *Loser!*" She said the last word in a singsong voice.

Francine guessed it was some kind of universal sign Charlotte had picked up from a television show.

Halfway into the first hour of bingo, Francine was getting better at playing the six cards she was working on. Despite having a couple of "casers," she did not win. She found herself frustrated and disappointed. Apparently six women down the table from her felt the same way. One of them picked up a miniature rag doll and threw it repeatedly against the table, yelling, "Dammit!"

Francine startled. "What is she doing?" she muttered to Mary Ruth.

"It's her Dammit Doll," Charlotte said, butting in. "She's trying to change her luck."

Mary Ruth, who hadn't had any casers since the first game, turned Flip the cat upside down on its back. It looked like a beached whale. "This is how I change my luck," she said. "Flip needs to be flipped."

Francine noticed that the thin young man had moved two tables closer to them, followed by Joy, followed by a kitchen runner, who brought him a beer. He handed the runner what appeared to be a five-dollar bill. In between games, Joy continued to talk at him. The young man did not seem to be interested in conversation.

Mary Ruth won the next game on the tenth call. "Bingo!" she yelled triumphantly, thrusting her flag in the air.

"Check her card!" yelled a man at the front.

"Dammit!" said the woman down at the end of their table. Several thuds followed. Other people followed suit. Francine could feel the reverberation at their end of the table.

While Mary Ruth's card was being checked by one of the monitors, Francine observed the young man picking up his bingo cards and advancing to a vacant seat at the table immediately to the left of theirs. He had strategically chosen a place with only one empty spot, leaving Joy completely out. She reluctantly moved next to Charlotte, to the spot with the chair still tilted against the table, showing it to be reserved.

"If he followed you, I have no idea why," she reported to Charlotte. She said it in the snappy, short voice that made her sound like a chirping bird. "The only thing I could get out of him was, 'It's a job.' He repeated it like a mantra, even when I wasn't asking about you. I couldn't figure out what kind of a job he was talking about. And he drank a lot. He ordered a beer every time we changed places. And we did that three times in the last hour."

"I'll trade you Ellie, my elephant, for your cat," said a plump woman in a dusty purple t-shirt who'd come up behind Mary Ruth. "I'll even sweeten the pot with a fiver." She flashed a bill at Mary Ruth. "It's been so long since I've won."

Mary Ruth shook her head. "Not a chance. Flip and me go back a long way."

"Can they rub noses, at least?"

She shrugged. "I guess."

The woman rubbed the trunk of her little stuffed elephant to the nose of Flip the cat, who remained upside down like it was dead, despite having won Mary Ruth a game. "I don't mean to be eavesdropping," the woman said as she pulled her elephant to her bosom, "but aren't you Joy McQueen, the reporter?" She looked at Joy.

Joy beamed. "I am."

"Well, that young man you were trying to talk to is Tripper." She said it as though that explained everything.

"I guess I don't know who he is," Joy said. "Is there something wrong with him?"

The woman gave a smile that stretched her wide mouth, "He hasn't quite been the same since he returned from Iraq. It's sad. You might find out more at the end of the first hour, depending on what he's here for." She returned to her seat.

"I wonder what she means by that," Joy said. "Aren't we all here to play bingo?"

"Tripper," Mary Ruth mused. "I may have heard something about him when I've been here before. Let me think on that."

The first hour of bingo ended with a coverall game. Since Francine hadn't bought the extra games, she was the only one of the four to sit it out. She eyed Tripper while the others listened intently to the caller and dobbed their cards like the world might end if they failed to mark a number forcefully enough. Tripper was dressed more smartly than most of the men around the room. Instead of a flannel shirt, he wore a red plaid woven shirt buttoned to the top of the collar. The shirt was slightly too large for his build and billowed around his thin waist.

Apparently Tripper wasn't into coverall bingo either. When something close to half the numbers had been called, he rose unsteadily from his chair and wobbled his way over toward them. He stood behind Francine and across from Charlotte.

"Hello, ladies," he said.

Francine could smell the booze on his breath wafting over her shoulder.

"Sure, now you want to talk to me," Joy said without looking up. "Now that I've got three casers on the coverall. Come on, G-45."

Francine tried to look over her shoulder at him without engaging in eye contact. She had never had good luck dealing with drunks when they thought she wanted to talk to them.

He had something in his hand. It wasn't a bottle of beer. Francine couldn't determine what it was without completely turning around, which she was loathe to do. She thought it might be a handheld microphone.

There was a minor disruption at the back of the room where Francine and Mary Ruth had entered. Francine checked it out and found Marcy Rosenblatt back there. She had a cameraman from Channel 6 with her. "Joy, did you tell Marcy that we would be here tonight?"

"Not me."

The caller said, "G-47."

Joy groaned. "So close."

Mary Ruth finished checking her coverall cards for the elusive G-47. "I might have mentioned it to her in passing. Why?"

"Because she's at the back of the room with a cameraman."

Francine thought back to Marcy's comment a day ago, which contained an implied threat to have a dancer show up for Charlotte. But it had been said in the same context as Marcy's meeting with Buckingham dancers, and Tripper was clearly not a Buckingham dancer.

"I-19," said the caller. "I-19."

"I won again!" said Mary Ruth. "Bingo!" She held up her flag.

A runner rushed to the table to check Mary Ruth's card. Dammit Dolls banged on tables around the room. The women from the end of the table rushed toward Flip the cat with their good-luck animals, hoping to touch noses. Though there weren't many men, most of them rose with a packet of cigarettes clutched in their fingers. They put on coats and beat a hasty retreat to the outside to smoke.

Francine studied Tripper with curiosity. The men's exit left Tripper standing alone among the women surrounding Mary Ruth. The pupils of his eyes were small, and Francine had to assume he had had other substances that evening in addition to several beers. She was no longer worried about catching his eye. She wasn't sure he was all there to begin with.

"The bingo is good!" declared the runner loudly.

Tripper flicked a switch on what Francine was now certain was a microphone. Music came over the public address system from somewhere. Francine knew the tune immediately. It was "Can't Take My Eyes off You." Tripper crooned into the microphone, "You're just too good to be true." He trained his eyes on Charlotte and began unbuttoning the top button of his shirt. Francine could see where this was going. She tried to stand, but there were too many people surrounding her, Charlotte, Joy, and Mary Ruth.

"You go, Tripper," said one lady.

"Tripper the Stripper," said Mary Ruth. "I remember now."

SIXTEEN

It was a train wreck waiting to happen. Francine again tried to get out of her seat but was held down by the women crowding in to reach Flip the cat.

In a continuous flowing move, Tripper hopped from the floor to a vacant chair and then to the top of an adjoining table. He never lost his place with the lyrics and continued his mesmerizing version of the song. Tripper had an ethereal voice that could have swept a woman away, Francine thought, were the setting not the Bingo Hall of the American Brownsburg Legion and the target woman, Charlotte, not more interested in the chili-cheese fries the table runner had just dropped off at her place setting.

Francine also noticed Tripper was adept at getting his clothes off. Before he reached the second stanza, he was down to his skivvies, which were noticeably Calvin Klein. The brand name was prominently on display around the waist band.

Marcy and the cameraman moved in for a close-up.

"Watch it," said the woman in the purple top. "He's going to do his electric table glide."

Devoid of shoes, in thin argyle socks whose colors did not match the red plaid shirt he'd discarded nor the navy blue parachute pants he'd pulled off, he leaped over the table where Charlotte sat. She spotted him in time to move her chili-cheese fries out of the way but not her bingo cards. He landed on them and continued sliding toward the end of the table.

Which buckled the minute his weight unbalanced it. Tripper realized he was going to take a dive and backpedaled, managing to fall backward instead of flat on his face. He rolled off to the side and almost knocked Joy off her seat. He managed to grab her chair and hold himself upright while his legs scrabbled to gain traction on the floor. Unfortunately, it was now slick with Pepsi products, wine, and plastic cups. He turned Joy's seat toward him as his legs went out from under him and he landed butt first on the floor. Joy popped out of the chair and onto his lap.

"Would have stuck the landing if the Pepsi had had time to dry," said one of the women, shaking her head. "It's a shame, that."

Francine was horrified, but no more so than Joy, who found herself with one arm around the neck of a nearly naked man. Her expression was one of shock. She slid off his lap, using her arms to propel herself in the opposite direction. She was still staring at him, however. His bared torso was so thin it was all rib cage and ab muscles.

Francine finally managed to pull her attention away from Joy to check her end of the table. Charlotte was no longer holding her cheese fries. The table must have come up and smacked them directly into her white curly wig, because chili, cheese, and fries were running down one side of her face. Mary Ruth had been smacked by a beer bottle. Flip the cat was upended and had set the women scrabbling to capture it and rub off its good luck. They were in a scrum surround the tiny stuffed animal.

Charlotte looked momentarily like she would cry, but then she got hold of herself. "What the hell is going on here?" she demanded.

"Can't Take My Eyes Off You" continued karaoke-style over the PA system. Tripper, who seemed to have been snapped out of whatever fog he was in, grabbed his shirt, pants, and shoes and ran from the room.

Marcy and the cameraman took one look at Francine's face and made a bee-line out the door into the outdoor smoking area.

The manager rushed over. "Are you all right?" he asked, concentrating on the women who had been downed by the incident. "Let's get you back to my office."

Several kitchen runners helped Mary Ruth, Joy, Charlotte, and Francine into a cubbyhole office adjacent to where the bingo cards and paraphernalia were sold. There was a table with boxes containing unsold pull tab gambling games, disposable bingo cards, and snack items on it. The manager cleared the table and sat them at chairs around it. "I'm so sorry."

"You ought to be," Charlotte grumbled. She swiped a muck of chili cheese off her wig. It left a yellow-ish brown stain across the blue-white hair. "Why did you let that happen? I understand it's probably not the first occurrence, given his nickname is Tripper the Stripper."

"He's a member. It doesn't happen often, and it's never happened like that before. He had a bad experience in Iraq."

"And now he has trouble keeping his clothes on in public?" Joy said. She said it in an accusing manner, but Francine noticed she had a smile on her face. The fact was, Joy did not give any indication she would be nauseous. It was a good sign.

"Usually not. But with the Buckingham dance troupe in Browns-burg now, he fancies that he could be one of them. I understand he's tried out."

Probably didn't get very far, Francine thought, comparing his skinny frame to the muscular dancers she knew Eric employed.

Charlotte continued to grumble. "I'm going to the restroom to clean up and then I'm headed home. I need to change my wig and recover from all this. And we're likely not going to talk to any veterans, like we'd hoped." She glared pointedly at the manager. "Tonight was a waste of time."

"Wait," said the manager. He pulled a handkerchief from his back pocket and wiped his bald head, which had begun to sweat. "I might be able to help. What did you want to talk to some veterans about? I'd hate to disappoint you all, especially a reporter from *Good Morning America*."

Francine remembered the videographer Marcy had dragged in right before Tripper started his routine. At first she'd been angry about it, but if Joy handled this right, it could turn out just fine.

She needn't have worried. Joy handled it like a pro. "No one will probably talk to me now," Joy sniffed. "At least not here. My camera-man is gone now anyway. But perhaps if you could get us a list…"

———

It had taken some fast talking even then. But by the time they left, the manager had compiled a list of the older veterans that were members of the Brownsburg post. They weren't specific to Vietnam, but they were before Desert Storm. He'd also written in some vets of similar ages he knew belonged to the Avon, Plainfield, and Danville posts. He didn't provide contact information and had sworn them to secrecy as to how they got the list. In return, Joy promised to make the earlier footage of Tripper's disastrous routine disappear.

"It better disappear," Charlotte said, "or Marcy's dead." The four women were back in Francine's kitchen around the island, having a late-night chamomile tea before returning to their homes.

"I think there have been enough deaths at this point," Mary Ruth said. She was still nursing a bruised spot on her cheek where she'd been clobbered by the beer bottle. Francine had provided some ice wrapped in a white washcloth. "Though I could kill whoever nabbed Flip in the melee that followed."

Francine was anxious to change the subject. She scoured the list. "Fuzzy Carter was a vet. Army, early eighties."

"I wonder if they were using knives like that then," Charlotte said. "Later wars were fought in deserts, not jungles. Plus, he and Camille were buddies on the Council. I'm still looking for a strong motive."

Francine returned to the list. "Tricky Dicky Raden is a vet."

"Army?" Mary Ruth asked.

"Looks like it," Francine responded.

Charlotte sipped her tea. "So maybe they were all in the Army together? They're roughly the same age, mid-fifties."

Joy nibbled on a cookie from a stash of slice-and-bake frozen chocolate chip cookie dough Francine had pulled out of the freezer and baked until slightly underdone. They were soft and gooey. "Dick and Vince side together most of the time. Fuzzy almost always votes with Camille and Janet Turpen. It would be interesting to find out if they're friendly when they hang out at the Legion."

"I guess it all goes back to the divorce, but why would Vince and Fuzzy be so radically different now in their views?" Francine wondered aloud. "If they grew up as friends, why would they be so opposite in how they look at things?"

"Politics," Joy said, "has nothing to do with reason. It has to do with relationships, and the ones between Fuzzy, Cass, Vince, and Myra are complicated."

Francine put her teacup down so she could use her hand to gesture. "So Fuzzy and Cass are unfriendly because of the divorce. I understand that. Vince is somewhat mad over the whole thing because Myra made him pick sides and he stuck with his wife instead of his best friend. I sort of understand that, but wasn't there some kind of neutral ground he could have taken?"

"As it so often does," Joy said, "it comes down to money. When Vince's parents passed away, he bought the part of the funeral home from his sister that he didn't inherit. It's Myra's money that enabled him to do that. He became the full owner, he and Myra."

Mary Ruth appeared to be savoring the last bite of chocolate chip cookie in her mouth, but Joy's comment interrupted her reverie. "Is that a fact? I didn't know that."

"It's true," Charlotte said, chiming in. "Myra and Cass are Old Bob's daughters. They sold his business when he died. Old Bob's Bail Bonds and Ice Cream Shop."

They all snickered at that. No one had any idea why the idea of bail bonds and ice cream went together, but the concept seemed to work. The firm had offices in Danville and Brownsburg. In Danville, the county seat, the bail bonds office was located on the square near the courthouse and did a lot of bond business during the week. Old Bob had been very liberal with free ice cream if you bought your bail bonds there, and that little item seemed to have given him the edge over everyone else. "I'll sweeten the deal," he'd say, and he became famous for it.

"What did Cass do with her half of the money?" Francine asked.

The women looked from face to face to face, but none of them seemed to have an answer. Almost simultaneous they all put their teacups to their lips, not knowing what to do next. That made them laugh.

"Maybe she invested it," Joy surmised. "Maybe she's another of Janet Turpen's clients. Does anyone know about Fuzzy's financial condition?"

"I know that teachers don't make a lot of money," Charlotte said. "But Fuzzy's from a farm family. His parents made money selling off parcels of land to developers. But as far as I know, it's still their money. Both of them are still alive."

Francine played off Charlotte's knowledge. "So Fuzzy's money is tied up in his parents' estate. Vince's funeral home may not be profitable if the rumors are true it's for sale, and he needed Myra's money to fully inherit it in any event. Certainly doesn't sound all that prosperous. Tricky Dicky is always going for the type of cheap growth the Council splits over. Camille had money. Is there anything big that all of them are involved in, something for them to tussle over?"

Francine, Charlotte, and Mary Ruth looked at Joy.

Joy examined her sweater. "Do I have something on me?"

"It's because you're the reporter," Francine said. "If anyone would know about something big, it would be you."

She brushed off a few cookie crumbs she discovered were on her sweater. "I haven't heard anything. I'm not sure any of us would have. Wouldn't it need to be something really hush-hush to justify murder? If it were out in the open, murder would be too obvious."

"Would Eric know?" Mary Ruth asked.

"Would he tell us if he did?" Charlotte countered. "He seems to be afraid of something."

"Not some*thing*, some*one*," Francine said. "He's afraid of some-one."

"He's going to feel a lot better if he gets it off his chest," Joy said.

Charlotte popped a last bite of her chocolate chip cookie into her mouth. "Then let's persuade him that we're the right people to tell."

SEVENTEEN

MAYBE THEY FELT BOLD because they were in a group, or maybe it was because they had survived an evening of bingo madness with Tripper the Stripper, or maybe it was because they'd successfully gotten what they'd wanted at the Legion Hall. Whatever the reason, Francine was amazed they'd decided to drive over to Eric's house and confront him to learn the truth.

When they got there and saw the police cruiser in the driveway, the wind went out of their sails.

"Jud," said Charlotte. "Why is he here?"

They sat in the car contemplating their next move.

"Maybe he won't stay long," Francine suggested. "Maybe once we get there, he'll leave. After all, he has a wife and kids to go home to. We'll stay until we get a little bit of time with Eric."

"I'll try to pull Toby aside and explain the situation to him," Mary Ruth said. "He'll help us."

Toby let them in and said Jud and Eric were in the back. "He's questioning Eric. The good news is, I've persuaded Eric to cooperate." He beamed at his grandmother. "I knew you'd be pleased."

He took all their coats and hung them up. "So, what are you here for?"

"We were looking to get a head start on the video," Charlotte said. "We have Joy with us tonight, and you know that she's better than the rest of us with video and writing and all that. So we came to see if we could gather up some of the material tonight."

Toby shrugged. "He may be back there a while."

"We'll wait," Charlotte said. She pushed her way toward the kitchen.

Camille's kitchen was in a galley formation, oblong with a refrigerator, sink, and stove at the shorter end and counter space along the length. A small kitchen island was opposite the counter space, creating a narrow pathway for navigation between the two. There were two barstools on the other side of the island. Mary Ruth took a seat at one of them.

Francine stood, pacing a bit. She was trying to figure out a way to get back to Camille's office. Charlotte's idea that they were here to get a head start on the video resonated with her. She hadn't had a chance to look at the files much the other day. If they were still in the office, why not just take them while Jud and Eric were in the back? She'd return them tomorrow. No harm done. But she needed to get them and then leave before Jud came out.

Charlotte found an electric teakettle and turned it on. When it got hot, she poured the water into a white mug that read *Jacqueline Consulting* and added a tea bag. Joy came around and joined her. She found another mug and did the same. The dark stain of tea spread out in the clear hot liquid. As Francine watched, the word *Jacqueline* on the mug disappeared.

Francine pointed to the mug. "Now it just says *Consulting*."

"What?" Joy asked.

"The mug."

Everyone stared at it. The word *Consulting* disappeared as well.

Francine reached over and ran her hand over the area where the words were. "I can feel the raised letters. Must be one of those trick mugs where words disappear when the mug gets hot."

"Yes, but it's strange that one disappears before the other."

Toby came over to look. "It's the difference in paint. They have two different temperature triggers."

Joy pulled a notebook out of her purse. "What is Jacqueline Consulting, anyway?"

"It was Camille's consulting firm," Francine said.

Joy began to take notes. "I didn't know she had a consulting company. I thought she worked for the cable company."

Toby said, "If I understood Eric right, she did both."

It hit Francine again that they were talking about someone who wouldn't sing, wouldn't laugh, wouldn't enjoy summer or spring or fall, wouldn't watch her nephew dance in a male revue anymore. It made her sad.

Joy paused to chew on the pencil. "This makes me realize I don't know a whole lot about Camille. What else don't I know?"

"What else don't *we* know," Francine amended. "Especially in light of the fact Charlotte and I are supposed to be creating a display for Eric to use." She stared off into the hall. "Do you think they'll be much longer?"

Toby shrugged. "Couldn't say."

Francine decided to take a chance. She knew her fellow Bridge Club members wouldn't rat her out, once they figured out what she was up to. Toby might, but she didn't think he was watching them that closely.

She stood up and self-consciously smoothed her sweater. She walked toward the hall.

"Where are you going?" Toby asked.

"Restroom," she answered. It was just past the office. To be truthful, she'd visit it after a brief stop in the office.

She walked purposefully into the hall and into the office, holding her breath as she got there. The hall took a bend farther down past the restroom, so she knew Jud couldn't see where she was even if the door to Eric's room was open, which she suspected it wasn't. She hoped he hadn't heard her footsteps and come out to investigate. A few long seconds later, there was still no reaction, so she decided she had a least a little bit of time. She ducked into the office.

The laptop computer was gone, as expected, and the files that were on top of it were also gone. Francine hadn't had time to rifle through the file cabinets or desk drawers the day before, but now they were the only things left. She tackled the desk drawers first.

She opened the top drawer a crack. Nothing in there but pens, pencils, erasers, paper clips, and the like. She pulled it open a bit more and found a stash of blank Jacqueline Consulting stationery. She extracted a sheet and folded it into fourths, cramming it into her back pocket.

Next she opened the side drawers. There were two of them. The top one had hanging files. They were tabbed. Francine looked for anything that had to do with business, either Brownsburg, the cable company, or Jacqueline Consulting. She found several that were marked for Brownsburg, but no papers were contained inside. *Thanks a lot, Jud*, she thought.

She opened the bottom side drawer. It was more of a mess, like a drawer where a person saved things they fully expected to organize at some point, but never got around to. She pulled out the chair so she could sit down and not have to bend over to look through it. She found a lot of newspaper clippings. Some had to do with Camille's election, some were about the cable company, and others appeared to be random stories that must have interested her. Francine decided they all revealed something about Camille that could be useful for a display. And perhaps other things. She took an emptied folder from the top drawer and put all the newspaper clippings in it. She closed up the two drawers and moved onto the file cabinet, taking the folder with her. She set it on top of the cabinet.

The file cabinet had three drawers. The first drawer had a lock on it. Francine yanked on the handle several times, but it wouldn't budge. She moved onto the second drawer, which opened easily. If the desk drawer with the newspaper clippings had looked unorganized, this drawer was total chaos. There were no dividers or anything in it, just mounds of photos in a heap at the bottom. Francine sifted through them pretty quickly. They appeared to have been taken over a long period of time. Some were of Camille, but not all. Francine noticed there were some of a girl that looked like Camille, but wasn't her. *Probably her sister*, Francine thought. She knew Camille's sister, Eric's mother, had died many years ago, which was how Eric had originally come to live in Brownsburg. There seemed to be a bunch of those strewn together in the heap.

Not wanting to take time to decide which one would be useful, Francine helped herself to the bunch. She added them to the file and went back to the drawer. More scavenging yielded another batch of photos, this time of a graveyard. Probably not useful for a display, but it got Francine's curiosity up. *Why so many of that particular graveyard?* She added them to the file, thinking Charlotte would be delighted. Back in the drawer she found some recent ones of Camille that could be used for the display—Camille being sworn in;

Camille and a shirtless Eric at a strip club; Camille and Eric hiking in a woods. They were good slice-of-life photos. Francine took of few of those and then opened the bottom drawer.

The bottom drawer was nearly empty. Francine wondered if it had been that way before Jud went through it. It was divided and organized, but did not contain much in the way of display materials or snooping materials. Some mailing supplies, blank notecards sent by nonprofit organizations hoping to spur donations, nothing much. She closed the drawer and tiptoed to the door of the room. She could hear Jud talking, then Eric. Taking a deep breath, she went back to work.

The office had one last thing to search. The bookcase. It was more upright than squat, which was good because Francine could search the top two shelves without having to bend over too much or get down on her knees. *The bottom shelf won't be fun*, she thought.

She perused the top shelf. Lots of business titles like *Who Moved My Cheese?* and Malcom Gladwell books like *Outliers* and *Blink*. She tipped a couple of books back to see if there were any scrap pieces of papers in between, but there were none. She moved onto the second shelf.

The second shelf was more personal. Francine found Camille's three-ring binder from Leadership Hendricks County, a class that trained leaders for service to the county and its communities. Both Francine and Jonathan were graduates. Francine hadn't remembered that Camille had been a student. She checked the date. Camille had only graduated a couple of years ago. It coincided with the year she was elected. *Not surprising*, she thought. Next to the binder was the blank notebook where students were encouraged to write down their thoughts. Francine was interested in Camille's free-thinking. *There might be clues in there as to what got Camille killed.* She added the notebook to her folder.

Francine had just gone down on one knee to examine the bottom shelf when she heard a cough from the door. She looked up and found Jud leaning against the doorframe with his arms crossed. "What are you doing?"

EIGHTEEN

FRANCINE CLUTCHED THE BOOKCASE to steady herself as she got up from the one-knee stance. "Just gathering some materials for the retrospective Charlotte and I are making for Camille's funeral. Eric asked us to do it. We were going to come by tomorrow, but since we had Joy with us this evening, we decided to come tonight. We didn't know you'd be here questioning Eric."

Jud worked his jaw. *He always does that when he's suspicious*, Francine thought.

"I wasn't questioning him as much as we were just talking. We were high school friends, remember?" He righted himself and walked into the room. "Can I see what you've got?" His casual shoes made a very soft sound that reminded Francine of her cat padding across the floor. No wonder he'd been able to sneak up on her.

"Sure." She backed up a few steps to the file cabinet and handed him the folder, now thicker because of the Leadership notebook. He began to flip through it.

Charlotte clomped into the room, her orthopedic shoes making a clacking sound on the floor. "I don't see how you could object to her taking what she's collected," Charlotte said. "I'm sure you've been through here and taken out everything that's useful to your investigation."

Francine was grateful she'd been watching and had come to help, but given that Charlotte chafed on most people, especially the police, she wasn't sure how much help she might be.

Jud glanced through the items she'd collected. "I understand you were at the Legion tonight," he said. "What were you doing there? Investigating?"

"We were playing bingo," Charlotte answered. "You are so suspicious."

"And you are so transparent," he answered. "You don't usually go to bingo. Not all together."

"How would you know?" Charlotte asked.

"Maybe we have a secret Sixty List item that involves bingo," Joy said.

They were saved by Eric, Joy, Mary Ruth, and Toby all coming into the room.

"Eric," Charlotte said, "please tell Jud that you have asked us to put something together about your aunt for the funeral."

Eric nodded. "It's true."

Francine worked the pretense. "We stopped by to get some photos and source material tonight since we had Joy with us. Do you mind if we take those, Eric?" She pointed to the folder Jud now held open. She appealed to Eric in the hopes Jud would be more amenable that way.

"It's okay with me if it's okay with Jud," Eric said.

Francine tried not to look like she was holding her breath, even though she was.

"C'mon, Jud," Charlotte said. "Your men have already looked through here. And you'll know where to find them if you need them."

Jud seemed to make a decision, but hesitantly. "Go ahead."

They beat a hasty retreat, gathered their coats, and left.

———

They all went back to Charlotte's house. They looked through the photos, but it was close to ten o'clock and they weren't coming up with anything but more questions, especially the photos taken in a graveyard. There seemed to be a significant number of them. Eventually they called it a night.

Francine returned home and went upstairs to the bedroom. Jonathan was still up. She expected that he'd heard about the incident at the bingo and maybe the confrontation with Jud. She thought maybe he'd give her grief. Instead he spread a computer printout on the comforter and pointed to it like he expected Francine to applaud him.

She examined what he'd brought. It looked like a Quicken summary of someone's financial situation. "What is that, and where did you get it?"

"Camille's records for last year. She gave them to the firm to use for taxes."

Francine felt her heart beat a little faster. She bent over the first page as though it were a clue-laden document. "Isn't it illegal for you to have it?"

"No. Camille gave it to us. I was pretty sure my partner was her tax accountant. Turns out I was right. We gave a copy of this to the police. Since we still need it to finish our task of preparing her taxes, it's okay."

"So this is all in the name of helping your partner out."

"In a manner of speaking. And helping us out."

"Us?"

He gave her a look that said not to ask too many questions.

Francine lifted the page she was looking at. She had hoped something would jump out at her. "It's a lot of data," she said.

"It's an itemized list of every transaction from her bank accounts. The one you're looking at is her business account for Jacqueline Consulting."

Knowing what it was allowed her to make some sense of the entries. She scanned the list for names she recognized. There were monthly payments to all the expected entities, like the gas company, electric company, cable company. "She must be using a home office deduction."

"My understanding is that she did much of her work at home, even for the cable company."

Francine hadn't known that. She wondered if Charlotte did. Living next door, she would have observed that Camille stayed home much of the time. She gathered up the next few sheets, trying to keep them in order. "Her income varies a lot from month to month."

"That's to be expected. She was dependent on when projects came in and how big they were, not to mention when clients paid."

"You know all about getting clients to pay."

"Oh, yes." Jonathan said it with the weight of truth. "Even the best clients have to be reminded from time to time about payments due."

Francine remembered the early years in their marriage when Jonathan was just getting his company started. Her steady income as a nurse had been critical to their financial stability. Now, decades later, his firm was established and had operating capital. He drew a regular paycheck. The company absorbed the month-to-month variability.

After letting her flip back and forth among the printed sheets, Jonathan got close so he could look over her shoulder. "Here," he said, pointing. "Do you see that she had some steady clients as well?"

Francine didn't recognize the company names but she did recognize the monthly numbers. "Jonathan, those are the same figures I saw in folders at Camille's house before Jud took them. I don't know how they link to who paid them, but she had these same amounts listed for Tricky Dicky and Vince."

"Which ones?"

She pointed to the $916.67 figures. "I remember them because they weren't rounded up." She looked into his face and could see his puzzlement.

"In what context did you see them?" he asked.

"Dick's amount was listed under Lizton State Bank. Vince's was listed at Old National. She had a file on Janet Tarpen, too, but all I could see in that file were records about some potential land deal at the Ronald Reagan Parkway interchange at I-74."

"Janet's had no numbers or bank accounts referenced?"

She shook her head. "Janet's file was more like a report or a memo. The files for Vince and Dick were slim, and the only records inside had those numbers."

"Let me see if I can trace those companies tomorrow."

She studied him. "Why are you doing this?"

"The sooner someone solves this, the better I'll feel."

Francine inferred that he was worried about her. There had been some close calls in the past year.

She sat on the edge of the bed. "What consulting work did she do for Dick and Vince? Would the firm have any idea? It surprises me that they would trust business to her, as much animosity as there was between them."

"There isn't a business these days that doesn't gain an advantage by having the latest and greatest tech tools for their industry. And they knew her. Better the enemy you know?"

"I suppose they could have been frenemies," Francine said. "But Camille certainly upset their lives with her coup of the Council."

"She did," he said. "The question is why she died. Was it the coup—the takeover of the Council by her and Janet and Fuzzy—or was it something else?"

The house phone rang. Francine and Jonathan had an extension in their bedroom. Jonathan was closest, so he walked over and glanced at it to see who was calling. "Charlotte."

"This late?"

He shrugged.

"Well, as Mary Ruth said to me, 'she has the scent of a killer in her nostrils.' I'm sure that's what's keeping her going."

"You should probably answer it."

"What took you so long?" Charlotte could sound really snippy when she wanted to.

Francine glanced at the clock on the nightstand, its digital numbers glowing green. "It's close to eleven o'clock. Jonathan and I are getting ready for bed."

Charlotte continued as though Francine hadn't said anything at all. "You should know I found out that Tricky Dicky is representing Fuzzy in a real estate transaction."

"Selling farmland for some kind of commercial development?"

"Exactly. It's in the area where the new I-74 interchange just got developed."

"At the Ronald Reagan Parkway?" The location made Francine do a mental double-take. Camille had a file on Janet Tarpen that also related to that interchange. She knew Fuzzy had some land in that area. Fuzzy's ex-wife had managed to get hold of the old Carter homestead as a result of the divorce settlement, something everyone knew always rankled Fuzzy. Her property was one of the things blocking full development of the site. It was adjacent to Fuzzy's farmland at the north end, and she refused to sell. It couldn't stop Fuzzy from selling what he had, though. But what was Dick doing representing Fuzzy?

"Yes, at the Ronald Reagan. How many new interchanges with I-74 are there in the Brownsburg area?"

"But how is any of that related to Camille's death?"

"I don't know that it is. But Toby told Mary Ruth who told me that Eric had lunch with Dick at Bob Evans a couple of days before the benefit."

Francine paused to digest that. "When did Mary Ruth tell you that?"

"A little while ago. I've been on the phone with her too."

Francine was more than a little annoyed that Mary Ruth had somehow forgot to mention it. But maybe she hadn't regarded it as important.

"Even if they did, how is that related to Camille's death?"

"Don't know. But we're going to get the chance to ask Tricky Dicky tomorrow morning. I'm arranging for us to see the land."

"We're not developers."

"Oh, forgot to mention—he's also selling a five-acre parcel across the street. It butts up against the old farmstead his ex-wife Cass owns. That's what we're going to see."

Francine was certain she wasn't going to be the one misleading Dick. "I didn't know you were interested in acquiring land for a new home."

"Ever since you began building a vacation home on those three hundred acres you inherited in Parke County, I've been insanely jealous. Haven't you noticed?"

"You've been hiding it well," Francine said drily.

"Look, just get some sleep and get over here tomorrow. We've got lots to do, what with figuring out where this graveyard is Camille had lots of photos of."

"You think you can figure out which cemetery it is?"

"You'll have to come over to see."

NINETEEN

FRANCINE HAD NO IDEA how Charlotte had managed to set up an appointment with Dick, late as it had been the night before, but she didn't ask too many questions. As it was, the appointment was near lunchtime. That meant they were able to get an early start on the display boards using the material they'd nabbed at Eric's. Despite the promise to tell her about the cemetery, Charlotte made Francine wait until after they had a mid-morning snack break.

"Let's be civilized about this," Charlotte insisted. "No discussing business over food."

"That's not like you."

"More coffee?"

"I'll switch to tea. I try to limit myself to no more than one shot of cognac in the morning."

"Since when?"

"Since you started adding it to the coffee."

Francine clipped another article from the *Hendricks County Flyer* and put it in a preliminary location on the white poster board she was working on. Charlotte had obtained three of them, and she and

Francine had tentatively planned them for "The Early Years," "Midlife," and "Recent." Francine was working on Midlife.

"I don't know if this will work," Francine told Charlotte. "I can't find much in the way of Midlife. This whole board is skewing toward Late Midlife. Are you sure you won't let me look through the pictures?"

"Nope. The cemetery pictures are in there. I don't want you to see those until later."

Charlotte was in the kitchen slicing up orange cranberry tea bread. She wore a red and white *Kiss the Cook* apron over her blue Indianapolis Colts sweatshirt and elastic waist jeans. Francine thought it was appropriate the jeans were elastic waist. She considered that maybe she should have worn hers. She'd done an awful lot of eating lately without much exercise.

Charlotte put the bread knife down and came over to see the poster board. "What article has you concerned?"

"This one." Francine showed her the clipping. "It's only ten years old but it's about the oldest one I can find that doesn't go back to her teen years. It was when she was involved in helping the police bust a child pornographer."

Charlotte tilted her head. "I knew about it, but only in a general sense. It was ten years ago?"

"She had been working for the cable company for quite a while back then."

Charlotte scanned the article. "She monitored the public WiFi at a coffee shop and found the guy downloading porn and reported it. What was she doing monitoring the WiFi?"

"The article doesn't say, but that was in the early days of public WiFi. It wasn't so widespread then, and some places charged for it. The owners of that coffee shop go to our church. I'm willing to bet they wanted to make sure it was being used for legitimate purposes."

"I miss that place. They just couldn't compete when Starbucks moved in right down the street."

Francine remembered the coffee shop. It was in a strip mall along Northridge Drive. Starbucks built just west of the strip mall, where it had more visibility from State Road 267, known locally as Green Street. The Starbucks name brought in a lot of traffic, and being that close, it drove the the local shop out of business. Francine thought they could have made it if they'd served better coffee, had free WiFi, and paid more attention to the ambiance. It had been a narrow, sterile place with stainless steel tables and chairs.

"A lot of Brownsburg public officials used to congregate there in the mornings when it was the only game in town."

Charlotte nodded. "I remember seeing Tricky Dicky oozing his homespun charm trying to put together real estate deals on the cheap. And boy, were they cheap. Dollar and Less is hardly a desired grocery store."

Francine laughed. "I wonder what beauties Camille would have found on *his* WiFi."

The two of them stopped laughing as the words sunk in. Then Francine held up a hand. "Let's not go there. Dick is hardly a techie. I doubt he would have been using WiFi back then. And he was cheap enough he certainly wouldn't have paid for it."

"They gave out the security password when you bought a drink, remember? So technically, it was free. He was cheap, but he always bought coffee."

The teakettle sang and Charlotte hurried to take it off the stove. She pulled out a selection of teas and let Francine choose one while she poured water in a mug.

Francine selected a black Oolong tea and tossed it into the mug to steep. She began to sort through the articles again. "Camille started her consulting business six months after the FBI made the porn arrest."

"Do you think the two are related?"

"Maybe. Not sure it means anything."

Francine carefully put double-stick tape on the back of the articles and secured them to the poster board. She had left space where she could put a few photos, when and if Charlotte would ever let her look at them.

Charlotte turned her back to Francine and took hold of the bread knife again. She had a chocolate zucchini tea bread yet to slice. While Charlotte's attention was diverted, Francine thought she might be able to check the photos.

The two were working on Charlotte's rectangular kitchen table, a solid maple Tell City product, and Charlotte had placed the stack of photos on her side in the corner farthest from Francine. But being a tall person with long arms, Francine had a good wingspan.

"I see you eyeing those photos," Charlotte said. "No peeking."

Francine snatched them anyway.

Charlotte trotted to the table with the two sliced mini loaves. "Put down the photos and slide your poster over so we can sit."

"How did you know I was going for them?"

"Easy. First, you got too quiet, and second, you were doing exactly what I would have done, only about a minute later."

Francine took two paper napkins from the dispenser and put them next to their plates. Charlotte took a seat at the corner Francine had cleared. Francine took the chair opposite her.

Charlotte sipped her tea. "I really needed something warm. It's cold enough outside to freeze Eric Dehoney's sexy body, and that boy is hot, hot, hot."

Francine deliberately rolled her eyes in front of Charlotte. There were certain phrases Charlotte would say that sounded rehearsed, like she'd be thinking of them for a long time and worked hard at concocting some kind of opening to use them. "You've been waiting for a tea break so you could use that line, haven't you?"

"Not necessarily. If you'd have gone for the second coffee with cognac, I would have used it then too."

Francine took a few sips and declared, "Done! I can look at the photos now."

She began to paw through them. Charlotte had placed the photos in chronological order with the cemetery photos at the end. Francine presumed it was because there was no way to date them.

In some ways, the photos were a disappointment. There were no closeups, no marked graves to go by. By anyone's standards, the cemetery was unkempt. Weeds and overgrown grasses obstructed any serious view.

"Got any ideas as to where this cemetery is?" Francine asked.

Charlotte sat back in the wooden dining chair and wrinkled her forehead. "Not a clue. It's got to be a private cemetery, because it's so overgrown. But it could be anywhere."

"There aren't any signs, either. I wonder why there are so many photos of the cemetery but none of the actual graves. I feel like the point of being at a cemetery is because of who's there."

"You're not looking close enough," Charlotte said. She dabbed her fingers on the napkin and pointed at a photo without touching it. "The photos are taken from different angles, but this one grave is in every photo."

Francine laid out the photos in a group next to her plate. "That's why you're a good detective. I would never have noticed. I was still trying to get my bearings."

"The gravestone on that one is particularly hidden from view. Even in the photos that are close, you can see how thick the rose bushes are. It looks like they were originally planted on the side of the tombstone but have grown up to surround it.

"Are you certain they're roses?"

"Fairly. And it provides me a clue as to what time of year the photo was taken. Late spring, probably April. The buds were out but they hadn't bloomed yet."

"I'm sorry, Charlotte, but you acted like these photos were going to be a source of major clues. I'm let down. Unless there's something you're not telling me."

Charlotte checked her watch. "Look at the time!" She licked her finger and used it to accumulate the crumbs of cranberry orange bread from her plate. "Think that'll hold you until lunch?"

Francine took a bite of the chocolate zucchini bread. "I should think so."

"Good. Let's go meet Tricky Dicky and see this five-acre property he's selling."

———

Francine drove to a part of Brownsburg near the border with Boone County. Land this far north wasn't actually in the Town of Browns-burg but rather in Brown Township. Most of the land was agricultural, and most of the houses were farmhouses that dated back to the early or mid-1900s. Any houses less than twenty years old were on large lots carved out of the farmland along county roads. Charlotte directed Francine to the place she'd agreed to meet Tricky Dicky, which turned out to be Cass Carter's driveway.

Francine pulled up on the concrete driveway. She stayed to the right. "What are we doing here? Why are we not meeting at the property you supposedly want to buy?"

"I think because the property in question may not have a driveway." Charlotte got out of the car. She wandered in front of it, walking over to the left side of Cass's driveway. "I think it might be where that For Sale sign is." She pointed to a large wooden sign painted white. Because it was angled so it was readable from the road, they couldn't see the letters from where the car was parked.

Francine got out and joined Charlotte. She turned up the collar on her coat to protect her neck from the freezing wind. "How do you know it's a For Sale sign?"

"I don't. But what else could it be?"

A white Cadillac came roaring down the street toward them from the direction of the sign. "That's Tricky Dicky's car," Charlotte said. "You have to help me remember not to call him Tricky Dicky."

"How am I going to stop you from doing that? I have trouble remembering myself."

The Caddy passed the sign, slowed down, and then eased into the driveway, allowing the two women to move to the side of the concrete for safety.

Dick got out. He was a self-important man, with a big belly and diamond-encrusted pinky rings on both hands. Jonathan joked that at Dick's funeral there would be handouts that read, "You can buy this coffin and gravesite for less money than a new car!"

"Hello, ladies," he called out, the wind making little ripples of the skin across his fat jowls. "Francine McNamara, I didn't know you were going to be here. Are you also interested in some land?"

"No, Dick, I'm just here to help Charlotte consider new locations for a home. Jonathan and I have our hands full with the land out in Parke County."

"I heard you inherited a big bunch of acreage out there. You interested in selling any of it off?"

Before Francine could answer, Charlotte said, "It's too cold for chitchat, Dick. Let's get down to business. Where's this land Fuzzy's selling?"

"Right there," he said. "Where that sign is."

"Five acres, you were telling me? I guess I don't know how big five acres is."

"That plot of land goes from the property line here with Cass Carter's house out to where that tree is down the road." He pointed in the same direction as the sign.

"So it goes to the edge of that field?" Charlotte pointed to a field that had been harvested in the fall. You could still see where the rows of soybeans had been.

"Yep. That's it. And the end is along the fence row."

Francine thought it looked rather barren.

"It doesn't have any trees?" Charlotte asked.

"Well, it includes that tree at the end of the field, and there are a few trees along the fence."

"Those are scrub trees, Dick. I want some kind of wooded lot. And maybe five acres is too small." She had a mischievous smile on her face.

"How much are you interested in?" Dick asked.

"Well, let me think." She looked admiringly at Cass Carter's house. "What about this one? How many acres come with this property?"

"Seventy. But it's not for sale. Boy, do I know that. We could get a lot of money for it with the development that's proposed for this area."

"Suppose I just want ten of it. Cass Carter doesn't need that much. I hear she's hired a cleaning lady to come in once a week to do the house, and she rents out fifty acres to one of those organic farmers. She got any wooded acres?"

Tricky Dicky's eyes shifted back and forth like he was formulating a plan. "I don't represent her, so I don't know. But Fuzzy's got some land that might suit you. It's not for sale that I know of, but at the right price, it might be."

Charlotte frowned. "I won't be taken to the cleaner's, Dick. Does it have some woods?"

"Nice woods, and about eight acres."

"Sounds nearly perfect."

"I have to warn you, though, it borders on a cemetery."

Francine and Charlotte looked at each other.

"Even better," Charlotte said. "How soon can we look at it?"

TWENTY

TRICKY DICKY HEMMED AND hawed a bit like he was running things through his mind.

Charlotte marched up to him. Dick wore a thick cable knit sweater under an unbuttoned long leather coat, his stomach stretching the sweater over the waistline of too-tight blue jeans. Charlotte, though a little round herself, looked diminutive next to Dick's bulk. She poked his stomach. "It's too cold to stand out here while you make a decision. Why don't you show me this property, and then if I like it, you can see if Fuzzy will sell it."

Dick seemed to make a decision. He rubbed his hands together, the pinky rings clacking when they met. "You've got me there, Ms. Charlotte. If the two of you want to get in my car, I'll drive you out there and you can take a look at it."

Charlotte didn't need a second invitation. She took Francine by the arm and steered her toward Dick's car. The motor was still running, and when they opened the back door, the heater blasted warm air on their faces.

"That feels good," Charlotte told her. "Why don't you ever keep your car this warm?"

"I'm just a conservationist at heart."

They slid into the back seat. Tricky Dicky heaved himself into the driver's seat, which was pushed way back to accommodate his expanded waist.

"Good thing you're behind him and not me," Francine mouthed to Charlotte. The passenger seat was scooted almost all the way forward, which allowed her to stretch out her legs. Charlotte, who was a good half foot shorter, had only a couple of inches of leg room thanks to Dick's seat position.

Dick burped. "Indigestion, sorry. I probably shouldn't have had a sack of White Castle egg and cheese sliders for breakfast." He forced a series of small burps, then got himself settled and put the car in gear. "Hold on, ladies. We'll be there in no time."

Charlotte tapped him on the shoulder. "Where is this acreage? Is it still in Hendricks County? I've heard bad things about trying to get permits to build in Boone County."

"Relax," he said, directing his comments back at her. "It's in Hendricks. It's on the next road running north-south. Just around the corner, really."

"Sounds good."

"It's on the east side of Cass's property. Fuzzy managed to hang on to the land around her in the divorce settlement, just to torment her." He tried to chuckle but it seemed to pain him to do that. He pounded his chest a few times with his fist. It made him cough like he had phlegm in his throat.

"I hope he doesn't cough up a loogie," Charlotte whispered to Francine.

Francine darted her eyes toward the rearview mirror. "He can see you," she mouthed back. Charlotte looked up at it in alarm, but she must not have detected him catching her because her expression relaxed immediately. She gave a slight shrug of her shoulders.

"How long have you been lookin' for land, Charlotte?" Dick said. "I haven't heard anything about it, and I hear just about everything that goes on around here. In real estate terms," he added.

Charlotte looked out the window as though she was finding creative license in the great outdoors. "I just started actively looking. Decided I shouldn't wait any longer to find a more stable investment than the stock market. It's been up and down lately."

"Down mostly," he replied "Land would be a good investment. You trying to set anyone up for an inheritance? I didn't think you had children."

"Only two things I cannot stand," Charlotte said in her best W.C. Fields impression, "dogs and little kids." She twitched her fingers to enhance the imitation.

"So who would you be leaving it to?" he asked.

"Possibly Francine. She's my best friend. And she's got kids. But I hope I'm not leaving God's good earth anytime soon."

"You'll be here for a long time," Francine said confidently. At least, she hoped so. Francine made her tea nearly every day using water from the special Parke County spring.

Tricky Dicky slowed the car and pulled onto a dirt road that ran perpendicular to the county road they'd been on. The private road had huge ruts reminiscent of what might be left over when a big harvester was using the road repeatedly in the rain. He drove slowly for about a quarter mile then put the car in park.

The area was remote in a sparsely populated part of the county. There were woods to the right and to the left with a wide path in between, big enough for a farm machine to use. If a murderer wanted to knock someone off, Francine reflected with alarm, this is where he would do it.

"I hope you're not thinking of doing away with us, Dick," Charlotte said. "Because it's kind of scary here in the woods."

"You're hardly Little Red Riding Hood," Dick said. "And I'm not the Big Bad Wolf."

I don't know, Francine thought. *He has a big snout. The better to smell you with, my dear.*

Charlotte kept staring into the woods on her side of the car. "Let's get out," she said.

Francine hesitated. Charlotte noticed it.

"Before it clouds up, while there's still good sunlight," she added. "And we can see the cemetery from here." She nudged Francine so Dick couldn't see.

"The cemetery, yes." Francine brightened. She opened the door. "Where is it from here?"

"It's on my side." The two women got out.

Dick snapped open his door. "The cemetery is not on the property you're buying."

"I never said I was buying it," Charlotte answered.

"Interested in buying then. You still can't go over there."

"Just trying to be neighborly. If anyone objects, I'll come back to the car."

Tricky Dicky swiveled in the front seat and pried himself out. "But it's not your property. It belongs to Cass Carter."

The cemetery was shrouded in the shadows of the trees. Francine could see headstones when slim beams of sunlight shined through the naked branches, but the canopy was dense. Some of the headstones looked to be rustic and weathered, like they'd been there a century or more. She assumed it was the family cemetery for the Carters, who'd been in the county practically since Indiana became a state.

Charlotte almost dared Dick to chase her through the forest. "If Cass objects," she said, already walking toward the cemetery at a good pace, "I'll come back. Trust me."

Dick staggered to his feet. "I don't trust you any farther than I can throw you. And that's not much anymore." He gave a loud burp. "This indigestion is killing me."

Francine watched Dick with alarm. He started toward Charlotte, then clutched his chest. He backed up a step and pulled a handkerchief out of his back pocket. He mopped his brow where beads of perspiration formed at his hairline. "I feel dizzy," Dick told Francine.

It's freezing out here, and he's sweating. She knew what that meant. "Dick, I think you better sit down."

Charlotte, oblivious to Dick's distress, was making good progress across the rutted pathway between the two properties. *Of all the time for her to show off the progress she's making with her knee.* Francine would have felt proud of her alchemy except for Dick's pale face and the shallowness of his breath.

"Charlotte!" Francine called. "That's not the best idea right now."

Charlotte held up a dismissive hand, not even turning around to look. "Nonsense. I mean, really, who's going to object?"

"If… if… Cass catches you on the property…" Dick wheezed, "she'll… she'll…" He fell to his knees. "Kill you." He croaked out the last words, put his hands out to brace his fall, and dropped over cheek first into the dirt, his closed eyes facing at Francine.

Francine rushed over. "Damn! Of all the times for you to have a heart attack, Dick Raden." She tried to flip him over but he was too heavy and too unresponsive. She patted his cheek. "Dick! Dick!" His eye lids fluttered, but he didn't seem to be registering.

"Charlotte," she yelled, "Dick's had a heart attack! I need your help!"

———

Charlotte paced while talking on her cell phone with the Hendricks County Communications Center. "I'm telling you, I have a retired nurse working on him and she says he had a heart attack. What more do you possibly need to know? Just send out an ambulance as fast as you can." She paused to listen. "Yes, I'll stay on the line until someone gets here."

Charlotte finally stopped pacing and stood on the other side of Dick. The two women had managed to get him onto his back. They'd found several blankets in the trunk of his car. Francine had fashioned a pillow by wadding up one of the bigger ones and with the rest covered Dick as best she could. Having detected a rapid, erratic heart rate, Francine had unbuttoned the top few buttons of his shirt. When the heart rate dropped to practically nothing, she'd begun performing chest compressions, which she was still doing. "You're sure I can't go over there?" Charlotte asked. "That looks exactly like the cemetery in the photos."

Francine was too busy to respond. She was angry anyway, because she was doing everything she could to keep Dick alive, and all Charlotte wanted to do was play detective.

Charlotte put her ear back to the phone. "Yes, I'm still here. No, I'm not the nurse. She'd talk to you but she's kind of busy trying to keep the victim alive right now."

"What do they need to know?" Francine asked.

"Just a minute, Francine." She listened to the dispatcher. "Yes, I searched his pockets and the car for nitroglycerin pills. I couldn't find any.

"You want me to ask her what?" Charlotte paused. "What? Under the best of circumstances I can't hear very well on this cell phone and we are out in the middle of nowhere with the wind whistling in my ears. You're going to have to speak distinctly or I will *not* be able to understand you. And why can't you just send an ambulance anyway? Oh, one's coming from Whitestown? That's the most sensible thing you've said since we started talking."

"Charlotte!" Francine said it sharply to get her attention. "Do you know how to do chest compressions? Because I could use some relief here."

"No, I don't. He's not going to die, is he, Francine?"

"He may already be dead. What I'm doing may be useless. We need the paramedics here as quickly as possible."

Charlotte covered the cell phone with her hand like it was a landline telephone and she could cover up the speaker. "This is going to ruin our chances of finding out whose gravestone that is in the picture, isn't it?"

"It is so wrong for you to be asking that question right now I'm not even going to answer it." She continued with her compressions.

"Is he going to remember any of this?"

"You mean before or after the heart attack?"

"Before. Did I really cause it? Because I don't like the idea that he's going to accuse me of anything."

"You didn't hear his last words before he fell."

"What were they?"

"Something to the effect that if Cass Carter caught you in the cemetery, she'd kill you."

"Really? He said that?"

"Yes."

Charlotte worked her mouth. "Do you hear sirens, Francine?"

"I wish I did, because then I'd know the paramedics would get here soon."

But the first vehicle with sirens to arrive was not an ambulance, it was Jud's police car. Fortunately, the ambulance was right on its tail.

TWENTY-ONE

THE PARAMEDICS ASSESSED THE situation and took over compressions from Francine. They loaded him in the ambulance and left for the hospital. Francine's hands were freezing and she got in Dick's car. The motor was still running, and the heater was still pumping out warm air. She shut the driver's door behind her and adjusted the air vent so it blasted her face. She held her hands in the stream of warmth to defrost them.

Jud shuttled Charlotte to Dick's car and had her get in the passenger side. He climbed in the back seat. When they were comfortable, Jud got out his ever-present notepad. "How is it that I find the two of you out here in the middle of nowhere with one of Camille's outspoken opponents on the Council having a heart attack?" he asked.

"How is it that you arrived here first?" Charlotte asked, countering.

"I have friends in the Dispatch center. They alert me whenever one of your names comes across their desk. In this case, both of them did. It was like hitting on a coverall bingo."

Francine didn't want to think about what happened after the last coverall bingo she'd been to. She rubbed her hands together and

186

flexed her fingers, trying to get her circulation back. "Charlotte is interested in purchasing some land. Dick was showing it to us."

Jud regarded Charlotte with suspicion. "You would move to a remote area of Hendricks County at your age, with no one around you to spy on or interrogate?"

"Who said I would move here? Maybe I just want to buy the property for investment purposes."

Jud dismissed the comment. "And while we're talking about coincidences, how about the coincidence that you are looking at purchasing some of Fuzzy Carter's land, and he just happens to be another suspect in this case?"

Charlotte sighed noisily. "That land over there," she said, pointing to their left, "belongs to Cass, not Fuzzy."

"Let's get to the point. Why are you here?"

"We didn't force Tricky Dicky to drive us here, and we didn't force him to have a heart attack," Charlotte said. "He was in the process of showing us the land when he suddenly went into cardiac arrest. He probably shouldn't have had that sackful of White Castle egg and cheese sliders for breakfast. And before you ask, we didn't force feed him the White Castles, either."

"I'm sure he ate those willingly." Jud put the notebook on the seat beside him and crossed his arms. He was wearing a warm, thick Brownsburg police jacket and he had to work at getting one arm to fold over the other. "I think it's time we talked about what you know about Camille's death."

Francine made eye contact with Charlotte, urging her to cooperate. Charlotte's stone-faced expression told Francine that it would not come easy. "What if we drove Dick's car back to Cass's house, picked up my car, and returned to Charlotte's house? We could talk there. Because Dick's car is going to run out of gas soon, and I don't want to be responsible for having it stranded here."

"Not to mention that we need to keep working on the display for Camille's funeral. It's tomorrow," Charlotte added.

Jud gathered his notebook. "Yet you somehow took time out from that very important task to come look at property with Dick Raden. Yep, I look forward to hearing why that is."

Despite Francine's offer to drive Dick's car back, Jud made them turn it off and leave it there. He drove them back to Cass Carter's driveway, where Charlotte's car had been parked, and then followed them home from there.

"Let me do the talking," Charlotte said as soon as they were en route.

"No problem. You're the one who arranged for the near-fatal real estate showing with Tricky Dicky."

Jud was quick to follow them inside Charlotte's house. Francine took him by the arm and led him to the dining room table while Charlotte hung up their coats. Charlotte asked Francine to show Jud the progress they'd been making on the three storyboards about Camille's life. Francine hoped it might help demonstrate their contention they weren't really investigating her murder, even though they were.

"So, as I'm sure Francine has been telling you," Charlotte announced triumphantly as she entered the dining area after hanging the coats, "we've divided Camille's life into three sections. Her early life, the middle years, and recent past." She pointed to each of them. Jud didn't seem at first like he was going to look at them. He'd come in with his notebook and opened it up, but something caught his attention in the photos they'd posted on the first board.

"Where did you get these photos?" he asked.

Charlotte, for having said she'd do the talking, turned to Francine. "I think Francine got them from Eric." She made a rolling motion with her hand to indicate Francine should elaborate.

Francine took a deep breath and plunged headlong into a defense. "You were there when I took them out of the house, Jud. Eric said it was okay. When Eric asked us to put this together, we knew we'd need to look through Camille's files. It's not like any of us would keep photos or articles about a neighbor."

Jud held up his hand. "It's okay, it's okay! I'm not saying you did anything wrong. I just wondered where they came from."

Charlotte must have caught his interest in the early photos because she indicated them with her hand, even though that poster was farthest away from her. "Are there any in particular you want more information about?"

"Not at all," Jud said. "It's just that I don't know much about her. She lived here in Brownsburg all her life, didn't she?" He took out his cell phone and snapped a photo of each of the storyboards.

Charlotte was quick to answer. "For the most part, yes. She did spend summers with a favorite aunt up in the Chicago area while she was growing up."

"I didn't know that," Francine said, annoyed that Charlotte had seemingly withheld information from her. "That must be where this photo was taken." She touched a picture on the first storyboard, which Charlotte had put together. The black-and-white photo featured a chubby young woman in a one-piece bathing suit standing by a Tastee-Freez stand holding an ice-cream cone. The smooth and creamy soft-serve was piled on top.

Jud nodded. "Is Tastee-Freez like a Dairy Queen?"

"Only better," Charlotte said. "I used to love their banana splits. At one time there were a lot of them in the Chicago area. I think there might be one or two left still."

Something about the photo bothered Francine. She got up close to the board and adjusted her glasses to get a closer look at the figure. "Are you sure that's Camille? It doesn't look like Camille to me."

Charlotte moved in for a closer look. "I'm pretty sure it's just because she was a lot younger then. We all looked different when we were that young."

"Maybe," Francine said.

Charlotte gave it one more cursory glance. "Who else would it be?"

The three of them stared at it for a few seconds, but no one appeared to have any better idea. Finally Jud asked, "Do you know where that stand was?"

"No. It looks like every other Tastee-Freez I remember."

"Just curious." He moved on to the second board, the one Francine had been working on. "I hadn't seen this article on her helping catch the child pornographer. Interesting."

Charlotte perked up. "What do you know about her consulting business, Jud? Anything?"

"It was profitable. She didn't have a big list of clients, but she made good money from it."

"Define 'good money,'" Charlotte said.

"Good enough to pay the expenses and make a profit."

"I imagine the expenses couldn't have been too great, what with it being mainly consulting. Intelligence business, you know."

"Are you getting at something?"

Charlotte reacted like he was accusing her of meddling in the affairs of the Police Department. Which, of course, she was. Francine had to suppress a smile. "Not at all, I was just trying to get an idea of scale. You know, how much she might have been worth."

"And how is that relevant to creating this retrospective of her life?"

Charlotte put her hands on her hips. "Okay, Jud. Let me just be totally honest here."

"It might be a first for you. You might find you like it."

She sputtered. "We—that is, Francine and I—have it on good authority that she was worth somewhere around two million. I'm looking for some kind of confirmation here."

"She lived next door to you for fifteen or more years, and you never had a clue how much she might be worth?"

Charlotte seized on that bit of information. "So you're confirming she was a millionaire two times over?"

"Not at all. You'll have to find that out for yourself."

Give Charlotte a breather, Francine thought. *Maybe it will help her calm down.* "Perhaps you can provide some information on a question I've been having that has nothing to do with the investigation," she said. "At least I don't think it does."

He turned to her. "Go ahead."

"Why is her business named Jacqueline Consulting?"

He stroked his chin. "I can be honest. We don't know."

Francine used her fingers to enumerate some points. "Her middle name is Josephine. I checked that. I found a family tree in her Bible. There were no relatives that I could see that had the name Jacqueline. And to the best of my knowledge, she never married."

Jud leaned against the table in thought, but his weight started to move it backwards. He straightened up. "Jacqueline is kind of an old-fashioned name, isn't it? I can't remember the last time I came across someone named that."

"It was popular in the sixties. Jacqueline Kennedy. She was the first lady when John F. Kennedy was president."

"Well, yes, but that was way before my time."

"Surely not," Charlotte interjected. "She married Aristotle Onassis and was Jacqueline Kennedy Onassis for decades after that. I bet you were alive then."

He whipped out his cell phone and punched in a few things. "She died in 1994. I was still in elementary school." He flashed the phone at her. "See?"

She didn't check to make sure. She looked at Francine. "Has it been that long, really?"

"I'm terrible at estimating how long ago something happened," Francine said, raising her hands palms up. "Everything seems like it was just a few years ago, and then I discover it was more than a decade."

Charlotte became dismissive. "I stand corrected."

Satisfied, Jud returned to perusing the middle board. "I see you've put some articles on here about Eric."

"There wasn't a lot of information she'd kept on her middle years," Francine said. "She mostly saved clippings about Eric's high school years. I decided to use one or two. She was clearly proud of him."

Jud smiled. "Those were good days. At first he wasn't close friends with Chad and me, but there's nothing quite like high school football to bring everyone together. I remember that Camille was at every game."

Francine could appreciate the memories. She had them too. "He was more like her son than her nephew."

Charlotte said, "He was young when he moved here. Second half of eighth grade, maybe. He needed someone and she'd been alone most of her life. They bonded tightly."

"Until first part of senior year, at least." Jud said it matter-of-factly and continued on to the third storyboard.

"Wait." Francine held up a finger. "What do you mean about senior year? I don't recall anything happening senior year."

"Eric got a little weird. He turned eighteen in September. Not that I think any of you adults noticed, but Camille did. He pulled away. Got a bit of swagger to his attitude."

"You all got a bit of swagger that year. You won conference and regional and went to state."

"It was different with Eric. We all thought there was something going on he wouldn't talk about. We suspected it had to do with a girl."

Francine frowned. That jibed with what her son Chad had told her only a few days before. "Like he was having relations with her?"

Jud snorted. "Relations?" He raised an eyebrow at her, half mocking the expression she'd used. "Yes, that's what we thought, but any normal guy would have bragged about that. And none of his girlfriends seem to last more than a few dates. We never did figure it out."

Jud moved on to the third storyboard. Charlotte had put it together, but since it contained the most recent information about Camille, it had been the easiest to do. At least, Francine thought it must have been. Like the first one Charlotte had done, it contained a lot of photographs. This was when Camille had become politically active.

Jud studied an article from six years ago, when Camille had first been elected to the Brownsburg Town Council. "What made her want to run for the Council? She was a political newbie, wasn't she?"

Charlotte traced a finger on the article. "She was upset about the deterioration of the downtown district. You remember when Harley's steakhouse was torn down?"

"No," Jud said. "That was a long time ago too. My understanding is that it was beyond repair, though."

"It was," Charlotte said, "but that didn't mean a Walgreen's had to be built in its place. Right across the street from a CVS pharmacy. What had been a corner of downtown Brownsburg now looked like every other street corner in every other suburb in America. Then the town went and built the Taj Mahal of Town Halls behind the strip of downtown that barely remained, and it looked nothing like the old downtown. She revolted against the establishment and was elected."

"She's been a fighter on the Council," Jud said. "I just didn't know what was behind it."

Francine looked at her watch. "I need to get the second storyboard done. I have to get to some other things this afternoon."

"But first, it's lunchtime," Charlotte added. "Would you like to stay, Jud?"

"No. My purpose in coming was to figure out why you got Dick Raden to show you a piece of Fuzzy Carter's property that wasn't even for sale on a bitterly cold day when you were otherwise occupied getting ready for Camille's funeral."

Charlotte went to the kitchen and looked in the refrigerator. "I could make grilled cheese."

"I don't have time. And you still haven't answered the question."

"I did. You just didn't like the answer. I'm interested in buying property."

"You're lying to me. I know it and you know it. Why are you making this hard on yourself? Admit you're investigating this case, share your information with me, and I'll go easy on you for obstructing justice."

"If I knew something, then I might be obstructing justice. But I don't know anything."

"You probably know more than you think." He shook his head in frustration. "My jacket's in the closet, right? I'll see myself out."

He left.

"That didn't go well," Francine said. "You shouldn't be making enemies with Jud."

Charlotte pulled wrapped slices of American cheese out of the refrigerator. "We're rivals, but hardly enemies."

The doorbell rang, startling both women. Charlotte frowned. "That couldn't be Jud again. It will take him at least another fifteen minutes to think of a clever retort."

"More likely he's thought of something to charge you with. He thinks of those faster." Charlotte started for the front of the house but Francine waved her off. "I'll get it."

Before she could take another step, though, they heard the door open.

"It's me, Joy!"

"Come on in! We're in the kitchen!" Charlotte called.

Joy entered a few moments later. She was wearing a zippered red cashmere sweater and skinny black jeans that flattered her thin frame. It looks like something Alice's personal shopper would pick out, Francine thought, though it would be in a larger size if it were Alice. The sense of fashion was similar.

Joy wielded her reporter's notebook like it was a winning lottery ticket. "I have news!" She pointed to a page with scribbling on it. "It's not a smoking gun, or anything, but if what I hear is true, Eric met individually with each of the other four members of the Council the week before Camille was killed."

TWENTY-TWO

FRANCINE TILTED HER HEAD to one side. "Why would he do that?"

"Why, indeed?" Joy asked, mocking herself in a conspiratorial manner. "Coincidence?"

Charlotte closed the refrigerator door. "Are you drawing a link between Camille's murder and his meeting with the Council members, or are you saying we need to find out what they talked about?"

"Either is good," she answered. "If his meetings caused the murder to occur, then we need to find out what was said so we can trace it back and figure out who did it. But in any event, it's kind of suspicious, isn't it? As Francine asked, why was he meeting with them in the first place?"

The women mulled that over in their minds. Charlotte spoke first. "Where did you get this information?"

"It started when I stopped at Hilligoss Bakery this morning to pick up some donuts to take to a meeting. You know how long the line can get? Well, I was at the back of the line and got into a discussion with Chief Cannon. Imagine that, cops and donuts. I don't like to stereotype, but it was classic. Of course, I didn't bring it up."

"I hope you brought up something about Camille's death," Charlotte said. She sounded anxious for Joy to get on with the story.

"Naturally. I tried to make it seem like I was interviewing him off the record, but he wasn't buying. In fact, he wasn't saying much of anything. He kept looking at his wife to bail him out."

"His wife was there?" Francine wasn't sure she'd ever seen the chief's wife before. She tried to remember if he'd been accompanied at the benefit. It didn't seem like it, but then she hadn't remembered seeing him at all until after Camille had been stabbed.

Joy nodded. "I think it was his wife. Although now that you mention it, I didn't look to see if he was wearing a ring. I guess it could have been someone on his staff. He bought three dozen donuts and she helped him carry them out to a police vehicle. Anyway, I kept chattering away, figuring sooner or later one of them would break. The line was pretty long. Finally, the chief excused himself and went to use the restroom. She said to me, kind of slyly, 'Why don't you ask Eric Dehoney why he met with each of the Council members individually before the benefit? No one seems to be interested in that.' I was pretty shocked."

"I bet she wasn't with the Police Department," Charlotte said. "They wouldn't be so free with information like that."

"I asked her where this had happened. She laid it all out for me. She'd seen Eric meet with Fuzzy Carter at Hilligoss, then with Janet Turpen at Bob Evans, Dick Raden at Flap Jacks, and finally Vince Papadopoulos at Starbucks. Then she turned and faced front—she was ahead of me in line. Chief Cannon came back, and they ignored me. But I hung in there until they picked up their donuts and left, hoping they might say something. They didn't."

"From a detective's standpoint, I would say this woman eats breakfast out too often," Charlotte said. "But it could be a lucky break if it's true."

"When I was buying a couple of their chocolate iced yeast donuts for myself," she held up the bag for evidence, "I asked the guy at the counter about Fuzzy meeting with Eric Dehoney there, and he said it was true. He knew who Fuzzy Carter was—Fuzzy is apparently a regular—but he hadn't known who Eric was until after the benefit and the story hit the media. Mind if I have some tea? I stopped at all three of the other places and talked to everyone until I had confirmation."

Charlotte put the kettle on. "You don't have to eat the donuts now. It's lunchtime. I'm making grilled cheese. Want one?"

"Are you kidding? I've been dying to eat these all morning. There's nothing like an old-fashioned Hilligoss yeast donut."

"Agreed," Charlotte said. "Say what you will about those hoity-toity artisan donuts with strange ingredients they sell in Indianapolis at Fountain Square, Hilligoss is the best. But what did you learn, other than he met with them?"

Joy extracted a donut from the bag. It had been fried to a perfect golden brown and sported a thick ring of chocolate icing around the top. Joy daintily held it between her index finger and thumb and took a small bite. She practically glowed when she chewed and swallowed it. She licked the sugar off her lips. "Sorry I didn't bring any to share."

"Just get to the point," Charlotte said. Francine noticed Charlotte was studiously avoiding Joy eating the donut by buttering pieces of bread for the sandwiches.

"Here's the thing," Joy said. "Neither the waitress at Flap Jack's nor the waitress at Bob Evans could recall any exact words, but they both were under the impression it was about money."

"Were any of them upset? Was it like they were arguing about money, or was it more like a contract negotiation?" Francine remembered Eric saying Camille had brought him into the business as a partner. She knew, too, that all of them had some kind of financial connection to Camille's firm, Jacqueline Consulting.

"The waitress at Flap Jack's remembered Dick Raden turned purple several times, but that could have been from the cream cheese–stuffed French toast slathered in maple syrup he ate with a double helping of sausage patties. She may not have remembered the conversation, but she remembered what he ordered. She said she couldn't watch him eat it."

Francine made a gulping noise. *No wonder the man had a heart attack.* She tried to rid herself of the image, now burned in her head, of Tricky Dicky eating the French toast breakfast. "Did you find out anything about anyone else?" She hoped none of the other reports came with graphic scenes.

"The baristas at Starbucks said Vince Papadopoulos was very nervous," Joy answered. "And they said he rarely came in."

"What about Eric?"

"*He's* a regular, but he usually comes in late, right before they leave at ten thirty, they said. But that day he came in early. And he was all dressed up, compared to normal."

Charlotte had finished assembly of the sandwiches and was now pressing them into a panini maker. "So let's see," she said, leaning on the handle. "Eric got up early four mornings in a row for meetings with his aunt's supporters and detractors on the Council. He dressed up for the appointment with Vince and made him nervous. He gave Tricky Dicky a case of indigestion. Or he accelerated it, at any rate. No word on his effect on Janet or Fuzzy?"

"They seemed more cordial, I guess." The teakettle whistled. Joy headed for it. "I'm freezing. A cup of tea will warm me up."

"I've got something that will warm you up even better," Charlotte said. "How about a little Jack Daniels in that tea?"

Francine was aghast. "What is it with you and hard liquor all of a sudden? You get a taste of Prunier cognac and suddenly you're buying brand-name liquor?"

Joy perked up. "She has Prunier?"

"You want some?" Charlotte asked. "I could put it in your tea or give you a snort."

"Where did you get it? I'm not sure where I would buy Prunier around here," Joy said.

"Camille gave it to her," Francine answered.

A light bulb went on in Charlotte's head. "Are you saying it's not readily available?"

Joy poured water into a teacup and added a tea bag. "I'm fairly sure it's not."

"Then, if we can find out where Camille bought it," Charlotte continued, "we might have an idea of when she got it and why."

Francine asked Charlotte, "How will that change anything?"

"It won't, but it's a good bet she didn't buy it for me."

"Maybe she regifted it," Joy suggested. "Although, who would regift Prunier?"

Francine shook her head. "That's the least of our mysteries."

"What's the most of our mysteries?" Joy asked.

Charlotte reached for the pile of photos, which were still sitting on the table from earlier in the day. "The next order of business, in my mind, is to get back out to this cemetery and find out why Camille had so many photos of it." She passed the photos to Joy, who had moved back to the table with her tea.

Joy sorted through the photos. "Where is this cemetery?"

Charlotte and Francine caught her up on the morning's events.

"Tricky Dicky had a heart attack?" Joy said, aghast. "Did you cause it?"

200

"I would like to say he had a Big Mac attack," Charlotte cracked, "but it was actually White Castle. A whole sackful." She told Joy about his indigestion comment.

"Between that and the cream cheese–stuffed French toast he had at Flap Jack's, no wonder he had a heart attack. He must eat like that all the time. Is he okay?"

"Francine gave him CPR. He was alive when the paramedics showed up."

"I'm pretty sure he'll be okay," Francine said. "But they'll likely have to do surgery to bypass his blocked arteries."

"I guess we can scratch another person from the list of funeral attendees tomorrow."

Charlotte finished making the grilled cheese sandwiches. She served one to Francine and the other to herself.

"I'd like to go with you to the cemetery," Joy said, sipping the hot tea. "It's strange, isn't it, how little we really knew about Camille? And she's lived here for a long, long time."

Charlotte took a seat. "She was a guarded person for so many years. I think it wasn't until Eric moved in and started high school that she had to connect with people."

Francine agreed in part. "She was starting to come out of her shell a little before that. According to the clippings I was working on for the funeral, she had already helped the police nail that child pornographer right before Eric came to live with her. But there's no denying it all seemed to happen about the same time."

Charlotte bit into her grilled cheese and had to deal with a long gooey string that wouldn't let go from the sandwich. Francine took a smaller bite. She thought about Eric's influence on Camille.

When Camille's sister and her husband died—Francine couldn't recall either name off the top of her head—Eric had come to live with Camille. The neighborhood knew about it because it was a fairly close-knit group, but Camille hadn't participated much. So it was a surprise when she'd shown up at the freshman football games to cheer for her nephew. In fact, if Jonathan hadn't reminded Francine who Camille was, she might have introduced herself, certain they'd never met.

Camille had been slow to get involved, but she'd done so. She proved to be adept at wrangling donations for the athletic booster club, a quality that everyone appreciated since only a few people seemed to like doing it. Once she was complimented on her handling of those duties, she began to be a better neighbor all around. She and Eric participated in the homeowners' association block party, where he won the pie eating contest, out-eating even Francine's sons—which was saying something, considering Eric was a good twenty pounds lighter. She'd also begun to take better care of her house, which lead to an escalation in curb-appeal wars, which lead Charlotte to the installation of the ill-fated irrigation system, which had started the cold war between them.

When Eric returned to Texas to attend Southern Methodist University, Camille focused her energies on the political system. She never outright accused anyone of wrongdoing, but she sat through each Council meeting like Carl Bernstein on the hunt in *All the President's Men*. Everyone knew there was animosity between her, Vince Papadopoulos, and Tricky Dicky Raden, but no one knew where it came from or why it built. The next election cycle she ran for a seat on the Council from her district, defeating the incumbent in the Republican primary. Though Fuzzy and Dick backed the independent candidate they set up to run against her, she still won the general election. The perception had been that there was cronyism on the Council and that the good ole boys' network was in charge. Under Camille's opposition platform, she began outing some shady dealings.

The next election cycle, she'd been elected President of the Council. She was the first woman on the Council and its first woman President. She and her majority party installed a new town manager and cleaned up many undesirable business practices. Vince and Dick, amazingly, remained on the Council, having been re-elected with the solid support of the ole boys' network and those who'd been around a long time and wanted Brownsburg to go backwards. At least, that's the way Francine regarded it.

Brownsburg was a growing, influential suburb of Indianapolis, no longer a sleepy little town on the outskirts. To try to stick one's head in the sand and turn back the clock to when it was a quaint village was not only impossible, but undesirable for the thousands of people who'd moved in for the excellent school system and quality of life. They weren't going away no matter how hard Vince and Dick and the ole boys wanted it. That network was no longer running the town.

So yes, Camille had changed because of Eric, and she'd led the charge that changed Brownsburg. But how close was Eric to that change? He'd only been back a year, and though he was developing some notoriety because of his growing popularity as a stripper with the Royal Buckingham revue, that wasn't affecting anything in the political realm where Camille was celebrated by most but feared and hated by a few. So what had he been doing talking to the other Council members? Mending fences or making deals?

"The cemetery photos are strange items to find in this pile of pictures," Joy admitted. "For the most part they're all about Eric and Camille, except these. Camille isn't related to the Carters, is she?"

"Not that I know of," Charlotte said. "Francine, you saw the family tree in the Ledfelter Bible, didn't you tell me that? Did you see any Carters in there?"

"I didn't study it looking for them, but I don't remember that off hand. Carter is a common name, though."

Charlotte got up from the table carrying her empty plate. "I like the grilled cheese made with part Asiago. It has a nice flavor. And grilling them panini-style makes them a little more special."

"You licked your fingers clean enough you probably don't need to wash your hands," Joy said.

Charlotte walked over and snagged Joy's empty donut sack. "I don't see any traces of chocolate donut icing on your hands, either, dearie." She tossed the sack in the garbage and placed the plate in the sink. "Let's get to the cemetery. It's not going to get much warmer than it is now, and I'd rather do this in the middle of the day, anyway."

"I'll drive if we can take your car, Charlotte," Francine offered. "We drove yours back here from my house."

Charlotte led them to the closet to get their coats. She grabbed her orange down coat, which might have been her way of saying she didn't want to blend in with the dead in the cemetery. Charlotte was sensitive about getting older.

Francine helped Charlotte get her arms into the coat. Its cuffs were tight and could be difficult. "Did anyone grab the photos?"

"Good idea," Charlotte said, zipping up the front of her coat. "We need them to check for the grave that's in the center of this photograph, even if it's taken from far away."

Joy wrapped the wool scarf around her neck before putting on her coat. "I'll get them."

The thought of going to the cemetery again made Francine pause. "Let's just hope the cemetery sheds some light on this case," she said. "I keep going over and over what we know, and there are too many pieces missing."

TWENTY-THREE

FRANCINE PULLED THE CAR to a stop near the place where the ambulance had picked up Dick Raden earlier in the day. She, Charlotte, and Joy climbed out of the car. Charlotte teetered right and left as though she'd gotten off a Tilt-A-Whirl at a summer carnival. "Could you have driven any faster over those ruts? You know how I get car sick."

The comment irritated Francine. They were in Charlotte's big Buick, not her car, and she had been extra careful to take it slow. "Quit complaining. This car is big enough to stay righted in the face of a tidal wave."

"If you're going to throw up," Joy said, "please do it over there in the brush so I don't have to hear it or smell it."

Charlotte clutched Francine's right arm. "I'll probably be okay, but hold on to me just in case."

Francine would have done that anyway. The divots in the path caused by farm machinery going to the fields were treacherous enough for someone with good stability, let alone Charlotte. "Joy, can you help on Charlotte's other side?"

Joy took up Charlotte's flailing arm and the three women picked their way toward the forest where the cemetery was.

Once they got off the rough path, the wooded environs returned. The grass was frozen by the dusting of snow and the cold temperatures, and it crunched under their boots. The trees were mostly maples, and they passed a station where a tap had been driven into the trunk of a tree that had to be ten feet in circumference. Charlotte held them back. "Maple syrup," she noted. "Cass Carter doesn't strike me as the type of person who would go to the trouble to make maple syrup."

Joy peered inside the wooden bucket that hung from the peg. "She probably rents the trees to someone who makes it from the raw sap. Can we move along here? I'm cold. I don't see how maple syrup is involved with the mystery anyway."

The women approached the cemetery slowly as if they expected a ghost to rise up any moment. "It looks peaceful," Joy said, "but it feels creepy."

Francine could understand that. On the one hand, the area looked serene. The powdery snow, sustained by the cold, sat on the branches of the trees. An occasionally slight breeze would cause a dusting to float to the ground. They went by a small stand of pines and it smelled like a Christmas tree farm.

But on the other hand, the quiet of the deserted area coupled with the limited light making its way through the bare branches made her feel insecure. The gravestones, only partially covered by snow, reminded her that this was a place of the dead.

She tried to observe it without letting her emotions get the better of her. The cemetery had been carved out of the woods and occupied about a half-acre. One populous section boasted gravestones that were mostly old and worn. They were laid out in lines that weren't straight. Other areas were devoid of upright grave markers. A few small monuments were interspersed throughout.

Francine noticed how long the grass was. Though partially covered by snow and ice, the cemetery looked unkempt. *Couldn't have been mowed any more recently than October*, she thought. *Who even takes care of it?* She found it ironic that Cass married into the family, divorced her way out of it, and still ended up with a family cemetery in which she had no relatives buried. *I guess there's not much motivation to take care of it.* "I wonder if the township should take responsibility for it," she said aloud.

"What?" Charlotte asked.

"This cemetery. The township is required to care for private cemeteries under certain conditions. I can't remember what they are now, but being private and not cared for is part of it."

Charlotte had moved ahead and was studying the gravestones. "Some of these are so weathered you can't read the names or dates anymore." She moved down a few gravestones until she found one she could read. "Here's one that goes back to 1902."

"Long time ago," Joy said. "I'm guessing the ones that are short and weather-damaged are all from about that time. Which one was centered in the photograph?"

Charlotte pulled the photos from the depths of her orange down coat. She was wearing mittens, and after a few fumbled attempts to sort through the photos, handed them off to Francine, who was wearing gloves. "Can you figure it out?"

Francine sorted through them trying to get her bearings. She backed up to the point in the graveyard where her view matched that of the photograph. "The headstone we're looking for is more to the right," she said. "Joy, move toward me, then go to the end of that short row. It's probably second or third from the end."

Joy did as she was instructed. "This one?"

"Next one or the one after. Can you read either?"

Joy stopped in place. "The grass has matted over the stone. With the snow and ice on top of it, I can't make anything out. Let me brush it off."

She bent down and extended her glove toward it.

And the sound of a rifle shot split the serenity of the cemetery.

Francine screamed. At least, she thought it was her. It could have been Joy or Charlotte or all three of them. The sound echoed in her ears as she crouched to the ground. Her heart pounded in her chest. She hadn't heard the bullet hit anything. She wondered if it had been a warning shot, maybe fired in the air.

She checked on her companions. Joy, who had been bent over the gravestone, was now on her hands and knees trying to make herself as small as possible. Charlotte had ducked behind one of the small monuments. She peered out from behind it looking back to where they'd left the car. Joy was also staring in that direction.

Francine held her breath and listened. The sound of the shot still echoed in her ear, but she could also hear the brush of someone walking through the snow and ice. She looked around trying to find the source of it.

Charlotte spoke up first. "Who are you?" She didn't shout but spoke louder than normal. The words carried in the stillness.

The walking ceased. There was no response. The three of them held their positions. Slowly Joy stood. She used the grave marker to brace herself. As she did, the snow and ice fell off it. She swept the overgrown grass and weeds aside to look at what it said.

And a second blast was fired. This time Francine was certain they all screamed. The bullet hit in Joy's vicinity, pinging off a grave to her right. Joy dove back on her hands and knees.

Charlotte called again, this time louder, "Who are you?"

"Who are *you*?" the voice responded. "And why're you on my property?"

It was a woman's voice with a slight rural Indiana accent, soudning a bit countryish. Although she didn't know Cass Carter well, Francine was certain it was her. She didn't know who else would claim ownership and be female.

"Cass Carter, is that you?" Charlotte said. "It's me, Charlotte Reinhardt. We worked together at Brownsburg High a long time ago."

Francine hoped Charlotte would be able to make a connection before Cass fired again. She struggled to stand, trying to keep her hands raised in a surrender position.

"What brings you to my woods, Charlotte?" The woman asked it like she didn't recognize Charlotte but used her name because it had been given to her. She strode into view from behind a clump of evergreens on the west side of the cemetery. She wore dark sunglasses that hid her eyes, and her long black hair rested silky-smooth along the cut of her fur-lined winter coat. Her slim leather gloves gripped the rifle.

"We're not armed and we're not dangerous," Francine announced. "I'm Francine McNamara. You've met Charlotte; the other woman is Joy McQueen." Joy and Charlotte leveraged their way to standing positions.

Cass shifted her rifle so it pointed at Francine. "You're not the usual troublemakers."

Usual troublemakers? Francine wondered who those would include. "We're here to see your cemetery."

"Point of fact is, it's not mine, although I guard it for the Carters. And even if it was mine, who told you it was okay to come?"

Francine couldn't come up with good answer, and apparently neither could Joy or Charlotte. They remained silent.

Cass continued to advance. She entered the cemetery near Joy. "I recognize you," she said. "You're that reporter from *Good Morning America.*"

Joy brightened and stood taller. "Yes, I am."

"That's not a thing to be proud of, darlin'. I don't like reporters." Cass shifted the rifle so it pointed at Joy, making her raise her arms to show she had no weapon.

"We're just interested in one particular grave. If you'll let us look at it, we'll be on our way in no time," Joy said.

"You'll be on your way in no time if I let you see it or not," Cass answered. "What grave is it?"

"This one right here," Joy answered. Francine could hear the tremble in her voice. She was scared. They were all scared.

"Back away from that grave."

Joy did it slowly, carefully looking behind her as she stepped. Francine thought she could see a cell phone in Joy's hand.

"What are you doing here?" Cass asked.

"Looking into the death of Camille Ledfelter," Francine answered.

"Ah, Camille. Now she *is* one of the usual troublemakers. I'd like to say I'm sorry she's gone, but that'd be a lie."

"Usual troublemakers?" Charlotte asked. "What did she do?"

"She was an unwelcome visitor to this cemetery. She was told not to come back, but she did, time after time after time."

Francine could smell the gun's discharge of the bullet casing. It made her nervous, but she couldn't stop now. "It would help our investigation if you'd just let us look."

Cass swung the rifle barrel toward her. "First, why're *you* looking into the investigation? Shouldn't that be a police matter? And second, what's this grave got to do with Camille's death?"

The rifle being pointed at her chest stopped Francine in her tracks. "We don't know that it does," she said. "We found a series of photographs in her possession. They pointed to that grave."

Cass worked her jaw. "I want you out of here. Now!" She clamped the rifle between the crook of her arm and her body on one side and slid back the coat sleeve on the other hand. She looked at her wristwatch. "Go!"

None of them needed further invitation. They scurried back to the car.

TWENTY-FOUR

JOY SPEED-WALKED OUT OF the graveyard. Francine hooked Charlotte's arm in hers and steered the two of them into Joy's wake.

Despite their retreat, Cass shouted, "Time's up!" and fired the rifle into the air.

Joy had the lead by a good thirty seconds. She was nearing the rutted path between the two properties by the time Francine and Charlotte made it out of the cemetery. Cass must've thought they still weren't moving fast enough because she fired the rifle again. The bullet nicked a tree not too far from Francine. It gave added spring to her step. She felt like she was dragging Charlotte.

"Slow down," Charlotte whispered. "She talks big, but she wouldn't actually shoot us."

"Maybe not this time, but she might next. Not that there will be a next time."

Joy was yanking on the door handle to the car. "It won't open!" She continued to pull on it. "You locked the door. Why did you lock the door in a God-forsaken place like this? Who did you think would steal it?"

Francine pulled out the key to Charlotte's car and used the remote to open the door. The rear driver's side door flew open under Joy's continued yanking and Joy jumped inside. She slunk down in the seat and peered out the window. Francine could only see her head from the nose up.

Despite Charlotte's drag on her forward progress, Francine managed to get to the Buick quickly. She let go of Charlotte's arm and got in the driver's side. Charlotte tried to show no fear, but one more shot from Cass's gun made her duck into the car as well. The shot went over her head and ricocheted off a tree behind her.

Joy's head popped up from the back. "Good thing this car is built like a tank. Her rifle doesn't stand a chance of penetrating the side."

"It could still shatter the window," Francine said. "Better not let her see you thumbing your nose at her, Joy."

Joy slid down until her knees pushed into the driver's seat. "I'll sit up and put on my seat belt when we get out on the road. Just drive."

Francine put the car in gear and they took off, slowly at first because of the farm machinery ruts, and much faster after she pulled onto the paved county road. Though no one said anything, Francine heard a great exhale as though all three ladies let out a breath at once.

"Jacqueline Carter," Joy said finally. "That was the name on the grave. I got a look at it, I just couldn't tell you with her standing there."

Francine sucked in a breath. "Jacqueline is the name of Camille's consulting company. What do you make of it?"

Joy fumbled with her camera. "I managed to get a photo too. Not sure how well it might have come out."

Charlotte turned as much as she could in the front passenger seat to face both Joy and Francine. "Can I look at it?"

Francine glanced at Joy through the rearview mirror. She was already on her cell phone examining the photo. She squinched her fingers together on the screen and pulled them apart to enlarge the photograph.

"No date," she said. "I don't see a date on this gravestone. In fact, all it says is 'Jacqueline Carter'." She passed the phone up to Charlotte.

Charlotte fumbled around with the phone. She pushed a finger up the screen and down the screen, squinting at it. "Let's face it. The only function I can get one of these things to perform is make a phone call. I can't even see the name on the gravestone." She handed the phone back to Joy. "We should look at it on the computer when we get back."

"It has to mean something," Francine said. "But how does that grave tie to Camille? If she hadn't had photos of it in her possession, I wouldn't think the two names being the same was anything but a coincidence."

"Any detective worth their salt would investigate it," Charlotte assured her.

"Any fictional detective investigating a fictional crime might," Joy said. "But this is real life."

"It's practically the only thing we have to hang a hat on," Charlotte snapped back.

Francine suddenly realized there was a sharp turn in the country road up ahead. She was going too fast and braked, but she was already in the turn. She gripped the steering wheel hard and pushed on the brake even harder. The three of them gasped as the rear wheels slid into the other side of the road. Charlotte and Joy grabbed whatever they could find to stabilize them. Francine struggled with the wheel but managed to regain control of the car. She slowed to a stop. No one was behind her or ahead of her on the road, for which she was grateful.

When their breathing had returned to normal, Charlotte said, "We need to relax. Cass Carter is far behind us. Unless she ran, got her truck, and is now following us." The thought made her and Joy swivel to look out the back window.

"No," Francine assured them. "She's not there. I already checked." She felt her face flush with embarrassment. "I just got caught up in trying to figure this out. I was going too fast and not looking ahead. I'll drive slower now." She put the car in gear and cautiously accelerated to the speed limit.

"Good," Charlotte said. "Because I think too much of this heart racing might make me go into cardiac arrest."

"None of us has a pacemaker, right?" Joy asked.

It took a moment, but they finally chuckled.

Charlotte put her hands out as if to slow down their thinking as well as Francine's velocity. "Let's review the facts as we know them. Fact one: Camille was killed in a daring manner with lots of people around because someone turned the lights off in the Crown Room and someone else stabbed her with a knife. And not just any knife. A pilot's knife issued during the Vietnam War."

"Which leads us to believe it was probably a Vietnam veteran," Joy added. "And we have a list of those who live in Hendricks County."

"It's not a fact that it was a Vietnam vet," Charlotte said. "That's a supposition on our part. You're getting ahead of me."

Joy, who had been leaning forward in her seat, slunk back. Francine could hear the seat belt retract. "Sorry."

"It's okay," Charlotte said. "To continue with the facts, we know that all of the Council members were customers of Camille's IT consulting business, with the exception of Janet Turpen. Camille kept records of their bank transfers to her account. But Janet was her investment advisor. Camille's transfers went the other way in that case, into Janet's bank account."

"Girl power?" Francine asked.

"Maybe, but again, that would be supposition."

Joy chimed in. "We know for a fact that there was animosity between Camille and Vince Papadopoulos and Tricky Dicky."

"We do," Charlotte agreed. "It's long-standing, and we don't really know the source."

"For a long time Camille lived in the background of Brownsburg politics," Francine added. "It's been only recently, and I say that in relative terms, that she's become a political force."

Charlotte sounded dismayed. "Unfortunately, we don't know the why of that one, either."

"It could be the animosity she feels for Vince and Dick that fueled it," Joy said, shivering. "But you're going to tell me that's conjecture too."

"It is."

"For as big as this boat is," Joy said, pulling her coat tight around her, "it sure heats up slowly."

Francine checked the heater controls. She pushed the fan to its highest setting, and cold air blew out the front vents. She turned them back down. "We're almost to Charlotte's house. You'll be fine."

"Fine and frozen." Joy buried her nose in the top of her coat.

Francine could feel Charlotte rolling her eyes. "More facts. Eric was worried almost immediately after Camille's death that he was in danger as well. He's been using Toby like a bodyguard."

"Let's get to the part about Jacqueline Consulting." Joy's voice was muffled through the upturned lapel on her coat.

Charlotte glanced back at her. "We know that Camille has been working for CableFirm for a long time, that she helped the police obtain evidence to arrest a child pornographer, and that she subsequently opened a side business, Jacqueline Consulting."

Joy's mouth momentarily popped out of the warm enclave created by the coat. "Do we know if it's successful?"

"She accumulated a lot of money somehow," Francine said. "All I know is Jonathan's firm handles her tax returns. It provided a steady stream of revenue that allowed her to be fairly generous to Eric. She just paid off the student loans he accumulated at college."

Charlotte frowned. "When did you learn that? Have you been holding out on me?"

"Nonsense." Francine thought she could feel a bit of warmth coming out of the heater. It was about time. Of course they were only about a minute from Charlotte's house at that point. "I just found that out this morning." *Or maybe yesterday*, she muttered inaudibly.

"I'm not sure that changes anything," Joy said. "Do I detect heat?"

Francine nodded. "Finally."

Charlotte waved a finger in the air. "According to Eric, Camille is worth two million dollars. Eric's been out of college what, ten years? And she's just now paying off his loans? So when did she accumulate the money?"

Francine thought again of the timeline. The child pornography case was the start of the clippings Camille kept of her recent history. Was there something about that case that made her a lot of money? She floated the idea out loud to the others.

Joy turned down the collar on her coat so she could talk freely, clearly excited. "Francine, that's a great question! I'm thinking blackmail. What if she blackmailed the child pornographer?"

"I'm pretty sure he's in jail," Charlotte said. "And what could she possibly blackmail him for? They already know what he did."

"I'm the reporter here," Joy said. "Nowadays, they break one child pornographer, and one leads to another and another. It's like a bunch of them are networked. Maybe Camille knew of the others, and she kept it to herself."

There was something about Joy's theory Francine didn't like, but she couldn't put her finger on it. Child pornographers were the lowest of the lows, but what to think of someone who took advantage of that to make money? Maybe just as low. Camille had her flaws, but in the course of this investigation Francine had come to admire Camille in many ways and didn't want to think of her like that.

But blackmail would certainly explain how she could accumulate a bunch of money in a short period of time.

Charlotte wasn't buying this. "Why would a pornographer want to kill Camille in such a public way, even if she were blackmailing him? What would he have to gain?"

"She has a point," Francine said. "Didn't we agree somewhere along the line that Camille's death was probably meant to send a message to someone? Who would that message have been sent to?"

"It had to be Eric," Joy said.

Francine pulled the Buick into Charlotte's driveway. The back end slid just a bit when she did, giving her a bit of déjà vu from when they'd left the cemetery. "You need to get your driveway shoveled," Francine said. "Either that, or your tires are getting close to bald and need to be changed."

"It's the ice," Charlotte answered. "I tried calling someone to come do it, but no one wants to do a single driveway anymore. The kids don't even want to shovel their parents' driveways, let alone mine, and drivers with blades on their trucks only want to do big parking lots where they can make a lot of money."

Francine used Charlotte's remote control and opened the garage door. She drove in. "If you don't get it done soon, you'll slip and fall going out to the mailbox and that will set back all the progress we've made—I mean, you've made—with your bad knee."

Francine turned the engine off and heard the doors unlock. Charlotte threw open the door and stepped out. "Let's get inside and get that photo of the gravestone up on the computer where I can see it. There may be something we've overlooked on the small screen."

TWENTY-FIVE

"SHE DIED ON NOVEMBER 22nd," Charlotte said. "That's the same day John F. Kennedy was assassinated. But there's no birthdate."

"Odd, isn't it," Joy said. She'd emailed the photo to Francine, who got on her email account and pulled it up online at Charlotte's computer. She'd enlarged the engraving, which had been sculpted into the black stone, so it could be seen better. "It's no wonder we missed the date earlier, though. The shadows were terrible."

"That, and we had Cass Carter breathing down our necks with a rifle pointed at our bellies," Francine said.

Charlotte peeked over Francine's shoulder, trying to get a better look. "Speak for yourself. She had it pointed at my head."

Joy had a bemused look on her face. "It's because you're short. For the rest of us, that was belly height."

Charlotte sputtered.

Francine tried to steer the other two away from sniping. "Good thing you had the presence of mind to snap a picture, or we wouldn't be able to examine it now."

"To Charlotte's point about John F. Kennedy's death being on November 22nd," Joy said. "Does that mean anything as it relates to Jacqueline Carter? Jackie Kennedy was JFK's wife, and the death date may remind someone of Kennedy's, but you don't name a person on the date of their death. You name them on the date of their birth, and this doesn't give one."

"So who *was* Jacqueline Carter?" Francine asked. "That grave certainly wasn't the oldest one there, but with them all so neglected, it's hard to be sure. I don't think it's from the early 1900s, though, or why would Camille even care about this person?"

Joyce nudged Francine off the chair. "Let me on the computer. I'll Google the name."

Francine steadied herself as she got bumped off and had to stand. "I could have done it."

Joy's hands flew over the keyboard. "Yes, but I'm faster. Years of working in public relations makes you pretty speedy on the computer."

Joy searched for ten minutes and investigated several websites. "Nothing," she concluded. She stood up, interlaced her fingers, and cracked her knuckles.

"I hate it when you do that," Francine said, wincing at the cracking noise.

The computer was in the middle bedroom, which Charlotte called her office, though the computer was the only hint of it. Otherwise it held a twin bed with a patchwork quilt serving as a bedspread, an upright chest of drawers, and a closet full of books that didn't fit in Charlotte's large library. There were even frilly white lace curtains on the windows.

Joy circled the room, thinking. "Could it be that this person died the same day and same year JFK died? We don't have a year for either the birth or death."

"No matter when she lived or died, it still has to answer the question of why there's this mysterious grave with 'Jacqueline Carter' on the gravestone, why Camille was obsessed with it to the point of having taken pictures of it, and why she presumably named her consulting company after this person," Francine said.

Charlotte rubbed her forehead like she was getting a headache. "Maybe we're getting ahead of ourselves. What if this were the gravestone of a baby that died in childbirth? That would account for the single date."

They all thought about that. "It would, I guess," Joy said. "But why avoid putting a year on it? Those usually have a year."

"What if they wanted to keep it a secret?" Charlotte said. "It's a private cemetery. No one would even know a burial took place out there."

Joy sat down and perched on the edge of her chair. She faced Charlotte. "Now we're getting somewhere. Why would someone keep a burial a secret?"

"What if the baby was unwanted?" suggested Francine, coming over to where the two of them sat. "What if the birth mother was underage, or had an abortion? Depending on what decade it was, an abortion would have been an illegal act."

"Abortion may turn out to be the reason," Joy said, "but that doesn't necessarily narrow the time frame. While it's legal today, among many people it's still unspeakable. I know I couldn't do it, let alone leave evidence that it happened. I'd keep the grave a secret."

"That's still conjecture, though," Francine said, rising to the challenge of being the devil's advocate. "She may have been a person who lived and breathed in Brownsburg but was so unnoticed that there're few records of her. It could have been before websites and social media."

Charlotte blew out a breath. "Can we all agree that the key to unlocking this mystery hinges on the choice Camille made in selecting the name Jacqueline for her consulting company? And if we're going to do that, we need to figure out who Jacqueline Carter was."

"If she wasn't a baby, we could check the Brownsburg High School yearbooks at the Brownsburg library," Joy suggested. "It's close to dinner, and Roy's coming in from Rockville for a dinner date, but I could talk him into stopping by the library after that."

Much as she was happy Joy was still dating the detective she'd met at the Covered Bridge Festival, Francine didn't want her to drag Roy to the library when they were researching a murder. They'd only get another lecture from another law-enforcement officer about how they should stay out of investigations. The ladies already knew that. It wasn't going to stop them. "Why don't you let me do that after supper?" Francine offered. "You and Roy should enjoy your time together."

"I'll do it," Charlotte said. "I'm the one who has the time. I don't even need to wait. I could just go over there now and stop at McDonald's on my way home. They serve breakfast all day, and I've been thinking about an Egg McMuffin all afternoon."

"Even after all the calories you consumed at lunch with those grilled cheese sandwiches?" Joy asked.

Charlotte scoffed. "When has that ever stopped me before?"

Francine knew that was the truth. "Okay, you'll cover the library. Here's a thought: We haven't asked Eric about the company name yet. That could be the easiest and best solution."

They all could have smacked their foreheads like people did in the old V-8 commercials. "Oy vey," Charlotte said. "I should have thought of that. He might know. We know she brought him into the business as a partner. He might have asked and she might have said. If you'll check that, Francine, I'll check the library for the yearbooks, and we'll all compare notes. Let's get together in the morning. We need to go over to Vince's funeral home to get set up for the visitation anyway."

————

Francine walked home in the cold. The sidewalks were mostly cleared of the snow, but she took note of whose homes were responsible for the icy ones. She didn't want to make trouble, but many people in the neighborhood walked for exercise, and not having a shoveled path was dangerous. Most of them were like her, of a certain age.

Jonathan had been working on dinner, and when she came through the front door, the house smelled of cumin and chili powder. "What are you fixing?" she asked, leaving her coat in the closet and entering from the swinging door. "Smells spicy."

She caught him getting ready to taste it. "White chicken chili," he said, blowing on a spoonful. "I've made some corn muffins to go with it." He tried the chili and his eyes opened wide. "It might be a little hot."

"Temperature-wise or spicy?"

"Both, actually. Needs a little salt, though." He sprinkled salt from the shaker into the pot. "We can eat in about fifteen minutes. Would you make a fruit salad?"

She busied herself chopping fruit while he checked the muffins.

Francine thought about the two million dollars Camille reportedly had accumulated. If she had started her nest egg ten years previously, when she began her consulting company, she would have needed two hundred thousand a year, or about seventeen thousand dollars a month, rounded. That was a mind-boggling amount.

"Do you have any idea yet how Camille was able to accumulate so much money? If she started socking money away at an early age, and then throw in the idea that she supplemented her savings with everything she earned from her consulting company, I could see that she might have managed to collect that much. But it would have required a lot of discipline."

Jonathan closed the oven door, leaving the corn muffins inside. Francine had seen him test them with a toothpick that did not come out clean. "She didn't do it in the steady fashion you're suggesting. She had a few large deposits in the early years. And no, I can't go into detail."

She peeled an orange and used kitchen scissors to snip the sections into smaller pieces. "Can you tell me if the years of the large deposits were spread out or clumped together?"

"Clumped together. But don't ask me which years. I won't tell you. Client confidentiality."

"For heaven sakes, Jonathan, she's dead. And you are as interested in solving this mystery as I am. Don't pretend you're not investigating, too, because it's obvious that's not true."

"Perhaps, but the results of *my* investigative work are going right to Jud."

"Why have you not mentioned that before?"

"You didn't ask." The stove timer went off and Jonathan lightly touched the muffins. He seemed satisfied, put on an oven mitt, and took the muffin tin out of the oven. "Jud got a search warrant issued and so we had to turn over the records from all the years we've been doing her taxes. We spent time this afternoon putting them together. I came home and found you were still gone. What have you been doing?"

Francine wasn't sure where to start. Tricky Dicky's heart attack, giving him CPR until the paramedics got there, dealing with an angry Jud, a return to the cemetery, getting shot at by crazy Cass Carter, or discovering that at one time there existed a Jacqueline Carter who apparently so affected Camille that she named her consulting company after her. Where to start? Or should she even start, knowing he was keeping stuff from her?

"It wasn't that eventful," she said. "We were at Charlotte's most of the afternoon. Joy came over to tell us she learned that the week before Camille died, Eric met with each of the Council members individually. We discussed a lot of things, like why he might have done that, if that had anything to do with Camille's death, and why she named her firm Jacqueline Consulting."

He pulled a cooling rack out of a cabinet and placed the muffin tin on it. "Get anywhere?"

She quartered an apple, cut out the core, and diced up the rest of it. "No, but I thought I might ask Eric if he knows why her firm is called Jacqueline Consulting."

"How is that related to the murder?"

Again, Francine decided not to go into detail about the photos of the cemetery and the discovering of the Jacqueline Carter grave. "We don't know. Yet." She switched topics to avoid saying any more. "Did you know that Fuzzy Carter is trying to sell land out by the I-74/Ronald Reagan Parkway interchange for a major real estate deal? Janet Turpen is involved, and we think Camille may have been involved in some way too."

Jonathan put his hands on his hips. "I hadn't heard that. Do I even want to know how you learned about it?"

"It's better if you don't, trust me."

"I think you are getting too involved in this."

"And you're not?" she threw back at him. She continued to cut fruit for the fruit salad. "We ought to invite Eric to have dinner with us sometime," she said. *So I can interrogate him,* she thought. *In a nice way, of course.*

"I thought of that too. In fact, I called and invited him tonight, but he said he and Toby were meeting a couple of the dancers at Scotty's Brewhouse for a drink."

"I'm surprised. He's been avoiding going out, at least from what I've been told. I suppose Scotty's is a public place, though. No one would try anything in a public place."

"You seem to act like the Crown Room where Camille was stabbed was not a public place."

Francine diced up a small portion of a banana and added it to the fruit mixture. "You're not making me feel any better. At least Toby will be with him." She stirred the contents of the bowl. "This is ready."

"We've still got a few minutes on the chili," Jonathan said.

"Good. I've been meaning to look for Camille's obituary in the paper. Was it in today's? I would have expected it before today, but Eric didn't seem to know what to do."

"Would you have when you were his age?"

"No, I guess not. It's still a shock to me."

They found the paper in the living room where Jonathan had read it earlier in the day. *The Indianapolis Star* had the obituaries in the front section. Francine flipped through it. "Here it is." She read through the obituary. It didn't highlight anything she didn't know. It was a good three paragraphs. For not knowing what to say, Eric had done a pretty good job of improvising. At the very end, it listed those who had preceded her in death, and it gave the name of her sister and brother-in-law, Eric's parents. That was what Francine was looking for. It occurred to her that Camille's sister's name or middle name might have been Jacqueline, which could have accounted for the consulting firm name if not Camille's interest in the grave.

"I couldn't remember the sister," Francine said. "That was a tragic thing, when they died in Texas. This says her name was Claudia Lee Ledfelter Dehoney. I had thought her middle name might be Jacqueline."

"Are you surprised it isn't?"

Relieved was more like it. "Maybe a little." Her phone dinged. She checked the text message. *Charlotte.* Charlotte rarely texted her two days in a row.

I found something interesting at the library. It doesn't relate to Jacqueline Carter or the gravestone we found in the Carter cemetery today, but it still puts a new wrinkle in what we know about the Council members. I'm back home. Can you come over?

TWENTY-SIX

FRANCINE SLID THE CELL phone back in her jeans pocket.

"What is it?" Jonathan asked.

"What is what?"

"Your hand went to your chest and you sucked in a breath like you'd just read something surprising."

Francine tried to think fast, something she wasn't always good at. "No, not at all. I felt a touch of heartburn is all. You know that happens from time to time."

"Will you be able to eat the white chicken chili?"

Francine realized Jonathan had just thrown her a lifeline. "You know, probably not. I really appreciate you making it, though. That was Charlotte texting me. She mentioned she just got home from the library and has something she wants me to see. Why don't I skip out and go see her? Go ahead and eat the chili, and hopefully my system will be settled tomorrow and I can have some for lunch."

She went to give him a kiss, but he caught her by the wrist and held on. "Fran, you are a terrible liar. Anyone could see through that lie, but especially me. What message did Charlotte send?"

She didn't want him to know about the gravestone and their visit to the cemetery. It would only lead to more questions about their investigation. She tried to pull away. He wouldn't let go of her wrist. "I really need to go see Charlotte," she insisted.

"Perhaps if we talked through it, you could convince me."

"It will take a long time to explain, and I'm not sure I have that kind of time."

"Try me. I'm not letting go until I hear you out."

Francine knew he wasn't being unreasonable, but it didn't make her any less angry. "Let go of my wrist." She said it low and threatening through gritted teeth. She hoped it would make Jonathan give up.

He lifted the forearm so it was between the two of them. It was like he wanted her to see him holding it. Then he let go. She wasn't ready, and her arm dropped a few inches before she regained control.

He said, a little hurt, "I am not a monster. I am someone who loves you very much. But if you won't tell me, go ahead and leave."

Francine paused. This wasn't like her. Maybe she was becoming a clone of Charlotte. Would too many mysteries do that to her? She reminded herself that this *was* her third dead body in less than a year.

She took a deep breath and tried to regain her composure. "Let's have some chili," she said. "My heartburn is suddenly better."

They sat down to dinner and she spilled it all, including Tricky Dicky's heart attack and the encounter with Cass Carter. She finished with the discovery of the November 22 date on the tombstone of Jacqueline Carter with no year. "I'm not sure what it means, but it feels like too much of a coincidence. The question is whether it's linked to Camille's death."

"Why didn't you tell me all this at the beginning?"

"I was mad at you for not telling me more about Camille's finances. You deliberately told me you had the information and then withheld it. What was I supposed to think?"

Jonathan pursed his lips. "I'm sorry. I shouldn't have mentioned it if I wasn't going to tell you about it."

"That's right. Now that I've been forthcoming, why don't you? Jud won't find it out from me."

She had been learning just recently that Jonathan had secrets and was pretty good at burying them. Before, she hadn't figured he had any secrets, let alone that he would keep them from her. After over forty years of marriage, this was an unexpected development. He seemed to have a reverence for authority, too, when it came to being quiet about things he knew. The information he and his business partner had gleaned from Camille's tax records was an example of the new status quo.

Jonathan crossed his arms and studied Francine. She waited him out.

"I won't do this all the time," he said, "but I'll do it now. Camille had four lump sum payments of a quarter of a million dollars each. They occurred once a year beginning six years ago. She hasn't had any for two years now."

"Were they the same time of year each time?"

"Yes. And they were all in late November."

Francine had been ready to take a final bite of the white chicken chili in her bowl, but she lowered the spoon when she registered what time of the year he said the payments took place. "Is this just one big coincidence?" she asked.

"I don't know. We don't have enough information. We know a portion of it was used to pay off Eric's student loans. Did Charlotte really go to the library, or were you making that up?"

"She really went. Her plan was to look through the yearbooks and see if she could come up with anything on Jacqueline Carter. We figured if Jacqueline was middle school age or older in 1964, she'd have an entry in the yearbook."

"That's a good assumption. I probably wouldn't have thought to check yearbooks."

"Women are like that. We want to know what was said about us. Men probably don't care."

"I don't know that I've looked at a yearbook even once since I left high school. Or college." The doorbell rang. "I'll get it." He wiped his lips with his napkin as he left the kitchen, returning through the swinging door with Charlotte in tow. "I think Charlotte has some news," he said, "but she wouldn't tell me until she had a chance to consult with you."

Charlotte didn't bother to take off her coat. She pulled a folded sheet of paper from the pocket. "Get a load of that," she said, tossing it to Francine. "I copied it out of the yearbook from when Fuzzy was a senior."

The paper turned out to be not a single sheet but three sheets folded together in quarters. Francine unfolded them and smoothed out the creases. Charlotte had copied several photographs, but the reproductions weren't very good. Francine had to squint to determine who was in the pictures and even then had to read the captions to figure out what Charlotte was getting at. When she did, her reaction was one of quiet reflection.

She shrugged. "It's just proof that Fuzzy and Vince were best friends back then. We knew that."

"You might have, but look at the girl Fuzzy is holding hands with," Charlotte said, taking off her coat finally. "She's only an eighth grader."

Jonathan studied the photographs over Francine's shoulders. "She doesn't look like an eighth grader."

"Nonetheless, she is," Charlotte said. She plopped into a chair at the table.

"Fuzzy always had an eye for the younger women. Remember that Cass is ten years younger than him. She was a new teacher at the high school when he started dating her."

"It's not illegal then. She would have been twenty-one or more."

"But she probably looked sixteen. She's always looked young. I'm just saying it's a pattern with Fuzzy. The women he dates now are all much younger than he is."

Francine turned behind her to look at Jonathan. She was trying to determine if anything she'd learned fit with this new information. Of course, she couldn't very well reveal to Charlotte the payments she'd learned Camille had received from a mysterious source, especially with Jonathan standing right there. But they didn't seem to fit anyway. Francine could feel Charlotte watching the two of them.

"Okay, what is it?" Charlotte asked. "You act like the cat who swallowed the canary, Francine. If you open your mouth, will I see feathers? What is it you don't want me to know? Because I'll get it out of you. If not now, then later when Jonathan isn't around."

"I'm not hiding anything. I was only processing your information."

Charlotte folded her arms over her chest. "Well, what about you?" she asked. "You were supposed to ask Eric if he knew why his aunt named her consulting company Jacqueline Consulting. What did you find out?"

"Nothing yet."

"You haven't found out anything new?"

She shrugged nonchalantly. "I found out that Camille's sister Claudia's middle name was Lee."

Charlotte thought a moment, then laughed. "I'd forgotten her name was Claudia. That makes the link to Jacqueline Consulting interesting."

"How?"

"Claudia was Lady Bird Johnson's real name. Lady Bird was Lyndon Johnson's wife, of course, and she became first lady…"

"…after JFK died," Francine finished.

"And Lee was Jackie Kennedy's middle name," Jonathan added. "I didn't think of the 'Lee' connection until just now, when Charlotte mentioned the Claudia thing."

Francine frowned. "How is it the two of you can remember things like that? I only remember the press using 'Bouvier' for Jackie Kennedy. I know that was her maiden name, not her middle name, but still." She turned to Charlotte. "And how the heck do you remember Lady Bird Johnson's real name?"

Charlotte leaned over and pilfered a piece of corn muffin left uneaten on Francine's plate. "I don't know how my memory works. I can't remember today's date but I can name a tune from 1967 in five notes. It's crazy."

Jonathan absentmindedly massaged Francine's shoulders. "More importantly, is this just coincidence, or does it mean something?"

"What do you mean by *coincidence*?" Charlotte cracked. "I would have dumped 'Claudia' for 'Lady Bird' in a heartbeat."

"You know what I mean. Significance."

"I don't see how it could have any," Charlotte said, thinking. "Camille's sister was older than her, so I think she was born before Lady Bird Johnson or Jackie Kennedy were first lady. It has to be a coincidence."

Francine, who had clipped the articles about Camille's election for the display board, thought otherwise. "But even given the unlikelihood of a link between Camille's sister's name and the Johnson/

Kennedy connection, there is this: after Camille won the race, she said she was a Kennedy admirer. Even though she ran as a Republican."

Jonathan was matter-of-fact about that. "We all know why she ran as a Republican. A Democrat hasn't been elected in Hendricks County for decades. A lot of people just pull the party lever, especially if they don't have time to study the candidates."

"Or won't take the time to learn about them," Charlotte said. "Once you've won your primary, you're a lock."

Francine handed the yearbook copies back to Charlotte. "But it could still account for the Jacqueline name."

"I think we should just ask Eric," Charlotte said, looking at Francine. "Where is he?"

"He and Toby went to Scotty's Brewhouse to meet some of the other male strippers."

Charlotte's eyebrows went up. "That sounds like fun! Let's go."

Francine tried to think of a reason not to go. She wasn't successful. "I guess we could do that."

"Hot dog!" Charlotte said. "I like hanging around male strippers. It's fun. Except when someone dies. Then it's a real downer."

"It shouldn't be a downer tonight."

Charlotte picked up her purse. "Coming Jonathan?"

"No. It doesn't sound like that much fun to me. Besides, I don't think you'll be there long."

"Suit yourself."

Before she left the house, Francine excused herself to go upstairs. She went to the study and extracted the ampule of formula number 58. It had a small hole in the tip, and she attached it to her necklace. *Just in case*, she thought.

TWENTY-SEVEN

SCOTTY'S BREWHOUSE WAS LOCATED on Northfield Drive in a strip mall just west of Green Street. Francine drove herself and Charlotte there in her Prius. She'd already done enough driving of Charlotte's boat of a car in the last couple of days. She realized too late that she should have at least checked to see if they were being followed. Although, as dark as it was, she wasn't sure she would have been able to determine anything.

This being a Monday, Francine was able to find a parking spot not too far from the door. She elected to park rather than drop Charlotte at the door first. She reasoned that with Charlotte's improvement in her knee, the walk would do her good.

They opened the door, and the drone of sporting events on the many televisions spilled out and assaulted their ears. *Sports announcers sound alike in all manner of sporting events except golf*, Francine thought. Golf announcers whispered like raising their voices would wreak havoc on the concentration of the competitors, even though they were located in studios far from where any golf swings were taking place. These were not golf announcer voices, though, not on a Monday night. These were basketball announcers and hockey announcers and professional wrestling announcers. Their voices were loud and brash, and they blended into a cacophony of noise amid the bright lights of a half dozen or more LED televisions glowing in the dark spacious serving room while smells of delicious food rolled out of the Brewhouse's kitchen. It was an atmosphere that worked, and not just for young people. Francine and Jonathan and their friends had eaten there many times.

The women peered through the darkness and located the men, grouped around a couple of tables on the left side of the restaurant near a television broadcasting two scantily clad women about to engage in a professional wrestling bout. The men appeared to be only half watching the screen. They were more involved in ESPN *SportsCenter*, which was being televised on an adjacent set. On the table were beers and food.

Francine saw Toby notice them. He tilted his head to the side as if to ask if they were here to see him. Francine nodded and he waved them over.

He gave them a hug. The other men nodded in acknowledgement. "What are you two doing here?" he asked.

"We came to see Eric," Francine said.

Eric seemed surprised. Since he was on the other side of Toby and there was no way the women could maneuver their way around to him, Eric traded places with Toby so they could talk without having to shout too loudly. "What do you need?" he asked.

"We need to know why your aunt named her firm Jacqueline Consulting," Charlotte blurted out.

Eric wrinkled his nose. "You do? Why?"

Francine didn't want Charlotte to say too much too soon, so she jumped in with a simple explanation. "We think it might shed some light on who killed her."

"I don't see how it could," he said. "To the best of my knowledge, she took it after my middle name, which is Jack. I thought she just feminized it."

"But she never confirmed that?" Charlotte pressed. "She never actually told you that?

Eric continued to look puzzled. "No. Do you know otherwise?"

Francine and Charlotte looked at each other.

Francine spoke hesitantly. "Does the name Jacqueline Carter mean anything to you?"

"Carter," he repeated with just a touch of defensiveness. "It's a common name. Or are you implying it's somehow connected to the local Carters?"

Again the two women made eye contact. This time Charlotte spoke.

"Camille seemed to have a special fondness for a grave in the Carter cemetery that's on Cass Carter's land. The gravestone has 'Jacqueline Carter' on it. We thought that might be it."

Eric stared at them. He had a distant look in his eyes.

"Uh, oh," Toby said. Francine glanced over at him. But he wasn't looking at her. He was squinting at a figure whose silhouette was framed by light coming from the kitchen area. He was holding a microphone and advancing toward their table. "Francine," he said, "did you check to see if you were followed on your way over?"

"No," she answered. "Why?"

"Because a certain individual who knows how to hack his way into electronics and thinks he is destined to be a stripper is on his way over here."

There was a blip over the sound system and all the audio went dead except for the karaoke strains of a song.

"I can name that tune in five notes," said Charlotte. "It's Whitney Houston's version of Dolly Parton's 'I Will Always Love You.' It's from *The Bodyguard*."

Tripper the Stripper began to sing as he slowly unbuttoned his shirt. Francine wasn't sure how he had managed to do it, but the lights in the Brewhouse had come up in a sequence that highlighted his slow approach toward Charlotte. Lights elsewhere had dimmed.

"Hoo-wee!" said Charlotte. "He's got an unbelievable voice. He could sing to me all day long." She waved to him as though he weren't already coming this direction. "Over here, Tripper!"

"This is way too creepy," Toby said. "We need to get you two out of here before this gets any worse."

But it's already getting worse, Francine thought. Charlotte was climbing onto one of the chairs so she was tall enough to see Tripper coming. Once she reached it, her eyes searched for a way to get even taller. She eyed the table.

"I don't think that's a good idea, Charlotte," Francine called, trying to raise her voice above the audio recording.

Tripper launched into the drawn-out chorus.

The crowd seemed mesmerized by what was going on. Every face in the restaurant was focused on the voice that came from the pipes of the skinny man slowly threading his way through the maze of tables toward someone standing on a chair. They seemed to not notice he was singing to a short, elderly woman with a crooked silvery wig.

Charlotte sang loudly in unison, her arms waving with abandon. She made no real attempt to hit the same notes Tripper was hitting. She didn't care, and no one else seemed to, either.

"Train wreck," Toby muttered, his eyes wide with alarm. "You don't suppose Charlotte is going to ..."

Francine knew what he was thinking. "She might."

Charlotte began unbuttoning the sweater she was wearing. She didn't look steady but at least she wasn't dancing on the table. Though Francine worried she might try that next.

Then the music picked up. It morphed into a disco version of the song Francine had never heard before. It had a strong beat, and the tempo picked up. The crowd began to clap to the new rhythm.

Francine gripped Toby by his arm. "Please get her down before she hurts herself!" *Or embarrasses herself*, she thought. *Or us.* But she felt her face blushing and knew it was too late for the latter.

Toby got closer to the chair Charlotte was standing on. He was so much taller than her that his arms were at the same height as hers. He tried to stop her hands from fumbling with the buttons.

In one swift motion Tripper jumped onto an empty table, still some distance away from them.

One thing's for sure, Francine thought, *that Tripper is an agile guy.*

The karaoke music moved on to the second verse, Tripper's hypnotic voice crooning over the hijacked speakers.

Charlotte batted at Toby's hands. He became more insistent. He shifted his gaze from Charlotte to the person she was focused on. Tripper had now removed his shirt to reveal his skinny torso.

Francine watched Charlotte become unbalanced on the chair as she fought off Toby's hands. "Can you just pick her up and get her down?" she asked.

"I'll try." He swooped an arm under her legs, tilted her back, and caught her with his other arm as she fell. She was laughing. She put her arms around his neck and kissed him on the cheek.

A black man in a Scotty's uniform walked rapidly toward Tripper. He carried a snifter glass in one hand. Francine recognized him as "Isaac Washington," the stripper who'd been auctioned off first at the benefit. *So he really is a bartender*, she thought.

"Tripper, please get down from the table," Isaac said.

He continued crooning until he reached a spot where Whitney Houston would have taken a breath. "Can't," he said. "I've been hired to do a job, and I won't rest until I complete my mission."

Then he shifted back into song. He jumped one table closer to Charlotte and removed his belt.

Isaac advanced on the next table and held up the snifter glass. "If you come down now," he shouted over the music, "we're prepared to give you two complimentary glasses of cognac."

Then quickly before the next line started, Tripper asked, "On the house?"

The refrain started up. Tripper didn't sing. But everyone else in the restaurant did.

"It's Prunier," Isaac yelled.

Prunier? Francine thought. *Really?*

Isaac nodded. "But you have to come down before you take your pants off. If we see any underwear, the deal's off."

Everyone in the place was staring at the spectacle that was developing at the north end of the building. And they continued to sing, completely amused.

Tripper jumped to the next table. Unlike the former tables, this one had been occupied and not yet bussed. Glasses slid off and crashed onto the floor, splintering into glass shards that skittered in all directions. Isaac reached the table in time to nab an appetizer platter with his free hand as it teetered on the edge. His quick action prevented remnants of a Macho Nachos feast from splattering the ground like a Pollack masterpiece, but his shoes took a hit from the salsa. The sound of glass crunching under his feet made his eyes widen, but his attention never wavered from Tripper.

"No underwear," he cautioned.

Tripper was now only one table length away from Charlotte and Toby. Finding the table to be mostly empty now, he hopped on one foot and removed a slip-on shoe from the other. The karaoke machine moved on to the third stanza. He breathed the words into the microphone, going for a husky, pity-me effect.

Isaac slid the platter onto another table and showed Tripper the snifter again. "I'm losing my patience, but if you get down now you can still have the cognac."

Toby, wrestling with a squirming Charlotte in his arms, tried to back away from the action. Unfortunately he hadn't accounted for Charlotte's leg sweeping across the table Tripper was on. Tripper saw it coming and hopped on one foot again, but the movement made him tip to one side and lose his balance. He hit the table, rebounded with a jump, and launched himself toward Isaac. To his credit, he did a somersault in midair, missed Isaac, and stuck the landing.

The music might have gone on, but Francine couldn't hear it. The applause in the room for Tripper was deafening. As it died down, Tripper picked up the end of the third stanza.

The crowd joined Tripper once again with the refrain. They sang so loudly that when the song ended, Francine couldn't hear him, though she was standing right next to him. Tripper took Charlotte from Toby, held her in his arms, grinned ear to ear, and sang a capella, just as Whitney had done at the end of the song, only faster. He wore no shirt, only one shoe, and both socks, but he still had his pants on.

Isaac looked relieved.

Tripper set Charlotte back on her feet. "Mission accomplished," he said, and saluted her. "I'll have that drink now." He took the snifter from Isaac.

Francine saw the spinning lights of two Brownsburg Police cars pull up in front of the restaurant. Officers came through the front door, guns drawn.

"It's okay, officers," Isaac said. "I think the situation's under control."

"Darn tooting we're okay," said Charlotte. "This is one of the most fun nights I've had in a while." She waggled her eyebrows at Tripper. "*I'm your baby now*," she sang, slightly off key and off lyric, but giving a fair rendition of another Whitney hit. This brought more laughter from the throng.

"A few broken glasses," Isaac recounted to the older of the policemen, "but nothing that couldn't have happened with a careless server. We won't file any charges. And I'm hoping this is the last we'll see of him attempting to be a stripper."

"I don't know about that," Tripper said. "I thought I did a pretty good job. And I don't have any other talents."

"You have your voice," Francine answered. "You have an amazing singing voice. It's like Jim Nabors performing 'Back Home Again in Indiana' at the Indianapolis 500. All anyone could think of when they looked at him was Gomer, the character he played on *The Andy Griffith Show*, but then he opened his mouth and this beautiful, confident, melodious voice came out. That's you! You do the same thing."

Tripper blushed.

Somewhere, Tripper's hacking into the sound system was undone. The noise of the televisions and their various sporting events roared back over the audio channels. Servers rushed out to clean up the mess that had been made, which didn't appear to be too bad.

Francine breathed a sigh of relief. She'd have to talk to Marcy about finding some singing gigs for Tripper. Maybe the women could help him with whatever demons still plagued him from being in the war. She hoped so. *He may be troubled*, she thought, *but he certainly feels the call to duty. He could probably hold a job. And what a voice!*

Francine found she still had her purse slung over her shoulder. She dug out her keys and started toward Charlotte, who'd been offered a margarita by a group of young people watching *American Ninja Warrior*. "It's going to be tough pulling her away from all this attention," she said. She'd intended to mutter it to herself, but then she discovered Toby was standing next to her.

"That's our Charlotte," he said, rolling his eyes. "Have you seen Eric?"

Francine looked around. She didn't see him, but the lights had gone dim again for watching television. "Maybe the restroom?"

Toby shrugged. "Maybe." He didn't sound convinced. He looked worried. "I'm going to go check."

That was when she realized that she hadn't seen Eric since they'd told him about the gravestone for Jacqueline Carter. Tripper's escapade might have provided the perfect cover for his exit.

She wondered if he'd taken it.

TWENTY-EIGHT

WITHIN A FEW MINUTES Toby came back from the restroom zig-zagging through the restaurant scouting for Eric. The rest of the male dance troupe didn't know Francine, and they were conversing among themselves. She thought about trying to pry Charlotte from the group of Millennials who were encouraging her with a margarita, but she wanted to hear what Toby had to say about Eric. Since Toby appeared to be still searching for him, it didn't look good.

Then she remembered that Isaac, who'd returned to bar duty, had tried to tempt Tripper with Prunier cognac. The coincidence of Camille having given Charlotte a bottle of it and Tripper being of-fered it made her curious. She left Charlotte to her margarita and Toby to his search and walked over to the bar area. There were no empty barstools near the center of the bar, where Isaac was stand-ing, but she didn't want one near other people. She wanted to be out of whispering range so she could ask about the cognac. She sat at the far end of the bar, near the wall.

Isaac walked over. "What can I get you, Mrs. McNamara?" he asked, placing a small napkin in front of her.

"A glass of white wine, please."

"Chardonnay?"

"That works. And I'd like some information."

He gave a throaty chuckle. "I've heard that about you. Is the wine order for real, or do you just want the information? I'd tell you what I can even without the order."

She looked back at Charlotte, who seemed to be enjoying herself, and Toby, who was now in conversation with the male strip group. "I think a glass might do me some good."

"Then let me get that first." He returned to the center, pulled a bottle of wine out of a small refrigerator below the bar, and poured a glass. A hefty man with a beard gestured for another mug of whatever beer he was drinking. Isaac pulled a draft from the tap and set it down next to the not-quite-empty one. He took the man's money, gave him change, and then returned to Francine with her glass of wine. He set a glass on the white cocktail napkin he'd left in front of her.

He leaned against the bar on his right side so he could see the bar and notice if anyone needed to be served, but was close enough to Francine that they could have a quiet conversation. "What do you need to know?"

"You tried to bribe Tripper with Prunier cognac. I'd like to know who else drinks it. Cognac seems like an unusual thing for you to serve here, especially a name brand."

"It *is* a bit unusual. I confess I'd never served it until I started working here. I had a special request, which is how we came to stock it."

"Do you remember who asked you for it?"

He nodded. "Do you know the owner of the funeral home?"

Francine's eyes shot up. "Vince Papadopoulos?"

"Yep. He's the one."

"Does he come in here often?"

Isaac nodded again. "I think we're his go-to stop for dinner after evening visitations. Prunier is his preferred aperitif. Sometimes he buys the rest of the bottle from us. I give it to him at a good discount, since he's about the only one who drinks it."

That could explain the bottle Camille gave Charlotte, Francine thought, *if Vince had given the bottle to Camille opened, and she'd regifted it.* Francine would question Charlotte about the bottle's condition later.

"What about Tripper? He must like it or you wouldn't have tried to bribe him with it."

Isaac snorted. "Tripper's a draft beer guy, and *cheap* beer at that. He and Vince had a drink one night after a veteran's funeral. Vince bought him cognac. It's all Tripper could talk about after that. At least, until he ordered one and discovered it was more expensive than his usual."

Francine sipped her wine. It was sweeter than what she usually liked, but it was good. "Is Tripper okay? Everyone talks like he's a little ... off."

"He's had a rough go of it since he returned home from Iraq. He'd probably get better if he were evaluated and treated by the Veterans hospital, but he refuses to go. Mostly he wanders from one job to another."

"What's the obsession with stripping?"

"I figure it's symptomatic of something that happened during the war. He struggled with it for a while after he got back. Most of us thought he'd conquered it until he found out about our dance troupe. Now he thinks it's okay to do that, if someone pays him."

"I wouldn't think he'd get much business."

"I wouldn't think he'd get *any.* But those of us in the troupe are so busy now, trying to fit in gigs around our regular jobs, that I guess there's a market even for him."

"Do you think this will last?"

He gave her a wry smile. "No. We're just the latest fad around here. It'll run its course until the next fad takes over. I just want to make as much extra money as I can while we have the public's attention."

Francine took another sip. "Let me ask you something about the troupe. Has Eric said anything to you about creating a permanent location here in Brownsburg?"

Isaac laughed. "In Brownsburg? You must be kidding. Since he brought the group up from Texas a year ago, he's talked about returning. I haven't heard him talk about it for a while, though."

"Would you go?"

"I wouldn't, but I'm from around here. The two transplants who came up here with him might. I think they like the lower cost of living here, though. We might not have as many gigs, but we manage pretty well. One of them got a job with a high-tech company in downtown Indy, and he may drop out altogether."

A customer down the bar motioned for him. "Anything else?" Isaac asked.

"No. Thanks for your time."

He nodded and headed down to the other end of the bar. Francine picked up her wine, left a five-dollar tip, and went to find Charlotte, who was back with Toby and the remaining strippers.

"She's back from the world's longest potty break," Charlotte said. Her words slurred together like ingredients in a frozen margarita, which Francine suspected she'd had one too many of. The words were no longer distinct, yet the sentence was understandable.

Francine displayed the half-full wine glass she'd carried with her. "I went to the bar," she said. "Not the restroom."

"Eric's gone," Toby said.

"I didn't need to go to the bar," Charlotte said as if Toby hadn't spoken. "Those nice young people over there bought me this." She indicated an empty glass in front of her. Then she realized it had nothing in it. Her face hovered over it disbelievingly, like she couldn't comprehend why it was empty. "Well, it had a strawberry margarita in it."

"Those fruity drinks go down easy," Francine said. "Are you sure you had only one?"

Charlotte frowned at her. "I am not drunk."

"You're maybe a little tipsy, then." She turned to Toby. "Where do you think he went?"

"Don't know, but his car isn't in the parking lot. So I need a ride."

Francine began hunting through her purse for a key. "Are you ready to go? Because I think I might need to get Charlotte home."

Stieg, the blond, chiseled-cut dancer she remembered from the benefit, waved her off. "We'll get him home," he said, indicating Toby. "It's early yet."

Francine pulled out the key to the Prius. "Not for us older folks," she said with a smile. "C'mon, Charlotte."

When Charlotte hesitated, Francine took her arm. "It's time for us to review the facts of the case, anyway."

"Then I'm on it." Charlotte said. She slipped off the high bar-stool and had to grab onto the table to steady herself. "Maybe I've had a bit too much to drink."

Francine steered her toward the exit. "With margaritas, the alcohol doesn't catch up to you until after you've had more than enough."

"Good night," Toby called after them.

Francine walked Charlotte out. She was glad to get into the cold night air. She hit the remote button on the key to her car and the Prius came unlocked. For a moment, she wondered if she might find Eric in the back seat. She glanced through the back window just to be sure. The light from the parking lot street lamp illuminated the seat. He wasn't there. She was both relieved and disappointed.

The women got in the car. "So to recap," Charlotte said, slipping on her seat belt, "Here's what we know. I'll do this chronologically. We know Fuzzy and Vince were best buds back in the day, in high school. We know Fuzzy dated girls younger than him, which may well have led to his later relationship with Cass, her being much younger than he."

"We don't really *know* that about Fuzzy." Francine adjusted the rearview mirror before she put the car in drive. "That's conjecture on your part."

Charlotte shrugged off the criticism. "We have demonstrated proof of two instances where that was true, but have it your way. We'll call it an educated guess."

Francine drove out of the Scotty's parking lot and turned south on Green Street. "We know that he married Cass in the early nineties, and they didn't have kids."

"To my point about younger women," Charlotte said, interrupting, "she was only twenty or twenty-one at the time, while he was in his early thirties. She graduated from college the year after they were married."

"He worked at the high school, didn't he?"

"Right. He was the shop teacher."

"So she wouldn't have had him as a teacher?"

Charlotte seemed taken aback by the implication. "I see where you're going with that. But no, he wouldn't have been her teacher. Girls didn't take shop back then."

"Okay. But after college she joined the faculty teaching phys ed."

"She did." Charlotte shifted in her seat so she could better face Francine. "Fast forward fifteen years. Cass and Fuzzy get a divorce.

Vince and Myra side with Cass, which forces Fuzzy and Vince's friendship to fracture."

"Which is natural," Francine continued, "since Myra and Cass are sisters. When did Vince and Myra marry?"

"About a year after Fuzzy and Cass. Myra is the older sister by five years, so the age difference wasn't as big. I'm not sure Vince even noticed Myra until Fuzzy started dating her sister."

Francine reached the railroad tracks and slowed as they went over the bumpy grade. She accelerated and reached a red light at Main Street. She put on her turn signal to make a left. "Then we have another big gap, don't we, until Fuzzy and Vince both get elected to the Council? When was that?"

"Just before the turn of the century. Although, we *do* know the divorce was messy and that somehow Cass ended up with land that included the Carter family cemetery."

"With the Jacqueline Carter headstone."

"Exactly. Though we still don't know when Jacqueline was born or died."

The light turned green. Francine turned east onto Main. "If I remember right, Camille was elected to the Council around 2010, right after the capture of the pornographer, which was what got her name out there and probably made her electable."

"Right."

"Was the Council contentious before Camille arrived, or did she somehow instigate it?" Francine hadn't paid much attention to politics or gossip before she retired.

"There was some dissention, but when Camille came on board, it escalated. Vince in particular became set against whatever she wanted . . ." her voice trailed off.

Francine looked at her friend. Her white glasses were smudged and her blue eyes were staring into another land. Francine knew

Charlotte was at her free-thinking best. Francine couldn't watch because she was driving, but she'd seen that look before. It usually happened when Charlotte pieced together a difficult puzzle, a puzzle that involved a leap in logic. More times than not, though, its basis was sound. She imagined Charlotte's brain crowded with plots from Agatha Christie to James Patterson, and the facts of this case pinging against them until an answer emerged.

There was silence in the car for a while. Francine was afraid to disturb Charlotte while she was thinking like this.

Finally Charlotte came out of the trance-like state. "We'll be passing by Papadopoulos Funeral Home, won't we?"

"We already did. I can take a right at the next light and circle back. Do you want me to?"

"Yes."

"Why?"

"I want to see if Eric's car is in the parking lot."

TWENTY-NINE

THE PAPADOPOULOS FUNERAL HOME was in an old Victorian house one street off of Main and several blocks east of Town Hall in a historic area of Brownsburg. Since it wasn't located directly on Main, the Papadopoulos family had purchased the rundown house between it and the chief thoroughfare in the 1960s, cleared the lot and paved it for parking. The grand old mansion then looked like it was a part of the Main Street corridor. Over the years, Papadopoulos's had become *the* place to have a funeral. Francine remembered Charlotte's report on rumors that the funeral home was having difficulties and was for sale. She hoped not. It was part of the fabric of the community.

The parking lot had a fair number of cars in it, but it was not full by any means. *Must be a small funeral tonight*, Francine thought.

"Is that Eric's car over there?" Charlotte asked, pointing to a blue Mustang parked in a dark corner of the lot.

"Looks like it."

"Park. Let's go in and find him."

"I'm not dressed for a funeral," Francine protested.

"It's okay. We're here to find Eric. He's not here for the funeral, either."

"What's he here for? And how did you know he'd be here?"

"I think he's here to see Myra Papadopoulos. I just don't know what it's about."

"How do you know he's here to see Myra?"

"There's a certain pattern to Camille's work. She was all about finding out secrets. I think she used them for blackmail. All she had to do was sit in a coffeehouse, troll around on the very public WiFi, and discover what people were doing. Most of it was probably droll. But every once in a while, she'd hit the jackpot. At least, she'd have to, to get all that money. I got to thinking, what's worth that much to Fuzzy or Vince? It'd have to be pretty damning."

"What about Janet Turpen?"

"Janet was on the sidelines. She got paid by Camille, not the other way around."

"What does any of this have to do with Jacqueline Carter?"

"I think Camille was investigating that when she got killed. I think she smelled a new victim when it was clear Cass wasn't going to sell the property she got in the divorce settlement. That property is worth a lot of money. It's the last piece needed to develop that area at the interchange into a retail center. A lot of people want it to develop, including most of the Council."

"So what's the big secret that ties all of them together, and why would Eric seek out Myra?"

"Because he knows something about Cass Carter and Jacqueline Carter. It's why he took off after we told him about the grave. Myra is her sister, and Camille had something on the Papadopouloses that Eric likely also knew. The two must be linked, but I have no idea how. Let's go find out."

The women exited the car. Francine looked back at Eric's car. They were parked far enough away from it that she didn't have a good view. "Wait," she said, clutching Charlotte's arm. "I thought I saw something in Eric's car."

Charlotte studied the scene. "It's just shadows from that tree over there near the street light, the one with the spooky branches blowing in the wind."

"I don't think so."

"Sure it is. Let's get inside and figure out what's going on. I'm going to turn into a popsicle if we stay out here much longer. My buzz is already wearing off."

The two of them walked arm in arm headed for the entrance, Francine steadying Charlotte where the sidewalk seemed a little slick. They both took in a breath as they reached the front steps that led up to the entrance. The spotlights in the yard lit up the old mansion in a sepia-toned way that daylight couldn't.

"At night it's almost like you can read the history of the house," Francine said.

"Vince certainly has a good eye for restoration work," Charlotte said, agreeing. "This is a pristine example of twentieth-century Victorian mansions."

"I've always admired the fact that he preserved the diamond pane window," Francine said. "I heard he had to re-create the gable fretwork."

As the two stood there, a woman Francine recognized as a cheerleader from many years ago descended the steps with her husband. They nodded to Francine and Charlotte but didn't attempt to engage in conversation. They reached the sidewalk and continued into the parking lot. The women watched them go.

Charlotte nudged Francine. "I'm nervous, too, but we can't put this off. We need to go in."

"You have a plan?" Francine asked.

She shook her head. "We'll make it up as we go along. Just remember that no one's likely to question us as to how well we know whoever's dead. That would be impolite. This is Brownsburg after all."

Francine hooked her arm solidly in Charlotte's and they walked the steep steps from the street up to the front wraparound porch. The entry door was made of solid oak stained dark with an etched glass window that had lace curtains behind it. The light from the front parlor shone through the lace. Together they navigated the threshold.

They hung their coats on the rack that had been wheeled in for visitors to use. Francine had a brainstorm. "We're here to see about Camille's funeral tomorrow, right? Mary Ruth is catering, and she sent us here to see what the setup is. That way we can talk our way into the rest of the house if we don't see Eric out front."

Charlotte's brow creased as she considered it. "It's a bit late in the evening to be claiming that, but we'll go with it. The first thing to do is get our name on the guest list and see what the old guy looks like. Get the lay of the land."

Francine glanced around the room, checking to see who she knew. They were in the foyer next to the parlor. The parlor was always where they placed the casket and rows of chairs for people to sit. The receiving line didn't stretch into the foyer, so it was easy to walk up to the guest book and sign it without being seen. Francine wanted to start looking after that, but Charlotte stuck her head in the parlor. "Eric's not in there," she whispered, after scanning the crowd for him. "Let's snoop. You have to use the restroom, don't you? I know I do."

Francine nodded. "Nothing makes me need to use the toilet quite like snooping through an old house searching for an elusive stripper and clues as to why Camille Ledfelter was murdered at a fund-raiser featuring half naked men."

"Don't get snippy, Francine. You know why I asked. There're restrooms in the back."

The two went past the coatrack and into the back part of the house. The hallway was long and had several sets of doors on each side. The first two rooms were across from each other and had placards marking MEN and WOMEN. Charlotte reached for the antique crystal doorknob on the dark wooden door marked WOMEN. She rattled it but didn't actually turn the knob to open it. "Too bad it's already occupied," she said with a wink. "We'll have to look farther for another."

They were headed for the next entryway when they heard a noise in a room with a closed door. Whatever was inside, it was clacking in a mechanical way, as though some machine were operating. Charlotte put an ear to the door, listening. She seemed to make an instant decision. Glancing both ways down the hall to make sure no one would see them, she turned the knob and went in.

Francine swiftly followed on Charlotte's heels, anxious to get out of the hall where she might be seen. The room was dark and she eased the door shut behind them.

THIRTY

CHARLOTTE FLIPPED A LIGHT switch. On the other side of the room, a desk lamp with a Tiffany shade came on. The orange and green of the shade made for a dim light, but it illuminated the room enough to maneuver. The lamp sat on a beast of a desk made of dark cherry wood. Three large floor-to-ceiling windows were behind the desk, each with its own set of drapes. The drapes were pulled. The room smelled musty.

"Vince's office," Charlotte said, sotto voce.

The sound in the room was a constant, low-level whirring, intermittently interrupted by a ratcheting clack that would go on for some time. Francine recognized it as the noise they'd heard from the hall. It came from a strange-looking machine sitting on a short table to one side of the desk. Charlotte advanced toward it.

Close-up, the strange machine was a black rectangular box with open sides. It was taller than it was long, maybe three feet high and two feet across. Francine estimated its depth to be about a foot and a half. A thin mechanical arm came out from the back, bent over into the open top, and moved around the internal space of the box. It spun some kind of plastic material that it extruded. It seemed to be creating an object. The bottom of the machine reminded Francine of the laser printer they had at home. That was when it hit her.

"It's a 3-D printer."

"You know that for sure?" Charlotte asked, examining the device up close.

"No, but what else could it be?"

She continued to stare at it. "I suppose you're right. How does it work?"

"My understanding is you have to feed a digital blueprint of the object you want to copy into its memory. Then the arm spits out a plastic string as it re-creates the shape of the object it's supposed to duplicate."

"If this is a 3-D printer," Charlotte said, "That would explain a lot."

"About where the sheath was made for the Vietnam-era knife that killed Camille?"

Charlotte nodded. "That and a lot more. Let's hope it still has the knife loaded into its memory."

The two women watched the mechanical arm continue its journey across the internal space in the box. creating something they didn't yet recognize. "What is it making, do you think?" Francine asked.

"No idea," Charlotte answered. "But we've seen all we need to see. Let's get out of here."

"Here meaning this room?"

"And the funeral home."

"What about Eric?" Francine asked.

"We can question him tomorrow. I think we should let Jud know we've located a 3-D printer. Maybe he can do something."

The women crept out of the room, turning off the light before they opened the door into the brightly lit hallway.

Charlotte took a couple of steps out and stopped abruptly. Francine bumped into her from behind, propelling her forward. Charlotte stopped inches from an apron-clad Myra Papadopoulos, who was leaned against the wall opposite Vince's office, watching them, her arms crossed over her chest.

"Hi Myra," Charlotte said, as though there were nothing suspicious about her behavior. She backed up so she and Francine were standing side by side. "Francine and I were looking for a restroom, and that one was already occupied." She gestured to the women's room down the hall toward the entryway.

"Ya'll could have tried the public restrooms outside the parlor. We provide those for the convenience of our funeral guests." Myra unfolded her arms. Unlike Cass, who projected feminine strength, Myra projected power. Her body was sturdy, and she stared at them with unplucked eyebrows and black eyes that glared threateningly. Her accent, while still Indiana-rural, had gotten a little more refined from her role as a funeral home director's wife.

"We should have thought of that," said Charlotte, snapping her fingers at Francine.

"But actually," Francine chimed in, "we were looking for the kitchen, which is why we were back here. We're helping Mary Ruth cater tomorrow's bereavement dinner for Camille Ledfelter, and we thought we'd check out the kitchen ahead of time."

"Mary Ruth came earlier," Myra said.

Charlotte thought quickly. "She sent us to double check refrigerator space."

Myra didn't look convinced. "Well, I suspect you've been to enough funeral dinners here to know where the kitchen is."

Francine smiled. "Down the hall on the right?"

Myra gave a little bow and gestured for them to go first.

Charlotte led the way, turning in the entryway. Francine's mind was already throwing up red flags. They knew Myra, like Cass, was familiar with guns, and it would be prudent to assume she was carrying under that apron. As soon as they were in the kitchen, she took in as much of the surroundings as she could with a glance.

The kitchen was serviceable but cramped. It had been modernized with new appliances that only served to take up more space. The stove, refrigerator, and pantry were to the right. To the left of the sink was a long row of cabinets attached to the wall. In front of it was a table with six chairs around it. At it sat Vince Papadopoulos, helping himself to food set out for the family of the deceased to eat. He was the only other one in the room.

"I found some visitors in the hall." Myra said. "Were you expecting company?"

Vince used his fork to split a small meatball in half. He looked up. "No, but let's be welcoming. Make yourselves at home, ladies. Have a seat." He put the half meatball in his mouth, chewed, and swallowed.

Charlotte didn't sit, though. She picked up a plate and began to put food on it.

"What are you doing?" Vince asked her.

"You said to make ourselves at home. This is what I do at home."

Vince eyed her with a great deal of suspicion.

Francine watched Charlotte concentrate on the desserts. There was a banana cream pie, a peanut butter pie with meringue, and a cherry pie. Charlotte took larger pieces of the banana and peanut butter and a smaller piece of the cherry. She picked up a fork and napkin and sat down.

Francine was stunned at her nonchalance. *Doesn't she feel the danger?* She was about to reassess the situation when Myra jammed something hard and metallic into her back.

She didn't need to rethink anything.

"Help yourself to some food like your friend has," Myra said, her voice mixed with faux hospitality. "Then sit down. You're going to be here a while."

It struck Francine that Myra sounded much like her sister Cass had in the graveyard when she'd threatened them with a shotgun. "I think I'll pass on the food."

"Too bad," Charlotte said. "It looks like a pretty good spread." She used a dessert fork to spear a bite of the cherry pie. She chewed it thoughtfully. "This is canned pie filling, though."

Myra ignored her and focused on Francine. "Where's Jonathan?"

"He didn't come," Francine said. Too late she realized she should have made them think he was there. It might have distracted them for a while. She tried to cover. "But he knows we're here. If we're not home soon, he'll come looking for us."

Myra jerked her thumb toward the front of the house. "He might be in with the funeral crowd. Start there and then check the rest of the house."

"You sure you want me to leave you here alone with them?"

Myra pulled the gun out of the folds of her skirt. She trained it on Charlotte now. "I don't think they're likely to try anything."

Vince wiped his mouth, making sure he'd cleaned any food off his mustache. He gave a quick laugh and left.

Francine wondered how much time they had before Vince came back. Myra took the seat Vince had vacated, which was next to her. She sat just out of Francine's reach.

"So," Charlotte said, almost as if she was having a regular conversation with Myra, "you asked us about Jonathan. You want to tell us where Eric is?"

"Don't flatter yourself, Charlotte. We know you don't know anything about what's going on. You're only trying to goad me into revealing information."

"We know about Jacqueline Consulting," she answered, matter-of-factly.

Myra seemed curious but as of yet, still unconcerned. "What do you know?"

"Enough."

Myra studied her. "Meaning you know nothing."

Francine wasn't sure where to take this from here. She didn't know much, but she wasn't sure about Charlotte. Charlotte had guessed something back in the car. She wasn't sure convincing Myra they had insight was a good idea, but they needed to keep her talking.

Charlotte finished up the small piece of cherry pie. "We know that Jacqueline Carter died on November 22nd, the same day John F. Kennedy died."

Myra's eyes registered a controlled alarm. "Who's Jacqueline Carter?"

"Jacqueline Carter is the reason your sister divorced Fuzzy," Charlotte answered.

Myra thought a moment. "And you think there's a connection to Jackie Kennedy?"

Now it was Charlotte's turn, and she took her time like they were playing chess. "Did I say there was?" she said eventually, keeping her tone nonchalant. "Maybe it's more important that Jack is Eric's middle name. Can I get some tea or something to go with the rest of the pie?"

Myra's expression tightened. Francine presumed Charlotte had struck gold with the last one. Myra gripped the gun and pointed it at Charlotte.

"The tea?" Charlotte asked. "Can I get some tea?"

263

"We don't have any." Myra said it through clenched teeth.

"How about coffee then?" She pointed to the two insulated coffee carafes sitting in the middle of the table.

This seemed to fluster Myra. She looked from the carafes to Charlotte and back again.

Charlotte took a small bite of the banana cream pie and her face lit up. "Francine, this is wonderful. I know you love bananas. You would really enjoy this pie."

There was some kind of code going on here that Francine didn't understand. She liked bananas okay, but didn't love them. "How is the peanut butter pie?" Francine asked, trying to decode whatever message Charlotte was sending. Maybe the whole purpose was to unsettle Myra.

Charlotte sampled the other piece. "Delicious, but it's rich. We'll need coffee or tea to cut the sweetness." She looked at Myra for approval.

"No," Myra said. "No coffee or tea."

Charlotte let out an exasperated breath. "Really, Myra? I thought you were supposed to be hospitable."

She waved the gun at Francine. "You get the coffee. I don't trust her."

"Okay." Francine got up. She lifted a Styrofoam cup from the small tower of them on the table. She faced Myra as she lifted the carafe and poured coffee into the cup. She handed the cup to Charlotte.

"Thanks. You should pour one for yourself so that you can try the pie too."

"No more pie is getting cut!" Myra announced. "I want you both seated."

"Fine. No pie," Francine said. She poured herself a coffee. "Want one?" she asked their host.

Myra was getting more and more anxious. "No. Now sit down."

Francine sat. Her best friend half stood. Myra leaned forward in her chair, training the gun on Charlotte. "Easy, now. What are you doing?"

"You said we couldn't cut any more pie, so I'm passing the rest of mine to Francine so she can try it."

Myra was suspicious, but she nodded anyway. Charlotte reached across the table holding the plate containing a large piece of banana cream pie and a larger piece of peanut butter pie, each with one small bite out of them.

Myra watched the pie plate carefully. She was seated close enough to Francine that it went nearly in front of her nose. As it crossed, Charlotte flicked the plate with her wrist and the pies slapped Myra in the face. Charlotte followed through with the plate, smacking her nose with it. The plate came off and Myra's eyes were covered with cream and meringue.

Francine hadn't known this would happen, but she took advantage of it. She jumped Myra, grabbed the gun away from her and knocked her to the floor. Myra fell backward in the chair, her mouth full of creamy substances.

Charlotte grabbed a dish towel and threw it to Francine. "Stuff it in her mouth before she decides to scream."

By this time Myra was thrashing around, her thick arms trying to strike Francine in the face. Francine leaned on the overturned chair to control the flailing arms, but she couldn't stuff the towel in her mouth at the same time. Charlotte was almost in place to do it for Francine when Myra let out a scream.

"Damn," Francine said. She pushed the chair into Myra's throat, producing enough of a choke hold that the scream died abruptly. Charlotte shoved the towel in, and the two of them wrestled her into a sitting position back in the chair as Francine held the woman's hands behind her back.

"Can you find me something to tie her hands with?" Francine asked.

Charlotte looked around but didn't see anything. She searched the drawers and the cabinets under the countertops. "How about this?" She pulled out a ball of twine. It looked like the kind of thing to tie turkey legs together before roasting the bird on Thanksgiving.

"It's worth a try."

Myra struggled but Francine held tight to her arms.

Charlotte hurried over with the twine and a pair of scissors. She cut some rope and tied her hands together as best she could. It was messy looking, but it held.

Francine examined the handiwork. "I think it may be worth double tying this." She snipped another piece and did a neater job.

"Well, sure, now that I've already tied them together it's easier to do," Charlotte said.

"I was about to say that."

"We've got to find someplace to stash her. Vince'll be back any minute."

They looked around. The only place big enough for Myra to fit was the pantry. Charlotte opened the door. It was full of food staples.

"The restroom!" Francine said.

She peeked out into the hall. It was deserted. Francine whispered a thank you to the heavens, gripped Myra's upper arms, and dragged her down the hall.

She immediately began kicking. Francine put a hand to Myra's throat and looked her in the eyes. "I will not hesitate to squeeze if necessary. Understand?" She hoped Myra was sufficiently scared because she wasn't sure she could actually choke the woman.

Myra's eyes bulged and she stopped fighting. Charlotte maneuvered around her in the hall and opened the door to the women's restroom. Francine was relieved to find no one in it. She pushed her in, and Charlotte hit the lock on the inside doorknob before she pushed it shut.

"That won't hold her too long," Francine said, wiping her brow. She was sweating from the exertion and the excitement. "Let's get out of here."

"What for?"

The women heard a new voice and froze. The voice sounded a lot like Myra's.

"Cass," Charlotte said without turning around.

Francine felt the barrel of Cass's shotgun jab her in the back. Involuntarily, her hands went up. Charlotte noticed it and followed suit.

Cass double-jabbed Francine. "Move. Now."

"If you shoot me right here, Charlotte will scream before you can do her in with a second bullet. Witnesses back in the parlor will come in and see you. They'll testify that you were here, were seen going down the hall, and there will be all kinds of messy evidence that you killed us."

Charlotte chafed. "Speak for yourself, Francine. I don't want to be 'messy evidence.'"

"She might have the gun, but she really doesn't have a choice," Francine said. *Surely Cass can't do anything without jeopardizing herself. There's no way for her to get away if she makes good on her threat.*

But she didn't like gambling with their lives. She tried to figure out the next move. Trying to overpower Cass would only get the two of them shot. That would happen instinctively. Plus, she knew taking Cass down wouldn't be as easy as it had been with Myra. They had no props. They needed a miracle.

Muffled noises came from the women's restroom.

"What's going on in there?" Cass asked.

Did she not see us stuff Myra in there?

"Constipation," Charlotte answered quickly. "I feel for the woman."

More thumping and banging came from inside. "She's got it bad," Cass said.

The door flew open, and Myra lurched out, her hands still tied behind her back, her face still covered with whipped cream and meringue. She slammed into Cass, taking them both down.

Cass's shotgun clattered down the hall toward the parlor.

THIRTY-ONE

FRANCINE STAGGERED TOWARD THE gun, tripping over Cass and landing on Myra. She heard the breath whoosh out of Myra when she fell. Myra head-butted Francine, spreading whipped goo all over Francine's face. It covered her glasses. She couldn't see, but she knew she was closer to the gun than Cass. She stretched out her hand and felt for it.

"Move your feet, Francine! I'm trying to get past you," Charlotte said.

Francine swiped at the mess on her glasses hoping to clear them enough to see Charlotte. She spotted her best friend edging her way down the hall. Francine pulled her knees to her stomach to keep them out of the way so Charlotte could slip past.

Cass scrabbled over Francine and Myra and latched onto one of Charlotte's ankles, trying to trip her. Francine jumped Cass and made her let go. Charlotte stayed upright, although Myra staggered to her feet and looked like she would try to fight again. Charlotte pushed her back in the open women's restroom. Myra tripped and fell, her head crashing into the toilet tank. Charlotte slammed the door shut. She turned and kicked Cass hard.

Vince Papadopoulos pounded down the stairs at the other end of the hallway. He made a quick assessment of the situation and lurched toward them, pulling a gun from his holster. Grabbing Charlotte roughly, he pushed her up against the wall while simultaneously aiming the gun at Francine's face. She froze immediately.

He glanced around. "Where's Myra?"

Cass got to her feet and opened the restroom door. "In here."

They all looked inside. Myra, her arms still tied behind her back, had managed to get to her feet enough to sit on the stool. Her legs were splayed and she was only semi-coherent. Her face was still covered with pie goo.

"What happened?" Vince demanded.

"Don't ask me," Cass said. "All I know is Myra called and told me to get over here. I came in through the back and found these two planning to search the place. They had Myra trapped in the restroom."

"We don't have time for this," Vince said. "There's still a wake going on. One of the family members could wander back. We have the food back here!"

"Need to clear the hall," Myra mumbled.

Cass pushed Charlotte over to a fire alarm, grabbed her hand and used it to set off the alarm. "Fire!" she yelled. It didn't take long before they heard others pick up the cry. Next they heard the thunderous noise of people running out of the building.

"Nice going," Vince said. "Now the Fire Department will be here as soon as they can."

"It worked for you on Friday," Cass said.

The noise seemed to have made Myra snap to consciousness. "Untie me. Now!" she ordered.

"Just a minute," Vince said. He handed the gun to Cass and disappeared into his office. He came out carrying a knife that Francine thought looked like an exact duplicate of the knife that killed Camille. It sliced through the rope so easily Francine almost gasped at its sharpness.

"See?" he said to Myra. "This knife has its uses. You keep wanting me to get rid of it, but it's just like the one my brother used in Vietnam."

Myra rubbed her wrists. "You shouldn't have bought a second one. You should have let it be for a while."

The fire alarm continued to scream. "We've got to get out of here," Cass said.

Myra turned to Francine and Charlotte. "Give me your keys! Cell phones too!"

The two did as she asked.

She handed the gun back to Vince. "Tie them up," she said, indicating Francine and Charlotte. "Load them into the hearse and drive them out to the cemetery. We're going to have to get rid of them." Then she started down the hall toward the front entrance.

"Where are you going?" Vince asked.

"To get their coats. I'm going to take their car, run over to Dick Raden's office, and make it look like they broke in looking for clues."

"How's that going to work?" Vince asked.

"Do I have to spell out everything for you?" Myra said, disgusted. "We'll say they came over here first, tried to sneak into your office, and when we caught them, they set off the fire alarm and escaped in the confusion. Then they went over to Dick's."

Vince looked stunned. "Won't that implicate Dick?"

"I never liked him anyway," offered Cass.

"Just leave it to me," Myra said. "I'll walk two blocks west from his office so I'm near Green Street. Swing by in the hearse and pick me up on your way out to the cemetery. Just hurry!"

She turned and strode down the hall.

Cass picked up her shotgun and held it on them while Vince hurried into the office and returned with some proper rope. He began binding their hands behind their backs.

Francine tried to think. She could tell Charlotte was panicking too.

"So you don't know about Eric?" Charlotte said to Cass.

"Eric?" Cass's voice had the unmistakable sound of concern. "What about him?"

"He's here. We saw his car outside."

It made Cass pause. "Is that true?" she asked Vince.

"He's just another blackmailer, like his aunt." Vince spit out the words like he'd eaten something rotten. He finished tying Francine and moved on to Charlotte.

Charlotte worked Cass's unease. "He knows about Jacqueline Carter."

That made her take in a sharp breath. "What does he know about Jacqueline Carter?"

"About the abortion," Charlotte said. Francine had been around Charlotte enough to know a bluff when she heard it, but to anyone else it probably sounded like she knew what she was talking about.

"He knows?" Cass said faintly.

Charlotte's eyes widened for a moment. Then she shrugged. "He does."

"No, he doesn't," Vince said, finishing binding Charlotte's hands. "Now stop listening to her. We've got to get out before the Fire Department gets here." He holstered his gun and used the knife to push Francine toward the exit.

Cass went along but was clearly wrestling with her emotions. "What he must think of me," she said, mostly to herself. It echoed fear and regret.

Francine resisted Vince's efforts. He shifted the knife he was holding so it was in the same place on her body where Camille had been stabbed. "Don't think I won't hesitate to gut you," he said, "because I will."

"Just like you killed Camille?"

He didn't answer, other than to ease the knife against her shirt so that she felt the sharpness of it. Much as she wanted to goad him into an answer, that changed her mind.

Charlotte took up the cause. "Just like you did in cold blood."

He swiveled, still holding the knife against Francine. "It wasn't my idea," he hissed.

"Then whose was it?" Charlotte asked.

"Just move."

They arrived at the rotunda, where the funeral home received caskets. The hearse was parked outside the back door under an overhang. A small parking lot lay beyond it.

"I can't go out there!" Charlotte said. "It's below freezing and my coat is in the front room."

"Get used to the cold," Vince said. "That's how the ground feels this time of year."

Francine braced herself for the cold blast when Vince pushed her outside.

Cass opened the back of the hearse. She and Vince shoved Francine in, then Charlotte. "I'll be watching you from my seat so don't try anything funny," Cass said.

Doors slammed as their captors got in the big vehicle. The engine started up, and the hearse pulled away.

The two women lay side-by-side, Francine on the left, Charlotte on the right. Francine wiggled until she was next to Charlotte. "We've got to stay warm until they get the heat going," Francine said. "I don't think they'll deny us that."

Charlotte's wig was coming off. The silver curls were no longer attached to the left side of her head and it was starting to look like some kind of half-dead animal crawling off her scalp onto the floor. Francine could see wispy strands of iron gray hair bobby-pinned beneath. If they survived this thing, she resolved to reattach the wig before any press got there. She was sure the press would eventually find them. Somehow they always showed up.

Actually, at this moment in time she would relish anyone showing up.

Charlotte was shaking. Francine wasn't sure if it was the cold or the situation.

"I only half understand what's going on," Charlotte said, her teeth chattering. She kept her voice low so only her friend could hear it. "Camille had blackmailed Vince and Myra because she discovered something about them when she was monitoring Internet activity in the Brownsburg coffee shop. I'm guessing it had to do with an abortion, because they're such staunch opponents. I mean, what else about them could be blackmail-able? That's all I can come up with."

"I thought they wanted to have kids but couldn't," Francine whispered back. "Why would they have an abortion?"

"I'm not sure it was theirs. I think they arranged it, and I think they did it for Cass."

Francine was puzzled. "So Cass was pregnant? You're saying the two sisters weren't the ones who were infertile?"

Charlotte nodded. "At least Cass wasn't. If I'm right."

"I had assumed all these years it was the women, since neither couple had children."

"Everyone was under that impression," Charlotte agreed. "We must have assumed wrong."

Vince's voice carried to the back. "What are you two doing back there? You're awfully quiet."

"Don't respond," Francine whispered in Charlotte's ear. "Let them think we're up to something."

They lay in the dark. Francine sent up a prayer that somehow they'd survive this.

The hearse stopped somewhere, and Myra got in. "Are they in the back?" Myra asked.

"Yeah," Vince responded. "Cass is watching them."

"I've been thinking," Cass said. "We shouldn't go to the cemetery right away. Cars are on the road still and the hearse is too noticeable. Let's park it in my garage. It'll go in easily. Fuzzy's family built that thing for storage. We can go later when the coast is clear."

"That's a good point," Myra said. "This is risky enough as it is. Head for Cass's," she ordered Vince.

Francine took this as a good sign. At least this bought them more time.

After a half minute of silence in the hearse, the radio came on. It was a golden oldies station. Dean Martin sang about the "little old winemaker, me." Francine thought she could use the glass of wine she'd only sipped at earlier in the evening. "You worked with Cass at the school for a long time," she told Charlotte. "When could Cass have been pregnant?"

Charlotte thought a moment. "The most logical time would have been fourteen or fifteen years ago, when she took a semester off and went to Chicago. That would explain a lot."

"So is that who Jacqueline Carter is? Cass and Fuzzy's baby?"

The hearse went over a pothole, jolting the two women. If her hands hadn't been tied, Francine would have clung to Charlotte in fear. "For a moment, all I could think of was that they'd brought us to the cemetery already," Francine confided, letting out a breath she didn't know she'd been holding.

"I only wish it were farther away than it is."

They were silent for a couple of minutes, letting the warmth of their bodies support each other. Francine shifted her weight around, trying to get comfortable. "Do you suppose Eric knew that Camille was a blackmailer?" Francine asked.

"Eric told us she'd brought him into her consulting business, and we know he met with each of the Council members the week before Camille was killed. I'm wondering if he let something slip that caused Vince and Myra to want her dead."

"I'm still confused about why Cass would want an abortion. Fuzzy was older than her by quite a bit. If he wanted children, you would have thought he'd be in a hurry by then."

"Maybe it wasn't Fuzzy's baby."

Francine drew in a breath. "Do you know that for a fact, or are you guessing?"

"Guessing, but maybe it makes sense. Fuzzy had a thing for younger girls. You remember that yearbook photo I showed you? Fuzzy was a senior and the girl he was with was in junior high. What if he thought Cass was already too old for him..."

"...and she became pregnant by someone else? It could explain the abortion."

"Not to mention the secrecy, especially if Fuzzy already knew he couldn't father kids." Charlotte let her head rest against Francine's shoulder. Her glasses poked into Francine, but she didn't care. "I don't want to die," Charlotte whispered, half to herself.

"Then we need to think of how to get out of this." Francine tried to sound more assured than she felt. "Either we've got to find a way to stay alive until someone rescues us, or we need to rescue ourselves. I thought your pie-in-the-face idea back at the funeral home was brilliant."

"Back then it was just you and me against Myra. Now it's the two of us against three of them."

Francine tried to rally her friend. "But we know Eric was there. Maybe he saw them put us in the hearse. Maybe he'll contact the police."

The vehicle slowed and went over a curb, then pulled to a stop. Francine heard the sound of a motor grinding and something moving. She figured it was a garage door opening. The hearse's transmission engaged, and they pulled to a smooth stop a few moments later.

Doors slammed as the other passengers got out.

The doors to the back of the hearse swung open. Cass stood with her shotgun trained on them. "Get out," she said.

Behind her a garage door closed automatically.

THIRTY-TWO

"I'M AN OLD LADY. I can't get up with my hands tied," Charlotte said grumpily.

"Fine." Cass nodded to Vince. "No funny business."

Vince sliced the ropes to free Francine and Charlotte's hands, and Francine climbed out of the hearse. She turned to help Charlotte to her feet as well. Then they were pushed along and shoved into the house by Vince and Myra. Vince carried the large knife in one hand. Myra had a handgun. They were followed by Cass with her shotgun.

"It's Cass's house," Charlotte confirmed, leaning just close enough to Francine so that only she could hear.

The women were ushered into a large room with windows. While Myra drew the curtains, they were directed to sit in front of the fireplace. The chairs were vintage French antique oak chairs with padded fabric seats. Charlotte slumped in hers and gave their captors a stony glare. Francine tried her best to sit up and stay alert for any chance to escape.

Vince got a fire going in the fireplace, but Francine knew it would be a while before the room heated up. She glanced around. The room was rectangular and had wooden paneling along one wall. Over the fireplace was a portrait of a woman with her hair in a bun. She wore a grim expression that seemed straight out of the Depression. Her face had a familiar long, hang-dog look and it took only a second for Francine to register that it was likely Fuzzy's mother. Francine couldn't imagine why Cass would have left a portrait of her ex-mother-in-law over the fireplace when the divorce had been nasty. Perhaps she admired the woman. She certainly looked formidable.

The front door opened, and Fuzzy Carter walked in. He brushed the snow off his skiff of a hairline and unbuttoned his leather coat. He took off the coat and hung it on a rack inside the front door.

"What are you doing here?" Cass asked.

Vince shrugged, trying to appear casual. "I asked him to come."

Francine didn't know what to make of Fuzzy's sudden appearance. Having him there didn't make sense in light of Charlotte's latest theory.

Myra pulled up one of the vintage chairs and sat at Francine's right facing the fireplace. Cass did the same on Charlotte's left. Cass laid her shotgun across her lap, and Myra cradled a handgun. Vince sat on the hearth by the fire, warming himself. His knife was laid on the hearth next to him. Francine could also see he had his gun holstered.

"Well, this is cozy," Charlotte said, trying to provoke a reaction. No one bit.

Fuzzy took a seat on the hearth and crossed his arms over his chest. He looked from Francine to Charlotte and back again, and then addressed Vince. "You didn't tell me you had company."

"They're an inconvenient set of guests," Vince replied.

"We're gonna move them to a more *permanent* location else-where on the property," Myra added.

Fuzzy processed that. He frowned. "No, you're not. Not in my family's cemetery. We're not a dumping ground for inconvenient bodies with no trace of Carter blood. Bad enough I don't own it any-more." He sounded bitter.

"Relax," Vince said. "Once Cass sells the land, the developers have promised to move all the graves to a new location. You can have it back on your own property."

Cass gritted her teeth. "I told you, I'm not selling the land."

"You have to sell it," Fuzzy said. "I don't like it any more than you do, but that's how it's got to be."

Myra got angry at her sister. "We've been over this again and again. Do you know how much money there is to be made?"

Cass blinked back tears. "You keep talking like I need the money. You might, but I don't."

"What makes you think you don't need the money?" Vince ar-gued. "The same secrets Camille knew, Eric knows now."

Francine thought that Cass was biting her tongue. *So Eric does know something. And she must have made some kind of arrangement with him not to be worried like the others.*

Charlotte perked up as though what Vince had said made her think of something. "It didn't start out as blackmail," she began. "Did it?"

Everyone looked at Charlotte like she had blundered into a fam-ily picnic pretending to be a long-lost relative. Vince's posture went rigid. The tension in the room became palpable.

"What blackmail?" Fuzzy asked. Francine recognized a feigned innocence on Fuzzy's part.

"She doesn't know anything," Myra said.

Charlotte persisted. "I know that you all make or have made payments to Camille's company, Jacqueline Consulting. And I know who she named the company after."

Cass turned in anger. "Who?"

"Jacqueline Carter."

Myra frowned, but her head held an inquisitive tilt as she spoke. "And who was she?"

"She was Cass's baby."

"Cass never had a baby," Fuzzy said.

Everyone ignored him. "Jacqueline Carter was a long time in the past," Myra said.

Vince nodded. "Absolutely." Francine thought it came too quickly, like he was trying to shut down any speculation.

"Stop pretending it was that long ago," Cass said. She was on the verge of tears. "Especially you, Myra. You're my sister. I expect you to understand. It *wasn't* a long time ago, not for me."

In her best sympathetic voice, Charlotte said, "And it never will be, either, will it?"

Myra pointed the gun at her. "That's enough prying from you."

"It must have been difficult to make that decision," Charlotte said to Cass. It was clear she wasn't going to let go of this thread. "You knew Fuzzy couldn't give you a child."

Fuzzy leapt to his feet. "Will everyone stop acting like I am not in the room? And what's this about Cass having a baby?"

"He was unfaithful too," Cass said, sniveling a bit, not looking at Fuzzy.

Vince stood up. "This is not the place to air dirty laundry."

"It was complicated," Cass said, continuing as though neither Vince nor Fuzzy had spoken. "I didn't want anyone to know. Even with *his* cheating, I was still ashamed of what *I* did. If I could have made him believe the baby was his, I would have had her anyway.

But I knew he wouldn't. And the father was too young to take on the responsibility. No matter how much I loved him."

Fuzzy opened and closed his mouth like a fish. He seemed too stunned to say anything.

Francine was fairly certain her own mouth hung open in surprise, but Charlotte seemed to take the matter in stride. "Fuzzy always had an eye for the young ones, didn't he?" Charlotte said. "You were one of them once. Is that the reason you went after a student too?"

"You don't what you're talking about," Myra said. "Or who."

Charlotte held her hand out toward Cass as if to give her the option of answering first. It implied that Charlotte knew who the father was. Francine thought it was a good bluff on Charlotte's part, but she also might have guessed it.

Cass put her head in her hands.

Everyone turned to Charlotte. She shrugged and said, "It was Eric Dehoney."

Eric? Francine thought. *Eric and Cass, teacher and student? And she said she loved him. Did he love her back? No wonder it was complicated.* Francine looked around the room. Apparently she wasn't the only one shocked. Vince's eyes were wide with surprise and Fuzzy's face turned beet red. Myra seemed to have known, though.

Cass pulled her head out of her hands and went on talking. She sounded miserable, but words spilled out of her like she'd needed to tell someone the truth for a long time. "He had just turned eighteen, so it wasn't like he wasn't of age. He was cute and shy and sexy. I'd watch him in the weight room. He was so different from Fuzzy."

In one swift move, Fuzzy seized Vince's knife and pointed it at Cass. "That's enough. I don't want to hear anymore."

Myra pointed her gun at Fuzzy. "She'll talk if she wants to."

Vince pulled his gun and aimed it at Cass. "I agree with Fuzzy. We don't need to hear anymore. Not with these two in the room."

Charlotte smiled at the division that was happening among their captors. "She probably doesn't know about the payments Vince made to Camille. The big ones."

"That's enough from you too," Vince said. With all the weapons pointed at other people, though, no one shifted theirs toward Charlotte.

Myra seemed to grow bolder and more defensive of her sister with each new revelation. "What payments? How big?"

Francine wasn't sure how Charlotte knew all that she'd revealed so far, but the financial data was information she'd gleaned from Jonathan. This seemed a good time to share it. "A quarter of a million dollars. Four times."

She looked at Vince. "Our savings? Gone? That's why we have to sell the funeral home?"

"It was never his money to begin with," Fuzzy spat out. "He'd bullied that amount out of my parents over a period of years. I didn't know until later. I still haven't forgiven him. The only reason I came tonight is so we can work on Cass to sell the land to the developers. Then I'm out."

"Wait a minute!" Cass said. She stood up and pointed the rifle at Vince. "What were you blackmailing his parents about?"

"It wasn't blackmail. Fuzzy got a young girl pregnant. It was before you married him. There could have been a lot of collateral damage if anyone found out. So his parents asked me to arrange for an abortion. Me! Who'd been so outspoken against abortion. So I faked them out. I sent the girl away where she could have the baby in peace and put it up for adoption. She did like she was told."

"We had a funeral!" Fuzzy protested. "There was a baby in that casket."

"I faked it."

Myra was sputtering she was so upset. "You told me that was Fuzzy's baby, that the girl had miscarried. You liar!"

Vince dug a fist into his hip. "We arranged for your sister to have an abortion several years later. You seemed to think it was okay that time."

Meanwhile Fuzzy grappled with the information. "So I'm a father?"

Vince shrugged.

"And you charged my parents?" Fuzzy asked his former friend and brother-in-law.

"I sent some of the money to the foster family, for the baby."

Francine noted he'd said *some* of the money. She was willing to bet it was a small percentage.

Cass stomped her feet, angry. "*He* got a girl pregnant. How is that possible?"

"It was before he got the mumps that made him sterile," Vince said.

"But how did Camille know all this?" asked Myra. "How did *she* get hold of our money?"

At first no one answered, but Charlotte was happy to keep stirring the pot. "I'm guessing here, but Fuzzy and Dick were regulars at the same coffee shop where Camille busted the child pornographer. She was monitoring all the Internet connections being made. If Vince was blackmailing Fuzzy's parents during that time, and it sounds like he was, she would have intercepted any emails he sent. From there, she could have blackmailed him."

Myra rose from the chair, walked over to Vince, and slapped her husband in the face. "That's for not telling me the truth from the start."

Vince interrupted. "You didn't care so much when we had all that money, did you? It didn't even matter to you where it came from. Not until now."

"Why were you paying Camille?" Francine asked Fuzzy. "She was already getting the money from Vince. But you were a customer too. You gave her a monthly stipend."

"Stipend? It was blackmail all the same. It was her way of keeping me from going after younger girls. I thought maybe when I retired it would stop. But it didn't. My entire paycheck as a Council member went to her to keep the school from finding out the truth."

Francine wondered if Camille thought of herself as a crusader. In some ways, she'd been exacting justice. Even from a certain perspective, her blackmail of Charlotte could have been considered dogooding. Charlotte didn't step outside her marriage again; Camille never asked for a penny more. But if Camille was monitoring the public Internet, she could have uncovered lots of unsavory things about people who sat at the coffee shop, the Town Hall, or anywhere else there was WiFi. Who knew how many of them had been blackmailed?

"If she had something on a lot of different people, then who killed her?" Francine asked. She was thinking maybe it wasn't any of her captors.

Fuzzy looked to Cass. Cass shook her head. Myra stared accusingly at Vince. He didn't make eye contact.

Myra slapped Vince again. "You are stupid."

He pumped his fist like Jackie Gleason threatening to knock Audrey Meadows to the moon, but he didn't hit her. "She's not blackmailing us anymore, is she?" he said.

That makes it sound like he did her in, Francine thought. Or maybe it was both him and Fuzzy. Maybe this was *Murder on the Orient Express.* Maybe she had something on Tricky Dicky too. Francine wouldn't have doubted that. And all of them were seated at the table with Camille.

"Eric," Charlotte blurted out. "How much of this did Eric know? Why did he want to meet with you before Camille died?"

"Looking for a handout," Vince said. "The little worm. He claimed he wanted a lump sum payment and that would be it. One payment and he would make it good with Camille. He'd see to it she never asked for money again."

"Maybe he was sincere?"

"Blackmailers are never sincere."

There was a knock on the front door. All faces turned toward it. The knock came a second time.

Vince got up. There was a small round window about a third of the way from the top of the door. He snuck a swift glance through it. "It's Eric."

Fuzzy joined him and peeked out the window. "It looks like he's alone. He's holding up his hands like he's surrendering."

"He's probably trying to show us he has nothing in his hands."

"Good point," Fuzzy said. "He's wearing a coat, though. He might have a weapon in it."

"That'll be easy enough to find out."

Vince stood to one side of the door. He took the knife from Fuzzy and gave him the gun. Fuzzy unlocked the deadbolt with a click and yanked open the door.

Francine felt the cold air sweep into the room as Eric stepped in, still holding his hands in the air. Vince jumped out from behind the door. He accosted Eric, wrapped an arm around him, and brought the cold steel of the knife to Eric's throat with the other hand. Fuzzy put the barrel of the gun in front of his face. Eric stared at it and then at Fuzzy. There was fear in his eyes.

Fuzzy went outside and made sure Eric had come alone. Satisfied, he backed in and closed the door. Eric's coat was bulky. He clearly wasn't carrying anything in his hands, but the coat was large enough to hide a small assault rifle strapped to his chest. Eric didn't move. Vince pushed him hard into the front room. Eric stumbled but regained his balance.

"I'm here to exchange myself for Francine and Charlotte," he said. The words sounded brave but his voice wavered. "This is between me and the rest of you. Let them go."

"How did you know we were here?" Myra asked.

"I was outside the funeral home sitting in my car. I'd seen Francine and Charlotte go in, so I waited to see what would happen. Then the fire alarm went off and people came running out, but they didn't. I saw the hearse tear away from the funeral home and followed it."

Cass asked, "Does anyone else know you're here?" She sounded almost hopeful.

He nodded. "Jonathan McNamara. I told him to stand by for a call. He's nearby. If you let Francine and Charlotte leave, he'll come pick them up."

Vince stood up. "Just like that? You expect us to let them go, just like that?"

He shrugged. "As I said, they're innocent bystanders. They may have been trying to solve a mystery, but that's what they do. What's at stake here is between us. What we know, that they don't."

Vince worked his jaw. He looked at Myra, looked at Cass, looked at Fuzzy. "They know everything now," he said. He pulled out a concealed gun and in one smooth move shot at Eric. At the last second Eric realized what was happening and dodged left, but not enough. The bullet hit him. He crumpled to the floor. Cass, horrified, aimed the shotgun at Vince. Myra knocked it out of her hand. Cass grabbed Myra's gun, aimed at Vince's hand, and pulled the trigger.

Francine looked away just as Vince clutched his bleeding hand, screamed, and fainted.

THIRTY-THREE

THE HORROR OF WHAT just happened stunned Francine for only a second before she realized she had to do something. Vince would probably survive. He might lose his hand, but he wasn't in danger. Eric was her first priority.

He lay on the floor, in agony but conscious. Blood pooled on the edges of his sweater. She lifted it. The bullet had hit him square in the stomach. She did a quick examination and determined the bullet was still embedded in his body. "Call 911 now!" she said. "He needs to get to an emergency room."

Cass rushed over and knelt beside her and Eric. She pulled out her cell phone. "What should I say?"

"Just give them the location. I'll talk you through the rest of it."

"What about Vince?" Myra said.

Francine noticed that Myra was now on the floor cradling her husband's head in her lap and trying to wipe away the blood with her shirt. Fuzzy and Charlotte seemed rooted in their spots. "He needs to get to an emergency room too," Francine told Myra. She noticed Cass's hands were shaking so bad she couldn't seem to hit the right numbers on the phone.

Charlotte, meanwhile, roused herself and scouted the room for a phone. "Doesn't anyone have a good old-fashioned landline anymore?" she asked, hands on hips.

Cass finally hit the jackpot on the numbers. While the phone call went through, Francine directed Charlotte elsewhere. "I need to stop the bleeding, Charlotte. Please get me some towels."

With Charlotte looking, she turned her attention back to Eric. She felt for a pulse at his neck. It was still strong, but beating very fast.

Cass took Eric's hand. "I meant to tell you about the baby when we met in secret the other night, but it just didn't seem like the right time. I never suspected that you still loved me. I broke it off fifteen years ago because it was wrong. I knew it was wrong. I shouldn't have seduced you. I'm sorry for everything. But I'm not sorry about where we are right now, that I love you and you love me."

Eric squeezed her hand. His eyes were closed and he licked his lips. They were dry. "Water," he said. His voice was raspy.

Cass got up and ran to get water.

Francine knew what she had to do. She couldn't take any chances on Eric dying. She reached into the neckline of her shirt and pulled out her necklace. On it was the ampule containing formula Number 58 from Doc Wheat's supply of medicines, the one she couldn't duplicate. The ampule contained only a few milliliters of the liquid, but she believed it would do the trick. She put it to his lips. "Drink this," she said. When he opened his mouth, she poured it in. It was gone in a swallow.

"Please, more," he said.

She had just tucked the tiny container away when Cass returned with a glass of water. She propped his head while Cass helped him sip from the glass.

Charlotte entered the room carrying a stack of towels. "Found 'em. Finally." She left a couple with Myra and dropped the rest next to Francine.

Francine pushed the towels into the wound.

Five minutes later when the paramedics arrived, the bleeding had slowed and almost stopped.

———

Since Camille's death had been Jud's case from the start, the county prosecutor called on him to assist even though Cass's house wasn't located in Brownsburg. Jud arrived at the scene, took everyone's statement, and helped process the crime scene. Francine and Charlotte were eventually sent home, but he'd warned them he wanted to see them the next day.

And so, after a restless night where she found herself reliving the horror of being thrown in the back of a hearse, fearing for her life, and then seeing two people shot, she had already anticipated Jud's phone call. When it came, she dragged herself out of bed and into a hot shower. She got ready, picked up Charlotte, and headed for Brownsburg's Town Hall.

Jud's office had changed little since the last time they'd been there, which Francine reminded herself was only a couple of days ago. The multitude of picture frames on the wall had still not been dusted. She wondered when they would be. Maybe never.

He offered them a cup of coffee, which they both gratefully accepted. She half expected Charlotte to pull out a bottle of cognac and spike them up because you really never knew what Charlotte would do, but thankfully no such thing happened.

Jud returned with a tray of three mugs. He leaned back in his chair and took a sip of his. "Weak," he said, "but hot. The Kuerig machine is out this morning, and no one remembers how to use the coffeemaker. We were lucky to find some ground coffee in the freezer."

Francine sampled hers and agreed with Jud's assessment. It was weak.

"So, Jud," Charlotte said, "how can we help?"

"I find this convoluted. It would appear that blackmailing ran rampant. Even you were a victim, Charlotte. Is that your assessment?"

Charlotte's eyes grew wide. "No, not me! I mean, I suppose I had been, in the past. A long time ago. You found that out?"

"Your name showed up in the paperwork we took out of Camille's house after she died. We've been watching you, though we doubted you had anything to do with her death. From past experience, we know you and dead bodies go together like coffee and donuts."

She chuckled. "Spoken like a true policeman, though you don't look like you spend much time in donut shops. It's true I made a tribute payment to her after my husband died. I don't really want to talk about it, other than she never asked for more."

"So why did she do it at all?" Jud interlocked his hands behind his head and stretched. "What motive did she have?"

"Francine has a theory," Charlotte answered, nodding toward her. "I think you should share it with him." She looked back at Jud. "She really is on to something."

"I think Camille came to think of herself as a vigilante," Francine said. "Like a superhero who had the ability to see the wrongs people were committing and could administer justice."

Jud righted himself in his chair and leaned forward. "You have an example?"

"One you already know about. She discovered the child pornographer while monitoring Internet activity from the Bulldog Coffee House. What I think happened—and I only have circumstantial evidence—is that she uncovered some other things about people she was able to use against them. Like Vince Papadopoulos and the 'abortion' he arranged for the student Fuzzy got pregnant. He didn't really have an abortion done. He made the girl disappear until the baby was born and given up for adoption. What he did was technically blackmail, since he extracted a million dollars out of Fuzzy's parents. But some of it was so he could provide money to her foster parents for support."

Jud's mouth twisted as though he wasn't sure how much to reveal. He seemed to decide in favor of continuing the discussion, though. "He wasn't completely philanthropic with that money. Only about half of it went to the foster parents. He kept the rest."

"Which is what made Camille's sense of justice kick in," Charlotte said, butting in. "If he had been sending all of it to the foster parents, he might not have cared if all had been revealed. He might even have looked like a good guy. But he got greedy."

"She was blackmailing Fuzzy too," Francine said. "I think she was holding what she knew about his previous wrongdoing over his head. Yes, she was extracting his pay as a Town Council member, but she was also trying to keep him from doing it to any other young girls."

"What about Dick Raden?" Jud asked.

Charlotte scoffed. "We don't know exactly what she had over him, but with all the bad deals he's made—at least, bad for Brownsburg—we bet you'll be able to track something he did that was illegal."

"What we don't know," Francine said, "is why she really chose to run for the Town Council in the first place. All we can figure is that she knew their good ole boys' network was not helping the Town, and, in do-gooder mode, knew she had the goods on them to break up their control. Between her and Janet Turpen and Fuzzy, who might have been hoping she would stop blackmailing him if he supported her, she was getting the job done."

Jud nodded. "That would make sense. Then who killed her?"

"You don't know?" Charlotte asked, frowning.

Jud shook his head. "No one's confessed. We have Cass, Vince, and Myra on charges of abducting you; Vince on attempted murder charges with regards to Eric; and Fuzzy on some minor charges. But no one on Camille's death."

Charlotte and Francine locked eyes. Francine wasn't about to answer that one. She knew who shot Eric because she'd been a witness. But who knifed Camille was a different story.

Charlotte took a deep breath and plunged ahead. "I'm pretty sure it's Vince. I think he and Camille had gotten to the point of real animosity. When Eric presented him with the alternative of giving him a lump sum in return for getting Camille off his back, he viewed him as just another blackmailer. Eric was younger and stronger, and so Vince decided he could kill Camille and send a message to Eric that he was not to be trifled with."

Francine shuddered when she remembered finding Camille gasping for breath because the knife had penetrated one of her lungs. It was worse than almost anything she'd encountered during her days as a nurse. No wonder Eric hadn't wanted to be left alone after that. And yet, he'd slipped away from Toby, whom he'd recruited as a protective roommate, to be with Cass at least one night they knew of. "Do you know if Cass's baby was Eric's?"

"That's what she claims," Jud said. He habitually took another sip of the coffee, remembered it was weak, and made a face. "The only way to know for sure is to exhume it, but we don't think it will come to that. She says she regrets having the abortion, and both of them have professed their love for each other. Apparently they've been meeting in secret during the last two months. In the end, it doesn't matter. He was eighteen even back then, so there was nothing illegal going on."

Francine turned to Charlotte. "I've been meaning to ask, how did you guess last night that Jacqueline Carter was Cass's baby?"

"Mostly I just wanted to keep them talking," she said. She exhaled shakily as if recalling how frightening it had been. "Cass wouldn't let go of the land, so there had to be a strong motive that involved who Jacqueline Carter was. Plus, I remembered that photo of the chubby girl at the Tastee-Freez taken in Chicago. You said you said you thought it wasn't Camille, even though it was in with her pictures. I realized that Chicago was where Cass had gone the summer before she and Fuzzy divorced. It seemed possible."

Francine was always amazed at how Charlotte's mind bordered on clairvoyance. "Was Fuzzy ever in love with Cass do you think?"

Charlotte shook her head, but it was Jud who answered. "My opinion is no. When she was young, he may have been in lust with her, but when she got older he was just using her as a cover for his predatory habits."

"I'm guessing the only reason they were cooperating was to make the shopping mall at the I-74 interchange a reality," Charlotte said. "And Cass was frustrating them all."

"She held a key piece of land," Jud agreed. "Fuzzy's parents are in a nursing home, so he had control of the surrounding parcels. Vince and Myra had purchased a five-acre plot from him many years ago for a retirement home, but they were willing to sell at a high price. Vince was looking to replace some of the money he'd obtained from Fuzzy's parents that Camille had extracted from him. Dick Raden was going to make a killing if he could arrange the deal, and Janet Turpen was working on the financing piece. Cass was the only one they had to convince."

"But she wouldn't sell because she couldn't let go of her daughter Jacqueline?"

Jud nodded. "Exactly. She's at an age now where having children would be very tricky, so it looked like Jacqueline would be her only child. She knew the cemetery was going to be moved. Since she had fought Fuzzy for that land during the divorce, she didn't want to give in. She didn't want the grave disturbed, knowing her daughter was buried there. Money wasn't enough of a motive."

Charlotte thought a moment. "What strikes me is the number of people who thought they were doing the right thing, or at least a good thing. Vince, in not allowing an abortion but instead arranging for an adoption, and then sending some of the money to the foster parents. Camille, in making Vince pay for what she perceived as blackmail and also controlling Fuzzy's impulses. Dick Raden and Janet Turpen in creating the outlet mall that would bring people to Brownsburg. And even Eric, who says he told his aunt Camille that blackmail was wrong no matter what reasons she had for it. He tried to buy her off with a lump sum payment extracted from all the players to end the scheme."

Francine agreed that it was surprising how wrong things had gone and how many secrets had been spilled, not to mention the life that was lost and the life that was almost lost. She wondered about the secret she was carrying—of the rejuvenative powers of the spring she'd inherited in Parke County and the curative formulas that could be created from its waters. She took a contemplative deep breath before asking a question she really wanted an answer to. "Any information you can share on Eric's condition?"

"Since it's good news and they're doing a press conference in a half hour, I don't see why I can't. He's out of intensive care, and the hospital expects him to make a complete recovery," Jud said. "They said it's a good thing he was in excellent physical condition because his body is healing quickly. That's the only way they could account for it. They told me it's as if his body knows exactly how to make the repairs it needs to get better."

Francine put a hand to her neckline and subconsciously twirled the necklace containing the now-empty ampule that had held the last remnants of Doc Wheat's formula No. 58, which she had yet to duplicate, and wasn't sure she ever could.

Not unless she could find the elusive second spring.

THIRTY-FOUR

"THIS IS A PIP of a wedding," Charlotte remarked. "I can't wait for the bride and groom to get here. We need to get this party underway!"

Francine and Jonathan, Charlotte, Mary Ruth, Joy and Roy, and Alice and Larry sat at a table in the Crown Room of the Schrier Building in Brownsburg. The men were dressed in suits, and the ladies were dressed in either skirts with jackets or long evening gowns. The June wedding, just a few months after they'd solved the murder of Camille Ledfelter, was being held in the same place the mystery started. It seemed fitting somehow. Camille's death had been mourned, but the community had been purged of wrongdoing in the name of righteousness, and now it was time to move forward.

Francine nudged Mary Ruth, whom she was sitting next to. "Toby looks very handsome as the best man."

"I'm just glad that he's no longer looking to be a male stripper," she said. "Cass made it a condition that Eric sell the revue, even though she wanted to marry him as much as he wanted to marry her. I still find it a surprise that he never resented her in later life for having relations with him."

Joy perched on the edge of her seat, always anxious to share information when she knew something the others didn't. "When I did a post interview followup for Channel Six, he told me it was as much him as it was her back in high school. That's why there was never any blame. He had real feelings for her. He was hurt when she cut off the relationship. I'm surprised he carried the torch for her all those years."

"Could we not talk about this?" Alice asked in her nasally voice. "It makes me feel creepy just thinking about it. And I wasn't even here for it!"

"Be glad you and Larry were out seeing one of Jake's races," Francine advised. "It wasn't that pretty."

Charlotte perked up her ears. "What's that song?"

Francine had earlier figured out that the music being played by the DJ as they awaited the arrival of the wedding party was karaoke versions of songs the Royal Buckingham Male Revue used to dance to.

"Tripper's doing a great job with the vocals," Mary Ruth said. "Who knew he'd turn out to be so talented?"

"That's the guy who wanted to be a stripper?" Alice asked, wrinkling her nose at the idea. "He doesn't look like a stripper."

Francine smiled. "What he lacked in ability he made up with enthusiasm and persistence. But he does have a dreamy voice."

"I'll say," Charlotte said. "Joy's feature on him ended up on *Good Morning America* and netted him a try out for *The Voice*. He could be the next Josh Kaufman!" Charlotte referred to another Indianapolis area resident who'd grabbed the top spot on the vocal talent reality show.

Joy beamed when Charlotte mentioned her role in helping rehabilitate Tripper. "He's working hard at keeping this new career going. And his clothes on," she added. They laughed. Roy took her hand in his and kissed it.

Francine noted that Joy and Roy looked very much in love. They had snuggled close throughout the ceremony and kept exchanging meaningful glances at key points. Joy had confided to her that she and Roy had discussed marriage and she expected he would propose any day now. She intended to go for it when Cass tossed the bouquet, even though she'd be the oldest one competing for it. Probably by a lot of years.

Francine surveyed the room. The new Council members who'd replaced Vince Papadopolous and Camille Ledfelter were there with their spouses. Fuzzy Carter was in jail and would be for a long time. Two of his victims had come forward and testified that he'd molested them when they were underage. The charges against Cass were reduced because she had tried to keep the two older women from getting killed. Eric had texted her from the parking lot of the funeral home to ask what had happened, and when he found out, he had persuaded her not to be a part of it. That was why Cass had suggested moving the ladies to her house instead of going to the cemetery. And her shooting Vince in the hand was to prevent him from doing any more harm.

The Royal Buckingham troupe had been sold and moved out of town, and Eric had taken over Jacqueline Consulting. Camille may have made the company a big success through blackmail, but there were legitimate sources of income in there, too, and Eric was focused on that. He'd been persuaded it was more stable than starting a male dance club site in Brownsburg. This idea was pushed as hard as anyone by his fiancé, who didn't appreciate others seeing him nearly naked.

Jonathan stood up and held out his hand to Francine. "Shall we dance?"

There were few people on the dance floor. Francine thought more people should be dancing to the fine vocals Tripper was providing.

He was singing "Love is a Many Splendored Thing," a song that meant something to the two of them. "I would love to dance," she said.

"How is the effort going to re-create Formula No. 58?" he asked once he'd whisked her away from their table of friends. "You've been working on it intently for a number of days now."

"Not so good." She could hear the regret in her own voice. "I know it's not right because the pale blue color doesn't appear. I don't think there's a substitute for the 'second spring,' wherever it might be."

"I was there last weekend checking on the retreat house and did some more searching. I swear we've been over every inch of the property. But with three hundred and some odd acres, it's quite possible we've overlooked it."

"Or it doesn't exist."

"Or it might be on an adjacent property," Jonathan said, moving her around the floor. "Or somewhere else in the county."

"In other words, a needle in a haystack." Francine sighed. "We need a clue."

"Well, you seem to find clues every time you come across a mystery. You and Charlotte."

"We do, don't we?"

"Speaking of the formula, you've managed to achieve your top bucket list item, haven't you? Save a Life All by Myself." He hugged her close.

"I could argue I didn't do it by myself, that I used a formula I can't even reproduce or replace. But that would be pulling a Charlotte. I still want to recreate Doc Wheat's cure, but I feel like I've accomplished my number one item."

Jonathan looked over at Tripper. "I'd say you've saved more than one life."

She winked at him. "Saving Tripper was a bonus."

"How about Joy? Wasn't going to a strip club on her list?"

Since more couples were now on the small dance floor, she leaned in close. "She checked off Go to a Male Strip Club when Tripper pulled off his clothes at the bingo and then fell on her. It wasn't technically a strip club, but it did the trick."

Joy danced by them with Roy Stockton. She was beaming, and his eyes were fixed on her. Since his head wasn't covered with his usual Stetson, Francine could see the wispiness of his white hair. It looked almost like Joy had been mussing it with her hands. *Maybe she has.* "Joy's also checked off her number five, which was simply listed as Romance!"

"Roy seems to be a good match."

They finished their dance and Tripper asked everyone to return to their seats. Once the room was settled, he pointed them toward the main entrance to the room, where Eric and Cass were now standing. He introduced them, and they bounded into the room arm in arm, smiling broadly.

How remarkable, Francine thought. *Their love started off in such a wrong way and they've had to deal with so many tragedies, but somehow they've come through it.*

Of course, it helped that only a few people knew the truth. Those closest to it—like Fuzzy and Myra and Vince—had no choice but to accept it, because revealing the truth would open themselves up to more scrutiny than they could handle. Especially Vince, since he was already in jail for Camille's murder. As for the Summer Ridge Bridge Club, they would keep the secret. Everyone else would have to accept that Eric had moved back to town and fallen for an older woman.

Time heals, she thought.

Then the music started up, Tripper sang "Can't Take My Eyes off You," and Eric and Cass danced their first dance together.

They used the Frankie Valli version, and no one took any clothes off.

Yet.

THE END

ABOUT THE AUTHORS

Elizabeth Perona is the father/daughter writing team of Tony Perona and Liz Dombrosky. Tony is the author of the Nick Bertetto mystery series and the standalone thriller *The Final Mayan Prophecy* (with Paul Skorich) and coeditor and contributor to the anthologies *Racing Can Be Murder* and *Hoosier Hoops and Hijinks*. He is a member of Mystery Writers of America and has served the organization as a member of the Board of Directors and as Treasurer. He is also a member of Sisters in Crime.

Liz Dombrosky graduated from Ball State University in the Honors College with a degree in teaching. She is currently a stay-at-home mom and teaches preschool part-time. *Murder at the Male Revue* is her third novel.